W9-BCU-780

The Essential
SHAKESPEARE

*an annotated bibliography
of major modern studies*

A
Reference
Publication
in
Literature

James L. Harner
Editor

The Essential
SHAKESPEARE

---

an annotated bibliography
of major modern studies

LIBRARY
BRYAN COLLEGE
DAYTON, TN 37321

LARRY S. CHAMPION

G.K.HALL&CO.

70 LINCOLN STREET, BOSTON, MASS.

102831

All rights reserved.
Copyright 1986 by Larry S. Champion.

Library of Congress Cataloging-in-Publication Data

Champion, Larry S.
  The essential Shakespeare.

  (A Reference publication in literature)
  Includes index.
    1. Shakespeare, William, 1564–1616—Bibliography.
  I. Title.   II. Series.
  Z8811.C53   1986   [PR2894]   016.8223'3   86-9994
  ISBN 0-8161-8731-2

This publication is printed on permanent/durable acid-free paper
MANUFACTURED IN THE UNITED STATES OF AMERICA

Contents

Contents

Contents

The Author

    Educated at Davidson College, the University of
Virginia, and the University of North Carolina, Larry
S. Champion is currently professor of English at North
Carolina State University, where he served as head of
the department from 1971 to 1984. He has published
numerous books on Shakespeare and Renaissance drama.
An examination of Ben Jonson's late comedies (Kentucky,
1967) was followed by studies of Shakespeare's comedies
(Harvard, 1970), Shakespeare's tragedies (Georgia,
1976), Shakespeare's histories (Georgia, 1980),
Jacobean and Caroline tragedy (Tennessee, 1976), and
Thomas Dekker's dramatic works (Lang, 1985). He also
compiled a two-volume annotated bibliography of King
Lear, published in 1981 as number 1 in the ongoing
Garland Shakespeare Bibliographies. His articles have
appeared in such journals as Publications of the Modern
Language Association, Studies in Philology, Shakespeare
Quarterly, Studies in English Literature, Modern Lan-
guage Quarterly, Texas Studies in Literature and Lan-
guage, and English Studies.

Preface

Far more is written about Shakespeare than about any other literary figure. The <u>daily</u> rate of production varies from 1.5 to 8.8 articles/books, depending on which bibliography one uses for a point of reference. The <u>MLA International Bibliography</u>, for example, includes 5,038 Shakespeare items during the past decade, 586 for 1983 alone. The more inclusive World Shakespeare Bibliography, covering such things as reviews of recently published books, productions, and notices of conferences and colloquia, cites 3,218 entries for 1983; and major plays like <u>Hamlet</u> and <u>King Lear</u> require literally hundreds of entries in each annual listing. For the Shakespeare specialist the task of covering this progressively burgeoning production is overwhelming. For the student and the more eclectic reader or scholar it is virtually impossible. Equally difficult for most--if for no other reason than the time required--is the selection of the most significant material from the hundreds of thousands of pages that each year appear in specialized journals, newspapers, and books both from university presses and commercial printing houses.

While this volume cannot address the difficulties of currency or inclusiveness, it does aim to provide a convenient and annotated checklist of the most important criticism on Shakespeare in the twentieth century. Obviously, any project limited to around fifteen hundred entries cannot pretend to include every item of merit; just as obviously one person's list of inclusions will differ in some detail from another's. The effort to cover the entire canon, moreover, imposes certain restrictions on the number of entries for any individual title or phase of the playwright's work. So, too, does the need to limit the number of books dealing with Shakespeare in broad and general terms in favor of a representative number of articles and chapters addressing individual plays, issues, or characters in order to make the bibliography as helpful as possible for users interested in investigating particular ideas in a given play or poem. In a word, this bibliography attempts to address the needs and interests both of the casual reader and the student with a specific and limited agenda. The entries as a body represent what is generally accepted as essential Shakespearean scholarship, and the annotations are developed in a manner that clearly reflects the content in

sufficient detail to provide helpful guidance for more selective
reading. Cross-references within the annotations focus on particular
matters of agreement or disagreement among critics or guide the user
to significant parallel studies, and a list of references at the end
of a category or an individual work provides convenient access to
additional titles of related interest.

The material of the bibliography is organized in a relatively
simple and straightforward manner. A major section on general studies is subdivided into the categories of greatest importance and
interest--reference works, editions of the entire or major portions
of the canon, biographies, history of criticism, dating and textual
studies, generalized source studies, investigations of Shakespeare's
language and style, discussions of the Elizabethan stage and of the
stage history of Shakespearean productions and of the artistic development of Shakespeare on film, and a lengthy number of thematic and
topical studies. By design, however, the chief focus is on the individual works--arranged under poems and the sonnets, the English histories, the comedies, the tragedies, and the romances. Each of these
divisions includes a selected group of general studies followed by
the individual titles and, for each, specific reference works, significant individual editions, critical studies of the individual
work, and (for the plays) studies of the stage history.

The sections on critical studies of the individual works are
intentionally reflective of the larger body of criticism they represent, both in quantity and in the variety of critical approaches.
That for _Hamlet_ there are ninety-two items and for _The Two Gentlemen
of Verona_ there are thirteen, for example, is not an inaccurate reflection of general critical interest and activity. Moreover, while
the items representing an individual work have been chosen, first and
foremost, for their significance, they at the same time are reasonably representative of the diversity of critical opinion and method-
ology. The _Hamlet_ section, for instance, features those critics
approaching the play through its language, whether the rhetoric
(Maurice Charney--entry 1073, Madeleine Doran--entry 1078), the
dramatic imagery (Alan Dessen--entry 1077), the iconographic associations (Roland Frye--entries 1087-88, Bridget Gellert Lyons--entry
1112); those critics with psychoanalytic concerns (Avi Erlich--entry
1083, Ernest Jones--entry 1098); those who insist that the historical
context provides a key for analysis, whether in the matter of Elizabethan pneumatology and the nature of the ghost (Robert West-entries
133-34, Geoffrey Hughes--entry 1095, Eleanor Prosser--entry 1122) or
those concerned with the play as reflective of the profound philosophic transition occurring during the Renaissance (Maynard Mack--
entry 1116, Walter King--entry 1101, Francis Fergusson--entry 1084,
Ruth Levitsky--entry 1108); those who focus on structural features of
the play, whether its metadramatic qualities (James Calderwood--
entry 1071, P.J. Aldus--entry 1065, Thomas Van Laan--entry 1135) or
its relationship to conventions of popular revenge tragedy (Fredson
Bowers--entry 1070, Charles and Elaine Hallett--entry 1092); those

who view the play as fundamentally reflective of Christian precepts (Roy Battenhouse--entry 1069, Sister Miriam Joseph--entry 1119, S.F. Johnson--entry 1097); those whose interest is in the developing Hamlet saga (Kemp Malone--entry 1118, William Hansen--entry 1094); those who focus on textual matters, whether the first quarto is corrupt (G.I. Duthie--entry 1062), for example, or sound (Albert Weiner--entry 1060). In pursuing any investigation of critical method or concern with particular issues or structural components of the play, one should be mindful of those studies cited by entry number at the end of the division that, by virtue of their larger focus, have been relegated to the section on general thematic and topical studies or the section of general studies of the particular genre.

Since the principal aim of this bibliography is to identify the specific essays and books of greatest significance and since limitations of space are so critical, I have not included, as individual entries, collections of essays such as Prentice-Hall's Twentieth Century Interpretations series (for instance, Ronald Berman's on Henry V, Hallett Smith's on The Tempest, Walter Davis's on Much Ado About Nothing, David Young's on 2 Henry IV, Jay Halio's on As You Like It, Walter King's on Twelfth Night, Mark Rose's on Antony and Cleopatra, Terence Hawkes's on Macbeth), Crowell's Casebook series (for instance, Gerald Willen's and Victor Reed's on the sonnets, Leonard Dean's on Othello), Heath's Discussions of Literature series (for instance, J.C. Levenson's on Hamlet, Robert Ornstein's on the problem comedies, R.J. Dorius's on the histories, Maurice Charney's on the Roman plays, Herbert Weil's on the romantic comedies), the Norton Critical Edition series (for instance, Cyrus Hoy's on Hamlet, James Sanderson's on 1 Henry IV), Scribner's Research Anthology series (for instance, Julian Markel's on Julius Caesar), Houghton Mifflin's Research Series (for instance, Rolf Soellner and Samuel Bertsche's on Measure for Measure), or individual collections like Laurence Lerner's on the comedies and on the tragedies for Penguin, Helmut Bonheim's on King Lear for Wadsworth, Clair Sacks and Edgar Wahn's on Hamlet for Appleton-Century-Crofts, Russell Leavenworth's on Hamlet for Chandler, Leonard Dean and James McPeek's on Twelfth Night for Allyn and Bacon, Leonard Dean's on modern essays for Oxford, or Clifford Leech's on the tragedies for Chicago. The list is only a small sampling of the numerous reprint materials and study guides available on Shakespeare, and I cite them (and selected reprint information in the entries themselves) merely as reflective of this larger body of material. Any attempt to include information on every reprint of an article--with some appearing in four of five locations--or to indicate extensive reprint information on book-length studies would severely limit the space available for annotated entries and, since such information is readily available in libraries, would serve no particular need. Limitations of space also permit no attempt here to trace the major developments in Shakespearean criticism, but various entries indicate the availability of such studies (Augustus Ralli--entry 67, D. Nichol Smith--entries 70, 71, Arthur Eastman--entry 64, Paul Siegel--entry 69, Paul Conklin--entry 1074,

Terence Hawkes--entry 65, Raymond Powell--entry 66, T.M. Raysor--
entry 68, the introductions to the Garland Shakespeare Bibliogra-
phies--entries 461, 482, 658, 694, 1058, 1174, 1420.

    This bibliography, more specifically, annotates the most sig-
nificant items of Shakespeare scholarship from 1900 through 1984.
The individual plays and poems are arranged alphabetically, as are
the entries within each of the subsequent categories. The material
has been indexed by both author and subject; the bulkiness resulting
from duplication of entries in this instance seems far less important
than the attempt to provide reasonably convenient access for the wide
variety of readers who may find this bibliography useful. While
numerous individual bibliographies have been consulted, I have
been primarily dependent on the annual listings in the World Shakespeare Bibliography (Shakespeare Quarterly), in the MLA International
Bibliography, in Shakespeare Jahrbuch (Weimar and Heidelberg), and in
the Modern Humanities Research Association Annual Bibliography of
English Language and Literature. The entries in this study are limited to works published in English and to those works that should be
reasonably accessible in most libraries, either directly or through
interlibrary loan. I am grateful to Garland Publishing for permis-
sion to reprint, with appropriate modifications, many of the Lear
items from my "King Lear": An Annotated Bibliography (entry 1174).

    A project of this nature would simply be impossible without the
cooperation and support of numerous individuals, and I would be un-
grateful beyond measure were I not to thank those who have helped me
along the way. I am pleased to record my genuine appreciation to
Ann Smith, Margaret Sugg, Peggy Cole, and Bonnie Baker, members of
the staff at the library of North Carolina State University who were
instrumental in locating books and materials both efficiently and
courteously. I appreciate, as well, support from the Department of
English in the form of a semester of release from teaching duties so
that I might bring this project to fruition. Above all, I am grateful to my wife Nancy and son Stephen, whose patience and encourage-
ment (to say nothing of the card filing, alphabetizing, and proofing)
were especially valuable during those moments when the task seemed
indeed endless.

Larry S. Champion
North Carolina State University
Raleigh, North Carolina
May 1985

I. General Studies

REFERENCE WORKS

1   ALEXANDER, MARGUERITE. Shakespeare and His Contemporaries:
     A Reader's Guide. London: Heinemann; New York: Barnes &
     Noble, 1979, 386 pp.
         Provides a plot summary and a synopsis of critical commen-
     tary for each of Shakespeare's plays and poems, in addition to
     brief essays on comedy, dark comedy, poetry, the English history
     play, the Roman history play, tragedy, romance, and Shakespeare
     and his critics. Also discusses twelve major Elizabethan-Jacobean
     tragedies (Norton and Sackville, Kyd, Marlowe, Tourneur, Webster,
     Ford) and five comedies (Jonson, Beaumont and Fletcher).

2   BARTLETT, HENRIETTA C., and POLLARD, ALFRED W. A Census of
     Shakespeare's Plays in Quarto, 1594-1709. Rev. and extended
     ed. London: H. Milford; New Haven: Yale University Press,
     1939, 165 pp.
         Describes the 144 extant copies of Shakespeare's quartos
     ranging from a single copy of Titus Andronicus (1594) to thirteen
     copies of Othello (1622). The introductory essay provides an
     analytic history of the quarto publications, distinguishing be-
     tween the good and bad quarto texts. In the body of the study
     the plays are arranged alphabetically, and each copy is closely
     described as to location, size, condition, binding, and pressmark.

3   DORSCH, T.S. "William Shakespeare." In The New Cambridge
     Bibliography of English Literature. Edited by George Watson.
     Vol. 1, 600-1660. Cambridge: Cambridge University Press,
     1974, columns 1473-1636.
         Lists books and selected articles in Shakespearean scholar-
     ship under the following categories: general bibliographies,
     concordances, glossaries, dictionaries; Shakespeare societies and
     periodicals; collections; the quarto texts, the plays by indi-
     vidual titles; the poems by individual titles; Shakespeare's
     life; Shakespeare's personality and interests; technical criti-
     cism (sources; influences; transmission of the text; textual
     criticism; language, vocabulary, style, prosody); aesthetic

criticism; Shakespeare's influence; and Shakespeare abroad
(France, Germany, other countries). A rigorous compression of
the material was edited by George Watson in "William Shakespeare,"
in The Shorter New Cambridge Bibliography of English Literature
(Cambridge: Cambridge University Press, 1981), pp. 199-224.

4   BERGERON, DAVID M. Shakespeare: A Study and Research Guide.
     New York: St. Martin's Press, 1975, 145 pp.
        Projects an overview of the development and present state
of Shakespeare scholarship and the variety of critical approaches.
Part 1 features a discussion of criticism in Shakespeare's time,
in the eighteenth and nineteenth centuries, and in the twentieth
century, Shakespeare in the classroom, critical approaches, historical criticism, genre criticism, language and imagery, character, psychological criticism, thematic and mythic criticism,
textual criticism, major scholars and critics, and the future of
Shakespearean studies. Part 2 features a guide to the resources.
Listings are divided into bibliographies and reference guides,
literary histories, editions, studies in the genres, studies of
groups and movements, interdisciplinary studies, journals, and
biographical studies. Part 3 carries the student step by step
through the preparation of a research paper.

5   BERMAN, RONALD. A Reader's Guide to Shakespeare's Plays.
     Rev. ed. Glenview: Scott, Foresman, 1973, 167 pp.
        Cites some 3,000 books and articles on Shakespeare, with
synoptic comment on many of them. A chapter is devoted to each
play, and the entries are divided into sections on texts, editions, sources, criticism, and staging.

6   CAMPBELL, OSCAR JAMES, ed., and QUINN, EDWARD G., assoc. ed.
     The Reader's Encyclopedia of Shakespeare. New York: Thomas
     Y. Crowell, 1966, 1014 pp.
        Offers essential information on aspects of Shakespeare's
life and works with entries arranged alphabetically. Material
is included on individuals Shakespeare is thought to have known,
on playwrights who influenced him or who have been influenced by
him, on characters from the plays, and on notable actors, critics,
and editors. Comment by well over 100 authors is cited in discussion of the plays themselves. A selected bibliography is also
included.

7   CUNLIFFE, RICHARD JOHN. A New Shakespearean Dictionary.
     London: Gresham Publishing Co., 1922, 346 pp.
        Contains an alphabetical listing of Shakespearean words no
longer current or with meanings that have become obsolete or
archaic. Following each definition is at least one contextual
citation from Shakespeare's plays or poems. Etymologies are
normally not provided.

8   DENT, R.W. Shakespeare's Proverbial Language: An Index.
     Berkeley: University of California Press, 1981, 289 pp.
          Revises and expands the six-page "Shakespeare Index"
     appended to Morris P. Tilley's A Dictionary of Proverbs in
     England in the Sixteenth and Seventeenth Centuries (Ann Arbor:
     University of Michigan Press, 1950). The index itself cites
     4,684 proverbs or proverbial references from the plays and poems
     and is followed by three interrelated appendixes. "A" lists the
     citation for the great majority of references in the index; "B"
     provides for each the Oxford English Dictionary location and
     earliest date; "C" lists all references excluded in "A" and ex-
     plains the reason for the exclusion.

9   EBISCH, WALTER, and SCHÜCKING, LEVIN L. A Shakespeare Bibli-
     ography. Oxford: Clarendon Press, 1931, 294 pp.
          Provides bibliographical listings for all titles "indis-
     pensable for scientific Shakespearean study." The section on
     general studies is divided into categories on bibliography,
     Elizabethan literature, Shakespeare's life, personality, text:
     transmission and emendation, sources, the art of Shakespeare, the
     stage and the production of his plays, literary taste in Shake-
     speare's time, aesthetic criticism, his influence through the
     centuries, civilization in Shakespeare's England, and the
     Shakespeare-Bacon controversy and similar theories. The section
     on the works themselves is divided into categories on the chron-
     ology of the dramas, the individual plays, the poems, and the
     apocrypha. An author index is included. A Supplement for the
     Years 1930-1935 (Oxford: Clarendon Press, 1937), 104 pp. cate-
     gorizes material in similar fashion.

10   No Entry

11   ELTON, WILLIAM R. Shakespeare's World: Renaissance Intel-
     lectual Contexts, 1966-1971. Garland Reference Library of the
     Humanities, 83. New York: Garland Publishing, 1979, 464 pp.
          Emphasizes contextual significances in the interpretation
     of Shakespeare's work. Although covering only a six-year period
     the volume includes almost 3,000 entries. The twenty divisions
     feature such categories as economic-social contexts, educational
     contexts, humanist-classical, iconographical, military, and
     musical. A final section on research tools extends the reader
     beyond the coverage of this single volume.

12   EVANS, GARETH LLOYD, and EVANS, BARBARA. The Shakespeare
     Companion. New York: Charles Scribner's Sons, 1978, 368 pp.
          Features sections on Shakespeare and his times (the bio-
     graphical record), Shakespeare in performance (the stage record
     through the centuries in England and North America), his works
     (commentaries on each of the plays and poems with discussion of
     the printing of the text), and Stratford (the town, Mary Arden's
     house, the birthplace, the grammar school, Anne Hathaway's

cottage, New Place, Nash's house and Hall's Croft, and Holy
Trinity Church). Also included is a review of the achievements
of the major artists who have performed at Stratford.

13   FRYE, ROLAND M. Shakespeare: The Art of the Dramatist. Rev.
      ed. London: George Allen & Unwin, 1982, 271 pp.
         Features, in addition to extensive bibliographical guidance,
sections on Shakespeare's life and work, the types of plays, the
structure, the style, and the characterization. Concerning the
comedies, for example, Frye investigates the atmosphere of optimism, the festive endings, the nonsatiric and genial tone, the
predominance of young lovers and marriage, the background roles
for older characters, the muting of evil, and the green-world
environment. The discussion of "dramatic line" and "time line"
provides a concept of structure that effectively moves beyond
simplistic assumptions of plot summary.

14   GRANVILLE-BARKER, HARLEY, and HARRISON, G.B., eds. A Companion
      to Shakespeare Studies. Cambridge: Cambridge University
      Press, 1934, 390 pp.
         Includes original essays on Shakespeare's life by J.W.
MacKail, the theater and companies by C.J. Sisson, his dramatic
art by Harley Granville-Barker, Shakespeare the poet by George
Rylands, Elizabethan English by G.D. Willcock, music in the plays
by Edward J. Dent, the national background by G.B. Harrison, the
social background by M. St. Clare Byrne, sources by A.L. Atwater,
the drama of Shakespeare's time by Bonamy Dobrée, the text by
A.W. Pollard, criticism by T.S. Eliot and J. Isaacs, and the history of the theater from the Restoration to modern times by Harold
Child. Updated by entry 22.

15   HALLIDAY, F.E. A Shakespeare Companion 1550-1964. Rev. ed.
      New York: Penguin Books, 1964, 565 pp.
         Covers the major aspects of Shakespeare's work and the
individuals who have been significantly associated with it,
whether his contemporaries in the theater, printers and pub-
lishers, or later actors, editors, and critics. The material,
with entries arranged alphabetically, falls into three general
areas--Shakespeare's life and his most important associates; his
works, considered as manuscripts and as printed books and their
history; the theater, both the physical stages and the acting
history of the plays.

16   HARBAGE, ALFRED. William Shakespeare: A Reader's Guide.
      New York: Noonday Press, 1963, 498 pp.
         Includes a chapter on dramatic components followed by units
on each of Shakespeare's three major periods--1587-96, 1597-1606,
and 1607-13. Each unit describes Shakespeare's development in
general terms and provides brief surveys of the plays that comprise the period. Additionally, a separate section is devoted to
the four major tragedies. Attention is focused on language,

versification, prose style, implied stage business, developing
characterizations, significant juxtapositions, structural devices, and details of technique.

17   JAGGARD, WILLIAM. Shakespeare Bibliography: A Dictionary of
      Every Known Issue of the Writings of the Poet and of Recorded
      Opinion Thereon in the English Language. New York:
      Frederick Ungar, 1911, 729 pp.
           Describes itself as "an encyclopedia of Shakespearean in-
      formation and stage history" (p. xviii). In fact, it is a cumula-
      tive, partially annotated, catalog of what at the time were the
      world's twelve largest Shakespeare libraries, containing over
      36,000 entries and references. The material is presented alpha-
      betically without division and covers publications and commentary
      to 1909. Editions of the plays and poems are alphabetically
      arranged under "Shakespeare." The absence of a subject index
      sorely hampers the book's use as a research tool for a particular
      play or topic.

18   KOKERITZ, HELGE. Shakespeare's Names: A Pronouncing Dic-
      tionary. New Haven: Yale University Press, 1959, 100 pp.
           Features all proper names in Shakespeare's works, arranged
      alphabetically and through phonetic transcription indicating the
      proper English, American, and Elizabethan pronunciation, along
      with the metrical and phonological variants required by Shake-
      speare's rhythm. The work serves as a supplement to Shake-
      speare's Pronunciation (see entry 19).

19   _____. Shakespeare's Pronunciation. New Haven: Yale Uni-
      versity Press, 1953, 516 pp.
           Aims to present the student of Shakespeare a comprehensive
      account of the playwright's pronunciation along with relevant
      phonological evidence. Such knowledge of the three basic ele-
      ments of speech--vowels, consonants, stress--can be used to
      attack a wide range of textual and prosodic problems. Section
      one describes the linguistic situation in Shakespeare's England
      and describes the orthoepistic, orthographic, metrical, and rime
      evidence; section two discusses Shakespeare's homonymic puns; and
      section three presents the main body of material, the analysis of
      stressed vowels and dipthongs, of unstressed vowels, of conso-
      nants, of stress, and phonetic transcriptions of various Shake-
      spearean passages. (See also entries 18, 23, and 154.)

20   McMANAWAY, JAMES G., and ROBERTS, JEANNE A. A Selective
      Bibliography of Shakespeare: Editions, Textual Studies, Com-
      mentary. Charlottesville: University Press of Virginia (for
      the Folger Shakespeare Library), 1975, 309 pp.
           Includes 4,519 entries, with major emphasis on works since
      1930 and, with few exceptions, a cutoff date of 1970. All items,
      without annotation, are arranged alphabetically within the major
      categories of general reference works, bibliographies,

dictionaries and concordances, textual studies and critical
bibliography, special collections, biographies, and the individual works. In addition to the commentaries, the section on the
individual play or poem includes editions, adaptations, prompt-
books, and translations.

21   METZ, G. HAROLD, comp. Four Plays Ascribed to Shakespeare:
      "The Reign of King Edward III," "Sir Thomas More," "The History
      of Cardenio," "The Two Noble Kinsmen": An Annotated Bibliog-
      raphy. Garland Shakespeare Bibliographies, 2. New York:
      Garland Publishing, 1982, 193 pp.
          Contains 208 entries representing virtually all publica-
      tions on the plays from 1940 through 1980--books, chapters, arti-
      cles, reviews, and notices of stage productions, along with the
      most significant scholarship prior to 1940. The categories for
      each play are criticism, dates, sources, and texts and editions.

22   MUIR, KENNETH, and SCHOENBAUM, SAMUEL, eds. A New Companion
      to Shakespeare Studies. Cambridge: Cambridge University
      Press, 1971, 298 pp.
          Features original essays on Shakespeare's life (Samuel
      Schoenbaum), the playhouses and stage (Richard Hosley), the
      actors and staging (Daniel Seltzer), Shakespeare's reading (G.K.
      Hunter), Elizabethan English (Randolph Quirk), rhetoric (Brian
      Vickers), Shakespeare's poetry (Inga-Stina Ewbank), the narrative
      poems (J.W. Lever), the early plays (David Bevington), the late
      plays (Muriel C. Bradbrook), music (F.W. Sternfeld), the social
      background (Joel Hurstfield), the intellectual background (W.R.
      Elton), stage history (A.C. Sprague), the drama of Shakespeare's
      time (Peter Ure), Shakespeare's text (G.B. Evans), and Shake-
      spearean criticism (M.A. Shaaber and Stanley Wells). Update of
      entry 14.

23   ONIONS, C.T. A Shakespeare Glossary. Oxford: Clarendon
      Press, 1911, 264 pp.
          Aims to provide definitions of words in Shakespeare's
      canon now obsolete or surviving only in provincial or archaic
      use. An outgrowth of the analysis of Shakespeare's vocabulary
      conducted in the preparation of the Oxford English Dictionary,
      the work also supplies explanations of idiomatic usage, of words
      involving unfamiliar allusions, and of proper names with conno-
      tative significance. Some current words are included, primarily
      where there is textual obscurity or multiple ramifications of
      meaning. (See also entries 19, 154.)

24   PARROTT, THOMAS MARC. William Shakespeare: A Handbook. New
      York: Charles Scribner's Sons, 1934, 266 pp.
          Provides a narrative, interpretative account of Shake-
      speare's life as a playwright and actor and of his achievements
      in drama and poetry. Sections are included on his environment
      and family, his London years, his company and audience, his place

in the development of English drama, the textual problem, editors
and editions, a synopsis of Shakespeare criticism, and Shakespeare on the stage. Also includes a chronological table and
bibliography.

25   QUINN, EDWARD G.; RUOFF, JAMES; and GRENNEN, JOSEPH. The
      Major Shakespearean Tragedies: A Critical Bibliography. New
      York: Free Press, 1973, 293 pp.
          Provides a summary of major critical evaluations of Hamlet
      (101 items), Othello (153 items), King Lear (80 items), and
      Macbeth (82 items). An introductory essay for each play describes
      the significant approaches and places them in a chronological con-
      text. The annotated entries are also arranged chronologically,
      covering from the writing of the play to 1972. The material for
      each tragedy is divided under criticism, sources and date,
      textual criticism, editions, and staging.

26   SMITH, GORDON ROSS. A Classified Shakespeare Bibliography,
      1936–1958. University Park: Pennsylvania State University
      Press, 1963, 784 pp.
          Cites 20,527 items covering all aspects of Shakespearean
      scholarship that would appear in standard bibliographies. The
      work is divided into two basic sections, one on general items and
      one on the individual plays and poems. The latter in each case
      is subdivided under text, literary genesis, language, general
      criticism, characterization, miscellaneous, and history. The
      general section includes subdivisions on bibliographies, surveys
      of scholarship, Shakespeare's life and personality, textual stud-
      ies, sources, his art (language, vocabulary, prosody, style), his
      dramatic art, his stage and the production of his plays, Eliza-
      bethan literary taste, aesthetic criticism, his influence through
      the centuries, the modern stage, and the authorship controversy.

27   SPEVACK, MARVIN. A Complete and Systematic Concordance to the
      Works of Shakespeare. 9 vols. Hildesheim: Georg Olms Ver-
      lagsbuchhandlung, 1968–80, 11302 pp.
          Provides a comprehensive index to Shakespeare's vocabulary
      in a computer-generated word list. Volumes 1–3 comprise a series
      of interlocking concordances to the individual dramas and charac-
      ters for the most part in the order of appearance in the folio,
      with general statistical information at the beginning of each
      play. Volumes 4–6 comprise a concordance of the complete works;
      and volumes 7–9, a concordance of additional specialized mate-
      rials--the stage directions and speech prefixes, the bad quartos,
      and substantive variants. (See entry 28.)

28   _____. The Harvard Concordance to Shakespeare. Cambridge,
      Mass.: Belknap Press, Harvard University Press, 1973,
      1600 pp.
          Represents in substance if not in format volumes 4–6 of
      Spevack's A Complete and Systematic Concordance to the Works of

Shakespeare (see entry 28). This single volume locates each
appearance of the more than 29,000 different words used by
Shakespeare, along with information on the frequency of each
word, identification of the passage as prose or verse, and cross-
references. (See entry 27.)

29   STOKES, FRANCIS GRIFFIN. A Dictionary of the Characters and
     Proper Names in the Works of Shakespeare. London: George C.
     Harrap, 1924, 360 pp.
          Consists of annotations, arranged alphabetically, of every
     proper name that appears in the First Folio, Pericles, and the
     poems attributed to Shakespeare. The subjects included are char-
     acters from medieval history, Greek and Roman historical and
     legendary characters, purely fictitious characters, persons
     alluded to or mentioned but not appearing in the dramatis per-
     sonae, place names, and miscellaneous subjects such as festivals,
     seasons, planets, and the titles of books and songs.

30   SUGDEN, EDWARD H. A Topographical Dictionary to the Works of
     Shakespeare and His Fellow Dramatists. London and New York:
     Longmans, Green; Manchester: Manchester University Press,
     1925, 580 pp.
          Provides information on all place names in Shakespeare's
     poems and plays, in the work of other English playwrights to
     1660, and in Milton's works. The entry "East Cheap," for exam-
     ple, after indicating the precise location in London, traces each
     reference through the Henry IV plays, citing as well references
     in The Famous Victories of Henry V and in plays by Lydgate,
     Jonson, Dekker, Thomas Heywood, and Wager.

For handbooks, see entries 1, 4-6, 12-16, 22, 24; for bibliographies,
see entries 3, 9-10, 17, 20, 25-26, 94, 107; for dictionaries, see
entries 7, 23, 27-28, 30; for the history of Shakespearean criticism,
see entries 64, 67, 69, 70-71; for foreign sources, see entries 94,
102, 104-5, 107.

COLLECTED EDITIONS

31   ALEXANDER, PETER, ed. William Shakespeare: The Complete
     Works. London: William Collins Sons, 1951, 1376 pp.
          Includes, without introductions, the thirty-seven plays,
     along with the poems and a transcript of Shakespeare's contribu-
     tion to Sir Thomas More. The introductions to the individual
     plays may be found in Introductions to Shakespeare (see entry
     195). The general introduction describes Shakespeare's early
     life in Stratford and traces him in London through four periods
     of his active work as a playwright. A brief discussion of the
     folio and quarto publications is also included, as are reprints
     of the preliminary materials of the First Folio and a glossary.

32   BARNET, SYLVAN, ed. <u>The Complete Signet Classic Shakespeare.</u>
      New York: Harcourt Brace Jovanovich, 1972, 1776 pp.
          Features in a single volume the material that appeared in
      forty volumes between 1963 and 1968. Critical and textual intro-
      ductions are provided by individual editors for each play, the
      sonnets, and the nondramatic poems. The arrangement is generally
      chronological, and an extensive reading list is divided into
      thirteen categories. The general editor offers introductory com-
      ments on Shakespeare's life, the canon, the theaters and actors,
      the dramatic background, style and structure, Shakespeare's
      English, his intellectual background, the texts, Shakespeare's
      comedies, histories, and tragedies.

33   BEVINGTON, DAVID, ed. <u>The Complete Works of Shakespeare.</u>
      3d ed. Glenview, Ill.: Scott Foresman, 1980, 1745 pp.
          Abandons Craig's practice of chronological arrangement
      (entry 36) in favor of grouping by comedies, histories, trage-
      dies, and romances. The text has been completely reset, with
      spelling modernized and speech prefixes normalized and expanded.
      In addition to interpretative introductions to each of the plays,
      a general introduction covers life in Shakespeare's England, the
      drama before Shakespeare, London theaters and companies, Shake-
      speare's life and work, his language, editions and editors, and a
      survey of criticism. Appendixes include material on the canon,
      sources, doubtful and lost plays, a glossary, and a selective
      bibliography.

34   BROOKE, C.F. TUCKER, ed. <u>The Shakespeare Apocrypha: Being</u>
      <u>a Collection of Fourteen Plays Which Have Been Ascribed to</u>
      <u>Shakespeare.</u> Oxford: Clarendon Press, 1918, 456 pp.
          Considers the doubtful plays in general, the history of
      their ascription, and compares them in theme, style, and drama-
      turgic technique with those plays accepted as genuine. Specific
      comments are then provided on each of the apocryphal works, fol-
      lowed by the full text of <u>Arden of Feversahm</u>, <u>Locrine</u>, <u>Edward III</u>,
      <u>Mucedorus</u>, <u>Sir John Oldcastle</u>, <u>Thomas Lord Cromwell</u>, <u>The Puritan</u>,
      <u>A Yorkshire Tragedy</u>, <u>The Merry Devil of Edmonton</u>, <u>Fair Em</u>, <u>The</u>
      <u>Two Noble Kinsmen</u>, <u>The Birth of Merlin</u>, and <u>Sir Thomas More</u>.

35   CAMPBELL, OSCAR JAMES, ed. <u>The Living Shakespeare: Twenty-</u>
      <u>Two Plays and the Sonnets.</u> New York: Macmillan, 1949,
      1239 pp.
          Aims at readability and contemporaneity in moving the
      reader in the introductions to each play directly to matters of
      interpretation. Discussions of text, sources, date, and stage
      history are relegated to a position of secondary importance.
      The general introduction carries information on Shakespeare's
      youth and his professional career, Elizabethan London, pre-
      Shakespearean drama, the stage, Shakespeare's company, his text,
      and a chronological table. Included are the major comedies, his-
      tories, and tragedies, with the text based on that of the Globe
      Shakespeare.

36   CRAIG, HARDIN, ed. The Complete Works of Shakespeare.
      Chicago: Scott, Foresman, 1951, 1337 pp.
           Provides an extensive introduction covering life in Shake-
      speare's England, pre-Shakespearean drama, London theaters and
      acting companies, the order of the plays and Shakespeare's dra-
      matic development, editions and editors, actors, Shakespeare's
      English, and the doubtful and lost plays. The arrangement of the
      material is chronological within genres, and a separate intro-
      duction for each play or poem is concerned with the specific na-
      ture of the copy text, the publication record, the date, the
      sources, the dramatic techniques, and the stage history. A re-
      vised edition, updated by David Bevington, was published by Scott,
      Foresman in 1973. (See also entry 33.)

37   EVANS, G. BLAKEMORE, ed. The Riverside Shakespeare. Boston:
      Houghton Mifflin, 1974, 1902 pp.
           Features an introduction to Shakespeare's life and to major
      critical opinions and salient existing problems by Harry Levin,
      an essay on the plays in performance since 1660 by Charles
      Shattuck, and a discussion of the text and a glossary of biblio-
      graphical terms by G. Blakemore Evans. A note at the end of each
      work explains the basis for selecting the copy text and lists all
      textual variants among quarto and folio publications. Introduc-
      tions to the comedies are provided by Anne [Righter] Barton, to
      the histories by Herschel Baker, to the romances and poems by
      Hallett Smith, and to the tragedies by Frank Kermode. A unique
      feature, Annals 1552-1616, lists in parallel columns year by
      year principal data concerning historical events, Shakespeare,
      theater history, and nondramatic literature.

38   HARBAGE, ALFRED, ed. William Shakespeare: The Complete
      Works. Baltimore: Penguin Books, 1969, 1481 pp.
           Prints in a single volume the Pelican edition of the plays
      and poems that originally appeared in thirty-eight volumes be-
      tween 1956 and 1967. Introductory material is provided on
      Shakespeare's intellectual and political background (Ernest
      Strathmann), his life and canon (Frank Wadsworth), his theater
      (Bernard Beckerman), his technique (Alfred Harbage), and his
      original texts (Cyrus Hoy). The material itself is divided into
      comedies, histories, tragedies, romances, and the nondramatic
      poetry. Each title represents the work of an individual editor,
      who also provides a critical introduction.

39   HARRISON, G.B., ed. Shakespeare: The Complete Works. New
      York: Harcourt, Brace & World, 1948, 1666 pp.
           Features sections on the universality of Shakespeare,
      records of his life, the nature of his age and of Elizabethan
      drama, the Elizabethan playhouse, textual problems, the develop-
      ment of his art, the major eighteenth- and nineteenth-century
      critics, and Shakespearean scholarship in this century. Separate
      introductions to each play address salient critical points and

the nature of the copy text for the particular work. Appendixes
include both a reading list and a discussion of the great variety
of Elizabethan beliefs and traditions.

40   HINMAN, CHARLTON, ed. The First Folio of Shakespeare. New
     York: W.W. Norton, 1968, 928 pp.
     Reproduces a facsimile text from the corrected sheets of
the First Folio. The corrected sheets were determined through a
collation of the copies of the folio in the Folger Shakespeare
Library. Included are an introduction (the value and authority
of the First Folio, the printing and proofing, the facsimile) and
two appendixes (on the variant states of the folio text and on
the Folger copies used).

41   KOKERITZ, HELGE, and PROUTY, CHARLES T., eds. Mr. William
     Shakespeare's Comedies, Histories, and Tragedies. New Haven:
     Yale University Press, 1954, 889 pp.
     Features a preface by Kokeritz citing the copy text and
explaining the reduction in size, an introduction by Prouty describing the nature and quality of the extant folios, and the
general printing conditions of Shakespeare's day, and a facsimile
edition of the First Folio.

42   NEILSON, WILLIAM ALLAN, and HILL, CHARLES JARVIS, eds. The
     Complete Plays and Poems of William Shakespeare. Cambridge,
     Mass.: Houghton Mifflin, 1942, 1120 pp.
     Includes the complete text of Shakespeare's plays and
poems, divided by genre and arranged chronologically. A general
introduction features sections on Shakespeare's life, the chronology of the canon, Shakespeare's opportunities, and his achievements. A critical introduction to each play covers matters of
text, date, sources, and interpretation; notes are supplied
throughout the text. An index to the characters in the plays
concludes the volume.

43   RIBNER, IRVING, and KITTREDGE, GEORGE LYMAN, eds. The Com-
     plete Works of Shakespeare. Rev. ed. Waltham, Mass.: Ginn,
     1971, 1743 pp.
     Comprises a revision of Kittredge's 1936 edition, incorpo-
rating advances in the knowledge of Shakespeare's text, of dates,
sources, and general historical background. Kittredge's text and
many of his notes remain, though the general introduction and the
critical introduction to each play have been written anew by
Ribner. The introduction features discussion of Shakespeare and
the English Renaissance, his life, life in Elizabethan England,
the English drama before Shakespeare, Elizabethan theaters and
companies, the publication of the plays, a general survey of
criticism, a survey of plays in performance, and a bibliography.

BIOGRAPHIES

44   ADAMS, JOSEPH QUINCY. A Life of William Shakespeare. Boston
      and New York: Houghton Mifflin, 1925, 561 pp.
          Attempts, through the use of the wealth of biographical
      detail that became available in the late nineteenth and early
      twentieth century, to picture Shakespeare against a background of
      contemporary theatrical life--as a busy actor, a hired playwright,
      a theatrical proprietor--while avoiding needless contention on
      points that cannot be settled and on the numerous flights of bio-
      graphical speculation. The last four of thirty chapters deal
      with the nature of theatrical manuscripts, the quartos of Shake-
      speare's plays, the attempted collection in 1619, and the folio
      in 1623.

45   ALEXANDER, PETER. Shakespeare's Life and Art. New York: New
      York University Press, 1961, 247 pp.
          Provides a critical and biographical account of Shake-
      speare's life and work, with discussion of the plays and poems
      framed by chapters on his birth and youth in Stratford and on his
      retirement years. The critical analysis is divided chronologi-
      cally into four sections: (1) from Shakespeare's arrival in
      London to his joining the Lord Chamberlain's Men in 1594, (2) from
      his association with Chamberlain's Men to the opening of the Globe
      in 1599, (3) from the Globe to the access to the Blackfriar's
      Theatre in 1608, and (4) from the opening of Blackfriars to the
      burning of the Globe in 1613.

46   BENTLEY, GERALD EADES. Shakespeare: A Biographical Handbook.
      New Haven: Yale University Press, 1961, 256 pp.
          Depicts Shakespeare's life and artistic methods through the
      more than one hundred surviving Shakespearean documents. Follow-
      ing a description of the manner in which late seventeenth- and
      early eighteenth-century legends accrued detail by detail as they
      hardened into accepted fact and a discussion of the anti-
      Stratfordians, the study addresses the various phases of Shake-
      speare's professional career--the actor, the playwright, the non-
      dramatic poet, his relationship with printers, and the contempo-
      rary publication of his poems and plays. Included, as well, is
      a selective bibliography and a list of contemporary documents and
      books utilized in the preparation of the biography.

47   CHAMBERS, EDMUND KERCHEVER. William Shakespeare: A Study of
      Facts and Problems. 2 vols. Oxford: Clarendon Press, 1930,
      1024 pp.
          Includes in volume 1 a biographical and textual study of
      Shakespeare covering his origin, the stage in 1592, his company
      of players, the book of the play, the quartos and First Folio,
      plays in the printing house, the problem of authenticity, the
      problem of chronology, and the plays of the First Folio. The
      last section provides a separate description of the publishing

history of each play and the poems and sonnets, noting the
Stationers' Register entry, full head titles and running titles,
the printer and the publisher, reprints and modern editions,
along with a discussion of the principal textual characteristics
and a survey of textual scholarship. Volume 2 reprints all offi-
cial contemporary documents relating to Shakespeare, all known
contemporary allusions, materials documenting the development of
the "Shakespeare-Mythos" from 1625 to 1862, a record of the performances of the plays from 1588 to 1642, information on the name
Shakespeare and on Shakespearean fabrications, a table of quartos,
and an extensive bibliography. An index is provided by Beatrice
White in An Index to "The Elizabethan Stage" and "William Shakespeare" (Oxford: Oxford University Press, 1934), 161 pp. (See
entry 503.)

48 CHUTE, MARCHETTE. Shakespeare of London. New York: E.P.
    Dutton, 1949, 397 pp.
        Depicts Shakespeare, not as a gigantic and legendary fig-
    ure, but as a mortal man who belonged to the Elizabethan age.
    Focusing on Shakespeare as an actor, playwright, and theatrical
    entrepreneur, the study provides a wealth of detail about the
    country village of Stratford, Shakespeare's parents, his affilia-
    tion with the Lord Chamberlain's Men at the Theatre and the
    Globe, his relationships with fellow playwrights associated both
    with his own and other companies. Appendixes include a review of
    legends about Shakespeare that first became current during the
    Restoration and of the attacks on the authority of the First
    Folio editors that for a time earlier in this century led to a
    disintegration of the canon.

49 ECCLES, MARK. Shakespeare in Warwickshire. Madison: Univer-
    sity of Wisconsin Press, 1961, 182 pp.
        Recreates the life of Shakespeare's immediate environment
    during his Stratford years through the court record of wills,
    lawsuits, property transactions, and miscellaneous letters and
    papers. In addition to providing a kind of social history of a
    prosperous country town, the study traces what is known of
    Shakespeare's ancestors and the career of his father as well as
    details from some of Shakespeare's boyhood neighbors on Henley
    Street. The emphasis throughout is not on legend and inference
    but on the evidence of archival records.

50 FRIPP, EDGAR I. Shakespeare Man and Artist. 2 vols. Oxford:
    Oxford University Press, 1938, 939 pp.
        Provides an inclusive biographical record of Shakespeare
    along with critical analyses of the plays and poems. Volume 1
    focuses on Shakespeare's childhood in Stratford, his joining the
    players in London, his dramatic career through King John and
    Romeo and Juliet, and his purchase of New Place in 1597-98.
    Volume 2, with opening sections on the Henry IV plays and the
    building of the Globe, covers the height of Shakespeare's

romantic comedies, his major tragedies, and the romances. Concluding chapters deal with events following Shakespeare's death--
for example, the Stratford monument, the folio, the family line,
and the development of legends.

51   HALLIDAY, F.E. The Life of Shakespeare. London: Gerald
      Duckworth, 1961, 299 pp.
         Purports to be neither a study of Shakespeare's art nor a
      fanciful reconstruction of his lost years but an attempt to "fill
      in the gaps between the beads of biographical fact with as great
      a degree of probability as possible, yet without resorting to any
      extravagance of speculation" (p. 10). Following an introductory
      sketch of Restoration and eighteenth-century legends, Halliday
      chronologically divides the major sections of his narrative into
      the schoolboy, marriage, London, the Lord Chamberlain's servant,
      the death of Hamnet, the Globe, the man of property, the King's
      servant, a grandchild, and Stratford.

52   LEE, SIDNEY. A Life of William Shakespeare. Rev. ed. New
      York: Macmillan, 1909, 495 pp.
         Provides a turn-of-the-century account of Shakespeare's
      life and the development of his art. Chapters 1-3 and 16 concern
      his life at Stratford, but the major focus is on his London
      years--the London stage, his early dramatic work, the narrative
      poems and sonnets (and the nature of the conceits used in the
      sonnets), the patronage of the Earl of Southampton, the develop-
      ment of dramatic power in the final years of the sixteenth cen-
      tury and the full flowering of maturity in the early seventeenth.
      Final chapters concern portraits, autographs, memorials, and his
      posthumous reputation.

53   QUENNELL, PETER. Shakespeare: A Biography. Cleveland and
      New York: World Publishing, 1963, 352 pp.
         Notes that much factual information exists about Shake-
      speare, whether an attack by a fellow playwright, references to
      his increasing reputation, or allusions to his human qualities.
      When these facts are combined with the evidence provided in his
      plays and our general knowledge of the period, a clear portrait
      emerges. This study happily champions the ambitious Stratfordian
      as the author of the canon, tracing the various phases of his
      work and observing his ability to create onstage literary fig-
      ures who reflect not only his own times but the universal con-
      dition of man.

54   REESE, M.M. Shakespeare: His World and His Work. Rev. ed.
      New York: St. Martin's Press, 1980, 422 pp.
         Provides a full account of Shakespeare's life, age, and
      work through a topical rather than chronological approach. The
      basic divisions are Shakespeare's youth, his predecessors, the
      Elizabethan stage, the man as we know him, and his art. The
      inherited, traditional world picture, in the stages of dry rot

just preceding fragmentation, formed the background for Shakespeare's "artistic meditations about life" (p. 328); the age's
alternating conception of humanity as at one moment an angel,
at another a beast, was particularly well adapted to his dramatic
vision of man.

55   ROWSE, A.L. Shakespeare the Man. New York: Harper & Row,
     1973, 284 pp.
        Proclaims itself as the first three-dimensional biography
of Shakespeare, revealing fully his personal life as recorded in
the sonnets and placing his dramatic works in proper perspective.
The sonnets can be dated 1592-95 with Southampton as the patron
and Marlowe as the rival poet. The dark lady, whose identity was
discovered in the manuscript casebooks of the London astrologer
Simon Foreman, is Emilia Bassano, the daughter of Baptist
Bassano, one of the well-known Italian musicians of the Queen.
Emilia, pregnant by Lord Hundson, the Lord Chamberlain, was
married "for colour" to a minstrel, William Lanier.

56   _____. William Shakespeare: A Biography. New York: Harper
     & Row, 1963, 485 pp.
        Claims with the methodology of historical research to have
solved several basic issues that have confounded literary critics
for countless decades--the problem of the sonnets, the date and
occasion of A Midsummer Night's Dream, the significance of the
Southampton circle to a full understanding of Love's Labor's Lost
and Romeo and Juliet. Divided chronologically into seventeen
sections moving from "Elizabethan Warwickshire" to "New Place,"
the account of Shakespeare's life and work also includes numerous
illustrations.

57   SCHELLING, FELIX E. Shakespeare Biography. Philadelphia:
     University of Pennsylvania Press, 1937, 143 pp.
        Contains essays on the difficulty of writing Shakespeare's
biography as distinguished from collecting facts and dates, on
the characteristic qualities that make him human as compared with
the radical positions of many of his contemporaries, on his contemporaneity and his clear vision and practical wisdom in matters
of the world that know no historical period, on the festive
greatness of Elizabethan England and of Shakespeare's confrontation with the Puritans, and on the Shakespeare collection in the
H.H. Furness Memorial Library.

58   SCHOENBAUM, SAMUEL. Shakespeare's Lives. Oxford: Clarendon
     Press, 1970, 838 pp.
        Presents both a biographical account of Shakespeare and a
history of the efforts to construct Shakespeare's biography from
the seventeenth century to the present. The material is divided
into seven major sections--materials for a life, Shakespeare of
the legends, the first biographers, Edmond Malone, the earlier
nineteenth century, the Victorians, deviations, and the twentieth

century. The first section includes specific descriptions of the
Janssen monument and the Droeshout engraving along with sections
on Shakespeare's childhood, his London years, his reputation, and
the canon. Of special interest is the comprehensive account of
the various Shakespeare claimants, especially of Delia Bacon's
assertion of Francis Bacon's authorship and of her nocturnal
visit to Shakespeare's tomb in 1856, convinced that the hiero-
glyphics of Bacon's letters contained minute instructions for
locating a will and other relics in a hollow space beneath the
gravestone.

59 _____. William Shakespeare: A Documentary Life. New York:
   Oxford University Press, 1975, 273 pp.
       Includes a biographical sketch of Shakespeare, along with
reproductions of over 200 documents--records, public tracings in
parish register entries, records of investment, litigation, and
professional activity. Shakespeare's story, both in prose and
in picture, unfolds against the backdrop of Stratford and London.
A compact version of the book was published by the Oxford University Press in 1977. A companion volume, William Shakespeare:
Records and Images (New York: Oxford University Press, 1981),
reproduces and discusses more than 160 additional documents.

60 SPEAIGHT, ROBERT. Shakespeare: The Man and His Achievement.
   New York: Stein & Day, 1977, 384 pp.
       Sets a discussion of each of Shakespeare's poems and plays
within the context of his life on the premise that his works
constitute the best guide to his biography. If his dramas are
not merely veiled accounts of his personal crises or mirrors of
allegorical contemporary events, neither are they written in a
vacuum; and to understand the subject matter, the perspective,
and the level of achievement is in some measure to understand
the man.

61 SPENCER, HAZELTON. The Art and Life of William Shakespeare.
   New York: Harcourt, Brace, 1940, 495 pp.
       Provides a general discussion of Shakespeare's life and the
Elizabethan theater followed by a brief analysis of each play
grouped under experimental comedies, early and later histories,
the four great and last tragedies, the dramatic romances. Forty
illustrations, notes, and an extensive bibliography are also included. The analyses of the plays' structure and theme also de-
scribe productions and actors of special note.

62 WAGENKNECHT, EDWARD. The Personality of Shakespeare.
   Norman: University of Oklahoma Press, 1972, 190 pp.
       Draws from the known facts of his life, the comments of
his contemporaries, and the works themselves to develop a pattern
of Shakespeare's personality. All evidence suggests that he was
a warm and sunny individual but at the same time one who was
reticent of sharing his private life too openly. In general, we

know nothing of Shakespeare that contradicts the impression con-
veyed by the plays--a fundamental normality in psychology and
social perspective, a basic quality of culture and sensitivity,
and a reasonably pious Christian.

63   WILSON, JOHN DOVER. The Essential Shakespeare: A Biographi-
     cal Adventure. Cambridge: Cambridge University Press, 1932,
     148 pp.
         Believes that the essential Shakespeare is to be found in
the relationship to his times, issues, and figures, and in his
spiritual development as it can be traced in his poems and plays.
Following a chapter on Elizabethan social and political conditions are four chapters intermingling biography with analysis of
the plays. The Tempest is envisioned as the capstone of Shakespeare's career, achieving a dramatic and spiritual unity and
reflecting much of Shakespeare in Prospero.

See also entries 110-12, 116, 118, 251, 276, 284, 293.

HISTORY OF CRITICISM

64   EASTMAN, ARTHUR M. A Short History of Shakespearean Criti-
     cism. New York: Random House, 1968, 418 pp.
         Studies the shifting currents of Shakespearean criticism
through major critics reflective of the views of their age and
of various critical methods of interpretation--Johnson, Lessing
and Schlegel, Morgann and Coleridge, Goethe and Lamb and Hazlitt,
Gervinus and Lowell, Dowden and Swinburne and Pater, Shaw and
Tolstoy, Bradley, Bridges and Stoll and Schücking, Harris and
Jones and Lewis, Knight, Murry and Armstrong, Spurgeon and
Clemen, Spencer and Tillyard and Hubler, Granville-Barker and
Harbage and Spivack, Barber and Holloway and Frye, and Sewall.
The method throughout is to provide a framing commentary with
liberal quotations from the critics themselves.

65   HAWKES, TERENCE, ed. Coleridge's Writings on Shakespeare: A
     Selection of the Essays, Notes, and Lectures. New York:
     Capricorn, 1959, 256 pp.
         Aims to provide a fair and accurate text of Coleridge's
Shakespearean criticism, to overcome the occasional diffuseness
by a reasonable and usable kind of order, to achieve a measure
of conciseness and thus to be of value to the average student of
Shakespeare. The material is organized into chapters on general
principles regarding poetry and drama, Shakespeare as a poet,
Shakespeare as a dramatist, the individual plays (extensive
treatment for eight, less so for ten others). An essay on
Coleridge as a critic by Alfred Harbage is included. (See
entry 68.)

66   POWELL, RAYMOND. <u>Shakespeare and the Critics' Debate</u>.
      Totowa, N.J.: Rowman & Littlefield, 1980, 167 pp.
          Focuses on the "contradictoriness" of Shakespearean criti-
      cism as a reflection of the inexhaustibility of his plays, briefly
      explaining the concept of various critical approaches, then cate-
      gorizing further discussion under language; topical meanings;
      source, Christian, and impressionistic criticism; ritual, myth,
      and archetype; thematic, structural, and Marxist criticism; and
      twentieth-century (contemporary) criticism. Plays examined in
      detail from this variety of approaches are <u>Love's Labor's Lost</u>,
      <u>Henry IV</u>, and <u>The Tempest</u>; glanced at more briefly are <u>The</u>
      <u>Merchant of Venice</u>, <u>Henry V</u>, <u>Measure for Measure</u>, and <u>Coriolanus</u>.
      The key to the richest criticism is the emphasis on Shakespeare's
      ambiguity.

67   RALLI, AUGUSTUS. <u>A History of Shakespearian Criticism</u>.
      2 vols. Oxford: Oxford University Press, 1148 pp.
          Traces the course of selected criticism on Shakespeare from
      his own time to 1925 in England, France, and Germany. For each
      of the forty-two categories of critics, an introduction describes
      the individuals who comprise the group, their individual methods,
      and the intrinsic worth of their views; a conclusion to each
      section considers those critics as a group to determine the major
      analytic directions. The study is not only a compendium of
      criticism on Shakespeare; it is also a partial aesthetic record
      of the European mind for three centuries.

68   RAYSOR, THOMAS MIDDLETON, ed. <u>Samuel Taylor Coleridge:</u>
      <u>Shakespearean Criticism</u>. 2 vols. London: J.M. Dent & Sons,
      1930, 506 pp.
          Aims to restore from the original manuscripts the exact
      words of Coleridge's Shakespeare criticism, which shortly after
      Coleridge's death was published in garbled form by his nephew.
      The influence of Goethe, Lessing, Schiller, Herder, Richter, and
      Schlegel is described in the introduction, as is Coleridge's
      general defense of the effectiveness of the comic scenes and his
      defense of Shakespeare's violation of the dramatic unities, and
      his psychological analyses of characters. In volume 1 the mate-
      rial is arranged in the first section by plays and in the second
      by topics. Volume 2 focuses on lectures between 1811 and 1819.
      (See entry 65.)

69   SIEGEL, PAUL N., ed. <u>His Infinite Variety: Major Shake-</u>
      <u>spearean Criticism Since Johnson</u>. Philadelphia: J.B.
      Lippincott, 1964, 432 pp.
          Brings together a body of criticism that, although weighted
      toward the modern, reflects Shakespearean criticism since the
      mid-eighteenth century. The selections, while representing all
      historical periods, have been chosen primarily on the basis of
      critical substance. The organization is, accordingly, by sub-
      ject, with part 1 dealing with broad aspects of Shakespeare's

dramatic art. Succeeding portions deal with the various genres--
the history plays, the romantic comedies, the satiric comedies,
the tragedies, the romances. Each section moves from a general
discussion of the genre to treatment of particular plays and
characters. A brief introductory sketch preceding each section
provides an overview of critical trends.

70   SMITH, D. NICHOL, ed. Eighteenth-Century Essays on Shake-
      speare. Glasgow: MacLehose, 1903, 340 pp.
          Provides a survey of eighteenth-century opinion of Shake-
speare by Rowe, Dennis, Pope, Theobald, Hanmer, Warburton,
Johnson, Farmer, and Morgann. The essays represent the chief
critical phase between Dryden and Coleridge. The introduction
analyzes both the salient points of the criticism itself--on such
matters, for example, as the extent of Shakespeare's learning and
his attitudes toward the dramatic unities--and also the critical
methods brought to the editions. The third quarter of the century is described as one of major transition with emphasis on a
return to Shakespeare's text itself and a critical interest in
characterization.

71   _____. Shakespeare Criticism: A Selection. Oxford: Oxford
      University Press, 1916, 416 pp.
          Includes selections representing the major movements in
critical opinion and method from twenty-eight Shakespeare critics
from John Heminge in 1623 to Thomas Carlyle in 1840. The early
criticism consists of poems and comments comprising the prefatory
materials of the First Folio, with the criticism dealing with
principles and merits initiated some years later by Dryden.
Johnson in the mid-eighteenth century provides a summary of major
critical issues, and his judgments are marked by judiciousness
and impartiality. Character criticism begins with Whatley,
Richardson, and Morgann, culminating in the work of Hazlitt and
Carlyle.

72   WILSON, EDWIN, ed. Shaw on Shakespeare: An Anthology of
      Bernard Shaw's Writings on the Plays and Production of Shake-
      speare. New York: E.P. Dutton, 1961, 284 pp.
          Brings together from dozens of widely scattered sources all
of Shaw's significant Shakespearean material. Included are over
twenty reviews of Shakespearean productions along with letters to
Ellen Terry, Mrs. Patrick Campbell, and John Barrymore on the
playing of particular roles in the plays. Matters of acting and
production are also addressed. The material is arranged by plays
in part 1; part 2 deals with aspects of the playwright--his
philosophy, his dramaturgic techniques (weaknesses as well as
skills), and his interpreters.

DATING AND TEXTUAL STUDIES

73   BAYFIELD, M.A. A Study of Shakespeare's Versification: With
      an Inquiry into the Trustworthiness of the Early Texts.
      Cambridge: Cambridge University Press, 1920, 521 pp.
          Argues that the abbreviations found in Shakespeare's verse,
      provoking various kinds of irregularities, are textual corrup-
      tions, as are the abbreviations found in the prose. The contam-
      ination probably originates with the scribe, who wrote down the
      plays from the dictation of a second individual. Textually the
      folio is totally unreliable. The quarto and folio texts of
      several plays are examined at length, and the appendix carries a
      complete text of Antony and Cleopatra revised according to the
      principles of the study.

74   BLACK, MATTHEW W., and SHAABER, MATHIAS A. Shakespeare's
      Seventeenth-Century Editors 1632-1685. New York: Modern
      Language Association of America; London: Oxford University
      Press, 1937, 420 pp.
          Comprises an examination of all variants in the folios of
      1632, 1664, and 1685. Scholars have gradually come to realize
      that, excepting typographical errors, many of the changes in
      these folios are deliberate emendations meant to improve the
      text. The anonymous compositors and correctors engage in both
      acute, intelligent alterations and arbitrary, absurd ones. For
      each folio, analysis covers changes adopted by many or all sub-
      sequent editors, changes that restore the reading of an earlier
      text, superseded changes, intelligible changes not adopted by
      most modern editors, and mistaken and arbitrary changes.

75   BOWERS, FREDSON T. On Editing Shakespeare and the Elizabethan
      Dramatists. Charlottesville: University Press of Virginia,
      1966, 210 pp.
          Asserts that textual editing is one of the significant
      aspects of modern scholarship. For Elizabethan drama the funda-
      mental task is to establish the grounds for establishing the copy
      text--the text that most accurately represents the play as the
      author wrote it. An editor must also determine whether his edi-
      tion is to be facsimile, diplomatic, or eclectic (critical). The
      editor of Shakespeare must make distinctions among foul papers,
      fair copy, prompt copy, transcriptions, and corrupt texts (bad
      quartos); must distinguish, as well, among textual variants in
      equally acceptable texts; and must have an understanding of the
      printing process and of the types of errors to which it is
      subject.

76   BURCKHARDT, ROBERT E. Shakespeare's Bad Quartos: Deliberate
      Abridgments Designed for Performance by a Reduced Cast.
      Studies in English Literature, 101. The Hague: Mouton, 1975,
      124 pp.

Presents a detailed account of the nature of the abridgment in the "bad" quartos--2,3 Henry VI, Romeo and Juliet, Henry V, The Merry Wives of Windsor, and Hamlet. Argues that the texts are not pirated in any fashion. Instead, they have been artistically and effectively shortened to reduce both playing time and the cast. Abridged good quartos for provincial performance by touring companies, these publications are not textually corrupt. (See entries 77, 1061.)

77   CRAIG, HARDIN. A New Look at Shakespeare's Quartos. Stanford: Stanford University Press, 1961, 134 pp.
Attempts through reexamination to simplify the history and classification of the Shakespeare quarto texts prior to the First Folio. In particular, the theory of memorial reconstruction as an explanation for the so-called bad quartos is ingenious but specious. Nor is the theory necessary since normal conditions-- "namely, changes made by actors and managers in the texts of plays when they were acted on the stage" (p. 118)--fully account for alterations in the material. Other outmoded methods of textual criticism are also discussed. (See entries 76, 160.)

78   FEUILLERAT, ALBERT. The Composition of Shakespeare's Plays: Authorship, Chronology. New Haven: Yale University Press, 1953, 340 pp.
Argues, like John Dover Wilson (in the Cambridge introductions to the individual plays), that Shakespeare as a young playwright involved himself in recasting old plays owned by the company. To these works he brought his poetic ability and his interest in character and motivation. The result in 2,3 Henry VI, Titus Andronicus, Richard III, Richard II, and Romeo and Juliet is a series of plays reflecting in their quarto publications visible layers of the old and the new. To Richard III Shakespeare adds flexibility of dialogue; to Titus Andronicus, the sorrows of the old soldier that justify his vengeful action; to Romeo and Juliet, the exaltation of youthful love.

79   GREG, W.W. The Editorial Problem in Shakespeare: A Survey of the Foundations of the Text. Oxford: Clarendon Press, 1942, 210 pp.
Describes in the prolegomena the tenets basic to the study of Shakespeare's text concerning the aim of a critical edition and the significance of distinguishing between substantive and derivative editions in the selection of a copy text. Following a general discussion of the Shakespearean folio and quartos, chapters address the nature and types of theatrical manuscripts (foul papers, fair copy, promptbook, the actor's part, plots or "plats"), the bad quartos (2,3 Henry VI, Romeo and Juliet, Hamlet, The Merry Wives of Windsor, Henry V, The Taming of a Shrew, Pericles) and the theory of memorial reconstruction, two doubtful quartos (Richard III, King Lear), the ten good quartos, and the

First Folio (the Pavier forgeries, assembled texts, massed entries, and the nature of the text for the seventeen plays first printed in the folio of 1623).

80   _____. The Shakespeare First Folio: Its Bibliographical and Textual History. Oxford: Clarendon Press, 1955, 496 pp.
    Describes the planning and printing of Shakespeare's collected dramatic works in 1623. Individual chapters are devoted to those instrumental in the project (Heminge, Condell, Jaggard, Blount, the Lord Chamberlain) and to questions of copyright. The bulk of the volume discusses various editorial problems, both the nature of the copy text for each play and particular problematic features such as stage directions, irregular character designations, and indications of censorship or of contamination. A final chapter focuses on the printing itself--the compositors, the proofreading, the interruptions (involving especially Troilus and Cressida and Timon of Athens), and the standard of accuracy.

81   HART, ALFRED. Stolne and Surreptitious Copies: A Comparative Study of Shakespeare's Bad Quartos. Melbourne: Melbourne University Press, 1942, 478 pp.
    Investigates the problems associated with the bad quartos (the "stolne and surreptitious copies"), concluding that all six are derivative texts. A principal form of evidence is Shakespeare's vocabulary. Each of the bad quartos displays "garbling, petty larceny, solecisms, anacoloutha, irrelevance, vulgarity, fustian, and nonsense" (p. 441). Demonstrates that Shakespeare's version is the prior text and that the text of the bad quarto rests on the oral transmission of what an actor could remember of a part written out by a scribe from the acting version made officially from the author's manuscript.

82   HINMAN, CHARLTON. The Printing and Proof-Reading of the First Folio of Shakespeare. 2 vols. Oxford: Clarendon Press, 1963, 1067 pp.
    Scrutinizes bibliographical evidence concerning the publication of the folio of 1623. Evidence suggests that about one-half of the plays were printed from manuscripts, and not all of them from Shakespeare's holograph. Others were set from earlier quartos and from a combination of materials, part manuscript and part printed. The cardinal aim of this study is to determine the nature of the copy used by the printer for a particular play or poem and the kinds and amount of modification to which the copy was subject during the printing process. Volume 1 surveys the kinds of evidence and their uses; volume 2, the sections of the histories, tragedies, and comedies.

83   HONIGMANN, E.A.J. The Stability of Shakespeare's Text. London: Edward Arnold, 1965, 212 pp.
    Argues that editors have given too little thought to the vagaries of authors copying out their own work and that such

attention in Shakespearean textual study would provoke a fundamental redirection of editorial policy. Whereas the tendency
involving variants in Shakespeare is to assume that one or both
must be corrupt, we must not in the name of a single copy text
rule out the possibility that both may be Shakespeare's, especially where two authoritative texts exist as in Othello and
Troilus or Cressida. A critical edition, by citing all variants
in substantive texts, should make the reader aware of the full
range of textual possiblities.

84   HOWARD-HILL, T.H. Shakespearian Bibliography and Textual
     Criticism: A Bibliography. Oxford: Clarendon Press, 1971,
     pp. 1-177.
          Comprises volume 2 of the seven-volume Index to British
Literary Bibliography. This volume covers both Shakespearean
bibliographies and the literature devoted to the texts of Shakespeare's works, along with the circumstances of their production
and distribution. The 1,981 items are categorized under general
bibliographics and guides (periodicals, cumulative indexes,
serial bibliographies), works (bibliographies, collections and
libraries, general, quartos, folios), and textual studies (hand-
writing and paleography, collected emendations, individual plays
and poems).

85   McKERROW, RONALD B. Prolegomena for the Oxford Shakespeare:
     A Study in Editorial Method. Oxford: Clarendon Press, 1939,
     113 pp.
          Represents a body of rules developed for an old-spelling
edition of Shakespeare that itself never appeared. Individual
chapters are devoted to the basis of the reprint (determination
of the substantive text, derived texts), the degree of exactitude
to be aimed at in reproducing the copy text (orthographical and
grammatical irregularities, critical methods of earlier editors),
and the recording of readings of other editions than the copy
text (variant spellings, collation). Appendixes are included on
typographical abnormalities and the descent of editions, along
with two specimen pages of Shakespeare's text.

86   POLLARD, ALFRED W. Shakespeare's Fight with the Pirates and
     the Problems of the Transmission of His Text. London:
     A. Moring, 1917, 110 pp.
          Describes the process by which Shakespeare's plays were
pirated by journeymen actors hired for minor parts who acted in
conjunction with printers willing to take the risk of running
afoul of the law. Shakespeare's company responded to such
pirates by entering a play in the Stationers' Register so that
no pirate could obtain the copyright to it. Occasionally the
company would authorize a better text. In several instances
plays were sold directly to the printer to forestall piracy.

87   _____. Shakespeare's Folios and Quartos: A Study in the
        Bibliography of Shakespeare's Plays 1594-1685. London:
        Methuen, 1909, 176 pp.
             Refutes Sidney Lee's theory of piracy (entry 268) as the
        cause of textual contamination in virtually all early Shake-
        spearean quartos. The good quartos are not textually corrupt;
        they are regularly entered in the Stationers' Register, and the
        text generally agrees with that of the folio. The bad quartos
        (the first quarto of Romeo and Juliet, the first quarto of
        Hamlet, The Merry Wives of Windsor, Henry V, Pericles) are
        textually contaminated; they are not entered in the Stationers'
        Register or are irregularly entered, and the text differs sub-
        stantially from that of the folio. The bad quartos probably
        result from pirated copy derived from a shorthand transcription.
        Also discussed at some length are the quarto publications of
        1619 and the four folios.

88   ROBERTSON, J.M. The Genuine in Shakespeare. London: George
        Routledge & Sons, 1930, 170 pp.
             Contains a conspectus of the views contained in his multi-
        volume Shakespeare Canon, arguing in general the presence of
        collaboration or alteration in most of Shakespeare's plays. At
        the beginning of his career Shakespeare notes that he invented no
        work in full prior to Venus and Adonis (1593); Heminge and
        Condell did not hesitate to include non-Shakespearean material
        in the First Folio. Shakespeare's hand in 1 Henry VI, for
        example, is denied entirely, and it appears only briefly in
        2 Henry VI. Similarly, he wrote only parts of The Comedy of
        Errors. Individual chapters address the authorship of each play.

89   WALKER, ALICE. Textual Problems of the First Folio:
        "Richard III," "King Lear," "Troilus and Cressida,"
        "2 Henry IV," "Hamlet," "Othello." Cambridge: Cambridge
        University Press, 1953, 170 pp.
             Argues that the folio texts of the plays examined in this
        study were printed from corrected quarto copies. The principle
        is significant in light of the fact that modern editors still
        tend to mix texts in eclectic fashion as if they were independent
        prints. Such an argument generally asserts the quarto is the
        primary text; in King Lear, for instance, the quarto is much
        closer to Shakespeare than the First Folio even though in two
        scenes there is serious memorial contamination. The folio text
        of Hamlet, likewise, is edited, meaning again that the judgment
        and the accuracy of the collator or transcriber come between
        Shakespeare and the reader.

90   WALTON, JAMES KIRKWOOD. The Quarto Copy for the First Folio
        of Shakespeare. Dublin: Dublin University Press, 1971,
        306 pp.
             Investigates the nature of the copy used for the First
        Folio, specifically in cases where a prior good quarto exists--

whether the copy text was quarto or manuscript and the nature of the collation where that occurred. Textual analysis based on the evaluation of substantive readings reveals which quarto served as copy (where there is more than one). It reveals, as well, that a manuscript, not a quarto, stands behind 2 Henry IV, Hamlet, and Othello.

91   WELLS, STANLEY. Re-Editing Shakespeare for the Modern Reader. New York: Oxford University Press, 1984, 144 pp.

  Discusses textual problems involved in a modern edition of Shakespeare, drawn from his work as general editor of the newly initiated Oxford Shakespeare. Particular topics include the advantages and disadvantages of modernized spelling and punctuation, the appropriate manner of amplification of stage directions, and the limits of editorial prerogative in textual emendation.

92   WILLOUGHBY, EDWIN F. The Printing of the First Folio. Oxford: Oxford University Press (for the Bibliographical Society), 1932, 70 pp.

  Traces the history of the First Folio, specifically attempting to identify the typographical habits of the two (or three) compositors. Individual chapters focus on the incidentals of publication (the price of the book, the size of the edition, the rate of printing), the printing process itself, and the composition and proofreading. Issued in an edition of one thousand copies, the folio was, except for twenty-two quires, printed on one press with work proceeding at the rate of two three-sheet quires per week. Orthographic analysis is the basis for identifying the work of the individual compositors.

See also entries 2, 40-41, 181.

SOURCES

93   BULLOUGH, GEOFFREY, ed. Narrative and Dramatic Sources of Shakespeare. 8 vols. London: Routledge & Kegan Paul; New York: Columbia University Press, 1957-75, 4252 pp.

  Assembles the chief narrative and dramatic sources and analogues of Shakespeare's plays and poems. For each an introductory essay describes Shakespeare's use of source material; the texts of these sources then follow. Volume 1 includes the early comedies, the poems, and Romeo and Juliet; volume 2, the comedies (1597-1603); volume 3, the early English history plays; volume 4, the later English history plays; volume 5, the Roman plays; volume 6, the classical plays; volume 7, the major tragedies; and volume 8, the romances.

94   GUTTMAN, SELMA. The Foreign Sources of Shakespeare's Works:
      An Annotated Bibliography of the Commentary Written on This
      Subject Between 1904 and 1940 Together with Lists of Certain
      Translations Available to Shakespeare. New York: King's
      Crown Press, 1947, 168 pp.
          Cites items (many of them annotated) of English, French,
      and German commentary concerning Shakespeare's sources originally
      written in foreign languages--including 239 Latin sources, 117
      Greek sources, 68 French sources, 91 Italian sources, and 41
      Spanish sources. The entries cover scholarship from 1904 to
      1940. Baconians, whatever their eccentricities, were among the
      first to awaken modern criticism to the significance of the clas-
      sical influence on Shakespeare. Generally critics now assume
      Shakespeare to have had a basic working knowledge of Latin,
      Greek, and French.

95   HART, ALFRED. Shakespeare and the Homilies: And Other Pieces
      of Research into the Elizabethan Drama. Melbourne: Melbourne
      University Press, 1934, 262 pp.
          Reveals that Shakespeare's views on divine right and on the
      relationship between monarch and subject are drawn essentially
      from Certain Sermons or Homilies, first published in 1547. It is
      here declared that the king is God's immediate deputy on earth,
      not liable to deposition, that the subject's obedience is to be
      passive and without reservation, that rebellion is a most heinous
      sin. These views permeate Shakespeare's work from early to late,
      and he appears to accept them uncritically.

96   HOSLEY, RICHARD, ed. Shakespeare's Holinshed. New York:
      Capricorn Books; Toronto: Longmans Canada, 1968, 346 pp.
          Reprints with modernized spelling and punctuation the mate-
      rial from Raphael Holinshed's Chronicles of England, Scotland,
      and Ireland (2d ed., 1587) that Shakespeare used as a principal
      source for thirteen of his plays. The material is presented in
      Holinshed's chronological order, organized separately by play;
      and appendixes include an outline of English history (1154-1603),
      genealogical tables, and a bibliography. (See also entry 99.)

97   JONES, EMRYS. The Origins of Shakespeare. Oxford: Clarendon
      Press, 1977, 290 pp.
          Focuses on the "archeology" of Shakespeare's contributions
      to the theater. Shakespeare's education was extensive and
      thorough. A familiarity with Euripides, for example, explains
      Shakespeare's overall conception of tragic form. The chief
      dramatic model for Titus Andronicus was Hecuba; the argument
      between Cassius and Brutus has its source in the argument between
      Agamemnon and Menelaus in Iphigenia in Aulis. 1,2,3 Henry VI is
      a trilogy patterned after Thomas Legges's Richardus Tertius.
      King John is a paradigm of a morality like Mundus et Infans, in
      which the hero Faulconbridge encounters the baffling reality of
      worldly politics.

98   MUIR, KENNETH. The Sources of Shakespeare's Plays. New
     Haven: Yale University Press, 1978, 320 pp.
        Ascertains Shakespeare's sources for his plays and dis-
     cusses how he used them. Shakespeare's method was to read all
     accessible works relevant to his theme and to utilize one source
     to amplify another, complicating his story by adding elements
     from a variety of places. In King Lear, for example, he combines
     an old chronicle play, at least one prose chronicle, two poems,
     and a pastoral romance. The chronological arrangement reveals
     his increasing skills in transmuting his materials for the stage.

99   NICOLL, ALLARDYCE, and NICOLL, JOSEPHINE, eds. Holinshed's
     Chronicle as Used in Shakespeare's Plays. London: Dent;
     New York: Dutton, 1927, 233 pp.
        Presents selections of Raphael Holinshed's Chronicles of
     England, Scotland, and Ireland that Shakespeare drew upon in his
     plays. Contrary to the older view that he wrote on whatever
     story came to hand, he apparently read widely--especially in
     North's Plutarch and Holinshed--seeking for themes suitable for
     developing certain ideas or types of characters. Here the mate-
     rial is ordered by the thirteen Shakespearean plays, with marginal
     notation of the volume and page of the Chronicle from which the
     passage is taken and with further notation, when appropriate, of
     the act and scene of the play. (See entry 16.)

100 NOBLE, RICHMOND. Shakespeare's Biblical Knowledge: And Use
     of the Book of Common Prayer, As Exemplified in the Plays of
     the First Folio. London: Society for Promoting Christian
     Knowledge, 1935, 303 pp.
        Reveals Shakespeare's close knowledge of the Bible through
     listing identifiable quotations from and allusions to at least
     eighteen books of the Old and New Testaments and six from the
     Apocrypha. As Shakespeare matures as a playwright, such refer-
     ences--primarily from the Geneva Bible and the Bishops' Bible--
     become more idiomatic, more closely woven into the text. For
     each of the plays, arranged in presumed chronological order,
     Biblical quotations and allusions are identified and in many
     instances annotated.

101 POTTS, ABBIE FINDLAY. Shakespeare and "The Faerie Queene."
     Ithaca: Cornell University Press, 1958, 269 pp.
        Examines ethical action as a comparable term in the art of
     Spenser and that of Shakespeare. Specifically, the plays from
     1599-1604 (Much Ado About Nothing, Twelfth Night, All's Well That
     Ends Well, The Merry Wives of Windsor, Troilus and Cressida,
     Hamlet, and Measure for Measure) reveal many demonstrable analo-
     gies with the agents and actions of Spenserian allegory. To
     Jonson's theory of dominating humors Shakespeare is totally
     alien; he looks instead to the moral principles of Spenser's
     Book of Courtesy and the Blatant Beast, who operates at the

center of Much Ado, and to the legends of Friendship and Chastity
in the story of Helena and Bertram or Isabella and Angelo.

102   ROOT, ROBERT KILBURN. Classical Mythology in Shakespeare.
       New Haven: Yale University Press, 1903, 134 pp.
       Collects Shakespeare's allusions to classical mythology,
examines their source, and describes their dramatic function.
By far the greatest classical source is Ovid, followed by Virgil.
As Shakespeare develops and his tragedy darkens, his mythology
tends to disappear or, as in Antony and Cleopatra, to turn to
jest. Part 1 consists of a dictionary of mythological characters
with annotations indicating the Shakespearean play or poem in
which they appear. Part 2 discusses, work by work, Shakespeare's
use of mythology.

103   SATIN, JOSEPH. Shakespeare and His Sources. Boston:
       Houghton Mifflin, 1966, 623 pp.
       Aims to reveal how Shakespeare borrows and molds his mate-
rial by comparing thirteen plays with their sources. The choices
reveal a variety of treatment--from fairly close adherence to a
central source in Richard III, Richard II, and 1 Henry IV, to
selection and compression in 2 Henry IV and Antony and Cleopatra,
to major deviation in the resolution of Othello and King Lear, to
the fitting together of disparate segments in Macbeth, to shaping
a fragment into a whole in Hamlet. Shakespeare frequently uses
subordinate sources for complication or counterpoint. Perhaps
the most fascinating single point of comparison is in characterization, where Shakespeare demonstrably transforms his originals
to meet his own dramatic demands. At the end of each section is
a list of sources for further study.

104   SPENCER, T.J.B. Shakespeare's Plutarch. Harmondsworth,
       Eng.: Penguin Books, 1964, 365 pp.
       Includes North's translation of Plutarch's accounts of
Julius Caesar, Marcus Brutus, Marcus Antonius, and Marcius
Coriolanus. Plutarch's virtue was that he saw history in terms
of human character, interpreting ambiguity as a "state of existence in which outstanding men molded events by their personal
decisions and by the inevitable tendencies of their characters"
(p. 7). Shakespeare apparently began to read or re-read Plutarch
about the time he was writing Henry V. In Julius Caesar he was
clearly impressed both by Plutarch's emphasis on character and
by North's language. The development of Enobarbus in Antony and
Cleopatra reflects his later willingness to extend the material
of his source. In Coriolanus the deviations from Plutarch are
all in the direction of theatrical effectiveness, for example
the adding of Virgilia and the young son in the scene of suppli-
cation outside the walls of Rome or the added touch of Coriolanus's
not being able to remember the name of a friend in Corioli.

105   THOMSON, J.A.K. <u>Shakespeare and the Classics</u>. London:
      George Allen & Unwin, 1952, 254 pp.
         Points to the danger of overestimating Shakespeare's obli-
      gation to classical authors in the original, given the relatively
      low standard of classical scholarship in Elizabethan England.
      Following a general discussion of Shakespeare's education, the
      plays are individually examined for Shakespeare's use of classi-
      cal material. <u>Macbeth</u>, for example, is considered the most
      classical of Shakespeare's plays, with tragic irony through the
      audience's foreknowledge communicated through the witches and
      with Duncan's murder offstage reflecting the direct influence of
      Seneca and the indirect influence of the Greek playwrights'
      tragic spirit through Plutarch.

106   TYNAN, JOSEPH L. "The Influence of Greene on Shakespeare."
      <u>PMLA</u> 27 (1912):246-64.
         Investigates the distinctive characterisitcs of Robert
      Greene's comedy and the extent to which Shakespeare borrows from
      Greene in his romantic comedies. Greene's influence is found,
      not in specific borrowings of scenes, lines, or sources, but in
      the use and adaptation of a narrative formula--the struggle and
      ultimate victory of love against the opposition of parents,
      against differences of rank or apparent differences of rank, and
      against faithlessness.

107   VELZ, JOHN W. <u>Shakespeare and the Classical Tradition: A</u>
      <u>Critical Guide to Commentary, 1600-1960</u>. Minneapolis:
      University of Minnesota Press, 1968, 459 pp.
         Includes 2,487 annotated entries covering relevant criti-
      cism in English, French, and German concerning Shakespeare's use
      of classical materials. Boethius (524 A.D.) is set as a forward
      limit, but Shakespeare's paths to the classics (Erasmus, Lily,
      Susenbrotus, Palengenius, Manthuanus) are also included. Follow-
      ing a historical introduction to the topic, the material is clas-
      sified under bibliographies, general works, the comedies, the
      histories, the plays on classical themes, the tragedies, the last
      plays, the poems and sonnets, and Shakespeare's classics (a sec-
      tion devoted to modern editions of the originals that Shakespeare
      probably used).

108   WHITAKER, VIRGIL K. <u>Shakespeare's Use of Learning: An</u>
      <u>Inquiry into the Growth of His Mind and Art</u>. San Marino:
      Huntington Library, 1953, 366 pp.
         Charts Shakespeare's intellectual development through his
      use or adaptation of clearly defined sources and to allusions
      within the plays to contemporary learning. Generally, Shake-
      speare follows his sources faithfully in his early plays, adapt-
      ing character to meet the demands of plot. From <u>Hamlet</u> forward,
      however, he freely reshapes material to illustrate or conform to
      philosophic concepts. Similarly, a mark of his intellectual
      progress is the substituting of the regular operation of the

laws of nature as the moving force in events for a God who inter-
venes actively, an incalculable Fortune, and erratic human behavior.

See also entries 15, 97, 100, 107, 122, 148, 286, 328, 953.

BACKGROUND STUDIES

109   BALDWIN, THOMAS WHITFIELD. Shakspere's Five-Act Structure:
      Shakspere's Early Plays on the Background of Renaissance
      Theories of Five-Act Structure from 1470. Urbana: University
      of Illinois Press, 1947, 848 pp.
         Constructs through analysis of the body of critical com-
      mentary on classical writers, especially Plautus and Terence, the
      theory of dramatic structure as Shakespeare and other Renaissance
      dramatists would have understood it. Specifically, through
      Horace, Varro, Donatus, Servius, Landino, Latomus, Willichus,
      Melancthon, and Scaliger, Baldwin reveals the evolution of a
      five-act concept consisting of three basic movements--the
      protasis (1-2), the epitasis (3-4), the catastrophe (5). Shake-
      speare followed this structure closely in his early dramas, but
      by the mid-1590s and works such as Romeo and Juliet he outgrew
      strict adherence to these artistic constraints. (For a counter-
      view, see entry 127.)

110   _____. William Shakspere's Petty School. Urbana: University
      of Illinois Press, 1943, 240 pp.
         Describes the program of study in the petty school of
      Shakespeare's childhood. The early phases of study involved
      movement from the alphabet to the Catechism and thence to the
      Primer, Psalter, and perhaps the New Testament and movement gen-
      erally from the English to the Latin. Essentially, the petty
      school aimed to teach reading, writing, and casting of accounts;
      clearly it stressed in its religious orientation the Reformation
      far more so than the Renaissance.

111   _____. William Shakspere's Small Latine and Lesse Greeke.
      2 vols. Urbana: University of Illinois Press, 1944, 1525 pp.
         Presents information on the kind of formal education Shake-
      speare is likely to have experienced in sixteenth-century Strat-
      ford. Chapters on the formulation of the tradition in the
      Restoration and eighteenth century that he had only a minimal
      education are followed by an investigation of the grammar school
      curricula and their content in the time of Edward VI and Eliza-
      beth. Volume 2 analyzes the rhetorical training (Tully, Cicero,
      Erasmus, Quintilian) and describes study in the Latin poets
      (Ovid, Virgil, Horace), moral history, moral philosophy, and
      Greek. Certainly, Jonson's phrase reflected in the title must
      be taken only in relative terms.

112   BRADBROOK, MURIEL C. Shakespeare: The Poet in His World.
      New York: Columbia University Press, 1978, 272 pp.
         Places an account of Shakespeare's life and artistic growth
      in the wider context of the development of English theatrical
      history and of the spirit and major events of the Elizabethan-
      Jacobean period. Described as an "applied biography," the major
      focus is on the works themselves. Of particular interest is the
      identification of the rival poet in the sonnets as Marlowe and of
      Shakespeare's friend as Southampton, the discussion of Falstaff
      as at once a dramatic success and a political blunder, of the
      influence of Jonson as friend and rival, and of the effects of
      the Gunpowder Plot on the later tragedies.

113   BUSH, GEOFFREY. Shakespeare and the Natural Condition.
      Cambridge, Mass.: Harvard University Press, 1956, 135 pp.
         Notes the essential duality of Shakespeare's view of nature
      as a philosophic doctrine of divine order and as the physical
      process of life and death. Ultimately his characters strike an
      attitude in the face of the world, not in a moment of certainty
      but in a doubt that a natural philosophy is sufficient to be the
      core of a view of life. If they must ask whether life may be ex-
      plained by natural causes, they must also ask "what the conse-
      quence is to the human spirit of being compelled to ask this
      question" (p. 78). Shakespearean man is caught between the
      reality of surrender to time and the events of the world and the
      longing to be engaged in what is certain, absolute, and beyond
      the reach of time.

114   DORAN, MADELEINE. Endeavors of Art: A Study of Form in
      Elizabethan Drama. Madison: University of Wisconsin Press,
      1954, 482 pp.
         Devotes considerable space to Shakespeare, who was the
      master of architectonic design, creating unity out of great
      diversity through syntax, diction, imagery, and prosody. More so
      than his contemporaries, he refused to be bound by traditional
      concepts of form; he seemed to understand, for example, the ethi-
      cal basis of tragedy, focusing on man's responsibility for the
      effects of his action, no matter how little control can be exer-
      cised over his fate. Chapters are included on eloquence and
      "copy," verisimilitude, moral aim, dramatic forms, history and
      tragedy, comedy, tragicomedy, character, and complication and
      unraveling.

115   DRIVER, T.F. The Sense of History in Greek and Shakespearean
      Drama. New York: Columbia University Press, 1960, 231 pp.
         Views Shakespeare's work as the fulfillment of the dramatic
      question of man's action in a historical situation. The Greek
      dramatists, on the other hand, raised questions about the rela-
      tion of man to his world for which the Hellenic civilization had
      no satisfactory answers. Shakespeare, in addition to seeing man
      in a sequence of historical events, sees these events as

controlled by and relating to a purposeful design. Whereas Greek
action moves from the temporal to the nontemporal with a non-
existent or closed future, Shakespeare moves from event to knowledge to new event; the action is controlled by a sense of passing
time. Examined in detail are <u>Richard III</u>, <u>Hamlet</u>, <u>Macbeth</u>, and
<u>The Winter's Tale</u>.

116   DUSINBERRE, JULIET. <u>Shakespeare and the Nature of Women</u>.
       London and Basingstoke: Macmillan, 1975, 329 pp.
           Maintains that Shakespeare through the breeched heroines
    of romantic comedy and the gracious figures of forgiveness of
    the romances explores aspects of female emancipation. The
    Elizabethan-Jacobean society was basically sympathetic to the
    rights of women, in large part as a consequence of the Puritans'
    emphasis on the spiritual quality of Adam and Eve. The role of
    women was further enhanced by the presence of Queen Elizabeth on
    the throne and by humanistic educational doctrines. The nature
    of Shakespeare's women, in a word, is the result both of his
    genius and the philosophic climate of the age. (See entry 128.)

117   FARNHAM, WILLARD. <u>The Medieval Heritage of Elizabethan</u>
       <u>Drama</u>. Oxford: Basil Blackwell, 1936, 487 pp.
           Argues that Shakespeare's tragedy is essentially a deriva-
    tion of the medieval Gothic tradition. Whereas Greek tragedy
    limits its scope to the immediate events of the catastrophe,
    Gothic tragedy incorporates a more expansive view. The con-
    trolling <u>de casibus</u> narrative involves choral comment on the
    nature of the world and a conclusion in death (the <u>contemptus</u>
    <u>mundi</u> and the danse macabre). The tension between man's physical
    ignobilities and his spiritual nobilities takes effective shape
    in the morality play, with central emphasis on his freedom of
    choice; and in Shakespeare emerges the mature expression of
    "tragedy based upon inner struggle or spiritual civil war"
    (p. 51).

118   FORD, BORIS, ed. <u>The Age of Shakespeare</u>. The Pelican Guide
       to English Literature, vol. 2. Baltimore: Penguin, 1982,
       576 pp.
           Features, in the section on Shakespeare (pp. 277-403),
    essays by Derek Traversi on the young dramatist and the poet, by
    J.C. Maxwell on the middle plays, by L.C. Knights on the great
    tragedies, by Derek Traversi on the last plays, and by Kenneth
    Muir on changing interpretations of the playwright. In tracing
    the history of Shakespeare in the theater, Muir argues that the
    "best critics of our time have given us a better understanding
    of Shakespeare" than that of any previous generation (p. 386).
    Such critics, whether through language, character, or structure,
    have stressed the conscious artistry of the plays rather than
    the natural or uneducated genius of the playwright. Included
    are essays by L.G. Salingar on the social and intellectual back-
    grounds of Shakespeare and the Renaissance in England.

119   FRYE, ROLAND M. Shakespeare and Christian Doctrine.
       Princeton: Princeton University Press, 1963, 314 pp.
           Demonstrates that Shakespeare's personal beliefs cannot be
       deduced from the plays, that his drama is pervasively secular
       within its own structural constraints. Part 1 surveys the work
       of critics who have insisted on Christian archetypal interpreta-
       tions of Shakespeare. Part 2 discusses the historical Reforma-
       tion background, and part 3 provides a topical analysis and
       appraisal of Shakespeare's theological references. Unlike
       Milton's Samson Agonistes and Marlowe's Dr. Faustus, Shake-
       speare's plays are not patterned on a particular theological
       concept; to insist that they are is to engage in special pleading
       by distorting both the nature of drama and also the evidence.
       Certainly the plays attest to Shakespeare's theological literacy
       and to his impressive ability to adopt theological subjects to
       essentially dramatic purposes. His theological and ethical ref-
       erences are placed within a context accessible to either Chris-
       tian or heathen in dealing with universal human concerns. Shake-
       speare's literary endeavors are independent of theological
       constraints; within the context of such literary freedom, we are
       able to "understand Shakespeare's dramatically masterful and
       theologically appropriate use of Christian doctrine" (p. 272).
       (For counterviews, see especially entries 210, 920.)

120   HERNDL, GEORGE C. The High Design: English Renaissance
       Tragedy and the Natural Law. Lexington: University Press of
       Kentucky, 1970, 337 pp.
           Asserts that Shakespearean tragedy is not antinomian, that
       it reflects the cosmos of natural law. The tragic hero, con-
       fronted by evil and divided in his impulses between choice and
       action, is "able finally to survive in integrity, to control what
       he becomes and govern at least his inner and ultimately signifi-
       cant fate" (p. 42). The plays firmly reflect the psychological
       principle that passion must be kept within the control of reason.
       Shakespeare's tragedies, in general, display not a poetic justice
       but a profound revelation that moral laws are never intrinsically
       inexplicable, a revelation rooted in scholastic belief in a uni-
       fied cosmic moral order based on the reason of God.

121   HOLZKNECHT, KARL J. The Background of Shakespeare's Plays.
       New York: American Book Co., 1950, 482 pp.
           Concerns Shakespeare's art and the social, literary,
       theatrical, and philosophical climate in which it was created.
       Chapters are included on the facts and legends of Shakespeare's
       life, pre-Shakespearean drama, the Elizabethan theatrical com-
       panies, the public playhouses and the effect on Shakespeare of
       theatrical conditions, his audience and language and sources,
       his histories, comedies, and tragedies, the publication of his
       plays, his reputation, and a survey of Shakespeare on stage from
       the Restoration to the mid-twentieth century.

122   KEETON, GEORGE W.   Shakespeare's Legal and Political Back-
       ground. New York: Barnes & Noble, 1967, 417 pp.
           Explains the manner in which Shakespeare employed the lan-
       guage and content of the law in his plays and relates this in-
       formation to the playwright's political ideas. Part 1 deals with
       the extent of Shakespeare's legal knowledge and particular legal
       questions concerning the law of nature, local justice, the law of
       debt, the legal basis of the pound of flesh, trial by battle, and
       Ophelia's burial. Part 2 places Shakespeare's political thought
       within the context of his age, covering such matters as his view
       of English kingship and the title to the crown, the political
       background of King John, and the politics of the Greek and Roman
       plays.

123   KNIGHTS, L.C. Drama and Society in the Age of Jonson. New
       York: George W. Stewart, 1937, 347 pp.
           Asserts that the prevailing mode of economic production and
       the social organization it fostered formed the basis of the
       political and intellectual history of the era. Shakespeare's
       period was one of great economic confusion in that there were
       large-scale capitalistic enterprises on the one hand and tradi-
       tional forms of trade and industry (guilds) on the other. The
       dramatists directly reflect the society. Shakespeare's plays are
       referred to randomly throughout the study, especially concerning
       his topical satire and delineation of the trades.

124   MILWARD, PETER. Shakespeare's Religious Background. London:
       Sidgwick & Jackson, 1973, 312 pp.
           Examines the major religious currents of the Elizabethan
       age and Shakespeare's response to them through his plays.
       Shakespeare as a deeply religious man was apparently grieved at
       the break with Rome and the resultant religious chaos. The
       plays, more specifically, are an analogical form of this religious
       situation--from the theme of mistaken identity in the comedies to
       the schismatic strife threatening unity in the histories to the
       sin and suffering consequent upon alienation in the tragedies to
       the last plays with their hope of ultimate reunion. The theme of
       the last plays is the restoration of moral and social harmony
       possible only through forgiveness and love.

125   SIEGEL, PAUL N. Shakespeare in His Time and Ours. South
       Bend, Ind., and London: Notre Dame University Press, 1968,
       260 pp.
           Argues that, while we respond in terms of our own expe-
       rience, a full appreciation of Shakespeare requires some knowl-
       edge of Elizabethan culture as well. Just as Shakespeare's
       contemporaries could imaginatively accept Romeo and Juliet as
       achieving amoral bliss beyond the grave, so modern atheists can
       artistically conceptualize the afterlife adumbrated in Shake-
       speare's Christian tragedies. Cordelia's life and death, for
       example, assume greatest significance as the means by which Lear

achieves spiritual salvation. Other essays consider the disastrous effects of honor without principle and the Elizabethan
response to the stage figure of the Jew.

126 _____. Shakespearean Tragedy and the Elizabethan Compromise.
    New York: New York University Press, 1957, 243 pp.
       Examines Shakespeare's tragedy as a reflection of the
Elizabethan social, political, and religious order--an order
reflecting the uneasy relationships between the old aristocracy,
the new Tudor aristocracy, and the bourgeoisie. With the growth
in the power of the bourgeoisie following the defeat of the
Spanish Armada came new challenges to the Christian humanist
world view that provided rationalization for the dominant position of the new aristrocracy. Hamlet depicts both ideal prince
and malcontent with the Prince torn between acceptance and rejection of the Christian humanist's view. Iago typifies the
malcontent of low birth resentful of his superiors. Both Macbeth
and Lear are based on a conflict of new and old views. Lear is
saved by love, but the play reflects a degenerate contemporary
society.

127 SNUGGS, HENRY L. Shakespeare and Five Acts: Studies in a
    Dramatic Convention. New York: Vantage Press, 1960, 144 pp.
       Takes issue with T.W. Baldwin's claim (see entry 109) that
Shakespeare consciously worked within the concept of five-act
structure developed by classical scholars. Except for Ben
Jonson, all of whose plays reflect five-act division, only those
plays performed in private houses by children's companies are
generally divided into acts. Until around 1610 Shakespeare and
other playwrights involved with the adult companies employed the
sequential or natural-order plot of the popular or native
tradition.

128 SPENCER, THEODORE. Shakespeare and the Nature of Man. New
    York: Macmillan, 1949, 233 pp.
       Explores Shakespeare's vision of life through an examina-
tion of the intellectual, social, and religious background. The
conflict between medieval and Renaissance views created the
philosophic tensions inherent in his plays. From the medieval
period comes the belief in the three interrelated hierarchies--
in the universe, in the ranks of created beings, and in the
institution of government. In such a view nature is infused and
controlled by God. On the other hand, a counterview was also
developing, whether fostered by the Calvinistic assumption of
the depravity of man or by attacks upon the received traditions
by such men as Galileo, Machiavelli, Telesio, and Montaigne.
Nature in this view is devoid of God and teleological design.
Macbeth is Shakespeare's most extensive depiction of the break-
down of Nature's order, extending even to the animal kingdom.
The Tempest, like all the last plays, reflects a "re-birth, a
return to life, a heightened almost symbolic awareness of the

beauty of normal humanity after it has been purged of evil"
(p. 200). (See entry 116.)

129 SPIVACK, BERNARD. Shakespeare and the Allegory of Evil: The
     History of a Metaphor in Relation to His Major Villains. New
     York: Columbia University Press, 1958, 508 pp.
         Maintains that Shakespeare wrote in a period of profound
     transition from one dramatic mode to another, specifically that
     some of our difficulties with Shakespeare's villains are the
     consequences of our attempts to impose a purely naturalistic view
     of evil on what for the playwright has allegorical dimensions.
     In a word, Shakespeare's villains represent efforts to refashion
     figures from an archaic dramatic convention. The primary diffi-
     culty is implanting credible psychological motivation in a char-
     acter of pure and simplistic evil. Figures like Iago, Richard,
     Aaron, and Don John may horrify, but the drapery of conventional
     humanity never fits them. The father of all such characters is
     the Morality Vice.

130 TILLYARD, E.M.W. The Elizabethan World Picture: A Study of
     the Idea of Order in the Age of Shakespeare, Donne, and
     Milton. London: Macmillan, 1946, 116 pp.
         Sets forth the fundamental Elizabethan beliefs about the
     constitution of the world and the cosmos. Accepting a solidly
     theocentric concept of an ordered universe arranged in hierarch-
     ies, the Elizabethans were obsessed with a fear of chaos and the
     fact of mutability. They pictured universal order in three major
     forms: the chain of being, which stretched from the foot of
     God's throne and linked all forms of created matter in its proper
     place and function; a series of corresponding planes--the divine
     and the angelic, the universe or macrocosm, the commonwealth or
     body politic, man or the microcosm, and the lower creation; and
     a dance, a vision of creation as music with the "static bat-
     talions of the earthly, celestial, and divine hierarchies . . .
     sped on a varied but controlled peregrination to the accompani-
     ment of music" (p. 102). (See entry 253.)

131 WICKHAM, GLYNNE. Shakespeare's Dramatic Heritage: Collected
     Studies in Medieval, Tudor and Shakespearean Drama. New York:
     Barnes & Noble, 1969, 277 pp.
         Focuses on the concept of the tragic hero in Marlowe and
     Shakespeare. Early chapters trace how the subjects of the fall
     of man, the redemption, and the ju'~ment day were developed by
     the Church and by medieval drama and how the revival of classical
     learning affected these themes i.. .he early sixteenth century.
     The heart of the study is an analysis of Shakespeare's Richard III
     and Marlowe's Edward II as artistic blendings of these dramatic
     traditions. Attention is also directed to A Midsummer Night's
     Dream, Hamlet, Coriolanus, and The Winter's Tale.

132   WEIMANN, ROBERT. Shakespeare and the Popular Tradition in the
      Theater: Studies in the Social Dimension of Dramatic Form and
      Function. Edited by Robert Schwartz. Baltimore and London:
      Johns Hopkins University Press, 1978, 325 pp.
         Emphasizes Shakespearean drama as sociologically living
      theater. The governing literary trends (formalist, history of
      ideas) tend to remove Shakespeare from the theater and the
      theater from society at large. By tracing the origins and values
      of Shakespearean drama from the mimes and mumming plays, one
      gains new insights into his stagecraft and its traditions, into
      the clowning conventions, for example, or into such figures as
      Richard III, Hamlet, and King Lear. Originally published in
      German (1967).

133   WEST, ROBERT H. The Invisible World: A Study of Pneumatology
      in Elizabethan Drama. Athens: University of Georgia Press,
      1939, 275 pp.
         Investigates Elizabethan beliefs concerning ghosts and
      demonic spirits, the practice of ceremonial magic and witchcraft,
      and the dramatic use of this body of material. Demons function
      on stage primarily in feats of possession, revelation, and trans-
      formation. Central to the interpretation of Hamlet is the in-
      terpretation of the ghost as an objective or demonic figure; to
      some extent the same problem exists concerning the appearance of
      Banquo's ghost. This study provides coverage of the use of
      spirit lore in a wide range of Elizabethan-Jacobean drama. (See
      entry 134.)

134   _____. Shakespeare and the Outer Mystery. Lexington:
      University of Kentucky Press, 1968, 205 pp.
         Explores the philosophical and supernatural elements in
      five plays--Hamlet, Othello, King Lear, Macbeth, and The Tempest.
      Since for reasons of art Shakespeare never "fixes the great sur-
      round" for any of his tragedies, critics are equally wrong to
      envision the plays as expressions of either the absurd or
      Christian parable. Instead, the metaphysical backdrop, visualized
      through the characters' perceptions that like the spectators' are
      finite and limited, is ultimately ambiguous, maintaining a "vast
      reserve, a mysteriousness that should stop the critic from more
      than hesitant suggestions about how they may be read, or confine
      him to a modest statement of personal views" (p. 18). Shakespeare
      deliberately mixes the evidence concerning the nature of the
      ghost in Hamlet, for instance; however strongly we might come to
      accept Hamlet's ministry, we are never absolutely certain of its
      validity and thus dramatically comprehend the protagonist's
      mingled passion and caution. Shakespeare, in a word, belittles
      neither man nor the cosmos; the dignification of man's choices in
      turn dignifies the indeterminacy of the outer mystery. (See
      entry 133.)

See also entries 11, 37, 173B, 200, 217-18, 308, 334.

LANGUAGE AND STYLE

135   BAXTER, JOHN. Shakespeare's Poetic Styles: Verse Into Drama.
      London and Boston: Routledge & Kegan Paul, 1980, 255 pp.
         Perceives the power of Shakespearean drama to be the proper
      wedding of dramatic form and poetic style. In Richard II the
      playwright utilizes and at times intermingles four distinct
      styles--the golden, the moral, the metaphysical, and the Shake-
      spearean. These styles are defined not by individual characters
      but by the rhetorical demands of the stage situation. York in
      act 2 uses the plain didactic style in citing Richard's exotic
      excesses while Gaunt's response, ringing with both disgust and
      patriotism, represents a mixture of the moral and the golden.
      Richard himself utilizes a plain style in moments of resignation
      bordering on despair but a golden Petrarchism in contemplating
      his religious seclusion. Shakespeare's mastery of a multiplicity
      of styles provides one key to effective individualization of
      characterization.

136   BEVINGTON, DAVID. Action is Eloquence: Shakespeare's Lan-
      guage of Gesture. Chicago: University of Chicago Press,
      1984, 248 pp.
         Focuses on gesture in Shakespeare's plays as a language in
      itself with its own vocabulary of signs and rich symbolic poten-
      tial in staging. Nature, personality, social status, inner
      states of mind--such matters can be signaled to the spectators
      through a glance, a shrug, a turn of hand. In instances like
      Coriolanus's turning his back on Rome or Macbeth's start of fear
      at the sound of MacDuff's knocking, the gesture reinforces a
      highly significant dramatic moment. Ceremonial posturing fre-
      quently also serves to clarify character or suggest conflicts.
      (See entry 143.)

137   BURCKHARDT, SIGURD. Shakespearean Meanings. Princeton:
      Princeton University Press, 1968, 317 pp.
         Identifies key words, phrases, or sounds as those which,
      properly understood, can unlock a wealth of information about
      the meaning of the whole play. The striking clock in Julius
      Caesar, for example, far from being an error on Shakespeare's
      part, is his method of signaling as anachronistic Brutus's de-
      cision to kill Caesar in a classical, ritualistic manner. Simi-
      larly, the word nothing as diversely understood by Lear (who
      accepts it at face value) and Gloucester (who refuses to accept
      it and pursues the matter further) signals for both men the flaw
      that ultimately provokes their destruction--their unwillingness
      to gain truth by engaging in the mental struggle necessary to
      penetrate the veil of metaphor.

138   CERCIGNANI, FAUSTO. Shakespeare's Works and Elizabethan
      Pronunciation. Oxford: Clarendon Press, 1981, 432 pp.

Attempts to ascertain the extent to which Shakespeare's
works afford reliable evidence of the types of speech then current in London and to discuss the information provided by rimes,
puns, spellings, and metrical peculiarities. The study investigates both passages from Shakespeare's plays and poems and contemporary writers on orthography and pronunciation. It aims
further to correct Kokeritz's mistaken determination (see
entry 18) to prove Shakespeare's English virtually identical with
that of present educated Southern English. The body of material
analyzes accent, short vowels, long vowels, dipthongs, vowels in
unaccented syllables, and consonants.

139   CLEMEN, WOLFGANG H. The Development of Shakespeare's Imagery.
       Cambridge, Mass.: Harvard University Press, 1951, 236 pp.
          Pursues an analysis of Shakespeare's imagery in its dra-
       matic context in order to discover relations and connections to
       the play as a whole. As Shakespeare's art develops, so does his
       ability to use imagery for multiple effects in expressing charac-
       terization and dramatic theme. In the early plays Shakespeare's
       imagery is largely decorative and unorganic; in Richard II he has
       learned to wed imagery and character; in the major tragedies
       imagery has assumed manifold relevance in terms of mood, charac-
       ter, and theme. The emphasis throughout is on how the image or
       image patterns function to enhance the dramatic elements of
       style, diction, plot, and character.

140   _____. Shakespeare's Soliloquies. Cambridge: Cambridge
       University Press (for the Modern Humanities Research Associa-
       tion), 1964, 26 pp.
          Stresses the variety, style, method, and function of Shake-
       speare's soliloquies. The test for the effectiveness of this
       dramatic convention is not one of psychological naturalistic
       analysis but one of its credibility in context, delivered on the
       platform stage by an isolated actor for whom the barren setting
       is transformed into a metaphor of inner experience. In numerous
       instances a symbolic partner (for example, sleep, a dagger, a
       personified idea such as honor or conspiracy) creates a dialogic
       rhythm.

141   COLMAN, E.A.M. The Dramatic Use of Bawdy in Shakespeare.
       London: Longman, 1974, 230 pp.
          Emphasizes the dramatic function of Shakespeare's bawdy
       language. The simple farce of the Dromios in The Comedy of
       Errors, of Petruchio's household servants in The Taming of the
       Shrew, and of Romeo's foil Mercutio in Romeo and Juliet gives way
       to the sardonic jesting of Hamlet and the bitter raillery of
       Othello that directly reflect the state of the protagonist's mind
       and in turn to the grotesqueries of bestial figures in the late
       plays such as Cloten and Caliban. Also included is a glossary of
       Shakespeare's words and phrases with indecent connotations.

142   CRANE, MILTON. Shakespeare's Prose. Chicago: University of
       Chicago Press, 1951, 219 pp.
           Describes Shakespeare's prose as the first body of prose in
       English that contributes both to the depiction of character and
       the creation of atmosphere. Shakespeare's delighted awareness of
       Elizabethan speech is reflected in the excellence of Falstaff's
       language. He follows tradition by using prose for comic charac-
       ters, but he also utilizes prose in the characterization of his
       tragic heroes. Almost from the beginning Shakespeare uses prose
       for effective contrast--in Romeo and Juliet and Henry IV. Its
       excellence consists in its simplicity, ease, and naturalness and
       in the subtlety with which it contributes to the creation of
       character.

143   DANSON, LAWRENCE N. Tragic Alphabet: Shakespeare's Drama of
       Language. New Haven: Yale University Press, 1974, 200 pp.
           Concerns the tragic hero's difficulty in seeking for an
       adequate expressive mode--in a fully theatrical sense involving
       words, movement, costume, scenery--in the face of his dilemma.
       Traditional language fails, and he is forced to develop a new
       form of communciation adequate to articulate his experience. In
       Othello, for example, the words of various worlds collide un-
       intelligibly. When Othello succumbs to the Iago-world, he falls
       victim to perverted imagination masquerading as truth. Words of
       reality break through at the end, but Othello fears that Lodovico
       will never be able to speak of him as he really is. (See
       entry 136.)

144   DONAWORTH, JANE. Shakespeare and the Sixteenth-Century Study
       of Language. Urbana and Chicago: University of Illinois
       Press, 1984, 279 pp.
           Explores the relationship between five Shakespearean plays
       and Renaissance pedagogical theory concerning language and the
       art of communication. Love's Labor's Lost, King John, The Mer-
       chant of Venice, All's Well That Ends Well, and Hamlet are ex-
       amined as experimentations in the use and abuse of language for
       dramatic effect. Hamlet, for example, represents Shakespeare's
       consummate ability to render characters lifelike through lan-
       guage; in Hamlet's experience we come to realize that speech
       reflects the limitations as well as the transcendence of the
       human spirit.

145   ELAM, KEIR. Shakespeare's Universe of Discourse: Language
       Games in the Comedies. Cambridge: Cambridge University
       Press, 1984, 339 pp.
           Explores the "self-consciousness" of Shakespeare's lan-
       guage, more specifically language in the comedies as a dynamic
       and active protagonist. Focusing primarily on Love's Labor's
       Lost as Shakespeare's most sophisticated play of words, the study
       examines the function of verbal activities and language games--
       those involving gesture, scenery, and physical property, the

multiple meanings of words and the process of communication, and
rhetorical figures. This analysis is framed by reference to
sixteenth-century theories of meaning, language use, conversa-
tional decorum, and rhetoric.

146   EVANS, IFOR. The Language of Shakespeare's Plays. London:
      Methuen, 1952, 216 pp.
         Follows chronologically Shakespeare's development in lan-
      guage, direct statement as well as imagery, rhetorical devices of
      ornament and those of function. Love's Labor's Lost, for exam-
      ple, is examined as one of the earliest plays that live by words
      rather than by character and plot. Already in Berowne's knowl-
      edge of the value of "russet yeas and honest Kersey noes" the
      battle of words is set that will live with Shakespeare throughout
      his career--the temptations and opportunities of sumptuous dic-
      tion set against the dramatic strength found in simple and direct
      statement. Generally this study moves from the use of words as
      words to patterns of language with profound dramatic function.

147   HALLIDAY, F.E. The Poetry of Shakespeare's Plays. London:
      Gerald Duckworth, 1954, 194 pp.
         Argues that Shakespeare's superiority as a playwright re-
      sults in large part from his superiority as a poet. The develop-
      ment of the three major contrapuntal elements in his poetry (the
      words themselves, the rhythmic relationship of the words, and the
      imagery and image patterns) can be traced through five distinct
      periods--the early histories and comedies (1590-94), the sonnets
      and lyrical plays (1594-97), the historical and romantic comedies
      (1597-1601), the tragedies (1601-8), and the romances (1608-13).
      A lyric poet before he was a dramatic poet, Shakespeare moves
      from a largely derivative ornamental, diffuse style to imagery
      "subdued to the action" and metaphor "stripped of its elabora-
      tions" (p. 40).

148   HANKINS, JOHN E. Shakespeare's Derived Imagery. Lawrence:
      University of Kansas Press, 1953, 289 pp.
         Focuses on the sources of Shakespeare's imagery and their
      influences on his ideas, concluding that Shakespeare's genius was
      more adoptive and less inventive than has been commonly assumed.
      Almost inevitably the Shakespearean phrase is more concise and
      more intense than that of its source. The material is topically
      arranged--for example, the world as a stage, life as a brief
      candle, the internal struggle, love as a preserver, life as a
      dream, the golden world--and the major sources include the Bible,
      La Primaudaye's The French Academy, Montaigne, Aristotle, and
      Palingenius's Zodiacus Vitae. (See entries 139, 158-59.)

149   HULME, HILDA M. Explorations in Shakespeare's Language: Some
      Problems of Word Meaning in the Dramatic Text. London:
      Longmans, Green, 1962, 351 pp.
          Explores the common currency in Elizabethan speech in an
      attempt to draw the modern reader and spectator closer to the
      original idiom of Shakespeare's words and phrases. An examina-
      tion of manuscript local records of the sixteenth and seventeenth
      centuries often helps to clarify the meaning of troublesome words
      and phrases such as "aroint," "trammell," and "as thick as Tale/
      Can post with post" in the first act of Macbeth. Particular
      attention is directed to the proverb-idiom in Shakespeare's lan-
      guage, the vocabulary of Elizabethan bawdy, Latinate meanings,
      spelling habits, pronunciation variants, and Warwickshire
      provincialisms.

150   HUSSEY, S.S. The Literary Language of Shakespeare. London
      and New York: Longman Group, 1982, 214 pp.
          Examines Shakespeare's various uses of language to demon-
      strate rank and to establish genre, along with his divergent
      styles--for example, the rational man, the language of invective,
      metadramatic language, affairs of state, a Roman style, and the
      language of ultimate integrity. Shakespeare utilizes the solilo-
      quy from the beginning of his work, as in the expositional solil-
      oquies of Richard III. The full possibilities are developed
      relatively slowly, however. Juliet's soliloquies introduce para-
      dox; the Bastard's, mimicry; but it is Brutus who first articu-
      lates the psychological condition that points toward the major
      protagonists.

151   KENNEDY, MILTON BOONE. The Oration in Shakespeare. Chapel
      Hill: University of North Carolina Press, 1942, 270 pp.
          Points out the necessity, in studying the rhetoric of
      Shakespeare's plays, of distinguishing between the sophistic or
      Senecan rhetoric found in them and the older classical rhetoric
      whose principles Shakespeare came to employ. His mastery of
      rhetoric in the drama is visible in the substitution early in his
      career of climactic plot movement for episodic narrative, of his
      making the interplay of character and circumstance the essence of
      plot action, and his individualizing of character through empha-
      sizing the emotional state of mind as a logical expression of
      thought designed to persuade and to influence the action. He
      perfected oration as an artistic convention of plot development.

152   MAHOOD, M.M. Shakespeare's Wordplay. London and New York:
      Methuen, 1957, 192 pp.
          Examines the central themes of five plays and the sonnets
      through the pervasive wordplay. Among the dominant patterns
      discussed are the Liebestod motif in Romeo and Juliet, the
      phrases of disquiet at all levels in Hamlet, the doubly and
      triply ironic meanings in Macbeth, and the variation on grace in
      The Winter's Tale. Poetic truth emerges through multiple

meanings of words, and the richness of the dramatic experience
results in part from Shakespeare's ability to manipulate the
interplay of the various semantic levels.

153   MIRIAM JOSEPH, Sister. Shakespeare's Use of the Arts of
        Language. New York: Columbia University Press, 1947, 423 pp.
        Aims to help modern readers respond to devices of rhetoric
readily known to virtually every schoolboy in Renaissance Europe.
The book presents in detail the theory of composition current
during Shakespeare's time. His power and vitality of language
were due in part to his own creativeness, but also in part to
this knowledge of a body of precepts on the three arts of lan-
guage--grammar, rhetoric, and logic. Shakespeare would have
learned the precepts in grammar school, then have employed them
as a tool of analysis in reading, and finally have used them as
a guide to composition. His early plays and poems are marked by
an almost schematic use of rhetorical and logical devices; in his
mature work his use of such devices is more subtle and dramatically refined. Part 3 presents a handbook of the general theory
of composition and reading as defined and illustrated by Tudor
logicians and rhetoricians. An abridged version--Rhetoric in
Shakespeare's Time (New York: Harcourt, Brace, & World)--was
published in 1962.

154   PARTRIDGE, A.C. Orthography in Shakespeare and Elizabethan
        Drama: A Study of Colloquial Contractions, Elisions, Prosody
        and Punctuation. Lincoln: University of Nebraska Press,
        1964, 200 pp.
        Provides an orthographic analysis of Shakespeare's dramatic
and poetic texts--that is, accidentals such as spelling, punctuation, elision, syncope, and contractions. While interference by
the scribe or compositor is an ever-present danger in matters of
spelling and punctuation, it is less likely to occur in con-
tracted forms and idiosyncrasies of syntax. Generally Shakespeare's approach to language is humanistic and figuratively
imaginative; Jonson's is academic and logical. Attention is
directed to syllabic variation in the quarto and folio texts and
to editorial revision and corruption in the First Folio
Coriolanus and Antony and Cleopatra. Evidence also suggests the
presence of two hands in Henry VIII; most likely Fletcher revised and completed a work Shakespeare left unfinished. (See
entries 19, 23.)

155   PARTRIDGE, ERIC. Shakespeare's Bawdy: A Literary and Psycho-
        logical Essay and a Comprehensive Glossary. London: Routledge
        & Kegan Paul, 1947, 226 pp.
        Examines the bawdy in Shakespeare's work from literary,
psychological, and lexicographical angles. Shakespeare expresses
his views on love, passion, and sex "with a power and pertinence
unrivalled by other great general writers and with a picturesque-
ness unapproached by the professional amorist writers" (p. 7).

Part 1 is divided into a section on nonsexual bawdy, homosexual, sexual, general, and valedictory. Part 2 provides a glossary of some fifteen hundred words and phrases and briefly describes the bawdy connotations. Shakespeare is by turns witty, profound, idealistic, and cynical in his use of bawdiness. Only Jonson and Beaumont and Fletcher are as smutty, but in neither case is the usage as straightforward, natural, and provocative.

156   SHIRLEY, FRANCES A. Swearing and Perjury in Shakespeare's
         Plays. London: George Allen & Unwin, 1979, 174 pp.
            Examines the dramatic function of swearing in Shakespeare's
         plays--as a device for increasing tension, for shock, for satiric
         attack, for delineation of character. The plays up to 1606
         reflect his increasingly effective use of oaths. The self-
         excoriating attacks in Hamlet's soliloquies, for example, help
         to articulate his character and his inner tension. In act 5,
         though otherwise in self-control, he punctuates with an oath his
         forcing Claudius to drink from the poisoned cup. The anti-
         blasphemy statute in 1606 limited Shakespeare's freedom with words
         and forced him to search for surrogate terms and expressions in-
         offensive to the censor. (See entries 139, 148, 158.)

157   SIPE, DOROTHY L. Shakespeare's Metrics. New Haven and
         London: Yale University Press, 1968, 266 pp.
            Argues that Shakespeare, whatever the corrupting influences
         of Renaissance spelling and modern editing, wrote carefully con-
         structed iambic verse, the normative line thus being a succession
         of two-syllable feet. Evidence demonstrates such regularity in
         99.5 percent of the lines. In Shakespeare the metrical framework
         competes for predominance with the idea to be expressed and the
         semantic and morphological features of the language itself. Con-
         sistently he is able to make the constraints of and deviations
         from the meter enhance the power and grace of his verse.

158   SPURGEON, CAROLINE F.E. Shakespeare's Imagery and What It
         Tells Us. Cambridge: Cambridge University Press, 1935,
         425 pp.
            Assembles, sorts, and examines on a systematic basis all of
         Shakespeare's images--sensory, simile, metaphor--for what they
         can tell us about the man and about his plays. Following a com-
         parison of Shakespeare's imagery with that of Bacon and other
         playwrights (especially Marlowe), the study discusses imagery
         under such categories as nature, indoor life and customs, and
         classes and types of men and then describes the personality of
         Shakespeare that emerges. Part 2 devotes individual chapters
         to the leading imagistic motives in the histories, comedies,
         romances, and tragedies. Charts visually demonstrate both the
         general predominant images and those for the individual plays.

159   STAUFFER, DONALD A. <u>Shakespeare's World of Images: The Development of His Moral Ideas</u>. New York: W.W. Norton, 1949, 393 pp.

Reveals Shakespeare's moral views through a consideration of his choice of subjects, alteration of sources, character analyses, plot structure, and images. Assuming that all great works of art reflect the conviction of their creators, Stauffer is especially concerned with Shakespeare's reinterpretations of old themes as an insight into his valuations of worldly power, love, reason, and loyalty and with his images as the rhetorical means of conveying his thought. <u>Measure for Measure</u>, for example, was written when his intellect was most active, but his ethical sense was not at its most certain; love in the play becomes an unweeded garden for desecration and monstrosities. <u>The Tempest</u>, on the other hand, champions the imagination as the "servant of the 'nobler reason' in shaping images of natural beauty that vary from the delicate to the cosmic; and wondrous strange sea-music drifts through a life that is surrounded by sleep" (p. 302). (See entries 139, 148, 157.)

160   VICKERS, BRIAN. <u>The Artistry of Shakespeare's Prose</u>. London: Methuen, 1968, 452 pp.

Traces the steady growth in Shakespeare's use of prose through the early comedies and histories, reaching a peak in the prose comedy <u>The Merry Wives of Windsor</u> but dominant as well in <u>Much Ado About Nothing</u>, <u>As You Like It</u>, and <u>Twelfth Night</u>. Of particular significance is Shakespeare's juxtaposition of prose and verse in a given play. Movement to prose can underscore sincerity as in Vincentio's conversation with Isabella or intensify parody as in <u>Troilus and Cressida</u>. It can also reflect a character's shifting moods as in Coriolanus or Timon. Its most profound use is in the madness of Lear and Othello.

161   WILLCOCK, GLADYS D. <u>Shakespeare as a Critic of Language</u>. Oxford: Oxford University Press, 1934, 30 pp.

Examines the movement in Shakespeare from the mellifluous facility of the language of the early plays to the cloudy pregnancy of the language of the later plays. Shakespeare's mature comic dialogue by the last years of the sixteenth century has outgrown the earlier technique in which language is an end in itself. Benedick and Beatrice, for example, are intent, not on turning sentences inside out, but on turning each other inside out by means of language. Shakespeare was a leader in developing language for the stage, a supple blank verse and prose of almost unlimited range.

162   YODER, A. <u>Animal Analogy in Shakespeare's Character Portrayal: As Shown in His Reflection of the Aesopian Tradition and the Animal Aspect of Physiognomy</u>. New York: King's Crown Press, 1947, 150 pp.

Surveys and analyzes Shakespeare's use of more than four
thousand animal comparisons in character portrayal either by
delineating the foibles of man behind animal masks or judging
men by attributes of animals they supposedly resemble. Generally, characters through such comparisons gain in intensity,
whether the villains like the bottled spider Richard III or the
gilded serpant Goneril or the comic figures like Falstaff or
Malvolio or the satirically conceived portraits of Ajax and
Armado; gentle souls like Henry VI or MacDuff's children gain
in pathos. Shakespeare also uses animal analogies to heighten
the tone or atmosphere.

See also entries 7-8, 17-18, 23, 27-28, 197, 199, 265, 319, 932,
965; for discussion of imagery, see entries 139, 148, 159, 195.

STAGE, STAGE HISTORY, FILM

163 ADAMS, JOHN CRANFORD. The Globe Playhouse: Its Design and
     Equipment. Cambridge, Mass.: Harvard University Press,
     1942, 435 pp.
        Aims--with evidence from plays, dramatic entertainments,
     playhouse documents, letters, maps, pamphlets, and poems--to
     reconstruct as fully as possible the design and equipment of the
     Globe Playhouse. Sections of the theater discussed in detail
     include the frame, the auditorium (sign, yard, gallery sub-
     divisions, gentlemen's rooms), the platform stage, the tiring
     house (exterior and first, second, and third levels), and the
     superstructure.

164 ADAMS, JOSEPH QUINCY. Shakespearean Playhouses: A History
     of English Theaters from the Beginnings to the Restoration.
     Boston, New York, and Chicago: Houghton Mifflin, 1917,
     473 pp.
        Represents the first full attempt to provide a history of
     the playhouse in Shakespeare's time. Following a discussion of
     the inn yard as the forerunner of professional houses and of the
     general hostility of the city toward the players, individual
     chapters are devoted to seventeen regular theaters and to five
     temporary or projected theaters.

165 BALDWIN, THOMAS WHITFIELD. The Organization and Personnel of
     the Shakespearean Company. Princeton: Princeton University
     Press, 1927, 464 pp.
        Traces the development of Elizabethan acting companies as
     monopolies under license or patent, eventually limited to five
     companies of men in London at any one time. With the focus on
     the Lord Chamberlain's Men and the King's Men, individual chap-
     ters address membership in the Shakespearean company, the hired
     men and the permanent cadre, the economic operation and the
     division of labor, and the assignment of parts in Shakespeare's

plays. The study reveals the considerable extent to which the
development of Shakespeare's art was influenced by stage conditions (public and private) and by the strengths and ages of the
principal actors. (See entry 183.)

166   BALL, ROBERT HAMILTON. Shakespeare on Silent Film: A Strange
      Eventful History. London: Allen & Unwin, 1968, 403 pp.
         Discusses in part 1 the film productions of Shakespeare in
      chronological order from Herbert Beerbohm Tree's filming of King
      John in 1899 to an atrociously satiric German version of A Mid-
      summer Night's Dream in 1928. Part 2 provides more specific
      details for each production treated in part 1. In a sense,
      silent Shakespeare is a contradiction; hearing the language is
      an indispensable part of the theatrical experience. Moreover,
      the general public was not really ready for Shakespeare. Progress
      was made, though, in camera techniques and in gradually building
      a receptive public. (See entry 182.)

167   BECKERMAN, BERNARD. Shakespeare at the Globe 1599-1609. New
      York: Macmillan, 1962, 254 pp.
         Examines the Globe's repertory system, dramaturgy, stage,
      acting, and staging from 1599 to 1608-9, when it was home to
      Shakespeare's company (Chamberlain's, King's) as the only theater
      in which its plays were publicly produced in London. Not only
      was the theater architecturally regarded as the last word in
      efficiency and distinction; the company was controlled by rela-
      tively young men, shareholders in a perilous but exciting eco-
      nomic and artistic venture. Already Shakespeare was the leading
      playwright as well as part owner. The acquisition of Blackfriars
      provided a second (indoor) stage. The list of extant works pre-
      sented at the Globe during this period consists of fifteen Shake-
      spearean and fourteen non-Shakespearean plays. These twenty-nine
      plays form the basis for extensive analysis. All factors of the
      production were modified by the exigencies of the repertory sys-
      tem; and the script played the dominant part in shaping the style
      of production, a style characterized by the contradictory demands
      of convention and reality.

168   BENTLEY, GERALD EADES. The Jacobean and Caroline Stage.
      7 vols. Oxford: Clarendon Press, 1941-68, 2903 pp.
         Provides information on all aspects of English drama from
      1616 to 1642. Volume 1 discusses the acting companies, both
      adult and children; volume 2, the players; volumes 3-5, plays and
      playwrights (including several plays attributed to Shakespeare in
      his own day); volume 6, private, public, and court theaters, along
      with two projected theaters; volume 7 reproduces pertinent theat-
      rical documents and includes a general index. This study com-
      prises an encyclopedic source of information on later Jacobean
      and Caroline drama. (See also entries 170, 183.)

169   _____. Shakespeare and His Theatre. Lincoln: University of
       Nebraska Press, 1964, 128 pp.
          Focuses on the relationship of Shakespeare to his dramatic
       company, both at the Globe and at Blackfriars, and points to the
       fallacy of much current criticism that assumes the primacy of
       the reader rather than the spectator. Shakespeare wrote for the
       most part to accommodate the available personnel (patented mem-
       bers, hired men, boys) of the Lord Chamberlain's and King's Men.
       The action is continuous and episodic; the location, generally
       irrelevant. His romances demonstrably reflect the influence of
       the private stage with its greater emphasis on scenic spectacle
       and music.

170   CHAMBERS, EDMUND KERCHEVER. The Elizabethan Stage. 4 vols.
       Oxford: Clarendon Press, 1923, 1950 pp.
          Provides information on all aspects of English drama during
       the reign of Elizabeth and during the first thirteen years of the
       reign of King James (1558-1616). Volume 1 discusses the histori-
       cal period, the Revels office, the Mask and the Court play, the
       struggle between city and court, Puritanism and humanism, and
       the quality and economic conditions of the actors; volume 2, the
       history of the acting companies, both adult and children, and the
       actors; volume 3, the conditions of staging in the theaters and
       at court, the presenting of plays, and the actors; volume 4 of-
       fers reprints of various theatrical documents and a general in-
       dex. An index is provided by Beatrice White in An Index to "The
       Elizabethan Stage" and "William Shakespeare" by Sir Edmund
       Chambers (Oxford University Press, 1934), 161 pp.

171   COHN, RUBY. Modern Shakespeare Offshoots. Princeton:
       Princeton University Press, 1976, 426 pp.
          Concerns the manner in which Shakespeare's plays have been
       emended, adapted, and transformed for the modern theater in
       England, France, and Germany. Discussion covers modern adapta-
       tions of Macbeth, Hamlet, King Lear, and The Tempest as well as
       fiction stemming from Hamlet and essays inspired by Lear. An-
       other section focuses on Shakespeare's influence on the creative
       work of Shaw, Brecht, and Beckett.

172   DAVID, RICHARD. Shakespeare in the Theatre. Cambridge:
       Cambridge University Press, 1978, 263 pp.
          Provides detailed studies of the major English productions
       of Shakespeare during the 1970s, attempting not only to record
       those most strikingly successful individual moments but also to
       suggest the major trends in contemporary Shakespearean produc-
       tion. Twenty-two productions representing nineteen plays are
       discussed with Hamlet, Romeo and Juliet, and Richard II consid-
       ered and compared in two productions. Shakespeare works in a
       wide range from the naturalistic to the surrealistic, from bare
       stage to full; but a play is generally most successful when pre-
       sented on its own terms, "not rigidly or pedantically, but with

an eye to avoiding anything that is counter to the peculiarities
of its own nature" (p. 242).

173   FOAKES, R.A., and RICKERT, R.T., eds. Henslowe's Diary.
       Cambridge: Cambridge University Press, 1961, 368 pp.
           Provides the text of the Diary of Philip Henslowe, the
       chief source for theatrical history between 1590 and 1604.
       Henslowe's account falls into two sections: (1) the names of the
       companies who performed at his theater (the Rose?), the plays,
       and the amount he received for rent (one-half of the gallery
       takings); (2) records of advances he made to the Admiral's Men
       (after 1597) for the purchase of plays and costumes and of ad-
       vances to the players themselves. The introduction covers the
       history of the manuscript; and a general index, an index of plays,
       and an index of year-dates are included. This edition supersedes
       W.W. Greg's Henslowe's Diary, 2 vols. (London: A.H. Bullen,
       1904), 640 pp.

173A   FROST, DAVID L. The School of Shakespeare: The Influence of
       Shakespeare on English Drama, 1600-42. Cambridge: Cambridge
       University Press, 1968, 304 pp.
           Argues the pervasive influence on English drama until the
       closing of the public theaters in 1642. Not only did his plays
       continue to hold the stage; their popularity is reflected also
       in the number to appear in print. Moreover, in numerous in-
       stances the popularity of a Shakespearean play forces the work
       of later playwrights into its mold. In particular, Shakespeare
       revived and redeemed both the romance and revenge tragedy;
       Marston, Massinger, Fletcher, and Middleton all produced imita-
       tions. The majority of writers saw Shakespeare as a great re-
       pository of materials. (See entries 276, 1415.)

173B   GURR, ANDREW. The Shakespearian Stage 1574-1642. Cambridge:
       Cambridge University Press, 1970, 192 pp.
           Comprises a conspectus of background material for Shake-
       spearean drama, the Elizabethan society, the acting companies,
       the theaters, the mechanics of staging and acting, and the
       audience. One can trace a shifting population among the com-
       panies as, dictated by financial circumstances, players moved
       from group to group. Traveling companies generally were consid-
       erably smaller than those based in London. A playwright was
       normally hired for a particular play or was paid for a work he
       had for sale. Shakespeare, who wrote and acted for a single
       company from 1594 to 1613, is an obvious exception. An appendix
       lists major plays of the period, with author, date, company, and
       playhouse.

174   HARBAGE, ALFRED. Shakespeare and the Rival Traditions. New
       York: Macmillan, 1952, 393 pp.
           Concentrates on the organization of the Elizabethan theat-
       rical industry to serve its audience, the view of life common to

this audience, and the reflection of this view in the plays. The
theatrical tradition is decidedly dualistic, the public houses
and the adult companies evolving from the strolling players of
the fifteenth century, the private or coterie houses evolving
from the boy choristers and grammar school troupes. Shakespeare
was emphatically a participant in the public theater. The
coterie theater, catering to a wealthier and more highly educated
group, favored satiric comedy. The popular stage, operating
within more traditional moral constraints, provided more varied
fare, abounding in chronicle plays and romances. Writers for the
private stage performed an important service in carrying on the
earlier academic tendency to import and experiment, but most of
the plays are overwritten and underimagined. Shakespeare's
plays, to the contrary, possess a broad appeal, establishing
contact with significant numbers and kinds of people.

175   _____. Shakespeare's Audience. New York: Columbia Univer-
        sity Press, 1941, 201 pp.
        Refutes the popular misconception that the Elizabethan
audience was rowdy and uncouth, ready at a moment's notice to be
caught up in a passion in the pit at the expense of attention to
the actor on stage. Crowds averaging some two thousand per day
at the theaters are all too frequently attacked by disgruntled
poets or actors. Evidence suggests that the patrons came in
festive mood to mingle and to see a play; the "criminal or quar-
relsome or persistently noisy were a threat to their enjoyment"
(p. 113), and such trouble was relatively infrequent. An appendix provides information on attendance at the theaters by day of
the week, holiday, and season.

176   HILL, ERROL. Shakespeare in Sable: A History of Black
        Shakespearean Actors. Amherst: University of Massachusetts
        Press, 1984, 216 pp.
        Charts the history of Black Shakespearean actors from 1820
to 1970. The major focus is on Ira Aldridge and Paul Robeson,
each in his own way an innovator in past years, and on the present work of Gloria Foster, Earle Hyman, James Earl Jones, and
Jean White. Such a study inevitably deals with a significant
social dimension, in this instance tracing the difficulty of
Blacks to gain recognition as serious dramatic actors. Especially helpful in this regard among producers and directors have
been Joseph Papp and C. Bernard Jackson.

177   HODGES, C. WALTER. The Globe Restored: A Study of the Eliza-
        bethan Theatre. London: E. Benn, 1953, 190 pp.
        Combines evidence and conjecture to present a general re-
construction of the Globe Playhouse. Most probably both the
first Globe (burned 1613) and the second Globe (demolished in
1644) were polygonal in structure, a point clearly noted in
Visscher's engraving of the Bankside around 1616. Seventy pages
of plates include seventy-three historical documents such as

Visscher's view, Van Buchell's sketch of the Swan, and Hollar's
engraving of the Bankside, along with eight reconstruction
sketches.

178   HOTSON, LESLIE. Shakespeare's Wooden O. London: Rupert
      Hart-Davis, 1959, 335 pp.
      Claims that Shakespeare was originally played in the round.
The Globe did not have a scenic wall and inner and upper alcove
stages; instead it and other Elizabethan playhouses maintained
the form and method of the pageant or wagon-play. The dressing
room of Shakespeare's stage was still located under the stage;
the production was amphitheatrical, and the axis, like that of
the pageants, was transverse, extending in its long dimension
from left to right. The stage, in a word, resembled a tennis
court with its blank fourth wall removed and the second long side
opening to the yard below. Such an arrangement accommodated the
essence of drama--contrast, antagonism, conflict--and it maintained a clarity of place, the significant location of Heaven,
the World, and Hell enjoyed by the Middle Ages.

179   JORGENS, JACK J. Shakespeare on Film. Bloomington and
      London: Indiana University Press, 1977, 377 pp.
      Deals with the art of film adaptation of Shakespeare, both
literal and free, attempting to bridge the gap between theater
history, literary analysis, and film criticism and to reveal the
relationships between Renaissance visions and modern re-visions.
Individual chapters treat productions of A Midsummer Night's
Dream by Max Reinhardt and Peter Hall, of The Taming of the
Shrew and Romeo and Juliet by Zeffirelli, of Julius Caesar by
Mankiewicz, of Henry V, Richard III, and Hamlet by Olivier, of
Macbeth by Polanski and Welles, of Hamlet by Kozintsev, and of
King Lear by Brook and Kozintsev. Both literary and film critics
must recognize that cinematic adaptations of Shakespeare require
"complex triangulation between film, script, and life" (p. 25).

180   JOSEPH, BERTRAM. Elizabethan Acting. Oxford: Oxford
      University Press, 1951, 115 pp.
      Uses Renaissance writings on the art of action to supple-
ment the scanty surviving sketches of acting itself to examine
the form of Elizabethan acting. Generally, the Elizabethan actor
is praised for identification with his role, animating his speech
with action; the acting was not formal and stylized, but natural,
"familiar," and unaffected, even the monologues and asides. Attention was directed to emotion as the source of delivery, and
actors spoke with due attention to the literary quality of the
words. The source of much information is John Bulwer's Chirologia
and Chironomia, published in 1644.

181   KING, T.J. Shakespearean Staging, 1599-1642. Cambridge,
        Mass.: Harvard University Press, 1971, 163 pp.
            Surveys pre-Restoration staging techniques through an ex-
        amination of 276 texts (promptbooks, printed plays with prompter's
        notations, playbooks printed from prompt copy) dating from 1599
        to 1642. The aim is to reveal how the plays of Shakespeare and
        his contemporaries were staged, and the evidence--drawn from con-
        temporary architecture and pictures of early English stages and
        from the texts themselves--suggests the use of unlocalized
        facades with commonplace stage properties. The plays fall into
        four groups of ascending complexity in stage requirements:
        (1) eighty-seven require only floor space in front of an un-
        localized facade with at least two entrances, (2) forty-five
        also need an acting place above the stage, (3) one hundred two
        need an accessory stage from which actors and properties can be
        discovered, (4) and forty-two require a trapdoor, and hence a
        platform stage. References to Shakespeare are pervasive, and a
        full chapter is devoted to the conjectural staging of Twelfth
        Night as performed during Candlemas Feast 1601/1602 at the Middle
        Temple.

182   MANVELL, ROGER. Shakespeare and the Film. New York and
        Washington: Praeger, 1971, 172 pp.
            Examines the major films adapted from Shakespeare's plays
        during the period of sound film, from the early attempts of
        Douglas Fairbanks and Mary Pickford in The Taming of the Shrew
        and the Max Reinhardt production of A Midsummer Night's Dream to
        the achievements of Laurence Olivier, Orson Welles, Peter Brook,
        Sergei Yutkevich, Grigori Kozintsev, and Akira Kurosawa. Cine-
        matic techniques can lend an excitement not unlike the appeal to
        Shakespeare's contemporary audiences. In particular, the
        heightened atmosphere and the visual imagery of film can enhance
        the play's poetic imagery. (See entry 166.)

183   MURRAY, JOHN TUCKER. English Dramatic Companies 1558-1642.
        2 vols. Boston: Houghton Mifflin, 1910, 804 pp.
            Traces the history of English dramatic companies from the
        accession of Queen Elizabeth in 1558 to the closing of the
        theaters by the Puritans in 1642. Volume 1 covers the London
        companies (greater men's, lesser men's, children's), their
        affiliation with particular theaters along with Court and pro-
        vincial performances. Volume 2 covers the provincial companies,
        men's and children's under royal patronage, those under noblemen
        and commoners, those under players, and those under towns. Al-
        most 300 pages of appendixes include pertinent documents, mate-
        rials, and discussions, along with notices of dramatic companies
        in provincial record. Shakespeare's company (the Lord Chamber-
        lain's) is treated at length. (See entry 165.)

184   NAGLER, A.M. Shakespeare's Stage. New Haven: Yale Univer-
      sity Press, 1958, 117 pp.
           Attempts to describe, not yet another reconstruction of the
      Globe Theatre, but the "ideal type" of the Shakespearean stage.
      The documentary evidence simply is not sufficient to support
      Adams's (entry 163) and Hodges's (entry 177) reconstruction. One
      can safely infer a platform stage with traps. Henslowe's inven-
      tory in 1598 suggests that the stage was not barren, that indeed
      there were many free-standing scenic elements. Following a
      hypothetical staging of Romeo and Juliet, the study concludes
      with discussion of the actors, of the acting style, and of the
      private Blackfriars stage.

185   ODELL, GEORGE C.D. Shakespeare: From Betterton to Irving.
      2 vols. New York: Scribner, 1920, 954 pp.
           Examines the stage history of Shakespeare's plays from 1660
      to the early twentieth century with emphasis on major productions,
      alterations in dramatic representational technique, and altera-
      tions in the texts themselves. The material is divided into eight
      sections--in volume 1 the age of Betterton (1660-1710), the age
      of Cibber (1710-42), the age of Garrick (1742-76); in volume 2
      the age of Kemble (1776-1817), the leaderless age (1817-37), the
      age of Macready (1837-43), the age of Phelps and Charles Kean
      (1843-79), and the age of Irving (1879-1902). A final chapter
      describes recent trends and actors (Bensen, Tree, Granville-
      Barker, Greet).

186   SHATTUCK, CHARLES H. Shakespeare on the American Stage: From
      the Hallams to Edwin Booth. Washington: Folger Shakespeare
      Library, 1979, 170 pp.
           Provides a historical sketch of Shakespeare in the American
      theater, noting that from 1752 (with Lewis Hallam's London com-
      pany) until well into the 1820s Shakespeare was an entirely im-
      ported product both in the actors and in the eighteenth-century
      "improvements" on Shakespeare's plays. In the early nineteenth
      century a new wave of realistic characterization came in with
      George Frederick Cooke, Edmund Kean, and Junius Brutus Booth;
      and the first significant American actor emerged in Edwin
      Forrest. A more genteel tradition is found in the midcentury
      with William Burton, Edward Loomis Davenport, and John McCullough.
      American Shakespeare in the century climaxed in the work of Edwin
      Booth.

187   SMITH, IRWIN. Shakespeare's Blackfriars Playhouse: Its
      History and Its Design. New York: New York University
      Press, 1964, 577 pp.
           Concerns a portion of Blackfriars on the north bank of the
      Thames (originally founded by the Black Friars in 1275) and its
      use for two theatrical ventures--the first commercial indoor
      theater for children's performance and later the indoor playhouse
      for Shakespeare's company. The study reprints documents

pertinent to the topography of the Blackfriars precinct, the
relationship of the friary to the crown, and the history of the
two playhouses. The particular focus is on the theater as used
by the King's Men, with separate chapters on its auditorium,
platform, rear stage, and upper stage.

188   _____. Shakespeare's Globe Playhouse: A Modern Reconstruc-
         tion in Text and Scale Drawings. New York: Charles Scrib-
         ner's Sons, 1956, 240 pp.
         Results from the collaborative efforts with John Cranford
Adams to construct a scale model of the Globe. The acceptance of
the Elizabethan platform stage has freed actors and producers
from the tyranny--both economic and artistic--of stage settings
and has encouraged the current explosion of interest in Shakespeare festival theater. With information drawn from contemporary evidence, the study concerns the site and shape of the
Globe, its dimensions, fabric, auditorium, the stages (platform,
inner, rear, and second-level), the music gallery, and the super-
structure.

189   SPENCER, HAZELTON. Shakespeare Improved: The Restoration
         Versions in Quarto and on the Stage. Cambridge, Mass.:
         Harvard University Press, 1927, 406 pp.
         Describes Shakespeare on the stage during the Restoration
period from 1660 to 1710, the date that Betterton died and that
(one year after the publication of Rowe's edition) essentially
marks the end of a long sequence of altered independent quartos.
Part 1 sketches the stage history of the two licensed companies
at Drury Lane and Lincoln's Inn Fields and the first union in
1682. Part 2 deals with adaptations of Shakespeare--for example,
Davenant's Macbeth, Dryden's Tempest and All for Love, Tate's
King Lear, Shadwell's Timon of Athens, and Cibber's Richard III.
Adapted versions greatly outnumber unaltered productions, many of
them showing little regard for the nature of Shakespeare's plot,
diction, or stage methods.

190   STYAN, J.L. The Shakespeare Revolution: Criticism and Per-
         formance in the Twentieth Century. Cambridge: Cambridge
         University Press, 1977, 292 pp.
         Charts the movement of Shakespearean production from the
late Victorian period to the present time, from the full-scene
proscenium-arch stage to the empty stage and nonillusory presen-
tations, from the experimental work of William Poel and Harley
Granville-Barker to the revolutionary efforts of Jackson, Hall,
Guthrie, and Brook. Also examined is academic influence on the
stage (Bradley, Bradbrook, Knight, Knights, Leavis), especially
of Jan Kott on Peter Brook's King Lear (see entry 267).

191   _____. Shakespeare's Stagecraft. Cambridge: Cambridge
       University Press, 1967, 244 pp.
          Explores Shakespeare's stagecraft through the details of
       his work as a craftsman. Theatrical communication depends on a
       largely subconscious system of signals from actor to spectator
       through the script. Individual chapters address the Elizabethan
       stage (its flexibility, intimacy, and platform focus), staging
       and acting conventions (properties, symbols, the boy actor), the
       actor's movement (Shakespeare as director within the text, ges-
       ture, the soliloquy), grouping on the open stage (duologue, spa-
       tial distancing), the full stage (visual images, multiple en-
       trances and groupings), speech (tones, rhythm), and orchestration
       (contrasting patterns of sound).

192   THORNDIKE, ASHLEY H. Shakespeare's Theater. New York:
       Macmillan, 1916, 472 pp.
          Attempts to assimilate and focus the considerable body of
       knowledge concerning the Elizabethan stage that emerged in the
       early years of the twentieth century. Most significantly, the
       playing area is envisioned as threefold--a large stage jutting
       into the pit and surrounded on three sides by galleries, an inner
       stage, and a balcony stage directly above it. Indoor staging at
       court and later at private theaters such as Blackfriars provided
       a greater opportunity for decorative effects. Included also are
       discussions of Shakespeare's dramatic company and its leading
       rivals, of the Elizabethan acting style and the principal actors,
       and of the nature of the audience.

193   TREWIN, J.C. Shakespeare on the English Stage, 1900-1964: A
       Survey of Productions. London: Barrie & Rockliff, 1964,
       328 pp.
          Surveys productions of Shakespeare in the British theater
       since 1900, reflecting the theory and experimentation behind
       shifting representational fashions. While extensive discussion
       of individual performances is necessarily selective, an appendix
       cites a full list of West End, Old Vic, and Stratford-upon-Avon
       stagings. The general theatrical tendencies are suggested in the
       chapter headings--full dress (1900-14), scene changing (1914-30),
       moving fast (1930-46), nothing barred (1946-64).

194   WEBSTER, MARGARET. Shakespeare Without Tears. New York:
       McGraw-Hill, 1942, 240 pp.
          Approaches Shakespeare from a director's point of view in
       an assumption that Shakespeare can be kept alive in the fullest
       and most vivid sense only in the theater. The movement toward
       reconstructing the Elizabethan theater and the authenticity of
       Shakespeare's text, along with a renewed emphasis on dramatic
       criticism, now makes possible the establishment of a tradition
       against which Shakespearean productions can be measured. Part 1
       discusses the nature of the company, the actor and his methods,
       the stage, and the audience in Shakespeare's day. Part 2

provides critical insights on each play in the canon. The middle
comedies are especially noteworthy for their rich acting parts.
The great tragedies operate on a plane above the level of life,
allowing the actor scope and space for a diversity of different
psychological interpretations. The magic of the stage is its
duality, either evoking illusion or creating a penetrating search
for reality. Antony and Cleopatra is perhaps Shakespeare's
greatest piece of "theater craftsmanship" in the tragic vein.
His romances reflect the influence both of Beaumont and Fletcher's
tragicomedies and of the technical possibilities of the indoor
stage at Blackfriars.

See also entries 12, 14, 165, 168, 170, 176, 183, 222, 252, 929.

THEMATIC AND TOPICAL STUDIES

  195   ALEXANDER, PETER. Introductions to Shakespeare. London:
        William Collins Sons, 1964, 192 pp.
            Serves as a companion volume to Alexander's edition of
    Shakespeare (see entry 45). The material itself is drawn from
    his Tudor Shakespeare and the four-volume Collins Classics edi-
    tion. Included is an essay on Shakespeare's theater by E.A.J.
    Honigmann and Alexander's discussion of Shakespeare's life, the
    folio texts, the First Folio, and the Second Folio. Then follow
    critical introductions to each of the plays (arranged under
    comedy, history, and tragedy) and each of the poems. Topics
    generally addressed in each essay concern matters of source,
    date, text, and interpretation. (See entry 31.)

  196   ALLMAN, EILEEN JORGE. Player-King and Adversary: Two Faces
        of Play in Shakespeare. Baton Rouge and London: Louisiana
        State University Press, 1980, 347 pp.
            Asserts that Shakespeare employs the universality of human
    play as a mirror both for the character and the spectator in
    exploring, defining and educating human nature. The pattern
    makers are of two generic types, the Player-King and the Adver-
    sary. In the educative process the Player-King experiences a
    psychic shock--Richard II loses his name: Portia is bound by a
    casket; Hal mistrusts his political title; Vincentio fears his
    ability to rule; Prospero is stripped of authority and homeland.
    Whether in comic or tragic terms the characters and the specta-
    tors discover their true natures and regain psychic health.

  197   ARMSTRONG, EDWARD A. Shakespeare's Imagination: A Study of
        the Psychology of Association and Inspiration. London:
        Lindsay Drummond, 1946, 230 pp.
            Attempts to explain Shakespeare's compositional methods by
    examining the associative processes revealed in his imagery, in
    particular the nexus of images or image clusters. The creation
    of such clusters is a dynamic process utilizing memory, emotion,

and reason. Particular focus is on the image groups concerning
kites and coverlets, birds and beetles, the eagle and weasel, the
goose, the painted jay, fish, and fowl.

198   ARTHOS, JOHN. The Art of Shakespeare. London: Bowes & Bowes,
      1964, 198 pp.
         Explores a representative range of Shakespeare's plays to
display the consistent theme of the movement of a character
toward truth. In tragedy we move within the protagonist and engage in his dialogue of the soul; our own emotional involvement
is a part of the dramatic experience. In comedy the character's
ultimate discovery of truth also involves moments of bitterness
and rage, but Shakespeare forces the spectator to observe from a
distance and to grant emotional approval to the ending without
bloodshed. The final plays join to comedy the profound concerns
of romance and its setting in fantasy.

199   _____. Shakespeare: The Early Writings. Totowa, N.J.:
      Rowman & Littlefield, 1972, 264 pp.
         Examines Venus and Adonis, The Rape of Lucrece, and the
eight earliest plays in terms of Shakespeare's manipulation of
humanistic dramatic conventions and the infusion of elements from
the native tradition. Early in his career, for example, Shakespeare played with the Platonic doctrine at the heart of
Petrarchism, but the Platonism is matched and in some ways even
confined by the common sense of a Launce, a Speed, or a Dogberry
or by the conscious posing of a Feste. In his prodigality of
language and action, the wide expanse of contrarieties and similarities, he enriches the limits of drama in a manner that will
mature but not change in his major work.

200   BAILEY, JOHN. Shakespeare. English Heritage Series. London:
      Longmans, Green, 1929, 208 pp.
         Offers an analytic essay on Shakespeare's life and works.
The material is divided into a discussion of Shakespeare's life
and characters, of the poems, and of the earlier and later plays.
A brief survey is provided for each play in roughly chronological
order. A dominant strain throughout much of Shakespeare's work
is the monarch, whose necessity is not questioned, but whose
weakness, incompetence, and cruelty are depicted in particular
figures. The miracle of art, however, is that we are left not
with a sense of ruin and ugliness but with a conviction of man's
enigmatic grandeur and potential.

201   BAMBER, LINDA. Comic Women, Tragic Men: A Study of Gender
      and Genre Study in Shakespeare. Stanford: Stanford Univer-
      sity Press, 1982, 211 pp.
         Maintains that Shakespeare inevitably writes from the
masculine perspective (the self) and that the force that inter-
acts with it (the other) is the feminine perspective. This
interaction may involve genuine or apparent betrayal as in the

tragedies, demolition of the social hierarchies as in the comedies, or spiritual fulfillment as in the romances. While Shakespeare is not a feminist, he does--except for the histories--
associate the feminine with whatever man takes most seriously
outside of himself.

202   BARROLL, J. LEEDS. Artificial Persons: The Formation of
       Character in the Tragedies of Shakespeare. Columbia:
       University of South Carolina Press, 1974, 267 pp.
            Labels the theory of the humors an inadequate explanation
       for the dichotomy of passion and reason as basic to the concept
       of character in the Renaissance. The duality is more effectively
       perceived as the conflict within one's "affections" (his natural
       yearnings) of love of self and love of God. The former is
       destructive when for reasons of lust, greed, or ambition it pre-
       vents proper fulfillment of the latter. Generally Shakespeare's
       protagonists can be envisioned as individuals whose attempt to
       establish their identity or personality is thwarted by such dis-
       torted values and whose sense of psychological wholeness is
       realized only through the insights concomitant with their final
       disastrous moments.

203   BETHELL, S.L. Shakespeare and the Popular Dramatic Tradition.
       London: Staples Press, 1944, 164 pp.
            Discusses a variety of aspects of Shakespearean drama, for
       example, the range of production and critical interpretation from
       the highly stylized to the realistic, the Elizabethans' heightened
       awareness of play as play as a consequence of the nature of
       Shakespeare's theater and the psychological impact of that aware-
       ness, and Shakespeare's use of anachronism. The use of dialogic
       conventions emphasizes the double nature of character, and the
       generic mixing of comedy and tragedy reflects the audience's
       familiarity with rapid modal shifts in early popular drama.

204   BILTON, PETER. Commentary and Control in Shakespeare's Plays.
       New York: Humanities Press, 1974, 247 pp.
            Argues that the evolving sophistication of Shakespeare's
       dramaturgy is reflected in the changing nature of the "commenting
       characters" who "keep us emotionally and imaginatively on the
       right track" (p. 15). The commentators of the early plays
       (Exeter and Lucy in 1 Henry VI, Margaret in Richard III, Launce
       and Speed in The Two Gentlemen of Verona) are largely external
       to the action. Somewhat more integrated is the commentary of
       Feste and Touchstone in the mature comedies. The principal of
       the major tragedies is himself a commentator, revealing in
       soliloquies the various stages of his spiritual exploration while
       surrounding characters establish tension through their sympathy,
       praise, or condemnation.

205   BIRNEY, ALICE LOTVIN. Satiric Catharsis in Shakespeare: A
      Theory of Dramatic Structure. Berkeley and London: Univer-
      sity of California Press, 1973, 158 pp.
           Focuses on five Shakespearean figures who function as
      satirists--Margaret of Anjou in the Henry VI-Richard III
      tetralogy, Falstaff in 1,2 Henry IV, Jacques in As You Like It,
      Thersites in Troilus and Cressida, and Apemantus in Timon of
      Athens. Whereas Margaret employs the direct curse, Falstaff
      deals in witty invective and wordplay; Jacques is a fool-
      scapegoat whose rejection purges Arden of discordant emotions;
      Thersites infects his play with caustic views, transmitting his
      disease to others rather than purging; Apemantus drives Timon to
      rage, and in turn his death effects "a catharsis of such emotions
      of social censure that would have rocked the real world of 1609"
      (p. 17).

206   BRADBROOK, MURIEL C. The Living Monument: Shakespeare and
      the Theatre of His Time. Cambridge: Cambridge University
      Press, 1976, 287 pp.
           Concerns Shakespeare's contemporary theater, the "workshop"
      conditions that determined its direction, the playwright-audience-
      actor relationship, and the play's reflection of contemporary
      political and theological issues in a manner to which each of the
      elements of a stratified society could respond. The classical
      terms tragedy and comedy evolved as a consequence of particular
      combinations of actors and poets, just as the classical name
      theater came to be the customary term for the game or playing
      place. These forms in the last quarter of the sixteenth century
      "grew from a matrix of undifferentiated seasonal games, craft
      shows, and public entertainments, civic celebrations, private
      festivities, and polemics on social and religious questions"
      (p. 36). Members of the audience were not passive; their parti-
      cipation in a play promoted a sense of community and fulfillment
      present in the earlier ritual.

207   BRISSENDEN, ALAN. Shakespeare and the Dance. Atlantic
      Highlands, N.J.: Humanities Press, 1981, 145 pp.
           Concerns Shakespeare's use of dance, both literal and fig-
      urative, as a symbol of harmony throughout his plays. An opening
      chapter on the philosophic concept of dance in Renaissance
      thought and of the ubiquity of dance in Elizabethan society is
      followed by discussion of dance in the plays themselves. Literal
      and celebrative in the comedies, largely ironic in the tragedies,
      dance in the romances is thematically related to the movement
      from psychic bondage to freedom.

208   BROWER, REUBEN A. Hero and Saint: Shakespeare and the Graeco-
      Roman Heroic Tradition. Oxford: Clarendon Press, 1971,
      424 pp.
           Observes that the contrast between virtue in the sense of
      bravery and virtue in the sense of kindliness recurs constantly

in the plays of Shakespeare's maturity from Julius Caesar to The
Tempest. At times both virtues are depicted in the same play
(King Lear, Othello); at times the heroic predominates (Antony
and Cleopatra) and at times the saintly (The Winter's Tale).
They comprise for the morally sensitive and honest individual
two metaphoric ways of facing life at its most terrible moments.
The metaphors range, then, from the Christ type to the Graeco-
Roman type. No heroes in Shakespeare are absolute, but the image
of the ideal is the source for measuring their grandeur, con-
flicts, and sense of failure.

209   BROWNLOW, FRANK WALSH. Two Shakespearean Sequences:
      "Henry VI" to "Richard III" and "Pericles" to "Timon of
      Athens." Pittsburgh: University of Pittsburgh Press;
      London: Macmillan, 1977, 245 pp.
         Argues that Shakespeare's skeptical and analytical turn of
mind led him to write at the beginning and at the end of his
career genuinely experimental drama. Elizabethan plays are
filled with figuratively topical allusions; and the organizing
principle of Shakespeare's early histories, even while they pay
tribute to the past, reflects the reality of contemporary political problems. The second sequence provides an answer to the
corrosive evil of the tragedies and the problem comedies; the
late plays depict evil contained and turned to good by time,
nature, and patience.

210   BRYANT, JOSEPH A., Jr. Hippolyta's View: Some Christian
      Aspects of Shakespeare's Plays. Lexington: University of
      Kentucky Press, 1961, 239 pp.
         Demonstrates through analysis of eleven plays that Shake-
speare's view and practice of poetry derived from a Catholic
Christian perspective. Hippolyta, like the Christian, "recreates
the data of experience in a dream that is truth itself, or all we
shall likely get of truth this side of pardise" (p. 4). From
the literal tale the reader moves to the allegorical and from
thence to the moral or spiritual insight that lies behind it.
Shakespeare's plays, in a word, develop the great archetypal
myths of the human race, in each case working by analogy or
through transfiguration to embody and depict some aspect of the
Christian faith.

211   CALDERWOOD, JAMES L. Shakespearean Metadrama: The Argument
      of the Play in "Titus Andronicus," "Love's Labor's Lost,"
      "Romeo and Juliet," "A Midsummer Night's Dream," and
      Richard II." Minneapolis: University of Minnesota Press,
      1971, 192 pp.
         Argues that dramatic art--its materials of language and
theater, its generic forms and conventions, its relationships to
society--is a dominant Shakespearean theme. Various interior
playwrights like Aaron, Oberon, Iago, and Prospero underscore
the illusion of dramatic art as do the illusions controlled by

Poor Tom or Richard III or Hamlet. Each play generates its own
dramatic tensions--the barbarism of poetic language in Titus
Andronicus, the deposition of ceremonial language in Richard II,
a language that can bind lovers to each other but not to society
in Romeo and Juliet.

212   CAMPBELL, OSCAR JAMES. Shakespeare's Satire. Oxford: Oxford
       University Press, 1943, 227 pp.
          Argues that Shakespeare in the first decade of the seven-
       teenth century gave free rein to his satiric spirit. The mood
       darkens with Malvolio, and the spirit of derision fully controls
       Troilus and Cressida (see entry 855). While Troilus was designed
       for a private audience, Measure for Measure is a comical satire
       for the popular stage in which a conventional comic closure modi-
       fies and alters the derisive tone. Both Timon of Athens and
       Coriolanus are properly termed tragical satire. The heroes, as
       well as the surrounding figures, are hounded by caustic laughter,
       and a satiric ambiguity pervades both plays. The principles of
       sound polity and sane action must be inferred by the spectators.

213   CHAMBERS, EDMUND KERCHEVER. Shakespeare: A Survey. London:
       Sidgwick & Jackson, 1925, 325 pp.
          Reprints the introductions to each of the plays first pub-
       lished from 1904 to 1908 in the Red Letter Shakespeare. Per-
       sistent themes include Shakespeare's treatment of generic objects
       and limitations, the shifting phases of pessimism and optimism,
       and the apparent reflections of his personal experience upon the
       mirror of his art. The keynote of Hamlet is the "tragic in-
       effectiveness of the speculative intellect in a world of action"
       (p. 189), and, as with Brutus, Hamlet gets the worst of it and
       leaves us to wonder at the irony of why it must be so. All's
       Well That Ends Well, like Measure for Measure and Troilus and
       Cressida, is examined as a bitter comedy, Helena as degraded
       rather than triumphant, womanly love rendered ignoble by the
       imperious instinct of sex.

214   CLEMEN, WOLFGANG H. Shakespeare's Dramatic Art. London:
       Methuen, 1972, 236 pp.
          Covers such topics as the art of Shakespeare's exposition,
       his soliloquies, devices of anticipation, the theme of appearance
       versus reality in the plays, and Shakespeare in the modern world.
       The opening essay on Shakespeare's expository art deals with the
       dramatic use of omens, portents, dreams, supernatural appearances,
       irony, and prophetic imagery. Based on the assumption that a
       spectator's full experience involves his being drawn to antici-
       pate the action, Clemen notes that Shakespeare above all other
       playwrights is skillful in forcing the spectator to "watch the
       development of the play, the delusions, hopes, discoveries, the
       'false' and the 'right' actions of the characters on the stage
       with a mixture of pleasure, apprehension, and critical detach-
       ment" (p. 5).

215   COLIE, ROSALIE L. Shakespeare's Living Art. Princeton:
       Princeton University Press, 1974, 370 pp.
          Views Shakespeare's plays as explorations of his craft, as
       striking illustrations of an ability to interweave elements of
       farce, comedy, melodrama, and nightmarish tragedy. Such inter-
       action is present in his expansion of the Senecan model in Titus
       Andronicus, his enrichment of Plautine method in The Comedy of
       Errors, his exploitation of the range of language and his juxta-
       position of mirth and sorrow in Love's Labor's Lost. Perhaps
       this aspect of his artistry culminates in his merger of romance,
       epic, and derision in Troilus and Cressida and in the range of
       dramatic forms ("from interlude and morality to the most sophis-
       ticated forms of modern coterie plays" [p. 356]) in King Lear.

216   COUNCIL, NORMAN. When Honour's at the Stake: Ideas of Honour
       in Shakespeare's Plays. London: George Allen & Unwin, 1973,
       165 pp.
          Observes that honor in the Renaissance carried various
       meanings, ranging from the conferring of an external reward to a
       sense of obedience to what is due or right. In 1 Henry IV the
       action of the major characters is defined in terms of honor with
       Hotspur embodying the principles of a rigorous code of honor and
       Falstaff consciously and explicitly rejecting it; Hal, neither
       accepting nor rejecting, exploits it for his pragmatic purposes.
       Hamlet's dilemma is to discover a valid basis for action; basic
       to the play is the "assumption that there may exist an ideal,
       objective, and permanent system of moral value" (p. 110). The
       search for honor forms the structural basis for Lear as well; the
       old king must endure the stripping away of the position and the
       possessions inherent to his false concept of value in order to
       experience the honor at the heart of humanity.

217   CRAIG, HARDIN. An Interpretation of Shakespeare. New York:
       Dryden Press, 1948, 400 pp.
          Provides interpretive essays on each of the plays and poems,
       along with an introductory chapter on Shakespeare as an Eliza-
       bethan and a concluding chapter on him as a citizen of the world.
       As the context suggests, the primary focus is on understanding
       theme and structure through Elizabethan eyes, viewing the plays
       in terms of Renaissance psychology, politics, and philosophy. In
       matters of style, though Shakespeare is occasionally guilty of
       too much artifice, he rarely loses sight of his dramatic purpose.
       He skillfully employs the mannered style of his age, and his gift
       of lyrical beauty is second to none.

218   CRUTTWELL, PATRICK. The Shakespearean Moment and Its Place in
       the Poetry of the Seventeenth Century. New York: Columbia
       University Press, 1955, 262 pp.
          Examines the half-century from 1590 to 1640 that marks the
       social and cultural upheaval culminating in a transition from

the medieval past to the essentially modern mentality. Shakespeare's tragedies lie artistically at the heart of this profound
shift in thought and feeling, reflecting (like his sonnets before
them) the currents and cross-currents of the age--"lost innocence,
lost simplicity, lost certainty, all symbolized in a lost and re-
gretted past" (p. 37). Along with Donne, Shakespeare gives voice
to the spirit of the Renaissance that is founded on contrarieties,
simultaneously vulgar and intellectual, traditional and modern,
religious and secular.

219   CUTTS, JOHN P. The Shattered Glass: A Dramatic Pattern in
      Shakespeare's Early Plays. Detroit: Wayne State University
      Press, 1968, 153 pp.
          Suggests that Shakespeare in his early plays is moving
      through a series of experimentations in structure that culminate
      symbolically in the shattered glass in Richard II. It marks the
      point at which Shakespeare fully realizes a structure based on a
      dynamic figure who must shatter and be shattered, who must be
      broken into many people, and who must come to terms with the
      nature of his shattered personality. Earlier plays have dealt
      with mirror imagery (The Comedy of Errors), with shadow and
      substance (Titus Andronicus, Richard III), with fragmentation
      and synthesis (A Midsummer Night's Dream).

220   DASH, IRENE G. Wooing, Wedding and Power: Women in Shake-
      speare's Plays. New York: Columbia University Press, 1981,
      295 pp.
          Asserts that Shakespeare's plays offer insights into
      women's self-perceptions in a patriarchal world. Drawn with
      neither anger nor condescension, these female figures challenge
      accepted patterns for female behavior. The right to make one's
      own choices, for example, is at the center of Kate's confronta-
      tion with Petruchio, the rejection of the lovers' suits by the
      Princess of France and her attendants, Cleopatra's determination
      to live in adultery with Antony, and Isabella's unwillingness to
      sacrifice her virginity. Concentration on the female perspective
      will unfold for spectator and critic alike a greater appreciation
      of Shakespeare's ability to dramatize the complexities of the
      human situation.

221   DAWSON, ANTHONY B. Indirections: Shakespeare and the Art of
      Illusion. Toronto: University of Toronto Press, 1978, 194 pp.
          Focuses on Shakespeare's uses of illusion, deceit, disguise,
      and manipulation not only to incite the movement of the plot it-
      self but also to create a statement about the nature and function
      of the interaction between the character and the spectator. Dis-
      guise in the romantic comedies, for example, draws the characters
      into an illusion that is therapeutic for all the playgoers. Such
      comic manipulative devices are applied to morally ambivalent
      stage worlds in Hamlet, All's Well, and Measure for Measure.
      Hamlet's antic disposition is a disguise through which he intends

to set things right, both ethically and politically. As stage
manager, chorus, part author of the play-within-the-play, and
spectator the Prince counters Claudius's determination to gauge
his motives, but the impulsive slaying of Polonius irrevocably
deflects his efforts. The Tempest is envisioned as Shakespeare's
most stunning and most successful statement about theatrical
artifice.

222   DESSEN, ALAN C. Elizabethan Drama and the Viewer's Eye.
      Chapel Hill: University of North Carolina Press, 1977,
      176 pp.
         Asserts that a full appreciation of an Elizabethan play
requires a conjunction of the critic's interpretative perception,
the director's theatrical insights, and the historian's contextual knowledge. Unity in a play frequently involves all
three. The emphatic parallels between Hamlet and Pyrrhus as
avengers, for example, lend structural coherence, as do the
parallels between Hotspur's conspiracy and Falstaff's robbery at
Gadshill. Also discussed are the significance of symbols or
central images, the effect of metadramatic elements within the
play, and the pattern of stage psychomachia.

223   DRISCOLL, JAMES P. Identity in Shakespearean Drama.
      Lewisburg: Bucknell University Press; London and Toronto:
      Associated University Presses, 1983, 202 pp.
         Examines psychological, critical, and philosophical back-
grounds of identity anxiety to probe the four aspects of identity
found in Shakespeare--the conscious, the social, the real, and
the ideal. Hamlet's quest for self-knowledge, for example,
parallels in Jungian terms that of mythic heroes, whose dys-
functional view of society exposes the imbalance and the corruption. In Othello Iago cleverly manipulates the Moor's confusions
about his social identity to produce a fundamental alteration in
his conscious identity. Lear is viewed as a Jungian God-image
whose Job-like experience forces him to recognize on a cosmic
level the arbitrariness of his own will. Prospero achieves a
metastance or overview that, by dispelling fear of time and evil,
frees one to achieve ideal identity.

224   EDWARDS, PHILIP. Shakespeare and the Confines of Art.
      London: Methuen, 1968, 170 pp.
         Argues that Shakespeare consciously attempted to extend the
boundaries of his generic form by subjugating nature to art and
by creating an experience culminating in the reconciliation of
contraries, in a word, by making art an effective model of the
human experience. In his comedies Shakespeare seems to rewrite
with variation something of the same play structured on the
phases of separation, bewilderment, and harmony. The accumula-
tion of irony in the middle comedies enables him to build in a
dialectic that lends complexity to the form without repudiating
it. Hamlet explores in depth the limits of what an individual

with a sense of moral integrity can accomplish in a world of
anarchy. Shakespeare accomplishes his final vision of comedy,
love, and reconciliation through a form that itself blazons its
fictive nature and fragility of vision.

225   EGAN, ROBERT. Drama Within Drama: Shakespeare's Sense of His
       Art in "King Lear," "The Winter's Tale," and "The Tempest."
       New York and London: Columbia University Press, 1975, 128 pp.
          Examines how Shakespeare establishes the theme of King
       Lear, The Winter's Tale, and The Tempest through a character's
       effort to control and to alter reality through dramatic illusion.
       Prospero, Edgar and Lear, and Camillo and Paulina join the dra-
       matic art within the play to that of the play itself. The pietà
       tableau of Lear and Cordelia, for example, sets artistic control
       against life's worst realities, enacted by Lear and observed and
       commented upon by Edgar. The Winter's Tale depicts the fall of a
       cosmically ordered universe and, through the work of Paulina and
       Camillo, its regeneration through a renewed faith in essential
       human goodness. Prospero as artist pardons and embraces the
       human agents of disorder in his society.

226   ELLIS-FERMOR, UNA. The Frontiers of Drama. London: Methuen,
       1945, 154 pp.
          Observes that the frontiers of drama expand and contract
       from age to age and that truly great dramas are those that on
       rare occasions break through and transcend the genre's natural
       limits. Shakespeare's history plays, for example, achieve a
       reconciliation of epic material with dramatic form. Though gain-
       ing dramatic power through the conflict of individual figures,
       Shakespeare also throughout the series portrays a multifarious-
       ness of life that characterizes the development of England it-
       self. Troilus and Cressida is described as a great achievement,
       a succession of violently contrasted characters, events, and
       sentiments unified in the delineation of disjunction as the
       center of life in the universe.

227   _____. The Jacobean Drama: An Interpretation. London:
       Methuen, 1936, 345 pp.
          Surveys the range of moods and the dramatic technique that
       characterize English drama from 1598 to 1625. The heritage of
       this drama was spiritual uncertainty springing in part from the
       spread of Machiavellian materialism and fear of the impending
       destruction of a great civilization. After the spiritual nadir
       of the middle years of the period a slow return to a balanced
       view emerges. Shakespeare's transmutation of his sources in
       Julius Caesar and the Henry IV-Henry V plays signals this shift to
       a complex, ambivalent view of life; the full flood of Jacobean
       horror is reflected in the major tragedies and problem comedies,
       the return to balance in his romances.

228   FARNHAM, WILLARD. The Shakespearean Grotesque: Its Genesis
        and Transformation. Oxford: Clarendon Press, 1971, 175 pp.
        Describes the grotesque spirit in literature and art as
that which captures dramatically opposed forces in life. Falstaff
is a generous fulfillment of that spirit, a monstrous body in the
tradition of animal and man--an animal figure in whom "comicity"
joins with "cosmicity" (p. 50). His tavern world of thievery
joins with the political world of high endeavor. Hamlet's essential nature is invaded by the grotesque as he shares the role of
court prince and court fool. He mocks the comic in mankind
through Polonius and Osric, yet he in turn is ridiculed by the
grave digger. Also discussed as grotesque are Thersites, Iago,
and Caliban.

229   FERGUSSON, FRANCIS. Shakespeare: The Pattern in His Carpet.
        New York: Delacorte Press, 1970, 331 pp.
        Collects in a single volume the introductory essays written
over a period of eleven years (1958-68) for the Laurel Shakespeare series (Dell). Fergusson describes the early plays (to
1594) as deliberate efforts to cater to popular tastes--Plautine
farce in The Comedy of Errors, Senecan tragedy in Titus Andronicus, romantic comedy in The Two Gentlemen of Verona, and pageantic
chronicle in 1,2,3 Henry VI. The plays of the second period (to
1599) represent "ways to Eden" through either a beautiful mistress
or a monarch. In the period of the great tragedies and the problem comedies Shakespeare is "preoccupied with the hell, or loss
of faith, or the pronounced end which always threatens the human
scene" (p. 165). In the final years of The Winter's Tale and The
Tempest (to 1613) the fundamental pattern of the plays is a movement from innocence to experience to innocence.

230   FIEDLER, LESLIE. The Stranger in Shakespeare. New York:
        Stein & Day, 1972, 263 pp.
        Concerns the archetypal figure who, standing between "hero"
and "villain," defines the limits of the human in representing
that portion of life or culture that is seen as a threat and
hence must be symbolically cast out. Whatever marginal ambivalence Shakespeare might have felt, he subscribed to the public
mythology of his audience, and the "stranger" figure at various
stages of his career appears as woman (Joan of Arc), as Jew
(Shylock), as Black (Othello), and as new world savage (Caliban).

231   FITCH, ROBERT E. Shakespeare: The Perspective of Value.
        Philadelphia: Westminster Press, 1969, 304 pp.
        Stresses the moral order as the single consistent element
in Shakespeare's plays, whether depicted as operating under God,
nature, or time. So thoroughly had he assimilated the Bible that
it is woven by way of poetic paraphrase into all his works. At
times the religious imagery is used to enhance the spirituality
of love (Romeo and Juliet, Measure for Measure); at times it is
used to suggest temptation (Hamlet) or damnation (Macbeth). The

final plays see an emergence of the Hellenic over the Hebraic, especially in the metaphysical concern with nature and the cyclical, repetitive character of time.

232   FLY, RICHARD. Shakespeare's Mediated World. Amherst:
      University of Massachusetts Press, 1976, 164 pp.
          Isolates in five Shakespearean plays how "go-betweens"
      inadvertently distort communication and destroy both personal
      and social harmony. Such flawed mediation underscores the vul-
      nerability of the human condition whether through the futile
      efforts of the nurse, Benvolio, and Friar Lawrence in Romeo and
      Juliet or the specious adulteration of the truth by Thersites and
      others in Troilus and Cressida. Also considered are Flavius's
      role and other disjunctive elements in Timon of Athens and the
      ineffectiveness of communication at various levels in Measure for
      Measure and King Lear.

233   FOAKES, R.A. Shakespeare: The Dark Comedies to the Last
      Plays: From Satire to Celebration. Charlottesville: Univer-
      sity of Virginia Press, 1971, 186 pp.
          Examines the last plays as structures designed for perfor-
      mance for which the vision is the result of new techniques and
      possibilities that arose in the dark comedies in connection with
      the revival of children's companies. Above all, the problem
      comedies exhibit a stubborn energy for life that incorporates the
      desires of the flesh into the basic movement of the play, a min-
      gling of the satiric tone with the dramatic. The final plays
      exploit these techniques of distancing and disengagement that
      lead characters to accept and celebrate life on its own terms,
      unpredictable but wonderful.

234   FRENCH, MARILYN. Shakespeare's Division of Experience. New
      York: Summit Books, 1981, 376 pp.
          Insists on Shakespeare's primary concern with role playing
      as a concept of cultural programming, society's assigning of
      certain roles on the basis of gender and obliging individuals to
      play them out, the relationship between political power and the
      "division" of experience according to gender principles. Man's
      role encompasses law, authority, and legitimacy, and he views the
      end of sexuality as ultimate control or possession. While Shake-
      speare's comedies and tragedies contain similar events, emphasis
      in the former is on man's deadly power, in the latter on women's
      ability to neutralize and negate that power in the interest of
      love and harmony.

235   GARBER, MARJORIE B. Coming of Age in Shakespeare. London:
      Methuen, 1981, 248 pp.
          Examines Shakespeare's characters in terms of the socio-
      logical concept of the rites of passage. The character in each
      case must change and adapt as the situation changes. Those who
      fail to do so are banished, rejected, or destroyed--Don John, for

example, or Malvolio or Falstaff. Against these characters can
be measured the growth of Benedick and Beatrice, of Olivia and
Orsino, and of Hal. As Cordelia's failure to respond to her
father at the opening of King Lear provokes disaster, so her
conciliatory posture in act 4 issues in reconciliation. Perhaps
the quintessential rite of passage is that of the spectator, who
in tragedy is "at once isolated and chosen, privileged and obli-
gated" (p. 240).

236   _____. Dream in Shakespeare: From Metaphor to Metamorphosis.
        New Haven: Yale University Press, 1974, 226 pp.
        Concerns Shakespeare's consistent use of dreams or the
dream state, both literal and figurative. After surveying the
dominant Renaissance attitudes toward dreams, the author examines
the use of the device in Shakespeare's work for architectonic
structure--simultaneously foreshadowing events of the past and
establishing an atmosphere of mystery and apprehension. Of
ultimately more significance is Shakespeare's increasing ability
to subsume the metaphoric sense of dream and the concomitant
release of the imagination into the dynamics of the play. The
process culminates in the romance, in which the dream-state has
become metaphorically synonymous with the created artifact of the
stage world and the emphasis is directly upon the redemptive act
of metamorphosis and transformation. (See entries 312, 342.)

237   GODDARD, HAROLD C. The Meaning of Shakespeare. Chicago:
        University of Chicago Press, 1951, 694 pp.
        Argues that the passage of time is forever enriching for
society the meaning of Shakespeare's plays and the decisions that
his characters must face. The attempt is to consider Shakespeare whole, with each of the plays and poems envisioned as
chapters of a single work. Each play is discussed in the pre-
sumable order of composition. The Comedy of Errors is drama in
which the concept of character has not caught up with the dexterity of plotting; Richard III is exhuberance of invention and
excess of wit at its best; Romeo and Juliet champions a youthful
passion searing enough to cut through the bonds of familial
hatred. In Antony and Cleopatra Shakespeare is able to grasp the
full range of love, containing both God and the Devil. In the
romances the focus is on some shock just short of death that
awakens the full imagination of the personality.

238   GOLDMAN, MICHAEL. Shakespeare and the Energies of Drama.
        Princeton: Princeton University Press, 1972, 176 pp.
        Seeks for the meaning of a Shakespeare play primarily in
the response of the spectators and the manner in which it builds
upon their awareness and exposes their "closed selves" to urgent
and dangerous possibilities. We with the tragic protagonists
must travel from one form of isolation to another, must share
both the violence and the illumination of the love of Romeo and
Juliet, must analyze like Hamlet the various roles (scholar,

statesman, madman, critic, revenger) that he is forced to play, must admit the inadequacy of any single meaning in act 5 of King Lear, must perceive in the romances that--while human life is tragic--life itself is restorative and joyous. Shakespearean drama is a dynamic process binding both actor and spectator in an exchange of creative energies.

239 GOLDSMITH, ROBERT HILLIS. Wise Fools in Shakespeare.
     Liverpool: Liverpool University Press, 1955, 123 pp.
        Focuses on Shakespeare's use and transcendence of the con-
     cept of the fool from popular and literary traditions. Shake-
     speare's various fools culminate in four complex and individual
     figures--Touchstone, a comic realist astray in the forest of
     romance; Lavache, a conscious and modish humorist who jokes
     about sex and chastity through innuendo; Feste, an artist who
     observes the golden mean in loving and laughing; and Lear's Fool,
     who in following his sick king embodies the Christian doctrine
     of wise folly. (See entry 331.)

240 GRANVILLE-BARKER, HARLEY. Prefaces to Shakespeare. 4 vols.
     Princeton: Princeton University Press, 1946, 1026 pp.
        Features analytic essays on Hamlet (1), King Lear,
     Cymbeline, and Julius Caesar (2), Antony and Cleopatra (3),
     Love's Labor's Lost, Romeo and Juliet, The Merchant of Venice,
     and Othello (4). The principal aim is to discover the vitality
     of Shakespeare's dramaturgy by rediscovering the dynamics of the
     Elizabethan theater. The chief end of criticism, likewise, is
     to serve the end of supporting the living play on stage. The
     character of Hamlet, for example, despite incongruities in per-
     sonality, transports us into the "strange twilight regions of the
     soul" (1:131); the riches of his emotion and thought fall to
     those in the audience whose own are a touchstone for them, thus
     fulfilling the necessity of character in action. The text of
     Shakespeare's play is like a score awaiting performance. The
     soliloquy is one of the most important tools of Shakespeare's
     craft, the means by which he puts the spectator into both intel-
     lectual and emotional touch with the character. Essays on The
     Winter's Tale, Twelfth Night, A Midsummer Night's Dream, and
     Macbeth, along with "From Henry V to Hamlet," are available in
     More Prefaces to Shakespeare, ed. Edward M. Moore (Princeton:
     Princeton University Press, 1974).

241 GRUDIN, ROBERT. Mighty Opposites: Shakespeare and Renais-
     sance Contrariety. Berkeley and London: University of
     California Press, 1979, 217 pp.
        Observes that Shakespeare's dramatic vision is grounded in
     paradox, from individual phrases such as Desdemona as an "excel-
     lent wretch" and Iago as a "precious villain" to concepts of
     character such as Prospero as at once God-like revenger and fal-
     len man to concepts of an entire play such as Coriolanus as
     hideously heroic or Antony and Cleopatra as sublimely decadent.

The interaction of contraries is one of the major philosophic
traditions of the Renaissance; while Shakespeare at first uses it
within a moral and psychological perspective, it becomes the
structural basis or the metaphysics of his great tragedies.

242   HAMILTON, A.C. The Early Shakespeare. San Marino: Hunting-
       ton Library, 1967, 237 pp.
            Examines the early plays and poems to illustrate that the
       subtleties and comprehensiveness of Shakespeare's dramatic
       genius are present from the first. As a sophisticated literary
       craftsman, he shares the wit and critical awareness of the Eliza-
       bethan poet. The Henry VI plays are explored as experiments in
       the history play, in which 3 Henry VI moves very close to tragedy,
       while Richard III is indeed historical tragedy. The study con-
       tains individual chapters on each of the early works, concluding
       with sections on Richard II, Romeo and Juliet, and A Midsummer
       Night's Dream as the resolution of the early period.

243   HARBAGE, ALFRED. As They Liked It: A Study of Shakespeare's
       Moral Artistry. New York: Macmillan, 1947, 234 pp.
            Maintains that Shakespeare is moral without being a
       moralist, that his plays are designed to stimulate the imagina-
       tion in a fundamentally positive manner. This focus can be
       gauged quickly by Shakespeare's modification of his sources and
       analogues--Lear's ferocious pride that must be purged through
       suffering, Hamlet's moral questions about revenge, Othello's
       agony concerning what he sees as the necessity of destroying
       Desdemona, the mitigation of Shylock's villainy. His plays
       stimulate the spectators' basic assumptions of man's moral nature
       and provide for continuing audiences the comforting reassurance
       that justice and harmony are both desirable and attainable despite
       their bleak existence outside the Globe.

244   _____   Shakespeare Without Words and Other Essays.
       Cambridge, Mass.: Harvard University Press, 1972, 229 pp.
            In the lead essay admonishes critics and directors who
       reduce Shakespeare's plays to the level of theater of the absurd,
       declaring that the best proof of Shakespeare's limitless vitality
       is the number who read and enjoy the plays. Other essays in the
       first group also deal with excesses of critical interpretation,
       whether the claim of Marlowe's authorship or the excesses of New
       Criticism. The second group of essays deals with the history of
       Elizabethan drama and Shakespeare's place in its evolution.

245   HARTWIG, JOAN. Shakespeare's Analogical Scene: Parody as
       Structural Syntax. Lincoln and London: University of
       Nebraska Press, 1983, 243 pp.
            Stresses the significance of small scenes in Shakespeare--
       usually dismissed as breathers or comic relief or tone setters--
       in reorienting the spectator's perspective through parallelism,
       antithesis, and verbal echo. Specific attention is focused on

the scene with Cinna the Poet in <u>Julius Caesar</u>, on Elbow's trial
in <u>Measure for Measure</u>, on the apothecary's appearance in <u>Romeo</u>
<u>and Juliet</u>, on York's determination to expose the treachery of
his own son in <u>Richard II</u>, on scenes with the porter and the
murderers and Malcolm in <u>Macbeth</u>, on the parodic subplot in
<u>Twelfth Night</u>, on the parodic function of Polonius in <u>Hamlet</u>, on
Cloten and Caliban as parodic villains.

246   HASSEL, R. CHRIS, Jr. <u>Renaissance Drama and the English</u>
       <u>Church Year</u>. Lincoln and London: University of Nebraska
       Press, 1979, 215 pp.
            Observes that seventy percent of all the Court plays occur
       on one of the ten religious festival days and then investigates
       correlations between individual plays and the thematic, imagistic,
       and narrative facets of their festival occasion. <u>The Comedy of</u>
       <u>Errors</u>, for example, was performed on Innocents' Day, a feast day
       with Biblical readings on the dispersal and reunion of families,
       and the celebration of human absurdity has liturgical overtones.
       Similarly, <u>Twelfth Night</u>, an epiphany play, shares extensive
       similarities with the religious service. Also discussed are
       <u>Cymbeline</u>, <u>1 Henry IV</u>, <u>King Lear</u>, <u>Measure for Measure</u>, <u>The</u>
       <u>Mercant of Venice</u>, <u>A Midsummer Night's Dream</u>, <u>Othello</u>, <u>The</u>
       <u>Tempest</u>, and <u>The Winter's Tale</u>.

247   HIRSCH, JAMES E. <u>The Structure of Shakespearean Scenes</u>.
       New Haven and London: Yale University Press, 1981, 230 pp.
            Maintains that the scene, the interval between one cleared
       stage and the next, is Shakespeare's fundamental artistic unit.
       These units can be solo, duet, unitary group, two part, or
       multipartite. Paradoxically, Shakespeare achieves unity of dra-
       matic theme through a multiplicity of types of scenes. Fre-
       quently, the arrangment creates internal focus. In <u>As You Like</u>
       <u>It</u>, for example, juxtaposition of similar scenes indirectly pro-
       duces conflict between Duke Senior and Duke Frederick although the
       two never meet. Similarly, the five unitary duets in <u>King Lear</u>
       form a symmetrical pattern that provides a skeleton of the action
       as a whole.

248   HOLLAND, NORMAN N. <u>Psychoanlysis and Shakespeare</u>. New York:
       McGraw-Hill, 1966, 412 pp.
            Surveys major types of psychoanalytic criticism of Shake-
       speare's works, categorized by that which deals with the author's,
       with the character's, or with audience's mind. In his endeavor
       to illumine either the creative or the responsive aspect of the
       drama, the psychoanalytic critic must concentrate on how the
       intellectual meaning of a play grows from its emotional content.
       In <u>The Tempest</u>, for example, Prospero can profitably be viewed
       as a character successfully mastering his oedipal attraction to
       his daughter, or the other characters can be investigated as
       projections of his own psyche.

249   _____. The Shakespearean Imagination. London: Macmillan,
         1964, 338 pp.
         Includes chapters on Shakespeare and his theater, shifting
attitudes toward the playwright since 1616, and the textual studies and major critical methods of twentieth-century scholarship.
Then follow analyses of sixteen plays, representing the most
popular comedies, tragedies, and histories with emphasis on
structure, parallelism, recurring images, themes, characterizations, and the particular quality of each individual play.

250   HOMAN, SIDNEY. When the Theater Turns to Itself: The
       Aesthetic Metaphor in Shakespeare. Lewisburg: Bucknell
       University Press; London and Toronto: Associated University
       Presses, 1981, 238 pp.
         Concerns theatrical self-consciousness in nine Shake-
spearean plays, moving from early plays in which Shakespeare
comically celebrates the actor (the pageant of the Nine Worthies
in Love's Labor's Lost, Bottom as actor, Puck and Oberon as controllers in A Midsummer Night's Dream); to controllers as
playwright-surrogates in Rosalind, Iago, and Vincentio; to
Hamlet, who is concerned at once with staging and play and
manipulating the spectators' response and also with the artful
progression of the entire tragedy. As The Taming of the Shrew
is primarily concerned with the induction of the spectator into
the dramatic experience, so The Tempest is concerned with his
release or his departure.

251   HONIGMANN, E.A.J. Shakespeare's Impact on His Contemporaries.
       London: Macmillan, 1982, 149 pp.
         Challenges several traditional views concerning Shake-
speare's life and work. What we know of his commercial transac-
tions, for example, suggests that he was a hard-headed business-
man, not "sweet" and "gentle." Also, rather than being indif-
ferent to the publication of his plays, he may well have requested
the publication of good quartos to replace the reported texts.
Other points of significance include a rebuttal of the idea that
Shakespeare was a slow starter and a claim that Jonson was the
rival poet of the sonnets and that The Winter's Tale was a
response to Jonson's attacks upon his artistry.

252   HOWARD, JEAN A. Shakespeare's Art of Orchestration: Stage
       Technique and Audience Response. Urbana: University of
       Illinois Press, 1984, 216 pp.
         Challenges the conception that Shakespeare's plays can be
fully appreciated only through retrospective analysis of themes,
imagery, and structure. To the contrary, drama means performance;
and Shakespeare carefully controls the spectators' involvement
with the play as it progressively unfolds, forcing them to
imaginative participation in the events on stage. Specific
attention is directed to visual, aural, and kinetic elements of
performance by which Shakespeare creates this community of
responses.

253   HOWARTH, HERBERT. The Tiger's Heart: Eight Essays on
      Shakespeare. New York: Oxford University Press, 1970,
      210 pp.
          Consists of essays ranging from a discussion of Shake-
      speare's personality to the influence of Jonsonian method in
      Twelfth Night to significant dramaturgical experimentation in
      Henry VIII and the romances. An essay concerning The Merchant of
      Venice and Hamlet focuses on the movement of Shakespeare's mind
      as he depicts in the former those who claim to be Christian but
      are controlled by archaic, bestial thrusts and in the latter
      those who claim to be bound to pagan revenge but are controlled
      by Christian impulses. A final chapter discusses the stultifying
      effects on Shakespearean criticism of an overemphasis on
      Tillyard's Elizabethan world picture (see entry 130).

254   HUNTER, ROBERT GRAMS. Shakespeare and the Comedy of Forgive-
      ness. New York and London: Columbia University Press, 1965,
      272 pp.
          Investigates the denouement in forgiveness common to six of
      Shakespeare's plays--Much Ado About Nothing, Measure for Measure,
      Cymbeline, The Winter's Tale, All's Well That Ends Well, and The
      Tempest. The moment of forgiveness demands the approval and
      acquiescence of the spectators. That the issue is problematic
      for modern audiences and critics (with, for example, Bertram and
      Angelo) is a result of the fact that Shakespeare wrote in a now
      outmoded medieval and didactically Christian dramatic tradition
      inherited from the Middle Ages. A sympathetic understanding of
      the underlying doctrine is essential to a full appreciation of
      the plays.

255   JAMES, DAVID GWILYM. "The Failure of the Ballad Makers." In
      Scepticism and Poetry: An Essay on the Poetic Imagination.
      New York: Barnes & Noble, 1937, pp. 205-41.
          Maintains that the intense human joy expressed in Shake-
      speare's earlier work is a phenomenon of the unique time in
      history in which he lived. Because of such a genial sense of
      youth he was strikingly unprepared for his moment of crisis, and
      his failure to idealize and unify the world of human experience
      is reflected in his tragedies. His final plays are efforts
      through myth to convey a new imaginative apprehension of life;
      The Tempest, more precisely, is "the record of the final dis-
      solution, the ultimate destruction, of the world by the imagina-
      tion" (p. 241).

256   JOCHUM, KLAUS PETER. Discrepant Awareness: Studies in
      English Renaissance Drama. Neue Studien zur Anglistik und
      Amerikanistik, 13. Frankfurt: Peter Lang, 1979, 310 pp.
          Deals with the distribution of knowledge in Shakespeare's
      plays, the extent to which the spectator shares that knowledge,
      and the manner in which it determines or affects his attitude
      toward the characters and the action. Discrepant awareness in

Richard III, for example, stems from the fact that the spectators
share both the private level of Richard's ambition and his devil-
ish ability to dupe others and also the omniscient perspective
on the fate of the last Yorkist king in the pattern of pre-Tudor
history. In Romeo and Juliet only the characters are fully aware
of what happens; each character remains fatefully ignorant of
vitally significant events, and this very lack of knowledge--
rather than the actions of any particular individual--is the
negative force leading to the catastrophe.

257   JONES, EMRYS. Scenic Form in Shakespeare. Oxford: Clarendon
       Press, 1971, 269 pp.
          Claims that, quite apart from the verbal and poetic quali-
       ties, Shakespeare works with the structural unit of the scene.
       The rhythm within the scene can be one of repetition and accumu-
       lation or the character can be transformed from one polar extreme
       to another. The typical Shakespearean play has two units of
       action with each comprised of a tonally and thematically related
       cluster of scenes. Discussed in the final half of the book is
       the scene structure of four tragedies--Othello, King Lear,
       Macbeth, and Antony and Cleopatra.

258   JORGENSEN, PAUL A. Shakespeare's Military World. Berkeley
       and London: University of California Press, 1956, 345 pp.
          Views Shakespeare's concept of war and military personnel
       through Renaissance eyes, describing how Shakespeare frequently
       employs musical imagery, a kind of musical harmony in elevated or
       sonorous discourse, and literal music, especially the drum. Di-
       saster in war is traced strategically to discord, whether in lack
       of order in battle array and movements (Cymbeline), in dissension
       among the military personnel (1 Henry IV, Julius Caesar), or in
       insubordination (Troilus and Cressida). Generally, soldiership
       is depicted as an honorable occupation, though not infrequently
       military preeminence is no guarantee of success in a civilian
       context (Coriolanus, Othello).

259   KAHN, COPPÉLIA. Man's Estate: Masculine Identity in Shake-
       speare. Berkeley and London: University of California Press,
       1981, 238 pp.
          Questions the general critical posture that Shakespeare's
       plays present experiences identifiably equal with man and woman.
       To the contrary, the plays involve the masculine experience and
       perspective. The focus is on man's attempt to achieve social and
       psychological identity in a patriarchal world. The histories are
       viewed as a masculine world of war and politics in which man
       gains identity through relationships with other men; Romeo and
       Juliet and The Taming of the Shrew are tragic and comic versions
       of marriage as a passage to manhood; Othello features men uniting
       in cuckoldry against women as betrayers; and Macbeth and
       Coriolanus depict men who are "unfinished heroes" (p. 19) and who
       fight only because a woman has convinced them it will make them
       manly.

260   KERMODE, FRANK. Shakespeare, Spenser, Donne. New York:
      Viking Press, 1971, 308 pp.
         Devotes five of eleven essays to various aspects of
      Shakespeare's art. These essays include an analysis of Lear that
      tackles the reasons for the persistence of the play despite the
      shifts in cosmological perspective during the past four cen-
      turies, a discussion of Shakespeare's learning in general and
      education in particular, and separate pieces on the mature come-
      dies and the final plays. Kermode examines at some length what
      he calls Shakespeare's "patience," his power to absorb our ques-
      tions and to abide--in short, his universality.

261   KERNAN, ALVIN B. The Playwright as Magician: Shakespeare's
      Image of the Poet in the English Public Theater. New Haven
      and London: Yale University Press, 1979, 164 pp.
         Focuses on Shakespeare's reflection in his poems and plays
      of the evolution of the poet-playwright from one supported by
      courtly patronage to one dependent upon commercial success.
      Through the various plays-within-plays Shakespeare demonstrates
      the difficulties of communicating the theatrical intent to
      various kinds of audiences. The tensions between the poet's
      ideals and the nature of his marketplace are perhaps reflected
      most fully in Prospero as an exiled duke, practicing an illicit
      art on an isolated and barren island.

262   KIRSCH, ARTHUR C. Jacobean Dramatic Perspectives.
      Charlottesville: University of Virginia Press, 1972, 134 pp.
         Notes significant theatrical developments in the early
      Jacobean period--the rise of tragicomedy, satiric drama, and the
      private theater--changes occurring in part because of the decline
      of the aristocracy and the rise of economic individualism. All's
      Well That Ends Well, in particular, mixes the satiric with the
      romantic in a self-consciously paradoxical conception. The play
      celebrates the presence of grace in human life even while reveal-
      ing the desperate need for it. Cymbeline, too, is a conscious
      exploration of the techniques and implications of tragicomic
      dramaturgy. Its providential pattern is a dramatic rendition of
      the felix culpa.

263   KIRSCHBAUM, LEO. Character and Characterization in Shake-
      speare. Detroit: Wayne State University Press, 1962, 168 pp.
         Focuses on the dramatic function of Shylock, Albany,
      Edgar, Banquo, Othello, Hamlet, Ophelia, Cleopatra, Romeo,
      Angelo, Margaret, and Richard II. Angelo, for example, is de-
      scribed as two strikingly disparate characterizations; his im-
      portance to the plot is functional, a "pawn of theatricality"
      (p. 124). A Macbeth-like figure of conscience torn from within,
      he in the last part of the play is amorous, mean-spirited, and
      legalistic. To the contrary, Cleopatra is viewed as consistent
      in characterization, dazzling but a voluptuary to the end.

264   KNIGHT, G. WILSON. The Christian Renaissance. Toronto:
       Macmillan, 1933, 374 pp.
           Relates the works of Shakespeare, among others, to the
       Bible and Christian dogma. The Shakespearean play is spatial as
       well as temporal, and we must be prepared to see the play whole;
       story and atmosphere emanate from a single unity. This inter-
       pretation of Shakespeare looks beyond the external facts of the
       plot line to the inner significance. The plays are purgatorial,
       and we become a vital part of that experience. In every tragedy
       spirit and nature are wrenched apart through the experience of
       the protagonist, but the action moves toward a re-creation, a
       rebirth, a new harmony. Shakespeare in various ways entwines
       Christian eschatology with a pagan naturalism.

265   _____. The Shakespearian Tempest: With a Chart of Shake-
       speare's Dramatic Universe. Oxford: Oxford University Press,
       1932, 332 pp.
           Asserts that the principle of Shakespearean unity through-
       out his plays is found in the opposition of tempest and music,
       that critics obsessed with character, psychology, and metrical
       tests have blinded themselves to this larger symbolic quality.
       Whether historical, comical, or tragical, all of his plays re-
       volve on the axis of this imagistic tension. Analysis of the
       river, sea, tempest, and musical references throughout the canon
       reveals a movement from discord to harmony, whether in the pas-
       toral idealism of romantic comedy or in the depths of the indi-
       vidual soul in the tragedies.

266   KNIGHTS, L.C. Shakespeare's Politics: With Some Recollec-
       tions on the Nature of Tradition. Oxford: Oxford University
       Press, 1958, 18 pp.
           Observes that Shakespeare always makes political issues
       subservient to the personal and the specific; he never, that is,
       writes a drama of ideas except as they are embedded in his char-
       acters and their actions. In Julius Caesar and Henry V he raises
       the question of what statesmen are liable to accept without
       question. King Lear, Macbeth, and Coriolanus explore in par-
       ticular the nature of political order and its vulnerability to
       corruption. In effect, Shakespeare examines political concep-
       tions such as power, authority, honor, order, and freedom, but he
       forces us to view this examination in terms of the realities of
       human life and relationships.

267   KOTT, JAN. Shakespeare Our Contemporary. Translated by
       Boleslaw Taborski. Garden City: Doubleday, 1964, 372 pp.
           Claims that today's spectator views the cruelty, the
       struggle for power, and the mutual slaughter in Shakespeare far
       more comprehendingly than the nineteenth-century spectator be-
       cause we discover problems and actions relevant to our own time.
       The histories, for example, chronicle the operation of the Grand
       Mechanism, the emergence of one king after another from the

destruction of the previous ruler; every step of the way is
marked by murder, violence, and treachery. Hamlet is paramountly
a drama of political crime, Troilus and Cressida a sneering
political pamphlet set in a world with no place for love,
Macbeth a play without catharsis in which all the protagonist can
do is "to drag with him into nothingness as many living beings as
possible" (p. 97). King Lear, like Beckett's Endgame, mocks the
absolute by transforming it into a blind mechanism. In Coriolanus, one of Shakespeare's most profound plays, history is no
longer demonic but merely ironic and tragic, the scenes of battle
and looting reflect the external face of war and occupation.
Nihilistic values pervade the comedies as well, with the characters in A Midsummer Night's Dream reduced to mere animalistic
love partners, The Tempest a drama of lost illusions, and the
high romantic comedies latent manifestations of androgynous
myths. (See entry 409.)

268   LEE, SIDNEY. Shakespeare and the Modern Stage With Other
       Essays. New York: Charles Scribner's Sons, 1906, 251 pp.
          Deals with various aspects of the influence and traditions
of Shakespearean drama with emphasis on its relationship to current affairs. While the scholar in the study must welcome, not
scorn, the stage as a major avenue of appreciating Shakespeare's
talent, theater managers must recognize that the power of Shakespeare lies in the words, not in embellishments of costumes and
stage designs.

269   LEVIN, HARRY. Shakespeare and the Revolution of the Times:
       Perspectives and Commentaries. New York: Oxford University
       Press, 1976, 334 pp.
          Consists of addresses, essays dealing with general struc-
tural and ideological questions, and commentaries on individual
plays. The "revolution of the times" refers to the problem of
time in Shakespeare, and the initial piece concerns the sense of
a vital relationship between past and present in the history
plays and the diachronic tension between the affirmation of the
norms of society and the individual's defiance of those traditions that is central to the tragedies.

270   LEWIS, WYNDHAM. The Lion and the Fox: The Role of the Hero
       in the Plays of Shakespeare. London: Grant Richards, 1927,
       326 pp.
          Views the master-subject motif in Shakespeare as rooted in
the Machiavellian obsession of his time. An anarchist in comedy,
more the bolshevik than a figure of conservative romance, Shakespeare constantly mixes the humorous and the tragic, with one
foot in the crude humility of medievalism and the other in the
violent hubris of the Renaissance. The king in Shakespeare
represents the personal ego, the object of jealous solicitude
and disguised hatred from his subjects. Coriolanus--the lion--
is the ornament of a strong aristocratic system set against the
fox--the tribunes or Aufidius, as Othello is set against Iago.

271   LONG, JOHN H. Shakespeare's Use of Music: A Study of the
      Music and Its Performance in the Original Production of Seven
      Comedies. Gainesville: University of Florida Press, 1955,
      213 pp.
          Examines Shakespeare's use of choral and instrumental music
      in seven romantic comedies with the focus on how song intensifies
      the impact of the language and aids in developing the plot line
      and the character and in creating particular moods. Music also
      on occasion denotes off-stage action or a necessary lapse of
      time. The seventeen songs in these plays range in type from the
      elaborate song-dance-choral ayres of A Midsummer Night's Dream
      to the popular street song at the conclusion of Twelfth Night;
      and consort performances are featured in each play. The two art
      forms are fully integrated.

272   McALINDON, THOMAS. Shakespeare and Decorum. London:
      Macmillan, 1973, 227 pp.
          Examines five major plays in light of Renaissance concepts
      of decorum in verbal and nonverbal behavior as an important sig-
      nification of the mental health of the individual and the com-
      munity. Throughout Richard II, for example, actions leading to
      or constituting civil war are described as aberrations of natural
      behavior. In Hamlet the problem or evil of corruption "is vir-
      tually identified with the loss or abuse of 'form'" (p. 44)
      whether in Polonius's speech, Laertes' actions at Ophelia's
      grave, or Claudius's deceitful machinations. Similarly, the
      tragic fate of Othello and Desdemona is provoked, not merely by
      lie as a verbal abuse, but also by rashness and impatience,
      qualities best evinced in the Moor's sentence upon his innocent
      bride. In both King Lear and Macbeth Shakespeare is more intent
      upon exploring the basic principle that propriety is founded on
      harmony with nature.

273   No entry

274   No entry

275   MacKAIL, JOHN WILLIAM. The Approach to Shakespeare. Oxford:
      Clarendon Press, 1930, 144 pp.
          Cautions readers and scholars to focus on Shakespeare's
      essential artistry as a playwright, not on the byways of bio-
      graphical origins, textual criticism, political and social his-
      tory, the mechanisms of the Elizabethan stage, or the problems
      of modern stage productions. This reaction is not to Shake-
      spearean scholarship itself but to the virtual explosion of
      peripheral studies in the past twenty years and the potential
      danger of losing Shakespeare in a maze of academic detail.
      Individual chapters follow on the comedies, the tragedies, the
      romances, and on the general quality of Shakespeare's artistry.

276 McKEITHAN, DANIEL MORLEY. The Debt to Shakespeare in the
Beaumont and Fletcher Plays. Austin: Privately Printed,
1938, 233 pp.
     Identifies Shakespeare's influence in forty-five plays from
the Beaumont-Fletcher canon. Beaumont, especially, was steeped
in Shakespeare, the influence being a general one in style and
character rather than in individual lines. Fletcher actually
borrows more frequently in plots and incidents, but, unlike
Shakespeare, he is more concerned with sensational plot than
character. That Beaumont and Fletcher borrowed so extensively
indicates their high regard for his work; it was the tonal quality of Shakespeare's later work, especially Cymbeline, that was
of greatest significance.

277 MASEFIELD, JOHN. William Shakespeare. New York: Barnes &
Noble, 1954, 227 pp.
     Contains a biographical essay and brief analytic remarks
on the sonnets and each of the poems and plays. Helena in All's
Well That Ends Well is described as an ambitious vixen in a play
"that cannot now be liked" (p. 96); Parolles, the play's only
virtue, requires the kind of comic genius who can create
Falstaff. Hamlet is a play dealing with a welter of promptings
to kill and "seekings for a righter course than killing"
(p. 107). In King Lear, Coriolanus, Othello, and Antony and
Cleopatra the protagonist is destroyed in part by blindness in
a noble nature but more significantly by a cool, resolute individual who takes advantage of this blindness.

278 MATTHEWS, HONOR. Character and Symbol in Shakespeare's Plays:
A Study of Certain Christian and Pre-Christian Elements in
Their Structure and Imagery. Cambridge: Cambridge University
Press, 1962, 211 pp.
     Argues that, since Elizabethan audiences were the direct
inheritors of a drama reflecting a Christian unified view of
life, symbolic elements recur persistently in Shakespeare's
works. Their cumulative impact reveals something of Shakespeare's own values and provides a key to thematic interpretation. Progressively through his work can be traced a movement
from the Luciferian sin of pride and the irreconcilability of
justice and mercy to the difficulty of perceiving truth from the
error with which evil powers in the universe attempt to destroy
man and, finally, to the Christian archetype of redemption and
of a new life in a new world.

279 MAXWELL, BALDWIN. Studies in the Shakespeare Apocrypha.
New York: King's Crown Press, 1956, 233 pp.
     Discusses four of the seven plays included in the Third
Folio and now known as the Shakespeare apocrypha--The True
Chronicle History of Thomas Lord Cromwell (1602), The Puritan:
or, The Widow of Watling Street (1607), The Lamentable Tragedy

of Locrine (1595), and A Yorkshire Tragedy (1608). Following a
general discussion of the possible motives for attribution, a
chapter is devoted to each play, focusing on the theme, structure, and characterization and on the likelihood of Shakespeare's
having had a hand in the composition.

280   MERCHANT, W. MOELWYN. Shakespeare and the Artist. London:
      Oxford University Press, 1959, 254 pp.
         Examines in part 1 the significance of a visual tradition
      in the interpretation of Shakespeare through the history of stage
      setting, the contributions of individual artists (whether working
      within the theater or simply painting Shakespeare's subjects),
      and the great mass of book illustration (especially engraved
      frontispieces). Stage history, more particularly, is considered
      in three phases--that of architectural setting (through Garrick),
      that of landscape setting, and that of topographical and his-
      torical accuracy (nineteenth century). Part 2 includes essays
      on how the visual tradition has reflected or influenced six
      particular plays. (See entry 289.)

281   MIOLA, ROBERT S. Shakespeare's Rome. Cambridge: Cambridge
      University Press, 1983, 244 pp.
         Examines Shakespeare's changing conception of Rome in The
      Rape of Lucrece, Titus Andronicus, Julius Caesar, Antony and
      Cleopatra, Coriolanus, and Cymbeline. The various transforma-
      tions reflect Shakespeare's development as a playwright and the
      growth of his dramatic vision. In moving from a wilderness
      settlement (Titus) to a political arena (Caesar) to an empire
      (Antony), Shakespeare explores three basic Roman ideals--con-
      stancy, honor, and pietas. His view of these ideals becomes
      increasingly critical or paradoxical in Antony and Coriolanus.
      (See entry 928.)

282   MOULTON, RICHARD G. The Moral System of Shakespeare: A
      Popular Illustration of Fiction as the Experimental Side of
      Philosophy. New York and London: Macmillan, 1903, 381 pp.
         Defines Shakespeare's moral system as the perspective the
      figure brings to his fictional world and the perspective that
      world in turn reflects back to him as a result of his experiences.
      It is the mysterious motivational backdrop in the plays. The
      human will is far from free; it is acted upon from within by
      heredity and from without by the surrounding circumstances,
      superior human will, and supernatural agency. What appears to be
      accident may ultimately be controlled by human or divine law. In
      Shakespeare, though, man is the prime focus; the supernatural may
      accentuate what clearly exists, but man is the agent in whom
      choice of action is generated.

283   MURRY, JOHN MIDDLETON.   Shakespeare.   London: Jonathan Cape,
       1936, 448 pp.
       Describes Shakespeare as capable of shuffling off the
mortal coil of moral judgment, of revealing that man--to be
generous--must cease to be blind in any number of ways. His work
transcends any rigorous critical method. Following a biographical essay, the study proceeds to examine Shakespeare's poems and
plays in roughly chronological order. His early plays are viewed
as experimental, to a degree imitative but also pieces in which
he developed his individual style. Hamlet is described as a figure of the European consciousness; the final plays, defended
against theories of boredom, are championed as dramatic portray-
als of the miracles of nature.

284   NICOLL, ALLARDYCE.   Shakespeare: An Introduction.   New York:
       Oxford University Press, 1952, 181 pp.
       Justifies the rapid expansion of material on Shakespeare by
describing our growing awareness of Shakespeare's unique position
among the world's authors. Critical opinion, although fiercely
varied, is bringing us closer to a full understanding of his
achievement. Following a brief review of these "schools" of
critical thought are chapters on the chronological phases of
Shakespeare's work--the young dramatist, man and society, man
and the universe, and the inner life.

285   NOBLE, RICHMOND.   Shakespeare's Use of Song: With the Text of
       the Principal Songs.   Oxford: Oxford University Press, 1923,
       160 pp.
       Observes that the brevity of expression and the rapidity of
development distinguish Shakespeare's songs from those of his
contemporary dramatists. He also is the first fully to integrate
song into the dramatic action. "Who Is Sylvia?" for example,
connects the two plots of The Two Gentlemen of Verona; and the
songs in Twelfth Night characterize the discrepant moods of the
play, as even more philosophically do the songs in The Tempest.
Individual chapters for each play (or group of plays) present the
text of the songs and discuss their lyric qualities and thematic
relevance.

286   NOSWORTHY, J.M.   Shakespeare's Occasional Plays: Their Origin
       and Transmission.   New York: Barnes & Noble, 1965, 238 pp.
       Suggests that Hamlet, The Merry Wives of Windsor, Troilus
and Cressida, and Macbeth were originally designed for presentation before particular audiences on particular occasions (re-
spectively Oxford and Cambridge University, the Court of Elizabeth, one of the Inns of Court, and the Court of James) and that
a wide range of problems for each (dating, collaboration, adaptation, revision and textual variation) may be largely resolved by
this realization and close textual analysis. The plays were revised, most probably by Shakespeare himself, before they reached
the public stage.

287   ORNSTEIN, ROBERT. <u>The Moral Vision of Jacobean Tragedy</u>.
      Madison: University of Wisconsin Press, 1960, 299 pp.
      Views the early years of the seventeenth century as a time
in which the Elizabethan world view of hierarchial providential
control slowly defaults to a scientific, steady progress toward
the secular. Whereas the tragic inspiration in Shakespeare's
contemporaries is short-lived, with early scorn and indignation
fading into philosophic or religious conviction, Shakespeare's
vision persists; he "humanizes the categorical imperatives which
the stern didacticist offers as the senese of ethical truth"
(p. 223). His concern is with the few who through suffering become truly human, and he rejoices in the fulfillment of human
greatness despite the indifference of the universe.

288   PARKER, M.D.H. <u>The Slave of Life: A Study of Shakespeare and</u>
      <u>the Idea of Justice</u>. London: Chatto & Windus, 1955, 264 pp.
      Observes that Shakespeare, while in the early plays working
within the convention of justice in this world and mercy in the
next, in the last plays transfers mercy from the heavenly to the
earthly judge. <u>Measure for Measure, All's Well That Ends Well</u>,
and <u>King Lear</u> are essays in redemption. In the tragedies Shakespeare's villains are consumed by pride, while the tragic heroes
through suffering gain the self-knowledge that leads to redemption. Evil for Shakespeare is the defection of nature and being.
His dialectic process in the plays asks insistent questions about
the metaphysical dimensions, and ultimately he resolves his
doubts within the orthodox tradition.

289   PAULSON, RONALD. <u>Book and Painting: Shakespeare, Milton, and</u>
      <u>the Bible: Literary Texts and the Emergence of English Paint-</u>
      <u>ing</u>. Knoxville: University of Tennessee Press, 1982, 236 pp.
      Suggests that the major influence on the emergence of En-
glish painting as it developed in the eighteenth century was
neither a native graphic tradition nor a European tradition but
English literature. Shakespeare to the eighteenth century represented a freedom from rules and restrictive classical imitation.
Conventional Shakespearean illustrations tend to be constructed
on visual oppositions of good and evil, light and dark, but his
primary influence in art was the free interplay of individuals
and of character. In Hogarth, especially, one views the Shakespearean copiousness, the psychological and moral complexity.
(See entry 280.)

290   PRICE, HEREWARD T. "Shakespeare as Critic." <u>Philosophical</u>
      <u>Quarterly</u> 20 (1941):390-99.
      Maintains that Shakespeare was keenly sensitive to various
excesses in English literature and that his works incorporate a
kind of literary criticism. A principal method, for example, is
parody through which he attacks distortions in language
(Holofernes in <u>Love's Labor's Lost</u>, Hotspur in <u>1 Henry IV</u>), in
theatrical presentation (Bottom in <u>A Midsummer Night's Dream</u>),

and the literary convention of romantic love (<u>The Two Gentlemen of Verona</u>) and revenge (<u>2,3 Henry VI</u>, <u>The Merchant of Venice</u>).

291   RABKIN, NORMAN. <u>Shakespeare and the Common Understanding</u>.
        New York: Free Press, 1967, 267 pp.
        Defines Shakespeare's method of depicting human conflict as "complementarity," a concept in physics in which one is forced to live with paradoxes and contrarieties incapable of solution. The plays present a universe in which we must make value judgments concerning the action and the characters, yet simultaneously we are forced to realize that any such judgment is reductionistic. The true constant is the dialectical dramaturgy, and in this quality lies the essence of Shakespeare's power to create humanly ambivalent situations. Shakespeare structures his work in terms of polar opposites--reason versus passion in <u>Hamlet</u>, <u>Realpolitik</u> and traditional political order in <u>Richard II</u>, hedonism and responsibility in <u>Troilus and Cressida</u>, the world and the transcendent in <u>Antony and Cleopatra</u>, justice and mercy in <u>The Merchant of Venice</u> and <u>King Lear</u>.

292   _____. <u>Shakespeare and the Problem of Meaning</u>. Chicago:
        University of Chicago Press, 1981, 165 pp.
        Extols the value of recent trends in Shakespearean criticism that stress contrarieties in the interpretation of the plays and the characters. The reductionistic quality of some critical approaches is illustrated in <u>The Merchant of Venice</u>, in which Shakespeare draws the spectators' response in contradiction to the overtly established movement of the theme, and in <u>Henry V</u>, which at one level directs an immediate response either favorable or unfavorable to Henry, but at another requires the simultaneous acceptance of both. The final chapter explores the dual response inherent in the dramatic experience of the romances.

293   RALEIGH, WALTER. <u>Shakespeare</u>. London: Macmillan, 1927,
        232 pp.
        Describes Shakespeare in an appreciative essay as that "rarest of all things, a whole man" (p. 19), one who can see the many sides of virtue and vice and who can often reveal something of the truth by juxtaposing the two sides of the moral coin. The aim in the chapters that follow (on Stratford and London, on books and poetry, on the theater, and on story and character) is to see his mind at work on the raw materials of his craft and the nature of the tools he employed.

294   REED, ROBERT R., Jr. <u>Crime and God's Judgment in Shakespeare</u>.
        Lexington: University Press of Kentucky, 1984, 225 pp.
        Focuses on the Renaissance concept of divine retribution and on the significance of that concept in the two English tetralogies and in three tragedies--<u>Julius Caesar</u>, <u>Hamlet</u>, and <u>Macbeth</u>. The major concern is with Shakespeare's maturation in handling the theme, from the somewhat heavy-handed and repetitive

patterns of the Henry VI plays and the obvious character-agent of retribution, Queen Margaret, in Richard III to the subtle and ambiguous implications of Hamlet's relationship with Claudius or the mysterious nature of the witches and the extent and quality of Macbeth's free will. The concept of divine retribution, far more important than Shakespeare's providential view of history, is a method by which he envisions the dynamic process in a stage world in which moral order has been violated in its most heinous fashion, regecide.

295   RIGHTER [BARTON], ANNE. Shakespeare and the Idea of the Play. London: Chatto & Windus, 1962, 200 pp.
       Discusses Shakespeare's plays in relation to sixteenth-century concepts of drama and the evolution of a new relationship between actors and audience. The audience in medieval drama, which was poised between ritual and art, participated by attentive silence in the awesome affirmation of theological absolutes. The influence of the classical drama, in part, was to separate spectator and stage, to create a world altogether distinct, the play of illusion. By Shakespeare's day the illusion had become so standard that the metaphor of the stage as world becomes commonplace. Such a metaphor imbues Shakespeare's work and allows for a series of changing attitudes toward the relation of illusion and reality. In the early plays such imagery is usually rhetorical flourish. In the middle plays the player-king becomes the central metaphor. Apparently Shakespeare late in life--if we are to judge from the imagery--became disgusted with the stage; the actor cheapens life by dramatizing it, and the play is either corrupt or signifies nothing.

296   ROSE, MARK. Shakespearean Design. Cambridge, Mass.: Harvard University Press, 1972, 190 pp.
       Focuses on major structural features of Shakespeare's dramaturgy. While Shakespeare draws on his predecessors, he is the first to apply principles of scene design to the play as a whole--matters such as "structural echoes between scenes, the use of formal thematic liaisons and the function of the designed group of scenes as a structural unit" (p. x). A scene-by-scene analysis of Hamlet illustrates the method in detail; then follow briefer analyses of each play in roughly chronological order. Essentially Shakespeare's plays reveal "multiple unity" (p. 95); the scenic units may be relatively independent units, but only in context do they assume full coloration and meaning.

297   SANDERS, WILBUR. The Dramatist and the Received Idea: Studies in the Plays of Marlowe and Shakespeare. Cambridge: Cambridge University Press, 1968, 392 pp.
       Attempts to examine the relationship between the playwright and his culture, the transformation of received ideas into dramatic conflict by setting the fixity of cultural tradition against the concept of the evolutionary process. Richard III, for

example, would hardly fully please either the Tudor propagandist
or the monarchist; if Richard is the scourge of God, he is also
a chilling study in Machiavellian political amorality. Richard II
teems with the inextricability of justice as Richard's culpabili-
ties excuse Bolingbroke no more than Richard can take refuge in
the concept of divine right. Macbeth examines the inexorable
relationship between the "overwhelming potency of evil" and the
"concealed intention of nature" (p. 307).

298   SCHANZER, ERNEST. The Problem Plays of Shakespeare: A Study
      of "Julius Caesar," "Measure for Measure," and "Antony and
      Cleopatra." London: Routledge & Kegan Paul, 1963, 196 pp.
         Defines a problem play as one in which the audience loses
its moral bearings as the action unfolds. Shakespeare in these
works demonstrably manipulates the spectators' angle of vision
to the point that they perceive the futility of any attempt to
assume an absolutist posture. In Julius Caesar, for example, he
confronts the viewer with two essential problems--the psychological nature of the real Caesar and the justifiability of the
murder; by forcing us alternately to admire and disdain Brutus,
Cassius, Antony, and Caesar, Shakespeare avoids a definitively
clear answer to either. Isabella in Measure for Measure must
choose between the death of her brother and the sacrifice of her
virginity, and the orientation of the material renders it impossible for us to be fully sympathetic with her decision. Antony
and Cleopatra is the quintessential problem play; despite the
judgments of decadence and corruption that the spectators are
forced to bring against the royal lovers, by the close of act 5
we greet Cleopatra's death as glorious, her repudiation of the
material world as tiumphant.

299   SCHÜCKING, LEVIN L. Character Problems in Shakespeare's Plays:
      A Guide to the Better Understanding of the Dramatist. London:
      Harrap; New York: Henry Holt, 1922, 270 pp.
         Attacks the pluralistic post-Romantic tendency to read
subjective impressions into Shakespeare's characters rather than
attempting to understand them as Shakespeare's creations in the
context of the Renaissance. Shakespeare's was a popular art, and
many of his characters were bound in large part by tradition.
Character motivations are by necessity stated explicitly; critics
involved in hidden motivations exercise their ingenuity, not
Shakespeare's. Similarly, critics who attempt to allegorize
either the plot or the characters distort Shakespeare's theatrical practice of developing lifelike characters to enact events
in a plot imitating human action. (See entry 309.)

300   SEN GUPTA, S.C. The Whirligig of Time: The Problem of
      Duration in Shakespeare's Plays. Bombay: Orient Longmans,
      1961, 201 pp.
         Proposes that temporal sequence or duration is an integral
aspect of dramatic structure. The "unpsychological" concept of

Double Time does not account for the brilliance of Shakespeare's characters, which results from a genuine sense of time, past and future as well as present. In the early plays Shakespeare handles time in a conventional manner, compressing when desirable; in his greatest work he transcends time, creating a sense of duration in which the dramatic emphasis is on the changing emotional states rather than on any sense of the temporal.

301   SENG, PETER J. The Vocal Songs in the Plays of Shakespeare: A Critical History. Cambridge, Mass.: Harvard University Press, 1967, 314 pp.
       Includes an individual chapter on each play containing a vocal song. The text of each song is collated with all sixteenth- and seventeenth-century editions and with all major editions from Rowe forward. The material for each song includes a headnote indicating its source in the play, general and textual commentary arranged chronologically, information about the musical setting, information about sources or analogues, and a discussion of the dramatic function of the song in the play.

302   SKULSKY, HAROLD. Spirits Finely Touched: The Testing of Value and Integrity in Four Shakespearean Plays. Athens: University of Georgia Press, 1976, 288 pp.
       Notes that Shakespeare forces a violent collision in his major work between cherished beliefs and the reality of human experience, as in Hamlet's nightmare about how God works and whether God's justice is merely an anthropomorphic extension of man's vengefulness, in Angelo's equation of the law and brute power in Measure for Measure, in Othello's disturbing sense of justice and the glimpse of man's limitless potential for bestiality, in the abolition of justice, human dignity, and love in King Lear to see whether intrinsic value remains.

303   SMITH, MARION B. Dualities in Shakespeare. Toronto: University of Toronto Press, 1966, 252 pp.
       Examines the humanist's search for synthesis or order based on the reconciliation of opposition despite increasing philosophical disillusionment and social disruption. Tolerance, temperance, and charity manifest in the plays a harmonious ordering of differences in the personal and social spheres. The study specifically addresses the sonnets and six major plays, concentrating on the duality of love in the poems, the imagery of Romeo and Juliet, the inversions of Twelfth Night and Macbeth, the duality of order and justice in Measure for Measure, of structure in Antony and Cleopatra, and of intention in The Tempest.

304   SOELLNER, ROLF. Shakespeare's Patterns of Self-Knowledge. Columbus: Ohio State University Press, 1972, 454 pp.
       Concerns what Elizabethans and Jacobeans thought self-knowledge to be and the dramatic patterns Shakespeare created from this thought. Self-knowledge in some cases refers to the

control of passion by reason, in other cases to a moral way of
life. In truth, it was a vague and shifting concept that can be
identified only within the particular dramatic context. Shakespeare utilizes the concept in three distinct periods--the early
plays in which characters lose and find themselves in almost
formulaic ways (The Comedy of Errors, Love's Labor's Lost), the
middle plays in which characters, though they be noble, fail to
embody conventional humanistic ideals (Julius Caesar, Measure for
Measure), and a final phase that freely accepts diversity in an
attempt to synthesize theory and life (subjecting self in
Othello, stripping self in King Lear, losing self in Macbeth,
mastering the self in The Tempest).

305 SPENCER, THEODORE. Death and Elizabethan Tragedy: A Study of
     Convention and Opinion in the Elizabethan Drama. Cambridge,
     Mass.: Harvard University Press, 288 pp.
          Notes that conceptions of tragedy and comedy, of bravery
     and beauty and wisdom, all are constructed on the central fact of
     death. The conflict of attitude between the classical and Chris-
     tian concept of death is present from the beginnings of drama,
     but Marlowe is the first to discover how to use death dramati-
     cally. Likewise, Hamlet in his meditation on death, torn by the
     desire to escape the world and religious prohibition, is the voice
     of the Renaissance grown middle-aged. While Shakespeare's trag-
     edies are not marked by the intense atmosphere of mortality as
     sharply as those of his contemporaries, death is for his protago-
     nists the point against which their achievements are inevitably
     measured.

306 SPIVACK, CHARLOTTE. "Shakespeare and the Comedy of Evil." In
     The Comedy of Evil on Shakespeare's Stage. Rutherford, N.J.:
     Fairleigh Dickinson University Press; London: Associated
     University Presses, 1978, pp. 138-73.
          Stresses Shakespeare's inheritance of the medieval tradi-
     tion of depicting evil in comic or grotesque terms. The devil-
     porter in Macbeth, for instance, brings reverberations from the
     Harrowing of Hell scenes in the miracle plays. Aaron, Richard III,
     and Iago typify the use of craftiness, ingenuity, and verbal dis-
     guise; only the spectators know the villains' true nature for much
     of the play. With Falstaff the situation is reversed; Hal real-
     izes his true nature, but only later does the spectator come to
     share the view. The scene with Hamlet holding Yorick's skull
     treats the memento mori tradition with grim humor; and Malvolio,
     Shylock, Cloten, and Caliban are comic variations of evil's per-
     version. The remaining chapters deal with the "comedy of evil"
     in non-Shakespearean drama of the period.

307 STERNFELD, FREDERICK W. Music in Shakespearean Tragedy.
     London: Routledge & Kegan Paul; New York: Dover, 1963,
     334 pp.

Observes that tragedy utilizes far less music than comedy,
both because of the Senecan influence and because of the nature
of the tragic experience itself. Moreover, the use of instrumental music was greater than that of vocal music. Shakespeare
uses lyrics to supplement tragic speech (for example, Desdemona's
"Willow Song") and comic songs for particular effect (for example, the gravedigger's song in Hamlet, Pandarus's song in Troilus
and Cressida). Desdemona's character gains poignancy and pathos
through her brief song on marital infidelity, which Shakespeare
draws from popular stock. Ophelia's mad songs, giving emphasis
to her helplessness, become an integral part of the tragic scene
itself. The Fool in King Lear frequently mixes snatches of
lyric and prose in his dialogue with the king.

308 STEVENSON, ROBERT. Shakespeare's Religious Frontier. The
     Hague: Martinus Nijhoff, 1958, 97 pp.
     Observes Shakespeare's demonstrably secular cast of mind.
The playwright uses in his entire canon only a dozen technical
religious terms and portrays only fifteen high-ranking church
officials in his entire dramatis personae. The friars and
priests, while admittedly not vicious, generally fail to distinguish their calling. Shakespeare grew up in a world in which
religious zeal pit family member against family member and friend
against friend, and his association with professional players
again placed him in an environment where religious temper was
easily exacerbated. He must have learned at an early age the
desirability of an aloofness from partisan religious issues.

309 STEWART, J.I.M. Character and Motive in Shakespeare: Some
     Recent Appraisals Examined. London: Longmans, Green, 1949,
     147 pp.
     Reacts to the current critical overemphasis on "realistic"
and "psychological" approaches to Shakespeare and the concomitant derogation of dramatic poetry and symbolic association.
Pedestrian and unimaginative readings and performances with as
much business and spectacle and as little poetry as possible
depreciate Shakespeare's drama. Cases in point are Robert
Bridges, who advocates expurgating virtually at will since much
in Shakespeare is there merely to appeal to the masses, and
Levin Schücking (entry 299), whose historical approach would
eliminate the subjectivity of our response. Other critics discussed at some length include E.E. Stoll on Othello (entry 1328)
and John W. Draper on Falstaff (entry 418). (See entry 441.)

310 STIRLING, BRENTS. The Populace in Shakespeare. New York:
     Columbia University Press, 1949, 203 pp.
     Illustrates through numerous documents of the period that
the mob was viewed as a dangerous disintegrative and leveling
force, illiterate, disorderly, and vicious. This attitude persists throughout Elizabethan drama and in Shakespeare is most
clearly reflected in the Jack Cade scenes in Henry VI and the

mob scenes in Julius Caesar and Coriolanus. In large part, this sharply satiric view of the masses was reinforced by the con- servative reaction to growing political ferment in late Eliza- bethan England.

311   STOLL, ELMER EDGAR. Shakespeare Studies: Historical and Comparative in Method. New York: Macmillan, 1927, 502 pp.
      Collects the author's most significant articles and mono- graphs on Shakespeare and the Elizabethan theater. General mat- ters discussed include the folio; Shakespeare's life and the fallacy of viewing the periods of his work as reflections of his psychological state and of treating characters as extensions of his personality; Shakespeare's comic method; the ghosts in Macbeth, Richard III, and Julius Caesar, whether real or sym- bolic; and the criminals in the plays, especially the nature of the Elizabethan Machiavel. Individual chapters are devoted to Shylock, who is envisioned as a purely comic villain, and to Falstaff's perennial charm and the question of his cowardice. (See entries 423, 441-42.)

312   SUMMERS, JOSEPH H. Dreams of Love and Power. New York: Oxford University Press, 1984, 176 pp.
      Explores the primary concern with dreams in A Midsummer Night's Dream, The Winter's Tale, Hamlet, Measure for Measure, King Lear, Antony and Cleopatra, and The Tempest. At times the dream is literal, at times metaphoric; but in all cases it pre- figures the dramatic character's desires, hopes, and fears. Shakespeare's use of dream is thematic as well as structural. While its vision transcends the actual in Dream and Antony, it confronts harsh reality in Lear and disturbing ambiguities in Hamlet and Tempest. (See entries 236, 342.)

313   SUNDELSON, DAVID. Shakespeare's Restorations of the Father. New Brunswick: Rutgers University Press, 1983, 165 pp.
      Argues the centrality of the restored father to Shake- speare's vision of reconciliation, exploring both the presenta- tion of patriarchy in specific plays and the larger psychological context of the father's return. The significance of the loss or the weakness of the father or surrogate father figure is examined in detail in Richard II, 1,2 Henry IV, Henry V, The Merchant of Venice, Measure for Measure, and The Tempest. Ramifications of the argument also extend to the tragedies.

314   TALBERT, ERNEST W. Elizabethan Drama and Shakespeare's Early Plays: An Essay in Historical Criticism. Chapel Hill: University of North Carolina Press, 1963, 410 pp.
      Examines Shakespeare's early plays for methods by which he arouses and manipulates the spectator's response through famil- iarity with certain concepts such as multiplicity of plots, the use of rhetorical devices, the comedic element especially in the figure of the clown and courtly motifs, and through emotional

biases such as national patriotism and animosity toward France
and toward Roman Catholicism. Aspects of both native episodic
structure and the classical concept of five-act structure figure
in these early works. Perhaps most significant is the development in the spectator of an ambivalent response to the principal
figure.

315   TAYLOR, MARK. Shakespeare's Darker Purpose: A Question of
      Incest. AMS Studies in the Renaissance, 7. New York: AMS
      Press, 1982, 203 pp.
            Observes that in no fewer than twenty-one of Shakespeare's
      plays does a young woman who marries or plans to marry find her
      father or the memory of her father an obstacle. In these inter-
      actions a "degree of sublimated incestuous desire is nearly al-
      ways present in the mixture of concern, possessiveness, and love
      that Shakespeare's fathers feel for their daughters" (p. 72).
      Dread of losing the daughter in marriage provokes acts that are
      arbitrary, selfish, irrational, violent, and cruel. The Tempest
      is considered the culmination of the incest motif. While Alonso
      forces his daughter into a transracial marriage, Prospero must
      overcome his own subliminal desires in emancipating Miranda to
      mate with Ferdinand.

316   THALER, ALWIN. Shakespeare and Our World. Knoxville:
      University of Tennessee Press, 1966, 235 pp.
            Addresses the timelessness of Shakespeare, his dramaturgi-
      cal techniques, and his literary influence upon Milton. In
      part 1 the emphasis is upon the similarities of Shakespeare's
      world and our own, both possessing enormous capacities for good
      or ill, and upon the plays as charting adventures into both.
      Part 2 deals with such matters as Shakespeare's mute or off-stage
      characters and his use of delayed exposition, that is, the artful
      manner in which he incorporates significant expository details in
      the progress of his plot as well as at the beginning. Part 3
      includes a list of Milton's allusions to Shakespeare in tabular
      form.

317   _____. Shakespeare's Silences. Cambridge, Mass.: Harvard
      University Press, 1929, 279 pp.
            Focuses on Shakespeare's silences in characterization, at
      times calculated, at times oversights--for example, Sylvia's
      silence in The Two Gentlemen of Verona while being passed from
      Valentine to Proteus and back again, Isabella's silence to
      Vincentio's proposal in Measure for Measure, Hermione's silent
      forgiveness of Leontes in act 5 of The Winter's Tale, Iago's
      refusal to speak further at the conclusion of Othello. Another
      form of "silence" is the mysterious disappearance of Rosaline in
      Romeo and Juliet, of the Fool in King Lear, or the inconsistencies
      in Margaret's character in Much Ado About Nothing, or the un-
      spoken details of Macbeth's children.

318   TILLYARD, E.M.W. Shakespeare's Problem Plays. Toronto:
      University of Toronto Press, 1950, 156 pp.
         Views Shakespeare's problem plays as of two kinds--those
      that are genuinely abnormal like All's Well That Ends Well and
      Measure for Measure and those that deal with problems like Hamlet
      and Troilus and Cressida. They share a concern for religious
      dogma or abstract speculation, a serious but not pessimistic
      mood, realistic characterization, the common motif of a young man
      on the verge of adulthood receiving some form of traumatic shock,
      a nocturnal setting, and the juxtaposition of old and new genera-
      tions. Hamlet, more specifically, featuring a protagonist devoid
      of spiritual growth, is pervaded by problems rich and diverse,
      not solutions. Troilus and Cressida, likewise, is more display
      than order, Troilus's character fragmented by psychological in-
      consistency and the play itself fragmented by a multiplicity of
      planes of reality. The basic problem in both All's Well and
      Measure is an inability to fuse effectively romantic, fantastic
      plots with a vitality and realism of characterization.

319   TRAVERSI, DEREK A. An Approach to Shakespeare. 3d ed., rev.
      and expanded. Garden City, N.Y.: Doubleday, 1969, 674 pp.
         Proceeds from the word to the image in its verse setting,
      tracing the manner in which independent themes are woven into the
      dramatic action. The aim is to reveal a symbolic pattern through
      examining recurrent words, phrases, images, and themes, a pattern
      that provides subtle and suggestive unity. Shakespeare's early
      development takes place within dramatic conventions established
      by lesser artists--the revenge play, the chronicles, euphuistic
      or Plautine comedy. Virtually all of the themes of the great
      tragedies emerge in the problem comedies. Hamlet is treated as
      a problem play in which Shakespeare is still struggling to reduce
      to order a wide range of disturbing emotions. The mature trag-
      edies, exhibiting a greater linguistic range and power, firmly
      trace the theme of passion's dominance through a clash between
      contrasted and opposed personalities and orders. The romances
      give artistic form to a new symbolic purpose focusing on the
      marvel of forgiveness and healing.

320   TURNER, FREDERICK. Shakespeare and the Nature of Time: Moral
      and Philosophical Themes in Some Plays and Poems of William
      Shakespeare. Oxford: Clarendon Press, 1971, 193 pp.
         Stresses time in Shakespeare's plays as dynamic, a process
      and a becoming. Among the most significant aspects of time are
      the historical, the process of the personal experience, the
      natural or cyclic, and the secular. Whereas in the sonnets it is
      the great destroyer, destruction and restoration are juxtaposed
      in The Winter's Tale. With the appearance of the ghost from the
      outer world in Hamlet, the timeless world erupts ambiguously into
      the world of time; timeless forces also operate against Macbeth,
      but in that play they act as a kind of avenging angel. Shake-
      speare was interested in time as it affects human beings in its

single or combined forms, as a dramaturgical medium for the
development of character.

321   TURNER, ROBERT Y. Shakespeare's Apprenticeship. Chicago and
      London: University of Chicago Press, 1974, 293 pp.
          Studies Shakespeare's development as a playwright, not in
      the manner in which he adapts source materials, but in the in-
      creasingly sophisticated utilization of dramatic technique--
      rhetoric, dialogue, scene division and emphasis, irony, staging,
      the generic mixture of comic and tragic. In the plays up to A
      Midsummer Night's Dream, Shakespeare's progress can be traced as
      a phylogenetic recapitulation of "the main historical movement in
      drama of the sixteenth century from the generalized didactic
      morality play to the relatively literal drama as a distinctive
      art form" (p. 5).

322   VAN DEN BERG, KENT T. Playhouse and Cosmos: Shakespearean
      Theater as Metaphor. Newark: University of Delaware Press,
      1985, 192 pp.
          Explores Shakespeare's plays as a metaphoric experience, an
      imaginary world into which the spectator withdraws temporarily
      from actuality. The developing characterization prompts the
      spectator to participate emotionally in the activity shaped in
      the stage world, whether the progress of courtship, the heroic
      exploits on the battlefield, or the chilling isolation of self-
      hood in the alienation of the tragic protagonist. Shakespeare's
      overt attention to his theatrical medium ultimately discloses
      imaginative insights gained through this unique relationship
      between stage and spectator.

323   VAN DOREN, MARK. Shakespeare. New York: Henry Holt, 1939,
      302 pp.
          Includes essays on each of Shakespeare's plays and a sepa-
      rate essay on the poems, dealing flexibly with such matters as
      style, imagery, structure, and character analysis. The emphasis
      in Richard III, for example, is on character--the brilliant
      schemer-madman motivated by the sheer lonely force of his wit;
      in Titus Andronicus on the absurdities of plot; in Hamlet on the
      fiercely complex characterization of the protagonist and of those
      who serve as his foils; in the final plays on the common concern
      for the fundamental nature of family ties and their symbolic
      values.

324   VAN LAAN, THOMAS F. Role-Playing in Shakespeare. Toronto and
      London: University of Toronto Press, 1978, 267 pp.
          Argues that role playing through imagery or through actual
      misrepresentation abounds in Shakespeare's plays and directly
      affects the characterization and theme. This concern forces the
      spectators to perceive a character's fulfillment or violation as
      a role; whether a literal role, one of a stock tradition, or one
      imposed by society, it is a means of attempting to control his

situation. Titus, for example, assumes a revenger's role in
place of that of the suffering victim. Romeo enacts a Petrarchan
love drama. Hamlet swirls with various roles ranging from that
of lover to that of revenger; much of the play involves his
search for a psychologically compatible posture. In Antony and
Cleopatra a dream role triumphs, reducing history to insignifi-
cance. A final chapter focuses on the role of the internal
dramatist, especially in The Winter's Tale and The Tempest.

325   VELIE, ALAN R. Shakespeare's Repentance Plays: The Search
for an Adequate Response. Rutherford, N.J.: Fairleigh
Dickinson University Press, 1972, 127 pp.
    Traces Shakespeare's use of the theme of repentance from
early plays like The Two Gentlemen of Verona and Much Ado About
Nothing through the problem plays and into the romances. The
first comedies attempt no serious psychological examination of
characters who sin and repent. Instead, the characters merely
serve the demands of the plot. In Measure for Measure comedy
comprises the effect of psychological depth of character. In the
romances Shakespeare combines the serious and the comic through
variations of melodrama. Leontes views sin and repentance from
within, Prospero from without.

326   VYVYAN, JOHN. The Shakespearean Ethic. London: Chatto &
Windus, 1959, 208 pp.
    Argues that ethical problems exercised an increasing
fascination over Shakespeare and that frequently he deliberately
sacrificed stage effect to pursue a question of human nature and
human relationships. He, moreover, probably chose his plots
carefully to permit analysis of the various stages in the tragic
dilemma. Macbeth, for example, focuses on the aftermath of a
deed of horror, while Othello examines the stages of temptation;
Hamlet is concerned with the full impact of the inner conflict.

327   WAIN, JOHN. The Living World of Shakespeare: A Playgoer's
Guide. London: Macmillan, 1964, 268 pp.
    Aims to deepen the appreciation of theater goers and arm-
chair devotees of Shakespeare who lack a formal study of Elizabethan drama. Shakespeare had the advantage of working in an art
form that had come to involve active mental and emotional participation on the part of the spectators. Then, too, he is the
supreme artist in the use of the imaginative arts of language,
poetry, and figurative prose, and he was fortunate to have a
stage and a theater that could effectively accommodate this
artistic flexibility. Such principles constitute the major focus
in a series of essays on each of the plays, with emphasis constantly on the text and the performance.

328   WATKINS, W.B.C. Shakespeare and Spenser. Princeton:
        Princeton University Press, 1950, 339 pp.
            Includes discussion of Shakespeare and Spenser who, as
        embodiments of the narrative traditions, demonstrate the achieve-
        ment and potentiality of English poetry. The essays on Shake-
        speare cover his use of erotic verse ("spiritualized sensuality")
        in Venus and Adonis, Troilus and Cressida, Othello, and Antony
        and Cleopatra and, through a comparison of Richard II and King
        Lear, the evolution of his technique in the use of psychological
        realism and symbolic stylization and in the delineation of duali-
        ties both in matters transient and in matters universal. Yet
        another chapter compares Spenser's and Shakespeare's use of the
        concept of marriage.

329   WATSON, ROBERT N. Shakespeare and the Hazards of Ambition.
        Cambridge, Mass.: Harvard University Press, 1984, 360 pp.
            Views ambition, in the context of human inherited limita-
        tions, as the force that both drives and destroys Shakespeare's
        tragic characters. The morally ambiguous quality of ambition,
        more specifically, is painfully apparent in such key scenes as
        Richard II's recollections of time wasted, Hal's rejection of
        Falstaff, Macbeth's realization of the equivocation of the
        witches, or Coriolanus's capitulation to his mother. Attention
        is also directed to the psychoanalytic implications of a charac-
        ter's efforts to remake his identity.

330   WEISS, THEODORE. The Breath of Clowns and Kings:
        Shakespeare's Early Comedies and Histories. New York:
        Atheneum, 1971, 339 pp.
            Reveals Shakespeare's emerging abilities in the early plays
        to utilize the stage to depict an expansive view of life. The
        persistent motif of the comedies is that of love that, like a
        great school, enlightens young men; the women are both stimula-
        tors to love and also sane educators. In the history plays a
        second theme emerges, the relationship between word and deed.
        Richard III is frenetically active as he hacks his way to the
        throne, delighting in words only as an expression of his ego-
        mania. Richard II, to the contrary, loses himself in a "regime
        of words" that becomes an occupation in itself. In 1,2 Henry IV
        words felicitously join with action; at the same time, Hal, like
        the young men of the comedies, must be educated--in part through
        his father and the political problems of the realm, in part
        through his huge sack-ridden companion and the agony of tempering
        freedom with responsibility.

331   WELSFORD, ENID. The Fool: His Social and Literary History.
        London: Faber & Faber, 1935, 381 pp.
            Examines the origins of the role of the fool as entertainer
        and the relationship of the fool to comedy. Part 3 deals, in
        part, with the court-fool in Elizabethan drama, and part 4 with
        the stage-clown. The principal English clown actors are Richard

Tarleton, Will Kempe, and Robert Armin, transforming the type
from the guild-fool in motley into a mouthpiece for satire and
topical allusion. Shakespeare develops the role far beyond that
of his contemporaries with Touchstone as the authorized commen-
tator in As You Like It, the merry critic of the would-be prac-
titioners of the simple life; Feste as the sage fool who enter-
tains with the truth; and the Fool in Lear who cures with jest.
(See entry 239.)

332   WILSON, FRANK PERCY. Shakespearian and Other Studies. Edited
      by Helen Gardner. Oxford: Clarendon Press, 1969, 345 pp.
          Includes, among others, essays on the English history play,
      Shakespeare's comedies, his diction, his reading, his proverbial
      wisdom, the Elizabethan theater, and memorial accounts of the
      Elizabethan scholars E.K. Chambers and W.W. Greg. The opening
      essay defines the history play as one in which character is re-
      vealed through politics and its purpose as essentially instruc-
      tive. A survey of the stage histories of the early 1590s sug-
      gests that Shakespeare's seriousness of purpose is in sharp
      contrast with most others. The comedies are examined primarily
      in terms of Shakespeare's working out of his own theories of
      comic drama.

333   YOUNG, DAVID. The Heart's Forest: A Study of Shakespeare's
      Pastoral Plays. New Haven and London: Yale University Press,
      1972, 209 pp.
          Studies As You Like It, King Lear, The Winter's Tale, and
      The Tempest in terms of their stylistic, structural, and thematic
      relations both to each other and to the pastoral mode. Shake-
      speare utilizes pastoral to examine man's relationship to nature,
      in the alternate idealization of city and country, in the dream
      of an idyllic escape giving both sensual and spiritual gratifica-
      tion, in the relative good and evil in the civilized and the
      primitive worlds. The plays represent the great flexibility of
      the convention as well as the multiple meanings it can accommo-
      date in the hands of a consummate artist.

334   ZEEVELD, W. GORDON. The Temper of Shakespeare's Thought.
      New Haven and London: Yale University Press, 1974, 266 pp.
          Stresses the importance of historical context to the mean-
      ing of Shakespeare's plays--for example, the danger of the
      vestarian controversy in the sixteenth-century church and the
      English history plays, the topical implications of the differ-
      ences between monarchy and commonwealth in the Roman histories,
      actual legal questions argued in the courts of equity, and the
      central problems of The Merchant of Venice and Measure for
      Measure, questions of civility and barbarism in the romances
      stimulated by the Jacobean brush with new and strange worlds.

For discussion of metadrama, see entries 196, 221, 225, 250, 295,
324, 390. For discussion of gender studies, see entries 201, 220,

234, 259. For discussion of concepts of character, see entries 202, 235, 241, 263. For discussion of pointer or commenting characters, see entries 204, 232, 245, 252, 256, 295. For discussion of duality as a structural principle, see entries 270, 291-92, 303. For discussion of Christian allegory, see entries 100, 124, 210, 231, 255, 288, 294, 946; for a counterview, see entry 119. For discussion of the Christian philosophic background of the plays, see entries 113, 116, 126, 128, 130, 133-34, 218; for a counterview, see entry 267. For discussion of scenes as the principal structural unit, see entries 247, 257, 296. For discussion of music in the plays, see entries 271, 301, 306, 375, 1282.

II. The Poems and Sonnets

REFERENCE WORKS

335   TANNENBAUM, SAMUEL A., and TANNENBAUM, DOROTHY R. <u>William</u>
      <u>Shakespeare: "The Sonnets."</u> Elizabethan Bibliographies, 10.
      New York: Privately Printed, 1940, 88 pp.
          Cites 1,637 unannotated items covering major scholarship on
      the sonnets from the beginnings to 1938. The material is divided
      by the following categories and is arranged alphabetically by
      section--English editions, arrangements, anthologies; transla-
      tions; musical settings; book titles from the sonnets; commentary.
      The majority of the material (1,197 items) is loosely classified
      under commentary.

EDITIONS

336   BOOTH, STEPHEN, ed. <u>Shakespeare's Sonnets: Edited With</u>
      <u>Analytic Commentary.</u> New Haven and London: Yale University
      Press, 1977, 578 pp.
          Attempts through close analysis to resurrect the Renaissance
      reader's experience with the 1609 quarto, the only textual author-
      ity for all the sonnets except 138 and 144. A facsimile of the
      original publication and a modernized version are set on facing
      pages with the commentary on the individual sonnets following on
      pp. 135-538. Each commentary begins with general explicatory
      observations followed by specific notes on individual lines. A
      brief section in the appendix reviews major critical theories on
      the sonnets.

337   CAMPBELL, S.C., ed. <u>Shakespeare's Sonnets: Edited as a Con-</u>
      <u>tinuous Sequence.</u> London: Bell & Hyman; Totowa, N.J.: Rowman
      & Littlefield, 1978, 177 pp.
          Includes, in addition to the sonnets, introductory comments
      on the necessary rearrangement of the sonnet order, "A Lover's
      Complaint," and <u>The Phoenix and Turtle</u>. The principal argument
      of this edition is that the dark-lady sonnets describe a series
      of ailments--swallowing poison, fever, madness, perjury, danger

of death--all of which the poet notes in the past tense as something from which he has recovered. Yet, in the 1609 quarto the
latter sonnets precede the former. The rearrangement embeds the
dark-lady group in the sonnets to the friend, from which the
central theme emerges.

338   PRINCE, F.T., ed. The Poems. The Arden Shakespeare. London:
      Methuen; Cambridge, Mass.: Harvard University Press, 1960,
      201 pp.
           Includes discussion on the text and literary interpreta-
      tions, as well as appendixes featuring selections from Golding's
      translation of Ovid's Metamorphoses, Chaucer's The Legend of Good
      Women, Painter's The Palace of Pleasure, and Ovid's Fasti. The
      modernized texts of Venus and Adonis and The Rape of Lucrece are
      from the first quartos, for which the copy was probably Shake-
      speare's fair copies. The text of The Passionate Pilgrim is
      based on the first quarto for eight of the poems, the second
      quarto for the remainder. The text of The Phoenix and Turtle is
      from the edition of 1601.

339   ROLLINS, HYDER E., ed. The Poems: "Venus and Adonis,"
      "Lucrece," "The Passionate Pilgrim," "The Phoenix and Turtle,"
      "A Lover's Complaint." A New Variorum Edition of Shakespeare.
      Philadelphia: J.B. Lippincott, 1938, 667 pp.
           Uses the first quarto as the copy text in each case. The
      texts of the poems themselves are printed on pp. 1-368. On each
      page, for that portion of the text, are cited variant readings,
      textual notes, and general critical commentary. Following the
      texts are sections on varying critical opinions, the diverse
      copies, the dates of composition, sources, general criticism,
      musical settings, and a list of works consulted.

340   _____. The Sonnets. 2 vols. A New Variorum Edition of
      Shakespeare. Philadelphia and London: J.B. Lippincott,
      1944, 1010 pp.
           Uses the First Folio as the copy text. The text of the
      sonnets is printed in volume 1. On each page, for that portion
      of the text, are cited variant readings, textual notes, and
      general critical commentary. Volume 2 includes sections on
      varying critical opinions, the texts of 1609 and 1640, the
      authenticity of the 1609 text, the date of composition, the
      arrangement, sources, questions of autobiography, the dedication
      and Master W.H., the friend, the dark lady, the rival poet,
      musical settings, general criticism, and a list of works con-
      sulted.

341   WILSON, JOHN DOVER, ed. The Sonnets. 2d ed. The New
      Cambridge Shakespeare. Cambridge: Cambridge University
      Press, 1967, 273 pp.
           Includes, in addition to the sonnets, introductory essays
      on the multiple critical theories about the sonnets, the quality

of the Thorpe text, the friend and the poet, the identity of
Mr. W.H., the themes and sources, and a table of sonnet order.
The first quarto copy text, probably a transcript of Shakespeare's
autograph, is made up of two classes of sonnets--the framework
sonnets described by Meres in 1598 as in circulation among his
friends and the private sonnets concerning the young man's sexual
misadventures probably secured by Thorpe from the dark lady.
Authorities more than likely ordered Thorpe to discontinue further issues shortly after the 1609 quarto appeared in the book-
shops.

CRITICISM

The Phoenix and Turtle

342   ARTHOS, JOHN. Shakespeare's Use of Dream and Vision. Totowa,
      N.J.: Rowman & Littlefield, 1977, 208 pp.
          Considers the metaphysical dimensions of Shakespeare's work
      and the frequent use of dreams and visions to illumine the dark-
      ness of spirit. In The Phoenix and Turtle the poetic persona
      experiences a dream vision of love in which immortality is
      attained through sacrifice and resurrection; his friend appears
      as a phoenix, the turtle as her mate, and "their death through
      love becomes the means of entry into eternal life" (p. 64). This
      analysis of the significance of vision and allegory in Shake-
      speare's early work is used as a touchstone for exploring the use
      of dream in A Midsummer Night's Dream, Julius Caesar, Hamlet, and
      The Tempest. (See entries 236, 312.)

343   BATES, RONALD. "Shakespeare's The Phoenix and the Turtle."
      Shakespeare Quarterly 6 (1955):19-30.
          Examines The Phoenix and Turtle in relation to Shake-
      speare's work as a whole. Whereas the other poems in Chester's
      volume duly address the phoenix legend symbolizing union, love,
      and chastity, Shakespeare's approach is the opposite. In the
      plays of the period (Hamlet, Troilus and Cressida) Shakespeare
      is obsessed with inconstancy, unchastity, and lust; and he con-
      veys something of the same spirit to the poem, denying both the
      sexual act and posterity. The poem reads like the outline of a
      drama. The first five stanzas form the dramatis personae, the
      anthem is the substance in intellectualized form, and the threnos
      is the epilogue.

344   COPLAND, MURRAY. "The Dead Phoenix." Essays in Criticism 15
      (1965):279-87.
          Views Shakespeare in The Phoenix and Turtle as lightly
      mocking the Platonic joining of the idea of female beauty and the
      idea of male fidelity. In praising married chastity Shakespeare
      is intending to shock in the fashionable metaphysical manner.
      The entire poem seems to be his half-humorous, half-affectionate

"pastiche-tribute to the odd charm and elusive structure of the medieval dream-allegory form" (p. 283). The crowning metaphysical shock is to announce that the phoenix is indeed dead. The young are admonished to love and to be true and, above all, to relish this all-too-short human life.

345   CUNNINGHAM, JAMES V. "'Essence' and Phoenix and Turtle."
        ELH 19 (1952):265-76.
            Focuses on the statement of the relationship of the lovers in the central part of the poem as Love and Constancy, Beauty and Truth, the Phoenix and the Turtle. The beloved is the essence of the lover; they become one, yet neither annihilates the other. Consumed in flames, they have passed from mortal life into the real life of Ideas. The tradition from which this series of images derives is that of the Beatific Vision, not that of the scholastic doctrine of love. The mystery confounds reason and finds its solution in love.

346   EMPSON, WILLIAM. "The Phoenix and Turtle." Essays in Criticism 16 (1966):147-53.
            Finds the central problem to be locating the reason for Shakespeare's praise of the phoenix for extinguishing its breed through married chastity. The collection of poems in which it appears honors the knighthood of John Salisbury in 1601. While Shakespeare's poem expresses the martyrdom of chastity, it is joyously announced as a lie in the first line of the poem that follows by Marston proclaiming a new heir. A new phoenix has arisen. The meaning of Shakespeare's poem is clear only when it is seen as a part of the movement of thought in the collection as a whole.

347   GARBER, MARJORIE. "Two Birds With One Stone: Lapidary Re-Inscription in The Phoenix and Turtle." Upstart Crow 5 (1984): 5-19.
            Describes the poem as a juxtaposition of the elegy (or funerary inscription) and the epithalamium. The poem's curious diction underscores the paradox created by the union of inscription and wedding song. Three assumptions are basic to the progress of the poem: reason is useless in explaining the radical mysteries of love and death; the phoenix symbolizes a union of the temporal and the atemporal; the poem is about the condition of poetry. The love of the wedded pair is celebrated, but the actual event is a funeral. Shakespeare seizes in the phoenix the opportunity to fuse the two antithetical forms.

348   MATCHETT, WILLIAM H. "The Phoenix and the Turtle": Shakespeare's Poem and Chester's "Loves Martyr." Studies in English Literature, 1. The Hague: Mouton, 1965, 213 pp.
            Argues that the poem, in the context of Chester's Love's Martyr, depicts Elizabeth and Essex as the phoenix and the turtle. The subject concerns not personal love but the mutual

understanding that might have made Essex "the Queen's copartner in governing the country and determining the succession" (p. 194). A section of elaborate praise is countered by "Threnos," Reason's response in light of the sterile and tragic conclusion of the relationship. While Shakespeare was no doubt deeply shocked by Essex's disgrace, he uses Reason to mitigate and moderate this response; despite the magnitude of the loss, the world is not totally bereft of virtue and beauty.

349   UNDERWOOD, RICHARD A. Shakespeare's "The Phoenix and Turtle": A Survey of Scholarship. Elizabethan Studies, 15. Salzburg: Institut für englische Sprache und Literatur, Universität Salzburg, 1974, 366 pp.
        Systematically examines the history of previous scholarship. In general the critics speak for themselves as verbatim extracts comprise virtually half the text. The chronological survey of scholarship is followed by the varying opinions concerning the authenticity of the text, the date of composition, the allegorical meaning, the sources, and the relationship of the poem to the plays. The poem is not an anomaly in Shakespeare's work; it provides a distinctive tone and theme for the Chester collection much as Shakespeare's songs make a functional tonal and thematic contribution to their stage worlds.

The Sonnets

350   ACHESON, ARTHUR. Mistress Davenant: The Dark Lady of the Sonnets. London: Bernard Quaritch; New York and Chicago: Walter M. Hill, 1913, 332 pp.
        Argues that Shakespeare's sonnet writing extends over at least a three-year period between 1592 and 1599. Proper chronological arrangement reflects the growth in mental power and poetic facility. The publication in 1594 of Willobie His Avisa by Matthew Roydon is examined as an unsuccessful attempt to alienate Shakespeare and his patron, the Earl of Southampton, both of whom loved the same woman. The dark lady is identified as Mistress Anne Davenant, first wife of John Davenant.

351   _____. Shakespeare and the Rival Poet. London and New York: John Lane, 1903, 360 pp.
        Identifies George Chapman as the rival poet and Henry Wriothesley, the Earl of Southampton, as Shakespeare's patron. Specific attention is focused on Chapman's attacks on Shakespeare in 1594-95 and again in 1597-98, with Shakespeare's counter-attacks reflected in Love's Labor's Lost (Chapman as Holofernes) and in Troilus and Cressida (a travesty of Chapman's fulsome praise of the Greek heroes in the preface to his translation of Homer). The rival poet's attempt to secure the favor of Shakespeare's friend by capitalizing on their temporary alienation is a record of literary enmity that bursts forth in other forms as well.

352   _____. Shakespeare's Sonnet Story, 1592-1598. New York:
         Edmond Byrne Hackett, 1933, 680 pp.
             Attempts to arrange the sonnets in chronological order by
         "books" (each with twenty sonnets) and to demonstrate their auto-
         biographical nature, in part a comparison with similar personal
         phases in the plays. Anne Davenant, the first wife of John
         Davenant, is identified as the dark lady of the sonnets. The
         bulk of the sonnets were written to the Earl of Southampton be-
         tween 1592 and 1599. In the publication, pursued by John Florio
         and George Chapman as an attack on Shakespeare, the sonnets were
         "disarranged both sequentially and chronologically" (p. 35).

353   BOOTH, STEPHEN. An Essay on Shakespeare's Sonnets. New Haven
         and London: Yale University Press, 1969, 218 pp.
             Demonstrates the organization of Shakespeare's sonnets as a
         multitude of coexistent and conflicting patterns--"formal, logi-
         cal, ideological, syntactic, rhythmic, and phonetic" (p. ix). A
         part of the reader's pleasure derives from the movement of his
         ordered experience from one frame of reference to another. The
         sonnets depend upon a conflict in what is said and what the
         reader expects, the vocabulary of one kind of experience used to
         describe another. While the reader has the comfort of recogniz-
         ing these rhetorical patterns, he also confronts exaggerated
         predictability and surprise, pertinence and impertinence, and the
         collision of value systems.

354   FORT, JAMES A. "The Order and Chronology of Shakespeare's
         Sonnets." Review of English Studies 9 (1933):19-23.
             Observes that a test of the frequency of parallel phrases
         suggests that Thorpe's order of the sonnets is essentially a true
         chronological arrangement. Since we can date sonnet 107, from
         internal evidence concerning Queen Elizabeth and Henri IV of
         France, in late 1596 and since in sonnet 107 Shakespeare indi-
         cates that he has known the fair youth for three years, the pe-
         riod of composition for sonnets 1-107 was 1593 to 1596, with
         others written in the following year and a half.

355   GRAVES, ROBERT. "A Study in Original Punctuation and
         Spelling." In The Common Asphodel. London: Hamish Hamilton,
         1949, pp. 84-95.
             Describes Shakespeare's poems as having a more familiar
         appearance on the page than those of E.E. Cummings but being more
         difficult in thought. Certain printing errors in the 1609 edi-
         tion have led to unwarranted emendations and modernizations.
         Cummings safeguards himself against emendation by the very bold-
         ness of grammatical violation, but he sacrifices the fluidity
         Shakespeare achieves through light punctuation. An analysis of
         differences in sonnet 129 in punctuation, spelling, and diction
         between the original and the modern version in The Oxford Book of
         English Verse demonstrates the potential destructive quality of
         editorial emendation.

356   HAMMOND, GERALD. The Reader and Shakespeare's Young Man Son-
       nets. Totowa, N.J.: Barnes & Noble, 1981, 247 pp.
          Assumes that Thorpe's ordering of the sonnets in the 1609
       quarto is essentially correct and examines the carefully designed
       sequence of sonnets dealing with the poet's need to function
       biologically and artistically. The general movement of the poems
       is from Shakespeare's almost total dependence on a human rela-
       tionship to a realization of self-sufficiency in his verse. The
       reader is manipulated to a position of sympathy for the poet,
       disapproval of the young man, and scorn for the rival poet.

357   HOTSON, LESLIE. Mr. W.H. New York: Alfred A. Knopf, 1964,
       328 pp.
          Searches the sonnets themselves for identification of the
       "Mr. W.H." to whom the 1609 quarto is dedicated. The friend in
       the text is described as monarch, sovereign, prince, and king;
       his identity is William Hatfield of Lincolnshire, a noble youth
       of such beauty and character that he was chosen to be "True-
       Love," Gray's Inn's Christmas King for 1588-89. The dark lady
       was Luce Morgan; the rival poet, Marlowe. The order of the son-
       nets represents Shakespeare's own arrangement. The sonnets are
       poems of Shakespeare's youth; Love's Labor's Lost was written for
       the same Gray's Inn celebration.

358   _____. Shakespeare's Sonnets Dated and Other Essays. New
       York: Oxford University Press, 1949, 244 pp.
          Examines the topical sonnets against the principal events
       in England and Europe between 1585 and 1605. The "mortall Moone"
       sonnet (107) refers to the defeat of the Spanish Armada. The
       "pyramyds" of sonnet 123 refer to the re-creation of four obe-
       lisks from 1586-89. The "blow of thralled discontent" in son-
       net 124 refers to the assassination of King Henri III of France
       in 1588. Such references confirm that Shakespeare completed the
       main group of his sonnets by 1589 and that he reached a remark-
       able stage of maturity by twenty-five in the 1580s when the fad
       of the sonnet sequence was at its height.

359   HUBLER, EDWARD. The Sense of Shakespeare's Sonnets. Prince-
       ton: Princeton University Press, 1952, 169 pp.
          Observes that the sonnet, limited by its very form to the
       development of a single mood, image, or thought, provides a means
       for the expression of Shakespeare's major ideas before he was
       able to objectify and interweave them in the medium of drama--
       perceptions of friendship, the dynamics of personality in the
       experience of sin and expiation, the power of love and lust, the
       craft of the writer, the ultimate aims of poetry, the basis of
       reputation.

360   HUBLER, EDWARD, et al. The Riddle of Shakespeare's Sonnets.
       New York: Basic Books, 1962, 346 pp.
             Includes the text of the sonnets, introductory comments by
       Hubler, essays by Northrop Frye, Leslie Fiedler, Stephen Spender,
       and R.P. Blackmur, and the full text of Oscar Wilde's The Por-
       trait of Mr. W.H. Hubler presents a chronological sketch of the
       critical history, noting the various putative identifications of
       the personae in the sequence. Frye describes the sonnets as a
       poetic realization of the whole range of love in the Western
       world, from the idealism of Petrarch to the disillusionment and
       frustrations of Proust. Fiedler focuses on the pure masculine
       principle corrupted by the female, Spender on Shakespeare's power
       to universalize the most fundamental human emotions, Blackmur on
       the duality of voices in love--the conscious and the unconscious.

361   KAULA, DAVID. "'In War With Time': Temporal Perspectives in
       Shakespeare's Sonnets." Studies in English Literature 3
       (1963):45-57.
             Notes that Shakespeare uses the concept of time in the
       sonnets as thief, tyrant, devourer, and harvester. Instead of
       delimiting time by comparing it with the Platonic Idea or Chris-
       tian immortality, however, he describes it as a fierce antagonist
       against which he must assert the force and constancy of his devo-
       tion to his friend. Past and future are treated, not as objec-
       tive realities, but as modes of looking backward or forward to
       enhance the value of the present moment.

362   KNIGHT, G. WILSON. The Mutual Flame: On Shakespeare's Son-
       nets and "The Phoenix and the Turtle." London: Methuen,
       1955, 233 pp.
             Attempts, not to settle the problems of the sonnets in
       factual and biographical terms, but to investigate these poems as
       the spiritual principle behind all Shakespeare's work. The son-
       nets deal with issues of time, death, and eternity in the context
       of sexual drive and human aspiration. The bisexuality reflected
       in them is a window to his dramas--the reconciliation of the
       sexes in the romantic comedies, the interweaving of Apollonian
       and Dionysian principles in the histories and tragedies, the
       address to the miraculous youth's eternal significance in the
       romances.

363   KRIEGER, MURRAY. A Window to Criticism: Shakespeare's
       "Sonnets" and Modern Poetics. Princeton: Princeton Univer-
       sity Press, 1964, 224 pp.
             Suggests that the miracle of poetry is the tension between
       the presence of moral contradictions and the power of order, for
       the sonnet the interworking of the Petrarchan convention, the
       Courtly Love convention, and the image of the individual poem.
       Shakespeare's sonnets comprise a "memorial tomb of love to which,
       as a womb, it gives eternal life" (p. 193). The paradoxical
       quality of his literal image (the transforming power of love, of

youth, of spiritual union) functions as a mirror by which to
assume universal qualities. Serving as the "typological figura,"
they are the microcosm explaining the macrocosm of poetry.

364   LANDRY, HILTON. Interpretations in Shakespeare's Sonnets.
      Berkeley and Los Angeles: University of California Press,
      1963, 185 pp.
          Reviews the major themes of the sonnets, concluding that
      the order in the 1609 quarto is essentially correct, that the
      surrounding sonnets serve as the best gloss for an individual
      poem, and that Shakespeare consciously works for ambiguity of
      feeling, syntax, and descriptive meaning. Unlike either the
      Elizabethans or Donne, Shakespeare frequently scatters his
      imagery, gaining unity through subtle associative processes.
      The structure is as varied as the imagery with grammatical,
      rhetorical, and logical patterns in evidence. The couplet may
      reiterate, supplement, contradict, qualify, or render ironic and
      humorous. Shakespeare's sonnets, in a sense, are both Eliza-
      bethan and metaphysical.

365   _____, ed. New Essays on Shakespeare's Sonnets. New York:
      AMS Press, 1976, 276 pp.
          Contains essays on Shakespeare's sonnets by Rodney Poisson
      (on the theme of friendship in 18-26), Martin Seymour-Smith (a
      psychological reading of 1-42), W.G. Ingram (the quality of the
      Shakespearean sonnet as distinguished from the work of his con-
      temporaries), Winifred Nowottny (form and style in 97-126), Anton
      M. Pirkhofer (the dramatic character), Hilton Landry (on Ivor
      Winters's and John Crowe Ransom's dislike of the sonnets),
      Marshall Lindsay (on French translations), Paul Ramsey (on
      syllabic structure), and Theodore Redpath (on the punctuation).

366   LEISHMAN, J.B. Themes and Variations in Shakespeare's
      Sonnets. London: Hutchinson, 1961, 254 pp.
          Examines Shakespeare's sonnets within the context of the
      European poetic tradition. Part 1 surveys the dual themes of
      immortality through poetry for another and immortality for the
      poet himself as they appear in Horace, Ovid, Petrarch, Tasso,
      Ronsard, and the English sonneteers. Part 2 focuses on the theme
      of human transiency from classical times to Shakespeare; Shake-
      speare combines the theme of immortality with the theme of human
      transiency in a uniquely powerful manner. Part 3 concentrates
      on the use of hyperbole as a device for constructing a spiritual
      basis for evaluating the friend as the archetype of all beauty
      and excellence.

367   MARTIN, PHILIP. Shakespeare's Sonnets: Self, Love, and Art.
      Cambridge: Cambridge University Press, 1972, 169 pp.
          Believes that Shakespeare's feeling for self-hood under-
      lies the whole body of the sonnets, interacting with poetry, with
      mutability, and with love for others. A discussion of the themes

of destructive and constructive narcissism precedes a comparison
of Shakespeare's love poetry with that of his contemporary son-
neteers and that of Donne. Both Shakespeare and Donne transcend
rather than work within the Petrarchan tradition: Donne primarily mocking, while Shakespeare runs the gamut from parody to
a naturalistic revitalization of old themes. Both poets ultimately come to envision love itself as a power greater than the
art that creates it.

368   MELCHIORI, GIORGIO. Shakespeare's Dramatic Meditations: An
       Experiment in Criticism. Oxford: Clarendon Press, 1976,
       206 pp.
          Focuses on four sonnets as the best articulation of Shake-
       speare's thought and feeling. Sonnet 94, for example, deals with
       the ethics of power, juxtaposing the chivalric code to the new
       economic code of nature; sonnet 121 concerns the ethics of social
       behavior, exploring the possibility of an ethic of utter indi-
       viduality and then renouncing it as socially unacceptable; son-
       net 20 examines the polarities of good and evil through their
       confrontation with love; and sonnet 129 explores the ethics of
       sex, not renouncing desire but seeing its satisfaction as both
       bliss and woe. The connecting link in these meditations is that
       humanity is caught in a wearisome condition.

369   MIZENER, ARTHUR. "The Structure of Figurative Language in
       Shakespeare's Sonnets." Southern Review 5 (1940):730-47.
       Reprinted in A Casebook on Shakespeare's Sonnets, ed. Gerald
       Willen and Victor B. Reed (New York: Thomas Y. Crowell,
       1964), pp. 219-35.
          Constitutes a defensive response to John Crowe Ransom's
       attack (entry 374) on Shakespeare's sonnets. Shakespeare's
       method is fundamentally different from that of the metaphysical
       poet; whereas Donne uses an illogical image that requires logical
       analysis, Shakespeare uses a logical image that requires figura-
       tive interpretation. The unique power of Shakespeare is in the
       intense metaphoric interaction--for example, love in sonnet 124
       as time's blooming favorite, its hate, a worldly courtier, a
       house built in sand. His verbal construct requires a structure
       of figurative language that approaches the density and logical
       incompleteness of the mind itself.

370   MUIR, KENNETH. "The Order of Shakespeare's Sonnets." College
       Literature 10 (1983):244-50.
          Observes that the narrative line of the sonnets is erratic
       at several spots but that evidence suggests the order in the 1609
       quarto is Shakespeare's own. Basically the poet writes to a
       friend urging him to marry and promising to immortalize him in
       verse; other poets share the friend's patronage; at some point
       the poet's mistress seduces the friend; the poet reluctantly
       comes to acknowledge that the friend's character has serious

faults. Attempts to rearrange the order are successful in varying degrees, but each raises new problems even as it lays others
to rest.

371   ____. Shakespeare's Sonnets. London: George Allen & Unwin,
         1979, 179 pp.
         Discusses the date, text, and order of the sonnets, then
Shakespeare's greater indebtedness to Erasmus, Ovid, and Sidney
than to Petrarch. In addition to extensive focus on the several
groups of sonnets, individual chapters address the style, the
poetic quality, the links with his other work, and a brief history of critical interpretation. One of the most significant
features is Shakespeare's variety of structure within the three
quatrain-couplet pattern--from the rhetorical structure of
propositio, ratio, confirmatio, and conclusion to the couplet as
summarial or paradoxical, the quatrains as cumulative or qualifying.

372   PARKER, DAVID. "Verbal Moods in Shakespeare's Sonnets."
         Modern Language Quarterly 30 (1969):331-39.
         Suggests that the sonnets be considered, not in biographi-
cal terms, but in terms of their rhetorical qualities. Virtually
all of them are elaborate disguises of the imperative mood, and
some play off one mood against another; in the first quatrain of
sonnet 3, for example, the imperative mood ("Look in thy glass")
turns to subjunctive ("that face should form another") and in
turn shifts to the present indicative ("Thou dost beguile the
world"). The important point is the dramatic quality. The sonnets, not static, register the mind in process.

373   RAMSEY, PAUL. The Fickle Glass: A Study of Shakespeare's
         Sonnets. AMS Studies in the Renaissance, 4. New York: AMS
         Press, 1979, 242 pp.
         Focuses on the meter, rhetoric, structure, and major themes
(negation and Neo-Platonism) of Shakespeare's sonnets. Un-
deniably, critics unsympathetic with Elizabethan poetics can
find faults. There is a tautology because repetition of idea,
sound, imagery, syntactical pattern, and rhythm is built into
the form. There is metrical and rhetorical elaboration, in part
reflecting the Renaissance love of artistic copiousness. There
is at times obscurity, whether from vacillation, condensation,
or abused metaphor. Above all, however, the sonnets tell of love
in all its variations of ecstasy, grandeur, shame, and self-
humiliation.

374   RANSOM, JOHN CROWE. "Shakespeare at Sonnets." Southern
         Review 3 (1938):531-53. Reprinted in The World's Body (New
         York: Scribner's, 1938), pp. 270-303.
         Describes Shakespeare's sonnets as generally ill con-
structed and metrically deficient, bound by a too arbitrary
quatrain-couplet form. The imagery is often conventional or

literary, shaped more by cliche than by genuine observation; the
poetry is associative rather than behavioristic, filled with
pretty words and indefinite analogies. The sonnets are mixed in
effect. Some of the most successful are metaphysical in style;
not even his later plays provide examples of better metaphysical
effects. The lyric poem is the poet's microcosm whereas poetry
in drama must serve the prior and peremptory claims of the
stage. (See entry 367.)

375   STERNFELD, F.W.; NEJGEBAUER, A.; and LEVER, J.W. "Twentieth-
       Century Studies in Shakespeare's Songs, Sonnets, and Poems."
       Shakespeare Survey 15 (1962):1-30.
            Surveys major work in the twentieth century on Shake-
       speare's music, sonnets, and poems. In music perhaps the most
       significant developments are the bibliographic and photographic
       facilities that make possible a fine degree of accuracy and de-
       tail. The amount of writing on the sonnets is second only to
       that on Hamlet; on the whole, criticism of the sonnets will not
       bear comparison with that of the plays, but there is a marked
       increase in sobriety. Among the poems Venus and Adonis has
       passed from virtual disregard to genuine acclaim, and interest
       in The Phoenix and Turtle has passed from identification of
       personae to themes.

376   STIRLING, BRENTS. The Shakespeare Sonnet Order: Poems and
       Groups. Berkeley and Los Angeles: University of California
       Press, 1968, 317 pp.
            Argues that the extremely close linkages in several groups
       of Shakespeare's sonnets must be taken as Shakespeare's norm of
       cogency and that the place of thematic non sequiturs must be
       interpreted as a result of Thorpe's fragmentation. This re-
       construction of the sonnet chronology is based less on the con-
       fused riddles of continuous narrative than on principles of
       multiple interconnections (theme, recurring metaphor or phrase)
       and the consequences on the surrounding sonnets (the standard of
       coherence).

377   WAIT, R.J.C. The Background to Shakespeare's Sonnets. New
       York: Schocken Books, 1972, 221 pp.
            Examines the relationships and activities of Shakespeare
       and the Earl of Southampton as a key to understanding Shake-
       speare's sonnets. The poems poetically trace this relationship
       from Shakespeare's early idealization of his friend-patron to
       his disillusionment with the Earl's involvement with his own
       mistress, the political folly of Southampton's involvement with
       the Essex rebellion in 1601, and finally to the bitter self-
       reproach for failing to support his former patron in the dark
       years that followed (a mood also evident in the problem plays
       and tragedies). An eventual reconciliation with his friend pre-
       cedes publication in 1609 and emotionally frees Shakespeare to
       return to happier dramatic themes.

378   WILSON, KATHERINE M. Shakespeare's Sugared Sonnets. London:
      Allen & Unwin; New York: Barnes & Noble, 1974, 382 pp.
          Traces the major attributes of the Elizabethan sonnet to
      primitive song, the chivalric convention, and Platonic theory.
      Shakespeare's use of and references to the sonnet in his early
      plays suggests that he considered the form puerile. In the con-
      text of writing his sonnet sequence he was consciously moving
      from the old sugared Petrarchan style to a plain speech of real
      love. The quality of style that seems to have impressed Shake-
      speare's contemporaries is his ability to catch "reality-
      experience in a verbal structure with layers of association"
      (p. 321), a quality resulting in rich polyphonic verbal tone.

379   WINNY, JAMES. The Master-Mistress: A Study of Shakespeare's
      Sonnets. London: Chatto & Windus, 1968, 216 pp.
          Aims at an imaginative rather than biographical interpreta-
      tion of Shakespeare's sonnets. An understanding of such poems
      can perhaps be achieved by investigating the nature of the par-
      ticular imaginative experience that prompts him to write, "hap-
      penings inside . . . the private world which is the field of his
      creative consciousness" (p. 22). The key appears to be in
      Shakespeare's dualistic nature, in a continuous self-destructive
      struggle within a body too deeply divided against itself to
      achieve unity, a theme traceable in the sonnets, narrative poems,
      and early history plays.

380   WITT, ROBERT W. Of Comfort and Despair: Shakespeare's Sonnet
      Sequence. Elizabethan Studies, 77. Salzburg: Institut für
      Anglistik und Amerikanistik, Universität Salzburg, 1979,
      233 pp.
          Maintains that Neo-Platonism serves far better than auto-
      biography as a means of fruitfully exploring the sonnets. Love
      in this sense becomes both creator and revealer, the union of
      lovers being one of souls rather than of bodies. True love
      exists as a series of upward steps, and Shakespeare dramatizes
      this ladder in his sequence, using Castiglione's Il cortegiano
      as the primary source. Characteristic of the dramatist, he en-
      visioned and articulated these ideas in concrete terms. Reason-
      able love (the friendship) is the earthly ideal through which one
      achieves the disembodied idea.

See also entries 52, 55-56, 112, 147, 459, 656.

The Rape of Lucrece

381   HYNES, SAM. "The Rape of Tarquin." Shakespeare Quarterly 10
      (1959):451-53.
          Sees in the description of the tapestry depicting the fall
      of Troy an emblem of Lucrece's rape. Critics who have complained
      about its length and artificiality have failed to observe that
      the metaphor is reversed in 1. 715 to Tarquin not as the

besieger but as the besieged. We confront the rapist's soul torn
with guilt, and in this moment we glimpse something of the vision Shakespeare was to develop in his great tragedies.

382   SYLVESTER, BICKFORD. "Natural Mutability and Human Responsi-
      bility: Form in Shakespeare's Lucrece." College English 26
      (1965):505-11.
          Envisions the theme as a universe in which weakness and
      beauty are subject to the encroachments of evil. The irresponsi-
      bility of both Lucrece's husband and of Tarquin creates tragic
      disorder. The imagery stresses the mutability of the world, and
      the ubiquitous animal imagery focuses on the imminent destruction
      of beauty and gentleness. Lucrece's apostrophes to Time and
      Opportunity develop natural mutability into an explicit theme.
      Raped, she is a physical microcosm of the intolerably ambiguous
      world, but by suicide she can reaffirm the orderly absolutes
      necessary to man.

383   WADLEY, HAROLD R. "The Rape of Lucrece and Shakespearean
      Tragedy." PMLA 76 (1961):480-87.
          Views the poem as an illuminating document concerning
      Shakespeare's development and his coming of age as an artist.
      One of the "most laborious and studied" of Shakespeare's works,
      it is a revealing index to his mind. Significantly, the poem's
      narrative is a sequence of highly dramatic situations visualized
      as scenes to be staged. Major emphasis, though, is on the inner
      human conflict and the conditions and connotations of the physi-
      cal action. The moral issue is presented in purely personal
      tragic terms. This rationale of tragedy underlies the whole of
      Shakespeare's major tragic work.

See also entries 199, 281, 867, 937.

Venus and Adonis

384   LEECH, CLIFFORD. "Venus and Her Nun: Portraits of Women in
      Love by Shakespeare and Marlowe." Studies in English Litera-
      ture 5 (1965):247-68.
          Notes that, just as Shakespeare and Marlowe are instru-
      mental in the development of English drama, so they are also
      pivotal in the popularization of Ovidian love poems in the 1590s.
      To read the mass of them is to recognize anew the creative talent
      of these two writers in Venus and Adonis and Hero and Leander.
      Their influence may go beyond the cult of the epyllion; it may
      well have set the conventions and the modes for the delineation
      of women in love in the plays of 1592 and thereafter.

385   MILLER, ROBERT P. "Venus, Adonis, and the Horses." ELH 19
      (1952):249-64.
          Defends the episode of the courser and the jennet as
      thematically significant to the work as a whole. Considered

symbolically, it reflects a moral dimension in the poem and thus
heightens and enhances Shakespeare's concept of love. When
Adonis exhibits sound Renaissance morality in confronting
Venus's advances, she--by praising the courser (the beast, animal
man, conventional symbol of lust) as something for Adonis to
emulate--makes her own passion unmistakable, namely, that she
desires abandonment to sensual pleasure for its own sake, not for
propagation.

386   PUTNEY, RUFUS. "Venus and Adonis: Amour with Humor."
      Philological Quarterly 20 (1974):533-48.
           Asserts that Elizabethan readers delighted in the rhetori-
      cal hyperboles of Venus and Adonis and that it is a sparkling and
      sophisticated comedy, not a lascivious and erotic narrative.
      Shakespeare's alterations of Ovid, such as the notion of a coy
      Adonis and the inability of the goddess of love to win her prey,
      are decidedly comic. So, too, is Adonis's exclamation that he is
      too young for an amorous encounter, a claim denied by his sweaty
      palm. Recognition of the demonstrably comic Ovidian tradition
      frees Venus from much of the critical attack to which it has been
      subjected.

See also entries 88, 199, 328, 937.

III. The English-History Plays

387   BERRY, EDWARD I. Patterns of Decay: Shakespeare's Early
      Histories. Charlottesville: University Press of Virginia,
      1975, 130 pp.
          Focuses on a dominant theme in the Henry VI-Richard III
      sequence, expressed in language, character, and action, that both
      lends unity to the individual stage world and also marks a stage
      in the process of social and political organization that charac-
      terizes the entire series. The movement is generally away from
      the chivalric community idealized in Talbot in 1 Henry VI to the
      maniacal tyranny represented in Richard III. The vision of his-
      tory as process gives the series its meaning and form as distinct
      from the emphasis on personality that dominates the later
      histories.

388   BLANPIED, JOHN W. Time and the Artist in Shakespeare's
      English Histories. Newark: University of Delaware Press;
      London: Associated University Presses, 1983, 278 pp.
          Considers Shakespeare's English histories to be a nine-part
      sequence concerned with the evolving relationship between history
      and drama, the struggle between past facts and his creative
      imagination, which labors to cast the dramatic situation into
      compelling dramatic form. In the course of these plays he moves
      from an objective, passive scrutiny of facts to energetic in-
      sights into relationships between the dead past and the seething
      present. This progress toward generative drama also involves a
      movement in delineating the king-figure from "antic" to
      "Machiavellian."

389   BROMLEY, JOHN C. The Shakespearean Kings. Boulder: Colorado
      Associated University Presses, 1971, 138 pp.
          Notes that, unlike the ethical reconstruction in personal
      terms of Shakespearean tragedy, the histories involve a political
      solution. The Henry VI plays, for example, exemplify man-made
      chaos in the absence of a forceful ruler and the succession of
      figures who pay the price for the anarchy--Talbot, Humphrey,

113

Suffolk, York, Somerset, Clifford, and Henry VI. Richard III is
a union of iron will and superb intellect but ultimately is "too
moral" to be a successful Machiavellian. Henry IV and Henry V
are successful political animals without illusion; their remorse,
nothing but the rhetorical posturing of individuals who are aware
of the necessity of political performance.

390   CALDERWOOD, JAMES L. Metadrama in Shakespeare's Henriad:
       "Richard II" to "Henry V." Berkeley and London: University
       of California Press, 1979, 225 pp.
          Focuses on the manner in which Shakespeare in the second
       tetralogy examines metaphorically the nature and materials of his
       art. The major metadramatic plot centers on the fall of a "lan-
       guage instinct with truth and value" (p. 179), the collapse of
       sacramental language associated with Divine Right in Richard II,
       the corrupt secular language of Henry IV, and the establishment
       of a pragmatic rhetoric in Henry V. Recognizing the frailties
       of his own dramatic office, Shakespeare admits that truth and
       value do not reside in theatrical presentation.

391   CAMPBELL, LILY BESS. Shakespeare's "Histories": Mirrors of
       Elizabethan Policy. San Marino, Calif.: Huntington Library,
       1947, 346 pp.
          Argues that Shakespeare's history plays are best understood
       in relation to the methods of historiography current in sixteenth-
       century England. Specifically, there is in these plays a domi-
       nant political pattern characteristic of the political philosophy
       of Shakespeare's own age. While he does not produce polemical
       tracts, he is creating political mirrors, and each play "serves a
       special purpose of elucidating a political problem of Elizabeth's
       day and in bringing to bear upon this problem the accepted polit-
       ical philosophy of the Tudors" (p. 125). Individual chapters are
       devoted to King John, Richard II, Henry IV, and Richard III.

392   CHAMPION, LARRY S. Perspective in Shakespeare's English His-
       tories. Athens: University of Georgia Press, 1980, 226 pp.
          Examines the structure of each of Shakespeare's English
       histories with major attention to the particular devices through
       which the playwright controls the audience's angle of vision and
       consequently its responses to the pattern of historical events.
       The constant experimentation from one stage world to the next,
       particularly in King John and the Henry IV plays, culminates in a
       dramatic technique distinct from that of the major tragedies, a
       structure combining the detachment of a documentary necessary for
       a broad intellectual view of history with the engagement between
       character and spectator without which no drama can be emotionally
       effective.

393   CRAIG, HARDIN. "Shakespeare and the History Play." In Joseph
       Quincy Adams Memorial Studies. Edited by James G. McManaway,
       Giles E. Dawson, and Edwin E. Willoughby. Washington: Folger
       Shakespeare Library, 1948, pp. 55-64.
          Describes the history play as a result of the combined in-
       fluences of chronicle narrative, romantic drama, and Senecan
       tragedy. Shakespeare's approach to the chronicle play is pri-
       marily by way of Senecan tragedy as illustrated in the formal
       correctness and rhetorical ornament of 2 Henry VI. Throughout
       the Yorkist plays one finds tropes, schemata, and figures of
       expression in abundance. As his artistry develops, Senecan
       formalism wanes, its use becoming more closely connected with
       special situations and characters; and he develops a "soberer
       style, better adapted to the dramatization of history" (p. 64).

394   DEAN, LEONARD F. "From Richard II to Henry V: A Closer
       View." In Studies in Honor of DeWitt T. Starnes. Edited by
       Thomas P. Harrison and James H. Sledd. Austin: University of
       Texas Press, 1967, pp. 37-52. Reprinted in Shakespeare:
       Modern Essays in Criticism, ed. Leonard F. Dean, rev. ed.
       (New York: Oxford University Press, 1967), pp. 188-205.
          Refutes the concept that Shakespeare's second tetralogy
       delineates the traditional Tudor party line. Richard II for all
       his decadence possesses a rhetorical brilliance that counters
       Bolingbroke's cold efficiency. Such counterpointing of mode and
       language continues in the Henry IV plays in the juxtaposition of
       court and tavern scenes. In Henry V Shakespeare balances the
       heroic mode with moments of irony; the consequence is not to
       negate dramatic power but to intensify "emotional sympathy for
       the heroic to the point of feeling it as near-tragedy" (p. 51).

395   JENKINS, HAROLD. "Shakespeare's History Plays: 1900-1951."
       Shakespeare Survey 6 (1953):1-15.
          Observes the striking dissimilarities in the interpretation
       of Shakespeare's histories between nineteenth- and twentieth-
       century critics. For the age of vast commercial and industrial
       progress, the plays were foremost an expression of the national
       spirit, an immortal epic. Modern scholarship has focused on the
       history play as a genre and as a reflection of Elizabethan polit-
       ical thought. Among the most notable aspects of contemporary
       criticism is the argument that comic and serious materials are
       functionally and effectively integrated.

396   KELLY, HENRY ANSGAR. Divine Providence in the England of
       Shakespeare's Histories. Cambridge, Mass.: Harvard Univer-
       sity Press, 1970, 344 pp.
          Analyzes Shakespeare's use of supernatural references in
       the historical writings covering his double tetralogy (1398-
       1485). These references are manifested primarily in the workings
       of Providence in the lives and destinies of the kings. Whereas

Tillyard's thesis (entry 409) is that the providential view extends through the plays to the glory of Henry VII, in fact the providential interpretations of the chronicles followed more immediate political lines. Thus, for a time a Lancastrian God developed, only in turn to give place to a Yorkist God. Shakespeare's characterizations and moral attitudes are consistent within a play, but they likewise shift from one play to another.

397   LAW, ROBERT ADGER. "Links Between Shakespeare's History
       Plays." Studies in Philology 50 (1953):168-87.
       Takes issue with Tillyard's major thesis (entry 409) that Shakespeare wrote the two tetralogies on a single grand conception. Instead, Shakespeare worked his way tentatively from one stage world to another without a preconceived plan of thematic continuity. What links do exist are incidental and primarily serve the purpose of the given stage world that Shakespeare was creating. Such links, moreover, are usually Shakespeare's creation, having no source in the chronicles. Tillyard and Law engage in a further direct exchange in Studies in Philology 51 (1954):34-41.

398   MANHEIM, MICHAEL. The Weak King Dilemma in the Shakespearean
       History Play. Syracuse: Syracuse University Press, 1973,
       198 pp.
       Observes that Shakespeare's history plays reveal a growing awareness that effective political rule encompasses a willingness to exercise devious and ruthless Machiavellian tactics. Henry VI fails, for example, because he is no match for the treacherous tactics of those around him. Henry V, on the other hand, if not devious, possesses the ability to deceive others about his true intentions and the ability to threaten and use violence when necessary. The plays affect our own attitudes about political figures and represent a turning point in the public attitude toward the monarchic ideal.

399   ORNSTEIN, ROBERT. A Kingdom for a Stage: The Achievement of
       Shakespeare's History Plays. Cambridge, Mass.: Harvard University Press, 1972, 231 pp.
       Asserts that Shakespeare virtually created the history play whole cloth. For him order depends not on abstract Tudor concepts of hierarchy and degree but on the "fabric of personal and social relationships which is woven by the ties of marriage, kingship, and friendship" (p. 222). The major foe to political order is the individualist who in his search for power defies kinship and affection. Chaos results not when one questions the doctrine of obedience but when brother turns on brother. Henry V, in part, celebrates military victory; more importantly, it celebrates the human bond between Henry and his soldiers.

400   PIERCE, R.B. Shakespeare's History Plays: The Family and the
      State. Columbus: Ohio State University Press, 1971, 261 pp.
         Observes that family life plays a prominent role in the
      language, characterization, and dramatic situation of Shake-
      speare's history plays, at times functioning as a microcosm of
      the state, at times as direct or ironic contrast. The analogy
      between kingdom and family, king and father, was commonplace.
      The whole concept of nobility rests on the concept that sons
      inherit from their father an inclination toward virtue. Espe-
      cially notable is the chaos reflected in a father's discovering
      that he has killed a son and a son a father in 3 Henry VI, the
      Gaunt-Bolingbroke relationship in Richard II, and the troubled
      relationships of Henry, Hal, and Hotspur in the Henry IV plays.

401   PORTER, JOSEPH A. The Drama of Speech Acts: Shakespeare's
      Lancastrian Tetralogy. Berkeley and London: University of
      California Press, 1979, 208 pp.
         Traces Shakespeare's preoccupation with speech and language
      in Richard II, 1,2 Henry IV, and Henry V, a time when Shakespeare
      was developing from his poetic phase into more dramatic dialogue.
      Richard's language is theatrical, placing him within an inner
      imaginative world from which he is unable to communicate with
      others. His language eventually becomes tedious prattle to
      others. Henry IV's language, at times silence, rings with verbal
      practicality. Hal ascends the stage as a princely polyglot, uni-
      fying a kingdom "in which men can, and must, talk to each other,
      and in which their speech is morally intelligible" (p. 187).

402   REESE, M.M. The Cease of Majesty. London: Edward Arnold,
      1961, 350 pp.
         Surveys the development and artistry of Shakespeare's his-
      tory plays. Shakespeare was able in the period of history
      stretching from Richard II to Richard III (ca. 1390-1485) to
      explore the relationships of ethics and power and also to mirror
      contemporary problems in the late Elizabethan period. Most
      striking is the identification between Shakespeare's Queen and
      Richard II. While she was certainly her own person, it would
      seem that she could bring her country to the brink of disaster by
      whim. Serious political reflection occurs throughout Shake-
      speare's plays. Nowhere does he suggest that it is possible for
      a government to be sound without a leader who is dedicated,
      disciplined, and patriotic.

403   RIBNER, IRVING. The English History Play in the Age of
      Shakespeare. Rev. ed. London: Methuen; New York: Barnes &
      Noble, 1965, 356 pp.
         Surveys the development of the English history play as a
      separate genre with chapters devoted to Shakespeare's first and
      second tetralogies and with Henry VIII included in a final sec-
      tion. The emergence and popularity of the genre is the dramatic
      reflection of the extreme popularity of history in all literary

forms in the sixteenth century. More important is the playwright's intention to use the past for didactic purposes--the
glorification of England and the Tudor humanistic doctrines. The
Henry VI plays are a grim reminder of civil chaos; Richard III is
testimony to the futility of self-sufficiency; the second tetralogy depicts the triumph of the House of Lancaster and the emergence and education of the ideal prince.

404   RICHMOND, HUGH M. Shakespeare's Political Plays. New York:
       Random House, 1967, 241 pp.
            Observes that Shakespeare's history plays engage in a
       steadily evolving study of man as a political animal. Taken
       together, they represent a kind of epic statement of English ex-
       perience, exerting an influence on the Englishman's political
       self-awareness. Chapters on each of the English histories and on
       Julius Caesar and Coriolanus trace the maturation of his art in
       using political themes; the distinctive cathartic function of the
       plays is the focus on man as a complex individual forced to learn
       how to manage his personal relationships, often at the cost of
       political success, and the refusal to accept simplifying politi-
       cal judgments.

405   SACCIO, PETER. Shakespeare's English Kings: History, Chroni-
       cle, and Drama. London and New York: Oxford University Press,
       1977, 268 pp.
            Provides a historical guide to Shakespeare's ten plays on
       medieval history. For each of the plays the author interweaves
       discussion of the Tudor historiography concerning the particular
       ruler, the historical period as envisioned by modern scholarship,
       and the action as Shakespeare recreates it on stage. Also in-
       cluded are genealogical and chronological charts and a compila-
       tion of names and titles. The series of plays has "high coher-
       ence" as a chronicle of fifteenth-century England; more than any
       other source, Shakespeare's plays are "responsible for whatever
       notions most of us possess about the period and its political
       leaders" (p. 4).

406   SEN GUPTA, S.C. Shakespeare's Historical Plays. Oxford:
       Oxford University Press, 1964, 172 pp.
            Focuses on the creation of living characters within a
       historical contextual framework not intent upon propagating any
       particular idea, Tudor myth or otherwise. Individual chapters
       cover the first tetralogy, King John, the second tetralogy, and
       Henry VIII. There is an increasing tendency to subordinate his-
       torical event to movements initiated by character. Richard III
       is an extreme example; his defeat is not only a personal tragedy
       but the defeat of a philosophy as well. Henry V is a success at
       the other extreme; everything he does throughout 1,2 Henry IV is
       preparing him for his royal role.

407   SPRAGUE, ARTHUR COLBY. Shakespeare's Histories: Plays for
      the Stage. London: Society for Theatre Research, 1964,
      165 pp.
         Aims to bridge the gap between stage and study by bringing
      both academic theory and actual stage experience to bear on
      dramatic analysis. Individual chapters cover each of the English
      histories. These plays were commemorative for the Elizabethans,
      a glorious warring against time. They came in the eighteenth
      century to be viewed as a single grand work with King John as
      prologue and Henry VIII as epilogue. On the whole, the histories
      have been fortunate; the factual basis has tended to prevent
      extravagances of critics and fantastications of producers.

408   THAYER, C.G. Shakespearean Politics: Government and Mis-
      government in the Great Histories. Athens, Ohio, and London:
      Ohio University Press, 1983, 190 pp.
         Argues that Shakespeare in the second tetralogy is no
      spokesman for Tudor orthodoxy. Richard II, for example, under-
      mines the political theology of passive obedience through the
      inept and unprincipled Richard, whose deposition is virtually
      required for the good of the kingdom. Henry IV depicts an era
      of just and effective rule with emphasis on a kingly dignity
      that prepares for the ideal ruler. These essays in statecraft
      have a particular relevance for the politically anxious years
      1597-99, when all thoughts were focused on the question of
      Elizabeth's successor.

409   TILLYARD, E.M.W. Shakespeare's History Plays. London:
      Macmillan, 1944, 383 pp.
         Envisions Shakespeare's English history plays as a dramatic
      epic of England embodying the Elizabethan principles of world
      order and of God's retributive justice. Molding the chronicle
      play into authentic drama that is not merely ancillary to the
      form of tragedy, Shakespeare depicts a fundamentally religious
      scheme of history "by which events evolve under a law of justice
      and under the ruling of God's providence, and of which Eliza-
      beth's England was the acknowledged outcome" (p. 362). Behind
      the disorder traced through the two tetralogies, King John, and
      Macbeth lies a macrocosmic principle of control that lends
      philosophic direction both to the movement of the plays as a
      group and to the resolution of the conflict in the individual
      stage worlds. Part 1 deals with the cosmic, historical, and
      literary backgrounds, part 2 with explications of the individual
      plays. For counterviews, see entries 267, 396-97.

410   TRAVERSI, DEREK A. Shakespeare: From "Richard II" to
      "Henry V." Stanford: Stanford University Press, 1957,
      198 pp.
         Describes Shakespeare's second historical tetralogy as a
      movement from the concept of the royal office as divinely insti-
      tuted, to its interruption and disastrous consequences, and

finally to the restoration of order on a more secure, if more
limited, basis. Richard's failure to exercise his divinely
sanctioned authority provokes Henry's usurpation, and Henry in
turn is forced to rule without the support of traditional sanc-
tions. Henry V, following his education, is able to consolidate
a new political order combining his father's political capacities
with an authority not flawed by dubious origins.

411   WINNY, JAMES. The Player King: A Theme of Shakespeare's
      Histories. New York: Barnes & Noble, 1968, 219 pp.
          Insists that the history plays are essentially imaginative
      in character and that to read them as political statements is to
      distort their artistic design. While an imaginative view does
      not exclude moral awareness, his method is not one of homiletic
      commentary. The study traces the attempts of Richard II, Henry
      Bolingbroke, and Henry V to assume royal dignity, to deal with an
      identity larger than their own in a struggle to become the part
      they play--Richard as king in name, Bolingbroke as counterfeiter,
      Hal as true inheritor.

See also entries 130, 196, 199, 209, 211, 216, 219, 227, 242, 314,
321.

1, 2 HENRY IV

Criticism

412   BARBER, C.L. "From Ritual to Comedy: An Examination of
      Henry IV." In English Stage Comedy. Edited by W.K. Wimsatt,
      Jr. English Institute Essays, 1954. New York: Columbia
      University Press, 1955, pp. 22-51. Reprinted in Shakespeare:
      Modern Essays in Criticism, ed. Leonard F. Dean, rev. ed.
      (New York: Oxford University Press, 1967), pp. 144-66.
          Develops the analogies between the comic elements of
      1,2 Henry IV and the misrule of traditional saturnalian holidays.
      The creation of Falstaff combines the clowning customary on stage
      and the folly customary on holiday. Through his relationship
      with Prince Hal, Shakespeare dramatizes both the need for and the
      necessity of limiting holiday; unrestrained, the Lord of Misrule
      might issue into the anarchic reign of a dissolute king. Ulti-
      mately Falstaff is rejected, like the scapegoat of saturnalian
      ritual, an event more logical in pattern than it is emotionally
      successful in drama.

413   BARISH, JONAS. "The Turning Away of Prince Hal." Shakespeare
      Studies 1 (1965):9-17.
          Notes that our attitude toward the rejection of Falstaff
      tends to reveal us as either a moralist or a sentimentalist. It
      is likely that Shakespeare intended to provoke the latter re-
      sponse since the sanctimonious and dishonest retrospective vision

of Henry V imposes a sense of constriction rather than liberation
upon our dramatic experience. Certainly by progressively depicting revelry as misrule Shakespeare renders inevitable the moral
position and our transfer at the end from the spirit of comedy
to the grim reality of history.

414   BLACK, JAMES. "Henry IV's Pilgrimage." Shakespeare Quarterly
        34 (1983):18-26.
            Focuses on Henry IV's obsession with a voyage to the Holy
        Land as a pilgrimage neither of remorse nor of politics but of
        the heart. Bolingbroke speaks of his exile in Richard II as a
        long, weary, enforced pilgrimage; in the opening scene of
        1 Henry IV the theme begins anew with his pledge to march to
        Jerusalem to gain pardon for Richard's murder, and it continues
        until the final scene in the Jerusalem Chamber in which his
        speech to Hal is both confessional and advisory. With a wonder-
        ful irony this weary traveler finds his absolution in his own
        bed.

415   BOWERS, FREDSON T. "Shakespeare's Art: The Point of View."
        In Literary Views. Edited by Carroll Camden. Chicago:
        University of Chicago Press, 1964, pp. 45-58. Reprinted in
        1 Henry IV, ed. James L. Sanderson, rev. ed., Norton Critical
        Editions (New York: W.W. Norton, 1969), pp. 309-16.
            Maintains that drama is the most highly developed objective
        literary form in existence and that the plot--especially its
        climax--is the key to determining the dramatist's point of view.
        Perhaps the subtlest climax in drama occurs in 1 Henry IV, in the
        king's apparent weaning of Hal from his dissolute life and set-
        ting him on the path to Shrewsbury and political glory. In fact,
        however, we have known how Hal would react since his soliloquy in
        act 1. Shakespeare deliberately undercuts the climax to give the
        initiative to Hal, who, instead of being acted upon, manipulates
        others to the goal of his self-education.

416   BRYANT, JOSEPH A., Jr. "Prince Hal and the Ephesians."
        Sewanee Review 67 (1959):204-19.
            Asserts that Hal's reference to redeeming time in his "I
        know you all" soliloquy would remind Shakespeare's spectators of
        the command in Ephesians that Christians must walk circumspectly
        in evil, among fools, to redeem time. Throughout 1,2 Henry IV
        Hal is attempting to define for himself the proper sphere of
        honor. Hal in part 2 must come to terms with Falstaff, the
        embodiment of time and common humanity. He fails, in casting
        him off completely, to redeem time, and this impulse to condemn
        rather than struggle through to redemption is a mark of his
        immaturity. (See entry 433.)

417   DORAN, MADELEINE. "Imagery in Richard II and in Henry IV."
       Modern Language Review 37 (1942):113-22.
            Notes a greater maturity in Shakespeare's handling of
       images in Henry IV than in Richard II. Whereas the images in
       Richard II are direct, explicit, and self-contained, those in
       Henry IV are richer in implication, ambiguous, and fluid. More-
       over, the characteristics of the imagery in the earlier plays are
       adapted to the development of the personality of the central fig-
       ure; in Henry IV the poetic styles are as varied as the charac-
       ters themselves.

418   DRAPER, JOHN W. "Sir John Falstaff." Review of English
       Studies 7 (1932):414-24.
            Argues that Shakespeare's audience would see in Falstaff a
       mirrorlike delineation of actual Elizabethan soldier figures--
       army officers in peace insolvent, brawling, and involved with
       their lady-loves; in war self-motivated in preparation and in
       claiming the rewards of victory. More specifically, he typifies
       the two main types of speculation practiced by captains--corrupt
       recruiting and padding the muster-rolls. His companions Bardolph,
       Peto, and Pistol also typify the dominant traits of Elizabethan
       soldiers. (See entry 309.)

419   EMPSON, WILLIAM. "Falstaff and Mr. Dover Wilson." Kenyon
       Review 15 (1953):213-62.
            Questions the theory that the text of Henry V represents a
       major revision on Shakespeare's part in which he excised much
       Falstaff material. Wilson claims (entry 463), for example, that
       with Kemp's departure from the company there was no one to play
       the fat knight and that Pistol's marriage to Nell is a substitute
       for a union more natural for Falstaff. The argument that 1,2
       Henry IV form a single unit is untenable, as is the claim of
       general degeneracy in Falstaff's character in part 2.

420   EVANS, GARETH LLOYD. "The Comical-Tragical-Historical
       Method--Henry IV." In Early Shakespeare. Edited by John
       Russell Brown and Bernard Harris. Stratford-upon-Avon
       Studies, 3. London: Edward Arnold, 1961, pp. 145-63. Re-
       printed in 1 Henry IV, ed. James L. Sanderson, rev. ed., Nor-
       ton Critical Editions (New York: W.W. Norton, 1969), pp. 194-
       214.
            Observes that the plot strands of Henry IV encompass both
       the world of ceremony and kingship and the world of nature. Hal
       confronts a father in each world--Henry IV and Falstaff-and both
       must perish before he comes into his kingdom. In Hal's educative
       process both Falstaff's hedonistic world and Hotspur's rebellious
       world slowly disintegrate. Through reflections of the natural
       and political, the comic and serious, the private and public,
       Hal emerges as representative of an order more inclusive than
       either of those he has rejected.

421 FISH, CHARLES. "Henry IV: Shakespeare and Holinshed."
     Studies in Philology 61 (1964):205-18.
         Focuses on Shakespeare's intentions in the delineation of
     Henry Bolingbroke. Demonstrably he builds a sense of integrity
     into the character not found in Holinshed, for example in Henry's
     handling of the character of Edmund Mortimer. Also, unlike the
     situation in the Chronicles, Henry is never personally accused of
     usurpation until late in the action, when the rebels' denial of
     his offer of mercy justifies Henry's giving battle. Moreover,
     in Shakespeare the rebels are clearly planning war before they
     bring their demands to Henry. Shakespeare goes to some trouble
     to reflect Henry as worthy of his nation's respect. (See
     entry 430.)

422 HAWKINS, SHERMAN H. "Henry IV: The Structural Problem Re-
     visited." Shakespeare Quarterly 33 (1982):278-301.
         Maintains that the two parts of Henry IV are too different
     for part 2 to be, as Shaaber maintains (entry 455), a carbon copy
     of part 1 added to capitalize on the dramatic success, but that
     they are too alike to fit Jenkins's theory (entry 426) that the
     two parts form a single whole. The two parts do form a diptych,
     whether part 2 was conceived before or after part 1. By creating
     the two-part play Shakespeare balances the first tetralogy with
     the second. The two tetralogies themselves form a diptych, the
     one moving from epic to tragedy, the other from tragedy to epic.

423 HEMINGWAY, SAMUEL B. "On Behalf of That Falstaff." Shake-
     speare Quarterly 3 (1952):307-11.
         Observes that Falstaff accommodates controversy more than
     most Shakespearean characters because there are two figures, the
     Lancastrian Falstaff of Henry IV and the Tudor Falstaff of The
     Merry Wives of Windsor. While the latter is ignored, the former
     lives in books and articles because he is more than a synthetic
     character. To first-nighters he is a coward; later he is the
     huge foil that sets off the glory of Prince Hal. The real
     Falstaff is more than Morgann, Bradley (entry 991), and Stoll
     (entry 311) suggest; he is visible in fresh nuances in every
     performance.

424 HUNTER, G.K. "Henry IV and the Elizabethan Two-Part Play."
     Review of English Studies, n.s. 5 (1954):236-48.
         Calls the unity of 1,2 Henry IV a diptych with the pattern
     of the shape and design of part 1 repeated in part 2. Chapman's
     two-part play The Tragedy of Charles Duke of Byron is organized
     by parallelism, as in a more rudimentary sense is Marlowe's
     Tamburlaine and Marston's Antonio and Mellida. In both parts of
     Henry IV the theme is rebellion leading to order, both in the
     state and in the mind of the Prince. Whereas the emphasis is on
     the struggle of coming of age in part 1, it is on the evolving
     abstract view of kingship in part 2.

425   HUNTER, WILLIAM B., Jr.   "Falstaff."   South Atlantic Quarterly
       50 (1951):86-95.
           Perceives a pattern of moral allegory in the structure of
       1,2 Henry IV. Hal represents an Aristotelian mean between the
       extremes of Hotspur and Falstaff, who embody respectively the
       excess and deficiency of honor. Hal's full maturation as ideal
       king is signaled by his rejection of Falstaff and his ratifica-
       tion of the Lord Chief Justice.

426   JENKINS, HAROLD. The Structural Problem in Shakespeare's
       "Henry the Fourth." London: Methuen, 1956, 28 pp. Portions
       reprinted in Twentieth Century Interpretations of "2 Henry IV,"
       ed. David P. Young, Twentieth Century Interpretations (Engle-
       wood Cliffs: Prentice-Hall, 1968), pp. 99-101.
           Maintains that Shakespeare at the outset did not envision
       Henry IV as a two-part play but that, in the course of composi-
       tion, determined that a sequel would be necessary. Shakespeare's
       original plan would have involved Hal's defeat of Hotspur at
       Shrewsbury, his rejection of Falstaff, and his subsequent assump-
       tion of the throne. The new pattern of action involves the delay
       of Falstaff's fate until a later play emerges in act 4. To fill
       out part 2 Shakespeare is forced to reduplicate Hal's display of
       physical valor as a parallel to his achievement of moral valor in
       the banishing of Falstaff. (See entry 422.)

427   KERNAN, ALVIN. "The Henriad: Shakespeare's Major History
       Plays." Yale Review 59 (1969-70):3-32. Revised in Modern
       Shakespearean Criticism: Essays on Style, Dramaturgy, and the
       Major Plays, ed. Alvin Kernan (New York: Harcourt, Brace &
       World, 1970), pp. 245-75.
           Claims that Shakespeare's second tetralogy constitutes an
       epic--a large-scale heroic action involving the movement of a
       people or nation from one condition to another. In the movement
       from the rule of Richard II to that of Henry V Shakespeare traces
       England from the Middle Ages to the beginning of the Renaissance,
       from feudalism to the national state, from a closed world to an
       infinite universe. In the former Richard mistakes metaphor for
       science in his assumption of divine support; in the latter Hal
       banishes idealism and pleasure, losing his individual identity to
       assume the work that his role demands.

428   LAW, ROBERT ADGER. "Structural Unity in the Two Parts of
       Henry the Fourth." Studies in Philology 24 (1927):223-42.
           Argues for the structural integrity of the two parts of
       Henry IV as discrete plays. Demonstrably the central theme of
       part 1 is the rivalry between Hal and Hotspur and its resolution
       at Shrewsbury. Part 2 pushes Falstaff into the foreground; his
       comic adventures and his struggle for the soul of Hal provide the
       unifying motif. The two plays have distinctly different forms
       and aims, the first emphasizing a chronicle format, the second a
       morality format.

429   McLUHAN, HERBERT MARSHALL. "Henry IV: A Mirror For Magis-
      trates." University of Toronto Quarterly 17 (1947):152-60.
         Speaks of three themes and three groups in 1,2 Henry IV--
      the court, the Boar's Head crowd, and the rebels. Since the
      court is corrupt, ruled not by principle but by policy, Hal takes
      refuge in the tavern. There the commoners reflect the corruption
      emanating from the court. The rebels are also a part of that
      corruption, rendering Hotspur's honor ineffective. Henry, the
      source of evil, is finally poisoned by success. At his father's
      death it is perfectly natural for Hal to banish his erstwhile
      cronies and assert his true nature; the heroic mode has replaced
      the base.

430   MONAGHAN, JAMES. "Falstaff and His Forebears." Studies in
      Philology 18 (1921):353-61.
         Describes Falstaff as a composite of Sir John Oldcastle and
      Derrick the clown in The Famous Victories of Henry V. Derrick is
      the primary source as illustrated by a comparison of identical
      situations and incidents and similar turns of speech. When
      Shakespeare went to London, Richard Tarlton was acting the role
      of Derrick, and not improbably Tarlton added a great deal of
      stage business to the role as it is preserved in the text. The
      improvisation may well have played a large part in Shakespeare's
      conception and amplification of the part of John Falstaff. (See
      entry 421.)

431   MORGAN, ARTHUR EUSTACE. Some Problems of Shakespeare's
      "Henry IV." London: Oxford University Press, 1924, 43 pp.
         Suggests that the version of Henry IV including Oldcastle
      was radically different from the play as we have it and that it
      derived from a lost play from which The Famous Victories of
      Henry V also derived. 1,2 Henry IV represents revisions of that
      early version (ca. 1588). The original was all in verse and
      contained less comic material; to make room for the additional
      comedy Shakespeare abridged the historical plot. Sir John
      Oldcastle was but a dim foreshadowing of the richly humorous
      Falstaff.

432   NEWMAN, FRANKLIN B. "The Rejection of Falstaff and the
      Rigorous Charity of the King." Shakespeare Studies 2 (1966):
      153-61.
         Examines the sermon on charity from the Homilies to deter-
      mine that Henry in rejecting Falstaff reveals himself both as a
      devotee of sound government and as one possessed of Christian
      virtue. The homily specifically charges one to rebuke and punish
      vice without regard to persons. Metaphorically Shakespeare is
      purging from the kingdom that which might corrupt others. This
      reading will obviously not remove all ambiguities from an act as
      important symbolically as it is physically, but it provides
      further evidence of the context within which Shakespeare con-
      ceived it.

433   PALMER, D.J. "Casting Off the Old Man: History and St. Paul
       in Henry IV." Critical Quarterly 12 (1970):267-83.
          Observes that Hal's reference to redeeming time at the out-
       set of 1 Henry IV distinguishes the Prince in the spectators'
       eyes from the wild youth both Falstaff and the King thought him
       to be. Hal's allusion is to the admonition of St. Paul in
       Ephesians, who speaks of the old man as the unregenerate Adam
       who must be set aside. That Shakespeare consciously builds in
       the allusion is verified by the reference in 2 Henry IV (2.2) to
       the Eastcheap community as Ephesians of the Old Church and to
       Hal's exclamation, "I know thee not, old man," at the point of
       his rejecting Falstaff. (See entry 416.)

434   SCOUFOS, ALICE-LYLE. Shakespeare's Typological Satire: A
       Study of the Falstaff-Oldcastle Problem. Athens, Ohio: Ohio
       University Press, 1979, 378 pp.
          Argues that Shakespeare in his history plays inverts the
       medieval practice of typology and makes his characters "types"
       of contemporary Elizabethans, specifically in order to lampoon
       the Brooke family and Lord Cobham. The satire begins in
       1 Henry VI, continuing with the unfavorable depiction of Eleanor
       Cobham in 2 Henry VI. The major focus is on the Falstaff and
       Percy satirical material in 1,2 Henry IV and The Merry Wives of
       Windsor. Evidence of the attack shows up as late as Macbeth in
       reflections of the Gunpowder Plot involving the Ninth Earl of
       Northumberland (the "Wizard Earl").

435   SHAABER, MATHIAS A. "The Unity of Henry IV." In Joseph
       Quincy Adams Memorial Studies. Edited by James G. McManaway,
       Giles E. Dawson, and Edwin E. Willoughby. Washington: Folger
       Shakespeare Library, 1948, pp. 217-27.
          Argues against a unified artistic conception of 1,2 Henry IV.
       In every logical sense the action is complete at the end of part 1.
       The scene with the Archbishop of York (4.4) exists not to point
       to part 2 but to foreshadow Hotspur's defeat at Shrewsbury, and
       the reconciliation between king and prince appears genuine. The
       assumption that part 2 is an afterthought occasioned by the popu-
       larity of part 1 logically explains the carbon-copy structure of
       the two plays and the fact that Shakespeare has turned back his
       dramatic clock, estranging the father and son and thus necessi-
       tating another reconciliation.

436   SHIRLEY, JOHN W. "Falstaff, an Elizabethan Glutton." Philo-
       logical Quarterly 17 (1938):271-87.
          Observes that Falstaff has elicited diverse interpretations
       because he is essentially of a double nature, highly witty and
       also derisively obese. His physical characteristics are present
       in Gula, the Gluttony of the Seven Deadly Sins, while his mental
       characteristics are present in the Vice as it degenerates into a
       largely comic role and is merged with the character of the Glut-
       ton. Examples include Derrick the clown in The Famous Victories

of Henry V and Inclination in The Trial of Treasure. Falstaff is
the outgrowth of a dramatic tradition that evolves over a century
and a half.

437   SMALL, SAMUEL A. "The Reflective Element in Falstaff."
      Shakespearean Association Bulletin 14 (1939):108-21, 131-43.
         Observes that Falstaff uses his wit to charm away the
realities of life and that his humor arises in part from the in-
congruity of his youthful intellectual keenness and the age and
obesity of his body. Falstaff is aware of and sensitive about
his bodily infirmities, however, and at times evokes through
self-pity a sympathetic response from the spectators. In spite
of his lies he gains our understanding and even affection. The
reflective element is the counterpart to his roguishness, and
Shakespeare intended for us to have a degree of sympathy at his
banishment.

438   SPRAGUE, ARTHUR COLBY. "Gadshill Revisited." Shakespeare
      Quarterly 4 (1953):125-37.
         Maintains that Falstaff, notwithstanding the contrary
arguments of Maurice Morgann in 1777, is a coward. Given his
corpulence and his age, the spectators like him despite this lack
of courage. His military reputation is sheer bogus, and Hal provides him a "charge of foot" both to watch his immediate reaction
and to force him to lard the lean earth through "a march of
twelvescore." He is able to sleep behind the arras at the Boar's
Head because he knows the Prince will protect him. Above all,
his flight in the Gadshill robbery amounts to a dramatic demon-
stration of cowardice.

439   TOLIVER, HAROLD E. "Falstaff, the Prince, and the History
      Play." Shakespeare Quarterly 16 (1965):63-80. Reprinted in
      Twentieth Century Interpretations of "2 Henry IV," ed. David
      P. Young, Twentieth Century Interpretations (Englewood Cliffs:
      Prentice-Hall, 1968), pp. 58-79.
         Argues that Shakespeare involves the audience in a communal
rhythm, integrating concepts of providential order and pragmatic
political concerns with timeless human impulses. While Hal is
able to perceive history as a continuous succession of events
linking the present to past and future, Falstaff increasingly
loses himself in the present moment. In the course of the play
Hal incorporates and transcends the characteristics of Hotspur,
his father, and Falstaff. Falstaff's ultimate rejection coincides
with and contributes to the anagnorisis in the audience.

440   WATSON, ROBERT N. "Horsemanship in Shakespeare's Second
      Tetralogy." English Literary Renaissance 13 (1983):274-300.
         Views the literal and figurative equestrian references as
highly controlled by Shakespeare to delineate in one's lack of
mastery of horsemanship a failure of self-rule (for example,
Hotspur, Falstaff) and in one's ability (Henry IV, Prince Hal) a

political mastery of England. Specifically, Shakespeare transforms Plato's metaphor relating chariot driving with restraint
of unruly passions into one relating horsemanship and rightful
political authority. The king as horseman must restrain and
guide an unruly state.

441   WILLIAMS, PHILIP. "The Birth and Death of Falstaff Reconsid-
       ered." Shakespeare Quarterly 8 (1957):359-65.
           Defends J.I.M. Stewart's thesis (entry 309) that Hall fig-
uratively kills Falstaff rather than kill his father. Falstaff
becomes a father surrogate, sought out in part because of the
antagonism between the prince and King Henry. Note also that in
the tavern scene Falstaff in play actually assumes the paternal
role. In part 2 Falstaff becomes old, and Hal is not comfortable
as king so long as Falstaff is present. Stoll's theory (entry
311) that Falstaff derives from the miles gloriosus is curiously
similar in that both he and Stewart explain the figure through
his ancestry.

442   WILSON, JOHN DOVER. The Fortunes of Falstaff. Cambridge:
       Cambridge University Press, 1943, 143 pp.
           Insists that Falstaff is neither Bradley's succulent sinner
(entry 991) nor Stoll's stage butt descended from the Plautine
braggart (entry 311). Instead he is a character who, as a mixture of moral abandon and spontaneity of wit, is riding for an
inevitable fall. Such a vision of Falstaff also clears the focus
on Hal, who is both generous and lovable, but also faulty. Hal,
as he must, ultimately rejects Falstaff, but he provides well for
him. The embodiment of liberty lives on but is replaced at center
stage by the embodiment of order, with Hal representing the traditional ideals of public service.

443   _____. "The Origins and Development of Shakespeare's
       Henry IV." Library, 4th ser. 26 (1945):2-16.
           Notes the popularity of Henry IV on the stage in the 1580s
and 1590s, the clearest example being The Famous Victories of
Henry V, entered in the Stationers' Register in 1594 and extant
in a quarto of 1598. The play in part derives from Shakespeare,
but not from the version we have today. Shakespeare first
developed a verse play on Henry IV including Oldcastle, but he
was forced to put it aside when it incurred the wrath of old Lord
Cobham in 1596. When he took it back up, he changed the name to
Falstaff and developed his character to such an extent that it
encompassed two plays.

For discussion of the rejection of Falstaff, see entries 412-13,
432-33, 436, 441. For discussion of the structure of parts 1 and 2,
see entries 422, 424, 426, 428, 435, 460. See also The English History Plays (entries 387-411) and 30, 50, 66, 142, 162, 205, 227-28,
235, 306, 309, 311, 313, 330, 479, 548, 591, 622, 781, 878, 963,
1011.

Reference Works

444   KIERNAN, MICHAEL, comp. "Henry IV: Part I": A Bibliography
       to Supplement the New Variorum Edition of 1936 and the Supple-
       ment of 1956. New York: Modern Language Association, 1977,
       15 pp.
           Includes 280 items representing scholarship on 1 Henry IV
       from 1956 through 1972. The material is categorized alphabeti-
       cally under editions, text, criticism, sources, commentary, music,
       and staging and stage history. Books with general focus are
       placed in the criticism section; not included are collected edi-
       tions and book reviews. Supplements 445-46.

Editions

445   EVANS, G. BLAKEMORE, ed. Supplement to "Henry IV, Part I."
       A New Variorum Edition of Shakespeare. New York: Shakespeare
       Association of America, 1956, 121 pp.
           Follows the same format in providing a supplement to S.B.
       Hemingway's Variorum edition in 1936 (entry 446). All signifi-
       cant items of scholarship from 1935 through July 1955 are in-
       cluded. Other than the main sections on textual notes and criti-
       cal notes, material is categorized under the text, the date of
       composition, sources, general criticism, characters, style and
       language, and stage history.

446   HEMINGWAY, SAMUEL B., ed. Henry the Fourth, Part I. A New
       Variorum Edition of Shakespeare. Philadelphia: J.B. Lippin-
       cott, 1936, 554 pp.
           Uses the first quarto (1598) as the copy text (pp. 3-341).
       On each page, for that portion of the text, are provided variant
       readings, textual notes, and general critical commentary. Fol-
       lowing the text are sections on the text, the date of composi-
       tion, sources, the individual characters, the stage history,
       stage versions, and a list of works consulted. Supplemented by
       444-45.

447   HUMPHREYS, A.R., ed. The First Part of King Henry IV. The
       Arden Shakespeare. London: Methuen; Cambridge, Mass.:
       Harvard University Press, 1960, 202 pp.
           Includes discussion of the text, date, questions of revi-
       sion, sources, Falstaff, the unity of the play, the historical
       outlook, the spirit of the play, and the imaginative impact. The
       text is based on the first quarto (1598), for which the copy was
       probably a transcript of Shakespeare's foul papers. The date of
       composition is most likely 1596, with revisions of Falstaff's
       name occurring in 1597. Shakespeare's most striking modifica-
       tions of his source (primarily Holinshed's Chronicles) are in the
       characters of Glendower, Hotspur, and Hal. Falstaff himself is a

rich amalgam, a world of comic ingredients; thus he has responded
to source hunters from history, earlier dramatic tradition, and
theology. Although parasitical, he gives as much to life as he
takes from it and, symbolically, is like life itself. The basic
structure of the play is analogous to a morality--with vice and
virtue contending for the soul of a prince.

448   WILSON, JOHN DOVER, ed. The First Part of the History of
       Henry IV. Cambridge: Cambridge University Press, 1946,
       210 pp.
          Provides extensive textual notes, a critical introduction,
a discussion of the copy text, a section on stage history, and
a glossary. This edition is based on the first quarto (1598),
for which the copy was probably Shakespeare's foul papers.
1 Henry IV is patently only a part of a whole dramatic conception
in parts 1 and 2. The political and dynastic theme, the defeat
of the rebels and the repentance of the prince, is only half
concluded in this play. Moreover, to envision Hal as a cad or
a hypocrite destroys the centerpiece of the Lancastrian trilogy,
Henry V.

                              Criticism

449   BROOKS, CLEANTH, and HEILMAN, ROBERT B. "Notes on Henry IV,
       Part I." In Understanding Drama. New York: Holt, Rinehart &
       Winston, 1948, pp. 376-87. Reprinted in 1 Henry IV, ed. James
       L. Sanderson, rev. ed., Norton Critical Editions (New York:
       W.W. Norton, 1969), pp. 215-29.
          Envisions the question of unity as the central problem of
1 Henry IV in that one must accommodate the fortunes of Falstaff
to the resolution of the main plot at Shrewsbury. Falstaff at
the battlefield strips the pretensions from honor and courage
even as Hal displays those very qualities in confronting and
defeating Hotspur. The strength of the play's conclusion lies
in its rich ambivalence that forces the spectator to recognize
with a touch of irony that we live in a fallen world demanding
political compromises for survival.

450   KNOEPFLMACHER, U.C. "The Humours as Symbolic Nucleus in
       Henry IV, Part I." College English 24 (1963):497-501.
          Argues that Shakespeare's use of the humors theory provides
the basis for symbolically unifying the imagery of blood, sickness, and the elements. These images function to set Hal apart
from the other principals and to delineate his development into
the ideal Christian monarch. While the King is melancholic,
Hotspur choleric, and Falstaff phlegmatic, Hal is essentially a
sanguine person. The civil butchery has not yet ended, but a
new sun--a healthy individual--has arisen.

451   RENO, RAYMOND H. "Hotspur: The Integration of Character and
      Theme." Renaissance Papers (1962):17-25. Reprinted in
      1 Henry IV, ed. James L. Sanderson, rev. ed., Norton Critical
      Editions (New York: W.W. Norton, 1969), pp. 235-44.
            Notes that Hotspur, himself a figure of disorder in his
      inability to maintain self-control, reflects the play's major
      theme of disorder. For him honor is but rhetorical flourish
      without substance. This quality extends as well into the polit-
      ical center of the play, in which Henry IV, too, is obsessed with
      image and reputation rather than with actuality, and into the
      social center, in which Falstaff is a walking symbol of anarchy
      in the shape of appetite. The microcosmic disorder in Hotspur
      eventually extends into the larger pattern of the action and
      rends and deracinates the larger world of the state.

452   TRAVERSI, DEREK A. "Henry IV, Part I: History and the
      Artist's Vision." Scrutiny 15 (1947):24-35. Reprinted in
      1 Henry IV, ed. James L. Sanderson, rev. ed., Norton Critical
      Editions (New York: W.W. Norton, 1969), pp. 235-44.
            Argues that a significant part of Shakespeare's design in
      the second tetralogy is to trace a common destiny working itself
      out in the Lancastrian family. Whatever his desire for the
      general good, Henry IV--in calling for a crusade--is moved by
      motives essentially political. Hal in his opening soliloquy
      reveals himself as a true son of Lancaster. His false humility
      and amoral personality place him squarely in the service of
      political interests. Falstaff serves as a foil to Hal, in his
      human warmth, albeit sorely flawed, reflecting the cold, calcu-
      lating nature of his royal companion.

See also The English Histories (entries 387-411) and 103, 216, 222,
246, 258, 290, 481, 488.

2 HENRY IV

Reference Works

453   SHAABER, MATHIAS A., comp. "Henry the Fourth, Part Two": A
      Bibliography to Supplement the New Variorum Edition of 1940.
      New York: Modern Language Association, 1977, 18 pp.
            Includes 398 items representing the scholarship on
      2 Henry IV from 1940 through 1975. The material is categorized
      alphabetically under editions, text, date, criticism, sources,
      commentary, music, and staging and stage history. Books with a
      general focus are placed in the criticism section, and book re-
      views are not included. Supplements entry 455.

Editions

454   HUMPHREYS, A.R., ed. The Second Part of King Henry IV. The
       Arden Shakespeare. London: Methuen; Cambridge, Mass.:
       Harvard University Press, 1966, 242 pp.
           Includes discussion of the text, date, the extent of re-
       visions, the relationship to 1 Henry IV, the sources, major
       themes, Falstaff and the rejection, and style, as well as appen-
       dixes featuring selections from Holinshed, Daniel, Stowe, Elyot,
       and The Famous Victories of Henry V. The text is based on the
       first quarto (1600), for which the copy was probably Shakespeare's
       foul papers. The date of composition was most likely late 1596
       or early 1597, with revisions of the Falstaff name late in 1597
       and of the epilogue by early 1599. Shakespeare apparently in-
       tended two plays on Henry IV from the outset or very near it.
       One of the dominant themes of the play is miscalculation--from
       the introduction by Rumor to the pervasive list of surmises,
       jealousies, and conjectures. Falstaff continues to exercise
       comic prowess, but increasingly the play imposes its responsible
       moral tones. His rejection by Hal, though inevitable, is none-
       theless painful. Through the action Henry is deepened, not nar-
       rowed as the play achieves a balanced complexity not inferior to
       part 1.

455   SHAABER, MATHIAS A., ed. Henry the Fourth, Part 2. A New
       Variorum Edition of Shakespeare. Philadelphia: J.B. Lippin-
       cott, 1940, 715 pp.
           Uses the first quarto (1600) as the copy text (pp. 1-460).
       On each page, for that portion of the text, are provided variant
       readings, textual notes, and general critical commentary. Fol-
       lowing the text are sections on the text (the quarto, the folio,
       the copy text), the date of composition, the authenticity of the
       text, the sources, criticisms (the play as a whole, the rejection
       of Falstaff, local color, topical allusions, characters, identi-
       fications), the Dering MS, acting versions, stage history, and a
       list of works consulted. (See entry 422; supplemented by
       entry 453.)

456   WILSON, JOHN DOVER, ed. The Second Part of the History of
       Henry IV. Cambridge: Cambridge University Press, 1946,
       231 pp.
           Provides extensive textual notes, a discussion of the copy
       text, a section on stage history, and a glossary. This edition
       is based on the first quarto (1600), for which the copy text was
       probably Shakespeare's foul papers. The critical introduction
       for part 1 (see entry 448) covers both plays, which are accepted
       as a single thematic and dramatic unit. Everything points to
       the coronation of the prince and the mystery of how he will be-
       have at this critical moment. He emerges as the ruler of all
       England--nobleman, merchant, yeoman, peasant--able to cure
       Henry IV's, and by extension the kingdom's, sickness of soul.

Textual Studies

457   PROSSER, ELEANOR. Shakespeare's Anonymous Editor: Scribe and
      Compositor in the Folio Text of "2 Henry IV." Stanford:
      Stanford University Press, 1981, 219 pp.
           Argues for the rejection of eighty-six folio readings here-
      tofore considered canonical. Instead of valid alterations re-
      flecting stage practice, the first quarto (1600) represents
      changes made by the scribe and the compositor in Jaggard's print-
      shop. Changes made by the scribe result from his own stylistic
      affinities; changes made by the compositor--deletions, insertions,
      paraphrases--were functional, resolving problems of page makeup.
      Other folio texts set from good quartos should be carefully
      examined for similar contaminations.

458   WALKER, ALICE. "Quarto 'Copy' and the 1623 Folio: 2 Henry IV."
      Review of English Studies, n.s. 2 (1951):217-25.
           Maintains that the first quarto (1600) was printed from
      foul papers and the 1623 folio text from a copy of the quarto
      that had been collated with a fair copy of the foul papers.
      Errors and anomalies common to both texts are the result of con-
      tamination of the quarto by the folio. The massed-entry stage
      directions, representing little more than bookkeeper's jottings,
      have been exaggerated. The elimination of oaths from the First
      Folio 2 Henry IV (but not, for example, from the First Folio
      Much Ado About Nothing) suggests that, with the change of command
      in the Office of the Revels during the printing process, Jaggard
      anticipated a more rigorous attitude toward profanity.

Criticism

459   KNIGHTS, L.C. "Time's Subjects: The Sonnets and King
      Henry IV, Part II." In Some Shakespearean Themes. Stanford:
      Stanford University Press, 1959, pp. 45-64. Reprinted in
      Twentieth Century Interpretations of "2 Henry IV," ed. David
      P. Young, Twentieth Century Interpretations (Englewood Cliffs:
      Prentice-Hall, 1968), pp. 13-29.
           Sees 2 Henry IV as a transitional play, looking back to the
      sonnets and earlier history plays and forward to the great trage-
      dies. Like the sonnets 2 Henry IV is concerned with the theme of
      time and mutability and the various aspects of human frailty such
      as age, disappointment, and decay. The dying king, the repeated
      references to Northumberland's illness, the emphasis on Falstaff's
      age and diseases--all help to create the sense of a passing era
      that Hal must finally put behind him.

460   LEECH, CLIFFORD. "The Unity of 2 Henry IV." Shakespeare
      Survey 6 (1953):16-24. Reprinted in Twentieth Century
      Interpretations of "2 Henry IV," ed. David P. Young. Twentieth
      Century Interpretations (Englewood Cliffs: Prentice-Hall,
      1968), pp. 30-41.

Perceives in 2 Henry IV a tone distinctly different from that of part 1. The overt morality pattern pitting the Lord Chief Justice against Falstaff, the preoccupation with effects of time, the latent scepticism, and the striking objectivity in the presentation of the characters all contribute to a more sombre quality that in itself creates a sense of dubiety concerning basic assumptions in the great historical scheme. The probing and ambiguous quality of the play is not unlike that of the dark comedies.

See also The English Histories (entries 387-411) and 89-90, 103, 368, 475.

HENRY V

Reference Works

461   CANDIDO, JOSEPH, and FORKER, CHARLES R., comps. "Henry V": An Annotated Bibliography. Garland Shakespeare Bibliographies, 4. New York and London: Garland Publishing, 1983, 815 pp.
      Contains 2,103 entries representing virtually all publications on the play since 1940 through 1981 along with most significant items of scholarship prior to 1940. The categories, each arranged chronologically, are divided into criticism, individual editions, complete and collected editions, adaptations, textual and bibliographical studies, language, sources, influence, and staging. A brief introductory essay traces the history of recent criticism.

Editions

462   WALTER, J.H., ed. King Henry V. The Arden Shakespeare. London: Methuen; Cambridge, Mass.: Harvard University Press, 1954, 174 pp.
      Includes discussion of the text, date, the epic nature of the play, the conversion of Hal, the spiritual significance of the play, other plays on Henry V, the rejection of Falstaff, and critical interpretations, as well as appendixes featuring selections from Holinshed and The Famous Victories of Henry V. The text of this edition is based on the First Folio, for which the copy was probably Shakespeare's foul papers. The quarto publications are corrupt, representing a memorial reconstruction text. Only in our century has appraisal of the play become uncertain and contradictory. To many Henry is the ideal king, the consummation of the epic of England, a king both in ability and in right. To others he is the ultimate Machiavel, political son of his father willing to sacrifice friend and integrity for power.

463 WILSON, JOHN DOVER, ed. King Henry V. Cambridge: Cambridge
     University Press, 201 pp.
        Provides extensive textual notes and a discussion of the
     copy text (with sections on the first quarto [1600] and First
     Folio versions), the death of Falstaff, the origins of Henry V
     (and perhaps Fluellen), a discussion of the stage history, and a
     glossary. The copy text is the 1623 folio, which probably repre-
     sents Shakespeare's foul papers except for the act divisions and
     the purging of profanity. Shakespeare in all likelihood com-
     pleted the play shortly after Essex's departure for Ireland in
     1599. The quarto text is corrupt, a memorial production by
     "traitor-actors." This epic drama of Agincourt, frankly patri-
     otic, matches the national mood in the late sixteenth century.
     (See entry 419.)

Textual Studies

464 CRAIG, HARDIN. "The Relation of the First Quarto Version to
     the First Folio Version of Shakespeare's Henry V." Philo-
     logical Quarterly 6 (1927):225-34.
        Insists that the folio version of Henry V is a revision of
     the quarto version, that the quarto does not represent, as most
     critics believe, a shortened form of the folio. The folio text
     develops themes that are interwoven throughout in such a way that
     it is improbable they would have been omitted in a reduced ver-
     sion. Folio revision also explains why certain scenes in prose
     stand as blank verse in the quarto; revision would never move in
     the direction of prose to verse. The quarto represents a genuine
     manuscript of the play, not a shorthand account.

465 OKERLUND, GERDA. "The Quarto Version of Henry V as Stage
     Adaptation." PMLA 49 (1934):810-34.
        Claims that the bad quarto of Henry V is an unauthorized
     stage adaptation from the theater manuscript by pirates for pro-
     vincial performance. Virtually all of the differences between
     the quarto and folio texts are satisfactorily explained as the
     result of adaptation and errors of transcription. Both the
     length and the cast of characters are significantly reduced, and
     the style is compressed, made more simple and direct. The
     promptbook prepared for this production was the printer's copy
     for the first quarto.

466 PRICE, HEREWARD T. "The Quarto and Folio Texts of Henry V."
     Philological Quarterly 12 (1933):24-32.
        Defends the premise that the stage directions in the folio
     are textually superior to those in the quarto. The folio text
     names its characters more carefully, registers entrances, and
     notes musical signals and other calls. The stage directions of
     the quarto confront us with the same problems as the quarto as a
     whole, probably reflecting the contaminations of a note taker

working hastily during a performance, while the folio text represents Shakespeare's hand. Whether the stage directions are al-
together Shakespeare's must await more scientific analysis.

467   ____. The Text of "Henry V." Newcastle-under-Lyme: Mandley
       & Unett, 1921, 55 pp.
       Examines the three quartos (1600, 1602, 1608) and the folio
(1623) texts of Henry V to determine the proper copy text for
modern editions. The conclusion is that the first quarto, from
which the second and third quartos are derivative, is subsequent
to the folio, that it is not a first sketch, and that the folio
text is the work of Shakespeare alone.

Criticism

468   BATTENHOUSE, ROY W. "Henry V as Heroic Comedy." In Essays on
       Shakespeare and Elizabethan Drama in Honor of Hardin Craig.
       Edited by Richard Hosley. Columbia: University of Missouri
       Press, 1962, pp. 163-82.
       Describes Henry V as pervaded with irony, not the irony of
derisive subversion and derrogation but the tolerant irony of
that which is blandly content with itself and fails to perceive
its monolithic vision. Shakespeare is portraying a Henry and an
entire society as "admittedly illustrious but bounded within the
limits of a sub-Christian virtue" (p. 168). Spectators and
critics, blinded by the surface patriotism, admire the heroism,
but the more discerning perceive an emptiness in the pageantry
and a fulsomeness in the rhetoric. The crowning irony is that,
in act 5, Henry gains merely the title "heir" (not "king") of
France.

469   BERMAN, RONALD. "Shakespeare's Alexander: Henry V." College
       English 23 (1962):532-39.
       Observes that in the sources Henry is both chivalric and
patriotic and also ethical and Christian but that serious inconsistencies arise in the Henry of Shakespeare's play. The enigmatic tradition to which this Henry belongs is that of Alexander,
whose account in Plutarch may well have served as an additional,
albeit indirect, source. The life of Alexander is coupled with
and immediately precedes that of Caesar, his source for Julius
Caesar written in the same year 1599. Alexander, like Henry,
comes to know both the world of ideals and that of practical
reality. The death of each is a prelude to the rapid dissolution
of their achievements.

470   BOUGHNER, DANIEL C. "Pistol and the Roaring Boys." Shake-
       speare Association Bulletin 11 (1936):226-37.
       Suggests that living, not literary, models lie behind
Pistol and the realistic sketches of boisterous Elizabethan low-
life. The "bullying buck of the seamier side" (p. 226), Pistol
is a half-starved soldier driven to act as a pimp and a cutpurse.

This is a typical roaring boy of the period, pretending to
gentlemanly attributes but in actuality a common thief. Pistol
is not merely a braggadochio; he is modeled closely after an
Elizabethan type for whom the tavern served as refuge.

471   DANSON, LAWRENCE N. "Henry V: King, Chorus, and Critics."
      Shakespeare Quarterly 34 (1983):27-43.
           Suggests that Henry V was the first play at the Globe in
      the fall of 1599 and that the reference to Essex in the chorus
      of act 5 is a plucky defiance of temporary setbacks in Ireland.
      An English victory in late 1599 against the Irish would have been
      not unlike the victory at Agincourt. The interplay of the king
      as a representative of historical reality and of the chorus as a
      representative of theatrical reality creates a detached perspec-
      tive that allows the spectator to view Henry as hero or scoundrel.
      Henry can control the course of history no more than Shakespeare
      can control the fate of his play. (See entry 477.)

472   FLEISSNER, ROBERT F. "Falstaff's Green Sickness Unto Death."
      Shakespeare Quarterly 12 (1961):47-55.
           Examines the meaning of Mistress Quickly's reference to
      green in connection with Falstaff's death. Green sickness re-
      ferred to an anemic appearance and lack of vitality. He may well
      have died from a combination of the plague and a broken heart.
      More probably, he succumbed to a green death, the iron-deficiency
      anemia resulting from love, jealousy, and frustration that caused
      his nose to assume a greenish tinge. His death is bathetic, an
      ironic descent of the carefree knight to the absurdity of death.

473   GILBERT, ALLAN. "Patriotism and Satire in Henry V." In
      Studies in Shakespeare. Edited by Arthur D. Matthews and
      Clark M. Emery. Coral Gables: University of Miami Press,
      1953, pp. 40-64.
           Examines the three bodies of material that make up Henry V--
      The Famous Victories of Henry V, the Chronicles, and Shakespeare's
      additions--to determine why the play provokes such diversely
      opposed interpretations, Henry as ideal king or Henry as the
      exemplar of the blood-stained Machiavel. Whereas much of the
      action glorifies the pattern of princehood, Shakespeare delib-
      erately undercuts it through emphasis on the horrors of war.
      Shakespeare also adds the third theme of the king worn with care
      as a consequence of his concern for his subjects. These inde-
      pendent, even contradictory, elements form the artistic complex-
      ity of the play.

474   HOBDAY, C.H. "Imagery and Irony in Henry V." Shakespeare
      Survey 21 (1968):107-13.
           Suggests that the major critical disagreements concerning
      Henry V reflect a division in Shakespeare's own mind in which his
      emotions rebelled against his conscious intentions. Image clus-
      ters afford an insight into Shakespeare's emotions, and a major

cluster in Henry V is that associated with death. The fate of
Bardolph comments ironically on the nature of war. Shakespeare's
divided sympathies are most obvious at Agincourt where there is
much that is patriotic and bright but where there is also
Williams's moving indictment of Henry.

475   MENDILOW, A.A. "Falstaff's Death of a Sweat." Shakespeare
      Quarterly 9 (1958):479-83.
          Maintains that Shakespeare's reference in the epilogue in
      2 Henry IV to Falstaff's forthcoming death of a sweat in Henry V
      suggests death by plague or the sweating sickness. Dame
      Quickly's reference to Falstaff's "burning quotidian tertian"
      is not mere nonsense; it refers to that most serious of situa-
      tions in plague victims when the quotidian and the tertian are
      joined in one. Shakespeare's artistry was able to transmute
      grim medical details into a scene rich both in comedy and pathos.

476   PRICE, GEORGE R. "Henry V and Germanicus." Shakespeare
      Quarterly 12 (1961):57-60.
          Notes that Hal--when in the disguise of Sir Thomas
      Erpingham's cloak he encounters Pistol, Fluellen, and Gower--
      readily refutes them, meditating in the soliloquy that follows
      on the loneliness and responsibility of the king. The scene
      focuses merely on Henry's common touch, not his need to argue
      the morality of war. The incident appears in none of Shake-
      speare's sources. Possibly he drew it from an account of
      Germanicus's similar activity the night before he led his legions
      against the Germans, an account printed in 1598 in Richard
      Greneway's translation of Tacitus's Annales.

477   SMITH, WARREN D. "The Henry V Choruses in the First Folio."
      Journal of English and Germanic Philology 53 (1954):38-57.
          Argues that the choruses were not a part of the play as
      performed at the Globe in 1599, that they were added--possibly
      after the quarto publication in 1600 and possibly by someone
      other than Shakespeare--especially for a private performance at
      court. In at least two places the choruses create unfortunate
      breaks in the plot (choruses 3 and 4). Specifically, the play
      was probably performed at the reconverted Cockpit at Whitehall,
      its dimensions justifying the apologetic tones for depicting
      mighty actions in such small places. (See entry 471.)

478   STOLL, ELMER EDGAR. "Henry V." In Poets and Playwrights.
      Minneapolis: University of Minnesota Press, 1930, pp. 31-54.
      Reprinted in Discussions of Shakespeare's Histories, ed. R.J.
      Dorius (Boston: D.C. Heath, 1964), pp. 123-34.
          Views Henry V as in the tradition not of Marlowe but of
      earlier popular tragicomedy. Depicting Henry's triumphal pro-
      cession from Harfleur to Agincourt to the French crown and the
      Princess's hand, the play gains unity through its patriotic
      passion. If the patriotism is not particularly enlightened,

Shakespeare nonetheless sets forth the ideal of the practical
leader, the country's notion of a hero-king. At the same time he
manages to make this hero-king human with an individual voice
that expresses both joy and grief, happiness and apprehension.

479   TOLMAN, ALBERT H.   "The Epic Character of Henry V."   MLN 24
      (1919):7-16.
          Suggests that Shakespeare's sense of the stage's inadequacy
      for presenting large-scale historical plays developed through and
      after the writing of 1,2 Henry IV and in part in reaction to the
      influx of realistic drama spearheaded by Jonson. The aggravation
      was intensified by his desire to idealize and glorify his hero.
      Henry V is a heroic poem, using dramatic form for epic purposes.
      If it is at times strident to us, we must not forget its com-
      munal, national appeal.

480   WILLIAMS, CHARLES. "Henry V." In Shakespeare Criticism
      1919-35. Edited by Anne Bradby Ridler. Oxford: Oxford
      University Press, 1936, pp. 180-88. Reprinted in Twentieth
      Century Interpretations of "Henry V," ed. Ronald Berman,
      Twentieth Century Interpretations (Englewood Cliffs:
      Prentice-Hall, 1968), pp. 29-36.
          Notes the significance of the absence of Falstaff and
      Hotspur in Henry V so that Shakespeare through the protagonist
      can develop a new concept of honor as, in peace or war, the
      capacity to challenge the world and to endure the result of that
      challenge. Henry proves consistent whether in the brilliant
      light of victory or in the shadow of confronting conspirators or
      in facing potential defeat in battle. His was the last "legerity
      of spirit" before the tragedies, the development of a capacity of
      spirit that "thrills through the already poring dusk" (p. 188).

481   WILLIAMSON, MARILYN L.   "The Episode with Williams in
      Henry V." Studies in English Literature 9 (1969):275-82.
          Argues that Shakespeare does not suddenly transform the
      character of Hal into that of the ideal prince Henry V. In the
      Williams episode vestiges of the old Hal remain in his use of
      disguise to deceive those around him, in the soliloquy that re-
      calls his planned reformation in 1 Henry IV, in the exchange of
      gloves that travesties the chivalric values of Richard II, and in
      the attempt to pay off the common soldier. Clearly Henry is
      still learning to be a king and, thus, is a more complex figure
      than critics generally realize.

For discussion of the nature of Henry as king, see entries 468-69,
473-74, 478-79. See also The English Histories (entries 387-411) and
15, 66, 76, 79, 87, 104, 179, 196, 227, 266, 291, 313, 419, 427, 448,
504, 781.

1, 2, 3 HENRY VI

Reference Works

482   HINCHCLIFFE, JUDITH, comp. "King Henry VI, Parts 1, 2, and
      3": An Annotated Bibliography. Garland Shakespeare Bibliog-
      raphies, 5. New York and London: Garland Publishing, 1984,
      368 pp.
           Contains 981 entries, representing virtually all publica-
      tions on the plays from 1940 through 1982, along with the most
      significant items prior to 1940. The categories, each arranged
      chronologically, include criticism, authorship, textual studies,
      dating, sources, adaptations and influences, bibliographies,
      editions, and stage histories. A brief introductory essay traces
      the history of recent criticism and research.

Textual Studies

483   ALEXANDER, PETER. Shakespeare's "Henry VI" and "Richard III."
      Cambridge: Cambridge University Press, 1929, 229 pp.
           Establishes the first quarto (1594) of The First Part of
      the Contention Between the Two Famous Houses of York and Lan-
      caster and the first quarto (1595) of The True Tragedy of Richard
      Duke of York as bad quartos of 2,3 Henry VI. The texts are
      memorial reconstructions by the actor playing Warwick and the
      actor doubling as Suffolk and Clifford. These actors were lead-
      ing players in Pembroke's Company, which went bankrupt in 1593.
      Bibliographical and textual evidence suggests that 2,3 Henry VI
      are entirely by Shakespeare and not works of collaboration.

Criticism

484   BERMAN, RONALD. "Fathers and Sons in the Henry VI Plays."
      Shakespeare Quarterly 13 (1962):487-97.
           Suggests that a major unifying strand in the Henry VI plays
      is the relationship of fathers and sons reflecting tragically the
      refusal of the enlightenment of experience. Tainted by
      Richard II's murder, the royal family is deficient in the true
      qualities of kingship, the Lancastrians in political virtues,
      the Yorkists in moral virtues. In part 1 the death of the
      Talbots, father and son, contrasts nobly with bastardized royal
      kingship; the idea grows in parts 2 and 3 that blood relation-
      ships are inconveniences in the way of ambition. The idea of
      kingship is progressively debased both physically and
      spiritually.

485   BROCKBANK, J.P. "The Frame of Disorder--Henry VI." In Early
      Shakespeare. Edited by John Russell Brown and Bernard Harris.
      Stratford-upon-Avon Studies, 3. London: Edward Arnold, 1961,
      pp. 73-99.

Describes the Henry VI plays as a panoramic view of the
"plight of individuals caught up in a cataclysmic movement of
events for which responsibility is communal and historical, not
personal and immediate" (p. 73). From this sweep of events
emerge the two extremes of political man--the martyr Henry and
the Machiavel Richard. Part 1 stresses the disastrous consequences upon the English forces in France of political dissension
at home, part 2 the sacrifice of Gloucester and the dissolution
of the law, and part 3 the triumph of soldierly and political
anarchism and the creation of the power vacuum that will give
rise to Richard.

486   CANDIDO, JOSEPH. "Getting Loose in the Henry VI Plays."
       Shakespeare Quarterly 35 (1984):392-406.
       Suggests that through the large number of captures and
attempted escapes (whether literal or metaphorical) Shakespeare
was attempting to provide structural connections for disparate
episodes in the Henry VI plays. Such a motif artistically binds
the Talbot episodes, the relationship of Suffolk and Margaret,
the fortunes of the Duke of York, and the connection between
Henry VI and Edward IV. Increasingly the voice of the trapped
animal or the sense of achievement crushed in these episodes
underscore the cycle of brutality and anarchy that characterizes
the trilogy.

487   DEAN, PAUL. "Shakespeare's Henry VI Trilogy and Elizabethan
       'Romance' Histories: The Origins of a Genre." Shakespeare
       Quarterly 33 (1982):34-48.
       Considers many of the puzzling features in the Henry VI
plays to have their explanation in their indebtedness to romance
history, a popular type of play when Shakespeare came to London
that loosely incorporated historical personages within an imagi-
nary and usually comic framework. Material of this flavor is not
found in the chronicles--in part 1 the Temple Garden scene,
Joan's scene with the devils, the wooing of Margaret and Suffolk;
in part 2 the necromancy practiced by Eleanor, the Simpcox episode, the Jack Cade scenes. Such scenes constitute an ironic,
grotesque, or farcical amplification of the major political
themes and reveal the Henry VI plays to be among Shakespeare's
most powerful and richly textured work.

488   PRICE, HEREWARD T. "Mirror-Scenes in Shakespeare." In Joseph
       Quincy Adams Memorial Studies. Edited by James G. McManaway,
       Giles E. Dawson, and Edwin E. Willoughby. Washington:
       Folger Shakespeare Library, 1948, pp. 101-13.
       Describes Shakespeare's practice of inserting scenes that,
while having little or no narrative value, enhance and clarify
the emotional quality of the action. The fly scene in Titus
Andronicus, for example, both reveals Titus's approaching madness
and also reflects his emotional extremes of love and hatred. The
brief scene in 1 Henry VI in which representatives of the houses

141

of York and Lancaster pick white and red roses as emblems of
their cause is another example. So, too, is the gardener's
scene in Richard II. Shakespeare uses this technique throughout
his career.

489   QUINN, MICHAEL. "Providence in Shakespeare's Yorkist Plays."
      Shakespeare Quarterly 10 (1959):45-52.
          Suggests that Shakespeare's conception of Providence as a
controlling motif in the first tetralogy clearly marks his technical superiority over his contemporaries. Shakespeare received
from the chronicles the narrative of the War of the Roses as controlled by the general providential view that crime is eventually
punished and virtue triumphs. He was far more concerned, however, with cause and effect; by prophecies, explanation and judgment are wedded in the plays, and the spectators develop antici-
patory judgments that the action then fulfills. Thus, the
spectators see beyond a providential pattern to the individual
human deeds and decisions that form the larger pattern.

490   RICKS, DON M. Shakespeare's Emergent Form: A Study of the
      Structure of the "Henry VI" Plays. Logan: Utah State Uni-
      versity Press, 1968, 103 pp.
          Observes that critics now view the Henry VI plays not as
rude beginnings but as experimentation. 1 Henry VI, for example,
marks a revolutionary change in the nature of English drama in
its blend of the medieval and the naturalistic and in the imposi-
tion of a single controlling idea. The emphasis on strands of
action rather than on individual characters achieves a sense of
the sweep of history, juxtaposing contrasting scenes in part 1,
using a double plot to present the theme of dissolution of the
law in part 2, and synthesizing plot and design for a greater
organic focus in part 3.

491   RIGGS, DAVID. Shakespeare's Heroical Histories: "Henry VI"
      and Its Literary Tradition. Cambridge, Mass.: Harvard
      University Press, 1971, 194 pp.
          Suggests that Shakespeare set out to imitate the heroical
history play developed by Greene and his contemporaries, but that
he quickly came to understand the humanistic tradition better
than they. As he moves through the Henry VI trilogy, he progressively stresses the inherent anarchic elements in the tradition of history as "worthy and memorable deeds" in "lively and
well-spirited action" (p. 14). Indeed, Richard III is the final
distortion of heroic ideals. Hal, later, by insisting on his
freedom from the heroic tradition in his repudiation of the
style of Hotspur, frees himself to establish his own brand of
heroism for national, not personal, glory.

492   SWAIN, MATTIE. "Shakespeare's Henry VI as a Pacifist."
      College English 3 (1941):143-49.
          Notes that Shakespeare builds the character of Henry VI on
      the paradox that the prevalence of generous faith renders one a
      dupe to violence. His failure to prevail because he refuses to
      act in violence against his fellow countrymen, indeed his very
      political impracticality, is the key to his gaining the sympathy
      and admiration of the spectators. It is difficult to be highly
      critical of his material failures because of the personal misery
      occasioned by his regret and by his acknowledgment that he never
      wished to be king.

See also The English Histories (entries 387-411) and 15, 76, 78-79,
88, 97, 205, 209, 229, 242, 290, 294, 310.

1 HENRY VI

                              Editions

493   CAIRNCROSS, ANDREW S., ed. The First Part of King Henry VI.
      The Arden Shakespeare. London: Methuen; Cambridge, Mass.:
      Harvard University Press, 1962, 172 pp.
          Includes discussion of the text and of historical and lit-
      erary scholarship along with appendixes covering various source
      materials, a York-Lancaster genealogical table, and a list of
      "recollections" from 1 Henry VI in bad quartos. The text is
      based on the First Folio, for which the copy text was probably
      Shakespeare's autograph annotated by a stage-adapter. The likely
      date of composition is 1590, and current appraisals, unlike those
      of the eighteenth and nineteenth centuries, view the play as the
      work of a single mind. Instead of what used to be considered a
      stringing together of episodes from various chronicle sources,
      the play implies a comprehensive world picture "embracing the
      deposition of Richard II and its consequences as far as the suc-
      cession of Henry VII" (p. xxxix). The history plays form the
      epic of England rather than of individuals, and the unifying
      theme of 1 Henry VI is the breakdown of political order at home
      that in turn leads to the loss of France.

494   WILSON, JOHN DOVER, ed. 1 Henry VI. Cambridge: Cambridge
      University Press, 1952, 222 pp.
          Provides extensive textual notes and a discussion of the
      copy text. The critical introduction has sections on the rela-
      tionship of part 1 to parts 2 and 3, the date and occasion of
      composition, the possibility of Nashe's hand, the sources and the
      structure, and Shakespeare's hand and the Talbot scenes. A dis-
      cussion of the stage history and a glossary are also included.
      The copy text is the First Folio, which was probably set from
      Shakespeare's foul papers. 1 Henry VI is one of the worst and

most debatable plays in the canon; there are clear signs that it
was written after parts 2 and 3.

Criticism

495   BEVINGTON, DAVID. "The Domineering Female in 1 Henry VI."
       Shakespeare Studies 2 (1966):51-58.
          Observes that the theme of female domination in 1 Henry VI--
       in Joan of Arc, the Countess of Auvergne, and Margaret of Anjou--
       echoes the larger theme of division and discord throughout the
       play and the tetralogy. That much of this material is not in the
       chronicles indicates that the playwright was consciously organiz-
       ing his plot along these lines. The final seduction is that of
       Henry himself as he disregards wise advice and accepts a dower-
       less maiden sight unseen. It is the beginning of his self-
       indulgent withdrawal that characterizes his personality in
       2 Henry VI.

496   BOAS, FREDERICK S. "Joan of Arc in Shakespeare, Schiller and
       Shaw." Shakespeare Quarterly 2 (1951):35-45.
          Notes that the image of Joan of Arc in 1 Henry VI is in-
       consistent, reflecting her courage, shrewdness, and conviction
       of her divine mission to save France, on the one hand, and her
       lack of chastity, coarse mouth, and alliance with the devil on
       the other. Generally, though, Shakespeare does not distort the
       prejudicial view found in Holinshed. Joan in Schiller experiences
       a tragic purgation, but he falsifies history both in her love
       affair with an English soldier and in the manner of her death.
       Shaw announces her canonization and stresses the struggle of the
       Church against national unity.

497   GAW, ALLISON. The Origin and Development of "1 Henry VI" in
       Relation to Shakespeare, Marlowe, Peele, and Greene. Los
       Angeles: University of Southern California Press, 1926,
       180 pp.
          Studies the date, authorship, and early history of
       1 Henry VI. Evidence suggests a date of 1592 for what was then
       a wholly independent play for Lord Strange's Men by Marlowe (the
       kindred character studies of Winchester and York) and Greene (the
       Talbot story). Peele joined in order to hasten completion of the
       final scenes, and Nashe contributed the turret scene. After
       Shakespeare later joined the company, he recast the material to
       make it a third part of his own two-play sequence.

498   GREER, CLAYTON ALVIS. "The Place of 1 Henry VI in the York-
       Lancaster Trilogy." PMLA 53 (1938):687-701.
          Theorizes that there was a "Talbot" or "Harry the Sixth"
       play before 2,3 Henry VI and that there was a later revised form
       of this play. Demonstrably, however, the play was not revised as
       late as 1600, just after or just before the composition of
       Henry V, as Tucker Brooke argues. Metrical tests suggests a much

earlier revision; in no other play as late as Henry V do we find
the percentage of run-on lines, riming lines, and feminine endings. The revision probably took place immediately after Richard III.

499   KIRSCHBAUM, LEO. "The Authorship of 1 Henry VI." PMLA 67
       (1952):809-22.
            Argues against E.K. Chamber's removal of 1 Henry VI, Titus
       Andronicus and The Taming of the Shrew (entry 47), stating that,
       if we are correctly to understand the process of Shakespeare's
       artistic development, they must be brought back into the canon.
       The chief evidence for Shakespeare's authorship of 1 Henry VI is
       its inclusion in the First Folio. Moreover, 1 Henry VI was
       probably composed first, preparing the characters and the sequence
       of events for 2,3 Henry VI. A careful analysis of the language,
       metrics, and structure indicates nothing to prevent claiming
       Shakespeare's sole authorship.

500   PRICE, HEREWARD T. Construction in Shakespeare. Ann Arbor:
       University of Michigan Press, 1951, 42 pp.
            Derides the pervasive critical notion that Shakespeare was
       a child of nature and the manner in which it has for so long de-
       terred attention from the artistry of his dramaturgy. Shake-
       speare, in fact, was a meticulous craftsman with a Gothic ex-
       uberance in intricate design. In 1 Henry VI, for example, he
       imposes upon his material a controlling idea to which all directly
       or obliquely contributes--the effects arising from the strengths
       or weaknesses of the ruler. In scene 1 dissension breaks out
       even during the ritual of burying Henry V, and scene 2 offers a
       contrasting view in France. The play throughout exhibits a
       severely controlled design in its rhythmic patterns of repetition.

See also The English Histories (entries 387-411) and 204, 230, 434,
580, 586.

2 HENRY VI

Editions

501   CAIRNCROSS, ANDREW S., ed. The Second Part of King Henry VI.
       The Arden Shakespeare. London: Methuen; Cambridge, Mass.:
       Harvard University Press, 1957, 197 pp.
            Includes discussion of the text, the historical material,
       and literary interpretations, as well as appendixes covering
       source materials from Halle's Chronicle and Fox's Acts and
       Monuments, genealogical tables, and the relationship with the bad
       quarto, The First Part of the Contention Between the Two Famous
       Houses of York and Lancaster (1594). The text is based on the
       First Folio, for which the copy was probably a theatrical manu-
       script. The likely date of composition was early 1590, and the

current assumption is that Shakespeare was the sole author,
having written the play for Pembroke's Men as part of a planned
tetralogy. Central to the action is Henry's fatal marriage to
the increasingly manipulative Margaret of Anjou, the loss of the
French possessions, the love affair between Margaret and Suffolk,
the fall of Humphrey, and the progressive intensification of
Henry's almost abstract holiness.

502   WILSON, JOHN DOVER, ed. 2 Henry VI. Cambridge: Cambridge
       University Press, 1952, 221 pp.
           Provides extensive textual notes, a critical introduction
       covering both theatrical and literary origins (the hand of
       Shakespeare, the four candidates for authorship, dramatic incon-
       sistencies, classical learning in the play), a glossary, and a
       genealogical table. This edition is based on the First Folio,
       the play having first been printed in a bad quarto in 1594.
       Shakespeare's hand is surely present in all three parts of
       Henry VI, but the extent of his participation is unknown; the
       style is as debatable as the external evidence.

Textual Studies

503   DORAN, MADELEINE. "Henry VI, Parts II and III": Their Rela-
       tion to "The Contention" and "The True Tragedy." University
       of Iowa Humanistic Studies, vol. 4, no. 4. Iowa City:
       University of Iowa Press, 1928, 88 pp.
           Reviews the three theories of the relationship of the First
       Folio 2,3 Henry VI and The First Part of the Contention Between
       the Two Famous Houses of York and Lancaster and The True Tragedy
       of Richard Duke of York, concluding that the only viable one is
       that the last two are bad quartos of the first. Abridgment of
       nondramatic material, occasional patching, and accretion of comic
       material suggest adaptation for acting purposes put together from
       memorial reconstruction. Probably a traveling group in 1592-93
       included several who had played in the Henry VI plays and who
       communally reconstructed the texts, adding comic materials
       freely.

504   PROUTY, C.T. "The Contention" and Shakespeare's "2 Henry VI":
       A Comparative Study. New Haven: Yale University Press, 1954,
       157 pp.
           Concludes that the 1594 The First Part of the Contention
       Between the Two Famous Houses of York and Lancaster cannot have
       been derived from the version of 2 Henry VI in the 1623 folio.
       Thus, The Contention is not a bad quarto of 2 Henry VI; instead,
       the style of the unique material in the First Folio suggests that
       2 Henry VI was a later revision. We can no longer assume that
       Shakespeare wrote original history plays early in his career.
       All that we can assume, based on the reference to Henry VI in the
       epilogue in Henry V, is that Shakespeare had revised the play
       2 Henry VI some time before 1599.

Criticism

505   CALDERWOOD, JAMES L.   "Shakespeare's Evolving Imagery:
      2 Henry VI." English Studies 48 (1967):481-93.
          Notes that Shakespeare's imagery in this play begins to
      break its quality of set rhetorical speech and to acquire its own
      linear development in moving from the static and ornamental
      toward the active and functional. Four patterns of imagery are
      noteworthy, those dealing with trapping, sight, elevation, and
      hands. They are utilized to explore the kingly character of
      Henry himself and of two other regal figures, Gloucester the
      regent and York the claimant. Such imagistic patterns, while
      limited, suggest the texture of Shakespeare's rhetorical powers
      to come in the later plays.

See also The English Histories (entries 387-411).

3 HENRY VI

Editions

506   CAIRNCROSS, ANDREW S., ed. The Third Part of King Henry VI.
      The Arden Shakespeare. London: Methuen; Cambridge, Mass.:
      Harvard University Press, 1964, 187 pp.
          Includes discussion of the text, date, company, sources,
      and critical interpretations, along with appendixes featuring
      selections from Halle's Chronicle and Brooke's Romeus and Juliet,
      genealogical tables, and alternative passages from the bad quarto,
      The True Tragedy of Richard Duke of York (1595). The text is
      from the First Folio, for which the copy was probably Shake-
      speare's manuscript annotated by the prompter. The play is now
      considered to be wholly Shakespeare's, the date late 1590 or
      early 1591. 3 Henry VI is a study in anarchy--in the state, the
      family, and the individual mind as Richard develops into a living
      symbol of anarchy while Henry is a standing protest against the
      horrors of war.

507   WILSON, JOHN DOVER, ed. 3 Henry VI. Cambridge: Cambridge
      University Press, 1952, 225 pp.
          Provides extensive textual notes, a critical introduction
      (covering Shakespeare's early dramatic style and a comparison of
      the theme of the War of the Roses as handled by Shakespeare and
      Holinshed), a discussion of the copy text, a section on stage
      history, and a glossary. This edition is based on the First
      Folio, for which the copy was probably a draft supplied to the
      prompter for the original performances. The political view of
      the play is that usurpation like a poison works its way through
      the entire body politic. Most significant is the development of
      the character of Richard; he as a murderous Machiavel and Henry

as a saintly hero reflect the two poles within which anarchy and
chaos reigned in England between the battles of St. Albans and
Tewkesbury.

Criticism

508   KERNAN, ALVIN. "A Comparison of the Imagery in 3 Henry VI and
      The True Tragedie of Richard Duke of York." Studies in
      Philology 51 (1954):431-42.
          Observes that the imagery provides a striking contrast
      between 3 Henry VI and The True Tragedy, although in both the
      imagery is more decorative than functional. Typically Shake-
      spearean is the use of a comprehensive and recurrent central
      image, and such an image is the sea-wind-tide figure (the sea
      forcing against the land and blown back by the wind). Compared
      to the use of this image thirteen times in 3 Henry VI, it appears
      only twice in The True Tragedy. Facts such as these pose diffi-
      culties for those who consider The True Tragedy to be a memorial
      reconstruction of 3 Henry VI.

See also The English Histories (entries 387-411).

HENRY VIII

Editions

509   FOAKES, R.A., ed. King Henry VIII. The Arden Shakespeare.
      London: Methuen; Cambridge, Mass.: Harvard University Press,
      1968, 215 pp.
          Includes discussion of the text, authorship, date of com-
      position, sources, critical interpretations, and stage history,
      as well as an appendix on Henry VIII and the burning of the Globe
      Theatre. The text is based on the First Folio, for which the
      copy was probably a fair copy of the author's manuscript by a
      meticulous scribe. Despite the assumption that Fletcher was a
      collaborator, the textual peculiarities suggest a single writer.
      The date of composition was 1613, and Shakespeare drew from a
      variety of historical sources. Like the romances Henry VIII
      focuses not on one or two characters or problems but on the pros-
      pect of life's continuance through two generations. Structurally
      the play grows through a series of contrasts and oppositions, and
      its theme is "the promise of a golden future, after trials and
      sufferings, terminating in the attainment of self-knowledge,
      forgiveness, and reconciliation" (p. lviii).

510   MAXWELL, J.C., ed. King Henry the Eighth. Cambridge:
      Cambridge University Press, 1962, 251 pp.
          Provides extensive textual notes and a discussion of the
      copy text. The critical introduction has sections on the date
      and authorship, sources, and the play itself. A discussion of

the stage history and a glossary are also included. The copy
text is the First Folio, which was a carefully prepared manuscript. Included also is a discussion of the probable collaboration of Shakespeare and Fletcher and the various theories concerning that relationship. While the play has been a stage success, it is virtually devoid of dramatic life.

Criticism

511   ALEXANDER, PETER. "Conjectural History; or, Shakespeare's
      <u>Henry VIII</u>." <u>Essays and Studies</u> 16 (1930):85-120.
          Controverts the theory of Fletcher's hand in <u>Henry VIII</u> and
      argues for Shakespeare's sole authorship. The tone of the pro-
      logue suggests the weight of a Shakespeare with his career behind
      him; he may well have come from retirement to speak it. Simi-
      larly, the eulogy on Elizabeth spoken by Cranmer in 5.5 would
      have been tasteful and appropriate if written by Shakespeare but
      somewhat presumptuous by Fletcher. Moreover, the metrical tests
      used by Spedding and Hickson to substantiate Fletcher's author-
      ship fail adequately to take into account the nature of Shake-
      speare's metrical development from <u>Antony and Cleopatra</u> through
      <u>The Tempest</u>.

512   BERMAN, RONALD. "<u>King Henry the Eighth</u>: History and
      Romance." <u>English Studies</u> 48 (1960):112-21.
          Notes that <u>Henry VIII</u> is a symmetrical balance of themes
      and of modes of representation. It shares with the histories a
      concern for motive and heroic conflict while it shares with the
      romances a symbolic quality in which the principal figures are
      led to a new consciousness. The latter motif is greatly enhanced
      by the lavish quality of the staging; "full of state" and "noble
      scenes," the action involves twelve formal entrances, signs of
      power, music, and masquelike scenes. The final moments focus on
      Elizabeth as a child who will bring to the world a sense of
      blessedness. (See entries 516, 520.)

513   CESPEDES, FRANK V. "'We Are One in Fortunes': The Sense of
      History in <u>Henry VIII</u>." <u>English Literary Renaissance</u> 10
      (1980):413-38.
          Argues that critics who attempt to minimize Henry's
      hypocrisy neglect the fact that Shakespeare structures events to
      increase rather than to mitigate it. The final act does not
      vindicate Henry; to the end he is a thoroughly political self-
      aggrandizing monarch. The theme of the play is built on the
      conflict between the ends and means of history. The culminating
      irony is that events fall out beneficently, but not because men
      have done anything to guide them in that direction.

514   CLARK, CUMBERLAND. A Study of Shakespeare's "Henry VIII."
       London: Golden Vista Press, 1931, 218 pp.
          Observes that the theme of Rome versus the king is broached
       in King John but not resolved until Henry VIII with the christen-
       ing of the infant princess Elizabeth. Shakespeare's histories as
       a group constitute an immortal epic of the English nation.
       Henry VIII represents the culmination of the Tudor dynasty, and
       it turns on the ethical point of Protestantism. This study
       contains individual chapters on the date, the authorship, the use
       of the chronicles, the historical accuracy, Cardinal Wolsey,
       Archbishop Cranmer, the two queens Katherine and Anne, and the
       stage history of the play.

515   FELPERIN, HOWARD. "Shakespeare's Henry VIII: History as
       Myth." Studies in English Literature 6 (1966):225-46.
          Observes that critical attention to Henry VIII as drama,
       quite apart from the argument over who wrote it, has been
       patronizing and disappointing. In departing radically from his
       earlier uses of Holinshed and in subtitling the play "What Is
       Truth?" Shakespeare perhaps ironically hints that we should re-
       consider what historical truth is and what the truth of mimetic
       representation is. Henry VIII, more specifically, takes on the
       flavor of a myth. While the history plays set forth events for
       their own sake, Henry VIII is a metaphysical drama; the truth of
       the play resides in the eternal relevance of the Christian myth
       that the action re-creates.

516   HARRIS, BERNARD. "What's Past Is Prologue: Cymbeline and
       Henry VIII." In Later Shakespeare. Edited by John Russell
       Brown and Bernard Harris. Stratford-upon-Avon Studies, 8.
       London: Edward Arnold, 1966, pp. 203-34.
          Notes Shakespeare's use of past events to reshape the pres-
       ent as a motif in all of the romances. Cymbeline employs his-
       torical legend, romance, and fairy tale to create a royal eulogy
       through a veiled reconstruction of the Tudor myth. Henry VIII,
       likewise, is historical romance, at once sympathetic, interest-
       ing, and instructive. Through pageant and ceremony it meditates
       upon the dangers of pride and the ambivalences of ambitious
       kingship, atoning for Katherine's wrongs through her private
       vision, humanizing Henry by treating his love as lust, and glori-
       fying Elizabeth as a child designed by Providence to lead England
       to glory.

517   NICOLSON, MARJORIE H. "The Authorship of Henry VIII." PMLA
       37 (1922):484-502.
          Argues that Shakespeare was less original in his handling
       of the source material (Holinshed's Chronicles) in Henry VIII
       than in his other work and that it is not a work of collaboration
       but rather the product of Fletcher revising or completing a
       Shakespearean draft. Shakespeare's intention was to write a play
       dealing objectively with the buffets of fortune, but Fletcher

provided a sentimentalism of character and incident that almost
totally altered the tone and weakened the dramatic unity. (See
entry 519.)

518   PARKER, A.A. "Henry VIII in Shakespeare and Calderón: An
      Appreciation of La Cisma de Ingalaterra." Modern Language
      Review 43 (1948):327-52.
          Compares the treatment of Henry VIII in the history plays
      of Shakespeare and Calderón. To proclaim Shakespeare's histori-
      cal and Calderón's unhistorical is reductionistic. Shakespeare's
      play lacks a convincing central theme in its declaration that it
      was to England's advantage for the monarch to be a despot. Its
      flaw is the presentation of political theme in terms of royal
      despotism. Calderón, writing from a Catholic point of view,
      unifies the material and clarifies the moral. His most remark-
      able touch is in giving Henry a conscience; the king acts,
      blinded by passion, only after agonizing hesitation.

519   PARTRIDGE, A.C. The Problem of "Henry VIII" Re-Opened: Some
      Linguistic Criteria for the Two Styles Apparent in the Play.
      Cambridge: Bowes & Bowes, 1949, 35 pp.
          Argues that the stylistic strata in Henry VIII are differ-
      entiated by personal idiosyncrasy with fairly sharp transitions
      from one grammatical idiom to another. The style of one hand is
      involved, though poetically pregnant; the other is fluid and
      lucid in syntactical pattern. The evidence for Fletcher's hand
      is strong; it is based on metrical tests, linguistic criteria,
      iterative imagery, and internal matters of characterization and
      structure. Probably the play was left unfinished by Shakespeare
      and was completed by Fletcher for the company. (See entry 517.)

520   RICHMOND, HUGH M. "Shakespeare's Henry VIII: Romance
      Redeemed by History." Shakespeare Studies 4 (1968):334-49.
          Points out the irony in the fact that charges of the flawed
      nature of Henry VIII coincide with assumptions in the second half
      of the nineteenth century that the play was a work of collabora-
      tion with Fletcher. The artistry of Henry VIII is best under-
      stood in light of the romances as a similar attempt to contrive
      events to reveal human fallibility overridden by Providence. The
      action involves four successive trials of intimates of the king
      with Henry intervening to save the fourth, Archbishop Cranmer.
      This last episode is deliberately elevated to reflect Henry as a
      model magistrate. (See entries 512, 516.)

521   TILLYARD, E.M.W. "Why Did Shakespeare Write Henry VIII?"
      Critical Quarterly 3 (1961):22-27.
          Argues that Shakespeare's close familiarity in his early
      years as a dramatist with British history as recorded in Halle's
      Chronicle prepared him to write on the reign of Henry VIII. That
      reign was the culmination of Halle's account, and he spends vir-
      tually half of his book on it. Shakespeare probably stored in

his mind the idea and details for a play that he was finally
prompted to re-create in later life, whether by his conscience
or by a request for a play suitable for royal celebration. The
work reflects great technical skill but lacks the creative energy
at the center of his greatest work.

See also The English Histories (entries 387-411) and 15, 154, 253,
406-7, 1419, 1424.

KING JOHN

Editions

522   FURNESS, HENRY HOWARD, Jr., ed. The Life and Death of King
      John. A New Variorum Edition of Shakespeare. Philadelphia:
      J.B. Lippincott, 1919, 728 pp.
           Uses the First Folio as the copy text. On each page, for
      that portion of the text, provides variant readings, textual
      notes, and general critical commentary. Following the text are
      sections on the nature of the copy, the date of composition, The
      Troublesome Reign of King John, Cibber's adaptation, the charac-
      ters, criticisms, stage history, costumes, actors' interpreta-
      tions, dramatic versions, and a list of works consulted.

523   HONIGMANN, E.A.J., ed. King John. The Arden Shakespeare.
      London: Methuen; Cambridge, Mass.: Harvard University Press,
      1954, 176 pp.
           Includes discussion of the text, sources, date, stage his-
      tory, and critical interpretations, as well as appendixes featur-
      ing selections from Holinshed, consideration of the text of The
      Troublesome Reign of King John, and structural differences be-
      tween that play and Shakespeare's. The text is based on the
      First Folio, for which the copy was probably Shakespeare's foul
      papers; and the likely date of composition is 1590-91. While
      Shakespeare was familiar with The Troublesome Reign, he appar-
      ently searched painstakingly for details in other stories. In a
      sense, the play is a study in virtuoso politics. However short-
      sighted his strategy, John's tactics are brilliant; ultimately,
      though, the king collapses into ungovernable passion. Faulcon-
      bridge stands outside the inner framework as a commentator.

524   WILSON, JOHN DOVER, ed. King John. Cambridge: Cambridge
      University Press, 1936, 208 pp.
           Provides extensive textual notes, a critical introduction,
      discussion of the copy text, a section on stage history, and a
      glossary. This edition is based on the First Folio, for which
      the copy was probably Shakespeare's foul papers. Paradoxically,
      John lacks both reverence and a sense of personal dignity at a
      time when the power of the church and the glory of kingship were
      at their height. The play represents Shakespeare's reworking of

the anonymous The Troublesome Reign of King John, from which he
has carefully excised the violent anti-Catholic sentiment, focusing more sharply on John and Rome as the confrontation of temporal and spiritual powers.

Criticism

525   BONJOUR, ADRIEN. "The Road to Swinstead Abbey." ELH 18
      (1951):253-74.
          Notes that recent criticism has attacked the unity of the
      play in its lack of a central figure and a leading motive. To
      the contrary, Shakespeare achieves unity through a remarkable
      balancing of the development of two figures--John and the
      Bastard, their careers forming complementary panels of a diptych.
      Just as John's fall is epitomized in the scene in which he orders
      Hubert to murder Arthur, so the Bastard's rise is measured in
      terms of his reaction to this order. The scene measures his
      integrity in contrast to John's utter perfidy.

526   BURCKHARDT, SIGURD. "King John: The Ordering of This Present
      Time." ELH 33 (1966):133-53. Reprinted in Shakespearean
      Meanings (Princeton: Princeton University Press, 1968),
      pp. 116-43.
          Argues that Shakespeare in writing King John became a
      modern in the sense that he no longer accepted order as defined
      by the Christian medieval world view. In plot, style, and dia-
      lect the play directs attention to the falsity of this view.
      Arthur, for example, in pleading for Hubert to spare his life,
      never once mentions God; language must do its own work--and it
      works in that Hubert does not carry out the assassination. The
      Bastard's speech is another example, and John's counterclaim for
      the kingship strikes at a fundamental tenet of medieval divine
      sanction.

527   CALDERWOOD, JAMES L. "Commodity of Honour in King John."
      University of Toronto Quarterly 29 (1960):341-36.
          Describes the Bastard's commodity speech as more than evi-
      dence that Shakespeare is progressing from rhetoric to a more
      trenchant style of utterance; it is in its extremity suggestive
      of the imbalance that runs throughout the action. Shakespeare,
      more precisely, tests the two antagonistic ethical principles of
      honor and commodity, and its application to John and to the
      Bastard gives the play a unity of structure not generally recog-
      nized. Appropriately the Bastard delivers the final speech, in
      which honor dictates to commodity in confirmation both of loyalty
      to England and to an ethical principle.

528   ELSON, JOHN. "Studies in the King John Plays." In Joseph
       Quincy Adams Memorial Studies. Edited by James G. McManaway,
       Giles E. Dawson, and Edwin E. Willoughby. Washington: Folger
       Shakespeare Library, 1948, pp. 183-97.
            Examines the sources of the anonymous two-part The Trouble-
       some Reign of King John, itself a source of Shakespeare's King
       John, to determine the variety of materials behind Shakespeare's
       play. Not only Holinshed, but also Vergil's Latin chronicle,
       John Fox's Acts and Monuments, and John Bale's hybrid morality-
       history King John demonstrably provide details. The author of
       The Troublesome Reign simplifies and recasts the melange of de-
       tails into orderly dramatic sequences, making Arthur's death the
       provocation of the barons' revolt, enhancing the character of the
       Bastard, and retaining a fanatic Protestant spirit.

529   MATCHETT, WILLIAM H. "Richard's Divided Heritage in King
       John." Essays in Criticism 12 (1962):231-53.
            Envisions the plot of King John as built around the ques-
       tion of who should be the rightful king of England. Following
       Arthur's death and John's collapse, the Bastard seems to be mov-
       ing toward a rightful position; but, when Henry emerges as a
       candidate in act 5, Faulconbridge kneels in obeisance to him.
       Honor in the play is finally seen, not as a matter of prestige
       and power, but as a matter of duty and responsibility. As a
       symbol of a true subject in a unified England, he is more impor-
       tant than the king himself.

530   PETTET, E.C. "Hot Irons and Fever: A Note on Some of the
       Imagery in King John." Essays in Criticism 4 (1954):128-44.
            Notes that even the auditor in the playhouse can hardly
       miss the reiterated references to heat and fire. Shakespeare
       found no such imagistic predominance in his source play The
       Troublesome Reign of King John or in Holinshed. Central to the
       creative process is 4.1, which abounds with excruciating images
       of the hot irons with which Hubert threatens to blind Arthur,
       and 5.3, in which John in his last speech dies in burning agony
       from poison. Apparently these projected scenes exercised a com-
       pulsive force on Shakespeare's creativity throughout the play and
       are responsible for the pattern of associated images.

531   SIBLY, JOHN. "The Anomalous Case of King John." ELH 33
       (1966):415-21.
            Argues that Shakespeare placed great emphasis on John's
       being guilty of usurpation in order to minimize the effects of
       his final submission to the Papacy. He becomes permanently a
       usurper at the moment Arthur dies, and it is at precisely this
       moment that he surrenders the crown. To Shakespeare's contempo-
       raries John was giving to the Pope that to which he himself never
       had a right, and Pandulf "restored" that to which he never had a
       right. King John was "a detailed argument against the historical
       as well as the spiritual claims of the Papacy" (p. 421).

154

532   STEVICK, R.   "Repentant Ashes."   Shakespeare Quarterly 13
       (1962):366-70.
           Describes 4.1 as an experimental scene in which Shakespeare
      fuses drama and imagery in a powerful manner suggestive of his
      later mature work.   The scene involves Arthur's begging Hubert to
      spare his eyes, and the apogee of the appeal appears in Arthur's
      reference to repentant ashes.   The iron has grown cold; and the
      breath of heaven, by strewing the repentant ashes on it, makes it
      incapable of reheating.   The image functions synoptically for the
      language and action of the scene, while also describing the emo-
      tions imputed to Arthur and Hubert and directing the progress of
      emotions in the spectators.

533   VAN der WATER, JULIA C.   "The Bastard in King John."
       Shakespeare Quarterly 11 (1960):137-46.
           Notes that recent attention to Faulconbridge as protagonist,
      hero, and ideal figure has distorted the evidence of the play.
      While clearly he is the most vital figure, he can hardly be
      reconciled with the epitome of kingliness.   He is, more nearly,
      a slightly concealed Vice in the first three acts, bubbling with
      wit, cynical, yet basically a good, blunt fellow; in acts 4-5 he
      becomes the embodiment of active and outraged nationalism.   He
      never fully comes to life because the disparity of his roles is
      too great.

534   VAUGHAN, VIRGINIA MASON.   "Between Tetralogies: King John as
       Transition."   Shakespeare Quarterly 35 (1984):407-20.
           Asserts that King John is a vital transitional step between
      the first tetralogy, which focuses on a nexus of external actions
      to define the political process, and the second tetralogy, which
      probes the underlying causes of history in the political behavior
      of individual men.   In its emphasis on the political present of
      decision making, this play marks a critical stage of development
      in its experimentation with techniques to convey political com-
      plexities rooted in character.   Pretensions to majesty are under-
      cut by commodity at every turn, juxtaposing the desire for the
      perfect ruler with the grim realities of guile and treachery.

535   WIXSON, DOUGLAS C.   "'Calm Words Folded up in Smoke':
       Propaganda and Spectator Response in King John."   Shakespeare
       Studies 14 (1981):111-27.
           Argues that King John deserves an interpretation that frees
      it from the bondage of a political morality play and allows us to
      see it frankly as characters playing political roles.   The play's
      potential lies in such an open form, encouraging a spirit of
      detachment and scrutiny, and the spectators' response to it.
      Elizabethan pamphleteering provided a model for this polemical
      rhetoric and debate structure; the dialectical structure tends
      to draw the spectator's own experience into the ideological

context. King John has no hero, encouraging our engagement with
no single figure so that our own views will remain free and
active.

See also The English Histories (entries 387-411) and 50, 84, 97, 122,
144, 150, 166, 576.

RICHARD II

Reference Works

536   BLACK, MATTHEW W., and METZ, G. HAROLD, comps. "The Life and
       Death of King Richard II": A Bibliographical Supplement to
       the New Variorum Edition of 1955. New York: Modern Language
       Association, 1977, 31 pp.
          Includes 702 entries, representing the scholarship from
       1955 through 1973. The material is categorized alphabetically
       under editions, text, criticism, sources, commentary, music, and
       staging and stage history. Books with multiple focus are placed
       in the criticism section, and collected editions and book reviews
       are not included. Supplements entry 537.

Editions

537   BLACK, MATTHEW W., ed. The Life and Death of King Richard the
       Second. A New Variorum Edition of Shakespeare. Philadelphia
       and London: J.B. Lippincott, 1955, 655 pp.
          Uses the First Folio as the copy text. On each page, for
       that portion of the text, provides variant readings, textual
       notes, and general critical commentary. Following the text are
       sections on the six quartos and the folio, the date of composi-
       tion, the authenticity of the text, dramatic time, the sources,
       the play as a part of a series and as an individual entity, the
       influence of Lyly and Marlowe, style and imagery, the individual
       characters, stage history, the relationship to Elizabeth and
       Essex, and a list of works consulted. Supplemented by entry 536.

538   URE, PETER, ed. King Richard II. The Arden Shakespeare.
       London: Methuen; Cambridge, Mass.: Harvard University Press,
       1956, 210 pp.
          Includes discussion of the text, date, sources, the garden
       scene, the question of political allegory, and Richard's tragedy,
       as well as appendixes featuring selections from Holinshed,
       Daniel, John Eliot, and Sylvester. The text for this edition is
       based on the first quarto, for which the copy was probably Shake-
       speare's foul papers. The likely date of composition is 1595,
       and Shakespeare apparently drew on a variety of sources in addi-
       tion to Holinshed. The dominant focus is on Richard's nature
       and behavior; the first phase of the action demonstrates his

unfitness for kingly office, the second is concerned with the
transference of power, and the third focuses on his human suf-
ferings once he is deprived of political power and dignity. The
play has a powerful human dimension beyond the didacticism of a
spectacular fall of a weak and incompetent monarch.

539   WILSON, JOHN DOVER, ed. King Richard II. Cambridge:
       Cambridge University Press, 1939, 250 pp.
           Provides extensive textual notes, a critical introduction
       covering the Elizabethan and modern views of the historical and
       theatrical aspects of Richard and the sources, a discussion of
       the copy text, a section on stage history, and a glossary. Ex-
       cept for the deposition scene, this edition is based on the first
       quarto, for which the copy was probably the author's foul papers.
       The style of the play is deliberate and patterned; the most sig-
       nificant image is the sun as a symbol of royal majesty. The
       heavy ritualistic quality reflects something of the drama of the
       Mass. Richard himself combines the personal attractiveness of
       Mary with the wrongs of Charles.

                                Criticism

540   ALTICK, RICHARD D. "Symphonic Imagery in Richard II." PMLA
       62 (1947):339-65.
           Notes that certain words of multifold meanings recur
       throughout the play like a leitmotiv in music, with language
       having become a willing servant of structure. Each word theme--
       earth, land and ground, blood, sun, tears, tongues and words,
       plague and pestilence, a dark blot upon fair parchment, sweetness
       and sourness--symbolizes a fundamental idea of the narrative.
       Earth, for example, stands for England, also emblematizing the
       foundation of kingly pride, the vanity in human life, the un-
       tended garden, and the space one occupies at death. The itera-
       tive imagery lends the play a poetic unity unsurpassed in the
       major tragedies.

541   BERGERON, DAVID M. "The Deposition Scene in Richard II."
       Renaissance Papers, 1974, pp. 31-37.
           Argues that the deposition scene was not expunged from the
       first three quartos (1597-98), that indeed it did not exist until
       the early 1600s, probably not until the death of Queen Elizabeth.
       Neither the theory of political censorship nor that of textual
       corruption is persuasive. Moreover, the scene is not dramati-
       cally necessary; it does nothing to advance either the narrative
       or Richard's characterization. The scene was probably relatively
       new when first printed in the fourth quarto (1608).

542   BLACK, MATTHEW W. "The Source of Shakespeare's Richard II."
       In Joseph Quincy Adams Memorial Studies. Edited by James G.
       McManaway, Giles E. Dawson, and Edwin E. Willoughby. Washing-
       ton: Folger Shakespeare Library, 1948, pp. 199-216.
            Observes that in most instances Shakespeare prepared him-
       self for writing a play by consulting a variety of sources.
       Various slips or inconsistencies in Richard II are best explained,
       not by J.D. Wilson's theory that Shakespeare was revising an old
       play (entry 539), but by assuming that Shakespeare's mind was
       teeming with several accounts he had just been reading. He
       apparently worked directly from the chronicles, using Holinshed,
       Halle, Chronique de la Traison et Mort de Richart Deux Roy Dengle-
       terre, and Creton. Such preparation, while wide-ranging, would
       not have required an inordinate amount of time.

543   BOGARD, TRAVIS. "Shakespeare's Second Richard." PMLA 70
       (1955):192-209.
            Envisions Richard II as a milestone in Shakespeare's tragic
       dramaturgy. Whereas in Richard III the drama is explicit, in
       that our understanding of the action depends largely on the
       actors' explanations of their goals and motivations and the char-
       acter of Richard is essentially unpenetrated, Richard II is im-
       plicit drama. Richard's character grows out of the conflict with
       Bolingbroke. The first three acts depict Richard as an actor-
       king fascinated with ritual, but in the last two acts human suf-
       fering becomes the material of of tragedy.

544   BONNARD, GEORGES A. "The Actor in Richard II." Shakespeare
       Jahrbuch (Weimar) 87 (1952):87-101.
            Assumes that Shakespeare in Richard II dramatized material
       that he collected directly from a variety of sources. He planned
       it as a two-person drama of conflict with Richard II and Boling-
       broke, but the plan is upset in that Bolingbroke remains in the
       background as something of a silent enigma. Shakespeare's
       imagination seems to have caught fire with Richard and the
       exploration of his personality. The key to the spectators'
       fascination is Richard's histrionic nature; ever the actor, he
       betrays his lack of self-confidence, but he wins us as a poet and
       a dramatist.

545   BRYANT, JOSEPH A., Jr. "The Linked Analogies of Richard II."
       Sewanee Review 65 (1957):420-33.
            Considers Richard II a turning point in Shakespeare's
       career in a search for new dramatic form after the successes of
       Richard III and Romeo and Juliet. He develops in this play a
       metaphorical turn of mind, achieving an ability to set within a
       particular event a sense of universal analogy, a shaping of his-
       torical action into poetic symbol. The key appears to be his use
       of Biblical story as analogue for his secular fable, by which
       Richard becomes microchristus and microcosmos. The play draws
       references from Cain (Bolingbroke) and Abel (Richard) as well as
       from the crucifixion story.

546   CHAPMAN, RAYMOND. "The Wheel of Fortune in Shakespeare's
       Historical Plays." Review of English Studies, n.s. 1 (1950):
       1-7.
            Notes that the tendency to regard Shakespeare's histories
       as politicosocial documents has obscured the fact that they are
       dramatic versions of the medieval theme of the fall of kings, a
       theme involving the goddess Fortuna and her ever-turning Wheel
       of Fortune. The pattern of a relentless alternation of rise and
       fall underlies the histories, especially as a linking theme of
       the tetralogies. The deposition scene in Richard II is perhaps
       the most striking example, with Fortune compared to two buckets
       in a well with the rabble holding on to the wheel at Boling-
       broke's heels.

547   DEAN, LEONARD. "Richard II: The State and the Image of the
       Theater." PMLA 67 (1952):211-18.
            Observes that Richard II is about a sick state while
       Henry V reflects a healthy state unified in terms of the Eliza-
       bethan ideal of monarchy. A key sign of the diseased kingdom in
       Richard II is found in the implicit and explicit comparison be-
       tween the state and the theater, a comparison also found in More
       and Machiavelli. The theatricality of the opening scene reflects
       Richard's hypocrisy and his inability to handle dissension.
       Other examples include Richard's histrionic posturing, the garden
       scene compared to an unruly kingdom, and Richard's theater-like
       analysis of his moral dilemma.

548   DORIUS, R.J. "A Little More Than a Little: Prudence and
       Excess in Richard II and the Histories." Shakespeare Quarterly
       11 (1960):13-26. Reprinted as "Prudence and Excess in
       Richard II and the Histories," in Discussions of Shakespeare's
       Histories, ed. R.J. Dorius (Boston: D.C. Heath, 1964),
       pp. 25-40.
            Argues that Shakespeare's English history plays imply a
       standard of good kingship based on the virtues of kingly self-
       governance and political economy and prudence. Shakespeare
       broaches this theme in Richard II through image strands dia-
       metrically opposed to such a standard--carelessness, excess,
       waste, and disease. Richard through his imprudence creates a
       power vacuum that invites disaster. Falstaff in the later plays
       symbolizes both the sickness of the state and the caterpillars
       preying on the commonwealth. In banishing him Hal most nearly
       approaches the ideal of kingship; if he is not the kind of hero
       we would admire in the tragedies, he is clearly the hero-ruler
       postulated in the entire sequence of the history plays.

549   ELLIOTT, JOHN R., Jr. "History and Tragedy in Richard II."
       Studies in English Literature 8 (1968):253-71.
            Defines Richard II as a history play rather than as a
       tragedy because of the manner in which its political purposes
       influence the dramatic structure. Shakespeare carefully selected

his material from a wide range of sources in developing a primary
focus on the successive stages by which Bolingbroke threatens,
captures, and retains the crown. Gaunt's reaction to Richard's
incompetence marks the first stage of the action, York's ambiguity
the second, and his commitment to Bolingbroke the third.

550   GAUDET, PAUL. "The 'Parasitical' Counselors in Shakespeare's
      Richard II: A Problem in Drmatic Interpretation." Shakespeare
      Quarterly 33 (1982):142-54.
          Notes that, whereas in Shakespeare's sources Richard's
      parasites (Bushy, Bagot, Greene) openly declare their villainy
      and thus their guilt, Shakespeare's technique is more allusive,
      representing a more complex experience for the audience. Clearly
      Shakespeare does not depict the parasites as totally responsible
      for Richard's decadence. Hence, there is an undeniable touch of
      the equivocal and self-righteous in Bolingbroke's pronouncements
      and actions. To continue to speak of the "parasitic" favorites
      is to load the dice against Richard and to fail to appreciate
      that Shakespeare's ambiguity extends even to these minor figures.

551   HAMILTON, DONNA B. "The State of Law in Richard II."
      Shakespeare Quarterly 34 (1983):5-17.
          Asserts that Richard II on matters of kingship and its
      relationship to the law reflects the views of Shakespeare's, not
      Richard's, times. Specifically, Gaunt's charge that Richard is
      landlord rather than king does not question royal prerogative; it
      focuses on the well-being of those who are governed. It ques-
      tions the wisdom of a king to act as if divine right gives him
      the right to act in any way he wishes. The concepts that define
      the kingship and guide the spectators' response are precisely
      those that Shakespeare's contemporaries used to assess their own
      monarch; the careful design suggests that Shakespeare was not
      blind to the parallels between Richard and Elizabeth.

552   HARRIS, KATHRYN M. "Sun and Water Imagery in Richard II: Its
      Dramatic Function." Shakespeare Quarterly 21 (1970):157-65.
          Notes that the images of sun and water play an integral
      role in expressing the pattern of the action. In the development
      of their opposition emerges a metaphor of the play as a whole,
      of the political conflict of Richard and Bolingbroke, and of
      Richard's loss of royal identity concomitant with his self-
      discovery. Water and storm imagery, for example, are associated
      with Richard's arbitrary rule early in the play but come to
      symbolize Bolingbroke in the later action; conversely, the sun
      imagery used by Bolingbroke in act 1 to describe home and harmony
      becomes later the central symbol of Richard's divinity.

553   HENIGER, S.K., Jr. "The Sun-King Analogy in Richard II."
      Shakespeare Quarterly 11 (1960):319-27.
          Notes that the tension between the actual and the ideal,
      both in Richard and Bolingbroke, is suggested in large part

through cosmological imagery. The sun-king analogy at the end of
act 3, for example, occurs at the moment this tension is most
complete, restoring imagistically the political norm of natural
order in that the king must maintain order among his subjects as
the sun regulates the harmony of the planets. The image functions as a symbol of royal prerogative, as a mirror of the de-
ficiencies in both principals, and as an instrument of the transition of power.

554   KANTOROWICZ, ERNST H. "Shakespeare: King Richard II." In
      The King's Two Bodies: A Study in Mediaeval Political Theol-
      ogy. Princeton: Princeton University Press, 1957, pp. 24-41.
      Reprinted in Four Centuries of Shakespearean Criticism, ed.
      Frank Kermode (New York: Avon, 1965), pp. 309-29.
         Describes the king as twin-born, with both greatness and
humanity. Shakespeare may well have been familiar with the legal
definition of the king as having two bodies. In any case it is
the essence of his art in Richard II as he constantly plays the
human aspect against the divine; indeed, Richard II could be
described as the tragedy of the king's two bodies. Time and
again Richard refers to the image of sacramental kingship, even
as his corrupt mortal body undermines the concept. The mirror
scene completes the act of splitting his personality and assuring
his personal tragedy.

555   KELLY, MICHAEL F. "The Function of York in Richard II."
      Southern Humanities Review 6 (1972):257-67.
         Focuses on the central dramatic significance of the charac-
ter of York, who serves to regulate the audience's response by
functioning as a pivot upon which the transfer of power turns and
as a spokesman for the play's political message. After Richard
confiscates Gaunt's estate, York becomes a symbol for suffering
England, gaining the spectators' sympathy as a wise and realistic
man. In acquiescing to Bolingbroke's power, even condemning his
own son in act 5, York ultimately becomes a symbol of the ambiguity of human vacillation.

556   KLIGER, SAMUEL. "The Sun Imagery in Richard II." Studies in
      Philology 45 (1948):196-202.
         Observes that the significance of Shakespeare's imagery is
its function in the total design of the play. In this regard sun
images are applied to Richard in the rising action--with the
center of his kingdom like the center of the solar system. Quite
different are the sun images in the falling action; here his
kingship finds correlatives in an eclipse, the approaching night,
and the cold and sunless climate. These image patterns contribute directly to the tragic form of the play.

557   McPEEK, JAMES A.S.   "Richard and His Shadow World."   American
      Imago 15 (1958):195-212.
         Describes a part of Richard's fascination as his set of
      fantasies that in manifestations of action and speech constitute
      a God-complex. Since all men have such fantasies, Shakespeare is
      able to draw us closely to his protagonist. Whereas in normal
      men a sense of reality mediates this fancy, with Richard his
      sense of reality grows progressively weaker. Richard's narcis-
      sism, his exhibitionist tendencies, and his alternate cycles of
      euphoria and depression would lead him today to be classified as
      an ambulatory schizophrenic.

558   PHIALAS, PETER G.   "Richard II and Shakespeare's Tragic Mode."
      Texas Studies in Literature and Language 5 (1963):344-55.
         Calls Richard II the turning point in Shakespeare's devel-
      opment as a tragic playwright. As the first tragedy involving a
      character who receives tragic illumination, the play marks the
      transition from de casibus tragedy to tragedy of individual
      responsibility. This movement reflects Shakespeare's realization
      that a tragic protagonist must be largely responsible for his
      dilemma and that he must accept responsibility for the conse-
      quences of his actions. Richard's soliloquy at Pomfret Castle is
      the clearest example of this artistic growth.

559   QUINN, MICHAEL.   "'The King Is Not Himself':   The Personal
      Tragedy of Richard II."   Studies in Philology 56 (1959):
      169-86.
         Insists that to the Elizabethan Richard's tragedy is at
      once personal and political and that the issues of divine right,
      honor, and patience reflect the interaction of history and trag-
      edy, politics and ethics. Richard, for example, uses the religio-
      political theory of divine right to cover his own ethical mis-
      conduct, provoking division both within himself and among his
      subjects. Honor is equally ambiguous, as reflected in Mowbray's
      and York's difficulty in distinguishing between proper conduct
      and political allegiance. Patience, too, is double edged, a
      virtue turned vice when the situation demands political and moral
      redress.

560   ROSSITER, A.P.   Angel With Horns and Other Shakespeare Lec-
      tures. Edited by Graham Storey. New York: Theatre Arts
      Books, 1961, 316 pp.
         Examines Shakespeare's preoccupation throughout his plays
      with the equivocal nature of man. Richard III, for instance,
      juxtaposes a huge triumphant stage personality with a rigid Tudor
      schema of retributive justice; as the consummate actor and clown
      Richard draws us dangerously close to his side. Richard II,
      likewise, provokes an ambivalent response. In the half-fantasy
      world of the court, Richard's dream kingship reigns with angels
      at his command; in the world of curt reality he is a passive
      sufferer and king of woes. Whether in the characters who parade

through history, the heroes and villains of tragedy, or the figures of comedy, Shakespeare's view is the "double-eyed, the ambivalent: it faces both ways" (p. 292).

561   SCHOENBAUM, SAMUEL. "<u>Richard II</u> and the Realities of Power."
      <u>Shakespeare Survey</u> 28 (1975):1-13.
         Maintains that Shakespeare does not strictly adhere to the
      Tudor myth in <u>Richard II</u>, that he incorporates his own insights
      into the delineation of men in dangerous situations. In part,
      the diversity of available source materials encouraged an artis-
      tic eclecticism--legends depicting Richard as virtually a saint,
      chronicle accounts treating him as a weak and moody individual
      who abdicated of his own free will. In act 1 Richard acts with
      political acumen, not vacillation and caprice, in handling the
      argument between Bolingbroke and Mowbray.

562   STIRLING, BRENTS. "Bolingbroke's 'Decision.'" <u>Shakespeare</u>
      <u>Quarterly</u> 2 (1951):27-34.
         Notes that <u>Richard II</u> contains no unorthodox political doc-
      trine in that the bishop of Carlisle flatly condemns Bolingbroke's
      act of usurpation. But the effect of the play itself is more
      powerful and more mature. The political doctrine underlying
      Bolingbroke's moves is revealed progressively and succinctly, in
      terse comments on his action at the end of the Flint Castle scene,
      at the end of the deposition scene, and in the Exton scene at the
      end of the play. The doctrine evolves naturally and not without
      sympathy as the play and the characters develop.

563   SUZMAN, ARTHUR. "Imagery and Symbolism in <u>Richard II</u>."
      <u>Shakespeare Quarterly</u> 7 (1956):355-70.
         Describes the function of imagery in <u>Richard II</u> as a re-
      inforcement of the major theme, politically the fall of Richard
      and the rise of Bolingbroke, spiritually the fall of Bolingbroke
      and the rise of Richard. The centrally important moments are the
      throwing down of gages by Bolingbroke and Mowbray, Richard's
      throwing down his warder at Coventry, Richard's descent from the
      turret at Flint Castle, Bolingbroke's ascending the throne, and
      Richard's casting down the mirror and shattering his own image.
      The language, too, constantly reflects this dual theme.

564   TALBERT, ERNEST W. <u>The Problem of Order: Elizabethan Common-</u>
      <u>places and an Example of Shakespeare's Art</u>. Chapel Hill:
      University of North Carolina Press, 1962, 244 pp.
         Demonstrates Shakespeare's use of current concepts and
      representational methods to achieve within the theater a highly
      charged ambivalent effect in the Flint Castle scene and the
      deposition scene in <u>Richard II</u>. Like the entire play these
      scenes briefly contrast Richardian and Lancastrian interpreta-
      tions of history. At one moment Richard is God's agent, at
      another the fallen ruler; at one moment Bolingbroke is the proud
      and ambitious usurper, at another a Lancastrian nobleman. The

effect of the scenes is pervasively ambiguous. The deposition
scene also plays upon a diversity of religious attitudes, including those accordant with Aristotle's definition of the commonwealth.

565   ZITNER, S.P. "Aumerle's Conspiracy." Studies in English
      Literature 14 (1974):239-57.
          Observes that, while the Aumerle scenes are not central to
      the development of the narrative, they function in several sig-
      nificant ways. They provide necessary filler material to sepa-
      rate Richard's pathetic farewell scene and Exton's intent to
      murder him; they serve to convey a message of political necessity:
      that superior power must be obeyed; they furnish a commentary on
      the motifs of love, loyalty, treachery, and forgiveness. Pos-
      sibly their comical nature reflects Shakespeare's disenchantment
      with the traditionally sober presentations of historical material.

For discussion of Richard as a tragic character, see entries 543,
557-59; for a counterview, see entry 549. For a discussion of
imagery, see entries 540, 545, 552-53, 556, 563. See also The
English Histories (entries 387-411) and 78, 103, 135, 139, 172, 196,
211, 219, 242, 245, 263, 272, 291, 297, 313, 328-30, 414, 417, 427,
481, 488, 926, 942, 948, 953, 963.

RICHARD III

                            Editions

566   FURNESS, HENRY HOWARD, Jr., ed. The Tragedy of Richard the
      Third: With the Landing of Earle Richmond and the Battle at
      Bosworth Field. A New Variorum Edition of Shakespeare.
      Philadelphia: J.B. Lippincott, 1908, 641 pp.
          Uses the First Folio as the copy text. On each page, for
      that portion of the text, provides variant readings, textual
      notes, and general critical commentary. Following the text are
      sections on the nature of the quarto and folio texts, the date of
      composition, the sources, the text of The True Tragedy of Richard
      the Third, the character of Richard, English and German criti-
      cisms, stage history, the principal actors, and a list of works
      consulted.

567   HAMMOND, ANTONY, ed. King Richard III. The Arden Shake-
      speare. London and New York: Methuen, 1981, 382 pp.
          Includes discussion of the publication, the text, and date
      of composition, Richard III in performance, the sources, and the
      play itself. Appendixes consider longer passages unique to the
      First Folio and the first quarto and reprint source materials
      from Halle's Chronicle and The Mirror For Magistrates. The text
      is based on the 1623 folio but readings from the first quarto are
      allowed when they seem to represent an authoritative later stage.

The folio text was probably based on Shakespeare's foul papers
collated with the third and sixth quartos; the first quarto
represents a remarkably good memorial reconstruction.

568   SMIDT, KRISTIAN, ed. William Shakespeare, "The Tragedy of
      Richard III": Parallel Texts of the First Quarto and the
      First Folio with Variants of the Early Quartos. Oslo:
      Universitetsforlaget; New York: Humanities Press, 1969,
      221 pp.
         Describes the two substantive texts of Richard III, the
      first quarto of 1597 (with essentially derivative quartos in
      1598, 1602, 1605, 1612, 1622, 1629, 1634) and the 1623 folio.
      The latter contains 212 unique lines while omitting 35 lines from
      the quarto. Prints the quarto and folio texts on facing pages,
      the former from a transcript of Greg's Shakespeare Quarto
      Facsimile collated with the Huth copy in the British Library, the
      latter from the Folger First Folio # 42. Quarto variants are
      summarized on pp. 14-27.

569   WILSON, JOHN DOVER, ed. Richard III. Cambridge: Cambridge
      University Press, 1954, 280 pp.
         Provides extensive textual notes, a critical introduction
      (covering the text and date of composition, the sources--the
      chronicles, More, The Mirror For Magistrates, The True Tragedy of
      Richard the Third, and other pre-Shakespearean drama--style,
      character, and plot), a discussion of the copy text, a section
      on stage history, a glossary, and a genealogical table. This
      edition is based on the First Folio, but readings from the first
      quarto--possibly a joint memorial reconstruction--are also ad-
      mitted. The structural pattern centering on the villainous hero
      is serviceable because its very artificiality renders the charac-
      ter more credible and because the constant moral reiterations
      leave the audience comfortably free to enjoy his Machiavellian
      wickedness.

Textual Studies

570   PATRICK, DAVID LYALL. The Textual History of "Richard III."
      Stanford: Stanford University Press, 1936, 153 pp.
         Maintains that the first quarto and the First Folio do not
      represent two distinct texts. Instead, the quarto represents a
      piratical version of the play prior to 1597, incorporating
      deliberate alterations by the prompter or stage manager. The
      folio text represents essentially Shakespeare's original form.
      There is no indication that Shakespeare himself was involved in
      the variations preserved in the quarto. Hence, an editor is
      unjustified in producing an eclectic text based on both versions.

571   SMIDT, KRISTIAN. Iniurious Impostors and "Richard III."
      Oslo: Norwegian Universities Press; New York: Humanities
      Press, 1964, 213 pp.
            Maintains--through a study of transposition, anticipation
      and recollection, substitution, and omission--that the 1597
      quarto text of Richard III is not a bad quarto based on memorial
      reporting by one or two actors or by the entire company, that all
      evidence points to its authenticity. In all likelihood both the
      quarto and folio texts were set from an authoritative manuscript,
      with the quarto based on "a non-theatrical, or rather pretheatri-
      cal" version (p. 155).

572   WALTON, JAMES KIRKWOOD. The Copy for the Folio Text of
      "Richard III": With a Note on the Copy for the Folio Text of
      "King Lear." Auckland: Auckland University College Press,
      1955, 164 pp.
            Argues that the copy for the folio text of Richard III is
      not, as generally assumed, a corrected copy of the sixth quarto
      (1622) but a copy of the third quarto (1602) corrected with only
      sporadic accuracy by a collator. That the folio text of this
      play has the greatest number of variants of all of Shakespeare's
      texts printed from corrected quartos is demonstrably not evidence
      of the accuracy and thoroughness of the collation. A similar
      situation appears to exist in the use of corrected quarto copy
      for the folio text of King Lear.

                              Criticism

573   ARMSTRONG, W.A. "The Elizabethan Conception of the Tyrant."
      Review of English Studies 22 (1946):161-81.
            Points out that Elizabethans in their political and lit-
      erary documents drew sharp distinctions between usurper-tyrants
      and those who ruled by hereditary right. While the latter simply
      had to be endured until removed by God, the former were viewed
      as satanic creatures who could be justly overthrown. Such a
      tyrant, it was believed, lived constantly in fear of divine
      retribution, an offender against himself, country, and God; his
      tragic dimension is his dynamism, which sets him in conflict with
      the laws of God and man. Richard III was considered a prime
      example.

574   _____. "The Influence of Seneca and Machiavelli on the Eliza-
      bethan Tyrant." Review of English Studies 24 (1948):19-35.
            Focuses on the Elizabethan conception of a tyrant as a
      composite of Roman, Italian, and Christian ideas that was given
      shape by the humanistic theory of kingship. Seneca's villains
      are "super-human" creatures consumed by passion, immoral indi-
      viduals who are set in opposition to the gods. The Machiavel-
      lian, as popularly understood by the Elizabethans, combined the
      qualities of the lion and the fox; selfish and materialistic, he
      is "justified" in using whatever force is necessary. Such

Senecan and Machiavellian concepts were the dominant forces behind Elizabethan tyrant tragedy and revenge tragedy.

575   BEGG, EDLEEN. "Shakespeare's Debt to Hall and Holinshed in
       Richard III." Studies in Philology 32 (1935):189-96.
            Concludes that critics are incorrect in asserting that
       Holinshed is Shakespeare's main source for Richard III, that
       Halle is equally important, and that Shakespeare kept both vol-
       umes at hand when he wrote and revised his play. In instances
       in which Shakespeare bodily took material from his source, Halle
       outnumbers Holinshed eight to five; for borrowings of hints from
       which he developed a situation or scene, Halle outnumbers
       Holinshed four to nothing; and, for the borrowing of actual words
       and phrases, Holinshed outnumbers Halle eight to five.

576   BERMAN, RONALD. "Anarchy and Order in Richard III and King
       John." Shakespeare Survey 20 (1967):51-60.
            Observes that, among the histories, Richard III and King
       John are distinguished by tough, cynical, and realistic wit.
       Their heroes are characterized by a skeptical attitude toward
       matters treated quite seriously in the other histories--legiti-
       macy, honor, the sacredness of blood relationships. Richard's
       emancipation from morality is not unlike that of the Bastard's.
       Their minds are animated by a mixture of philosophical material-
       ism and Machiavellianism. In both plays the egocentric, anarchic
       nature of the individual confronts and eventually succumbs to the
       ideals of order.

577   BROOKE, NICHOLAS. "Reflecting Gems and Dead Bones: Tragedy
       Versus History in Richard III." Critical Quarterly 7 (1965):
       123-34.
            Views the conflict in Richard III as the gigantic force and
       pattern of moral history set against the tragic concept of an
       individual struggling against overwhelming odds. Whereas the
       language of the one is highly structured and ritualized,
       Richard's language is sparkling as he shares with the spectator
       his determination to defy the force of history represented by
       Margaret. As Richard is defeated, so is the force of human free
       will, albeit perverted, and the world "is poorer for his loss"
       (p. 134). (See entry 584.)

578   BROOKS, H.F. "Richard III, Unhistorical Amplifications: The
       Women's Scenes and Seneca." Modern Language Review 75 (1980):
       721-37.
            Finds Shakespeare's source for the women in Richard III in
       Seneca's Troades and, specifically, for the scene between Anne
       and Richard in act 1 in Seneca's Hercules Furens and Hippolytus.
       From Troades come the parallels of the Duchess of York and
       Hecuba, Elizabeth and Andromache, Anne and Polyxena, and Margaret
       and Helen. The hypnotizing of Anne by Richard corresponds to the

wooing of Megara by Lycus and Richard's proffer of his sword
by which Anne might kill him to Phaedra's similar offer to
Hippolytus.

579   CHURCHILL, GEORGE B. Richard the Third Up to Shakespeare.
         Palaestra, 10. Berlin: Mayer & Müller, 1900, 548 pp.
         Concerns the raw material available to Shakespeare at the
time he wrote Richard III. Part 1 provides the source materials
in the chronicles, tracing the growth of the legend of Richard's
wickedness in Warkworth, the Croyland manuscript, Rous, Commines,
André, Fabyan, More, Vergil, Rastell, Hardyng, Halle, Grafton,
Holinshed, and Stowe. Part 2 analyzes the earlier literary
treatments of Richard (Mirror for Magistrates, Legge, The True
Tragedy, Chute, Fletcher, Henslowe, Drayton) and their relationship to Shakespeare's play.

580   CLEMEN, WOLFGANG H. "Anticipation and Foreboding in Shake-
         speare's Early Histories." Shakespeare Survey 6 (1953):25-35.
         Views the element of anticipation and foreboding as an
important feature of both Shakespeare's technique and his art of
characterization. The Henry VI plays, much like pre-Shakespearean
drama, use prophecies, omens, and dreams to establish patterns of
anticipation for the spectators. More significant are the devices that structurally control the action in Richard III, whether
the purely choric scenes for atmospheric effect such as the
citizens discussing the dangers of a child king or the curses of
Margaret remembered successively by each victim.

581   _____. A Commentary on Shakespeare's "Richard III." Trans-
         lated by Jean Bonheim. London: Methuen, 1968, 247 pp.
         Develops a scene-by-scene analysis drawing upon multiple
critical approaches--stylistic, thematic, imagistic, dramaturgi-
cal--to provide a full analysis. The interplay between tradition
and originality is a major feature of the play, and from this
interaction Shakespeare develops a bold, new dramatic form. The
opening soliloquy announces the motivation for Richard's subsequent actions in nothing more or less than his aggressive will.
With careful rhetorical modulation Richard draws our eyes to
observe his deformity and his isolation. Throughout the play the
spectator is made to fluctuate between disgust at the horror of
Richard's machinations turned coldly and methodically into deeds
and admiration for his fiery will and resourcefulness.

582   _____. "Tradition and Originality in Shakespeare's
         Richard III." Shakespeare Quarterly 5 (1954):247-57.
         Notes that Shakespeare was more experimental than his fel-
low playwrights, that he sought his individual style by constantly reencountering existing modes of dramatic expression.
His originality is balanced by an amalgamation of inherited
forms. Richard III marks a decisive step in the evolution of
English drama in structure, style, and character. It gives a

unity to the chronicle play by focusing on the tragic history of
the individual man, with equal emphasis on the inner self. A
combination of natural and artificial styles also serves to enhance the characterization.

583   DOEBLER, BETTIE A. "'Despaire and Dye': The Ultimate Tempta-
       tion of Richard III." Shakespeare Studies 7 (1964):75-86.
          Focuses on the relationship between Richard III's death
       and the ars moriendi tradition. The appearance of the ghosts to
       Richard and Richmond in bed rings a variation on this icono-
       graphical tradition in that the spirits function like the good
       and evil angels to reenact the struggle for man's soul in life's
       final moments. Richard's cry about "coward conscience" is en-
       visioned as a form of internalized struggle, and his despair in
       battle signifies the damnation of his soul. (See entry 589.)

584   FRENCH, A.L. "The World of Richard III." Shakespeare Studies
       4 (1968):25-39.
          Considers Shakespeare's Richard III to be a more complex
       figure than the single-dimensional villain of Tudor propaganda.
       For one thing, Richmond is more a cypher than a Tudor hero; if he
       is morally without flaw, he is no emotional force in the play.
       For another, Stanley seems to point to the political climate of
       the play; a trimmer who does not openly oppose Richard, he plays
       both sides so as to be prepared for any political eventuality.
       Finally, Richard himself commands an almost perverse sympathy
       since the metaphysical dimension of the play seems so shallow and
       vindictive. (See entry 577.)

585   HILL, R.F. "Shakespeare's Early Tragic Mode." Shakespeare
       Quarterly 9 (1958):455-69.
          Considers the ornamental style of the early tragedies as
       representative of rhetorical tragedy derived from Seneca in which
       emotion is characterized by symbolic scenes, punning, repetition,
       and extended figures. At times Shakespeare slips into a natur-
       alistic style, for example in the speech of Richard III; as a
       consequence the other characters appear frigid and artificial.
       Rome and Juliet is pivotal in Shakespeare's development; while it
       employs the rhetorical style in the nurse's speech and the elabo-
       rate wit combats of Romeo and Mercutio, Romeo and Juliet grow
       consistently into a naturalistic style as the tragedy progresses.

586   McNEIR, WALDO. "The Masks of Richard III." Studies in
       English Literature 11 (1971):167-86.
          Considers Richard's role-playing talents, a mode of charac-
       terization Shakespeare prepares in 3 Henry VI in Richard's abil-
       ity to manipulate others and in the soliloquies in which he
       shares his motives and ambitions with the spectators. In
       Richard III he continuously performs for two audiences--his
       auditors on stage, who are duped by his incessant references to
       piety, humility, and integrity--and his auditors in the

galleries, whose moral scruples are dulled by his wit and virtuosity. The disintegration of his character in act 5 is signaled by the three roles of self-accuser, self-defender, and
conscience.

587   RICHMOND, HUGH M. "Richard III and the Reformation." Journal
      of English and Germanic Philology 83 (1984):509-21.
          Comments on the appropriateness of the many allusions to
      medieval drama in Richard III since in York, the seat of
      Richard's power, the popularity of such drama continued well
      after the development of Protestant opposition. Indeed, the
      vocabulary of the play suggests that Shakespeare is giving new
      life to the old dramatic tradition in light of just such opposi-
      tion, undercutting it with mocking irony and historical allusion
      generated by Puritan and humanist alike. Shakespeare's interest
      is not to discredit religion but to intensify it in Reformation
      terms; within Catholic terms it enhances the credibility of
      Richard's amorality.

588   SMITH, FRED MANNING. "The Relation of Macbeth to Richard III."
      PMLA 60 (1945):1003-20.
          States that the parallels between Macbeth and Richard III
      are so numerous and so complex as to require an explanation other
      than that of coincidence. Both protagonists are called hell-
      hounds, and the events in each play unfold as the fulfillment of
      prophecy. Moreover, the sequence of events and the general shape
      of the plot are strikingly similar. Shakespeare in writing
      Macbeth clearly turned to Holinshed, finding there the history
      and the outline of events; quite probably, he consciously was
      reminded of Richard III and drew from his own earlier play in
      matters of characterization, dialogue, and dramatic construction.

589   THOMAS, SIDNEY. The Antic Hamlet and Richard III. New York:
      King's Crown Press, 1943, 92 pp.
          Studies Richard III and Hamlet in relation to earlier
      dramatic types and to each other. "Antic" traditionally refers
      to a comic figure, a masked buffoon; and it is this figure to
      which Hamlet refers concerning his "antic disposition." As he
      is a mixture of the tragic and the comic, so Richard combines
      the villain and the comedian characteristic of the traditional
      vice character. Both are developments of these traditional roles
      in earlier native drama, not of Senecan influences as in Titus
      Andronicus. (See entry 583.)

                              Stage History

590   WOOD, ALICE I.P. The Stage History of Shakespeare's
      "Richard III." New York: Columbia University Press; Oxford:
      Oxford University Press, 1909, 186 pp.
          Examines the stage history of Richard III, reconstructing
      the likely conditions in Shakespeare's day and basing later

accounts on records of performances, conditions of staging,
scenery, properties, costumes, and acting style. The productions
of the early eighteenth century focus on the Cibber adaptation
and those of the latter half on the acting style introduced by
Garrick. Another chapter concerns the fortunes of the play in
America. Combining elements of the chronicle, Marlovian tragedy,
and Kydian revenge, Richard's perennial fascination is his reflection of that which in man is consummately evil.

See also The English Histories (entries 387-411) and 78, 89, 103,
115, 131-32, 150, 162, 179, 189, 204-5, 209, 219, 237, 242, 256, 263,
294, 297, 311, 323, 330, 483, 491, 498, 545, 560, 926, 933, 946, 963,
1250.

IV. The Comedies

GENERAL STUDIES

591   BARBER, C.L. <u>Shakespeare's Festive Comedy: A Study of Dramatic Form in Relation to Social Custom</u>. Princeton: Princeton University Press, 1959, 266 pp.
        Asserts that the fundamental structure of Shakespeare's festive comedies (those through <u>Twelfth Night</u>) derives from the saturnalian pattern of Elizabethan holiday. Whatever the variation, this pattern involves inversion, statement and counterstatement, and a general movement leading through release to clarification. Both the holiday festivity and the comic form to which it gives rise are "parallel manifestations of the same pattern of culture, of a way that men can cope with their life" (p. 6). <u>A Midsummer Night's Dream</u>, for example, imaginatively recreates the experience of the traditional summer holidays. In Falstaff Shakespeare fuses the clown's part with that of the Lord of Misrule, a festive celebrant. Shakespeare's theater was assuming on a professional basis the function of the amateur on celebrative occasions. (See entry 603.)

592   BAXTER, JOHN S. "Present Mirth: Shakespeare's Romantic Comedies." <u>Queen's Quarterly</u> 72 (1965):52-77.
        Describes Shakespearean comedy as a form that appeals both to the intellect and the emotion. With its setting in the human spirit, it makes no attempt to criticize life through satirically mirroring the vices and abuses or by a Jonsonian stage figure who expresses the author's judgments. The function of Shakespeare's comedy is to enlarge the dimensions of the spirit and to comprehend life as it may be lived in rich fulfillment under the law of nature and the law of God.

593   BERRY, RALPH. <u>Shakespeare's Comedies: Explorations in Form</u>. Princeton: Princeton University Press, 1972, 214 pp.
        Investigates the ten comedies through <u>Twelfth Night</u>. The overriding theme is illusion, whether the consequences of simple error (<u>The Comedy of Errors</u>), deception (<u>Much Ado About Nothing</u>) or self-deception (<u>Twelfth Night</u>). Opposed to this illusion is reality, most often depicted in the clowns, servants, rustics--

all in a sense extensions of the jester--who provide a commentary, often surprisingly tart, on the behavior of their social
superiors. The closure is frequently more interrogatory than
declarative, "clarifications" that must continue to be tested in
the imagination extending beyond act 5.

594   BONAZZA, BLAZE ODELL. Shakespeare's Early Comedies: A
      Structural Analysis. Studies in English Literature, 9. The
      Hague: Mouton, 1966, 125 pp.
         Views the evolution of Shakespeare's concept of comedy as
      the consequence of his working through several highly derivative
      plays in which he addressed practical stage matters. In The
      Comedy of Errors he followed the linear farcical comedy in the
      Plautine pattern but found it too uninvolved and unitonal; con-
      versely, in Love's Labor's Lost he followed Lyly's lead in roman-
      tic comedy but found the affectations of language and absence of
      dramatic intensity too restricting. An unsuccessful effort to
      blend the two in The Two Gentlemen of Verona precedes his first
      masterpiece in A Midsummer Night's Dream.

595   BRADBROOK, MURIEL C. The Growth and Structure of Elizabethan
      Comedy. London: Chatto & Windus, 1955, 254 pp.
         Traces the chronological development of Elizabethan comedy
      from its beginnings in medieval drama and the oral tradition to
      its fullest expression in Shakespeare, his contemporaries, and
      his immediate successors. Approximately one fourth of the study
      is devoted to Shakespeare, who in his characterizations most
      successfully engaged the audiences of his own day. His use of
      disguise or the assumption of a conventional role as a means of
      indicating maturation of character is an extension of the method
      of contrasted plot and subplot. Expecially significant is his
      development of the role of the heroine; his ladies sparkle with
      life, energy, and vitality compared with the stiff goddesses who
      stand to be wooed in duels of courtship or with the long-
      suffering "pieces of devotion" in sentimental comedy.

596   BROWN, JOHN RUSSELL. "The Interpretation of Shakespeare's
      Comedies: 1900-1953." Shakespeare Survey 8 (1955):1-13.
         Notes that studies of the comedies in this century have
      begun to focus on Shakespeare's working out of certain themes
      and patterns in the early and middle comedies, on the last plays
      as something more than idle recreations of boredom, and on the
      problem plays as the result of more than artistic melancholia.
      Much has been done in Shakespeare's sources both in identifying
      the works themselves and in analyzing the nature and intent of
      Shakespeare's modifications. By far the most popular approach
      has been in character analysis and in the language, especially
      the imagery, of the plays.

597   _____. Shakespeare and His Comedies. London: Methuen, 1957,
         253 pp.
         Observes that, except for three early intrigue comedies,
Shakespeare's plays follow the narrative tradition and are variations of the theme of true love. The Merchant of Venice reflects
the theme of love's wealth (the manner in which love transcends
mercantile values); A Midsummer Night's Dream and Much Ado About
Nothing, love's truth (the complexity of the lover's truthful
realization of beauty and the distinction between fancy and true
affection); As You Like It and Twelfth Night, love's order (the
power to infuse priorities issuing in harmony at both the social
and the individual level); the problem comedies, love's ordeal
(the conflict between the higher impulses of love and the instincts of man's corrupt nature). The romances, infused with the
same educative values, focus on love's ability to bring these
various elements into a stable relationship.

598   CHAMPION, LARRY S. The Evolution of Shakespeare's Comedy.
         Cambridge, Mass.: Harvard University Press, 1970, 241 pp.
         Views the development of Shakespeare's artistry in comedy
as a movement toward progressively more complex characters and
situations and the development of structural devices by which to
maintain an effective comic perspective. The early works are
essentially situation comedies; the humor arises primarily from
the action, and there is no significant development of character.
The romantic comedies of the late 1590s establish plots in which
emphasis is on identity rather than physical action; characters
who have assumed an unnatural or abnormal pose are forced to
realize and to admit the ridiculousness of their position. The
final comedies involve sin and sacrificial forgiveness, with
character development turning on a fundamental transformation of
values. The problem comedies represent partially successful
efforts to develop a comic perspective that can accommodate the
fully delineated characterization.

599   CHARLTON, H.B. Shakespearian Comedy. London: Methuen, 1938,
         303 pp.
         Maintains that Shakespeare elevated comedy to a mode of
grandeur and full maturity that will probably never be equalled.
Shakespeare's genius lies in the fusing of romance and comedy,
thereby enhancing both forms. From the early pieces that depict
life as a comic game of youthful passion, the playwright moves
to an examination of the enigmatic sources of true nobility and
the complex nature of the joy in life; in Much Ado About Nothing,
As You Like It, and Twelfth Night the heroine emerges in
Beatrice, Rosalynde, and Viola, "representations of the office
of love to lift mankind to a richer life" (p. 283).

600   COGHILL, NEVILLE. "The Basis of Shakespearian Comedy."
       Essays and Studies, n.s. 3 (1950):1-28.
           Distinguishes Jonsonian satiric comedy from Shakespeare's
       romantic comedy with its roots in the Middle Ages and the belief
       that comedy, the reverse of tragedy, involved a story that starts
       in sorrow and danger and by a happy turn of fortune ends in
       felicity. As the medieval formula for comedy led through love
       to the Beatific Vision, so Shakespeare's comedies are built on
       love stories that, following a series of misadventures, firmly
       espouse social and personal harmony.

601   EVANS, BERTRAND. Shakespeare's Comedies. Oxford: Clarendon
       Press, 1960, 337 pp.
           Analyzes Shakespeare's comedies in terms of their levels of
       discrepant awareness, the gaps in knowledge that develop between
       character and spectator or character and character. This ex-
       ploitation of dramatic irony is envisioned as the principal man-
       ner in which Shakespeare manipulates and controls his audience to
       achieve the maximum comic response. Of the 297 scenes in the
       seventeen comedies, the spectator holds the advantage in 177; of
       277 named characters, 151 stand in a condition of exploitable
       ignorance. As the early comedies yield to the mature ones, the
       problem comedies, and finally to the romances, the nature of the
       spectator's higher level of awareness and the control of his
       response become more complex, more concerned with psychological
       principles than with comic practice for its own sake.

602   FELHEIM, MARVIN, and TRACI, PHILIP. Realism in Shakespeare's
       Comedies: "O Heavenly Mingle." Lanham, Md.: University
       Press of America, 1980, 227 pp.
           Argues that it is reductionistic to view Shakespeare's
       comedies as sheer farce or as Kottian nightmare. Instead, they
       represent a consistent blend of youthful romantic passion and
       serious social or domestic concerns. Such a multiplicity of
       views is traditional on the Elizabethan stage, for example the
       juxtaposition of Egeon's dilemma with the knockabout humor of the
       Dromios and Antipholuses in The Comedy of Errors or the mixture
       of romantic and realistic views of pastoral existence in As You
       Like It.

603   FRYE, NORTHROP. "The Argument of Comedy." In English Insti-
       tute Essays 1948. Edited by D.A. Robertson, Jr. New York:
       Columbia University Press, 1949, pp. 58-73. Reprinted in His
       Infinite Variety: Major Shakespearean Criticism Since John-
       son, ed. Paul N. Siegel (Philadelphia: J.B. Lippincott,
       1964), pp. 120-29.
           Describes Shakespeare's comic form as a derivation of
       Menandrine New Comedy, with its material cause in a young man's
       sexual desire, a formal cause in the social order dramatized in
       the senex, and an efficient cause in the vice or clown (the
       Elizabethan version of the tricky slave). The final cause is the

spectator, who through applause becomes a part of the comic
resolution. Through a green-world experience a character gains
release from the psychological strictures of his grey world, and
society gains a renewed sense of social integration. Shakespeare's comic vision involves a "detachment of the spirit born
of [the] reciprocal reflection of two illusory realities"
(p. 73). (See entry 591.)

604   _____. "Characterization in Shakespeare's Comedies."
         Shakespeare Quarterly 4 (1953):271-77.
              Views Shakespeare's comic characters, though seemingly un-
         predictable and life-like, as derived basically from the three
         comic types described in the Tractatus Coislinianus of the third
         century B.C.--the alazon (a boaster or hypocrite), the eiron (a
         self-deprecator who exposes the alazon), and the buffoon (who
         amuses by his mannerism or rhetoric). Aristotle adds a fourth,
         the agroikos or rustic. The eiron is the hero-heroine, who at
         the center of the plot is engaged in conflict with the alazon;
         the rustic and buffoon polarize the comic mood.

605   _____. The Myth of Deliverance: Reflections on Shakespeare's
         Problem Comedies. Toronto and Buffalo: University of Toronto
         Press, 1983, 90 pp.
              Argues that the so-called problem plays are merely romantic
         comedies in which the chief magical device is a bed trick rather
         than an enchanted forest or identical twins. These comedies gen-
         erally fuse the human concerns for survival and deliverance in a
         teleological plot moving through an end that through some form of
         anagnorisis incorporates its beginning. Measure for Measure, for
         example, is a dramatic diptych combining a tragic and ironic
         section with one of elaborate comic intrigue. Like the other
         problem plays, it has both a constricted meaning within its his-
         toric context and also a limitless meaning within the structure
         of literature itself.

606   GORDON, GEORGE S. Shakespearian Comedy and Other Studies.
         London and New York: Oxford University Press, 1944, 158 pp.
              Observes that Shakespearean comedy juxtaposes two worlds,
         one occupied with those who play with words and the other with
         those who are played with by words. In another sense a world of
         poetic romance is countered by a world of comic realism, the two
         existing side by side without competing for attention. Charac-
         ters at the conclusion must frequently move from the poetic to
         the real world. Normally young lovers populate the one, workaday
         people the other. Shakespeare's comedies excel in the power to
         alternate the action "between Nowhere and England" (p. 51).

607   HART, JOHN A. Dramatic Structure in Shakespeare's Romantic
       Comedies. Carnegie Series in English, n.s. 2. Pittsburgh and
       London: Carnegie Mellon University Press, 1980, 126 pp.
            Finds in Shakespeare's five major romantic comedies (A
       Midsummer Night's Dream, The Merchant of Venice, Much Ado About
       Nothing, As You Like It, Twelfth Night) a love relationship set
       against the background of the relationship between father and
       daughter, between ruler and subject, and between master and
       servant. Genuine harmony can exist only in those situations in
       which a character through reason and imagination overcomes bar-
       riers of these social relationships and thus establishes a cli-
       mate in which the passion of love can flourish.

608   HASSEL, R. CHRIS, Jr. Faith and Folly in Shakespeare's
       Romantic Comedies. Athens: University of Georgia Press,
       1980, 255 pp.
            Claims that an understanding of the Pauline and Erasmanian
       paradoxes concerning the nature of foolishness and wisdom en-
       hances an appreciation of Shakespeare's comic artistry and en-
       larges our sense of the coherence of his comic vision. More
       specifically, the Pauline, liturgical, and Erasmanian principle
       that one is wise only in realizing and admitting his stupidity
       underlies the roles of Bottom and Feste, the juxtaposition of
       Touchstone and Jacques, the romantic relationship of Benedick and
       Beatrice, and the theme of edification through humiliation in
       Love's Labor's Lost, Twelfth Night, and The Merchant of Venice.

609   HAWKINS, SHERMAN. "The Two Worlds of Shakespearean Comedy."
       Shakespeare Studies 3 (1967):62-80.
            Observes in Shakespeare's comedies the recurrence of the
       two archetypal motifs of the journey or green world and the
       siege or closed world. The journey involves movement from a
       normal to a green world and back again, leading to self-knowledge
       and reconciliation (The Two Gentlemen of Verona, A Midsummer
       Night's Dream, The Merchant of Venice, As You Like It, The
       Winter's Tale). The siege deals with characters who are visited
       and changed by outside forces (The Comedy of Errors, Love's
       Labor's Lost, Much Ado About Nothing, Twelfth Night). The
       Tempest fuses the two; dream and reality are indistinguishable.

610   HERRICK, MARVIN T. "Shakespeare." In Tragicomedy: Its
       Origin and Development in Italy, France, and England.
       Illinois Studies in Language and Literature, vol. 39. Urbana:
       University of Illinois Press, 1955, pp. 249-60.
            Traces the movement in Shakespeare from tragical comedy to
       a near-tragic tragicomedy with a happy ending in tragicomedy.
       Most of the romantic comedies reflect tragicomic qualities, but
       in All's Well That Ends Well and Measure for Measure Shakespeare
       breaks new ground in variety of incident, characterization, and
       diction. There is anxious suspense, more in the minds of the
       spectators than in the minds of the characters. Cymbeline, like

Beaumont and Fletcher's Philaster, is more fully developed tragi-comedy, replete with surprising discoveries, romantic disguises, tragic complaints, and a happy ending.

611   KIRSCH, ARTHUR C. Shakespeare and the Experience of Love.
      Cambridge: Cambridge University Press, 1981, 194 pp.
          Focuses on the mystery and importance of love in forming
      the whole individual and a whole community, utilizing both
      Christian and Freudian analytic methods in five Shakespearean
      plays. Othello, for example, is highly resonant, representing a
      literal love story but also reflecting in its three central fig-
      ures a single moral and psychic entity. Similarly, the multiple
      plots of Much Ado About Nothing have a symbiotic relationship
      concerning the transforming power of love. While Posthumous's
      deception in Cymbeline provokes a virtual decomposition of his
      personality, the resolution of his inner guilt represents "a
      paradigm of spiritual and psychic transformation" (p. 176).
      Chapters are also devoted to All's Well That Ends Well and
      Measure for Measure.

612   LAWRENCE, WILLIAM W. Shakespeare's Problem Comedies. 2d ed.
      New York: Frederick Ungar, 1960, 259 pp.
          Argues that the problematic issues in All's Well That Ends
      Well, Measure for Measure, and Troilus and Cressida must be
      viewed in the context of the early seventeenth century, when
      vestigial remnants of medieval standards still obtained. Re-
      sembling each other in style and content, these plays combine
      romantic plots with serious and realistic attention to the darker
      complexities of human nature. Of particular significance are the
      medieval analogues that form the basis of Shakespeare's plot and
      help to condition the response of the spectators. Helena, for
      example, must be seen in light of Boccaccio's tale of the clever
      wench, Giletta of Narbonne; and the basic outlines of Isabella's
      actions are drawn from a story common in the south of Europe.
      What the modern critic sees as psychological inconsistencies
      Shakespeare's spectators would accept without question as a part
      of the conventions bound up in the old tale that the playwright
      was using. (See entries 728, 730.)

613   LEECH, CLIFFORD. "Twelfth Night" and Shakespearian Comedy.
      Toronto: University of Toronto Press; Halifax: Dalhousie
      University Press, 1965, 88 pp.
          Contrasts the comic formula of The Comedy of Errors (the
      Plautine single stage in which characters interact) with that of
      The Two Gentlemen of Verona (a journey with roots in the Hellen-
      istic romance). The early years of festive comedy culminate in
      Twelfth Night. In those that follow the darker tones suggested
      in Feste's epilogue prevail. Passing beyond the laughter of
      delight, Shakespeare depicts time's destruction in Troilus and
      Cressida and its reconstruction in The Winter's Tale, which

insists that by control of conduct and manipulation of natural experience man can achieve a degree of control over the flux of things.

614   LEGGATT, ALEXANDER. Shakespeare's Comedy of Love. London: Methuen; New York: Harper & Row, 1974, 272 pp.
        Seeks not the inner unity but the eternal variety of Shakespeare's comic artistry. At the center of the early plays is farcical comedy that, in turn, gives way to a more subtle humor based on the characters' response to their situation. Shakespeare sets the experience of being in love between contrasting poles of hostility and indifference and plays the theme off of various perspectives, including that of the clown as parodic. The study discusses each of the comedies through Twelfth Night.

615   MARTZ, WILLIAM J. Shakespeare's Universe of Comedy. New York: David Lewis, 1971, 146 pp.
        Argues that the interaction of Shakespeare's comic point of view (the framing structural principle creating the detachment appropriate to viewing life as spectacle) and his view of reality (a play's "rationally summarizeable" thematic content) constitutes the dynamics of his comedy. The Taming of the Shrew, A Midsummer Night's Dream, As You Like It, and Twelfth Night illustrate a range of laughter from hearty guffaws to provocative wit to quiet delight in the beauty of life. The unifying principle is the comic spirit of affirmation constant in the complexity of human experience.

616   NEVO, RUTH. Comic Transformations in Shakespeare. London and New York: Methuen, 1980, 242 pp.
        Observes that Shakespeare fused his comic form from the Donatan formula for plot and the battle of the sexes for motivation of the variegated romantic courtship stories. Since the journey toward self-knowledge and the reciprocal acceptance of love progresses at a slower pace for the character than for the spectator (whose perspective is at a higher level of awareness), the resolution is immediate for the one, holistic and integrative for the other. The characters in acting out their follies gain remediation, and the fools mediate through parody.

617   PALMER, JOHN. Comic Characters of Shakespeare. London: Macmillan, 1946, 135 pp.
        Includes chapters on Berowne, Touchstone, Shylock, Bottom, and Benedick and Beatrice. The key to Shakespeare's humor is his ability to delight in mocking the diverse misadventures of rascals at the same time he retains a kindred emotional fellowship with them. Berowne and Touchstone, foolish in their own right, share an ability to perceive the incongruities in the actions of those around them. Shylock is at once both comic villain and suffering human. Bottom for all his stupidity possesses a comic

unflappability we all cherish. Sympathy, not satire, is the
essence of Shakespeare's comic inspiration.

618   PARROTT, THOMAS MARC. Shakespearean Comedy. New York:
       Oxford University Press, 1949, 417 pp.
       Describes the medieval and classical influences on Shake-
speare's comedy and then chronologically surveys the canon, both
the comedies themselves and the comic elements in the histories
and tragedies. The comedy varies from the patterned structure of
Love's Labor's Lost to the lively farce of The Merry Wives of
Windsor, yet there is an element of realistic humor in both.
From the exclusive use of verse in the early plays, Shakespeare
moves to prose as the natural idiom of comedy. Advancement is
also visible in his fool figures as the early clowns (Launce,
Speed, Costard) become complacent citizens (Bottom, Dogberry)
and, in turn, professional jesters (Touchstone, Feste). Comedy
develops from action, language, and character, the latter being
the most sophisticated form.

619   PETTET, E.C. Shakespeare and the Romance Tradition. London:
       Staples Press, 1949, 208 pp.
       Views Shakespeare's romantic comedies as the assimilation
into drama of the historical and aesthetic climax of the romantic
heritage. Stories of farfetched adventures, they inevitably
center on young lovers and their struggles against adverse circumstances. The narrative culminates in the triumph of an ideal
poetic justice. The characters themselves are lightly sketched,
but love is presented as a transcendent experience. Through
overtly comic figures Shakespeare inserts a light antiromantic
thread. All's Well That Ends Well and Measure for Measure mark
his alienation from romance. He returns to romantic conventions
in the final plays, but the tone is more discursive, evil more
genuine, and the emphasis more sharply on reconciliation.

620   PHIALAS, PETER G. Shakespeare's Romantic Comedies: The
       Development of Their Form and Meaning. Chapel Hill: Univer-
       sity of North Carolina Press, 1966, 314 pp.
       Describes the goal of Shakespeare's romantic comedy as the
achievement of an ideal attitude toward love. To this end characters must overcome not only primarily external obstacles but
also a frustration or opposition to love from within--whether in
the form of utter rejection of it or of an overly romantic or
realistic view of it. Each comedy in its multiple plot strands
juxtaposes divergent attitudes toward love, and the resolution
builds toward a mutually qualifying relationship. The focus is
on the comedies through Twelfth Night.

621   SALINGAR, LEO. Shakespeare and the Traditions of Comedy.
       Cambridge: Cambridge University Press, 1976, 356 pp.
           Notes that Shakespeare's comedy represents a fusion of the
       native tradition--from which come the romantic elements in the
       plots, seasonal association, celebration, new beginnings--and the
       Roman tradition--from which stem his sense of comic irony, the
       trickster and clever servant, the deceptions. His comedies,
       moreover, seem aware of their place in the life of the nation,
       featuring a panorama of the public aspect of the national mon-
       archy in their emphases on aristocratic loyalty, good government,
       and proper education.

622   SEN GUPTA, S.C. Shakespearian Comedy. London: Oxford
       University Press, 1950, 281 pp.
           Traces the development of Shakespeare's comic art from its
       beginnings to its consummation in Falstaff. The genuine excel-
       lence lies in the unity and diversity, the vividness and in-
       comprehensibility, and the logic and inconsistency of the human
       personality. The plot of Love's Labor's Lost, for example, is
       merely the shell for the awakening of repressed emotion in the
       men. The point of Falstaff's exposure is not that he is crushed
       by laughter, but that like human nature he rises to build a new
       castle of comic protection. In the final plays the comedy arises
       from the juxtaposition of realism and fantasy, each forcing the
       other to appear unreal and in a sense comic.

623   SIDER, JOHN W. "The Serious Elements of Shakespeare's Come-
       dies." Shakespeare Quarterly 24 (1973):1-11.
           Traces the development of Shakespeare's use of serious
       material to the culmination of his comic artistry in the romances.
       In the early plays the ridiculous predominates, and mental and
       physical suffering are never taken seriously. In the romantic
       comedies dramatic events serve serious or sentimental purposes.
       In a third group, including The Merchant of Venice, Much Ado
       About Nothing, and the problem comedies, pity and fear are in-
       voked, but they are never carried to a satisfactory conclusion.
       Grave elements in the romances, on the other hand, provoke and
       sustain genuine emotion that in turn produces a more meaningful
       optimism than is implied in either tragedy or light comedy.

624   STEVENSON, DAVID LLOYD. The Love-Game Comedy. New York:
       Columbia University Press, 1946, 259 pp.
           Views Shakespeare's witty lovers as an adaptation and ex-
       tension of the conflicting religious and secular attitudes toward
       love in medieval literature and the Renaissance Petrarchan con-
       ventions. While the study also discusses the origins of the
       controversy and the manner in which writers preceding Shakespeare
       used it, the major focus is on this conflict in Love's Labor's
       Lost, As You Like It, Much Ado About Nothing, and Troilus and
       Cressida. The opposed attitudes are jocular in the first two,
       but grave overtones shadow the merriment in Much Ado and

overwhelm it in Troilus. Shakespeare's plays dramatize and uni-
versalize a conflict that is fundamental to the nature of love
itself.

625   SWINDEN, PATRICK.   Introduction to Shakespeare's Comedies.
      London and Basingstoke: Macmillan, 1973, 188 pp.
          Observes that Shakespearean comedy typically presents a
      medley of separate actions bearing on a central theme.   Unlike
      Jonson's comedy, its intent is not to correct but to endorse a
      sentiment.   In the course of the action, "Villainy and good sense
      manage to neutralise each other, leaving folly to blunder into a
      sort of happiness" (p. 21).   Each of Shakespeare's comedies is
      discussed, and a chapter is devoted to the place of Falstaff in
      Shakespeare's comic development.

626   THOMPSON, KARL M.   "Shakespeare's Romantic Comedies."   PMLA 67
      (1952):1079-93.
          Finds the essence of Shakespeare's romantic comedy in the
      courtly love tradition involving several central characteristics--
      the feudal metaphor of the vassal lover and the lord mistress, the
      religion of love in which a youth must perform noble deeds for
      the good will of a lady fair, the punishment of scoffers at love,
      and the training of such scoffers in a school of love.   Shake-
      speare added two distinct elements, a substitution of the romance
      of marriage for the romance of adultery and a humorous mockery of
      the conventions.   The plays covered in greatest detail are Love's
      Labor's Lost and The Two Gentlemen of Verona, with briefer atten-
      tion to Much Ado About Nothing, As You Like It, and Twelfth Night.

627   TILLYARD, E.M.W.   Shakespeare's Early Comedies.   London:
      Chatto & Windus; New York: Barnes & Noble, 1965, 216 pp.
          Describes Shakespeare's comedy as owing relatively little
      to classical theory.   The range of background materials includes
      medieval romance, folk tales, the Bible, classical narrative
      (especially Ovid), and the Greek romance.   While tragedy involves
      individual man's relation to the sum of things, comedy deals with
      man as a social creature, his relationship to his neighbor or to
      his society.   Individual chapters discuss The Comedy of Errors,
      The Taming of the Shrew, The Two Gentlemen of Verona, Love's
      Labor's Lost, and The Merchant of Venice.   Each play is discussed
      on its own terms with no overriding theme or motif.

628   TOOLE, WILLIAM A.   Shakespeare's Problem Plays: Studies in
      Form and Meaning.   Studies in English Literature, 19.   The
      Hague: Mouton, 1966, 242 pp.
          Argues that Shakespeare's problem plays share a structurally
      implicit Christian framework that he inherited from the mystery
      play and the morality cycle.   In All's Well That Ends Well and
      Measure for Measure the analogy is particularly close with both
      Bertram and Angelo akin to the morality protagonist.   While
      Hamlet is tragic, the implication of an afterlife for the central

figure is clear. In Troilus and Cressida the motif of retribution that comes to men of passion suggests a rational principle
in the universe, a framework central to the Elizabethan world
view.

629   VAUGHAN, JACK A. Shakespeare's Comedies. New York:
       Frederick Ungar, 1980, 249 pp.
           Includes an introductory chapter on comedy in Shakespeare's
       time, followed by individual chapters on each of Shakespeare's
       seventeen comedies. The Comedy of Errors is described as fine
       farce in which characterization is subordinate to the intricacies
       of plot. This comedy is set apart from Shakespeare's other
       comedies of mistaken identity in that only the spectator's level
       of awareness comprehends the multiple confusions. And these
       confusions occur, unlike those in the later comedies, with no
       deceiver, no schemer. The denouement, with the appearance of the
       abbess, is sheer deus ex machina, but the framing device adds
       depth and resonance to the antics.

630   WHEELER, RICHARD P. Shakespeare's Development and the Problem
       Comedies: Turn and Counter-Turn. Berkeley: University of
       California Press, 1981, 229 pp.
           Considers the problem comedies as a profound reorientation
       of Shakespearean comedy from the festive plays to the later stage
       worlds. These plays are marked by psychological conditions cen-
       tral to the tragedies and a preoccupation with the place of
       sexuality in the social order. Helena extends the controlling
       female role of the earlier plays, but here it becomes threaten-
       ing and ambiguous. The tension between the design of All's Well
       and its content is only intensified by the efforts to resolve it.
       Similarly, considering Angelo's sexual degradation, Isabella's
       frigidity, Claudio's fornication, and Vincentio's late-in-the-day
       proposal, the connecting theme in Measure for Measure is a de-
       graded relationship forced to take the stamp of official respec-
       tability--a theme parodied in the relationship of Lucio and Kate
       Keepdown.

631   WILSON, JOHN DOVER. Shakespeare's Happy Comedies. Evanston:
       Northwestern University Press, 1962, 224 pp.
           Notes that the critical neglect of Shakespeare's comedies
       not only has distorted our understanding of Shakespeare's artis-
       tic development but also has impaired our vision of the tragedies
       themselves. Unlike Jonson's, Shakespeare's comedy up to 1601 is
       not critical; his laughter is tolerant and delightful, and the
       clown is never far from the stage. In a word, his comedy is one
       of shared emotions. While each of the comedies through Twelfth
       Night has its distinct personality, they share a foreign setting
       with structured layers on domestic activities in the mercantile
       class and on the love affairs and friendship of the gentry in the
       class above.

For discussion of the comic structure, see entries 593-94, 598, 601, 621, 625. For discussion of the problem comedies, see entries 233, 262, 288, 298, 318, 612, 628, 630. For discussion of the theme of love, see entries 597, 600, 607, 611, 614, 619. See also entries 199, 209, 211, 219, 235, 240, 242, 250, 254, 314, 321, 325.

ALL'S WELL THAT ENDS WELL

Editions

632   HUNTER, G.K., ed. All's Well That Ends Well. The Arden
      Shakespeare. London: Methuen; Cambridge, Mass.: Harvard
      University Press, 1959, 152 pp.
           Includes discussion of the text, the source, critical
      interpretations, and the verse, as well as an appendix featuring
      selections from William Painter's Palace of Pleasure. The text
      is based on the First Folio, for which the copy was probably
      Shakespeare's foul papers. The theory that Love's Labor's Won
      was an earlier version of the play is now generally discounted.
      The ultimate source is "Giletta of Narbona" from Boccaccio's
      Decameron; Shakespeare's additions include the Countess, the
      clown, Lafeu, Parolles, and the subplot. All's Well is infre-
      quently read and acted. In a sense criticism has failed to pro-
      vide a context within which the virtues of the play can be ap-
      preciated. The play juxtaposes extreme romantic conventions with
      pragmatic and realistic ethical situations; every theme or motif
      is surrounded with ambiguities that render simplistic interpreta-
      tions reductionistic. Much of the perversity of interpretation
      is minimized if we view the play as an attempt to interweave the
      serious and the comic in a manner successfully accomplished in
      The Winter's Tale.

633   QUILLER-COUCH, ARTHUR, and WILSON, JOHN DOVER, eds. All's
      Well That Ends Well. Cambridge: Cambridge University Press,
      1929, 202 pp.
           Provides extensive textual notes, a critical introduction,
      a discussion of the copy text, a section on stage history and a
      glossary. This edition is based on the First Folio, for which
      the copy is unsatisfactory, probably a transcript of Shakespeare's
      Jacobean revision of an Elizabethan play. All's Well in style
      and thought is a mixture of Shakespeare's immature and mature
      manner. Parolles is perhaps the inanest of Shakespeare's inven-
      tions; Lavache serves no purpose. The moral dilemma of the play
      centers on Helena; the bed trick is a blot upon his plays.

Criticism

634   ADAMS, JOHN F.   "All's Well That Ends Well: The Paradox of
       Procreation." Shakespeare Quarterly 12 (1961):261-70.
          Suggests that the play's title is not one of comic non-
chalance but a kind of warning that an action can be judged right
or wrong only if it is considered in its entirety and in relation
to its consequences. The theme centers on how one is to know
what constitutes right action in a world of deceitful and duplica-
itous ambiguities. The major themes are the problem of the nature of honor (which becomes synonymous with human worth), the
problem of heritage (the responsibilities of youth to the past),
and the problem of sex and procreation.

635   ARTHOS, JOHN. "The Comedy of Generation." Essays in Criti-
       cism 5 (1955):97-117.
          Argues that comedy means more than the spectator's response
to humorous actions played out on a stage; it refers, as well, to
the enjoyment of a detached intellectual concentration on the
controlling idea of a play. One's enjoyment of the patterned
action of All's Well, with its relation of love to conquest, to
deceit, and to begetting, might be described as the comedy of
generation. The whole of the action focuses on confusion at the
very roots of love, and the conclusion is supported and given
coherence by this mood; we call on comic faith to support our
sympathies and hopes that Helena has achieved happiness.

636   BENNETT, JOSEPHINE WATERS. "New Techniques of Comedy in All's
       Well That Ends Well." Shakespeare Quarterly 18 (1967):337-62.
          Argues that All's Well was composed after Measure for
Measure and that it was consciously based upon the earlier play.
Helena, perhaps the most subtle and intricate female character
Shakespeare ever created, is consistent in her determination to
do anything to satisfy her overwhelming passion. The play incorporates the romantic, the comic, the inexperienced, the mature, the theatrical, and the burlesque. The skillful intermingling is the key to the comic perspective. (See entries 644,
648, 654.)

637   BERGERON, DAVID. "The Mythical Structure of All's Well That
       Ends Well." Texas Studies in Literature and Language 14
       (1972):559-68.
          Sees in All's Well Shakespeare's self-conscious awareness
of the myth involving the legendary struggle between Mars and
Venus. Helena epitomizes Venus's attributes of life and love,
triumphing over Bertram's (Mars's) characteristics of death and
war. Paradoxically Parolles, too, goes forth in the subplot to
fight, bragging that he was born under the sign of Mars. The
mythic structure behind the play is a fertility ritual fundamental to the renewal and re-creation of life.

638   BRADBROOK, MURIEL C. "Virtue Is the True Nobility." Review
       of English Studies, n.s. 1 (1950):289-301.
            Contends that the leading question in All's Well is
       "Wherein lies true honor and nobility?" Whereas Bertram deems
       nobility the consequence of descent or birth, Helena considers
       it to issue from noble deeds. Bertram, in lying and disobedience
       to his mother and his king, squanders any claim to nobility.
       Helena and Parolles are arranged as his good and evil angels, and
       his conversion is a miracle of Helena's true virtue. The charac-
       ters in this latter-day morality assume an extrapersonal signifi-
       cance.

639   CARTER, ALBERT HOWARD. "In Defense of Bertram." Shakespeare
       Quarterly 7 (1956):21-31.
            Observes that, if we see the justice of Bertram's cause,
       All's Well becomes a far more effective and more highly unified
       play. As a developing character in the action, he must grow up
       and gain his independence before he can surrender it. His con-
       flicts with Helena and later with the king arise from immaturity.
       The justice of Bertram's cause also arises from the manner in
       which Helena and others conspire against him. To whitewash
       Helena and darken Bertram (entry 646) is to diminish Shake-
       speare's artistry; Helena is far from a Patient Griselda.

640   COLE, HOWARD C. The "All's Well" Story from Boccaccio to
       Shakespeare. Urbana: University of Illinois Press, 1981,
       145 pp.
            Investigates pre-Shakespearean versions of the All's Well
       story in Boccaccio, an anonymous fifteenth-century French romance,
       Accolti's Italian play, sixteenth-century commentators on
       Boccaccio, and Painter's The Palace of Pleasure. Clearly Shake-
       speare did not inherit a monolithic and simplistic narrative; the
       main traditions had been characterized by wit, irony, cynicism,
       and, above all, intentional ambiguities. The ambiguity of
       Helena's motivation and our consequent inability to ascertain
       the precise nature of her character represents Shakespeare's
       determination to discover "new ways of capturing the old ironies"
       (p. 136).

641   DENNIS, CARL. "All's Well That Ends Well and the Meaning of
       Agape." Philological Quarterly 50 (1971):75-84.
            Views Helena's affection for Bertram as blind devotion to
       a man unworthy of her, as akin to agape in that it is given not
       in the expectation of reciprocation but in obedience to God's
       command. Bertram is depicted as totally unsympathetic until the
       very conclusion in order to emphasize the unconditional nature of
       this love. Agape stimulates moral growth in the recipient by
       encouraging a person to perceive his best self, and there is
       evidence in the final scene that such a change is occurring in
       Bertram.

642   HAPGOOD, ROBERT M.   "The Life of Shame: Parolles and All's
      Well." Essays in Criticism 15 (1965):269-78.
           Compares Parolles to Falstaff in his sheer zest for life
      and his unabashed acceptance of shame if necessary for life's
      continuance. His name suggests both word and verbal pledge, and
      indeed verbosity and empty promises bring him to his impasse.
      Other characters in the play also choose life before honor.
      Bertram, Helena, the King, and Diana all risk honor for life and
      love. If the result is not always "all's well" in the study, it
      is surely so in the theater where the sense of "felt life" pre-
      vails. (See entry 643.)

643   HUSTON, J. DENNIS.   "'Some Stain of Soldier': The Function of
      Parolles in All's Well That Ends Well." Shakespeare Quarterly
      21 (1970):431-38.
           Considers Parolles a curious combination of the corrupt and
      the commendable. If he is vain, deceitful, and foolish, he is
      also possessed of a tremendous energy that infuses his world with
      dramatic life. When he comes on stage, the world is heavy with
      the atmosphere of death and decay. At his suggestion Bertram
      pursues his honor on the field of battle, and at his suggestion
      Helena pursues her honor in the form of union with Bertram. (See
      entry 642.)

644   KING, WALTER N.   "Shakespeare's Mingled Yarn." Modern
      Language Quarterly 21 (1960):33-44.
           Notes that critics who labor to explain away the moral and
      aesthetic lapses of All's Well ignore the possibility that Shake-
      speare is intending to depict individuals as they behave incon-
      sistently in life as opposed to the way they behave consistently
      in traditional romantic story. The play may well be a psycho-
      logical study of the responses of Helena, Bertram, the King, the
      Countess, and Lafeu to a love problem that forces to the surface
      the wavering balance between vice and virtue in ordinary human
      nature. (See entries 636, 648, 654.)

645   LAGUARDIA, ERIC.   "Chastity, Regeneration, and World Order in
      All's Well That Ends Well." In Myth and Symbol: Critical
      Approaches and Applications. Edited by Bernice Slote.
      Lincoln: University of Nebraska Press, 1963, pp. 119-32.
           Observes that the play, in its movement from Bertram's
      unregenerate to regenerate condition, reflects the Renaissance
      interest in the idea of nature's renewal and man's worldly per-
      fectibility. Helena suggests a purity related to the divine
      world beyond nature; similarly, Parolles reveals a passionate
      nature, corrupted and imperfect. Helena is a redemptive force,
      and the play symbolically depicts in the reconciliation of the
      conflict of passion and purity in Bertram an image of the
      concordia mundi.

646   LAWRENCE, WILLIAM W.   "The Meaning of All's Well That Ends
        Well." PMLA 37 (1922):418-69.
             Cautions that we must temper our distaste for All's Well
        by attempting to understand how it was received in Shakespeare's
        day. Helena was meant to be wholly noble and heroic, fully
        justified in her actions; and Bertram's sudden conversion would
        have been accepted as a convention of medieval and Elizabethan
        storytelling. Traces the clever-wench story through numerous
        analogues to demonstrate the literary context in which Shake-
        speare worked and in which, while he was free to alter detail
        and emphasis, he was not free to change the basic direction and
        resolution.

647   LEECH, CLIFFORD.   "The Theme of Ambition in All's Well That
        Ends Well." ELH 21 (1954):17-29. Reprinted in Discussions
        of Shakespeare's Problem Comedies, ed. Robert Ornstein
        (Boston: D.C. Heath, 1961), pp. 56-63.
             Observes that each of the problem plays, establishing at-
        titudes strangely at variance with traditional values, lacks
        emplastic power or a sense of fusion. Such a juxtaposition in
        All's Well is Helena's love for Bertram and her raw ambition.
        Together with old characters rebuking the young and sighing at
        the state of corruption is a young woman who loves a man but who
        is also determined to bring him to heel. As a result the spec-
        tator is forced to observer her analytically, and this ambiva-
        lence reflects the conception of love at once as grandly noble
        and as a sickness needing to be cured.

648   LEGGATT, ALEXANDER.   "All's Well That Ends Well: The Testing
        of Romance." Modern Language Quarterly 32 (1971):21-41.
             Proposes that two dramatic modes, romance and realism, are
        juxtaposed in such a manner that they test each other. The ten-
        sion is genuine and the ending uncertain. The older aristocrats,
        Bertram, and Parolles are from a real and fallen world. Helena,
        as the upholder of romance, cures the king; but realism intrudes
        when Bertram refuses to marry her. She, in turn, pursues and
        wins him on his own terms, and romance seems victorious in the
        end. His qualified acceptance, however, leaves the issue in
        doubt and reflects the continuing tensions between the two
        generic forms. (See entries 636, 644, 654.)

649   LOVE, JOHN.   "'Though Many of the Rich Are Damn'd': Dark
        Comedy and Social Class in All's Well That Ends Well." Texas
        Studies in Literature and Language 18 (1977):517-27.
             Views the barrier of social class as the source of darkness
        in the play. Bertram, both when told to take Helena's hand and
        in the final moments of the play, presumes upon rank to shelter
        him from the consequences of his actions, denigrating Helena,
        Diana, and Parolles. Helena may be virtuous, but she acts from
        a position of social inferiority. Because of this pervasive

sense of class and its assumptions of a double standard, the play
is a mockery of reconciliation, repentance, and forgiveness.

650   MAXWELL, J.C. "Helena's Pilgrimage." Review of English
      Studies, n.s. 20 (1969):189-93.
           Believes that Helena, whatever her original intentions,
      never journeys to the shrine of St. Jacques, that she arrives in
      Florence by design, and that she is directly responsible for the
      report of her death by the rector of the shrine. Once the spec-
      tator or reader has a suspicion regarding Helena's motives, his
      imagination becomes a significant supplement to the plot struc-
      ture of the play.

651   NAGARAJAN, S. "The Structure of All's Well That Ends Well."
      Essays in Criticism 10 (1960):24-31.
           Argues that the love interest is the central focus, that
      the play follows the progress of a very young man who, subject to
      the base diversionary influence of Parolles, must come of age and
      accept the responsibilities of love and marriage. By refusing to
      consummate his marriage with Helena, Bertram makes the sexual act
      a symbol of marriage's meaning; and this meaning will be trivial-
      ized if he is allowed to engage in sex with Diana. Helena uses
      the bed trick both to preserve the honor of the sexual act and
      to shock Bertram into recognizing its value as well.

652   PARKER, R.B. "War and Sex in All's Well That Ends Well."
      Shakespeare Survey 37 (1984):99-113.
           Maintains that the play is built upon the concept of mascu-
      line honor in war and feminine honor in love and that the rela-
      tionship wryly forces the abandonment of the purity of both
      ideals. As Bertram must learn to accept sexual love and its
      responsibilities, Helena must learn to abandon self-abnegation
      in love and bring it to fruition through deliberate aggression.
      These lessons learned, Bertram and Helena return to Roussillon
      to confirm and rejuvenate family and state; but the tone of the
      end is not without the shadow of uncertainty.

653   PRICE, JOSEPH G. The Unfortunate Comedy: A Study of "All's
      Well That Ends Well." Toronto: University of Toronto Press,
      1968, 197 pp.
           Reviews the stage history and surveys the criticism from
      the seventeenth century to the twentieth. Whereas English
      Romantic criticism blossomed into a panegyric for Helena, fantasy
      gave way to tragicomedy in the interpretations of the mid-
      nineteenth century. From the turn of the present century criti-
      cism generally condemned the play as a failure, whether the con-
      sequence of inconsistency of characterization, of demands upon
      the audience, or of the incapability of the author. Critics of
      the midcentury engaged in a gradual reappraisal, balancing weak-
      nesses and merits with concepts of dark or satiric comedy, of
      high and serious romance, and of consistency of Shakespearean

theme. All's Well is a play of many but not incongruous elements. The most successful production or critical analysis will
exploit the diversity (the comic, the serious, the satiric)
rather than attempting to force the play into a single mood.

654   SHAPIRO, MICHAEL. "'The Web of Our Life': Human Frailty and
      Moral Redemption in All's Well That Ends Well." Journal of
      English and Germanic Philology 71 (1972):514-26.
            Views romantic love as the redemptive force that untangles
      the mingled yarn of life in the play. Both Bertram and Helena
      seek distinction, and the efforts of self-assertion produce
      disaster in both cases. The climax comes in 5.3 when Bertram
      begs forgiveness from a humble and contrite Helena. He implic-
      itly forgives her attempt to claim her love by a kind of force,
      and she forgives him for his obstinate perversity. While Helena
      is responsible for his redemption, he is also the agent of hers.
      (See entries 636, 644, 648.)

655   TURNER, ROBERT Y. "Dramatic Conventions in All's Well That
      Ends Well." PMLA 75 (1960):497-502.
            Describes All's Well as more of an age than for all time
      because in it Shakespeare adheres so closely to Elizabethan
      dramatic conventions. Shakespeare was adapting his material to
      the fashionable pattern of the prodigal son plays in which a hero
      undergoes a change of character preparing him, not for salvation,
      but for marriage. These plays do not normally test the heroine;
      All's Well is the only instance of a woman's being of lower
      social rank than the hero. Relating the play to terms of liter-
      ary scholarship rather than of psychological consistency demon-
      strates that it is a failure of one kind but not of another.

656   WARREN, ROGER. "Why Does It End Well? Helena, Bertram, and
      the Sonnets." Shakespeare Survey 22 (1969):79-92.
            Suggests that the relationship between Bertram and Helena
      reflects Shakespeare's personal relationship with the "friend"
      chronicled in many of the sonnets. Perhaps the saddest aspect is
      the sense of an inseparable difference in rank (especially son-
      net 26) and the probability that Shakespeare himself had to en-
      dure and forgive slights and insults. While Shakespeare provides
      no reassuring speech for Helena at the conclusion, it is likely
      that he considered that her single-minded love assures that all
      ends well.

657   WILSON, HAROLD S. "Dramatic Emphasis in All's Well That Ends
      Well." Huntington Library Quarterly 13 (1950):222-40. Re-
      printed in Discussion of Shakespeare's Problem Comedies, ed.
      Robert Ornstein (Boston: D.C. Heath, 1961), pp. 45-55.
            Argues that, for a modern audience unbiased by critical
      stricture, the play is skillfully contrived to render Helena
      appealing, Bertram's repentance credible, and the reconciliation
      of Bertram and Helena plausible. Shakespeare in making Helena

more appealing at the outset than Boccaccio runs the risk of her appearing conniving in the last half. Comic emphasis on the corruption of Parolles and on Bertram's recognizing his true nature, however, prepares the young count for his conversion and maintains the spectator's sympathy for Helena.

For discussion of the allegory, see entries 637-38, 641, 645. For discussion of the character of Helena, see entries 639-40, 646, 650, 657. See also The Comedies (entries 591-631) and 101, 144, 213, 221, 239, 254, 262, 278, 288, 318, 610-12, 619, 628, 630.

AS YOU LIKE IT

Reference Works

658   HALIO, JAY L., and MILLARD, BARBARA C., comps. "As You Like It": An Annotated Bibliography, 1940-1980. Garland Shake-speare Bibliographies, 8. New York and London: Garland Publishing, 1985, 744 pp.
        Contains 1,584 entries representing virtually all publica-tions on the play from 1940 through 1980, along with the most significant items prior to 1940. The categories, each arranged chronologically, are criticism, sources and background, dating, textual studies, texts and editions, translations, stage history, influence, and bibliographies. A brief introductory essay traces the history of recent criticism and research.

659   MARDER, LOUIS, comp. "As You Like It": A Supplementary Bibliography 1890-1965. The New Variorum Shakespeare. New York: American Scholar Publications, 1965, 19 pp.
        Includes representative scholarship on As You Like It from 1890 to 1965 and is intended to supplement H.H. Furness's Vario-rum edition of 1890. The material is categorized under biblio-graphical sources, modern editions, and critical studies (alpha-betically arranged). While not exhaustive, the material repre-sents every major category of scholarship and criticism.

Editions

660   KNOWLES, RICHARD, ed. As You Like It. A New Variorum Edition of Shakespeare. New York: Modern Language Association of America, 1977, 737 pp.
        Uses the First Folio (1623) as the copy text (pp. 9-303). On each page, for that portion of the text, provides variant readings, textual notes, and general critical commentary. Fol-lowing the text are sections on the nature of the text (press variants, the copy for the First Folio, the integrity of the text, theories of later revision, the staying entry of 4 August 1600), the date of composition, the sources--Lodge's Rosalynde, Gamelyn--a survey of criticism prepared by Evelyn Joseph Mattern

(the play as a whole, the tone, the technique, the characters,
the stage history, the music), and a bibliography.

661   LATHAM, AGNES, ed. As You Like It. The Arden Shakespeare.
      London: Methuen; Cambridge, Mass.: Harvard University Press,
      1975, 135 pp.
          Includes discussion of the text, date, sources, critical
      interpretations, and stage history. The text is based on the
      First Folio, for which the copy was probably good prompt material
      transcribed for the press. The play is distinguished by a high
      proportion of prose, and the blank verse reflects considerable
      metrical freedom. Featuring more songs than any other Shake-
      spearean play, As You Like It evokes a carefree mood and conjures
      up a woodland even on a bare stage. The date of composition was
      probably early 1599, and the primary source is Thomas Lodge's
      Rosalynde. The play endorses the values of romantic love through
      an agreeable exploitation of incongruities, whether through the
      contrast between Arden and the court or between the pragmatic
      fool Touchstone and the melancholy Jacques with the romantic
      lover Orlando.

662   QUILLER-COUCH, ARTHUR, and WILSON, JOHN DOVER, eds. As You
      Like It. Cambridge: Cambridge University Press, 1926, 181 pp.
          Provides extensive textual notes, a critical introduction,
      a discussion of the copy text, and a section on the stage his-
      tory. There is a staying or blocking entry in the Stationers'
      Register on 4 August 1600; the only publication is that of the
      First Folio, and this text—apparently based on the promptbook—
      serves as copy for this edition. The play probably represents
      two strata, the second involving extensive revision of material
      composed around 1593. Central to this play and to Shakespearean
      comedy in general is the woodland experience. Touchstone and
      Jaques are deliberately opposed commentators on the romantic
      transformations that occur in Arden.

Criticism

663   BARBER, C.L. "The Use of Comedy in As You Like It."
      Philological Quarterly 21 (1942):353-67. Reprinted in
      Shakespeare's Comedies, ed. Laurence Lerner (Baltimore:
      Penguin, 1967), pp. 227-44.
          Perceives Shakespeare's method as the interweaving of a
      serious theme (pastoral innocence, romantic love) with a layer of
      mocking accompaniment. The opposite of satire, which presents
      life and then ridicules its failures, Shakespeare presents ideal
      life and then mocks its shortcomings. Jaques and Touchstone are
      the principal figures in this comic machinery, which serves to
      reconcile the spectators to reality without cynicism or senti-
      mentality.

664   BARNET, SYLVAN. "'Strange Events': Improbability in As You
      Like It." Shakespeare Studies 4 (1968):119-31.
         Believes that Shakespeare intentionally heightens the
      improbabilities at the end--the personality changes of Frederick
      and Oliver, the quickly established love relationships of Oliver
      and Celia and of Orlando and Rosalind. This interest in improba-
      bility for its own sake is a tenet of comedy, and to achieve this
      tone Shakespeare consciously departs from the carefully articu-
      lated motivation in his source, Lodge's Rosalynde. There is a
      return to the court at the end, but the characters, strangely
      transformed, will never be the same.

665   BENNETT, JOSEPHINE WATERS. "Jaques' Seven Ages." Shakespeare
      Association Bulletin 18 (1943):168-74.
         Surveys the various attempts to find a source for Jaques's
      speech on the seven ages of man, noting that Shakespeare's
      account has little in common with medical and astrological con-
      vention, that he is satirically concerned with appearance and
      behavior. Not improbably Shakespeare had in mind Palengenius's
      Zodiacus Vitae, which describes the futility and folly of human
      life and places the idea of five ages in the context of life as
      a pageant. An associated source treating of seven ages and re-
      vealing numerous verbal parallels is the Onomasticon of Julius
      Pollux. (See entries 668, 675.)

666   BRACHER, MARK. "Contrary Notions of Identity in As You Like
      It." Studies in English Literature 24 (1984):225-40.
         Notes that, of the two types of comedy, one emphasizes the
      blocking figure, exclusivity, and the satiric tone while the
      other emphasizes discovery and reconciliation, inclusivity, and
      the romantic tone. As You Like It depicts two such comic types--
      the inclusive (Celia, Rosalind) and the exclusive (Oliver, Duke
      Frederick)--gradually leading the audience toward full acceptance
      of the inclusive self. On another plane the play juxtaposes two
      types of comedy, the romantic and the satiric. The satiric
      vision is contrary to Shakespeare's both because it denies the
      ultimate value of love and because it reinforces the attitude of
      exclusivity. (See entries 670-71.)

667   CIRILLO, ALBERT R. "As You Like It: Pastoralism Gone Awry."
      ELH 38 (1971):19-39.
         Suggests that, while the Forest of Arden is a pastoral
      retreat from life at court, the ideal must be tempered and in
      turn inform the world of the actual. Rejecting through irony
      the naive belief that the pastoral fiction is attainable in
      life, Shakespeare depicts Arden as able to correct the real
      world's problems involving young lovers and filial relationships.
      It is through Rosalind that the spectators come to realize the
      balance that must be established between ideal and actual.

668   FINK, Z.S. "Jaques and the Malcontent Traveller." Philo-
      logical Quarterly 14 (1935):237-52.
           States that Jaques is Shakespeare's delineation of the
      contemporary figure of a foreign traveller, something of the
      terrible Italianated Englishman of the 1560s who occasioned
      Ascham's diatribe in The Schoolmaster. His head filled with
      wrong notions and corrupted by licentious life, he dressed
      fashionably in black and was voguishly melancholy. In Jaques
      Shakespeare portrays such a traveller who rails against the world
      in melancholic guise, but he on a few occasions also deepens the
      figure into one who is not without sympathy in his disillusion-
      ment. (See entries 665, 675.)

669   GARDNER, HELEN. "As You Like It." In More Talking of Shake-
      speare. Edited by John Garrett. London: Longmans, Green;
      New York: Theatre Arts Books, 1959, pp. 17-32. Reprinted in
      Discussion of Shakespeare's Problem Comedies, ed. Robert
      Ornstein (Boston: D.C. Heath, 1966), pp. 52-66.
           Views As You Like It as a play to please all tastes with
      its romance, débat, pastoral, and burlesque. Idealizing life's
      possibilities by means of fantasy, Arden is juxtaposed to a
      corrupt court ruled by a tyrant. Yet, even the forest is a
      variable place, where one can find love or learn a bitter lesson.
      In the ultimate reconciliations only Jacques opts out of the
      human condition. The imagery suggests that possibly Shakespeare
      intends to depict the Christian ideal of loving kindness, gentle-
      ness, pity, and humanity.

670   HALIO, JAY. "'No Clock in the Forest': Time in As You Like
      It." Studies in English Literature 2 (1962):197-207. Re-
      printed in Twentieth Century Interpretations of "As You Like
      It," ed. Jay L. Halio, Twentieth Century Interpretations
      (Englewood Cliffs: Prentice-Hall, 1968), pp. 88-97.
           Believes that Shakespeare exploits timelessness in Arden by
      juxtaposing it to the time consciousness of the court and city.
      Orlando, fleeing from his tyrannical brother, becomes enamoured
      of the freedom of the forest; but he finds it to be a school in
      which he and others are prepared to discover their best selves by
      Rosalind, the agent for synthesizing the values of both worlds.
      The sense of timelessness in Arden links it with the sense of
      graciousness in the past that can serve to help regenerate a
      corrupt present. (See entries 666, 671.)

671   JENKINS, HAROLD. "As You Like It." Shakespeare Survey 8
      (1955):40-51. Reprinted in Shakespeare: Modern Essays in
      Criticism, ed. Leonard F. Dean, rev. ed. (New York: Oxford
      University Press, 1967), pp. 114-33.
           Views the structure of the play as basically a juxtaposi-
      tion of the golden with the real world, of the simple life with
      brittle refinements of the court. Each side, however, has its
      own dialectic. Of the immigrants to Arden, Rosalind, Orlando,

Duke Senior, and Amiens praise the life of the green world, but
Touchstone and Jaques humorously mock. Similarly, among the
natives, Sylvius, Phoebe, and William may be poetic rustics, but
Corin is a shepherd with rough and greasy hands. The constantly
shifting valuations, with reality dissolving illusions but ideals
ever newly creating, results in an all-embracing view of life
richer and more satisfying than any fragmented perspective. (See
entries 666, 670.)

672   KREIDER, P.V. "Genial Literary Satire in the Forest of Arden."
      Shakespeare Association Bulletin 10 (1935):212-31.
          Observes that As You Like It freely satirizes its own
      generic conventions--the unrealistic pastoral atmosphere through
      William and Audrey, the highly poetic language through Touchstone
      among others, the excessive sentimentality through Rosalind's
      mockery of Orlando, and the conventional happy ending through
      Jaques's observation that, with so many couples pairing off,
      there must surely be the imminent threat of another flood. The
      play is a lightly satiric view of romantic comedy, provoking
      laughter even while it engages emotionally.

673   MINCOFF, MARCO. "What Shakespeare Did to Rosalynde."
      Shakespeare Jahrbuch (Weimar) 96 (1960):78-89. Reprinted in
      Twentieth Century Interpretations of "As You Like It," ed.
      Jay L. Halio, Twentieth Century Interpretations (Englewood
      Cliffs: Prentice-Hall, 1968), pp. 98-106.
          Argues that critics overly stress pastoralism in As You
      Like It. Indeed, the pastoral tone is muted considerably from
      that in Lodge's prose romance. Shakespeare's concern is pri-
      marily to achieve a harmonious fusion of two themes--love's
      foolishness and the clash between appearance and reality. The
      concern for balance is evident in his simultaneous development
      of the love affairs of his several couples whereas in Rosalynde
      the romantic liaisons constitute separate and distinct portions
      of the narrative.

674   PALMER, D.J. "As You Like It and the Idea of Play."
      Critical Quarterly 13 (1971):234-41.
          Observes that the minimal plot in the play is merely
      enough to move characters in and out of the Forest of Arden.
      Once in Arden the characters engage in a world of play reflecting
      the impulse to create a better world and the releasing of ener-
      gies held in check by the real world. The game between Orlando
      and Rosalind is only the most significant of several activities
      and interrelationships designed to provoke self-awareness in
      preparation for encountering with resilience the challenges that
      lie outside the forest. Jaques and Touchstone are complementary
      figures, the one transparently foolish and the other wise in
      fooling.

675   SERONSY, CECIL C. "The Seven Ages of Man Again." Shakespeare
        Quarterly 4 (1953):364-65.
          Suggests Thomas Lodge's A Margarite of America as the
     source for Jaques's speech about the seven ages of man. This
     material consistently presents man in a ridiculous and painful
     condition, and it is precisely the indecorum at every stage that
     characterizes Jaques's speech. The fact that Lodge's Rosalynde
     is the principal source for As You Like It strengthens the pos-
     sibility that Shakespeare may also have used a second novel for
     smaller design. (See entries 665, 668.)

676   SHAW, JOHN. "Fortune and Nature in As You Like It." Shake-
        speare Quarterly 6 (1955):45-50.
          Observes that behind the lighthearted actions of the play
     exists a fundamental philosophic strife between Nature and
     Fortune that members of the Renaissance audience would quickly
     recognize. The rivalry is broached in Rosalind's witty repartee
     in act 1, epitomizing the situation in which Fortune's benefits
     have gone awry with Duke Senior and Orlando (and shortly will go
     awry with Rosalind). Bearing their situation with patience and
     wisdom, they will receive their just reward at the end of the
     play. Comments throughout the play as well as the pastoral
     setting emphasize the struggle and the ultimate power of Nature
     to counter Fortune's mischief.

677   SMITH, JAMES H. "As You Like It." Scrutiny 9 (1940-41):9-32.
          Suggests that both Shakespeare's comedies and tragedies
     address the same problems, the comedies less seriously in that
     the problems are not forced to an issue. As You Like It, more
     precisely, is essentially unromantic; Jaques's melancholy, based
     on a skepticism arguing that no experience is worth having,
     prompts him at the end to opt for a monastery instead of the
     world; Silvius and Phoebe darkly shadow the love of Orlando and
     Rosalind; and Corin proves by his very existence the harshness
     of a shepherd's life. The motifs of danger and evil that, though
     muted, give depth to Shakespearean comedy, are merely brought to
     center stage in the tragedies.

678   STAEBLER, WARREN. "Shakespeare's Play of Atonement."
        Shakespeare Association Bulletin 24 (1949):91-105.
          Calls As You Like It a play of felicity, not because it is
     marked by rapture or lovers' ecstasy, but because of an even-
     handed serenity resulting from a steady attitude toward life.
     The principal characters are at one with themselves and with each
     other--Celia and Rosalind, Adam and Orlando, Jaques and Duke
     Senior. Orlando, despite the wrongdoings he has endured, has no
     malice for the world. The world of nature acts further to har-
     monize all who enter it. As You Like It is the most down to
     earth of Shakespeare's comedies, free of preciosity, fantasy,
     barbed wit, cruelty, and magic.

679   TOLMAN, ALBERT H. "Shakespeare's Manipulation of His Sources
       in As You Like It." MLN 37 (1922):65-76.
           Explores Shakespeare's alterations of Lodge's Rosalynde in
       the composition of As You Like It. Aside from sharply compress-
       ing time, Shakespeare also focuses on one specific quarrel and
       its results between Orlando and his brother rather than three.
       He tightens another element of plot by making brothers of Duke
       Frederick and Duke Senior, in Lodge unrelated figures. Celia
       herself determines to accompany Rosalind into exile whereas she
       too is banished in Lodge's version. The subplot characters are
       original with Shakespeare. Such general transformation of mate-
       rial is a mark of Shakespeare's genius.

Stage History

680   SHATTUCK, CHARLES H. Mr. Macready Produces "As You Like It":
       A Prompt-Book Study. Urbana: Beta Phi Mu Chapbook Series,
       1962, 105 pp.
           Aims to provide in facsimile a significant specimen of a
       mid-nineteenth century promptbook of a Shakespearean play. As
       You Like It, transcribed by the stage manager George Ellis for
       the instruction of a young actor, Hermann Vezin, is significant
       both by virtue of its completeness of record and of its being
       Macready's restoration of Shakespeare's text. It also reflects
       his continuing struggle to practice reasonable restraint in the
       face of the lavish stage designs of Charles Kean. The version
       contains 2,458 lines (cutting only 387), and the playing time
       was two hours forty-nine minutes.

See also The Comedies (entries 591-631) and 160, 205, 239, 247, 250,
331, 333, 893, 1411.

THE COMEDY Of ERRORS

Editions

681   FOAKES, R.A., ed. The Comedy of Errors. The Arden Shake-
       speare. London: Methuen; Cambridge, Mass.: Harvard Univer-
       sity Press, 1962, 117 pp.
           Includes discussion of the text, the date of composition,
       sources, staging, stage history, and literary interpretations,
       as well as an appendix on the Gray's Inn performance in 1594.
       The text is based on the First Folio, for which the copy was
       probably Shakespeare's foul papers. In the manner of indicating
       localities, Errors is unique among Shakespeare's plays, preserv-
       ing a unity both of time and place and requiring only four play-
       ing areas. Any legitimate interpretation must skirt the dangers
       of making too much of the play (as more than farce) or too little
       (in comparison with the mature comedies). There is embryonic
       tragedy in Egeon, but overdoing it produces a killing solemnity.

Underlying the dexterity of plot is the theme of loss or change
of identity, the disruption of family, personal, and social
relationships. One is not likely to miss, however, the farce,
the clever exploitation of mistakes, of repartee, and talk at
cross purposes.

682   QUILLER-COUCH, ARTHUR, and WILSON, JOHN DOVER, eds. The
      Comedy of Errors. Cambridge: Cambridge University Press,
      1922, 127 pp.
         Provides extensive textual notes, a discussion of the copy
      text, a critical introduction, a section on stage history, and a
      glossary. The copy text is the First Folio, printed from an
      exceptionally clean composite copy in two hands, the second hav-
      ing reviewed the entire manuscript filling in stage directions
      and touching up speech headings. Shakespeare's propensity for
      fusing romance and farce is noted even at this early stage.

Criticism

683   ARTHOS, JOHN. "Shakespeare's Transformation of Plautus."
      Comparative Drama 1 (1967):239-53.
         Notes that Shakespeare in The Comedy of Errors warmly en-
      riches the Roman stage world. Whereas Plautus depicts a man's
      world in which everyone's attempt to outwit another issues in
      rough humor and physical byplay, Shakespeare's world is that of a
      more highly organized social hierarchy, and women and the roman-
      tic experience emerge as significant elements. The reunion at
      all levels at the conclusion (parents, sons and proper mates,
      servants) humanizes the material and lends it greater depth.

684   BALDWIN, THOMAS WHITFIELD. On The Compositional Genetics of
      "The Comedy of Errors." Urbana: University of Illinois Press,
      1965, 422 pp.
         Reconstructs and describes the process by which Shakespeare
      must have composed The Comedy of Errors. As Stratford sheep be-
      come London sheep, Shakespeare like the twin Dromios finds him-
      self much confused by the witchery of Ephesus-London. The polit-
      ical relations between Syracuse and Ephesus reflect those of
      England and Spain, and the setting of the play is demonstrably
      Hollywell Priory, where near the Theatre two priests had expe-
      rienced what for Egeon is only threatened. Blended with these
      local elements is Plautus's plot, subjected to the Erasmanian
      rhetorical device of analysis and synthesis and the additions of
      parody and doubling, and set within the obligatory five-act
      system.

685   _____. William Shakespeare Adapts a Hanging. Princeton:
      Princeton University Press, 1931, 202 pp.
         Argues that Shakespeare transmuted in The Comedy of Errors
      impressions from his witnessing the execution of William Hartley,
      a seminary priest, in Finnsbury Fields on 5 October 1588. In

depicting a priory or abbey ruled over by a lady abbess with the
gate of the priory opening into a street that leads, behind the
ditches of the abbey, to a place of execution, Shakespeare is
shadowing the reality of his firsthand knowledge of Hollywell
Priory. Such identification with place and event both give a
glimpse into his creative method and aid in dating one of his
earliest plays.

686   BARBER, C.L. "Shakespearian Comedy in The Comedy of Errors."
      College English 25 (1964):493-97.
          Describes The Comedy of Errors as a dazzling display of
      dramatic control in the manipulation of characters whose lan-
      guage, albeit sometimes tedious, exhibits genuine verbal energy.
      Shakespeare feeds Elizabethan life into the Plautine farce,
      forcing it to reveal universal traits of human character, espe-
      cially those arising from the tugs of marriage. The play, also,
      is filled with routine details of daily life. Shakespeare's
      sense of comedy as a moment in a large cycle leads him to frame
      the farce within action involving age and the threat of death.

687   BROOKS, C. "Shakespeare's Romantic Shrews." Shakespeare
      Quarterly 11 (1960):351-56.
          Notes that, whereas traditional literary shrews are gen-
      erally fools and monsters, Shakespeare's shrews (Adriana, Kate)
      are more humanly sketched as women unsure of their own hearts.
      Adriana, for example, has the will and the intelligence we admire
      in Shakespeare's heroines; she merely must learn to control these
      qualities more effectively. Both she and Kate in the course of
      the action come to realize that psychologically they have a need
      to submit, as a balance to their will to dominate.

688   COULTER, CORNELIA A. "The Plautine Tradition in Shakespeare."
      Journal of English and Germanic Philology 19 (1920):66-83.
          Concerns the influence of Plautus and Terence on English
      drama in general and on Shakespeare in particular. The "Plautine
      tradition" reached Shakespeare through both the classical revival
      itself and through German education drama. Specifically, the
      influence is seen in the stage setting of a street and three
      houses and the use of a prologue, in plot elements and plot
      motifs such as mistaken identity, in stock characters such as the
      clown servant and the amorous young man and the braggart soldier,
      and in stage devices such as horseplay and satiric asides. While
      Plautine elements are found throughout Shakespeare's work, they
      are especially noticeable in The Comedy of Errors.

689   ELLIOTT, G.R. "Weirdness in The Comedy of Errors."
      University of Toronto Quarterly 9 (1939):95-106. Reprinted
      in Shakespeare's Comedies, ed. Laurence Lerner (New York:
      Oxford University Press, 1967), pp. 19-31.
          Maintains that the success of The Comedy of Errors is due
      to a combination of excellent structure and a plot in which

comedy is tinged with horror, the fear of the loss of identity.
The romantic affair of Antipholus of Ephesus and Adriana is
saturated with fun that is swift, strange, and weird as
Antipholus of Syracuse becomes enchanted by Luciana even while
claimed by his "wife" and as the activities of Nell and Dromio
of Syracuse create a parodic parallel action. These antics,
characterized by farce bordering on terror, are humanized by the
pathos of old Egeon at the beginning, middle, and end.

690   GRENNAN, EAMON. "Arm and Sleeve: Nature and Custom in The
      Comedy of Errors." Philological Quarterly 59 (1980):150-64.
           Examines the dialectic of nature and custom that informs
      The Comedy of Errors and points forward to a continuing concern
      throughout Shakespeare's career. Luciana, for example, when
      pacifying her incensed sister, describes the traditional rela-
      tionship of the superior husband and the dutifully obedient wife;
      later, however, when lecturing the person she assumes to be
      Adriana's husband, she describes marriage as something that must
      be kept socially decorous at all costs. This disparity between
      reality and appearance is central to every situation in the play.

691   PARKER, PATRICIA. "Elder and Younger: The Opening Scene of
      The Comedy of Errors." Shakespeare Quarterly 34 (1983):
      325-27.
           Notes that Egeon's references in the opening scene to the
      positioning of the elder and younger sons, with each parent when
      the ship splits then being severed from the child he or she has
      been most careful for, is not a slip on Shakespeare's part and is
      significant to the structure of the entire play. The references
      echo the sibling rivalry between Jacob and Esau and make theatri-
      cally appropriate the conversation at the end between the Dromio
      twins as to who shall go through the door first and their deci-
      sion to walk through together hand in hand.

692   SANDERSON, JAMES L. "Patience in The Comedy of Errors. Texas
      Studies in Literature and Language 16 (1974-75):603-18.
           Notes that The Comedy of Errors, like Shakespeare's later
      comedies, embodies a sense of ignorance of death that gives way
      to a resolution projecting a renewal of life. More importantly,
      it sets forth the theme of patience, a motif upon which Shake-
      speare elaborates in a number of his later and greatest plays.
      The "errors" arise from individuals whose impotence in the face
      of frustrating circumstances generate activities that deepen
      their confusion and multiply the misconceptions. Patience is
      counseled both literally and figuratively throughout the play,
      and only its cultivation provides the means by which the errors
      can be resolved.

693   WILLIAMS, GWYN. "The Comedy of Errors Rescued From Tragedy."
      Review of English Literature 5, no. 4 (1964):63-71.
          Concentrates on the thin borderline between comedy and
      tragedy in The Comedy of Errors. Shakespeare's reason for dupli-
      cating Dromio was not merely to enhance the laughter but to save
      the play as comedy. The interaction of two Dromios not only pro-
      vides farce; it also prevents either the apprehension of the one
      Antipholus or the violent temper of the other from becoming dom-
      inant. For the masters the confusion of identity is painful and
      potentially dangerous, as it also is for Egeon. The servants tip
      the balance toward humor.

See also The Comedies (entries 591-631) and 88, 141, 215, 219, 229,
237, 246, 304, 808, 819.

LOVE'S LABOR'S LOST

                        Reference Works

694   HARVEY, NANCY LENZ, and CAREY, ANNA KIRWAN, comps. "Love's
      Labor's Lost": An Annotated Bibliography. Garland Shakespeare
      Bibliographies, 6. New York and London: Garland Publishing,
      1984, 220 pp.
          Contains 510 entries representing virtually all publica-
      tions on the play from 1940 through 1982 along with the most
      significant items of scholarship prior to 1940. The categories,
      each arranged chronologically, are divided into criticism,
      sources, dating, textual studies, bibliographies and concordances,
      editions, stage history and recordings, and adaptations and syn-
      opses. A brief introductory essay traces the history of recent
      criticism and research.

695   MARDER, LOUIS, comp. "Love's Labor's Lost": A Supplementary
      Bibliography 1904-1965. The New Variorum Shakespeare. New
      York: American Scholar Publications, 1965, 19 pp.
          Includes representative scholarship on Love's Labor's Lost
      from 1904 to 1965 and is intended to supplement H.H. Furness's
      Variorum edition of 1904 (see entry 697). The material is cate-
      gorized under reproductions of original folio editions of the
      play, bibliographical sources, and critical studies (arranged
      alphabetically). While not exhaustive, the material represents
      every major category of scholarship and criticism.

                           Editions

696   DAVID, RICHARD, ed. Love's Labour's Lost. The Arden Shake-
      speare. London: Methuen; Cambridge, Mass.: Harvard Univer-
      sity Press, 1951, 196 pp.
          Includes discussion of the text, date, sources, topical
content, and the possible occasion for the play. The text is

based on the first quarto (1598), for which the copy was probably
Shakespeare's foul papers that had undergone revision at least
once. The indication on the title page that the text is "newly
corrected and augmented" suggests the earlier publication of a
bad quarto. The date of composition of the play in its present
form is probably the autumn of 1597, but the original draft must
date from 1593-94. No source is known, but historical names,
journeys, and visits are woven into the original narrative. All
indications are that the play was "a battle in a private war between court factions" (p. 1) and that it was written for private
performance in court circles. In style it reflects the euphuis-
tic language popularized by Lyly. Of the numerous suggested
topical allusions, the most interesting, albeit fanciful, concerns Sir Walter Raleigh as Armado along with the possible references to his circle of friends in the "School of Night."

697   FURNESS, HENRY HOWARD, ed. Love's Labour's Lost. A New
      Variorum Edition of Shakespeare. Philadelphia: J.B. Lippin-
      cott, 1904, 401 pp.
           Uses the first quarto (1598) as the copy text. On each
      page are included, for that portion of the text, variant read-
      ings, textual notes, and general critical commentary. Following
      the text are sections on the nature of the quarto and folio
      texts; the date of composition; the sources; English, German, and
      French criticisms; Shakespeare's wordplay; imitations; and a list
      of works consulted. See entry 695 for a supplementary bibliog-
      raphy.

698   QUILLER-COUCH, ARTHUR, and WILSON, JOHN DOVER, eds. Love's
      Labour's Lost. Cambridge: Cambridge University Press, 1923,
      213 pp.
           Provides extensive textual notes, a critical introduction,
      a discussion of the copy text, a section on stage history, and a
      glossary. This edition is eclectic, based primarily on the first
      quarto but with readings also from the First Folio. A major
      concern of criticism of the play has involved the possible topi-
      cal allusions, with a disproportionate amount on the identifica-
      tion of the subordinate comic figures. In theme and phraseology
      the play is closely related to the sonnets; both include a con-
      centration of light imagery, especially that comparing women's
      eyes to stars. A comparison with Lyly's plays points up Shake-
      speare's superior artistry in the ability to develop a probing
      universal theme beneath a curiously frivolous surface.

Criticism

699   BABCOCK, WESTON. "Fools, Fowls and Perttaunt-Like." Shake-
      speare Quarterly 2 (1951):211-19.
           Focuses on the meaning of Roline's comment that she will
      oversway Berowne's state "perttaunt-like" (5.2.67). The passage
      begins with a reference to fools, pronounced much like fowls, and

the suggested associated meaning is "Partlet-like." Chaucer's
Partlet was Chaunticleer's favorite of seven, hence the sexual
association; moreover, she was scolding and domineering, much as
Rosaline in this passage. The series of puns and doubles
entendres would gratify the wit, intellect, and lustiness of the
young gentlemen of the Middle Temple.

700   BERMAN, RONALD. "Shakespearean Comedy and the Uses of Reason."
       South Atlantic Quarterly 63 (1964):1-9.
           Views the play as a comic attack on the Platonic Academy.
       The Platonic ideal of solitary contemplation espoused by the King
       of Navarre would deny basic humanity, and the other characters
       continually assert the power of the senses. Berowne, Longaville,
       and Dumaine assume the role of courtly lovers; far more earthy is
       the relationship between Costard, Jaquenetta, and Armado. The
       play, in a word, sets body against mind, man against woman, folly
       against pedantry. Similarly, The Taming of the Shrew is dis-
       cussed as a burlesque in its action of Platonic reason.

701   BERRY, RALPH. "The Words of Mercury." Shakespeare Survey 22
       (1969):69-77.
           Describes the theme of the play as a delicate and controlled
       movement toward the acceptance of reality. If it opens with an
       assault upon Time/Death, it closes with the acknowledgment of
       Time's victory in Marcade's entry and the news of the death of
       the Princess's father. As act 5 refutes act 1, so Winter's song
       refutes Summer's. Groups of characters use words in different
       ways--Navarre and his followers, the Princess and her retinue,
       the clowns, the pedants--but Marcade-Mercury, bringing news of
       death, announces the presence of a reality that must be mediated
       by words. (See entry 710.)

702   BOUGHNER, DANIEL C. "Don Armado and the Commedia dell'Arte."
       Studies in Philology 37 (1940):201-24.
           Illustrates the relationship of Don Armado to Andreini's
       Capitano Spavento and traces salient themes and conventions of
       the tradition within which Shakespeare was working--the capitano
       of the commedia dell'arte, the miles gloriosus of classical
       comedy, and the soldato of the commedia erudita. Shakespeare
       imparted new life into the tradition by decking Armado in the
       fashion of the fantastic courtier of Elizabethan London as one of
       the race of social climbers.

703   BRADBROOK, MURIEL C. The School of Night: A Study in the
       Literary Relationships of Sir Walter Raleigh. Cambridge:
       Cambridge University Press, 1936, 190 pp.
           Asserts that Love's Labor's Lost was Shakespeare's account
       of the "School of Night," Shakespeare's nickname for a group
       headed and patronized by Raleigh and including, among others,
       Thomas Hariot, the Earl of Northumberland, and Derby, Marlowe,
       and Chapman. This society studied theology, philosophy,

astronomy, and chemistry, and various members were accused of
atheism. The faction of Essex engaged in a literary skirmish
with the faction of Raleigh. Shakespeare's comedy mocked
Raleigh, who having been banished from court praised the solitary
life of study and contemplation. Armado parodies Raleigh, but
the satire is not sustained. On the whole the play is more concerned with theories of living than with personalities. (See
entry 711.)

704   CALDERWOOD, JAMES L. "Love's Labor's Lost: A Wantoning with
       Words." Studies in English Literature 5 (1965):317-32.
       Speaks of Love's Labor's Lost as a play in which words
become a fascination in themselves quite apart from their relevance to reality. Words function more to elicit aesthetic plea-
sure--through puns, metaphor, syntax, alliteration, coinage--than
to express ideas or feelings. The academic society of Navarre
ultimately breaks down because the language that creates it is
divorced from the truth of human nature. The movement in the
play is from self-aggrandizing and socially destructive uses of
language to words that provoke genuine human interaction.

705   CARROLL, WILLIAM C. The Great Feast of Language in "Love's
       Labor's Lost." Princeton: Princeton University Press, 1976,
       279 pp.
       Focuses on Love's Labor's Lost as a debate concerning the
proper uses of rhetoric, poetry, and the imagination, concluding
not with rejection of art for life but with the reassertion of
the need for sound art. Examples of rhetorical and theatrical
excesses appear in the sonnet-reading scene, the Masque of
Muscovites, the Pageant of the Nine Worthies, and in the six low
characters who constitute a kind of commedia dell'arte troupe.
The songs of spring and winter constitute an exemplum and model
for the right use of language and art, highly structured yet
direct in communication and functional in addressing time as
cyclical and thus offering the capability of renewal for the
characters in the play.

706   COURSEN, HERBERT R. "Love's Labor's Lost and the Comic
       Truth." Papers on Language and Literature 6 (1970):316-22.
       Notes that Love's Labor's Lost sets forth false values
gradually overtaken by truth. The men are manipulated by affec-
tation and ritual, and the ladies employ an even more intricate
counterritual, transforming the men's code of honor to absurdity.
The men's ploys involve the hypocrisy of foreswearing, while the
ladies' counterattack exploits the hypocrisy of the men's disguise and their misdirected love vows. With the social game
interrupted by news of death, the men are left to explore their
newfound realities in a "sixth" act.

707   ELLIS, HERBERT A. Shakespeare's Lusty Punning in "Love's
      Labour's Lost": With Contemporary Analogues. Studies in
      English Literature, 81. The Hague and Paris: Mouton, 1973,
      239 pp.
          Examines the more than two hundred discernible semantic and
      homophonic puns in Love's Labor's Lost as one means of appreciat-
      ing the dimensions of Shakespeare's comic artistry. Supporting
      evidence is drawn from dictionaries, works on Elizabethan pro-
      nunciation, and contemporary sources such as diaries, letters,
      broadside ballads, joke books, and the Bible. The study suggests
      that the humor of the play was intended for a more popular
      audience than critics have generally assumed and that Shake-
      speare's bawdiness is usually garbed in language that, through
      ambiguity, presents an outward semblance of innocence.

708   HOY, CYRUS. "Love's Labor's Lost and the Nature of Comedy."
      Shakespeare Quarterly 13 (1962):31-40. Reprinted in Shake-
      speare's Comedies, ed. Laurence Lerner (Baltimore: Penguin,
      1967), pp. 76-90.
          Describes the play as a satire of fine manners, pedantry,
      disguised love, and the infirmity of the human purpose. Intended
      to enlighten without destroying, the comedy plays upon the in-
      congruities inherent in the human condition--the spiritual and
      the material, the aspiration and the achievement. The basic
      pattern of Shakespearean comedy is a movement from the artificial
      to the natural, always with the object of finding oneself, a
      process achieved most effectively in a rural or natural setting.

709   KERRIGAN, JOHN. "Shakespeare at Work: The Katharine-Rosaline
      Tangle in Love's Labor's Lost." Review of English Studies,
      n.s. 33 (1982):129-36.
          Explains the confusions between Katharine and Rosaline in
      act 2 as the consequence of Shakespeare's mind in the act of
      creation. In the quarto Berowne and Katharine converse apart,
      and later he and Rosaline flirt. The conclusion must be that
      Shakespeare wrote the act originally with only the vaguest con-
      ception of particular relationships and that specific pairings
      emerged only later--Katharine and Dumaine, Rosaline and Berowne.
      After having completed the play, he overlooked the inconsistency
      in his last-minute revisions.

710   McLAY, CATHERINE M. "The Dialogue of Spring and Winter: A
      Key to the Unity of Love's Labor's Lost." Shakespeare
      Quarterly 18 (1967):119-27.
          Maintains that the concluding songs or dialogue of Spring
      and Winter, although probably a part of the additions to the play
      in 1597, are functional, holding the key to interpreting the
      central theme of Love's Labor's Lost. The men and the ladies
      throughout the play represent the forces of Art and Nature; cen-
      tral to the action is the hunting scene in act 4, in which the
      women become the pursuers, leading to the men's subjugation by

the force of Nature. Opposite to the pole of Nature, however, is
death; and true wisdom can come only with the full realization of
life's cycle, the theme of the concluding songs. (See entry
701.)

711   PARSONS, PHILLIP. "Shakespeare and the Mask." Shakespeare
      Survey 16 (1963):121-31.
            Describes Love's Labor's Lost as, like Romeo and Juliet, a
      play unfolding personal destiny in the characters' coming to
      realize a deeper and more vital self-awareness. Both use the
      theatrical images of a black visor, in Love's Labor's Lost when
      it becomes clear to the lords that love demands more than the
      sugared sonnets and in Romeo and Juliet when Romeo first views
      Juliet. The lords bent on "finding themselves" put on a masque
      and are met by the ladies wearing black visors. The scene leads
      to the lords' acknowledgment of their true natures, a moment
      concommitant with the intrusion of darkness with news of the
      death of the King of France.

712   PHELPS, JOHN. "The Source of Love's Labor's Lost."
      Shakespeare Association Bulletin 17 (1942):97-102.
            Suggests that the source of the play is a visit by
      Catherine de Medici, her daughter Marguerite de Valois, and her
      court ladies to Marguerite's estranged husband Henry, King of
      Navarre, at Nerac in 1578-79. Sidney Lee (entry 268) confused
      this meeting with one in 1586 at Saint Bris, which was a council
      of war concerning the civil wars and at which Marguerite was not
      present. Phelp's article is reprinted from the Baltimore News
      in 1899, in which he first suggested the Nerac meeting as the
      source.

713   TAYLOR, RUPERT. The Date of "Love's Labour's Lost." New
      York: Columbia University Press, 1932, 134 pp.
            Suggests a date of 1596 for the composition of Love's
      Labor's Lost. Individual chapters are devoted to the relation-
      ship between the masque of Muscovites and the Russian Episode
      presented at Gray's Inn in 1594-95, to the significance of the
      presence of the Venus and Adonis stanza in the play, to the
      relationship of the plot to events in France and England between
      1589 and 1596, and to references to the Thomas Nashe-Gabriel
      Harvey argument between 1592 and 1596.

714   YATES, FRANCES A. A Study of "Love's Labour's Lost."
      Cambridge: Cambridge University Press, 1936, 224 pp.
            Views Love's Labor's Lost as a play bristling with allu-
      sions to contemporary events and to living persons; more spe-
      cifically, the action reflects the struggle at court between the
      Essex-Southampton group and the Raleigh group. The core of the
      plot is drawn from the Gray's Inn Revels of 1594-95 and its mock
      speeches alternate in praise of study and of pleasure. John
      Florio, Gabriel Harvey, George Chapman, and the Earl of

Northumberland comprise Raleigh's "School of Night" group around
which the topical satire is developed. (See entry 703.)

For discussion of the language, see entries 145, 704-5, 707. See
also The Comedies (entries 591-631) and 56, 66, 144, 146, 162, 211,
215, 220, 240, 250, 290, 304, 351, 357, 594, 608, 609-10, 617-18,
624, 626-27, 878.

MEASURE FOR MEASURE

Editions

715   ECCLES, MARK, ed. Measure for Measure. A New Variorum Edi-
      tion of Shakespeare. New York: Modern Language Association
      of America, 1980, 555 pp.
          Uses the First Folio as the copy text. On each page, for
      that portion of the text, provides variant readings, textual
      notes, and general critical commentary. Following the text are
      sections, citing varying critical opinion, on emendations; the
      text; the date of composition; sources, analogues, and influ-
      ences; criticism--genre, character, style, technique, theme;
      stage history; music; and a list of works consulted.

716   LEVER, J.W., ed. Measure for Measure. The Arden Shakespeare.
      London: Methuen; Cambridge, Mass.: Harvard University Press,
      1965, 203 pp.
          Includes discussion of the text, date, sources, and criti-
      cal interpretations, along with appendixes on the songs and ex-
      tracts from the source materials. The text is based on the First
      Folio, for which the copy was probably Ralph Crane's transcript
      of Shakespeare's foul papers contaminated by prompter's inser-
      tions and scribal idiosyncrasies. Measure for Measure is, in the
      broadest sense, a drama of ideas that transcends labels like
      "problem play," "allegory," "morality," or "satire" in dealing
      with the polarities of justice and mercy in a social setting with
      contemporary relevance. The terrible encounter of absolutes dis-
      torts the human image to reptilian and simian proportions. The
      tense antagonisms of the first half are woven into a texture of
      issues reconciled through a sense of painfully acquired self-
      knowledge.

717   QUILLER-COUCH, ARTHUR, and WILSON, JOHN DOVER, eds. Measure
      for Measure. Cambridge: Cambridge University Press, 1922,
      176 pp. Introduction reprinted in "Measure for Measure":
      Text, Source, and Criticism, ed. Rolf Soellner and Samuel
      Bertsche (Boston: Houghton Mifflin, 1966), pp. 175-87.
          Provides extensive textual notes, a critical introduction,
      a discussion of the copy text and of time in the play, a section
      on stage history, and a glossary. This edition is based on the
      First Folio, for which the copy was probably an assemblage of

actors' parts. The play is not a genuine success, requiring
intricate psychological analysis; but for all its flaws it is
alive, exciting, and teeming with the power of poetry. The final
scene reflects its generic confusion, with the tragedy of Angelo
undercut by the comic ambles of Lucio.

Criticism

718   BACHE, WILLIAM B. "Measure for Measure" as Dialectical Art.
       Purdue University Studies. Lafayette: Purdue University
       Press, 1969, 66 pp.
           Finds the key in a dialectical argument that runs through-
       out the play concerning man's proper behavior and the proper
       function of the law in that regard. Reflecting a realistic view
       of life as uncontrolled, devious, and disordered, the play forces
       choices in a context ambiguously defiant of absolutes. In the
       process Duke Vincentio and Isabella, forced in differing ways to
       extend themselves, realize their finest potential as human beings
       and enact the Shakespearean ethic of love and duty.

719   BATTENHOUSE, ROY. "Measure for Measure and the Christian
       Doctrine of Atonement." PMLA 61 (1946):1029-59.
           Sees the theme of the Atonement as the formal structuring
       principle of Measure for Measure. Vincentio (Conqueror or God)
       reforms Angelo (fallen angel), saves Claudio (lame one or sinful
       man), rights the wrong done to Mariana (combining the names of
       Mary the mother and Anne the immaculate mother), tempers justice
       with mercy, and reconciles Isabella (devoted to God) to himself
       when he proposes marriage. Christ the Bridegroom woos the human
       heart and perfects it through suffering and sacrifice so that she
       may be his bride. Both the fishing metaphor (Christ as fisher of
       men) and the ransom metaphor (Christ as a ransom for man's soul)
       are prominent in the play.

720   BENNETT, JOSEPHINE WATERS. "Measure for Measure" as Royal
       Entertainment. New York and London: Columbia University
       Press, 1966, 208 pp.
           Attempts to illumine Shakespeare's intentions by placing
       the play within the context of a single year and a single day.
       Chosen as the first play for performance before King James during
       the gala Christmas season of 1604, Measure models the role of
       Vincentio on the King's own account of his principles of govern-
       ment. Angelo is depicted in the guise in which James describes a
       tyrant, and Lucio provides a comic instance of James's complaints
       about being libeled. Stylized comedy from beginning to end, it
       invites its contemporary audience from a reasonable distance to
       perceive James's self-proclaimed image.

721 BRADBROOK, MURIEL C. "Authority and Justice in Measure for
     Measure." Review of English Studies 17 (1941):385-99. Re-
     printed in "Measure for Measure": Text, Source, and Criti-
     cism, ed. Rolf Soellner and Samuel Bertsche (Boston: Houghton
     Mifflin, 1966), pp. 207-19.
          Considers the leading quality of the play to be analytic,
     pitting justice against mercy or false authority against truth
     and humility. Angelo (authority) usurps the place of the Duke
     (Heavenly justice and humility); Claudio and Juliet stand for
     original sin, and Mariana for eros. The debate between justice
     and mercy occurs primarily in the struggle between Isabella and
     Angelo. While the Duke is, in disguise, an external seemer,
     Angelo is a moral seemer. Ultimately, Measure for Measure is a
     problem play because its ethical values are controlled by
     doctrinaire imperatives.

722 CHAMBERS, R.W. The Jacobean Shakespeare and "Measure for
     Measure." London: Oxford University Press, 1938, 60 pp.
     Reprinted in His Infinite Variety: Modern Shakespearean
     Criticism Since Johnson, ed. Paul. N. Siegel (Philadelphia:
     J.B. Lippincott, 1964), pp. 162-92.
          Asserts that Shakespeare has transformed the crudities of
     Promos and Cassandra into a "consistent tale of intercession of
     sin, repentance from and forgiveness of crime" (p. 54). With the
     Duke symbolizing something of the mystery of providence, the play
     focuses primarily on the spiritual alteration of Angelo's nature,
     but Claudio and Isabella are stretched and refined in the process
     as well. To argue that Shakespeare created these characters with
     irony and cynicism is to stand the play on its head. While it
     has affinities with the tragedies, it also points to the romances
     in its growth in faith in the power of goodness.

723 COGHILL, NEVILLE. "Comic Form in Measure for Measure."
     Shakespeare Survey 8 (1955):17-26. Reprinted in "Measure for
     Measure": Text, Source, and Criticism, ed. Rolf Soellner and
     Samuel Bertsche (Boston: Houghton Mifflin, 1966), pp. 100-110.
          Interprets Measure for Measure as an allegory in the tradi-
     tion of the parables of Christ, reflecting a human world in an
     eternal situation. Vinentio, the primum mobile of the play,
     represents the anthropomorphic actions of God in effecting tests
     for Angelo, Isabella, and Caudio. Lucio, who through his unjust
     criticism of Vincentio functions as a device to retain the
     audience's sympathy for the Duke even when this tester seems to
     be manipulative, is himself a form of Satan on the anagogical
     plane. Measure for Measure, in a word, is not a dark comedy;
     instead it resembles a medieval comedy of Christian joy.

724 COLE, HOWARD C. "The 'Christian' Context of Measure for
     Measure." Journal of English and Germanic Philology 64
     (1965):425-51.

Asserts the impossibility of explaining the tone of
Vincentio's juggling of wrath and reconciliation that appears so
at odds with our expectation of straightforwardness in such a
morality framework. Bothersome, too, is the self-conscious
staginess of his manipulations in the final act. In fact,
Vincentio's actions merely reflect the larger theme of arbi-
tariness that unifies the plot and enforces the mood of general
injustice. Perhaps the real difficulty lies in Shakespeare's
having come to Cinthio's material through Whetstone the Puritan,
who developed his characters along lines more divine than
romantic.

725   COX, JOHN D. "The Medieval Background of <u>Measure for Mea-</u>
      <u>sure.</u>" <u>Modern Philology</u> 81 (1983):1-13.
          Considers the medieval dramatic tradition to be in the
broadest sense a source for <u>Measure for Measure</u>. In several
miracle and morality plays dealing with sexual sin are found
motifs not in <u>Promos and Cassandra</u>--the need to temper justice
with mercy, the need for self-examination in accusing others, the
problem of slander, the hypocritical abuse of authority, the contrast between the "old" and "new" laws, and the nature of sov-
ereignty. The Duke is humanized by being shown as less than
divine while his opponents are humanized by being made more than
abstractions.

726   DODDS, W.M.T. "The Character of Angelo in <u>Measure for Mea-</u>
      <u>sure.</u>" <u>Modern Language Review</u> 41 (1946):246-55. Reprinted in
      <u>Discussions of Shakespeare's Problem Comedies</u>, ed. Robert
      Ornstein (Boston: D.C. Heath, 1961), pp. 88-96.
          Views Angelo as a character fully conceived as capable of
experiencing tragic intensity and suffering. He typifies strict
justice and should not be viewed as hypocritical at the beginning
of the play. When lust paralyzes his will, Angelo's fall casts
no more doubt on the validity of his first estate than does
Macbeth's collapse to ambition. Angelo is Shakespeare's attempt
to handle in comedy a three-dimensional character comparable in
complexity to those in tragedy. (See entries 728, 737.)

727   DUNKEL, WILBUR. "Law and Equity in <u>Measure for Measure</u>."
      <u>Shakespeare Quarterly</u> 13 (1962):275-85.
          Explores the temper of the times concerning the idea of
justice with equity, especially James's actions involving the
trial of Raleigh and others in 1603 in which mercy came as a
climax to leading the defendants through agony and degradation to
produce repentance and James's ideas on the dispensation of mercy
in <u>Basilikon Doron</u>. Angelo's letter-of-the-law attitude and
Vicentio's humanitarian actions both miss the mark, the one with
severity and the other with lack of punishment. From their conflict arises the comedy in a theme dealing with the need for a
ruler to recognize the necessity of justice with equity.

728   FAIRCHILD, H.N. "The Two Angelos." Shakespeare Association
       Bulletin 6 (1931):53-59.
           Takes exception to W.W. Lawrence's assertion (entry 612)
       that Angelo is a smooth rascal who has concealed his baseness.
       While characters in drama do conceal their baseness from other
       characters, rarely if ever do they conceal it from the specta-
       tors; and baseness is never concealed in soliloquies. Until his
       fall there is no indication that he is anything but a harsh pre-
       cisian with a clear Puritanical conscience. There are two
       Angelos--the cold, harsh prig of acts 1-2 and the smooth rascal
       of 3 who results from the introduction of the Mariana plot. (See
       entries 726, 737.)

729   GLESS, DARRYL J. "Measure for Measure," the Law and the
       Covenant. Princeton: Princeton University Press, 1979,
       280 pp.
           Views the play as the movement of a series of flawed charac-
       ters toward forgiveness, reconciliation, and renewal. Emphasis
       is on the elusive and problematic nature of morality and on the
       inherent imperfections of human knowledge by which one individual
       must judge another. These ambiguities arise from diverse con-
       ceptions of evil/sin in civil law and theological law and of
       society's appropriate response to it, from the ambivalent impli-
       cations in the scriptural passage from which the title is drawn,
       and from the potential animosity of anti-Catholic sentiment in
       early seventeenth-century England. The complexity of the play
       is rooted in its cultural context.

730   HARDING, DAVIS P. "Elizabethan Betrothals and Measure for
       Measure." Journal of English and Germanic Philology 49
       (1950):139-58.
           Argues that W.W. Lawrence's interpretation of the bed trick
       (entry 612) has misled numerous critics, that to dismiss the
       ethics of this material is to do violence to the play. The para-
       dox lies in the fact that, on the one hand, the Church insisted
       on control over the institution of marriage and that, on the
       other hand, the Church had little choice but to recognize the
       validity of clandestine marriages. The morality of Measure for
       Measure is the morality of its time. No one, including the Duke,
       could be certain of whether the bed trick involved a sin; thus,
       we can hardly dismiss the issue as insignificant.

731   KNIGHTS, L.C. "The Ambiguity of Measure for Measure."
       Scrutiny 10 (1942):222-33.
           Observes that Measure for Measure is a disconcerting play
       because conflicting attitudes toward the characters are forced
       upon us. Isabella, for instance, is at one moment chaste
       serenity, at another frosty, self-regarding Puritanism. A
       major source of the spectator's uneasiness lies in the character
       of Claudio; he is not consistently created, living only in the
       intensity of his pleas to Isabella to be his savior. Admittedly

in the later plays Shakespeare offers no solutions, but he does
offer clarification and insight that are missing in Measure for
Measure. (See entry 735.)

732   KRIEGER, MURRAY. "Measure for Measure and Elizabethan
      Comedy." PMLA 66 (1951):775-84. Reprinted in "Measure for
      Measure": Text, Source, and Criticism, ed. Rolf Soellner and
      Samuel Bertsche (Boston: Houghton Mifflin, 1966), pp. 91-99.
         Considers Measure for Measure an unsatisfactory blending of
two comic fashions in dramatic construction. Whereas Shakespearean romantic comedy focuses on fanciful plot and demands
from the spectators a sympathetic concern for the fortunes of the
characters, Jonsonian comedy focuses on character types and demands an attitude of detachment and disdainful superiority. The
opposed patterns are mixed in Angelo; in one plot he is the gull
and Isabella the guller, and in the other he is the villain who
repents after he is overcome. The spectator's response is simply
unable to cope with such divergent demands.

733   LASCELLES, MARY. Shakespeare's "Measure for Measure."
      London: Athlone Press, 1953, 172 pp.
         Describes Measure for Measure as bewildering in large part
because critics have heightened our level of awareness of its
numerous ambiguities. Shakespeare in this play has filled the
vessel of tragicomedy "to capacity with thought and feeling"
(p. 159), and it spills over; his thought transcends the bounds
of his story. The characters refuse merely to play a role by
coming to life as ambiguously human--the Duke, powerfully involved with the problems of evil in Vienna but at times seemingly
cold and dispassionate; Isabella, deeply angered in a moral crisis
until she abdicates to the Duke's manipulations; Angelo, pushed
back from the threshold of tragic experience to two-dimensional
stylization.

734   LAWRENCE, WILLIAM W. "Measure for Measure and Lucio."
      Shakespeare Quarterly 9 (1958):443-53.
         Observes that Lucio in the first two acts is not without
redeeming traits, whereas in the last two acts he is an insulting
rascal. In like manner the play itself is essentially realistic
in the first half and romantic in the second. It is likely that
Shakespeare, in providing Christmas entertainment for the Court
in 1604, determined that a happy ending would be appropriate and
thus sacrificed consistency of character in order to develop an
overtly comic gull for the Duke to expose.

735   LEAVIS, F.R. "The Greatness of Measure for Measure."
      Scrutiny 10 (1942):234-47.
         Takes issue with L.C. Knights's assertion (entry 731) that
there is something distasteful about the play, an artistic un-
certainty and confusion of feeling. Complexity of attitude does
not necessarily mean conflict or confusion. Therein, in fact,

lies the greatness of Measure for Measure. Shakespeare's
approach requires subtler attitudes than those in the morality
tradition when we approach Isabella, Angelo, and the Duke. The
resolution is artistically fitting, not hastily contrived.
Angelo is stripped of his pretensions, but he is capable of his
redemption because he is not basically the criminal type.

736   LEECH, CLIFFORD. "The Meaning of Measure for Measure."
       Shakespeare Survey 3 (1950):66-73.
           Argues that it is a gross oversimplification to view
       Measure for Measure as built on Christian views of justice and
       mercy. Whatever the Christian coloring it wells up sporadically
       from Shakespeare's unconscious inheritance; it does not determine
       the fundamental nature of the action. The overt theme is, indeed,
       the governor's duty to practice mercy and requite evil, but the
       play is far richer through its thematic undercurrents. In the
       morality framework is found satire, a psychological probing into
       the motives of the action, and a profound sympathy for the un-
       fortunate and hard-pressed.

737   McGINN, DONALD JOSEPH. "The Precise Angelo." In Joseph
       Quincy Adams Memorial Studies. Edited by James G. McManaway,
       Giles E. Dawson, and Edwin E. Willoughby. Washington: Folger
       Shakespeare Library, 1948, pp. 129-39.
           Examines the religious and ethical concepts of Measure for
       Measure in light of sixteenth-century religious thought. Shake-
       speare's major alterations of his source involve the character-
       ization of Angelo, the treatment of the theme of adultery, the
       quality of the Duke's role, and the moral of the play. Generally,
       these changes reflect his distaste for Puritanism and his sympa-
       thy with the old faith. The major conflicts of the play seem to
       reflect the theological controversies regarding the Anglican or
       Roman Catholic position on the law of Christian love and the
       Puritans' desire to revive the harsh Mosaic laws. (See entries
       726, 728.)

738   MacKAY, EILEEN. "Measure for Measure." Shakespeare Quarterly
       14 (1963):109-13. Reprinted in "Measure for Measure": Text,
       Source, and Criticism, ed. Rolf Soellner and Samuel Bertsche
       (Boston: Houghton Mifflin, 1966), pp. 161-66.
           Asserts that the play comes into proper perspective only if
       we remember that the Catholic Church in England in the early
       seventeenth century stood in great disrepute. The play in its
       early stages exhibits a cynical attitude toward the Church
       against which Isabella shines as an idealist in her integrity
       and humility. Her attitude toward seduction is no more priggish
       than her acceptance of the Duke's offer of marriage is hypocrit-
       ical. Once we perceive that her leaving the nunnery is to be
       seen as a pivotal act, we are free to to envision her as a nubile
       young woman who rejects one man as a sinister and inhibited

creature and accepts another as an individual motivated by a
sincere affection for others.

739   MILES, ROSALIND. <u>The Problem of "Measure for Measure": A
      Historical Investigation.</u> New York: Barnes & Noble, 1976,
      349 pp.
            Locates the central problem of the play in the linking of
      a basically comic plot to Vincentio as a disguised duke cult
      figure artistically related to James I and his self-image. The
      Duke rules wisely but by stealth, and his concept of tempering
      justice with mercy in such a manner as to provoke a therapeutic
      response from his subjects is progressively revealed. The first
      half of the study is comprised of a critical and dramatic history
      of the play since its first production in 1604.

740   MINCOFF, MARCO. "<u>Measure for Measure</u>: A Question of
      Approach." <u>Shakespeare Studies</u> 2 (1966):141-52.
            Decries those who pick out certain aspects of the plot,
      rearrange them, and then proclaim that to be Shakespeare's in-
      tent--whether a satiric picture of a society under Puritan domi-
      nation, the theme of justice versus mercy, the nature of law in
      an imperfect world, or a dramatization of the Christian Atone-
      ment. We should accept the exciting story for what it is--the
      fall of a hypocritically proud man, a young girl whose hard
      choices suggest her initiation into full adulthood, and a brother
      whose idealistic vision of honor crumbles in the face of death.

741   NUTTALL, ANTHONY DAVID. "<u>Measure for Measure</u>: Quid pro Quo?"
      <u>Shakespeare Studies</u> 4 (1968):231-51.
            Points out the play's numerous "critical collisions"--
      Isabella's vowing chastity while condemning Mariana's sexual
      activity, the Duke's requirement both to love his subject and to
      punish him, his Machiavellian delegation of his punitive role,
      Angelo as both scapegoat and sinner, Vincentio as both heavenly
      and devilish in his methods. In these very collisions is the
      key to the ingenious structure, illustrating the Renaissance love
      of copiousness, of simultaneous multiplicity of seemingly para-
      doxical meanings. <u>Measure for Measure</u> is at once illusion pro-
      voking delight and shock, despair and consolation.

742   ORNSTEIN, ROBERT. "The Human Comedy: <u>Measure for Measure</u>."
      <u>University of Kansas City Review</u> 24 (1957):15-22.
            Describes <u>Measure for Measure</u> as a secular morality peopled
      with all-too-human figures; routine legality triumphs over com-
      passion, and tragedy is averted by politic strategems and un-
      heroic compromises. Characters (ruler, virgin, judge) forever
      put themselves at the center of their moral universe but lack the
      self-knowledge vital to wise judgment. The conclusion is un-
      satisfactory because, while the resolution sustains communal
      life, it avoids the moral problems inherent in the plot. Echoes
      of the morality suggest a touch of grace beyond the reach of
      mortal man.

743   PARTEE, MORRIS H. "The Comic Unity of Measure for Measure."
       Genre 6 (1973):274-97.
       Describes the tone of Measure for Measure as one of comic
seriousness rather than tragic gravity. As in other comedies the
characters through their experience come to a greater sense of
self-awareness and social fulfillment: Vincentio learns to gov-
ern well, Angelo learns the true measure of being human, and
Isabella is rescued from a religious life unsuited to her true
nature. Dramatic irony, the juxtaposition of the serious to the
bawdy, and the consistently hyperbolic reactions of characters to
the situation are the principal components of the comic perspective.

744   POPE, ELIZABETH. "The Renaissance Background of Measure for
       Measure." Shakespeare Survey 2 (1949):66-82.
       Explores the popular tenets of Christianity in the Renais-
sance as a means of illuminating Shakespeare's themes of law,
authority, and justice in Measure for Measure. Certainly, in
1603-4 with the accession of James I Shakespeare knew the topic
of good government would be timely and popular. Although a
ruler has the sanctity of person, he must enforce the law even if
it requires extraordinary measures. His highest duty is to over-
see the true administration of justice tempered by mercy. While
the Duke has erred from excess of good will, Angelo is a bitter
and uncharitable proponent of the law. The plot turns on the
disturbing discrepancy between the concepts of religious mercy
and secular justice.

745   PRICE, JONATHAN R. "Measure for Measure and the Critics:
       Toward a New Approach." Shakespeare Quarterly 20 (1969):
       179-204.
       Argues that Shakespeare consciously works for diversity and
complexity of response in Measure for Measure. Both Christian
exegesis and the Ibsenism inherent in the problem-play interpretation are ultimately reductionistic. By generic mixing and
clever plotting Shakespeare forces us time and time again to
shift our attention from one plane of reality to another. The
progressive revelation of contradictory information is, in effect, a structural principle that defies simplistic analysis
while it creates exciting theater.

746   SALE, ROGER. "The Comic Mode of Measure for Measure."
       Shakespeare Quarterly 19 (1968):551-61.
       Considers Measure for Measure to be experimental in nature
as Shakespeare comes to focus more directly on individual nature
and motive in the face of social institutions. More specifically, he insists on the stubbornness of human folly and iniquity
and on the inescapable necessity of authoritarian unscrupulous-
ness if society is to enjoy even a modicum of order and well-
being. The result is harsh comedy, strikingly different from

Shakespeare's earlier romantic comedy; the ending is equivocal
since Vincentio's methods are morally questionable.

747   SIEGEL, PAUL N. "Measure for Measure": The Significance of
       the Title." Shakespeare Quarterly 4 (1953):317-20.
            States that Shakespeare's central problem is how to achieve
       dramatic justice and yet reflect Christian mercy, how to arouse
       derisive laughter at the same time he provokes a sense of moral
       elevation. The key is not the absence of retaliation but the
       careful working out of it. The title refers simultaneously to
       Angelo's method of dispensing justice in precise relation to the
       crime, to Isabella's and the Duke's method of returning good for
       evil, and to the retribution visited upon the misdoers even
       though they are granted mercy.

748   SISSON, CHARLES JASPER. The Mythical Sorrows of Shakespeare.
       Oxford: Oxford University Press, 1934, 26 pp.
            Attacks those critics who attempt to recreate Shakespeare
       in their own image, specifically those who envision a poet shaken
       by personal passion and whose spiritual biography is traced in
       Jaques, Duke Vincentio, Lear, and Timon. Measure for Measure,
       usually a prime text for such critics, is not morbid and melan-
       cholic but rather a combination of superb dramatic poetry, ab-
       sorbing theme, and comic diversification setting forth the hero-
       ism of Isabella. The key to understanding Shakespeare is to
       examine the evolving phases of his artistic ability.

749   STEVENSON, DAVID LLOYD. The Achievement of "Measure for
       Measure." Ithaca: Cornell University Press, 1966, 169 pp.
            Refutes the concept that Measure for Measure is a flawed or
       obscure play penetrable only by a literary historian. Instead,
       it is a self-contained artistic achievement involving a complex
       set of ironies and reversals of both plot and character regarding
       moral behavior and human choice. A deliberately "uncomfortable"
       play compelling us to readjust our response to a greater level of
       apprehension than we are accustomed to, Measure for Measure
       forces the spectator to participate in a morally judgmental man-
       ner in its comic vision of the ineluctable evil in man.

750   _____. "Design and Structure in Measure for Measure." ELH
       23 (1956):256-78.
            Views the play as an intellectual tour de force on the
       Renaissance theme of the "monstrous ransom," intricately inter-
       weaving moral ironies concerning mercy and justice. Ironically,
       the legalistic Angelo is forced to judge himself by the same
       letter of the law he applied to Claudio, and the pristinely
       virtuous Isabella becomes a kind of panderer in the Mariana epi-
       sode after her zealous attack on Claudio. Both character rever-
       sals involve a transformation through which the spectator per-
       ceives the human potential for goodness despite the impossibility
       of moral absolutes.

751   VELZ, SARAH C. "Man's Need and God's Plan in Measure for
       Measure and 'Mark IV.'" Shakespeare Survey 25 (1972):37-44.
            Asserts that Shakespeare's principal source for Measure for
       Measure was the fourth chapter of Mark in the Geneva Bible, spe-
       cifically Christ's parable of the sower and the seeds. Angelo,
       Claudio, Lucio, and Mariana symbolize the various types of seeds;
       Angelo falls on stony ground, Claudio on shallow ground, Lucio is
       choked by thorns, and Mariana falls on fertile ground. Vincentio,
       like Christ asleep in the boat, is nearby to help his troubled
       followers, and both leaders trust subordinates who quickly prove
       unfaithful to the task.

752   WEIL, HERBERT, Jr. "Form and Contexts in Measure for
       Measure." Critical Quarterly 12 (1970):55-72.
            Stresses the consistency of comic perspective in Measure
       for Measure. Shakespeare carefully prepares the spectator for
       the sudden reversal in tone when the Duke emerges at the end of
       act 3 as an overt deus ex machina by allowing broad comedy again
       and again to undercut the serious theme in the early acts--the
       scene of comic gossip about venereal disease following Vincentio's
       delegation of power to Angelo, Lucio's interruption of Isabella's
       pious contemplation with "Hail virgin, if you be," Elbow and
       Pompey's interruption of the argument between Escalus and Angelo
       concerning the proper punishment for fornication. The energy of
       the early acts is thus transformed into joyous, mocking comedy.

753   WILSON, HAROLD S. "Action and Symbol in Measure for Measure
       and The Tempest." Shakespeare Quarterly 4 (1953):375-84.
            Argues that both Measure for Measure and The Tempest employ
       a duke as a controlling figure but for different dramatic methods
       calculated for different dramatic effects. Measure for Measure
       presents a story ab ovo, and Vincentio's firm purpose becomes
       clear only at the end of the play when several characters--
       Angelo, Isabella, Claudio--are led to make choices that intensify
       and enrich their humanity. Prospero, by contrast, carefully ex-
       plains his plan in advance, but here Shakespeare is presenting
       the end of a story; the question is not whether Alonso and
       Antonio will repent but whether Prospero will be able to exercise
       mercy instead of vengeance.

For discussion of the allegory, see entries 719, 721-23, 729, 751.
For discussion of the comic mode, see entries 731-32, 740, 743,
745-46, 752. See also The Comedies (entries 591-631) and 66, 101,
159, 196, 212-13, 220-21, 231-32, 246, 250, 254, 263, 298, 302, 304,
312-13, 317-18, 325, 334, 605, 610-12, 619, 628, 630, 636, 933, 1478.

THE MERCHANT OF VENICE

Reference Works

754   MARDER, LOUIS, comp. "The Merchant of Venice": A Supple-
      mentary Bibliography 1888-1965. The New Variorum Shakespeare.
      New York: American Scholar Publications, 1965, 25 pp.
          Includes representative scholarship on The Merchant of
      Venice from 1888 to 1965 and is intended to supplement H.H.
      Furness's Variorum edition of 1888. The material is categorized
      under reproductions and editions of Merchant quartos, biblio-
      graphical sources, modern editions, and critical studies (ar-
      ranged alphabetically). While not exhaustive, the material
      represents every major category of scholarship and criticism.

755   TANNENBAUM, SAMUEL A., and TANNENBAUM, DOROTHY R., comps.
      William Shakespeare: "The Merchant of Venice." Elizabethan
      Bibliographies, 17. New York: Privately Printed, 1941,
      140 pp.
          Cites 2,631 items covering major scholarship from the be-
      ginnings to 1939. The material is divided by the following cate-
      gories and is arranged alphabetically by section--English texts,
      adaptations; translations; selections; abstracts, synopses;
      operas; songs; incidental music; commentary on music; parodies,
      burlesques; theatrical history; sources, analogues; law and
      Merchant; Jews and Merchant; Shylock; Portia, Nerissa, Jessica;
      general commentary; bibliographical notes; continuations, imita-
      tions; illustrations, costumes; book titles from Merchant; elec-
      trical recordings. The majority of the material (1,015 items) is
      loosely classified under general commentary.

Editions

756   BROWN, JOHN RUSSELL, ed. The Merchant of Venice. The Arden
      Shakespeare. London: Methuen; Cambridge, Mass.: Harvard
      University Press, 1955, 174 pp.
          Includes discussion of the text, date, sources, stage his-
      tory, and critical interpretations, as well as appendixes featur-
      ing selections from Ser Giovanni, Anthony Munday, Alexander
      Silvayn, the ballad Gernutus, and the Gesta Romanorum. The text
      is based on the first quarto (1600), for which the copy was
      probably Shakespeare's foul papers; the second quarto, a Pavier
      forgery, was published in 1619 but falsely dated 1600. Shylock
      is essentially Shakespeare's creation, a character capable of
      evoking wrath, sympathy, or mirth. Appearing in only five
      scenes, he is for many the center of interest. Perhaps the chief
      marvel of the play is its ability, despite the panoply of fairy
      tale elements, to engage the spectator in a deeply emotional
      manner. Both Bassanio and Portia must learn that love is not
      like merchandise; its essence is in freely giving without thought
      of return.

757   QUILLER-COUCH, ARTHUR, and WILSON, JOHN DOVER, eds. The
      Merchant of Venice. Cambridge: Cambridge University Press,
      1926, 193 pp.
           Provides extensive textual notes, a critical introduction,
      a discussion of the copy text, a section on stage history, and a
      glossary. This edition is based on the first quarto (1600), for
      which the copy was apparently an assembled text made up of
      players' parts. Shylock has been badly overphilosophized and
      oversentimentalized. He is an intelligible, if not pardonable,
      man; Shakespeare tends to convey a degree of sympathy by giving
      him credible incentive for his vengeful desire. Antonio is high-
      minded and capable, but he is the indolent patron of a circle of
      wasters. The moral emptiness of Venice is set against Belmont as
      the Renaissance's dream of a golden age.

                              Criticism

758   AUDEN, W.H. "Brothers and Others." In "The Dyer's Hand" and
      Other Selected Essays. New York: Random House, 1948,
      pp. 218-37. Reprinted in Four Centuries of Shakespearean
      Criticism, ed. Frank Kermode (New York: Avon, 1965),
      pp. 240-51.
           Describes Shylock and Antonio as two alien creatures unable
      to enter the Arcadian world of Belmont. Shylock is a usurer;
      and, while the immorality of usury was not a settled issue in
      Shakespeare's day, Shylock acts unprofessionally in his role and,
      as a Jew who defies the Christian society, is branded an alien.
      Antonio, likewise, is unable to experience the love of women, and
      his fanciful backing of Bassanio constitutes a form of idolatry.
      Their presence ultimately reminds us that Belmont is an illusion,
      that in the real world no hatred is totally without justifica-
      tion, no love totally innocent.

759   BROCKBANK, J.P. "Shakespeare and the Fashion of These Times."
      Shakespeare Survey 16 (1963):30-41.
           Describes contemporary literary criticism as imaginatively
      exhausted, obsessed with objectively secured positions, and fre-
      quently overingeniously diverse. The trial scene of The Merchant
      of Venice, for example, has been the subject of flatly contra-
      dictory analyses. To the skeptical it is a magnificent exercise
      in lawcourt virtuosity, a consummate piece of Jew-baiting. To
      the allegorist Portia is an analogue of Christ, and the action
      issues in divine mercy. We would do well to remember the various
      treatises that speak directly of admitting equity into law, that
      Portia remains far on this side of the magical, that the stereo-
      typed Shylock is not tragically explored.

760   BURCKHARDT, SIGURD. "The Merchant of Venice: The Gentle
       Bond." ELH 29 (1962):239-62. Reprinted in Shakespeare's
       Comedies, ed. Laurence Lerner (New York: Oxford University
       Press, 1967), pp. 155-68.
            Perceives an exacting circular structure in that the bond,
       an instrument of destruction, becomes the source of deliverance.
       The circularity of the structure is reinforced by subsidiary
       metaphors of the bond and the ring. The ethic of the play is
       venture capitalism raised to a moral level; and Shylock, elevated
       by Shakespeare to a level of dignity, is the principal spokesman
       for this ethic. In order to gain, one must hazard one's posses-
       sions, material or emotional. The risks are genuine, and Shylock
       ultimately withdraws in the face of them.

761   COOPER, JOHN A. "Shylock's Humanity." Shakespeare Quarterly
       21 (1970):117-24.
            Views Shylock not as a Jew to be baited but as a represen-
       tative of the mind totally devoted to business and, like all men,
       desirous of revenge when wronged. As such he is a part of the
       commercial world of Venice committed to the law that is juxta-
       posed with the almost magical world of Belmont and its values of
       mercy. Shylock reflects the universal condition of fallen man,
       and his forced conversion illustrates the difficulty of man's
       understanding the New Law.

762   DANSON, LAWRENCE. The Harmonies of "The Merchant of Venice."
       New Haven and London: Yale University Press, 1978, 202 pp.
            Considers modern tendencies to play Shylock as a tragic
       figure or to read the play as an ironic attack upon uncharitable
       Christians a legacy of the romantic and Victorian periods. The
       play must be interpreted in its particular theological context.
       The music as reflective of individual and cosmic harmony, the
       marriage of Jew and Gentile, the ring as physical and spiritual
       symbol--such elements in act 5 are merely the culmination of
       drama that is simultaneously sexual intrigue comedy and symbolic
       comedy suggesting that the dictates of charity can be fulfilled
       only through the mutuality of concern central to Christian
       doctrine.

763   DONOW, HERBERT S. "Shakespeare's Caskets: Unity in The
       Merchant of Venice." Shakespeare Studies 4 (1968):86-93.
            Claims that the main plot of The Merchant of Venice is not
       the bond motif but the courtship of Portia and her marriage to
       Bassanio, with the elopement of Jessica a parallel and related
       plot. Both women are subject to the will of a father, but the
       world of Shylock (by extension the Venetian world) is antitheti-
       cal to that of Belmont. Portia's father has tendered love, and
       Portia accedes to his wishes; Shylock's failure as a father, in
       contrast, sets the stage for her repudiation of him. Portia's
       father in arranging the casket trial has inverted material values
       whereas Shylock pursues material wealth.

764   FREUD, SIGMUND. "The Theme of the Three Caskets." In
      Collected Papers. Translated by Joan Riviere. Vol. 4.
      London: Hogarth Press and the Institute of Psycho-Analysis,
      1949, pp. 244-56.
          Analyzes the secret motives behind Bassanio's unconvincing
      argument that he prefers the baser metal lead. By symbolic
      substitution Bassanio, like Lear later, is choosing among three
      women. He prefers the third, who is silent and unobtrusive and
      who by ambiguous extension is both the Goddess of Love and Death
      herself. In Lear's case Cordelia is Death; in Bassanio's she is
      the fairest and wisest of women.

765   GARNER, SHIRLEY NELSON. "Shylock: 'His Stones, His Daughter,
      and His Ducats.'" Upstart Crow 5 (1984):35-49.
          Concentrates on the impact of Jessica's elopement on
      Shylock--in his unwillingness to admit that she does not love
      him and in its place in his conflict with Antonio. Shylock's
      defeat strips him of his identity and darkens the play, reflect-
      ing the failure of humanity and love. Lorenzo and Jessica are
      reminiscent of tragic lovers; Portia must exorcise Antonio; and
      Gratiano distrusts Nerissa. Antonio strikes the final blow
      against Shylock by forcing him to become a Christian and thus
      isolating him from the Jewish community.

766   GOLLANCZ, ISRAEL. Allegory and Mysticism in Shakespeare: A
      Medievalist on "The Merchant of Venice." London: Privately
      Printed, 1931, 68 pp.
          Focuses on Shakespeare's ability to divine the myth behind
      the particular story in the tradition of the morality plays. The
      Merchant of Venice, more specifically, allegorically depicts
      Antonio as the Christian, Shylock as evil, and Portia as salva-
      tion. One of the most significant themes of the play is ex-
      pressed in Lorenzo's description to Jessica of the heavenly
      harmony in immortal souls cleansed of their "muddy vesture of
      decay." Just so, man divested not merely of corporeal flesh but
      of hatred, indignity, and narrowness shall comically participate
      in God's music of the spheres.

767   GREBANIER, BERNARD. The Truth about Shylock. New York:
      Random House, 1962, 369 pp.
          Examines the historical facts, sources, and primary themes
      of The Merchant of Venice, arguing that Shylock is paramountly a
      prototype of the banker whose only true god is money and, as
      such, is defeated by the comic forces of love and compassion.
      Repeatedly repudiating offers of mercy in the trial scene, he is
      ultimately banished as the exemplar of material as opposed to
      emotional value. The modern director and critic would do well
      to see beyond "the Jewish question" and to recognize that the
      play's real business is above distinction of race or creed.

768   HOLADAY, ALLAN. "Antonio and the Allegory of Salvation."
      Shakespeare Studies 4 (1969):109-18.
          Draws an analogy between Antonio's trial and the Parliament
      in Heaven allegory. Justice insists that man must die as a con-
      sequence of original sin; Mercy pleads that man, deceived by
      Satan, was innocent of evil intent; and the solution is salvation
      through Christ's death of atonement. In the analogy Portia rep-
      resents mercy while Shylock stands for the law; Antonio, guilty
      of pride, is fallen man. Morocco and Arragon in the casket scene
      are surrogates for Shylock and Antonio.

769   LEVER, J.W. "Shylock, Portia, and the Values of Shakespearian
      Comedy." Shakespeare Quarterly 3 (1952):383-86.
          Describes The Merchant of Venice as romantic comedy in
      which love is pitted against usury. Fittingly, the villain is a
      Jewish moneylender with a marriageable daughter. The bond plot
      transforms the Jewish usurer to a man challenging the pattern of
      recognized values, and Antonio's virtues have taken on harsh con-
      tours. When Jessica elopes, Shylock waives his final elements of
      Jewishness by calling for vengeance, not from the laws of the Old
      Testament but as a wronged man in Venetian society. He is ulti-
      mately defeated by commercial laws and customs that are hardly
      Christian. The struggle has totally transcended theological
      doctrine.

770   LEWALSKI, BARBARA. "Biblical Allusion and Allegory in The
      Merchant of Venice." Shakespeare Quarterly 13 (1962):327-43.
          Argues that patterns of Biblical allusion and imagery in
      The Merchant of Venice are too precise and pervasive not to be
      deliberate. Such patterns point to a significant theological
      dimension and unmistakable allegorical overtones. At the moral
      level the play explores and defines Christian love and its various
      antitheses. Antonio's practice of Christian love is in his "ven-
      turing." At the allegorical level the Shylock-Antonio opposition
      symbolizes the confrontation of Judaism and Christianity.
      Antonio's trial scene suggests literary and iconographical
      presentations of the Parliament of Heaven in which fallen man was
      judged. Shylock, having refused the opportunity to embrace the
      principles of Christianity, must undergo "schoolmastership" to be
      saved.

771   LEWIS, CYNTHIA. "Antonio and Alienation in The Merchant of
      Venice." South Atlantic Review 48 (1983):19-31.
          Focuses on the ambiguous discomforts Antonio provokes in
      spectators and readers. Certainly from the moment of his intro-
      duction Antonio is strange or alien; he is obsessed with a deep
      melancholy he cannot explain. He also seems to lack a depth of
      perception in dealing with the dangers of the world; and his
      knowledge of Venetian law, when he is caught in Shylock's bond,
      is superficial. At the play's end he walks slowly off stage, his
      best friend now married. He reminds us that alienation and

suppression are, for some, the consequence of social cohesion;
and the truth of his predicament disturbs us.

772   MIDGLEY, GRAHAM.   "The Merchant of Venice: A Reconsidera-
      tion." Essays in Criticism 10 (1960):119-33.
          Notes that any attempt to interpret The Merchant of Venice
      as either a love story or a study in the personality of the Jew
      is reductionistic. The two focal points of the play are Shylock
      and Antonio, and the two contrasting value structures are those
      of love and marriage and those of society, politics, and econom-
      ics. As Shylock is an outsider to the social values, Antonio is
      an outsider to the love values. The play is a study in twin
      loneliness. As act 4 covers the defeat of Shylock, act 5 covers
      the defeat of Antonio. The last we see of each is a solitary
      figure walking disconsolately off stage.

773   ROTH, CECIL.   "The Background of Shylock." Review of English
      Studies 9 (1933):148-56.
          Admits the fictional quality of Shylock but reconstructs
      the background that realistically formed the backdrop in trig-
      gering Shakespeare's creative imagination. Of the three Jewish
      colonies in Venice, Shylock would have belonged to the Nazione
      Tedesca, or German nation, since it was the only one allowing its
      members to practice moneylending. Like Shylock the Jews of the
      Ghetto period were not considered natives of the country. It is
      possible to speak with certainty also about the location of his
      home and dress.

774   SIEGEL, PAUL N.   "Shylock and the Puritan Usurers." In
      Studies in Shakespeare. Edited by Arthur D. Matthews and
      Clark M. Emery. Coral Gables: University of Miami Press,
      1953, pp. 129-38.
          Argues that Elizabethan spectators would have seen in
      Shakespeare's depiction of the villainous moneylender of folk
      tradition reflections of contemporary Puritan usurers. Judaism,
      Puritanism, and usury were connected in the popular mind. Puri-
      tans, because of their emphasis on Old Testament law, were fre-
      quently charged with returning to Judaism. Shylock like the
      Pharisaical Puritan is intolerant of others, attributing his own
      spiritual defect to others. In the final act charity, friendship,
      and love triumph over the Puritan individualism and its "cash
      nexus."

775   SIEMON, JAMES E.   "The Merchant of Venice: Act V as Ritual
      Reiteration." Studies in Philology 67 (1970):201-9.
          Notes that The Merchant of Venice stands between the festive
      and the optimistic comedies and the problem plays or tragi-
      comedies. The signal difference, first observed in Shylock, is
      the increased role of the villain and a greater focus on his
      motivation. Structurally the framing tale of Bassanio's wooing
      of Portia is raised to major prominence and becomes the efficient

cause of the comic resolution. Act 5 recapitulates the action
of acts 1-4 on a different level of awareness and meaning; in its
comic lesson in the nature of harmony and the music of the
spheres, it recapitulates Shylock's conversion in symbolic terms.

776   SMITH, JAMES H. "Shylock: 'Devil Incarnation' or 'Poor
       Man . . . Wronged?'" Journal of English and Germanic Philol-
       ogy 60 (1961):1-21.
           Surveys the widely divergent interpretations of Shylock and
       proposes to explore Shakespeare's intentions through his arrange-
       ment of incidents. The first quarto describes Shylock's actions
       on the title page as "extreeme cruelty"; and the resolution of
       the Shylock material at a relatively early stage makes certain
       that it will not cloud the romantic denouement. Shylock's bond
       motif becomes serious only after Jessica's elopement. He is
       neither comic butt nor tragic; he is a developing villain who
       progresses from human status in act 1 to that of savage monster
       in act 4.

777   STOLL, ELMER EDGAR. "Shylock." Journal of English and Ger-
       manic Philology 10 (1911):236-79. Reprinted in His Infinite
       Variety: Major Shakespearean Criticism since Johnson, ed.
       Paul N. Siegel (Philadelphia: J.P. Lippincott, 1964),
       pp. 131-51.
           Asserts that Shakespeare in his portrayal of Shylock
       depicts for the Elizabethan the prototypic Jew, moneylending,
       miserly, and hook-nosed. Played in a red beard and embodying
       widely prevalent social antipathies, he is both villain and comic
       butt. Attempts to make him a martyr or a sympathetic rejected
       father are far afield. Any human traits are undercut by passages
       depicting his villainously comic nature. References to Jews
       elsewhere in Shakespeare's plays are consistent with this inter-
       pretation.

778   TILLYARD, E.M.W. "The Trial Scene in The Merchant of Venice."
       Review of English Literature 2, no. 4 (1961):51-59.
           Notes that Portia in dictating right or wrong and speaking
       with more authority than the Duke himself becomes allegorical,
       but she stands not for mercy alone but for mercy and justice
       reconciled. As Christian mercy she is concerned with the soul
       of all men, Shylock as well as the unfortunate Venetian. In
       lecturing Shylock she is imploring him to recognize his own peril
       and to mind the salvation of his own soul. Having given him
       every opportunity, she finally turns her attention to justice
       alone, leaving any mercy at that point to the Duke and Antonio.

779   WERTHEIM, ALBERT. "The Treatment of Shylock and Thematic
       Integrity in The Merchant of Venice." Shakespeare Studies 6
       (1970):75-87.
           Asserts that Shylock's importance is primarily as a dra-
       matic statement of a play involving the examination of certain

values and morals. He epitomizes the disproportionate position
of monetary over spiritual concerns. Portia counteracts his
mercenary legalism, inculcating new values in Bassanio as well.
The forced conversion of Shylock is an act of the highest mercy,
the opportunity to find grace and Christian salvation. The characters are forced to realize that they cannot serve both God and
Mammon.

Stage History

780   LELYVELD, TOBY. Shylock on the Stage. Cleveland: Western
      Reserve University Press, 1960, 149 pp.
           Traces the stage history of The Merchant of Venice, more
      particularly the characterization of Shylock with emphasis upon
      those actors who have created significant changes in the role.
      Elizabethans viewed Shylock with comic opprobrium. George
      Granville in 1701 adapted Shylock's role in the vein of lowest
      comedy in The Jew of Venice. Charles Macklin in 1741 was the
      first to set the tragic tone so many later actors were to follow.
      Individual chapters are devoted to Edmund Kean, Edwin Booth, and
      Henry Irving, with some attention to the twentieth-century roles
      of George Arliss, John Gielgud, and John Carradine.

See also The Comedies (entries 541-631) and 66, 144, 240, 243, 246,
253, 263, 291-92, 307, 311, 313, 334, 597, 607-9, 617, 623, 627, 847,
933, 1395.

THE MERRY WIVES OF WINDSOR

Editions

781   OLIVER, H.J., ed. The Merry Wives of Windsor. The Arden
      Shakespeare. London: Methuen; Cambridge, Mass.: Harvard
      University Press, 1971, 149 pp.
           Includes discussion of the text, the relationship and
      printing of the quarto and folio, and the probable occasion of
      the play, along with theories of personal satire, the relation-
      ship to Shakespeare's histories, and the literary sources or
      analogues. The text is based on the First Folio, for which the
      copy was almost surely a transcript by the professional scribe
      Ralph Crane. Theories have been advanced that The Merry Wives of
      Windsor was written to gratify Queen Elizabeth's desire to see
      Falstaff in love and that it was written for the Garter Feast in
      1597. Similar attempts to relate the material to the history
      plays have focused on when the action occurs in relation to
      Henry IV and Henry V. The likely date of composition is 1597
      after the production of 1 Henry IV and before the completion of
      2 Henry IV.

782   QUILLER-COUCH, ARTHUR, and WILSON, JOHN DOVER, eds. The
       Merry Wives of Windsor. Cambridge: Cambridge University
       Press, 1921, 149 pp.
            Provides extensive textual notes, a critical introduction,
       a discussion of the copy text, a section on stage history, and a
       glossary. This edition is based on the First Folio, for which
       the copy was "made up by standing together players' parts with
       the aid of the theatrical 'plot' of the play" (p. 93). While the
       main intrigue is handled effectively, the play abounds in loose
       ends and threads, and the quality of the small amount of verse is
       especially weak. These inconsistencies are possibly explained by
       the fact that Shakespeare, working under royal command to display
       Falstaff in love, was hastily reworking an old play now lost, The
       Jealous Comedy.

                            Textual Studies

783   BRACEY, WILLIAM. "The Merry Wives of Windsor": The History
       and Transmission of Shakespeare's Text. University of
       Missouri Studies, vol. 25, no. 1. Columbia: Curators of the
       University of Missouri, 1952, 154 pp.
            Examines the quarto (1602) and folio (1623) texts of The
       Merry Wives of Windsor, focusing on the medium of transmission
       and the nature of the copy text for each. The theories of
       short-hand reporting, of a pirate-actor, and of memorial recon-
       struction are described as untenable, and the quarto text is
       considered an authorized stage version drastically abridged and
       adapted for special conditions of performance. The cutting is
       systematic--minor characters are eliminated, long speeches are
       reduced sharply, the plot is streamlined for effect--but it is
       dramatically consistent.

                              Criticism

784   BENNETT, A.L. "The Sources of Shakespeare's Merry Wives."
       Renaissance Quarterly 23 (1970):429-33.
            Surmises that Shakespeare felt compelled, because of
       Falstaff's popularity, to develop a domestic comedy with the fat
       clown as the butt of the jests and that he turned to Ralph
       Roister Doister for his principal source. Both plays place a
       braggart soldier center stage, and in both the soldier woos a
       citizen's wife, with money and not love as the prime motive.
       Both braggadochios are led to believe their passion is returned;
       and, following their comic exposure, both are forgiven.

785   FELHEIM, MARVIN, and TRACI, PHILIP. "Realism in The Merry
       Wives of Windsor." Ball State University Forum 22 (1981):
       52-59.
            Considers The Merry Wives of Windsor a blend of farce and
       realism, permeated with the details of small-town society and
       the concern for wifely honor in such a close community. The

language is filled with urban slang. Ford's jealousy is credibly
depicted, as the extremes of an Othello or a Corvino attest;
highly animated by nature, Ford becomes jealous by degrees in the
face of what appears to be overwhelming evidence. Falstaff's
carnal pursuits parody the romantic affair of Anne and Fenton;
money is a motivating force in both, though Fenton has tran-
scended material concerns.

786   GREEN, WILLIAM. Shakespeare's "The Merry Wives of Windsor."
      Princeton: Princeton University Press, 1962, 239 pp.
          Examines the events surrounding the composition of The
      Merry Wives of Windsor and how these events shaped the text from
      its initial performance to the printing in the folio. The play
      was apparently written to order and was first performed at the
      Feast of the Order of the Garter on St. George's Day, 1597. At
      this time both Shakespeare's patron Lord Hunsdon and the German
      ruler the Duke of Wurttemberg were made Garter knights. Writing
      at Hunsdon's commission a comedy depicting Falstaff in love,
      Shakespeare also incorporated material that would serve as a
      tribute to the Order of the Garter. The folio represents the
      authentic text; the quarto text is a memorially reconstructed
      version for acting in the provinces.

787   ROBERTS, JEANNE ADDISON. "The Merry Wives: Suitably Shallow,
      but Neither Simple nor Slender." Shakespeare Studies 6
      (1970):109-23.
          Argues that to dismiss The Merry Wives of Windsor as simple
      farce is to neglect the play's skillful design and genuine comic
      impact. The structural coherence and social orientation are
      antithetical to the spirit of farce; it is a world of cause and
      effect, human interaction, and rational principle. Thematically
      the play deals with the problems of achieving and maintaining
      marriage. In the ending, with Falstaff as a kind of sacrificial
      scapegoat, with contrast between strict justice and mercy, and
      with the establishment of a new order in the younger generation,
      The Merry Wives shares central affinities with Shakespeare's
      other comedies.

788   _____. Shakespeare's English Comedy: "The Merry Wives of
      Windsor" in Context. Lincoln and London: University of
      Nebraska Press, 1979, 169 pp.
          Encourages a new evaluation of The Merry Wives of Windsor
      in its full context. Following individual chapters on the text,
      date, and sources, directs attention to the generic form, and
      sets the play squarely within the tradition of Shakespearean
      comedy and of Shakespeare's work in the middle 1590s. The Merry
      Wives, more specifically, is experimental and transitional, com-
      ing between the histories and tragedies and sharing the bold comic
      developments of his finest romantic comedies. Of particular in-
      terest is the use of prose, the focus on married love, and the
      play-within-the-play.

789   SCHELL, J. STEWART. "Shakespeare's Gulls." Shakespeare
       Association Bulletin 15 (1940):23-33.
           Finds the precursor to Shakespeare's gulls in the epigram
       literature of the 1590s (Davies, Guilpin) in which the virtuoso
       touch was added to the standard characteristics of a foolish and
       credible simpleton. While Thurio in The Two Gentlemen of Verona
       is the first clear Shakespearean example, perhaps the most sig-
       nificant one is Abraham Slender in The Merry Wives of Windsor.
       The incompetent lover with "imperfect" speech, he boasts pride-
       fully of family and status but melts into cowardice when con-
       fronted. Other gulls mentioned briefly are Aguecheek, Osric,
       Roderigo, and Cloten.

790   SEWELL, SALLIE. "The Relation Between The Merry Wives of
       Windsor and Jonson's Every Man in His Humor." Shakespeare
       Association Bulletin 16 (1941):175-89.
           Conjectures that Every Man in His Humor directly influenced
       The Merry Wives of Windsor. Jonson's play preceded Shakespeare's
       by a few months to three years, and Shakespeare also had a chance
       to become familiar with Jonson's play by acting in it. The in-
       fluence was one of character (Stephen--Slender, Bobadil--Falstaff,
       Kitely--Ford), plot (the theme of the guller gulled in the main
       plot and of elopement and the cure of a jealous husband in the
       subplot), and identical targets of satire (heraldry, dueling,
       hunting, humors). Shakespeare, perhaps because royal command
       necessitated haste, followed Jonson's relatively simple intrigue
       plot structure.

See also The Comedies (entries 591-631) and 76, 79, 87, 101, 160,
286, 423, 434, 618.

A MIDSUMMER NIGHT'S DREAM

Reference Works

791   MARDER, LOUIS, comp. "A Midsummer Night's Dream": A Supple-
       mentary Bibliography 1895-1965. The New Variorum Shakespeare.
       New York: American Scholar Publications, 1965, 18 pp.
           Includes representative scholarship on A Midsummer Night's
       Dream from 1895 to 1965 and is intended to supplement H.H.
       Furness's Variorum edition of 1895. The material is categorized
       under bibliographical sources, modern editions, and critical
       studies (arranged alphabetically). While not exhaustive, the
       material represents every major category of scholarship and
       criticism.

Editions

792   BROOKS, HAROLD F., ed. A Midsummer Night's Dream. The Arden
       Shakespeare. London: Methuen; Cambridge, Mass.: Harvard
       University Press, 1979, 165 pp.
           Includes discussion of the text, the date, the occasion of
       composition, the poetic style, the sources, and critical inter-
       pretations, as well as appendixes on textual cruces, mislineation
       in the first quarto, and the proper punctuation of Quince's pro-
       logue. The text is based on the first quarto (1600), for which
       the copy was Shakespeare's foul papers, with occasional readings
       from the second quarto (a Pavier forgery printed from the first
       quarto in 1619 but falsely dated 1600) and from the First Folio
       (based on prompt copy). This most lyrical of Shakespeare's plays
       may well have been written to grace a wedding in a noble house-
       hold, probably that of Elizabeth Carey and Thomas, the son of
       Henry, Lord Berkeley, on 19 February 1596. It is unlikely that
       there was any comprehensive source; instead, Shakespeare drew
       upon at least a dozen identifiable works. The result is a work
       of imagination in which the comprehensiveness, balance, and
       coherence make of fancy's images a vision of truth.

793   QUILLER-COUCH, ARTHUR, and WILSON, JOHN DOVER, eds. A Mid-
       summer Night's Dream. Cambridge: Cambridge University Press,
       1924, 176 pp. Introduction reprinted in Shakespeare's Come-
       dies, ed. Laurence Lerner (New York: Oxford University Press,
       1967), pp. 95-99.
           Provides extensive textual notes, a critical introduction,
       a discussion of the copy text, a section on stage history, and a
       glossary. This edition is based on the first quarto (1600), for
       which the copy was a theatrical promptbook. The deft interweav-
       ing of the triple plots of the play structurally mark Shake-
       speare's artistic coming of age. Floating hints may have sug-
       gested an individual plot, but the combination is entirely his
       own. The possibility is strong that the play was originally
       written, or was later revised, to celebrate a marriage in a great
       house.

Criticism

794   ALLEN, JOHN A. "Bottom and Titania." Shakespeare Quarterly
       18 (1967):107-17.
           Focuses on the significance of the tableau scene in which
       the ass-headed Bottom lies in the arms of the Fairy Queen.
       Bottom is amusing in this situation both because it is comedy of
       the grotesque and because he represents the universal combination
       of asshood and humanity. This quality for the spectators is
       represented in the chase taking place in the woods. Bottom's
       presence tends to short-circuit any attempt to moralize by choos-
       ing between the reasonable and the fanciful as a basis for every-
       day action. (See entries 801, 808.)

795   BETHURUM, DOROTHY. "Shakespeare's Comment on Medieval Romance
      in A Midsummer Night's Dream." MLN 60 (1945):85-94.
         Suggests that Chaucer's "The Knight's Tale" provides the
      direct source for A Midsummer Night's Dream and that Shakespeare,
      in heightening the irony implicit in Chaucer's story, produces a
      lightly satirical view of medieval romance. Shakespeare raises
      the amorous center of the plot to farce by having two men contend
      for two girls in dizzying fashion; he also directs laughter upon
      the conventions of courtly love. The idea of the story may well
      have come to him through his seeing a production of the anonymous
      Palemon and Arcette.

796   COHEN, RALPH ALAN. "The Strategy of Misdirection in A Mid-
      summer Night's Dream and Bartholomew Fair." Renaissance
      Papers, 1982, pp. 65-75.
         Admits the diametrically opposite types of comedy written
      by Shakespeare and Jonson, Jonson striving for a kind of scien-
      tific detail in the setting whereas Shakespeare moves with aban-
      don through time and space. Both authors, though, go to great
      lengths to break down the barrier of illusion by framing the
      action within multiple levels of even more unbelievable percep-
      tion that amounts to a strategy of misdirection calculated to
      break down the spectator's disbelief. Once the spectator has
      moved from the rational to the irrational--to the dream world of
      Oberon's woods or the license of Smithfield--both plays reinforce
      the acceptance through a play-within-a-play.

797   FABER, M.D. "Hermia's Dream: Royal Road to A Midsummer
      Night's Dream." Literature and Psychology 22 (1972):179-90.
         Believes that Hermia's dream is the psychoanalytic center
      of A Midsummer Night's Dream. The theme, more specifically, con-
      cerns the movement of the various characters through dissociation
      to a new identity. Hermia's dream depicts classic characteris-
      tics of dissociation--with a snake (a phallic substitution for
      Lysander) attacking her breasts instead of her genitals. As a
      metaphor of the entire dramatic action, it realistically captures
      the "scope of unconscious causation in human experience" (p. 190).

798   FISHER, PETER F. "The Argument of A Midsummer Night's Dream."
      Shakespeare Quarterly 8 (1957):307-10.
         Views the major conflict of the play as the irrational
      force of sublunary passion (the four lovers) set against the
      rationally ordered world of Theseus and the Athenian court.
      Flanking each is the extreme of the grotesquely mundane world of
      Bottom and the fantastic world of Oberon. All four meet in the
      woods and through the action of the play are placed in proper
      perspective. The Theseus world is accepted as the controlling
      power; passion and desire are placed within the orbit of its con-
      trol; the world of common life approvingly sports itself for their
      amusement; and the world of imagination provides impetus for the
      interplay.

799   HEMINGWAY, SAMUEL B. "The Relation of A Midsummer Night's
       Dream to Romeo and Juliet." MLN 26 (1911):78-80.
           Argues that parallels in plot and character strongly sug-
       gest that A Midsummer Night's Dream was written after Romeo and
       Juliet, that in its spirit and its attitude toward love and life
       Dream is a natural reaction of Shakespeare's mind to Romeo. In
       particular, the Pyramus and Thisbe play is a direct burlesque of
       Romeo; the two catastrophes are virtually identical. Wall and
       Moon, moreover, might reflect Shakespeare's difficulty in staging
       the balcony scene effectively.

800   HERBERT, T. WALTER. Oberon's Mazed World: A Judicious Young
       Elizabethan Contemplates "A Midsummer Night's Dream" with a
       Mind Shaped by the Learning of Christendom Modified by the New
       Naturalist Philosophy and Excited by the Vision of a Rich,
       Powerful England. Baton Rouge: Louisiana State University
       Press, 1977, 200 pp.
           Applies Elizabethan dramatic, philosophical, and scientific
       issues to A Midsummer Night's Dream through the eyes of an in-
       formed sixteenth-century English theatergoer. This spectator
       discovers that the romantic comedy brings into focus diverse
       segments of society, diverse temperaments, and diverse ages of
       the world's history. His dramatic experience through the play's
       multiple worlds results in a sense of expansive love, "extending
       beyond the ignorant fictional Athenians to encompass his live,
       earnest, philosophic friends, himself, and even the world predic-
       ament they shared. He understood them with a new patience. He
       understood them with a newly compassionate heart" (p. 164).

801   HUSTON, J. DENNIS. "Bottom Waking: Shakespeare's 'Most Rare
       Vision.'" Studies in English Literature 13 (1973):208-22.
           Views Bottom's dream as reflective of both the theme of A
       Midsummer Night's Dream and of Shakespeare's art. The "dream"
       involves love's tyranny in the form of Titania's enslaving Bottom
       and of his childlike acceptance of it. Love's tyranny is also
       the theme of the action involving the dominance of Egeus and the
       ruler Theseus in the romantic affairs of the confused Athenian
       youth. Bottom's dream also, however, is a liberation into self-
       knowledge and, as such, is a metaphor for the action of the play
       as a whole. (See entries 794, 808.)

802   NEMEROV, HOWARD. "The Marriage of Theseus and Hippolyta."
       Kenyon Review 18 (1956):633-41.
           Describes the marriage as a symbolic as well as physical
       union. The poetic style of Theseus is rational and discursive,
       frequently tending toward prose. Hippolyta's, to the contrary,
       is magical and highly musical, drawing constantly from the
       fabulous. Theseus tends to see the literal and the obvious,
       Hippolyta the imaginary and the allusive. Their wedded life
       metaphorically reflects the history of poetry in the English
       language.

803 OLSON, PAUL A. "A Midsummer Night's Dream and the Meaning of
     Court Marriage." ELH 24 (1957):95-119. Reprinted in Shake-
     speare's Comedies, ed. Laurence Lerner (New York: Oxford
     University Press, 1967), pp. 110-16.
          Describes A Midsummer Night's Dream, not merely as a shim-
     mering fabric of moonlight, but as a carefully crafted work de-
     picting the Renaissance philosophy of the nature of love in both
     its rational and irrational forms. Oberon's curing of Titania's
     obsession is central to the meaning of the play; similarly,
     through leading the Athenian youth alternately to mock and dote
     on each other, he purges their passionate view of love, freeing
     them from the fond fancy that misdirects the will.

804 RICKERT, EDITH. "Political Propaganda and Satire in A Mid-
     summer Night's Dream." Modern Philology 21 (1923):53-87,
     133-54.
          Suggests that Shakespeare's plays abound with political
     purpose and that it is possible to identify the political alle-
     gory and satire in A Midsummer Night's Dream. Specifically, in
     its original form Shakespeare's play was an attempt to persuade
     Queen Elizabeth to follow the express desires of her father in
     legitimizing the Suffolk heir, Edward Seymour, Earl of Hertford,
     and to suggest that the abnormal weather of 1594-95 may be a sign
     of supernatural wrath. The Pyramus and Thisbe material takes its
     cue from a poem James sent Elizabeth and satirizes his preten-
     sions to the English throne. This version of 1595 was thoroughly
     revised before the quarto publication of 1600.

805 ROBINSON, JAMES E. "The Ritual and Rhetoric of A Midsummer
     Night's Dream." PMLA 83 (1968):380-91.
          Describes A Midsummer Night's Dream as a combination of
     realistic comedy, from both the primitive and medieval tradi-
     tions, and of rhetorical comedy, from the Plautine-Terentian
     tradition. The one affirms a renewal of life by perceiving a
     reality beyond the physical world; the other reaffirms the sig-
     nificance of a stable social order. While the humans with their
     concern for law, hierarchy, and authority represent the rhetori-
     cal world, the fairies represent the ritualistic world. The gods
     of nature become measure and mirror of human folly and love, and
     the result is both satiric and celebrative. (See entries 809-10.)

806 SCHANZER, ERNEST. "The Central Theme of A Midsummer Night's
     Dream." University of Toronto Quarterly 20 (1951):233-38.
          Notes that the events of the play take place not on Mid-
     summer Night but on Walpurgisnight. Shakespeare probably used
     Midsummer Night in the title because of beliefs that flowers and
     herbs possess magical powers at that time and because of its
     association with madness. The theme involves a kind of love in
     which reason is subordinate to the senses, and Shakespeare's
     dramatic method is to parody it. In the relationship of Theseus
     and Hippolyta love and reason are reunited, and it is appropriate

they should provide the resolving statements that give to these
relationships a sense of permanence and sanity.

807   WEINER, ANDREW D.   "'Multiformities Uniforme': A Midsummer
      Night's Dream." ELH 38 (1971):329-49.
         Views the play as an ordered sequence of events by which to
      provoke emotional responses with the power to affect the will.
      As the scene shifts from city to wood, day to night, pragmatic to
      magical, the spectator moves "from joy to uncertainty to wonder
      and finally back to joy" (p. 340). In such a manner Shakespeare
      forces the audience to respond fully to the central theme--the
      mystery of God's grace in marriage, the culmination of the action
      in the union of the four sets of lovers who share a new percep-
      tion of life's potential.

808   WYRICK, DEBORAH BAKER. "The Ass Motif in The Comedy of Errors
      and A Midsummer Night's Dream." Shakespeare Quarterly 33
      (1982):432-48.
         Observes that the word ass, whether as simile, metaphor, or
      pun, frequently conveys connotations that radiate outward from
      speaker or hearer to subplot and to theme. A Midsummer Night's
      Dream provides the most striking example. Bottom, ass-headed, is
      a walking metaphor, the apotheosis of asininity; and his presence
      comments upon the interconnected themes of metamorphosis, imagi-
      nation, and love. His hybrid nature (half-man/half-beast) sym-
      bolizes the basic pattern of the play--the Apollonian-Dionysian
      dialectic, Theseus's world representing the former and Oberon's
      the latter. (See entries 794, 801.)

809   YOUNG, DAVID P. Something of Great Constancy: The Art of "A
      Midsummer Night's Dream." New Haven and London: Yale Uni-
      versity Press, 1966, 190 pp.
         Views A Midsummer Night's Dream as a skillful synthesis of
      comic materials from courtly or coterie comedy and from popular
      comedy, as a structural blend of elements previously considered
      incompatible. The two worlds of the play--Theseus's orderly
      society and Oberon's confusing wilderness, with characters from
      each world discovering themselves temporarily lost in the fan-
      tastic one--correspond both to the moralities (the fall leading
      to reconciliation) and the romances (the grey world wandering
      leading to reunion in the green world). (See entries 805, 810.)

810   ZITNER, S.P. "The Worlds of A Midsummer Night's Dream."
      South Atlantic Quarterly 59 (1960):397-403.
         Identifies six different worlds in A Midsummer Night's
      Dream that coalesce to produce a comic inversion of the duties,
      responsibilities, and danger normally associated with them--the
      world of temporal power (Theseus and Hippolyta), the world of the
      lovers (Hermia, Helena, Lysander, Demetrius), the world of work
      (Bottom and his companions), the world of the fairies (Oberon and
      Titania), the world of illusion (the play-within-the-play), and

the world of nature (the elemental conditions). The interaction
of these worlds recalls for the Elizabethans a delightful illusion of their rustic past. (See entries 805, 809.)

See also The Comedies (entries 591-631) and 56, 131, 166, 179, 182,
211, 219, 242, 246, 250, 267, 271, 290, 312, 321, 342, 847, 893,
1450.

MUCH ADO ABOUT NOTHING

Reference Works

811   MARDER, LOUIS, comp. "Much Ado About Nothing": A Supplemen-
      tary Bibliography 1899-1965. The New Variorum Shakespeare.
      New York: American Scholar Publications, 1965, 19 pp.
         Includes representative scholarship on Much Ado About
Nothing from 1899 to 1965 and is intended to supplement H.H.
Furness's Variorum edition of 1899. The material is categorized
under reproductions of original folio editions, bibliographical
sources, modern editions, and critical studies (arranged alphabetically). While not exhaustive, the material represents every
major category of scholarship and criticism.

Editions

812   HUMPHREYS, A.R., ed. Much Ado About Nothing. The Arden
      Shakespeare. London and New York: Methuen, 1981, 237 pp.
         Includes discussion of the publication, the date of compo-
sition, the significance of the title, the sources, the style,
the stage history, the world of Messina, the form and structure,
the text, and a critical résumé. Appendixes cover source analogues, the evolution of wit style, William Davenant's adaptation
The Law Against Lovers, the proxy wooings, and the songs. The
text (with copious notes) is based on the first quarto (1600),
for which the copy was apparently Shakespeare's foul papers.

813   QUILLER-COUCH, ARTHUR, and WILSON, JOHN DOVER, eds. Much Ado
      About Nothing. Cambridge: Cambridge University Press, 1923,
      174 pp.
         Provides extensive textual notes, a critical introduction,
a discussion of the copy text, a section on stage history, and a
glossary. This edition is based on the first quarto (1600); the
folio text represents acting accretions between 1600 and 1623.
There is much witty rubbish in the opening scenes; but, when
Benedick and Beatrice fight their way through it and find their
true hearts, the effect is the more startling because their
natural style shines through the earlier artificiality. The play
is highly Italianate in feeling and is the closest to the spirit
of the Renaissance. See entry 820.

Criticism

814   ALLEN, JOHN A.   "Dogberry."   Shakespeare Quarterly 24 (1973):
       35-53.
            Describes Dogberry as a comic Everyman in whom bland self-
       ignorance rules supreme.   In his egotism he resembles Leonato,
       Don Pedro, and Claudio, whose pride blinds them to Borachio's
       villainy.   He also parodies their excessive sense of self-esteem
       and reputation.   His transformation into a vengeful fury at being
       called an ass parallels Leonato's all-too-tardy determination to
       defend Hero's wronged name.   Dogberry is a comic deus ex machina
       who functions like Vincentio and Prospero as a moral philosopher
       and champion of justice.

815   BERGER, HARRY L.   "Against the Sink-a-Pace: Sexual and Family
       Politics in Much Ado About Nothing."   Shakespeare Quarterly 33
       (1982):302-13.
            Views Much Ado About Nothing as a play about two "wars,"
       one between generations and one between genders.   Hero, a male-
       dominated heroine, is a willing participant in the sexual poli-
       tics of Messina, docile and submissive in her assumption that Don
       Pedro is to be her wooer and equally so when it turns out to be
       Claudio.   Beatrice in this respect is her foil, continually mock-
       ing the norms of arranged marriage and parental authority that
       Hero has been trained to respect.   The play celebrates the ending
       of bachelor happiness, the approach of the social tradition of
       marriage; as comedy it ends in the nick of time.

816   CRAIK, T.W.   "Ado."   Scrutiny 19 (1953):297-316.
            Admits that there is some disharmony of tone in Much Ado
       About Nothing but challenges a critical misconception concerning
       acts 4-5.   Virtually everyone condemns Claudio's cruelty and his
       public repudiation of Hero and proclaims the justice of
       Beatrice's vengeful move against Claudio.   To the contrary,
       Claudio is exonerated both in that Don Pedro is also fooled and
       in that Don Pedro draws all censure upon himself; Friar Francis's
       plan establishes reason over passion.   Beatrice's response, how-
       ever correct about Hero's innocence, is mistaken about Claudio's
       guilt, and her mandate to Benedick to kill Claudio represents
       passion in ascendance over reason.

817   CRICK, JOHN.   "Much Ado About Nothing."   Use of English 17
       (1965):323-27.   Reprinted in Twentieth Century Interpretations
       of "Much Ado About Nothing," ed. Walter R. Davis, Twentieth
       Century Interpretations (Englewood Cliffs: Prentice-Hall,
       1969), pp. 33-38.
            Describes Messina as reflective of the shallowness, com-
       placency, and inhumanity of a society that has turned upon itself
       in a stultifying manner.   The evil in such a society lies, not in
       a cardboard villain like Don John, but within, in the "consuming
       egotism which expresses itself in a studied artificiality, and at

times flippancy, of both language and attitude" (p. 227). Benedick and Beatrice, in their merry antagonisms and verbal bombard-
ments, provide an outlet for the normal instincts that have been
repressed in such an environment.

818   EVERETT, BARBARA. "Much Ado About Nothing." Critical
      Quarterly 3 (1961):319-35.
          Perceives Much Ado About Nothing as a less popular play
      than its predecessors in that it focuses on the mundane fact of
      life that men and women have different social planes, functions,
      loyalties, characters. It is the first play to treat the clash
      of these two worlds with a degree of seriousness and the first
      in which a woman dominates. The company of young bloods held
      together by a cheerful masculine solidarity is essentially dis-
      placed, a fact most clearly evident in Beatrice's mandate for
      Benedick to kill Claudio.

819   FERGUSSON, FRANCIS. "The Comedy of Errors and Much Ado About
      Nothing." Sewanee Review 62 (1954):24-37.
          Views Much Ado About Nothing as an interweaving of three
      plot lines unified by the theme of man's laughability as a con-
      sequence of a failure of insight. The theme is most vividly
      established in the festival scenes--Leonato's masked ball, the
      wedding scene in the church, the mourning scene at the tomb, the
      double marriage at the conclusion. Such ceremonial scenes shift
      attention from the individual to a more general, communal level.
      The final scene brings together the contrasting elements by which
      the theme has been adumbrated--true and false marriage, masking
      and unmasking, love as genuine and deluded.

820   GAW, ALLISON. "Is Shakespeare's Much Ado a Revised Earlier
      Play?" PMLA 50 (1935):715-38.
          Considers and rejects critical arguments that Much Ado
      About Nothing is Shakespeare's revision of an earlier play.
      Major attention is directed to the claim of revision in the New
      Cambridge edition (entry 813) based primarily on the "two strata"
      in the play and the inferior verse reminiscent of The Two Gentle-
      men of Verona and Romeo and Juliet. The application of the
      standard verse tests to the metrical sections and the superior
      quality of the prose strongly support the assumption that the
      play was composed shortly before its publication in 1600.

821   GILBERT, ALLAN. "Two Margarets: The Composition of Much Ado
      About Nothing." Philological Quarterly 41 (1962):61-71.
          Proclaims that there are two Margarets in the play, the one
      of witty dialogue and unimportant to the plot, the other never on
      stage but essential to it. Shakespeare probably initially devel-
      oped his plot and the role of the first Margaret from Bandello,
      later adding from Orlando Furioso or elsewhere the story of the
      disguised waiting woman. This latter function for simplicity's
      sake he gave to the Margaret of the former draft, but he failed

to revise further and thus fully integrate the two. Thus arises
the crux: why did Margaret not defend Hero against what she
knows to be a false charge? If it is a flaw, it is bothersome
only in the study, not in the theater.

822   HOCKEY, DOROTHY C. "Notes, Notes, Forsooth. . . ." Shake-
       speare Quarterly 8 (1957):353-58.
          Views Much Ado About Nothing as a dramatization of mis-
noting, a dramatized pun involving human frailty in observing,
judging, and acting sensibly. The entire church scene, for
example, turns on the idea that seeing is believing. Much is
made also of the verbal pun on notes and noting or overhearing.
To compound the confusion, Shakespeare places the principals
behind masks that further confuse the issues. The Elizabethan
pronunciation of "nothing" as "noting" reflects the centrality
of this theme of misperception. (See entry 823.)

823   HOROWITZ, DAVID. "Imagining the Real." In Shakespeare: An
       Existential View. New York: Hill & Wang, 1965, pp. 19-36.
       Reprinted in Twentieth Century Interpretations of "Much Ado
       About Nothing," ed. Walter R. Davis, Twentieth Century Inter-
       pretations (Englewood Cliffs: Prentice-Hall, 1969), pp. 39-53.
          Argues that Much Ado About Nothing, in its persistent pur-
suit of the question of appearances, reflects the multiplicity of
human truth from an ontological perspective, that is, that phenomenal reality to any given individual is only what he appre-
hends. Reality is multiple and opalescent. The title of the
play suggests the action that arises from different angles of
seeing and understanding, whether at the level of Benedick and
Beatrice in their wit combat, of Claudio in his manipulation by
Don John, or Dogberry and Verges in their bumbling attempts to
apply the law to villainy. Benedick and Beatrice, empowered by
imagination, are ultimately able to move beyond appearances and
to restore content to form. (See entry 822.)

824   KING, WALTER N. "Much Ado About Something." Shakespeare
       Quarterly 15 (1964):143-55.
          Advocates the reading of Much Ado About Nothing as a comedy
of manners, central to which is the critical inspection of a
leisure class intellectually lethargic from long acceptance of an
inherited social code. Shakespeare's two plot strands explore,
more specifically, love and courtship as verbalized but not
actually felt in such a society and the absurdity of elevating
wit to the position of a primary value in life. The love that
Benedick and Beatrice discover may be nothing, but it is the
vital something that can give genuine meaning to a life otherwise
stereotyped and impotent.

825   LEWALSKI, BARBARA.   "Love, Appearance and Reality: Much Ado
      About Something." Studies in English Literature 8 (1968):
      235-51.
           Argues that Bembo's Neoplatonic scale of love and knowledge
      provides a framework by which to gauge the development of Bene-
      dick and Claudio. In moving from a position of love's scorner to
      one in which he perceives all excellencies in Beatrice, Benedick
      approximates movement through the ladder from the lowest rung
      involving mere physical attraction and the judgment of the senses
      to the highest involving an imaginative concept of love that
      transcends the physical and finds beauty in the mind's eye.

826   McCOLLOM, WILLIAM C.   "The Role of Wit in Much Ado About
      Nothing." Shakespeare Quarterly 19 (1968):165-74. Re-
      printed in Twentieth Century Interpretations of "Much Ado
      About Nothing," ed. Walter R. Davis, Twentieth Century Inter-
      pretations (Englewood Cliffs: Prentice-Hall, 1969), pp. 67-79.
           Asserts that the kind of wit a character possesses and the
      manner in which he employs it in Much Ado About Nothing are the
      means by which the audience comes to understand and judge him.
      Shakespeare employs four types of wit in the play--puns and
      quibbles, allusive understatement and sophistic logic, flights
      of fancy, and short parodies and burlesques. Generally, the
      theme is the triumph of true wit and harmless folly (Benedick,
      Beatrice, the friar) over false or pretentious "wisdom" (Don
      John, Don Pedro, Claudio, Leonato).

827   NEILL, KERBY. "More Ado About Claudio: An Acquittal for the
      Slandered Groom." Shakespeare Quarterly 3 (1952):91-107.
           Examines the issue of Claudio's moral blame incurred for
      believing the slander against his bride in the sources and ana-
      logues for Shakespeare's plot. Shakespeare removes all traces
      of carnality from Claudio's love just as he eliminates any dif-
      ference in social position. By the addition of Don John and the
      false confession of Borachio he strengthens the credibility of
      Hero's improprieties, and he thus tends to transfer the blame
      from the hero to the villain who perpetrates the ruse. Claudio,
      moreover, is a virtuous character on the stage; no one assumes
      he has sinned and thus he accrues no moral blame. (See entry
      828.)

828   PAGE, NADINE. "The Public Repudiation of Hero." PMLA 50
      (1935):739-44.
           Argues that the repudiation of Hero at the altar is not
      morbid and distasteful but a reflection of Elizabethan social
      concepts and actualities. Woman was considered inferior to man
      intellectually and physically. The prevailing masculine attitude
      toward marriage was that it should be avoided as potentially
      destructive (Benedick) or that it should bring a wife with chaste
      reputation and a generous dowry (Claudio). Claudio's reaction

was traditional, and Shakespeare carefully stresses the devices
by which he later could be convinced of her innocence. (See
entry 827.)

829   PROUTY, CHARLES T. The Sources of "Much Ado About Nothing":
      A Critical Study, Together with the Text of Peter Beverley's
      "Ariodanto and Ieneura." New Haven and London: Yale Univer-
      sity Press, 1950, 142 pp.
         Maintains that Shakespeare's dramatic intentions can be
      determined by close examination of his modifications of his
      sources. Instead of the traditional romantic wooers, Claudio and
      Hero are realistic lovers following the way of the world with
      marriages arranged by parents or patrons. By adding Benedick and
      Beatrice, who search for emotion that is real, Shakespeare under-
      scores his reaction against such social tradition. Through
      eavesdropping in both plots he achieves a unity of tone to match
      the unity of theme.

830   ROSE, STEPHEN. "Love and Self-Love in Much Ado About Nothing."
      Essays in Criticism 20 (1970):143-50.
         Observes that the manner in which Claudio and Benedick
      respond to romantic hearsay is a measure of pride in one and
      essential humility in the other. Hearsay is at the narrative
      center of the play. It is what Hero is wooed by, what provokes
      suspicion in Claudio, what brings Benedick and Beatrice together,
      and what plays out and resolves the plot in the watch's overhear-
      ing the scheme against Hero and Benedick and Beatrice's overhear-
      ing their own stolen love poetry. Claudio's ready assumption of
      Hero's guilt reveals the very element of self-love that Benedick
      and Beatrice are able to repudiate in their declaration of love.

831   STAFFORD, T.J. "Much Ado and Its Satiric Intent." Arlington
      Quarterly 2 (1970):164-74.
         Claims that Shakespeare's major satiric thrust is against
      the courtly lover, specifically Claudio, who substitutes verbiage
      for genuine feelings and who judges entirely by appearances.
      Benedick functions as a foil to Claudio, and Dogberry serves to
      parody him. Benedick's "prosaic honesty" contrasts with Claudio's
      hyperbolic rhetoric. Dogberry, similarly, reflects the potential
      emptiness of language. The play demonstrates that genuine human
      communication must go beyond words alone, whether in matters of
      the heart or in matters of mundane social interaction.

832   STOREY, GRAHAM. "The Success of Much Ado About Nothing." In
      More Talking of Shakespeare. Edited by John Garrett. London:
      Longmans, Green; New York: Theatre Arts Books, 1959,
      pp. 128-43. Reprinted in Discussions of Shakespeare's Romantic
      Comedies, ed. Herbert Weil, Jr. (Boston: D.C. Heath, 1966),
      pp. 37-51.
         Notes that, while some twentieth-century critics complain
      of an incongruous mixture of comedy, tragedy, and farce,

Shakespeare's contemporaries viewed Much Ado About Nothing as an
exciting Italianate melodrama enlivened by two variegated sets of
humors in the wit combat of Benedick and Beatrice and the mental
intoxication of Dogberry. Any attempt to force a concept of
naturalistic realism upon the characters destroys the comedy,
which finds its center not in character but in the theme of deception, miscomprehension, and man's "giddiness" at every level
of society. The play's deliberate theatricality firmly estab-
lishes its comic perspective.

833   THOMSON, VIRGIL. "Music for Much Ado About Nothing." Theatre
      Arts 43 (1959):14-19. Reprinted in Twentieth Century Inter-
      pretations of "Much Ado About Nothing," ed. Walter R. Davis,
      Twentieth Century Interpretations (Englewood Cliffs: Prentice-
      Hall, 1969), pp. 88-95.
          Describes music in a Shakespearean production as something
      that should accentuate and underline the chosen background. Thus,
      it should not be considered until the period references of the
      production have been determined. A case in point was the John
      Houseman-Jack Landan production of Much Ado About Nothing at
      Stratford, Ontario, starring Katherine Hepburn and Alfred Drake.
      Once it was decided to use a northern Mexican setting, music was
      assembled from old popular tunes from the area utilizing a seven-
      member ensemble and a countertenor. (See entry 838.)

834   WAIN, JOHN. "The Shakespearean Lie-Detector: Thoughts on
      Much Ado About Nothing." Critical Quarterly 9 (1967):27-42.
          Considers the play to be a brilliant failure in that Shake-
      speare is bored with the Hero-Claudio plot and thus is unable to
      give that strand of action consistent artistic attention. Shake-
      speare is at the point in his career at which he begins to de-
      velop three-dimensional characters, a quality evident in the
      dynamic figures of Benedick and Beatrice. On the other hand, the
      narrative requires a melodramatic Claudio who quickly falls vic-
      tim to hearsay, deserts and denounces his bride at the altar, and
      shockingly agrees to a second marriage with wife unseen. Shake-
      speare finds himself creatively at odds with characters utterly
      devoid of psychological realism.

835   WEY, JAMES J. "'To Grace Harmony': Musical Design in Much
      Ado About Nothing." Boston University Studies in English 4
      (1960):181-88. Reprinted in Twentieth Century Interpretations
      of "Much Ado About Nothing," ed. Walter R. Davis, Twentieth
      Century Interpretations (Englewood Cliffs: Prentice-Hall,
      1969), pp. 80-87.
          Discusses the manner in which actual on-stage music and
      allusions to musical properties in the dialogue are incorporated
      thematically into the play's circle of meaning. Both music and
      musical allusions occur at moments of harmony and happiness in
      the action; conversely, they disappear at moments of disharmony
      and social disruption, even in the wooing scene itself. In the

final movement the action swells to harmony through Benedick's
love lament without accompaniment, Claudio's mornful dirge, and
the full burst of pipers. (See entry 836.)

See also The Comedies (entries 591-631) and 101, 160, 199, 235, 254,
317, 325, 458, 893.

THE TAMING OF THE SHREW

Editions

836   MORRIS, BROWN, ed. The Taming of the Shrew. The Arden
      Shakespeare. London and New York: Methuen, 1981, 316 pp.
          Includes discussion of the text, The Shrew compared to A
      Shrew, the date of composition, the authorship and sources, and
      the play itself (the stage history and adaptations). Appendixes
      cover the evidence to establish the relationship between A Shrew
      and The Shrew, the Sly scenes in A Shrew, and sources and ana-
      logues. The text, with copious notes, is based on the First
      Folio. Katherine's ostensible testing and humiliation at the
      conclusion of the play is, in fact, a "willing 'display' . . . in
      response to a series of coded messages from her husband, which
      have a secret meaning for the two of them alone" (p. 148).

837   QUILLER-COUCH, ARTHUR, and WILSON, JOHN DOVER, eds. The
      Taming of the Shrew. Cambridge: Cambridge University Press,
      1928, 194 pp.
          Provides extensive textual notes, a critical introduction,
      a discussion of the copy text, a section on stage history, and a
      glossary. This edition is based on the First Folio, for which
      the copy was probably a transcript made for Pembroke's Men in
      1592. The Taming of the Shrew is "primitive, somewhat brutal
      stuff" (p. xv). To call it a masterpiece is both to cheapen
      criticism and to lower one's level of judgment. It belongs to an
      earlier period; even so, behind Petruchio's blustering front we
      see a determined delicacy, and in Kate we recognize the typical
      Shakespearean woman, a Beatrice facing a more serious obstacle
      but willing, even seeking, to surrender.

Criticism

838   ALEXANDER, PETER. "The Original Ending of The Taming of the
      Shrew." Shakespeare Quarterly 20 (1969):111-16.
          Argues that the original ending of Shakespeare's play is
      not that found in the First Folio (spotlighting an obedient
      Katherine) but that of the 1594 quarto of The Taming of a Shrew
      (featuring a drunken Sly who prepares to go home, convinced that
      he now knows how to handle his shrewish wife). The quarto,
      pirated from Shakespeare's play, retains the final scene of what
      in The Shrew had been deleted by 1623. The importance of the

scene is that those who have been carried away by Petruchio's
triumph are returned to reality by the realization of what awaits
Sly at home.

839   DUTHIE, GEORGE IAN. "The Taming of a Shrew and The Taming of
       the Shrew." Review of English Studies 19 (1943):337-56.
           Analyzes the three major theories concerning the relation-
       ship of the anonymous A Shrew and Shakespeare's The Shrew--that
       the first is a source of the second, that the first is based on
       the second, that the two derive from a common source. Evidence
       suggests that A Shrew is memorially dependent upon The Shrew as
       it stood in an earlier form. The later revision of A Shrew,
       primarily in the full development of the subplot, resulted in
       The Shrew as we now have it. The main plot is almost entirely
       Shakespeare's work.

840   GREENFIELD, THELMA N. "The Transformation of Christopher
       Sly." Philological Quarterly 33 (1954):34-42.
           Notes the multiple levels of dramatic irony operating in a
       production of The Taming of the Shrew as a play about Petruchio
       and Katherine on a public stage pretending to be the hall of a
       great house pretending to be performed for a drunken slob of whom
       it is pretended that he is a nobleman. The Sly material of the
       Induction has an organic relationship to the shrew story. In
       dropping the emphasis of A Shrew, in which Sly indicates that he
       has found the moral of the story for a married man, Shakespeare
       makes the Induction more than a farcical setting for a farce; it
       becomes part of a subtle comic juxtaposition of two contrasting
       worlds, the real and the imaginative.

841   HOUK, RAYMOND A. "The Evolution of The Taming of the Shrew."
       PMLA 57 (1942):1009-38.
           Asserts that both The Taming of a Shrew and The Taming of
       the Shrew derive from the same source. This earlier play had
       interludes and an epilogue, but no rivalry elopement or shortened
       chronology. Shakespeare's The Shrew makes full and direct use of
       Ariosto's I Suppositi in developing the rivalry for Bianca's hand,
       and this material in turn forces a shortening of the chronology
       of the latter part of the play. The earlier form may have been
       either a completed play or a set of sketches. If the former, A
       Shrew is probably a bad quarto. Shakespeare may possibly have
       authored this hypothetical common source.

842   HUSTON, J. DENNIS. "'To Make a Puppet': Play and Play-Making
       in The Taming of the Shrew." Shakespeare Studies 9 (1967):
       73-88.
           Asserts that Shakespeare, by thwarting our expectations
       with a series of false starts (the drunken Sly, the lord's prac-
       tice through a troupe of players, Lucentio's pursuit of knowl-
       edge), jolts us into a fresh response to the theatrical expe-
       rience of Kate's "Taming." She, like the audience, is transformed

by a series of shocks, with Petruchio responding to each situation in a manner diametrically opposite to her expectations.
Petruchio makes a puppet of her (as she claims), but it is so
that she might lose her "woodenness of response."

843   KUHL, ERNEST P. "The Authorship of The Taming of the Shrew."
      PMLA 40 (1925):551-618.
         Regards the various linguistic, metrical, and stylistic
      tests claiming multiple or non-Shakespearean authorship of The
      Taming of the Shrew to be unconvincing. The play is simply a
      work of Shakespeare's youth. Much of what are called pedantic
      touches could be Shakespeare's conscious effort to create an aca-
      demic atmosphere. The plot itself is skillfully developed, and
      the characters are of a piece throughout. The Shrew, in a word,
      contains no marks of doubtful origin, and there is no reason to
      assume collaboration.

844   ROBERTS, JEANNE ADDISON. "Horses and Hermaphrodites:
      Metamorphoses in The Taming of the Shrew." Shakespeare
      Quarterly 34 (1983):159-71.
         Suggests that the Ovidian concept of metamorphosis under-
      lies the surface of The Taming of the Shrew and helps to provide
      a subtle interaction of human and natural worlds. Whereas in
      Ovid people turn into animals, in Shakespeare's play metaphoric
      animals are turned into people. Sly is through allusion changed
      from a swinish beast into a happy and wealthy lord and husband.
      More importantly, Kate and Petruchio move through a series of
      animal metaphors before finding full human identity in marriage;
      especially significant is their development in the progressive
      image of the horse.

845   SCHLEINER, WINIFRED. "Deromanticizing the Shrew: Notes on
      Teaching Shakespeare in a 'Women in Literature' Course." In
      Teaching Shakespeare. Edited by Walter Edens, Christopher
      Durer, Walter Eggers, Duncan Harris, and Keith Hull. Prince-
      ton: Princeton University Press, 1977, pp. 79-92.
         Examines the role of women in Shakespeare's comedies, espe-
      cially that of Kate in The Taming of the Shrew. Normally Kate is
      envisioned as a shrew broken to either a literal or ironic
      obedience by the male of superior strength and will. Instead,
      Kate in terms of Elizabethan psychology suffers from a humoral
      disease that often afflicts young virgins; and Shakespeare's
      spectators, familiar with the medical condition, would view her
      "cure" as an illustration of the beneficial relationship of the
      traditional hierarchical marriage.

846   SERONSY, CECIL C. "'Supposes' as the Unifying Theme in The
      Taming of the Shrew." Shakespeare Quarterly 14 (1963):15-30.
         Maintains that the unity of The Taming of the Shrew in-
      volves far more than the mere fitting together of triple plots
      and that the subplot (the "supposes" plot) provides the material

by which the organic interaction is achieved in its theme of the
suppositions or expectations concerning love. All three plots
involve the interplay of love and illusion. In the Induction
Sly's desire for his "boy wife" is pure illusion; in the subplot
love is little more than infatuation; the shrew plot holds the
possibility of happy wedded love because the love has grown from
within.

847   STETNER, S.C.V. "Baptista and His Daughters." Psychoanalytic
      Review 60 (1973):223-38.
           Maintains that Baptista is a recurring figure in Shake-
      speare's comedies, the father who, ostensibly willing to allow
      his daughter's marriage, places obstacles in her way because of
      unacknowledged incestuous feelings. Variations on such a charac-
      ter occur in Antiochus in Pericles, Portia's dead father in The
      Merchant of Venice, the Duke of Milan in The Two Gentlemen of
      Verona, and Egeus in A Midsummer Night's Dream. Typically the
      father does not recognize his incestuous proclivities, and he is
      eventually reconciled with his son-in-law.

848   WELLS, STANLEY. "The Taming of the Shrew and King Lear: A
      Structural Comparison." Shakespeare Survey 36 (1980):55-66.
           Asserts that Shakespeare in writing a play must have been
      alert to both the complementary and opposing functions of the
      mind and the body in the layout of the overall narrative design,
      the characterizations, and the sentiments. In The Taming of the
      Shrew Petruchio determines to use his mind to suppress Kate, just
      as mind has confused Sly in the Induction. The taming of Kate
      involves both her mind and her body. The process serves to bring
      her to full realization of herself as a woman. Lear's mental
      process, though far more complex and tragic, is structurally
      similar.

See also The Comedies (entries 591-631) and 79, 141, 179, 182, 220,
250, 259, 499, 687, 700, 1134.

TROILUS AND CRESSIDA

Reference Works

849   TANNENBAUM, SAMUEL A., and TANNENBAUM, DOROTHY R., comps.
      William Shakespeare: "Troilus and Cressida." Elizabethan
      Bibliographies, 29. New York: Privately Printed, 1943, 44 pp.
           Cites 919 unannotated items covering major scholarship on
      Troilus and Cressida from the beginnings to 1941. The material
      is divided by the following categories and is arranged alpha-
      betically by section--editions, adaptations, abstracts, transla-
      tions, theatrical history, commentary, bibliography, addenda.
      The majority of the material (669 items) is loosely classified
      under commentary.

Editions

850   HILLEBRAND, HAROLD N., ed. Troilus and Cressida. A New
      Variorum Edition of Shakespeare. Philadelphia and London:
      J.B. Lippincott, 1953, 613 pp.
         Uses the First Folio as the copy text. On each page, for
      that portion of the text, provides variant readings, textual
      notes, and general critical commentary. Following the text are
      sections, citing varying critical opinion, on the printing of the
      two quartos and the folio; the early stage history; the date;
      authorship; Troilus and contemporary affairs; sources; structural
      analysis; Troilus on the modern stage; the individual characters;
      and a list of works consulted.

851   PALMER, KENNETH, ed. Troilus and Cressida. The Arden Shake-
      speare. London and New York: Methuen, 1982, 337 pp.
         Includes discussion of the text, the date, sources, and the
      play itself (crucial scenes, time and time's subjects, treason
      and prophecy, identity and attributes, pride and envy, styles and
      methods) as well as appendixes covering disturbances in sheet F
      in the First Folio, the possibility of the play's being written
      for a performance at one of the inns of court, a discussion of
      degree, and selections from the source materials. This edition
      is eclectic, based primarily on the first quarto (1609) but with
      readings also from the folio. Troilus and Cressida is, quite
      frankly, a generic anomaly--at once comedy, tragedy, satire,
      tragic farce. The men, while they await engagement in battle,
      question and argue; and it is the form of those questions that
      gives the play its peculiar dramatic idiom. It is essentially
      "a schematic play, an exercise in dramatic paradigms" (p. 83),
      again and again juxtaposing similar or opposed attitudes and
      forcing the spectator to draw a comparison. The play invites and
      then frustrates judgment; it has recently grown in popularity
      because it "hits the temper of the times" (p. 93).

852   WALKER, ALICE, ed. Troilus and Cressida. Cambridge:
      Cambridge University Press, 1957, 254 pp.
         Provides extensive textual notes, a critical introduction
      (covering discussion of the generic confusion, Shakespeare and
      the Troy story, the audience, the satire, the integrity of the
      play, the date, and the sources), a discussion of the copy text,
      a section on stage history, and a glossary. This edition is
      eclectic, based primarily on the folio but with quarto readings
      allowed. The major thrust of the play is satiric, the intent
      somewhat like Jonson's to reform manners through the ridicule of
      folly; with the last words assigned enigmatically to Pandarus,
      the correction of folly is left to the audience's good sense.

Criticism

853   BAYLEY, JOHN. "Time and the Trojans." <u>Essays in Criticism</u> 25
      (1975):55-73.
           Speaks of Shakespeare's ability to provoke a sense of com-
      pressed time that we bring to the play--our entire range of
      accumulated impressions of a character, his culture, and that
      which has made him what he is--as the playwright's most singular
      achievement. Anomalously, <u>Troilus and Cressida</u>, by disregarding
      the beginning and the ending of the war, creates an intensity of
      focus upon the present. The nightmarish world of the present is
      given no meaning by a context of time. Thersites speaks for the
      play in a kind of Brechtian way.

854   BOWDEN, WILLIAM R. "The Human Shakespeare and <u>Troilus and
      Cressida</u>." <u>Shakespeare Quarterly</u> 8 (1951):167-77.
           Argues against interpretations of <u>Troilus and Cressida</u> that
      stress the supremacy of reason. Clearly, Shakespeare in his
      plays does not subscribe to the doctrine that a man's passion
      should always be ruled strictly by his reason. Such an approach
      forces us to either an apologetic or a scornful attitude toward
      Troilus, either of which leaves us emotionally unsatisfied. The
      Greeks and Trojans do not represent opposing values; they simply
      form the backdrop for a sympathetic portrayal of Troilus and
      Hector. Even though neither survives, the important thing is the
      value the world places upon them.

855   CAMPBELL, OSCAR JAMES. <u>Comicall Satyre and Shakespeare's
      "Troilus and Cressida</u>." San Marino, Calif.: Huntington
      Library, 1938, 246 pp.
           Establishes a direct relationship between <u>Troilus and
      Cressida</u> and Jonson's "comicall satyres," by which comedy is
      converted into dramatic satire "devoted to the denunciation,
      exposure, or derision of some kind of folly and abuse" (p. viii).
      Probably written for a private audience at one of the inns of
      court, <u>Troilus</u> pictures social disintegration by combining the
      excoriation of sexual indulgence with the derisive delineation of
      the Homeric heroes. Both Thersites as railer and Pandarus as
      leering pimp function as choric figures to direct the spectators'
      caustic laughter, which in turn reflects a kind of moral enlight-
      enment. (See entry 212.)

856   FARNHAM, WILLARD. "Troilus in Shapes of Infinite Desire."
      <u>Shakespeare Quarterly</u> 15 (1964):257-64. Reprinted in
      <u>Shakespeare: Modern Essays in Criticism</u>, ed. Leonard F. Dean,
      rev. ed. (New York: Oxford University Press, 1967),
      pp. 283-94.
           Argues that Troilus as both soldier and lover is shaped by
      a concern for infinite desire. As a lover of fire and air he
      fantasizes about impossible deeds to prove his love, but Shake-
      speare undercuts the dignity of his passion through the imagery

of his "wallowing" in delight. Similarly, Troilus's role in the
Trojan debate reflects an intensity of honor that is at least
partially a form of self-indulgence. By the end of the play
Troilus the lover falls tragically, but ironically Troilus the
warrior "rises to lead Troy in outfacing the 'discomfort' of
Hector's death" (p. 263).

857   GAGEN, JEAN. "Hector's Honor." Shakespeare Quarterly 19
      (1968):129-37.
          Observes that Hector's decision in the Trojan debate to
      allow the arguments of Troilus and Paris for keeping Helen to
      prevail has provoked both critical praise and condemnation. To
      one it reflects the superior value structure of the Trojans; to
      another it is a surrender to decadent honor freed from the re-
      straints of justice and reason. The key to this diversity is
      that the Renaissance recognized two forms of honor—an outward
      form based on reputation and public esteem and an inner form
      based on virtue or justice. Hector's dilemma was one shared by
      many in the Renaissance.

858   GREENE, GAYLE. "Language and Value in Shakespeare's Troilus
      and Cressida." Studies in English Literature 21 (1982):
      271-85.
          Calls attention to Ulysses's prophecy that in a world in
      anarchy the meaning of right and wrong in action and in word will
      be lost. Just such a situation has come to pass in the play's
      culminating action when Troilus perceives Cressida's vows to be
      meaningless and words to have become mere words without designa-
      tion. While Ulysses sees the dissolution of language as conse-
      quence and Troilus as cause, they both believe that the validity
      of verbal communication depends upon a knowable reality. Troilus
      and Cressida reflects not only the crisis of values in the late
      Renaissance but also the linguistic revolution that it was pre-
      cipitating.

859   HARRIER, RICHARD C. "Troilus Divided." In Studies in the
      English Renaissance Drama in Memory of Karl Julius Holzknecht.
      Edited by Josephine W[aters] Bennett, Oscar Cargill, and
      Vernon Hall, Jr. New York: New York University Press, 1959,
      pp. 142-56.
          Attempts to explain the dramatic logic in the play's con-
      cluding scene with a bitterly vibrant Troilus, having found no
      release in violent death, yearning for vengeance as a means of
      meliorating his agony. Troilus is intended to evoke an equal
      mixture of sympathy and condemnation. He has some claim to our
      affection if only by comparison with those around him. His claim
      that all value is in the prizer does not repel as much as
      Achilles' insistence that all value is in the prized.

860   KAUFMANN, R.J. "'Ceremonies for Chaos': The Status of
      Troilus and Cressida." ELH 32 (1965):139-57.
            Notes that great drama is philosophical in the sense that
      it constructs a dialectic for testing the utility and integrity
      of inherited, communal illusions. Troilus and Cressida is a
      play about competing modes of knowing and the final view, instead
      of upholding any single mode, is pluralistic. The organizing
      theme is the self-consuming nature of all forms called vice or
      virtue by one scale of value or another. It fails to provide a
      secure vantage from which to evaluate the action, whereas high
      tragedy focuses on the emotional cost of specific commitment.

861   KAULA, DAVID. "Will and Reason in Troilus and Cressida."
      Shakespeare Quarterly 10 (1961):272-76.
            Speaks of Troilus as someone between a sensualist and an
      idealist. He appears to be moved by two wills, sexual passion
      and rational choice, and the word will as used in the play vacil-
      lates between these two senses. The religious quality of his
      imagery reveals his tendency to elevate his position of the
      moment to sacred and inviolable terms. This tendency to deifica-
      tion is fatal for him because it renders him incapable of dealing
      in war or sex with contingencies inherent in the human condition.

862   KIMBROUGH, ROBERT. Shakespeare's "Troilus and Cressida" and
      Its Setting. Cambridge, Mass.: Harvard University Press,
      1964, 208 pp.
            Views Troilus and Cressida as Shakespeare's not wholly
      successful attempt to combine elements of the new drama of the
      private theaters with characteristics of popular drama as a means
      of offsetting the competition with the newly established chor-
      ister companies. Following a consideration of how the Trojan
      story would appear to an Elizabethan playwright, compares its
      major areas (the love story, the war as viewed from the opposing
      sides) to analogous aspects of the preceding Shakespeare canon.
      If the result is not cohesive, in part because of the attempt at
      inclusiveness of perspective, there are a dazzling variety of
      characters and a medley of profound themes.

863   KNOWLAND, A.S. "Troilus and Cressida." Shakespeare Quarterly
      10 (1959):353-65.
            Observes that overattention to the diverse values of the
      Greeks and the Trojans and to the theme of time is equally re-
      ductionistic. Both result from neglecting the total pattern of
      action in favor of certain scenes or speeches. The juxtaposition
      of the ornate language of Ulysses, Hector, and Nestor with the
      prosaic style of Cressida, Helen, and Paris underscores a similar
      contrast in the pattern of events; it becomes a part of the sharp
      contrasts that make up the play, an inevitable ignoble and
      prosaic denigration of the ideal. The play also demonstrates,
      though, that, if the achievements are transient, the impulse to
      accomplish endures.

864   LAWRENCE, WILLIAM W. "Troilus, Cressida and Thersites."
       Modern Language Review 37 (1942):422-37. Reprinted in
       Shakespeare's Problem Comedies, 2d ed. (New York: Frederick
       Ungar, 1960), pp. 118-59.
           Focuses on the diverse critical interpretations of the
       characters of Troilus and Cressida and of the function of
       Thersites. There is no evidence that the characters are intended
       as personifications of abstract types, and it is dangerous to
       evaluate the play as a philosophic poem. Shakespeare to some
       extent was bound by the interpretations of the material current
       at the time. Both Troilus and Cressida are debased as lovers,
       and Thersites functions to provide comic relief and to expose
       caustically the weaknesses of the Greeks. Shakespeare probably
       wrote the play for a special audience that would enjoy the sordid
       flavor.

865   McALINDON, THOMAS. "Language, Style, and Meaning in Troilus
       and Cressida." PMLA 84 (1969):29-41.
           Views the disappointingly anticlimactic nature of the duel
       between Hector and Ajax (4.5), in which Hector's bombast and
       Latinized diction and neologisms appear utterly out of character,
       as a key to understanding the play as a whole. Throughout the
       action Shakespeare employs elements of stylistic dissonance to
       undermine the heroic and romantic characters, violations of
       decorum that reflect the graver maladies afflicting them. The
       aubade, for example, is evoked only to be degraded on the morning
       of the lovers' parting. Oaths and vows are spoken in one scene
       only to be broken in the next.

866   MORRIS, BRIAN. "The Tragic Structure of Troilus and
       Cressida." Shakespeare Quarterly 10 (1959):481-91.
           Observes that the failure to conform to traditional modes
       of tragedy has led Troilus and Cressida to be labeled some form
       of comedy. Shakespeare uses two relatively static plots to
       balance the climactic construction of the play; the monolithic
       war story forms the backdrop for a series of scenes revealing
       various stages of the love story. The conflict of honor and
       reason is focused on Troilus, whose passionate nature betrays
       him as surely as does Othello's. The peculiar tragic effect
       results from the use in the climactic scene of the comic device
       of multiple levels of perception--Diomedes and Cressida, Troilus
       and Ulysses, Thersites.

867   MUIR, KENNETH. "Troilus and Cressida." Shakespeare Survey 8
       (1955):28-39.
           Compares Shakespeare's delineation of Troy in The Rape of
       Lucrece and Troilus and Cressida. In both Shakespeare is sympa-
       thetic to the Trojans and critical of the Greeks, but in the
       latter both sides are presented more critically. Troilus is as
       unwise in idealizing Helen as in idealizing Cressida; his love
       is thwarted both by Cressida's wantonness and his environment.

Hector is doomed in his failure to realize that the age of
chivalry is dead. In general, the play deals with the foolish-
ness of both war and love for unworthy purposes, an exposure of
idealism from multiple perspectives.

868   NOWOTTNY, WINIFRED M.T. "'Opinion' and 'Value' in Troilus and
        Cressida." Essays in Criticism 4 (1954):282-96.
            Views Ulysses, in his ability to preserve social stability
        among individuals intent on self-gratification, and Troilus, who
        espouses the view that a thing is valuable only as it is valued
        by others, as the polar thematic opposites in Troilus and
        Cressida. The idea is central both to the Trojan debate, in
        which Troilus argues the relative worth of Helen, and to the
        Greek debate, in which Ulysses argues that only fixed law pre-
        vents the collapse of society. The play is acted out against the
        backdrop of this antithesis between the world views, that of the
        statesman and that of the individual creative imagination.

869   OATES, JOYCE CAROL. "The Ambiguity of Troilus and Cressida."
        Shakespeare Quarterly 17 (1966):141-53.
            Argues that the play is a tragedy deliberately aborted by
        the savagery of its comic insight. It refuses to yield to analy-
        sis because of the incomplete assimilation of tragic and anti-
        tragic elements. Three strains work against tragedy--the use and
        rejection of ritualistic elements, the corruption and mockery of
        tragic values, and the incongruity of a tragic hero in an anti-
        tragic environment. The play has a distinctly modern quality in
        its existential insistence on man's inability to transcend his
        fate in a shabby, illusion-ridden world.

870   PRESSON, ROBERT K. Shakespeare's "Troilus and Cressida" and
        the Legends of Troy. Madison: University of Wisconsin Press,
        1953, 165 pp.
            Notes the continued popularity of the Troy legend in the
        reign of Elizabeth, but especially the intense interest that
        developed between 1598 and 1602 when a new interpretation was
        placed upon the material. Shakespeare drew his narrative from a
        variety of sources, in large part from Chapman's Illiad--for the
        characterization, the narrative flavor--but also from the
        Recuyell, Lydgate, and Chaucer. The theme is the destructive
        quality of passion: in Achilles, pride; in Hector, love of per-
        sonal fame and glory; in Troilus, infatuation. It is reduction-
        istic to call this "gateway to the later tragedies" (p. 142) a
        problem play, a dark comedy, or a comical satire. (See entry
        873.)

871   RABKIN, NORMAN. "Troilus and Cressida: The Uses of a Double
        Plot." Shakespeare Studies 1 (1965):265-82.
            Maintains that a successful interpretation of Troilus and
        Cressida must come to grips with the underlying idea that relates
        its several discrete elements, the relationship between theme and

plot. The play, more specifically, illustrates a double-plot
structure (the affair between Troilus and Cressida and the Greek
ruse to renew Achilles' participation in the Trojan War) to convey a complex theme implicitly through action and ironic language. As a symphonist sets theme against theme before resolving
them in a stasis, so Shakespeare by developing the two plot
strands forces upon us the theme of man's value and its relationship to time.

872   RICHARDS, I.A. "Troilus and Cressida and Plato." Hudson
      Review 1 (1948):362-76.
         Observes that Troilus and Cressida is not without power and
      that it in many ways reflects Plato at his height. Troilus is a
      young man who in the course of the play must confront his own mad
      idolatry, must watch the division within himself of will and
      reason. When he describes the gods as so angry that they will
      take Cressida from him, the reference is to Lachesis in The
      Republic, who sees to it that mortals reap the rewards of their
      choices. In more general terms, the central thought of the play
      accords closely with Plato.

873   ROLLINS, HYDER E. "The Troilus-Cressida Story from Chaucer to
      Shakespeare." PMLA 32 (1917):383-429.
         Notes that Shakespeare found the characters and incidents
      of the Troilus-Cressida legend far degraded from the Chaucerian
      treatment. The story is traced through Lydgate, Caxton's
      Recuyell, Elderton, Turbervile, and Gascoigne. In Robert
      Henryson's Testament of Creseyde (1532), Creseyde is regarded as
      a wanton who ends in misery, struck down at the height of her
      folly by retribution. Subsequent authors (Howell, Whetstone,
      Thomson, Heywood) follow Henryson in firmly establishing this
      literary tradition. (See entry 870.)

874   SCHWARTZ, ELIAS. "Tonal Equivocation and the Meaning of
      Troilus and Cressida." Studies in Philology 69 (1972):304-19.
         Maintains that disagreement concerning the theme of Troilus
      and Cressida stems from an intentional ambiguity as the tone
      changes abruptly from mock heroic to bathetic to farcical to
      pathetic to brutally satiric to near tragic. The result is a
      generic mixture envisioning the world as a meaningless chaos to
      which the characters (and the spectators) respond in various
      ways. Each in his own way attempts to create value where no
      value does or can exist; each realizes that time one day will end
      all.

875   SOELLNER, ROLF. "Prudence and the Price of Helen: The Debate
      of the Trojans in Troilus and Cressida." Shakespeare Quarterly
      20 (1969):255-63.
         Maintains that the Trojan debate is of central significance
      to the theme of Troilus and Cressida and that the philosophic
      dialectic of the scene is not borrowed from Caxton or Lydgate but

is original with Shakespeare. The voice of passion is pitted
against the voice of prudence; Helena is only nominally the subject in a debate centering on the relevance of traditional morality. Hector argues from a traditional philosophic position,
while Troilus reveals both contempt for reason and a skepticism
that sees all values as subjective. Shakespeare uses the haunt-
ing figure of Cassandra to point up man's inability to foresee
the tragic consequences of action based on passion.

876   STEIN, ARNOLD. "Troilus and Cressida: The Disjunctive
       Imagination." ELH 36 (1969):147-67.
          Describes Pandarus's cynical view of love in the opening
scene of Troilus and Cressida as a countervoice that prevails
over Troilus's exclamations. The second scene reinforces this
mood in Cressida's lack of refinement in her conversation with
Pandarus and her outright admission of fashionable reluctance
aimed primarily at intensification of Troilus's lust. Similarly,
the Greeks debate the grand mechanism of war but avoid mention of
the rotten core of Helen that has produced it. The play engages
our minds but deliberately keeps our sympathies at a distance,
thereby becoming "a dramatic form of the disjunctive imagination
deploying mutually exclusive alternatives" (p. 167).

877   TATLOCK, JOHN S.P. "The Chief Problem in Shakespeare."
       Sewanee Review 24 (1916):129-47.
          Explores the Elizabethan background of Shakespeare and the
age in order to come to terms with the puzzling nature of Troilus
and Cressida and the modern response to it. The Trojan story was
extremely popular both among the learned and the illiterate. The
play is made up of nobility and scurrility, but they are not
mixed. The satiric tone is embedded in Thersites, Ajax, and the
love story, and this material Shakespeare apparently added to
appeal to the masses. There appears to be no validity in attempting to use biographical theory to explain the play's sar-
donic tone.

878   TAYLOR, GEORGE C. "Shakespeare's Attitude Towards Love and
       Honor in Troilus and Cressida." PMLA 45 (1930):781-86.
          Observes that the theory that Shakespeare was working
within a fixed literary tradition does not explain why one's
reaction to the play involves a sense of revulsion. The problem
centers on Shakespeare's untypical bitter and cynical treatment
of love and honor. In all of his work the balance between
romanticism and realism is delicately maintained. Characters
like Berowne, Mercutio, Faulconbridge, Falstaff, Iago, and
Enobarbus with slightly different emphasis might invoke a mood
of cynicism and prurience. Troilus and Cressida is simply one
play in which Shakespeare fails to maintain this balance.

879   URE, PETER.   "Troilus and Cressida."   In William Shakespeare:
      The Problem Plays.   London: Longmans, Green, 1961, pp. 32–44.
      Reprinted in Four Centuries of Shakespearian Criticism, ed.
      Frank Kermode (New York: Avon, 1965), pp. 257–67.
            Speaks of Troilus and Cressida as problem tragedy, noting
      structural peculiarities of the debate scenes and multiple prin-
      cipal characters.   The interwoven war and love themes are given
      a sardonic tone by Thersites's crude commentary.   The debate
      scenes provide the keys to the meaning and construction of the
      entire play.   Typical is the irony inherent in Ulysses' emphasis
      on degree in his great speech coupled with his plan to invert
      rank for politicomilitary purposes in elevating Ajax over
      Achilles.   The play ends in a minor key of melancholy with
      Hector's death and Troilus's meaningless commentary.

For discussion of the satiric nature, see entries 855, 864, 874, 876,
878. See also The Comedies (entries 591–631) and 80, 83, 89, 101,
160, 162, 205, 212–13, 215, 226, 228, 232, 258, 267, 286, 291, 307,
318, 328, 343, 351, 612–13, 624, 627, 937, 964, 973, 1029, 1376.

TWELFTH NIGHT

Reference Works

880   MARDER, LOUIS, comp.   "Twelfth Night": A Supplementary Bib-
      liography 1901–1965.   The New Variorum Shakespeare.   New York:
      American Scholar Publications, 1965, 22 pp.
            Includes representative scholarship on Twelfth Night from
      1901 to 1965 and is intended to supplement H.H. Furness's Vario-
      rum edition of 1901 (see entry 882).   The material is categorized
      under reproductions of original folio editions, bibliographical
      sources, modern editions, and critical studies (alphabetically
      arranged).   While not exhaustive, the material represents every
      major category of scholarship and criticism.

881   McAVOY, WILLIAM C., comp.   "Twelfth Night, or, What You Will":
      A Bibliography to Supplement the New Variorum Edition of 1901.
      New York: Modern Language Association, 1984, 57 pp.
            Supplements the Variorum edition of 1901 (see entry 882),
      citing the most significant items published on the play between
      1901 and 1981.   The material is classified under editions, text,
      date, commentary, criticism, sources, music, staging, and stage
      history.

Editions

882   FURNESS, HENRY HOWARD, ed.   Twelfth Night, or, What You Will.
      A New Variorum Edition of Shakespeare.   Philadelphia: J.B.
      Lippincott, 1901, 434 pp.

Uses the First Folio as the copy text. On each page, for
that portion of the text, provides variant readings, textual
notes, and a generous sampling of general critical commentary.
Following the text are sections on the nature of the text, the
date of composition, the sources, criticisms, the characters,
stage history, costumes, and a list of works consulted.

883   LOTHIAN, JOHN M., and CRAIK, T.W., eds. <u>Twelfth Night</u>. The
      Arden Shakespeare. London: Methuen; Cambridge, Mass.:
      Harvard University Press, 1975, 188 pp.
          Includes discussion of the text, sources, critical inter-
      pretations, and stage history, as well as appendixes on the songs
      and a selection from the source <u>Riche His Farewell to the Mili-</u>
      <u>tary Profession</u> by Barnabe Riche. The text is based on the First
      Folio, for which the copy was probably a transcript of Shake-
      speare's foul papers. The date of composition is 1601, and the
      source is the Italian play <u>Gl'Ingannati</u> as utilized by Riche in
      his prose tale of Apolonius and Silla. Contrary to criticism of
      the eighteenth and nineteenth centuries, which generally found
      the play to be delightful and sunny, modern critics tend to be
      divided between the assumption that it is a happy comedy and the
      assumption that it is not only a farewell to comedy but an out-
      right rejection of mirth and romance. The character of Malvolio
      reflects a Jonsonian influence, and efforts to render him sympa-
      thetic arise from reflecting on his personality rather than from
      experiencing its impact in the theater. Feste's concluding song
      strikes a distinctly somber note and prepares the members of the
      audience for the transition between the fanciful world of comedy
      and the realistic world to which they must return.

884   QUILLER-COUCH, ARTHUR, and WILSON, JOHN DOVER, eds. <u>Twelfth</u>
      <u>Night or What You Will</u>. Cambridge: Cambridge University
      Press, 1930, 193 pp.
          Provides extensive textual notes, a critical introduction,
      a discussion of the copy text, a section on stage history, and a
      glossary. This edition is based upon the First Folio, for which
      the copy was probably the promptbook or a transcription of it.
      <u>Twelfth Night</u> is, in a sense, Shakespeare's farewell to comedy.
      It is replete with characters and situations proved effective in
      earlier stage worlds, but they are somehow transmuted into a
      wistful vision of life that, even while it acknowledges the
      necessity of sentiment and illusion, also points to its dangers;
      the mirth abides, but it comes through a tissue of shadowed
      reality.

Criticism

885   BARNET, SYLVAN. "Charles Lamb and the Tragic Malvolio."
      <u>Philological Quarterly</u> 33 (1954):177-88. Reprinted in
      <u>Twentieth Century Interpretations of "Twelfth Night</u>," ed.
      Walter N. King, Twentieth Century Interpretations (Englewood
      Cliffs: Prentice-Hall, 1968), pp. 53-62.

Observes that the nineteenth-century conception of Malvolio
as a tragic character is essentially the responsibility of
Charles Lamb, who in recollecting in 1822 his memories of the
role as played by Robert Bensley wrote of the "dignity" and
"gravity" of the character: "I confess that I never saw the
catastrophe of this character, while Bensley played it, without
a kind of tragic interest." Not only is Lamb writing twenty-six
years after Bensley retired; his recollection in no way agrees
with contemporary accounts of the actor's role. Just possibly
Lamb's view was colored by the fact that his father was a kind of
steward in the household of Samuel Salt.

886   BERRY, RALPH. "Twelfth Night: The Experience of the
      Audience." Shakespeare Survey 34 (1981):111-19.
      Argues that Shakespeare in the course of Twelfth Night
forces the audience to reevaluate festive comedy itself, that the
tensions between gulling and romantic action, between the joke
gone too far and the sense of playful abandon translate into the
ideas of rain, aging, and labor in Feste's final song. The tension is best visualized in the characters of Sir Toby and Malvolio, polarized extremes. It is a critical mistake not to admit
that the spectators with some degree of sympathy sense in Malvolio's dark-house experience a form of human debasement. His
calling the group "pack" is a key; we have unwittingly become
involved in a kind of bear-baiting. (See entries 891, 896.)

887   DOWNER, ALAN S. "Feste's Night." College English 13 (1952):
      258-65.
      Notes that Feste's satiric jibes are both direct and in-
direct. In his first appearance, for instance, he overtly ad-
dresses Olivia as a fool. With Orsino in act 2, however, the
mockery is subtle as—in response to a call for an old song that
dallies with love—Feste sings of unrequited love in terms of the
extravagant imagery of a mournful lover reduced to a thousand
sighs searching for his grave. In both such cases, Feste's mocking function is central to the action, involving the exposure of
hypocrisy and self-delusion.

888   DRAPER, JOHN W. The Twelfth Night of Shakespeare's Audience.
      Stanford: Stanford University Press, 1950, 280 pp.
      Insists on a thorough understanding of the characters—
their inner psychology and outer social relationships—as the key
to coming to terms with Shakespeare's structure and theme in
Twelfth Night. Belch, for example, seems drawn from actual
Elizabethan life, a younger son who could not hope to inherit
lands and who became something of a soldier in his earlier years;
of choleric humor, he has become a parasite in Olivia's household. Individual chapters are devoted, as well, to Aguecheek,
Mary, Malvolio, Orsino, Olivia, and Feste. The episodes of the
plot arise from the interactions of these personalities on their
several social planes.

889   EAGLETON, TERENCE. "Language and Reality in Twelfth Night."
      Critical Quarterly 9 (1967):217-28.
            Stresses the power of language to shape reality in Twelfth
      Night. It can serve to clarify the truth as in the opening
      dialogue between Viola and the sea captain. It can distort
      reality as in the conversation between Maria and Sir Andrew. It
      can create an illusion as in Maria's forged letter to Malvolio.
      It can regulate reality as in Orsino's self-persuasion that he is
      deeply in love, or as in Belch's and Feste's practice upon others.
      Indeed, the entire play is an overlapping series of verbally
      created unrealities.

890   HOLLANDER, JOHN. "Musica Mundana and Twelfth Night." In
      English Institute Essays 1956. Edited by Northrop Frye. New
      York: Columbia University Press, 1957, pp. 55-82.
            Comments on the Renaissance conception of music as of three
      types--mundana, humana, instrumentalis. The first two were
      actually not forms of music at all but figurative ascriptions of
      a regularity to nature. Musica mundana, more precisely, referred
      to the harmony of the universe as observable in the cosmological
      order of the elements, astral bodies, and seasons; of cardinal
      importance is the notion of due proportion. In Twelfth Night the
      role of music is fundamental to the spirit of the play. A play
      about parties and feasting and what they do to people, it is also
      a play of the application of Boethian order and proportion to
      human behavior.

891   _____. "Twelfth Night and the Morality of Indulgence."
      Sewanee Review 68 (1959):220-38. Reprinted in Modern Shake-
      spearean Criticism, ed. Alvin B. Kernan (New York: Harcourt,
      Brace & World, 1970), pp. 228-41.
            Maintains that Twelfth Night is consciously written as a
      counterpart to Jonsonian satiric comedy. Instead of merely pre-
      senting humor characters--static emblematic personality distor-
      tions--the play literally dramatizes the metaphor. The opening
      scenes introduce the characters and establish their active na-
      tures. Feste embodies not the spirit but the action of revelry
      as Malvolio does that of the scapegoat. The prank played on
      Malvolio is a condensed representation of the entire action, and
      the play--celebrating the Feast of the Epiphany--issues in the
      characters' realization and acceptance of their true natures.
      (See entries 886, 896.)

892   HOTSON, LESLIE. The First Night of "Twelfth Night." London:
      Rupert Hart-Davis, 1955, 256 pp.
            Asserts that Twelfth Night was first performed on Twelfth
      Night, 6 January 1601, for Queen Elizabeth at Whitehall where her
      guest of honor was Virginio Orsino, Duke of Bracciano. These
      festive events have been long obscured by the notoriety of
      Essex's rebellion a few weeks later. In this most musical of his
      plays, Lady Olivia is a shadow of the Queen in her youth, Orsino

a shadow of her courtly guest. Since it is a moment of licensed
saturnalia, the play makes sport with Knollys, the "sergeant
major" of the household.

893   HUNTER, G.K. "Twelfth Night." In Shakespeare: The Late
       Comedies: "A Midsummer Night's Dream," "Much Ado About
       Nothing," "As You Like It," "Twelfth Night." London:
       Longmans, Green, 1962, pp. 43-55. Reprinted in Discussions
       of Shakespeare's Romantic Comedies, ed. Herbert Weil, Jr.
       (Boston: D.C. Heath, 1966), pp. 92-101.
            Observes that, while it is similar to As You Like It in its
       mechanics, the effects of Twelfth Night are far different. Af-
       fectation and self-indulgence in Illyria cannot be so lightly re-
       garded; here debilitating affectation is everywhere, among the
       central characters and the marginal, the presumably wise and the
       foolish. All of the characters are victims of the need to hide
       from some form of truth and self-identity. The title itself
       suggests that the season of misrule is at its very limits. The
       tentative impetus toward reconciliation and the melancholy mood
       point toward the tragic vision of the later plays.

894   HUSTON, J. DENNIS. "'When I Came to Man's Estate': Twelfth
       Night and the Problems of Identity." Modern Language
       Quarterly 33 (1972):274-88.
            Describes Viola's decision to disguise herself as a page
       rather than a eunuch as an indication of her gradual acceptance
       of the fact that her brother might be alive and of her search for
       identity through a borrowed masculinity. She must play out
       various roles to discover what she is not, attempting to inte-
       grate Sebastian's masculinity into her own personality. When
       Sebastian reappears, she puts aside her usurped masculine freedom
       and accepts her role as woman and wife.

895   LEWALSKI, BARBARA. "Thematic Patterns in Twelfth Night."
       Shakespeare Studies 1 (1965):168-81.
            Asserts that Twelfth Night, reflecting the spirit and form
       of traditional Christmastide festivities at court and in the
       great houses of England, is informed as well by the religious
       significance associated with the Epiphany and the Christmas
       season. Typologically the story draws into itself and embodies
       larger meanings. Illyria is an Elysium-like setting of good
       will to which is opposed Malvolio or bad will, but it sorely
       needs the restoration and peace promised by the Christmas tid-
       ings. Maria and Feste are restorative forces of wit, while
       Viola and Sebastian function as restorative forces of love.

896   LOGAN, THAD JENKINS. "Twelfth Night: The Limits of Fes-
       tivity." Studies in English Literature 22 (1982):223-38.
            Suggests that Twelfth Night is saturnalian comedy that
       calls the spectators' attention to the reasonable limits of
       festivity by abolishing those very limits in the stage world of

Illyria. As such, the play merges the two major comic traditions, that of the celebration of festivity in which characters
grow and discover more about their true nature and that of
realistic didactic and satiric cast. The play discovers for us
through its action the dangers of life without something of the
principle for which Malvolio stands; Feste's concluding song is
one last vivid reminder. (See entries 886, 891.)

897   MARKELS, JULIAN. "Shakespeare's Confluence of Tragedy and
      Comedy: Twelfth Night and King Lear." Shakespeare Quarterly
      15 (1964):75-88. Reprinted in Twentieth Century Interpreta-
      tions of "Twelfth Night," ed. Walter N. King, Twentieth Cen-
      tury Interpretations (Englewood Cliffs: Prentice-Hall, 1968),
      pp. 63-69.
          Notes that the fool's function is in many ways similar in
      Twelfth Night and King Lear. Both perform a corrective social
      function for the characters who least know themselves--Malvolio
      and Lear; and in both instances the spiritual experience involves
      an obsession with the clothing they wear. Both at the outset are
      affected asses. In his tragic world Lear must actually be driven
      to madness by the Fool, whereas Malvolio's refusal to yield to
      madness when prompted by Feste disguised as Sir Topas signifies
      the opportunity for the continuation of a healthy society.

898   MEUSCHKE, P., and FLEISHER, J. "Jonsonian Elements in the
      Comic Underplot of Twelfth Night." PMLA 48 (1933):722-40.
          Focuses on the direct relationship between Jonson's humor
      characters in Every Man in His Humor and Every Man out of His
      Humor and the Shakespearean characters of Sir Toby and Sir Andrew
      (victimizer and gull) and Malvolio. Andrew, more particularly,
      is an unadulterated fool and gull, blindly imitating Toby, aping
      Viola's poetic speech, and claiming to be a great lover. Mal-
      volio, a social pretender and hypocrite, is only incidentally a
      Puritan. Shakespeare in these figures adapts the Jonsonian humor
      character to his own larger dramatic purposes.

899   NAGARAJAN, S. "'What You Will': A Suggestion." Shakespeare
      Quarterly 10 (1959):61-67.
          Suggests that self-deception as it manifests itself in love
      is the key to what is comic in the play and that the subtitle
      "What You Will" describes the ability for the individual to con-
      trol or to be controlled by the passion. The lovers unrequited
      in love have previously deceived themselves and no longer compre-
      hend their true personality. This theme will extend into more
      serious situations with Helena and Marina and will require a new
      comic form to accommodate the theme; the style in Twelfth Night
      is on the edge of being inadequate to the intrinsic demands of
      the theme.

900   PRESTON, DENNIS R.   "The Minor Characters in Twelfth Night."
       Shakespeare Quarterly 21 (1970):167-76.
           Views the minor characters in Twelfth Night as orchestral
       accompaniment to the solo passages, thereby preventing the prin-
       cipals from bogging down in tiring repartee. In the opening
       scene, for example, Curio and his prosaic nature and Valentine
       with his flourishing rhetoric verbally frame the pining Orsino
       in love with love. The sea captain and Antonio through their
       affection enhance the characters of Viola and Sebastian respec-
       tively. Fabian, a "well-born servant" useless in the overstaffed
       household, seems to be a social extension of Feste, reveling with
       Sir Toby and aiding in the tricks on both Sir Andrew and
       Malvolio.

901   SALINGAR, LEO.   "The Design of Twelfth Night." Shakespeare
       Quarterly 19 (1958):117-39. Reprinted in Discussions of
       Shakespeare's Romantic Comedies, ed. Herbert Weil, Jr.
       (Boston: D.C. Heath, 1966), pp. 102-10.
           Perceives in Twelfth Night a combination of romantic story
       and comic realism with both controlled by the spirit of satur-
       nalia. The subplot literally pictures Toby's long season of mis-
       rule, while the main plot figuratively expresses carnival in the
       lovers' mistaken identities, their psychological masking, and the
       reversal of roles with ladies as wooers. By consciously making
       his plot more improbable and illogical than that of his sources,
       Shakespeare shifts attention to sentiment rather than to story,
       to the triumph of natural love over affection and melancholy.
       (See entries 904, 906.)

902   SCHWARTZ, ELIAS.   "Twelfth Night and the Meaning of Shake-
       spearean Comedy." College English 28 (1967):508-19.
           Points out the differences between satiric comedy, which
       delineates characters who disobey the norms of social conduct and
       provoke a derisive laughter communally binding the spectators,
       and Shakespearean comedy, which sets forth characters with whom
       we identify and form a sympathetic bond because we recognize in
       them our own flaws, either actual or potential. This foolishness
       in the course of the action is not castigated but celebrated.
       In Twelfth Night all of the characters, save Sir Andrew and
       Malvolio, recognize their affectations; our response is "whole-
       souled" (p. 519) rather than merely intellectual.

903   SEIDEN, MELVIN.   "Malvolio Reconsidered." University Review
       28 (1961):105-14.
           Calls Twelfth Night a triumphant hoax. Shakespeare treats
       the confused and somewhat myopic lovers quite compassionately and
       without satire; they time and again escape involvements in em-
       barrassments and humiliation. The playwright develops this tone
       for the romantic strain by diverting our promiscuous and destruc-
       tive laughter to the figure of Malvolio. He, moreover, carefully

avoids a direct clash between Malvolio and the lovers, using,
instead, secondary characters to bait the steward. Malvolio is
a comic Coriolanus, baited not only by his enemies but also by
those who should, socially, be his friends.

904   SUMMERS, JOSEPH H. "The Masks of Twelfth Night." University
       Review 22 (1952):25-32.
            Notes that in Twelfth Night there is no conflict of genera-
       tions; instead, the members of the younger generation create
       their own barriers through a lack of self-knowledge. Each char-
       acter wears a mask--some unconsciously like Olivia (that of a
       grief-stricken lady) and Orsino (that of a literary lover), some
       consciously like Feste (that of a professional jester) and Viola
       (that of a young man). Generally we laugh at the former and with
       the latter. By the end of the play all save Feste are unmasked
       and comically forced to recognize their true identity. (See
       entries 901, 904.)

905   TILLEY, MORRIS P. "The Organic Unity of Twelfth Night." PMLA
       29 (1914):550-56. Reprinted in Shakespeare: Modern Essays in
       Criticism, ed. Leonard F. Dean, rev. ed. (New York: Oxford
       University Press, 1967), pp. 134-43.
            Argues that, beneath the romantic story of a love at cross
       purposes, Shakespeare sets forth an attack on the Puritan's
       tendency to disclaim against all forms of pleasure. Amidst the
       Puritans' sweeping reforms and the follies engaged in by their
       opponents, Shakespeare composed Twelfth Night in praise of the
       much-needed well-balanced approach to life. Viola and Feste
       stand for such humane moderation while Malvolio, Sir Toby, and
       Sir Andrew represent the extremes on both sides.

906   WILLIAMS, PORTER. "Mistakes in Twelfth Night and Their
       Resolution: A Study in Some Relationships of Plot and Theme."
       PMLA 76 (1961):193-99. Reprinted in Shakespeare's "Twelfth
       Night," ed. Leonard F. Dean and James A.S. McPeek (Boston:
       Allyn & Bacon, 1965), pp. 130-42.
            Views the characters' mistakes, not merely as devices to
       incite superficial laughter, but as relations of subconscious
       patterns of human behavior. While the basic action moves through
       masking, the resulting deceptions and errors, and unmasking, the
       truly significant developments occur beneath the surface. The
       characters, wearing psychological masks that block their normal
       behavior and render them incapable of experiencing love, must be
       comically purged in order to achieve the richest fulfillment of
       both their physical and spiritual capacities. (See entries 901,
       904.)

See also The Comedies (entries 591-631) and 101, 160, 162, 199, 235,
239, 245-46, 253, 271, 285, 302, 306, 331.

THE TWO GENTLEMEN OF VERONA

Editions

907 LEECH, CLIFFORD, ed. The Two Gentlemen of Verona. The Arden
     Shakespeare. London: Methuen; Cambridge, Mass.: Harvard
     University Press, 1969, 122 pp.
        Includes discussion of the text, date, sources, stage
     history, and critical interpretations. The text is based on the
     First Folio, for which the copy was probably a transcription of
     Shakespeare's foul papers. The material was apparently written
     in four stages with the earliest section dating from 1592 and the
     play in its present form from late 1593. It derives from the
     mass of friendship literature extending from the Middle Ages to
     the seventeenth century, especially Damon and Pithias, Diana
     Enamorada, and Brooke's Romeus and Juliet. The Two Gentlemen of
     Verona adheres closely to Terentian formula, making use of parody
     again and again in the juxtaposition of scenes. The play builds
     in its own dialectic, mocking love without denying either its
     power or value. Its seminal nature—anticipating characters and
     motifs in several later plays—suggests Shakespeare's own view
     of its significance.

908 QUILLER-COUCH, ARTHUR, and WILSON, JOHN DOVER, eds. The Two
     Gentlemen of Verona. Cambridge: Cambridge University Press,
     1921, 110 pp.
        Provides extensive textual notes, a critical introduction,
     a discussion of the copy text, a section on stage history, and a
     glossary. This edition is based on the First Folio, for which
     the copy was probably an assembled text by the scrivener Ralph
     Crane. While the play is admittedly early, the action of the
     final scene is so deeply flawed that it is impossible to ascribe
     it to Shakespeare; the outlandish coup de theatre possibly repre-
     sents some botcher's later revision. Otherwise the play is light
     Italianate comedy, and it appears to be the earliest play in
     which Shakespeare begins to weld character into plot.

Criticism

909 ATKINSON, DOROTHY F. "The Source of The Two Gentlemen of
     Verona." Studies in Philology 41 (1944):223-34.
        Claims that the major source of The Two Gentlemen of Verona
     is the fifth story of Henry Wotton's A Courtly Controversy of
     Cupid's Cautels (1578), a translation of Jacques d'Yver's Le
     printemps d'Yver. Jorge de Montemayor's Diana provides the
     source for only the Julia parts of the plot that Shakespeare
     grafted onto Wotton. The numerous parallels in narrative and
     character reflect Shakespeare's tendency to use materials close
     at hand; he may well have been introduced to the volume by Thomas
     Kyd, who used the first story as the source for the play scene in
     The Spanish Tragedy and for the whole of Soliman and Perseda.

Supplemented by Jim C. Pogue, "The Two Gentlemen of Verona and Henry Wotton's A Courtlie Controversie of Cupid's Cautels," Emporia State Research Studies 10, no. 4 (1962):17-21.

910   BROOKS, H.F. "Two Clowns in a Comedy (To Say Nothing of the Dog): Speed, Launce (and Crab) in The Two Gentlemen of Verona." Essays and Studies, n.s. 16 (1963):91-100.
        Asserts that Speed and Launce contribute directly to the thematic unity of The Two Gentlemen of Verona. Launce, for example, in each of his scenes burlesques the major themes; his monologue of impersonation with the aid of props is far from irrelevant clownage in its underlining of Proteus's love and friendship. Similarly, Speed, in having to explain Sylvia's ruse in confessing her love for Valentine, underscores the blind infatuation of his master. Later, Crab's indiscretions hilariously reflect Proteus's transgressions. The subordinate characters are in no way allegorical, but their actions contribute to and humorously reinforce Shakespeare's deliberate thematic design.

911   DANBY, JOHN F. "Shakespeare Criticism and The Two Gentlemen of Verona." Critical Quarterly 2 (1960):309-21.
        Defends The Two Gentlemen of Verona as thematically a straightforward and serious dramatic treatment of the confrontation of love and friendship, an issue popular in sixteenth-century literature. Our modern lack of sympathy with issues in this debate has led to a wide variety of distorted critical evaluations of the play.

912   GODSHALK, WILLIAM. "The Structural Unity of The Two Gentlemen of Verona." Studies in Philology 66 (1969):168-81.
        Argues that, despite critical charges of structural flaws, The Two Gentlemen of Verona is firm in its construction. By utilizing three recurring elements--classical myths, letters, and journeys--Shakespeare initiates schemes of dramatic irony that mirror the action of previous events, thereby providing architectonic continuity of action and unity of purpose. The emphasis on classical myths with tragic outcomes and on the failure of communication in a series of letters adds psychological tension and suspense. Through the layered structure of the journeys, on the other hand, Shakespeare focuses on the theme of the educative process and points to a comic resolution.

913   LINDENBAUM, PETER. "Education in The Two Gentlemen of Verona." Studies in English Literature 15 (1975):229-44.
        Maintains that, despite an unevenness of tone, Shakespeare's intent in The Two Gentlemen of Verona is thematically serious--to dramatize man's moral education. Both Valentine and Proteus are adept in the social arts, but neither has experienced love. While romantic passion confuses Valentine, he never loses his nobility of character. Proteus, however, is transformed into a liar both to his mistress and to his friend. Valentine and

Sylvia join in act 5 in revealing a truly noble pattern of conduct to him, thus producing a therapeutic shock of repentance.

914   PERRY, THOMAS A.   "Proteus, Wry-Transformed Traveller."
      Shakespeare Quarterly 5 (1954):33-40.
          Asserts that Proteus's faithlessness must be viewed against
      the background of an inexperienced youth's travelling abroad and
      his transformation into an Italianate courtier. In choosing
      Milan as Proteus's destination Shakespeare draws on its popular
      reputation both as an imperial court and as a fashion-conscious
      community. The play was written in the 1590s when a wave of re-
      action set in against the Italianate as well as the French and
      Spanish. Proteus, in a word, is no villain; he is corrupted by
      the Italian influence, but is finally brought to his senses.

915   SARGENT, RALPH M.   "Sir Thomas Elyot and the Integrity of The
      Two Gentlemen of Verona." PMLA 65 (1950):1166-80.
          Suggests that the flurry of action at the end of The Two
      Gentlemen of Verona--involving Proteus's repentance for attempt-
      ing to rape Sylvia and, in turn, Valentine's offering her to his
      erstwhile friend--closely adheres to its source in Elyot's The
      Book of the Governor, which also juxtaposes the superior claim
      of friendship to love. Shakespeare focuses on Proteus's fall
      and Valentine's offer of salvation, an offer not without danger
      to Sylvia and to Valentine himself. The confidence in friendship
      and love provides the means by which the characters can achieve
      durable human relationships and by which Proteus is redeemed.
      (See entry 917.)

916   SCOTT, WILLIAM D.   "Proteus in Spenser and Shakespeare: The
      Lover's Identity." Shakespeare Studies 1 (1965):283-93.
          Focuses on Shakespeare's intentions in the characterization
      of Proteus, tracing the significance of his name not only to the
      mythical god of shapes but also to another shape changer identi-
      fied with him--Vertumnus, more flagrantly a wooer who utilizes
      lust, deceit, and trickery. The associations are implied by
      Spenser in the Proteus of book 3 of The Faerie Queene. The theme
      of identity with delineations of the true and false self, the
      subordinate theme of love and friendship, and the heroine who
      brings her man to a reconciliation with his true nature will be
      important elements of many Shakespearean comedies to come.

917   SMALL, SAMUEL A.   "The Ending of The Two Gentlemen of Verona."
      PMLA 48 (1933):767-76.
          Views the conclusion of The Two Gentlemen of Verona as an
      artistic failure primarily because Shakespeare complicated the
      narrative by adding a new character, Valentine, and a new the-
      matic motif, the conflict between love and friendship. Romantic
      love traditionally was regarded as superior to the bond of
      friendship. By offering Sylvia to Proteus and never acknowledg-
      ing his affront to her, Valentine violates this primacy of love

and distorts the conventional ending of romantic comedy. (See
entry 915.)

918   TETZELI von ROSADOR, KURT. "Plotting the Early Comedies: The
      Comedy of Errors, Love's Labor's Lost, The Two Gentlemen of
      Verona." Shakespeare Survey 37 (1984):13-22.
           Reaffirms the primacy of plot in Shakespeare's dramatic
      craftsmanship, especially the importance of precipitation or
      prefiguring both the middle and end of a play within its protasis.
      The protasis of The Two Gentlemen of Verona introduces the theme
      of love and two attitudes toward it in Valentine and Proteus,
      their reversal of attitude prefigured in their very names. So,
      too, honor is contrasted with love in the opening dialogue. The
      characters' attitudes will change as often as their locales. The
      protasis fails, however, to establish a meaningful relationship
      between plot, theme, and structure.

919   WEIMANN, ROBERT. "Laughing With the Audience: The Two
      Gentlemen of Verona and the Popular Tradition of Comedy."
      Shakespeare Survey 22 (1969):35-42. Reprinted in German in
      Shakespeare Jahrbuch (Weimar) 106 (1970):85-99.
           Analyzes the dramatic function of laughter in The Two
      Gentlemen of Verona as an essential means of organizing and
      evaluating through a larger comic vision. Control of the laughter
      rests primarily with the various levels of the awareness manipu-
      lated by Speed, Launce, and Julia in their role as a kind of comic
      chorus. Launce and Speed provide a burlesque kind of parallelism
      with farce interwoven with the romantic scenes. In such a fashion
      the audience is drawn into and participates in the comic vision.
      Laughter is not so much a weapon of ridicule as it is an agent of
      communal ritual.

See also The Comedies (entries 591-631) and 199, 204, 229, 285, 290,
317, 325, 789, 820, 847.

V. The Tragedies

920   BATTENHOUSE, ROY W. Shakespearean Tragedy: Its Art and Its
      Christian Premises. Bloomington and London: Indiana Univer-
      sity Press, 1969, 466 pp.
          Believes that mainstream Christianity was the heritage that
      provided Shakespeare his fundamental premises concerning the
      value of life and the symbolism for signaling its meaning. Romeo
      and Juliet, for example, is envisioned as the tragic triumph of
      carnal love or eros leading both principals to suicide and damna-
      tion. The scene at the Capulet tomb, in particular, is developed
      as an upside-down analogy to the Easter story. Hamlet, too, is a
      story of damnation in which Hamlet wilfully chooses to pursue
      physical revenge and is in act 5 with Claudius a cocelebrant in
      a Black Mass. In a word, the tragedies can be more fully under-
      stood through a "knowledge of Shakespeare's background in medi-
      eval Christian lore—which includes theology, symbolism, and the
      principle of analogy" (p. 46).

921   BAYLEY, JOHN. Shakespeare and Tragedy. London: Routledge &
      Kegan Paul, 1981, 228 pp.
          Views Shakespearean tragedy as rising above conventional
      form and idea to achieve an unparalleled degree of artistic
      vitality. Not overtly concentrating on showing "how stark and
      awful life is" (p. 50), King Lear, nonetheless usurps life,
      achieving its supreme quality through the "free satisfactions
      both of delight and sorrow that seem unrelated to the tragic
      necessities" (p. 63). Similarly, Hamlet moves beyond a moral-
      istic focus on the avenger's mission; here the paradox is "to
      find that life is too involved with [Hamlet's] own instincts and
      affections for him to be avenged on it" (p. 176). Shakespeare,
      in a word, reveals the incompatibility of the protagonist with
      his situation in Hamlet, King Lear, and Othello by drawing the
      spectators as close as possible to the protagonist's conscious-
      ness and in Julius Caesar, Antony and Cleopatra, Coriolanus, and
      Timon of Athens by setting the central figure apart as "something
      from which a moral can be drawn, a case can be studied" (p. 73).

922   BOWERS, FREDSON T.   Elizabethan Revenge Tragedy 1587-1642.
       Princeton: Princeton University Press, 1940, 288 pp.
           Traces the background, origin, and chronological develop-
       ment of revenge tragedy as practiced in England between 1587 and
       1642.   The major classical motivation was Seneca, whose tragedy
       strongly emphasizes blood-revenge for murder or flagrant injury.
       Kyd's The Spanish Tragedy popularized the type on the public
       stage, establishing the fundamental formula--the motive of re-
       venge by a male blood relative, a ghost to incite the action,
       hesitation on the part of the hero, madness, a Machiavellian
       villain.   Titus Andronicus conforms closely to this Kydian
       formula; additionally, Aaron in his delight in villainy for its
       own sake reflects the influence of Marlowe's Barabas.   Hamlet is
       the supreme achievement in the form, differing from other revenge
       tragedies only because of Shakespeare's superior sense of drama-
       turgy; all of the elements are present, but the tragedy is made
       to turn upon the character of the revenger.

923   BRADBROOK, MURIEL C.   Themes and Conventions of Elizabethan
       Tragedy.   Cambridge: Cambridge University Press, 1935,
       275 pp.
           Describes, in the first half, the assumptions that an
       Elizabethan would bring to a tragic performance based on the
       traditions and conventions of the public theater.   The power of
       Elizabethan drama lies more in the words than in the action; the
       chief characteristics of the stage are its flexibility, its
       natural locale, its fast and slow time, its emotive gestures,
       and its symbolic groupings.   The action, hovering between the
       realistic and the allegorical, is cumulative rather than logical,
       and the speech is frequently patterned.   Part 2 focuses on the
       work of Shakespeare's major contemporaries.

924   BRADLEY, A.C.   Shakespearean Tragedy.   New York: St. Martin's
       Press, 1904, 448 pp.
           Describes the substance of Shakespearean tragedy as a story
       of exceptional calamity set in a world in which the ultimate
       power is a moral order and leading to the death of a man of high
       estate.   Constructed in three movements (exposition, central
       action, catastrophe), the plot features movement toward decisive
       success by one set of forces, then to destruction by the reaction
       the success provokes.   The key to Hamlet is not the burden of
       moral scruples, an effete personality, or an overly contemplative
       nature; instead, he is a figure whose love for Ophelia is weak-
       ened and deadened by melancholy; he returns from his sea voyage
       convinced that he is in the hands of Providence.   Othello, for
       all his poetry, is little experienced in the corrupt products of
       civilized life; he faces in Iago a creed that absolute egoism is
       the only rational and proper guide to action.   Lear is Shake-
       speare's greatest achievement but, as a consequence of vagueness
       of scene and darkness of atmosphere, not his greatest play.
       Macbeth is a tragedy with characters almost superhuman in nature

in which the protagonist is a soul "tortured by an agony which
admits not a moment's repose, . . . rushing in frenzy towards its
doom" (p. 265).

925   BRANHAM, GEORGE C. Eighteenth-Century Adaptations of Shake-
       spearean Tragedy. Berkeley and Los Angeles: University of
       California Press, 1956, 220 pp.
           Notes that the altered Shakespearean plays illustrate in
       their diction, dramatic theory, and dramatic practice the liter-
       ary tastes of the eighteenth century. The first chapter provides
       an overview of the three clusters of adaptations in the century,
       while later chapters discuss the influence of critical theory,
       the neoclassical rules (the unities, decorum, verisimilitude),
       the language (prosody, elevation of diction, reduction of
       imagery), character and moral, and stage effectiveness (action
       and report, female roles, play endings).

926   BROOKE, NICHOLAS. Shakespeare's Early Tragedies. London:
       Methuen, 1968, 214 pp.
           Claims that the early tragedies have failed to receive
       their due share of estimation. Titus Andronicus, not wholly
       successfully, attempts to adapt the techniques of poetic styliza-
       tion to the stage; its central theme is--like Ovid's--the de-
       terioration of individuals to bestial states under the dictates
       of vengeful passion. History in Richard III becomes imagina-
       tively felt as a huge impersonal force against which Richard,
       despite his villainy, struggles with a strange degree of heroism.
       The contrasted uses of verse and prose in Romeo and Juliet is a
       highly organized dramatic instrument; the play is brilliant if a
       bit cloying in its controlled multiplicity. Richard II ambiva-
       lently sets Richard's rhetorical abilities against a new and
       calculating concept of divine order. Julius Caesar also manipu-
       lates the audience's sympathies by juxtaposing the roles of
       haughty conqueror, conscience-torn conspirator, and Machiavellian
       opportunist. Hamlet contrasts an honorable, active, and creative
       world with one that is negational, chaotic, and diseased; to the
       very end the protagonist is ambivalent, orderly and disorderly,
       creative and destructive.

927   CAMPBELL, LILY BESS. Shakespeare's Heroes: Slaves of Passion.
       Cambridge: Cambridge University Press, 1930, 296 pp.
           Argues that Shakespearean tragedy is rooted in the Eliza-
       bethan psychological concepts of popular moral philosophy, the
       most significant aspect of which is that the healthy body and the
       healthy mind are dependent upon the maintenance of a proper
       relationship between the spirits, the natural heat, and the vital
       moisture or humors. Subjection of the vital moisture to un-
       natural heat, the consequence of permitting passion to transcend
       reason, results in the unnatural humor known as melancholy adust.
       All of Shakespeare's major protagonists suffer some form of such
       melancholy adust that transforms the healthy individual into one

capable of evil action. Hamlet, for example, is a study in
grief; Othello, in jealousy; Lear, in wrath in old age; Macbeth,
in fear as it consumes both him and his wife. These tragedies
represent one aspect of the general effort in the Renaissance to
understand man's nature and his relationship with divine will.
Their lesson is that the protagonists, by failing to balance
passion by reason, render themselves Fortune's puppets.

928   CANTOR, PAUL A. Shakespeare's Rome: Republic and Empire.
       Ithaca: Cornell University Press, 1976, 228 pp.
          Views Julius Casear as central to a historical trilogy
       chronicling the tragedy of the fall of Rome, with Coriolanus as
       its historical antecedent and Antony and Cleopatra as its suc-
       cessor. The blending of aristocracy, monarchy, and democracy
       reflects the eclectic political situation in Rome, which never
       strictly epitomized one particular form. Julius Caesar explores
       prominent imperial heroes while Coriolanus focuses on Rome in its
       founding phase. Antony is a companion piece to Coriolanus; both
       protagonists are embodiments of the values of their times. The
       Rome of Caesar occupies a balance between the "spirited" and the
       "erotic" city of the other plays. (See entry 281.)

929   CARLISLE, CAROL JONES. Shakespeare from the Greenroom: Actor
       Criticisms of Four Major Tragedies. Chapel Hill: University
       of North Carolina Press, 1969, 493 pp.
          Presents comments on the playwright by English-speaking
       actors from the eighteenth century to the present. Chapters on
       Hamlet, Othello, King Lear, and Macbeth include actors' general
       views of the play; their consideration of particularly enigmatic
       aspects of the plot such as the question of Hamlet's age, or his
       madness, or his attitude toward his mother; the intensity of
       Othello's passion, the degree of his blackness; the question of
       the appropriate setting for King Lear, the shifting interpreta-
       tions of the philosophic center; the nature of Macbeth's internal
       struggle as "demon incarnate" or "conscience in anguish," the
       method of presenting the supernatural machinery. The book pro-
       vides a wealth of theatrical opinion from personalities in a
       unique position to offer insights and to convey a sense of
       shared pleasure in Shakespeare's creations.

930   CHAMPION, LARRY S. Shakespeare's Tragic Perspective.
       Athens: University of Georgia Press, 1976, 279 pp.
          Directs attention to the various structural devices by
       which Shakespeare creates and sustains in the spectators the
       necessary pattern of anticipation and double vision that pro-
       vokes them simultaneously to participation in the protagonist's
       anguish and to judgment of his actions. Chapters on each of the
       tragedies examine such devices as tragic pointers, character
       parallels and foils, subplots and diversionary episodes, cosmic
       ramifications, and analytic asides and soliloquies. The middle
       tragedies are envisioned as those in which the spectators most

closely identify with the central figure, largely the consequence
of soliloquies that reflect his spiritual experience. In the
final tragedies Shakespeare, in developing a societal perspective, seems deliberately to force the spectators to view the
character from a greater distance and thus to recognize that the
causes of tragedy exist not in isolation but as a combination of
equally significant internal and external destructive forces.

931   CHARLTON, H.B. Shakespearian Tragedy. Cambridge: Cambridge
       University Press, 1948, 246 pp.
          Asserts that Shakespearean tragedy, while not religious, is
       intensely spiritual. In the early plays man accepts easily the
       laws of God; in the later, more vividly portraying man's im-
       measurable spiritual potentiality, he must shape from within him-
       self those values and relations that are "God-like." Man is a
       part of the animal kingdom; the beast is within, and the world
       often appears to be amoral; but the faith in man permeates the
       tragedies--faith in the vitalizing influence of human kindness,
       fellowship, and love despite the adversities and atrocities of
       life.

932   CHARNEY, MAURICE. Shakespeare's Roman Plays: The Function of
       Imagery in the Drama. Cambridge, Mass.: Harvard University
       Press, 1961, 250 pp.
          Investigates Julius Caesar, Antony and Cleopatra, and
       Coriolanus through verbal and nonverbal images that are set in
       a context not only of words but also of the dramatic situation,
       the interplay of characters, and the sequence of time. While
       Caesar illustrates a limited and controlled Roman style, Antony
       is characterized by hyperbolic and sensually evocative imagery.
       The imagery of Coriolanus depicts a cold and objective world with
       only Meninius comfortable with figurative language. Like Clemen
       (entry 139), Charney is paramountly concerned with the dramatic
       function of such language.

933   COE, CHARLES NORTON. Shakespeare's Villains. New York:
       Bookman Associates, 1957, 76 pp.
          Analyzes the effectiveness of Shakespeare's delineation of
       the villain by the criteria of the degree of psychological accu-
       racy in motivation, the degree of verisimilitude established by
       revelation of the character's background and antecedent action,
       and the general complexity of characterization. To this end he
       compares Aaron and Iago, Shylock and Angelo, and Richard III and
       Macbeth. Aaron, more specifically, is considered a stage vil-
       lain, the stock figure of the Machiavel; as such he lacks credi-
       bility and complexity.

934   COURSEN, HERBERT R., Jr.   Christian Ritual and the World of
       Shakespeare's Tragedies. Lewisburg: Bucknell University
       Press, 1976, 441 pp.
           Argues that the Elizabethan, regardless of religious per-
       suasion, went to the theater with a close familiarity with the
       Eucharist that deepened his response to Shakespeare's drama. The
       distinct pattern of this religious ritual is seen in several
       tragedies; the comic pattern moving from sin and alienation to
       contrition and thence to reconciliation is aborted in each
       instance by a tragic hero, who through a flagrant act of defiant
       self-will drives himself away from the possibilities of Communion.
       Hamlet, for instance, interrupts the play-within-the-play at a
       critical moment when Claudius might have confessed his murder,
       succumbing to a passion that preempts sacramental potentiality.
       Othello's critical moment is his parodic marriage with Iago,
       which reflects the discrepancy between what he believes he is
       doing and what he is actually doing. Lear's abdication parodi-
       cally mirrors "God's giving the earth to unfallen man" (p. 212),
       and Macbeth imagistically reenacts the fall of man (Macbeth and
       Lady Macbeth) and the coming of the Messiah (Malcolm).

935   CREETH, EDMUND. Mankynd in Shakespeare. Athens: University
       of Georgia Press, 1976, 192 pp.
           Argues that Macbeth, Othello, and King Lear represent re-
       creations of the morality plays The Castle of Perseverance, Wis-
       dom Who Is Christ, and The Pride of Life. The passion-flawed
       nobility of Brutus and Hamlet develops into a true duality of
       character in the protagonists who follow, and the subordinate
       figures are sharply divided into factions of good and evil. The
       design of moral drama reestablishes itself, but Shakespeare
       transmutes the material in such a way that what is central to the
       theological drama becomes overtone and what is figurative or
       metaphorical becomes real.

936   CUNNINGHAM, JAMES V. Woe or Wonder: The Emotional Effect of
       Shakespearean Tragedy. Denver: University of Denver Press,
       1951, 134 pp.
           Addresses the question of what emotional effects Shake-
       speare intends to evoke through the catastrophe of his major
       tragedies. By imagining the reality of the events the spectators
       achieve the emotional experience of woe or pity. Anticipation
       of the tragic catastrophe is fearful; the catastrophe itself is
       woeful. The tragic fact itself for Shakespeare is death. Wonder
       results from the tragic incident or the marvellous turn of
       events. As a consequence of a willed act or moral choice the
       irrational is ordered and presented in such a way as to evoke
       these emotions.

937   DICKEY, FRANKLIN. <u>Not Wisely But Too Well: Shakespeare's</u>
      <u>Love Tragedies</u>. San Marino, Calif.: Huntington Library,
      1957, 205 pp.
          Focuses on <u>Romeo and Juliet</u>, <u>Troilus and Cressida</u>, <u>Antony</u>
      <u>and Cleopatra</u>, and the poems <u>Venus and Adonis</u> and <u>The Rape of</u>
      <u>Lucrece</u>. Shakespeare as a Renaissance playwright conceived of
      love as a rational force or a passionate force. The latter type
      upsets the balance of the body humors, producing a form of
      melancholia and leading in extreme cases to rash and bloody
      deeds. While <u>Romeo</u> utilizes many comic aspects of love, the
      protagonists themselves are morally responsible for their actions
      and ultimately for their suicides. Similarly, while Antony and
      Cleopatra provoke extreme terror and pity from the spectators,
      Shakespeare forces us to view their relationship, albeit glorious,
      as tarnished, "examples of rulers who threw away a kingdom for
      lust" (p. 179).

938   DOLLIMORE, JONATHAN. <u>Radical Tragedy: Religion, Ideology and</u>
      <u>Power in the Drama of Shakespeare and His Contemporaries</u>.
      Chicago: University of Chicago Press, 1984, 312 pp.
          Challenges the accepted Christian and humanist readings of
      Renaissance drama, arguing that the playwrights--actively sub-
      versive in their critique of ideology, the demystification of
      political and power relations, and the decentering of man--
      developed a "subliteral encoding which bypasses the perfunctory
      surveillance of the censor" and is "reactivated in the perfor-
      mance" (p. 28). A manifestation of the struggle in that period
      between residual, dominant, and emergent conceptions of reality,
      the dramas through the irony encoded in their closures defy the
      central assumption of a harmonious telos and a retributive provi-
      dentialism. <u>King Lear</u> is, above all, a play about power, prop-
      erty, and inheritance. In the events of the conclusion that
      sabotage the attempt at recuperation, the tragedy nullifies the
      vision of the humanist, who represents suffering as a mysterious
      ground for man's self-redemption. Both <u>Antony and Cleopatra</u> and
      <u>Coriolanus</u> "effect a skeptical interrogation of martial ideology
      and in doing so foreground the complex social and political
      relations which hitherto it tended to occlude" (p. 204).

939   EVANS, BERTRAND. <u>Shakespeare's Tragic Practice</u>. Oxford:
      Clarendon Press, 1979, 327 pp.
          Analyzes the structure of Shakespeare's tragedies in terms
      of the varying levels of discrepant awareness, that is, the
      variation in the amount of knowledge the characters hold concern-
      ing themselves, their situation, and the other characters.
      Whereas exploitation of the gap in the characters' knowledge is
      the primary concern in comedy, the emphasis in tragedy is equally
      on the means by which the discrepancy is created and the disas-
      trous consequences. In most instances, then, major emphasis is
      directed upon the villain and his practice. Interestingly, only

in Antony and Cleopatra do the spectators fail to hold a significant information advantage over the principal figure.

940   FARNHAM, WILLARD. Shakespeare's Tragic Frontier: The World
       of His Final Tragedies. Berkeley: University of California
       Press, 1950, 289 pp.
            Examines the paradoxical nobility in the protagonists of
       Shakespeare's final tragedies--Timon, Macbeth, Antony, and
       Coriolanus. The world of these plays is carefully distinguished
       from those of the earlier tragic heroes in that these last fig-
       ures are pervasively tainted but also possess a nobility that
       appears to emanate from their very ignobility. In a world devoid
       of conventional villains, these characters seem bent on destroy-
       ing themselves, provoking simultaneous sympathy and antipathy.
       The tragic form is extended to its widest limits in these chill-
       ing analyses of deeply flawed human greatness.

941   FELPERIN, HOWARD. Shakespearean Representation: Mimesis and
       Modernity in Elizabethan Tragedy. Princeton: Princeton Uni-
       versity Press, 1977, 199 pp.
            Asserts that any dramatist must utilize the conventions of
       his art to establish a contextual frame of reference even though
       spectators cannot fully identify with and respond to a character
       overtly recognized as a product of literary tradition. Shake-
       speare, like other successful playwrights, resolves this paradox
       by "subsuming within his work a recognizably conventional model
       of life, repudiating that model, and thereby creating the illu-
       sion that he uses no art at all, that he is presenting life di-
       rectly" (p. 66). Shakespeare's plays, in other words, burst the
       traditional mold and produce a startlingly naturalistic character
       or situation. Such a view accommodates the immediate response of
       the spectator or critic who brings no specialized historical
       knowledge to the playhouse as well as that of the scholar fully
       attuned to the literary tradition upon which the play is
       constructed.

942   FOREMAN, WALTER C., Jr. The Music of the Close: The Final
       Scenes of Shakespeare's Tragedies. Lexington: University
       Press of Kentucky, 1978, 228 pp.
            Examines the shape that Shakespeare gives his tragic fig-
       ures through their encounter with death and the kind of figures
       who become the center of a new community when this death occurs.
       Whether by suicide (Romeo and Juliet, Brutus, Othello, Antony and
       Cleopatra), murder (Titus, Coriolanus, Hamlet, Macbeth,
       Richard II), or heartbreak (Lear), death is visualized by the
       spectators and in most instances by the characters themselves as
       either a rest from suffering or as the only possible thing con-
       sistent with their integrity. The tragic figure is the play's
       "center of energy," and his actions disrupt the prevailing system
       of order and value. His death wish is a response to both specific

and existential grief, to the inexorable limitations which in one way or another bind and restrict his aspirations.

943   FRYE, NORTHROP. Fools of Time: Studies in Shakespearean Tragedy. Toronto: University of Toronto Press, 1967, 121 pp.
      Observes that tragedy is the consequence of juxtaposing with the pattern of man's natural movement toward death a heroic movement involving a man's capacity for suffering that transcends the ordinary. In Hamlet the three concentric tragic spheres of Laertes, Fortinbras, and Hamlet interweave an ironic tragedy of blood and de casibus tragedy with the tragedy of moral imperative. In Lear Shakespeare interweaves a moral pattern with a pattern of the absurd. Lear's death parallels the absurdity of Christ's death and prompts a similar act of faith in the spectator.

944   HOLLOWAY, JOHN. The Story of the Night: Studies in Shakespeare's Major Tragedies. Lincoln: University of Nebraska Press, 1961, 187 pp.
      Berates those critics who insist on reading Shakespearean tragedy as a didactic metaphor depicting man as transcendent in some fundamentally moral struggle. The consistent pattern is rather that of a protagonist who moves from being the cynosure of society to being estranged from it and whose fall and death conveys something of the expulsion of the scapegoat. The evil of society takes shape in this protagonist and eventually is eradicated. The spectators vicariously experience this process, and it serves to deepen their sense of community with their fellows.

945   HONIGMANN, E.A.J. Shakespeare: Seven Tragedies: The Dramatist's Manipulation of Response. London: Macmillan, 1976, 215 pp.
      Examines in seven major tragedies the structural features by which Shakespeare manipulates and directs the spectator's response to achieve a profound sense of ambivalence. Brutus in Julius Caesar is the first clear example; the spectator, on the one hand forced to a detachment from which he judges the character in terms of his own and the play's value structures, is on the other hand drawn emotionally to the character and forced to share both the agony of his decisions and the insights that the tragic experience on occasion provokes. Cleopatra is a later example; critical attempts at overly neat clarification can only reduce the fascination of her character and minimize the profound mystery of the tragedy by forcing the spectator to a position not compatible with Antony's final vision.

946   HUNTER, ROBERT GRAMS. Shakespeare and the Mystery of God's Judgments. Athens: University of Georgia Press, 1976, 208 pp.

275

Asserts that Elizabethan tragedy results in part from a "desire to embody in art the mysteries that were forced upon the consciousness of intelligent artists and their audiences by the controversies of the Reformation" (p. 18). Shakespeare's audiences were made up of semi-Pelegians, Augustinians, and Calvinists; and his tragedies reflect the various attitudes toward the nature of God's judgment. In Richard III the mystery of God's election is contained within the mystery of His providence. Hamlet represents God's artifice for catching consciences, both Claudius's and Hamlet's. King Lear dramatizes the final possibility that there is no God.

947   IDE, RICHARD S. Possessed With Greatness: The Heroic Trag-
       edies of Shakespeare and Chapman. Chapel Hill: University
       of North Carolina Press, 1980, 253 pp.
           Centers on the "heroic tragedies" of Shakespeare and Chap-
       man that in the early years of the seventeenth century address
       the tragic plight of the soldier-hero cast into a society that
       neither recognizes nor accommodates his heroic qualities. Both
       playwrights were deeply shocked by just such an event--Essex's
       fatal confrontation with society and with Queen Elizabeth in
       1601--and their plays constitute a creative dialogue through
       which they examine from divergent points of view this disastrous
       conflict between martial conduct glorified in epic myth and that
       appropriate to social reality. Whereas Chapman attempts to draw
       the spectator's sympathy toward the pagan heroic ethos, Shake--
       speare's heroes gain tragic grandeur only through renouncing their
       idealism as a delusion and understanding their human frailties.

948   KIEFER, FREDERICK. Fortune and Elizabethan Tragedy. San
       Marino, Calif.: Huntington Library, 1983, 354 pp.
           Insists that Shakespeare and his contemporaries reflect the
       profound fear that--whatever his degree of wisdom--man is subject
       to unexplainable and horrendous calamity. Richard II openly
       views himself as Fortune's victim, for example; and Brutus un-
       successfully attempts to assert his individual will. If Hamlet
       succeeds in expunging Fortune from his world view, it reappears
       with a vengeance in the pattern of upheaval that characterizes
       King Lear. The societal implication of the final tragedies is
       that man's relationship to other men is a consequence of
       Fortune's activity.

949   KNIGHT, G. WILSON. The Imperial Theme: Further Interpreta-
       tions of Shakespeare's Tragedies Including the Roman Plays.
       Oxford: Oxford University Press, 1931, 367 pp.
           Focuses largely on the Roman tragedies with individual
       essays on Hamlet and Macbeth. The common thread is the search
       for "life themes," positive effects transmitted to the imagina-
       tive consciousness. The vision of Julius Caesar, for instance,
       is sensuous in the vivid apprehension of physical detail and
       spiritual in the sense of a dynamic energy in man that enriches

the action from first to last. <u>Hamlet</u> is centered on a struggle
of life and death forces; indeed, the Prince becomes so obsessed
with evil in himself and in others that he becomes--like Macbeth--
a "death-force" (p. 123), and the play forces us to look for a
solution outside the action to the gospel ethic of forgiveness.
Both <u>Antony and Cleopatra</u> and <u>Coriolanus</u> are viewed as the opposition of war and love. Whatever the positive values of nobility
and ambition, in <u>Coriolanus</u> their immoderate pursuit leads to
isolation and pride; in <u>Antony and Cleopatra</u> transcendental
humanism totally obviates the world and material values.

950   _____. Shakespeare's Dramatic Challenge: On the Rise of
         <u>Shakespeare's Tragic Heroes</u>. London: Croom Helm; New York:
         Barnes & Noble, 1977, 181 pp.
           Argues that Shakespeare's dark tragedies, culminating in
<u>Timon of Athens</u>, celebrate a poetic rise rather than any type of
fall. The supposed critical discrepancy between Shakespeare's
depraved figures and the poetry they utter is actually his dramatic challenge and achievement. Romeo's triumph, for example,
is his supreme poetry at the sight of Juliet in her tomb; death-
shadowed, he has "grown an eternity" (p. 46). Timon's final
moments also poetically transcend the narrative as his naked,
twisted body reflects all broken and desecrated bodies resulting
from wars and sadistic horrors perpetrated for centuries by man
upon man.

951   _____. The Wheel of Fire: Interpretations of Shakespearian
         <u>Tragedy</u>. Oxford: Oxford University Press, 1930, 343 pp.
           Stresses symbolic overtones and poetic atmosphere, the
blend in Shakespeare of the temporal (individual plot) with the
spatial (mysterious, universal reality). Hamlet, in "The Embassy
of Death," is described as a sick soul suffering mental and
spiritual death who brings death to all he touches. Othello
("The Othello Music") is set between the forces of divinity and
hell. Two essays on Lear, "<u>King Lear</u> and the Comedy of the
Grotesque" and "The <u>Lear</u> Universe," depict humanity as tortured
and cruelly impaled; but suffering is also seen to be purgatorial:
the good are sweetened by it while the evil are brutalized and
demoralized by their success.

952   LAWLOR, JOHN J. <u>The Tragic Sense in Shakespeare</u>. London:
         Chatto & Windus, 1960, 186 pp.
           Asserts that the worlds of Shakespeare's tragic protagonists
are in no sense mechanistic; to the contrary, once the tragic
choices are made, events run to their natural conclusions despite
any illumination that the central figure might experience. Lear,
for example, is purged of his guilt by suffering; forgiveness is
asked and freely given; yet utter disaster still occurs. Macbeth's
awakening to life comes only as he becomes inalterably separated
from it. The logic of tragic suffering escapes us, but the nature of tragic experience is not so much to reconcile as to reveal.

953   McCALLUM, M.W. Shakespeare's Roman Plays and Their Back-
       ground. London: Macmillan, 1910, 666 pp.
          Observes that Shakespeare in the Roman histories focuses
       on the interaction of individuals but that these individuals are
       exhibited in relation to the great mutations of state. Chapters
       on Shakespeare's treatment of history and on Plutarch, Amyot,
       and North are followed by individual sections on Julius Caesar,
       Antony and Cleopatra, and Coriolanus with emphasis on Shake-
       speare's alteration of his sources. Caesar is the first great
       tragedy; while Brutus is the central character, Caesar's spirit
       dominates the play. Antony is at once history, tragedy, and love
       poem; passion is the dominant force in Antony's character, and
       Cleopatra is ambiguously beauty without duty, impulse without
       principle. Coriolanus juxtaposes a depressed and famished popu-
       lace with a prejudiced and unorganized aristocracy. The one
       great aristocrat fails in part because his virtue is out of har-
       mony with the times and in part because it is corrupted by in-
       ordinate pride.

954   McELROY, BERNARD. Shakespeare's Mature Tragedies. Princeton:
       Princeton University Press, 1973, 256 pp.
          Focuses on the collapse of the tragic hero's subjective
       world in Hamlet, Othello, King Lear, and Macbeth. After such a
       collapse, each figure experiences extreme distortion (indeed, for
       Lear madness), and each must struggle to reaffirm a sense of
       meaning for his identity and his role in society. The Hamlet
       world is dominated by intrigue and deception; the Lear world by
       naked power and violent energy. In the final analysis these
       plays paramountly are about psychic, not physical, confronta-
       tions.

955   MacFARLAND, THOMAS. Tragic Meanings in Shakespeare. New
       York: Random House, 1966, 179 pp.
          Asserts that tragedy, in revealing a form of emotion while
       freeing us from the consequences of or the responsibility for it,
       pushes us to the vicarious experience of death or nonbeing; its
       movement from disharmony to a transcedent affirmation parallels
       the movement of Christianity. The focus is on four major Shake-
       spearean tragedies. Hamlet, by questioning the commandment to
       revenge, both fulfills and abolishes the Senecan revenge code.
       Othello transmutes to tragedy the comic possibilities of a social
       mismatch. The opposition of love and the world points early to
       the moral bankruptcy of Antony and Cleopatra, but the Machiavel-
       lian Octavius forces our sympathy back to those whose interests
       transcend the material. The theme of Lear is the search for a
       meaningful self by several major characters.

956   MACK, MAYNARD, Jr. Killing the King: Three Studies in
       Shakespeare's Tragic Structure. New Haven and London: Yale
       University Press, 1973, 310 pp.

Observes that, as in Greek tragedy, the killing of a king
is the central fact of several Shakespearean tragedies. Examination of Richard II, Hamlet, and Macbeth reveals a progressive
movement from the literal to the symbolic significance of the
act, the latter encompassing not only national politics and
social consequences but also psychic tension, religious and
metaphysical dimensions, and mythic structures. In each play the
Tudor fiction of the king's two bodies collapses into a dramatic
conflict of philosophic ideas and personal ambitions. Both the
king killers and the audience are engaged in the common effort
to achieve a balance between these forces of conflict.

957   MARSH, D.R.C. Passion Lends Them Power: A Study of Shake-
      speare's Love Tragedies. Manchester: Manchester University
      Press; New York: Barnes & Noble, 1976, 240 pp.
         States that the central issue in Romeo and Juliet, Othello,
      and Antony and Cleopatra is whether the destruction of the pro-
      tagonist by love is to be seen as the consequence of mere sexual
      attraction or as a splendid, if brief, victory over the eroding
      forces of time. Generally Shakespeare depicts the latter; the
      attempt to establish values in life not dependent on duration
      calls ultimately for admiration rather than censure. Such ad-
      miration is combined in each case, however, with a pathetic sense
      of waste. Romeo is described as a tragedy of love's intensity;
      Othello, of love's vulnerability; Antony, of love's triumph.

958   MASON, H.A. Shakespeare's Tragedies of Love: An Examination
      of the Possibility of Common Readings of "Romeo and Juliet,"
      "Othello," "King Lear," and "Antony and Cleopatra." London:
      Chatto & Windus; New York: Barnes & Noble, 1970, 290 pp.
         Examines the role of love in Shakespeare's plays and dis-
      tinguishes those circumstances when the treatment can be con-
      sidered tragic. In Romeo and Juliet love fails to make the young
      principals a cohesive whole; the nature of its passion is such
      that it isolates them from their society rather than enriching
      their function within it. In Othello the problem is one of
      balance; the passion of love is greater than the substance of
      character Shakespeare gives to either Othello or Desdemona. King
      Lear and Antony and Cleopatra explore variations of the paradoxi-
      calness of love in its ripest condition.

959   MAXWELL, J.C. "Shakespeare's Roman Plays: 1900-1956."
      Shakespeare Survey 10 (1957):1-11.
         Surveys the main critical work of the century on Shake-
      speare's Roman plays, centering on three periods--substantial
      studies culminating with McCallum's Shakespeare's Roman Plays in
      1910 (entry 953), Granville-Barker's stage-oriented study in 1927
      (entry 240) and the responses it provoked, and the eclectic stud-
      ies of the midcentury. Current studies are noticeably wary of
      the extravagant, and the view is emerging that Shakespeare's

basic approach is ambivalent. Separate sections deal with canon-
text-chronology and sources and analogues.

960   MORRIS, IVOR. Shakespeare's God: The Role of Religion in the
       Tragedies. New York: St. Martin's Press, 1972, 496 pp.
          Argues that tragedy is most powerful, not when it is pri-
       marily concerned with abstract doctrine, but when metaphysical
       values must be inferred by the character and by the spectator
       from purely human disaster. Beneath the character's primary
       awareness, concerned with the operation of ambition and jealousy,
       the workings of passion and the grip of obsession, tragedy re-
       veals a state of radical guilt--a pride or hubris that impels the
       hero to self-assertion. The catharsis is not so much a libera-
       tion from the tyranny of emotion as it is a liberation from the
       tyranny of the self, the recognition that wisdom comes only
       through suffering.

961   MUIR, KENNETH. Shakespeare's Tragic Sequence. London:
       Hutchinson University Library, 1972, 207 pp.
          Observes that Shakespeare's tragedies defy generalizations
       despite the psychological efforts of Lily B. Campbell (entry 927)
       or the theological analysis of R.W. Battenhouse (entry 920). If
       the governing principles are moral, each is its own unique world;
       and each is analyzed in a series of chapters. Hamlet's dilemma,
       for example, is the necessity of avoiding killing in rage lest it
       be revenge rather than justice coupled with his inability to kill
       in cold blood. In Lear questions concerning God's justice or the
       existence of an afterlife are irrelevant in the face of the na-
       ture of human behavior and the principles of a civilized society.

962   NEVO, RUTH. Tragic Form in Shakespeare. Princeton: Prince-
       ton University Press, 1972, 412 pp.
          Views Shakespearean tragedy as a five-phased sequence that
       is cumulative and consummatory and for which the tragic hero is
       the axis of development. The phases, correlating closely with
       the act divisions of the folio, are artistic extensions of the
       classical concept of five-act structure. The first phase--the
       "predicament"--forces the protagonist to confront an impossible
       choice. In phase two the terms of the conflict (the nature of
       the dilemma) become apparent. Phase three involves the psycho-
       machia, and phase four the renunciation of values viewed ironi-
       cally from outside the principal figure. In the final phase the
       protagonist through his dying mediates the survival of human
       value. Individual chapters pursue this structural pattern in
       each of the tragedies.

963   PALMER, JOHN. Political Characters of Shakespeare. London:
       Macmillan, 1945, 335 pp.
          Includes chapters on Brutus, Richard III, Richard II,
       Henry IV, and Coriolanus. The leading quality of the plays in
       which they appear is not the political issue but the character

and his human responses to the motives and pressures that mold
him--those qualities in Brutus that have forever rendered the
conscientious liberal ineffective in public life, the gesture
and flourish in Richard III of an intellect untrammelled by conscience, the equally self-centered Richard II doomed to destruction by his withdrawal to a false world of his own creation, the
fatal conflict in Coriolanus between personal pride and family
affection.

964   PHILLIPS, JAMES E. MERSON, Jr. The State in Shakespeare's
       Greek and Roman Plays. New York: Columbia University Press,
       1940, 230 pp.
          Examines Shakespeare's view of the nature and purpose of
the commonwealth as described in the political action of the
Greek and Roman plays. The idea of the state was a popular issue
in Shakespeare's day largely because of Tudor dictatorial rule
and the interpretation such a government imposed on earlier
English history. In the Roman plays Shakespeare focuses on
order, degree, vocation, and "specialty of rule." In Coriolanus
democracy is found wanting as is aristocracy in Julius Caesar and
Antony and Cleopatra. In Troilus and Cressida and Timon of
Athens society degenerates in its failure to recognize authority.
The movement is slowly toward monarchy, the form of state considered by the Elizabethans to be divinely authorized.

965   PRIOR, MOODY E. The Language of Tragedy. New York:
       Columbia University Press, 1947, 430 pp.
          Devotes a large portion of chapter two, "The Elizabethan
Tradition," to a discussion of Shakespeare's unequaled virtuosity
in the use of language in tragedy. His development generally is
toward a muted form of imagery in highly charged metaphorical
language. Romeo and Juliet in its wide variety of styles characterizes Shakespeare's language at a fairly early state. The
later King Lear in its forceful metaphoric unity reflects the
full maturation of Shakespeare's power. The pervasive image of
the play is nature and its derivative forms natural and unnatural as seen from such varying perspectives as Lear's,
Gloucester's, and Edmund's. Other dominant image patterns are
those of storm, of animals, of strain, of torsion and sharp
bodily contact, and of the rending of an organic structure.

966   PROSER, MATTHEW N. The Heroic Image in Five Shakespearean
       Tragedies. Princeton: Princeton University Press, 1965,
       254 pp.
          Examines Julius Caesar, Macbeth, Othello, Coriolanus, and
Antony and Cleopatra as tragic studies in the discrepancy between
a character's self-image and his social reality. Through his
actions he attempts to sustain the heroic persona built on a
mental illusion, and his ultimate death becomes symbolic of the
nobility to which he unsuccessfully aspires. Macbeth's experience, for example, involves the progressive brutalization of

soul and the suppression of prohibitive conscience, an enacting
without moral reservation of the ethic of pure desire. The focus
of delusion is in Brutus the image of the patriot, in Othello and
Coriolanus the image of the warrior, and in Antony the image of
the martial hero.

967   RACKIN, PHYLLIS. Shakespeare's Tragedies. New York:
      Frederick Ungar, 1978, 184 pp.
          Illustrates the variety of ways to approach the plays by
      utilizing for an individual play a method that can productively
      be applied to the remainder of the canon. The essays on Romeo
      and Juliet, Macbeth, and King Lear, for example, focus on sym-
      bolic language; that on Hamlet emphasizes plot; that on Othello
      character; that on Antony and Cleopatra, theatrical strategy.
      Julius Caesar and Coriolanus examine corrupt political systems;
      whereas Brutus fails to realize that the plebeians require gov-
      ernment from above for their own good, Coriolanus, blinded by
      pride, "fails to recognize that the higher orders are bound to
      the lower by obligations of love and duty as well as prerogatives
      of rule" (p. 138).

968   RIBNER, IRVING. Patterns in Shakespearian Tragedy. London:
      Methuen, 1960, 205 pp.
          Considers Shakespeare's growth in moral vision from the
      inherited dramatic forms with conventional morality to the suc-
      cessive visions of his major works that embody the emotional
      equivalent of an intellectual statement. Symbolic of human
      nature the tragic protagonists face critical choices arising from
      a condition of both faith and dubiety. Ultimately each tragedy
      explores man's place in the universe and implicitly affirms a
      metaphysical justice and benevolence. While Hamlet, Othello,
      King Lear, and Macbeth end in a great affirmation, Antony and
      Cleopatra and Coriolanus end in paradox; but there is nonetheless
      an artistic sense of reconciliation, altruism, and self-
      sacrifice.

969   ROSEN, WILLIAM. Shakespeare and the Craft of Tragedy.
      Cambridge, Mass.: Harvard University Press, 1960, 231 pp.
          Investigates the dramatic techniques of point of view in
      King Lear, Macbeth, Coriolanus, and Antony and Cleopatra. In
      each case Shakespeare clearly demonstrates the nature of the
      protagonist's personality before his world begins to crumble.
      Hamlet, Othello, and Macbeth fall away from an idea, whereas Lear
      grows to it. The spectators view the events of Lear and Macbeth
      from within the central figure's own conscience. Coriolanus,
      Antony, and Cleopatra, on the other hand, lack insight, and the
      values are imposed from without. For the former our concern is
      with the conditions of the spirit as a universal symbol; for the
      latter it is with public life and the world's opinion.

970   SIMMONS, J.L.   Shakespeare's Pagan World: The Roman Trage-
      dies. Charlottesville: University Press of Virginia, 1973,
      202 pp.
         Contends that the essentially unique feature of Shake-
      speare's Roman tragedies is that they antedate Christian revela-
      tion. Rome was the last world empire to emerge before Chris-
      tianity, and Shakespeare simultaneously re-creates the historical
      reality of Rome's glory alongside the perception of the imper-
      fection of that reality from a Christian perspective. The fully
      tragic experience involving the insight or self-illumination that
      lend dignity to human suffering is impossible because man's
      struggle to endure in his allegiances to two worlds, the real and
      the ideal, has not yet been clarified by the Christian experience.
      Coriolanus, more specifically, represents the plight of man as a
      combination of artistic integrity, aristocratic inflexibility,
      and fatal hubris; the counterclaims of the working class are
      equally extreme. Antony and Cleopatra captures the essential
      tension between Petrarchism and Neoplatonism; the situation de-
      mands the principals' deaths, and we share in the purging and
      reconciliation.

971   SNYDER, SUSAN.   The Comic Matrix of Shakespeare's Tragedies:
      "Romeo and Juliet," "Hamlet," "Othello," and "King Lear."
      Princeton: Princeton University Press, 1979, 185 pp.
         Focuses on Shakespeare's use of comic conventions, struc-
      tures, and assumptions in his major tragedies. Moving through
      three phases--the comic and tragic as polar opposites (Romeo and
      Juliet), as two sides of the same coin (Hamlet), and as two ele-
      ments in the same compound (King Lear)--Shakespeare provokes
      comic expectations that, when proven false, reinforce the sense
      of tragic inevitability. The shadow side of comic events occa-
      sionally points toward the tragic; and, when comic elements
      threaten the hero with absurdity as in King Lear, the two have
      become generically fused into a single artistic force.

972   SPEAIGHT, ROBERT.   Nature in Shakespearian Tragedy. London:
      Hollis & Carter, 1955, 189 pp.
         Examines the aspects of nature that appear in six tragedies
      as, variously, Divine Law, the voice of conscience, and the seat
      of sin. Hamlet is forced to address social adultery; the cor-
      rupted nature of Elsinor feeds the political and carnal lust of
      Claudius, and the Prince ultimately sacrifices himself to purge
      it. Macbeth's sin is against nature, against the loyalty of a
      subject, and against the conduct of a host to his guest. In
      Othello the divinity of love is transformed into a parody of God.
      Lear portrays the entire spectrum of nature as it is defined at
      one pole by Lear and Gloucester and at another by Edmund. In
      Antony and Cleopatra the dialectic of human nature is resolved
      by the sheer superabundant power of poetic image in the triumph
      of a transcendent humanism.

973   STAMPFER, JUDAH. The Tragic Engagement: A Study of Shake-
      speare's Classical Tragedies. New York: Funk & Wagnalls,
      1968, 336 pp.
           Notes that, whereas the Christian tragedies involve a hero
      purged through pain, the classical tragedies (Titus Andronicus,
      Julius Caesar, Troilus and Cressida, Antony and Cleopatra, and
      Coriolanus) depict a hero who loses his role or his identity for
      want of equilibrium. In these plays the ability to adapt oneself
      to the flow of politics counts more than moral depravity or re-
      demption. Julius Caesar is the first play in which the "willful
      hero" (Octavius) wins rather than the "ethical hero" (Brutus).
      In later plays the ethical hero disappears, and the struggle is
      between the willful hero and the political hero (for example,
      Coriolanus and Aufidius).

974   STIRLING, BRENTS. Unity in Shakespearian Tragedy: The Inter-
      play of Theme and Character. New York: Columbia University
      Press, 1956, 212 pp.
           Investigates for each tragedy the "state of mind" that
      governs both the principal figure and the play as a whole, the
      dominant motifs or themes and the selective use of materials,
      exposition, and cumulative repetitions by which they are estab-
      lished. In this relationship between the character and the
      larger action lies Shakespeare's principle of unity and the best
      evidence of his dramatic intention--for example, the variations
      of being played upon like a recorder in Hamlet, the theme of
      reputation in Othello, of ritual dedication in Julius Caesar, of
      "raptness" to evil in Macbeth.

975   TRAVERSI, DEREK A. Shakespeare: The Roman Plays. Stanford:
      Stanford University Press, 1963, 288 pp.
           Examines Julius Caesar, Antony and Cleopatra, and
      Coriolanus as works combining an acute perception of the his-
      torical process with a distinctive tragic vision. In Caesar the
      issue centers on the conflict inherent in the evaluation of
      Caesar as a tyrant and the human abhorrence of murder; in Antony
      human and political elements are held in balance in which "ripe
      universal intuitions of empire turn persistently towards decay"
      (p. 13); in Coriolanus the conflicting elements in the hero's
      nature are juxtaposed to a society divided against itself. Each
      play depicts an ordered society at the head of which stands a
      hero forced to choose between those elements which produce polit-
      ical harmony and those inherent to individual integrity.

976   WALKER, ROY. "The Northern Star: An Essay on the Roman
      Plays." Shakespeare Quarterly 2 (1951):287-93.
           Treats Shakespeare's development of the idea of Rome
      through several plays beginning with Titus Andronicus, in which
      the threat is external and the problem is to get the right man
      in control. In Julius Caesar Rome is a bane unto herself, and
      Antony and Cleopatra depicts the fatal quarrel of the victorious

triumvirate. <u>Coriolanus</u> probes the baseness of the people themselves in their banishment of the best from their own city, while
in <u>Cymbeline</u> Rome is defeated by Britain, but Britain submits and
from this union ultimately springs the hero-king Henry V.

977   WATSON, CURTIS BROWN. <u>Shakespeare and the Renaissance Concept</u>
      <u>of Honor</u>. Princeton: Princeton University Press, 1960,
      471 pp.
         Discusses in part one the moral values and political con-
      victions attached to honor by the Elizabethans and Jacobeans and
      in part two Shakespeare's use of these concepts in his poems and
      plays. Of major importance are the aristocratic ideals of glory,
      magnanimity, and heroic sacrifice that make honor and virtue vir-
      tually synonymous; but, relating both inwardly to moral rectitude
      and self-esteem and outwardly to reputation and public approba-
      tion, honor found at its center a fundamental pagan-humanist
      moral dualism. It is this ambivalence that Shakespeare capital-
      izes on in figures such as Brutus, Hamlet, Othello, Lear, Antony,
      and Coriolanus.

978   WHITAKER, VIRGIL K. <u>The Mirror Up to Nature: The Technique</u>
      <u>of Shakespeare's Tragedies</u>. San Marino, Calif.: Huntington
      Library, 1965, 332 pp.
         Aims to reveal in Shakespeare's craftsmanship why his
      tragedies differ from those of his contemporaries both in quality
      and in kind. Only Shakespeare, in his "Quasi-Aristotelian" trag-
      edies, provides effective metaphysical depth by which aestheti-
      cally to accommodate a morality grounded in natural law and the
      psychology of human sin. In the early plays he is experimenting
      within established forms--revenge tragedy, <u>de casibus</u> tragedy,
      tragic romance. In <u>Julius Caesar</u> he moves toward his greatest
      plays by making moral choice central to the action. The tremen-
      dous ambiguities of <u>Hamlet</u> result from the fact that it is a
      pagan revenge play in a distinctly Christian setting. <u>Lear</u>,
      likewise, is cosmic tragedy in a pagan world, but Lear's sense of
      peace comes only through a concept of patience and resignation
      originating in Christian doctrine. <u>Antony and Cleopatra</u> and
      <u>Coriolanus</u> reflect a falling off from the great tragedies; they
      are characterized by the episodic structure of the chronicle his-
      tories or narrative tragedies.

979   WILSON, HAROLD S. <u>On the Design of Shakespearian Tragedy</u>.
      Toronto: University of Toronto Press, 1957, 256 pp.
         Divides Shakespeare's tragedies into those dealing with the
      "order of faith," in which the Christian conception of the sig-
      nificance of human actions is the governing principle, and those
      dealing with the "order of nature," in which the governing prin-
      ciple is man's relationship to a concept of natural order without
      reference to a supernatural force. In each play the structural
      pattern is thesis, antithesis, and synthesis. In the last move-
      ment the mystery of human love and magnanimity balances the

mystery of human wickedness. The tragic vision of human love as
the summum bonum is most profoundly expressed in King Lear and
Antony and Cleopatra.

For discussion of the Roman plays, see entries 104, 281, 928, 932,
955-56, 970, 975-76. For discussion of Christian archetypes, see
entries 920, 934-35, 960. For discussion of the tragic perspective,
see entries 930, 939, 945. For discussion of the Elizabethan psychology of character, see entries 927, 937. See also entries 202,
209, 211, 216, 223, 240, 287, 291, 305, 329.

ANTONY AND CLEOPATRA

Editions

980   FURNESS, HENRY HOWARD, ed. The Tragedie of Anthonie and
      Cleopatra. A New Variorum Edition of Shakespeare. Phila-
      delphia: J.B. Lippincott, 1907, 614 pp.
          Uses the First Folio as the copy text. On each page, for
      that portion of the text, provides variant readings, textual
      notes, and general critical commentary. Following the text are
      sections on the date of composition, the sources, the text of
      Dryden's All for Love, English, German, and French criticisms,
      dramatic versions, the principal actors, costumes, and a list of
      works consulted.

981   RIDLEY, M.R., ed. Antony and Cleopatra. The Arden Shake-
      speare. London: Methuen; Cambridge, Mass.: Harvard Univer-
      sity Press, 1954, 285 pp.
          Includes discussion of the text and critical interpreta-
      tions along with appendixes covering specific textual cruces and
      selections from North's Plutarch. The text is based on the First
      Folio, for which the copy was probably Shakespeare's foul papers.
      The date of composition was most likely 1607 or early 1608, and
      the major source was Plutarch by way of Sir Thomas North's trans-
      lation. For all his corruption, Antony develops in the course
      of the play a capacity for devotion and self-forgetfulness that
      he pitiably lacked earlier, and Cleopatra dilates to tragic
      proportions through her exultant cunning. If Antony and Cleo-
      patra is a lesser tragedy than Othello or King Lear, it is none-
      theless highly successful, "a brilliant tour de force, perhaps
      Shakespeare's high-water mark of sheer technical brilliance"
      (p. 1). Ultimately, the peculiar glory of the play is not so
      much in its dramatic quality as in its poetry.

982   WILSON, JOHN DOVER, ed. Antony and Cleopatra. Cambridge:
      Cambridge University Press, 1950, 262 pp.
          Provides extensive textual notes, a critical introduction,
      a discussion of the copy text, a section on stage history, and a
      glossary. This edition is based on the First Folio, for which

the copy was probably Shakespeare's foul papers. While the defeat of Antony and Cleopatra at Actium irreparably tarnished their reputations among historians, Shakespeare through his penetrative power of sympathetic imagination conveys profoundly ambivalent delineations of human beings at once grandly victorious and morally culpable. His monument to these lovers has an Egyptian quality that transcends the temporal and legalistic powers of Rome.

Criticism

983   ADELMAN, JANET. The Common Liar: An Essay on "Antony and Cleopatra." New Haven: Yale University Press, 1973, 235 pp.
      Insists that multiplicity of perspective, forcing us to move simultaneously among the comic, the satiric, and the tragic, is the key to the structure of Antony and Cleopatra. A series of conflicting judgments both by the protagonists themselves, the surrounding characters, and the spectators, the play forces us to judge and also to realize the foolishness of judging. Antony and Cleopatra stands between tragedy and romance; "poetry and action conflict, and each makes its own assertions and has its own validity" (p. 167).

984   ALVIS, JOHN. "The Religion of Eros: A Re-Interpretation of Antony and Cleopatra." Renascence 30 (1978):185-98.
      Maintains that Antony and Cleopatra, in their ostentatious display of and argument for their love, make a religion of erotic passion. Their love grows monotonous in its very need constantly to be reaffirmed, not in privacy, but on the center stage of crowded events. Antony and Cleopatra is unique in the adulterous relationship of the protagonists. Whereas true love is the metaphoric killing of oneself in a new identification with the beloved in marriage, the love of Antony and Cleopatra leads to physical death and draws others after them.

985   BARROLL, J. LEEDS. "Antony and Cleopatra and Pleasure." Journal of English and Germanic Philology 57 (1958):708-20.
      Argues that in Antony and Cleopatra, as in his other tragedies, Shakespeare intends to depict the protagonist as flawed, as directly responsible for his tragedy because of a failure in reasoning and a moral weakness. The Renaissance was almost unanimous in condemning Antony and Cleopatra, and the imagery in the play supports a similar attitude on Shakespeare's part. Antony was too much subject to the vices of fleshly pleasures. He is a figure loved by friends, feared by enemies, magnetic in personality, but he is destroyed by his passion and dies unreclaimed and deluded.

986   ____. "The Characterization of Octavius." Shakespeare
         Studies 6 (1970):231-88.
         Argues that Octavius is a serious and complexly conceived
character.   Since he never speaks in soliloquy and since surrounding characters never draw out his inner thoughts, he remains
morally a vacuously ambiguous figure.   One, moreover, is never
certain of his motivations concerning Antony or Octavia.   While
he is the military victor, he is dwarfed by the more fully developed humanity of Antony and Cleopatra, and he fails miserably
in his efforts to keep Cleopatra alive for his greater glory.

987   ____. Shakespearean Tragedy: Genre, Tradition, and Change
         in "Antony and Cleopatra." Cranbury, N.J., and Washington:
         Folger Shakespeare Library, 1984, 312 pp.
         Focuses on the nature of tragic drama, the idea of the
tragic hero, and the problem of ethical argument in tragedy.
Specifically, Shakespeare inherited from both classical and
Christian nondramatic traditions the concept of tragedy as the
representation of an indivudal who destroys himself by violating
his society's highest moral values.   While transplanting this
concept to the stage is difficult because authorial commentary
and guidance are removed, Shakespeare succeeds in depicting his
tragic figures as responsible agents and in constricting the
ethical framework by which their defeat must be measured. Antony
and Cleopatra is analyzed in detail to illustrate the theory with
greater specificity.

988   BECKERMAN, BERNARD. "Past the Size of Dreaming." In
         Twentieth Century Interpretations of "Antony and Cleopatra."
         Edited by Mark Rose.   Twentieth Century Interpretations,
         Englewood Cliffs: Prentice-Hall, 1977, pp. 99-112.
         Maintains that the sprawling spectacle belies the heart of
the action, the development of thought and feeling between Antony
and Cleopatra.   This action falls into two halves--that in which
Antony attempts to accommodate his amorous desires to his political world and that in which he attempts to accommodate his alle-
giance to Cleopatra.   Only following his commitment to the East
does Antony begin to display the first signs of tenderness rather
than lust.   Throughout act 4 he mounts in stature, not as a
soldier, but as a man; and in act 5 Cleopatra achieves a state
of spiritual identity with him.

989   BEREK, PETER. "Doing and Undoing: The Value of Action in
         Antony and Cleopatra." Shakespeare Quarterly 32 (1981):295-
         304.
         Notes that the three uses of the verb "do" in the play
(2.2.201-5, 4.14.47-49, 5.2.4-8) are paradoxical; a character in
doing one action is undoing another.   This paradoxical quality is
central to the play's presentation of Cleopatra and the love
relationship of Antony and Cleopatra.   They embrace paradox in
choosing life only to die; they simply discover that there are no

successes worth having, and their deaths are rewards for this
knowledge. In "undoing" their lives they "do" something better
for their souls. (Compare entry 1014.)

990   BLISSITT, WILLIAM. "Dramatic Irony in Antony and Cleopatra."
      Shakespeare Quarterly 18 (1967):151-66.
         Argues that Shakespeare employs dramatic irony as a struc-
      tural device to suggest the impression of two worlds, the cult of
      pleasure in the East and of Roman stoicism in the West. By dis-
      crediting that which represents Rome and enhancing that which
      represents Egypt, he draws the spectator to accept pleasure over
      duty. Actually Egypt comes to represent more than mere pleasure.
      While imagery of angels and stars cluster about Antony, Cleopatra
      is transmigrated from the harlot of the Apocalypse to the New
      Jerusalem. (See entry 992.)

991   BRADLEY, A.C. "Shakespeare's Antony and Cleopatra." In
      Oxford Lectures on Poetry. London: Macmillan, 1909,
      pp. 279-308.
         Argues that Antony and Cleopatra in acts 3-4 is defective
      in its short, choppy scenes. More significantly, there is a dif-
      ference in substance between this play and the great tragedies.
      The first half is not decisively tragic in tone, and it lacks
      both an explosion of passion and exciting bodily action. Shake-
      speare chooses not to portray either an inner struggle in
      Antony's attempt to break his bondage or the magnitude of the
      fatal step. A pervasive irony constantly undercuts any sense of
      tragic dignity. We do not, for example, consider Antony to be
      the noblest type like Brutus, Hamlet, and Othello. Cleopatra, in
      effect, destroys him, but she does attain tragic stature in act 5.
      Though a great tragedy, Antony and Cleopatra is distinctly below
      the level of the great four. (See entries 423, 442.)

992   COUCHMAN, GORDON W. "Antony and Cleopatra and the Subjective
      Convention." PMLA 76 (1961):420-25.
         Attacks Shaw's polemical pronouncements on Antony and
      Cleopatra as a play about a whore and without a moral. Seizing
      on Shakespeare's exaltation of the lovers as material for a
      Puritanical and antiromantic attack, Shaw totally misses the
      moral and the realism under his nose. Just as much as the play
      eulogizes love as the supreme emotion transcending time and
      death, it also is a tragic rendering of an individual incapaci-
      tated and destroyed by passion set against the backdrop of a
      society itself in the advanced stages of decay. (See entry 990.)

993   DAICHES, DAVID. "Imagery and Meaning in Antony and Cleopatra."
      English Studies 43 (1962):343-58.
         Observes that the brilliant power of the poetry in Antony
      and Cleopatra compels an intensity of attention and empathy that
      normally would be afforded only a play with a challenging moral
      pattern. The chain of events that drives Antony to suicide

brings together, in terms of the poetic imagery, the man of
action and the lover. Similarly, Cleopatra's development in the
final act is viewed essentially through the imagery as Shakespeare combines the roles of mistress and wife, courtesan and
queen, Egyptian and Roman. Ultimately we are left with the feeling that there is no known morality by which we can determine
whether the play is about human frailty or human glory.

994   DANBY, JOHN F. "Antony and Cleopatra: A Jacobean Adjust-
       ment." In Poets on Fortune's Hill: Studies in Sidney,
       Shakespeare, and Beaumont and Fletcher. London: Faber &
       Faber, 1952, pp. 227-33. Also published as Elizabethan and
       Jacobean Poets: Studies in Sidney, Shakespeare, Beaumont and
       Fletcher (London: Faber & Faber, 1964). Reprinted in Modern
       Shakespearean Criticism, ed. Alvin Kernan (New York:
       Harcourt, Brace & World, 1970), pp. 407-26.
            Argues that Antony and Cleopatra depicts neither the down-
       fall of an infatuated soldier nor the epiphany of a soldier in
       love; instead, the play's meaning is to be found in the Shake-
       sperean dialectic, in the reality expressed through the con-
       traries that are juxtaposed and mingled. Rome and Egypt, Cleo-
       patra and Caesar, the soldier and lover--such opposites create
       for the spectator a swinging ambivalence as ultimately the
       ambiguous alternatives destroy each other. In a sense, the play
       like Timon of Athens appears to have been written in the after-
       math of King Lear in that it is a deliberate construction of a
       world without a redeeming Cordelia-principle.

995   DONNO, ELIZABETH STORY. "Cleopatra Again." Shakespeare
       Quarterly 7 (1956):227-33.
            Asserts that the Christian readings of Antony and Cleopatra
       arise from injudicious suppressions or misinterpretations of
       certain portions of the text. It has been argued, for example,
       that Enobarbus repeatedly calls attention to Christian principles
       that inform the play. Such an argument distorts both what he
       says and what he does. An even greater distortion is to presume
       that Cleopatra's actions in act 5 are in their main outline com-
       parable to the Christian penitent. Her shifting ideas, instead,
       reflect her psychological state, not her faith in anything be-
       yond herself.

996   FICHTER, ANDREW. "Antony and Cleopatra: The Time of Univer-
       sal Peace." Shakespeare Survey 33 (1980):99-111.
            Views Antony and Cleopatra as a fully conscious artifice
       that obliquely invokes a Christian vision chronologically and
       metaphysically uniting the quest traditions of Roman epic and
       Christianity. Because the play does not conform to the norms of
       tragedy, the spectators are encouraged to seek a vision of ref-
       erence beyond the physical action itself. Enobarbus in such a
       vision suggests Judas, and Antony suggests John; Antony's strug-
       gle with death bears a metaphoric correspondence with Christ's
       struggle.

997   FISCH, HAROLD. "Antony and Cleopatra: The Limits of
      Mythology." Shakespeare Survey 23 (1970):59-67.
         Suggests that Antony and Cleopatra deals directly with myth,
depicting Venus as the goddess of love and Mars as the god of
war. This theme is merged later into the myth of Isis as goddess
of fertility and Osiris as the sun god who dies and is resur-
rected. The Roman emphasis on history tends to reduce the tragedy of Antony and Cleopatra to an "incident," but their love
grows to a point of transcending both the Roman and Egyptian
worlds, indeed the entire pagan world, giving meaning not only
to human relationships but to history itself.

998   FITZ, L.T. "Egyptian Queens and Male Reviewers: Sexist Atti-
      tudes in Antony and Cleopatra Criticism." Shakespeare Quar-
      terly 28 (1977):297-316.
         Argues that almost all critical approaches to Antony and
Cleopatra have been colored by chauvinistic assumptions made by
male critics who feel threatened by Cleopatra. Response may take
the form of disdain for a woman who attempts to rule and thus to
usurp man's role (Daniel Stempel, entry 1014) or of distaste for
the carnality of the play and Cleopatra's sexual frankness (J.W.
Lever, entry 375) or of the assertion that Antony is the sole
protagonist. Cleopatra's role and function as protagonist should
be reassessed with greater fairness and objectivity.

999   HARRIS, DUNCAN. "'Again For Cydnus': The Dramaturgical
      Resolution of Antony and Cleopatra." Studies in English
      Literature 17 (1977):219-31.
         Claims that Shakespeare affirms the value of the lovers'
relationship in life and in death through a technique called
"framing" in which characters utter choric judgments that tend to
focus attention more sharply on the action. Examples are the
comments of Philo and Demetrius in 1.1, Enobarbus's observations
about the doting Antony and his desertion, and Caesar's words
following Cleopatra's suicide. While the first two prove to be
largely inaccurate or inadequate observations, the audience sus-
pends judgment in the final scene because the conflict between
telling and showing is resolved in Caesar's reminiscent eulogy.

1000 HOMAN, SIDNEY R. "Divided Response and the Imagination in
      Antony and Cleopatra." Philological Quarterly 49 (1970):
      460-68.
         Asserts that Antony and Cleopatra illustrates a grand
moment in Shakespeare when aesthetics and theme are one. The
play contains both praise and ridicule of acting, the theater,
the use of illusions, the artist and his profession. These
issues enrich the more obvious dichotomy between Rome and Egypt.
Cleopatra, paradoxically, is sex, sensuality, and art, possessing
the ability to transform imaginatively every element of her world
into an extension of herself. The supremacy of imagination in

Egypt directly contrasts with its absence in Rome; this contrast
links the theme and the artistic vision in the play.

1001   JONES, GORDON P. "The 'Strumpet's Fool' in Antony and
        Cleopatra." Shakespeare Quarterly 34 (1983):62-68.
        Suggests that possibly Antony's transformation into the
strumpet's fool should be symbolized in the opening scene by
Antony and Cleopatra wearing each other's clothes. Such a scene
would emphasize both the sportiveness of the lovers and Antony's
military and sexual degeneracy. It would also explain Enobarbus's
comment that Antony is coming on stage in scene 2 when, according
to the stage direction, Cleopatra enters first. The theme and
the tone of the unmanning of Antony by the power of love would
thus immediately take on the tone of heroic comedy so typical of
the play throughout.

1002   LEAVIS, F.R. "Antony and Cleopatra and All For Love: A
        Critical Exercise." Scrutiny 5 (1936-1937):158-69.
        Argues that Antony and Cleopatra is manifestly more power-
ful in poetry (metaphor, tone, movement) and tragic effect than
All for Love. Shakespeare's verse enacts its meaning while
Dryden's is merely descriptive eloquence. Moreover, Shakespeare's
characters have a life corresponding to the verse, his overall
drama a richness and depth that dwarf Dryden. In a word, Antony
and Cleopatra is a very great dramatic poem and All For Love can
be compared with it only in the sense of "setting off the character of the Shakespearean genius" (p. 168).

1003   LLOYD, MICHAEL. "Cleopatra as Isis." Shakespeare Survey 12
        (1959):88-94.
        Observes that Shakespeare's knowledge of the cult of Isis
may have suggested major aspects of Cleopatra's characterization.
Cleopatra's intent is to dominate and control Antony and ultimately, even though her method is destructive, to create. She
destroys Antony the soldier at Actium, and the next time he goes
to war the lover and the soldier are irrevocably fused. The concept of a militant sexual love from which emerges wifely fidelity
is central to the invocation to Isis at the end of Apuleius's
Golden Ass. Plutarch's account of Isis in Moralia was also published in translation in 1603.

1004   MARKELS, JULIAN. The Pillar of the World: "Antony and
        Cleopatra" in Shakespeare's Development. Columbus: Ohio
        State University Press, 1968, 191 pp.
        Observes that Shakespeare, by forcing the spectator simul-
taneously to hold morally contradictory notions of both Antony
and Cleopatra, slowly renders them amoral. Since the play has no
villains, the evil that must be conquered is within the self, but
it is irrevocably fused with the goodness as well. Both principals come to view death as not only a physical action but also an
apotheosis in which vision moves beyond the naturalistic world of

providential order. This is a key element of Shakespeare's
romances, and in this sense Shakespeare in this play moves beyond
(not above) King Lear.

1005   MOORE, JOHN REES. "The Enemies of Love: The Example of
        Antony and Cleopatra." Kenyon Review 31 (1969):646-74.
            Defends the love of Antony and Cleopatra against the
charges that they are too old, that they abandon religion and
morality, and that they are too self-centered and worldly wise.
Their theatricality masks genuine passion that becomes a gauntlet
flung in the face of the Roman ideals of power and ambition.
Throughout the play various forces tempt them to compromise their
love; but the reverse occurs, and the affection is driven to
greater heights.

1006   NEVO, RUTH. "The Masque of Greatness." Shakespeare Studies
        4 (1968):111-28.
            Views Cleopatra's final act as the dramatization of her
imagination working toward its resolution. She dies neither as
strumpet nor as ennobled queen but as the epitome of her own
voluptuous Egyptian nature. Her reference to the "eloquence of
Masques" is indirectly a reference to what she creates in "high
Roman fashion." She removes herself physically from the possibility of being exhibited in Caesar's triumph by a grand spectacle of her own. The clown provides the antimasque and dramatizes Cleopatra's transcendence of a baser life.

1007   ORNSTEIN, ROBERT. "The Ethic of the Imagination: Love and
        Art in Antony and Cleopatra." In Later Shakespeare. Edited
        by John Russell Brown and Bernard Harris. Stratford-upon-
        Avon Studies, 8. London: Edward Arnold, 1966, pp. 31-46.
        Reprinted in Shakespeare: Modern Essays in Criticism, ed.
        Leonard F. Dean, rev. ed. (New York: Oxford University Press,
        1967), pp. 389-404.
            Insists that the honesty of the imagination and its supe-
riority to matters of political conquests demand our sympathetic
perception of Cleopatra in the final act. Shakespeare faces full
front the paradoxical ironies in the lovers, but their relationship is elevated in that it is juxtaposed to a sadly decayed
Roman idealism in which treachery is ubiquitous. While morally
there is little to choose between Rome and Egypt, they are polar
opposites in matters of the heart.

1008   RACKIN, PHYLLIS. "Shakespeare's Boy Cleopatra, the Decorum of
        Nature, and the Golden World of Poetry." PMLA 87 (1972):
        201-12.
            Asserts that Shakespeare's strategy in writing Antony and
Cleopatra is daring to the point of recklessness, a quality
characteristic both of the love of the principals and also of the
dramatic technique. The episodic structure shifting from continent to continent and leaping years directly defies the growing

demands for neoclassical unities. The language, too, is reckless
in its mixture of Latinisms, slang, and mixed metaphors. Most
daring of all is the inconsistency of Cleopatra as the heroine.

1009   ROSE, PAUL L. "The Politics of Antony and Cleopatra."
       Shakespeare Quarterly 20 (1969):379-89.
            Notes that Caesar's trimph preserving society at the end of
       Antony and Cleopatra was reassuring to the Elizabethan spectator,
       while for modern audiences the emotional dislocation far out-
       weighs political reassurance. In Shakespeare's day, with fear of
       anarchy at a fever pitch, Antony, Caesar, and Cleopatra were
       archetypes of conflicting views on kingship. Caesar is the ideal
       ruler, Antony exploits war for personal valor, and Cleopatra is a
       hereditary despotic power. The play, most assuredly, is not a
       political treatise; the dynamic of history is the human character
       torn between impulse and reason.

1010   SEATON, ETHEL. "Antony and Cleopatra and the Book of Revela-
       tion." Review of English Studies 22 (1946):219-24.
            Focuses on the oft-noted cosmic quality of the imagery of
       Antony and Cleopatra in acts 4-5, a quality that provides an
       artistic backdrop for the transcendent experiences of the pro-
       tagonists. Not noted is the fact that much of the imagery comes
       from the Book of Revelation--the guard's description of the
       falling star and time at its end, Cleopatra's reference to the
       sun's having burnt itself out, and her description of her dream
       of Antony. Possibly Shakespeare's conception of the mystery and
       power of Antony and Cleopatra, their determination to form a new
       heaven and a new earth, led him to describe them in such apoca-
       lyptic fashion.

1011   SIMMONS, J.L. "The Comic Pattern and Vision in Antony and
       Cleopatra." ELH 36 (1969):493-510.
            Asserts that Antony and Cleopatra is delightful tragedy in
       which death has lost its sting and the sense of triumph is over-
       powering in love's aspiration for a new heaven removed from im-
       perfect realities. The play is structured more like romantic
       comedy than conventional tragedy, the worlds of Egypt and Rome
       functioning somewhat like the tavern and court of Henry IV, and
       Egypt having a quality of Saturnalia. Even without grace the
       play points upward, suggesting that death is not the final
       reality.

1012   SNYDER, SUSAN. "Patterns of Motion in Antony and Cleopatra."
       Shakespeare Survey 33 (1980):113-22.
            Notes Shakespeare's use of images of fixity set against
       images of flux to express the opposition of Rome and Egypt and
       to express the nature of Antony's tragic dilemma. Rome is the
       land of rigid immobility and measured temper, Egypt the land of
       shifting movements, overflow, and fanning. The clearest example
       is on Pompey's barge where the Romans reel and stagger, out of

their element. In their deaths Antony and Cleopatra both attain
a stillness, but Cleopatra's mode combines Egyptian means with
Roman ends.

1013   SPENCER, BENJAMIN T. "Antony and Cleopatra and the Paradoxi-
        cal Metaphor." Shakespeare Quarterly 9 (1958):373-78.
            Suggests that the recurrent use of paradoxical metaphor
        throughout Antony and Cleopatra provides a clue to its meaning.
        The play begins on this rhetorical note--with the beat of
        Antony's Roman heart having become the bellows to cool Cleo-
        patra's lust, and the technique recurs in virtually every scene.
        The reiterated paradox holds contradictions in solution; it is
        the staple utterance of characters in the play familiar with one
        culture and alien to another. The issue of the play is equally
        paradoxical--with "nobility in failure and pettiness in success,"
        "magnanimity in passion and calculation in reason" (p. 378).

1014   STEMPEL, DANIEL. "The Transmigration of the Crocodile."
        Shakespeare Quarterly 7 (1956):59-72.
            Argues that Antony and Cleopatra is paramountly concerned
        with the restoration of health to a diseased state. Antony's
        domination by Cleopatra reverses the natural roles of male and
        female, corresponding on the psychological level to reason's
        domination by will in his character. The mysogynic hostility
        toward Cleopatra in the play is not playful but deadly serious.
        When Octavius successfully resists her in act 5 and Cleopatra
        commits suicide, the death scene is dominated by the theme of the
        nature of woman; her death is the transmigration of the crocodile,
        the death of the serpent of the old Nile. (Compare entry 989;
        see entry 998.)

1015   STEPPAT, MICHAEL. The Critical Reception of Shakespeare's
        "Antony and Cleopatra" from 1607-1905. Bochumer anglistische
        Studien, 9. Amsterdam: Grüner, 1980, 619 pp.
            Surveys the criticism of Antony and Cleopatra from the
        beginning through Bradley in 1905 with the aim not only the
        elucidation of the play but also, through its impact on a wide
        range of critical expectation, the exploration of the transitori-
        ness of critical taste and standards. Chapters focus on the
        seventeenth and eighteenth centuries (nature and art, dramatic
        structure, poetic justice, rhetoric and style) and the nineteenth
        century (the moral approach, the romantic view, continental
        criticism after the romantics). A concluding section contrasts
        Bradley's emphasis on character (see entry 991) and Schücking's
        emphasis on the ethical traditions and conventions.

1016   STOLL, ELMER EDGAR. "Cleopatra." Modern Language Review 23
        (1928):145-63. Reprinted in Shakespeare's Tragedies, ed.
        Laurence Lerner (Baltimore: Penguin, 1963), pp. 237-44.
            Describes Shakespeare's vision of Cleopatra as sympathetic
        but austere; viewed from every angle, she both fascinates and

bewitches. Shakespeare's concern with character is its dramatic
function; it must be judged from what it says and does. Cleopatra is clearly a figure of vanity and amorous indulgence, living for pleasure and neglecting her duties of state. Shakespeare,
though, holds the balance evenly; he disapproves of the relationship of Antony and Cleopatra, but he does not refuse the glorification of their love in poetry.

1017   WILLIAMSON, MARILYN L. "Patterns of Development in Antony and
       Cleopatra." Tennessee Studies in Literature 14 (1969):129-39.
            Argues for a design in Cleopatra's "infinite variety,"
       perceptible stages in her development that lend unity to the play
       as a whole. This development is not so much basic changes in her
       personality as in her moving, wavelike, through experiences of
       increasing intensity to the final act of death. The mixture of
       her motives for suicide--love of Antony and fear of Caesar's
       triumph--is only the culmination of other motives we have seen
       in her earlier. She rises to death in the high Roman fashion as
       she rose to parting with Antony in act 1.

1018   WILSON, ELKIN CALHOUN. "Enobarbus." In Joseph Quincy Adams
       Memorial Studies. Edited by James G. McManaway, Giles E.
       Dawson, and Edwin E. Willoughby. Washington: Folger Shake-
       speare Library, 1948, pp. 391-408.
            Describes Enobarbus as vital to the structure of Antony and
       Cleopatra. The privileged friend of Antony, a Roman at ease in
       the Egyptian world, Enobarbus with his realistic asides provides
       something of a choric function. As Antony's military fortunes
       wane, Enobarbus counsels his master as Antony's own better self
       would, finally deserting him as beyond hope. Like Lear's Fool
       Enobarbus is a translation of the classical chorus into a human
       figure, a translation poignantly demonstrated by his remorse pro-
       voked by Antony's response to his desertion and by his own death
       of a broken heart.

1019   WIMSATT, W.K., Jr. "Poetry and Morals." Thought 23 (1948):
       281-99. Reprinted in The Verbal Icon (Lexington: University
       of Kentucky Press, 1954), pp. 85-100.
            Distinguishes moral value from poetic value in that the
       business of poetry is not to think but to present the feelings
       connected with thinking. Antony and Cleopatra, for example,
       pleads for certain evil choices; it involves the victory of pas-
       sionate, illicit love over practical political and moral con-
       cerns. These countervalues, on the other hand, are embodied in
       a corrupt, deceitful Roman world characterized by treachery and
       infidelity. In this instance the poetic value of love transcends
       narrowly defined moral values.

1020   WOLF, WILLIAM D. "'New Heaven, New Earth': The Escape From
       Mutability in Antony and Cleopatra." Shakespeare Quarterly 33
       (1982):328-35.

Traces Antony and Cleopatra's escape through suicide from a world of passion, turbulence, and change--a world of carnal love and lust--to a more lasting bond of love and affinity. With Egypt and Rome as the magnetic poles around which irreconcilable differences cluster, the love of Antony and Cleopatra develops to a point of rejecting both. Stripped of his armor, his suicide bungled, Antony responds to Cleopatra's trickery with a new patience and stoicisim; Cleopatra, in turn, dons her robes for death, symbolizing her rejection of subjectivity to Caesar and her immortal longings for Antony.

Stage History

1021   LAMB, MARGARET. "Antony and Cleopatra" on the English Stage. Rutherford: Fairleigh Dickinson University Press; London and Toronto: Associated University Presses, 1980, 241 pp.
Covers forty-two productions of Antony and Cleopatra from the first performance at the Globe with Richard Burbage, probably in 1606, to the Peter Brook Royal Shakespeare Company production at Stratford in 1978 with Alan Howard and Glenda Jackson. Among the most revealing aspects of changing tastes, theatrical and ethical, are the difficulties of production during the "Age of Scenery" with the proscenium-arch stage and the disturbance at times of what appears to be the glorification of illicit love. Characterizations have ranged from the sexy to the cerebral, from the humanly weak to the regally strong.

For discussion of the spectator's attitude toward the love of Antony and Cleopatra, see entries 1007, 1016, 1019. See also The Tragedies (entries 920-979) and 73, 102-4, 154, 189, 194, 220, 237, 240-41, 257, 263, 277, 281, 291, 298, 302, 312, 324, 328, 511, 878, 1049, 1052, 1055, 1262, 1416.

CORIOLANUS

Editions

1022   BROCKBANK, PHILIP, ed. Coriolanus. The Arden Shakespeare. London: Methuen; Cambridge, Mass.: Harvard University Press, 1976, 370 pp.
Includes discussion of the text, date, sources, language of the play, stage history, and critical interpretations, as well as appendixes featuring selections from North's Plutarch and Camden's Remains. The text is based on The First Folio, for which the copy was probably Shakespeare's foul papers, at least partly prepared by the playwright for the theater. The manifest maturity of the play's verse and its political insights suggest a date of 1607-8. Shakespeare's play will not yield to an exclusively political analysis; instead it is a coinciding of personal crisis with political. Coriolanus's tragedy arises from the fact that

his pride is coextensive with patrician prerogatives of honor and
power, the conviction that valor is the whole of virtue. The
tragedy is firmly established in the modern repertory, largely a
consequence of an Old Vic production in 1938 with Laurence
Olivier and Sybil Thorndike.

1023   FURNESS, HENRY HOWARD, Jr., ed. The Tragedie of Coriolanus.
       A New Variorum Edition of Shakespeare. Philadelphia: J.B.
       Lippincott, 1928, 762 pp.
          Uses the First Folio as the copy text. On each page, for
       that portion of the text, provides variant readings, textual
       notes, and general critical commentary. Following the text are
       sections on the nature of the text, Collier's trilogy, the date
       of composition, the source, criticisms, the characters, Shake-
       speare and the masses, dramatic versions, stage history, actors'
       interpretations, and a list of works consulted.

1024   WILSON, JOHN DOVER, ed. The Tragedy of Coriolanus.
       Cambridge: Cambridge University Press, 1960, 274 pp.
          Provides extensive textual notes, a critical introduction,
       a discussion of the copy text, a section on stage history, and a
       glossary. This edition is based on the First Folio, for which
       the copy was either Shakespeare's foul papers as touched up
       slightly by the prompter or bookholder or a transcript of the
       foul papers. Coriolanus, like Antony, is a soldier cast in the
       heroic mold and subject to vehement fits of passion that brought
       him to ruin. But, whereas Antony is a courteous, middle-aged
       sensualist, the other--little more than a boy in years--is a
       giant in strength, contemptuous of everything and everyone who
       fails to measure up to his idea of honor.

                              Criticism

1025   BRITTIN, NORMAN A. "Coriolanus, Alceste, and Dramatic
        Genres." PMLA 71 (1956):799-807.
          Observes that, just as a hair divides the comic character
       from the pathetic or tragic (Alceste in Molière's Le Misanthrope),
       certain characters have a tendency to cross over from the tragic
       to the comic (Coriolanus). Coriolanus's colossal egotism pre-
       vents our sympathetic engagement and retains a sense of intel-
       lectual detachment. More so than most Shakespearean protagonists,
       Coriolanus is unadaptable in a social sense. In his perversity
       at times almost approaching the level of caricature, he is
       diminished from tragic magnitude more nearly to comic size.

1026   BROWNING, I.R. "Boy of Tears." Essays in Criticism 5 (1955):
       18-31.
          Notes that Plutarch provided Shakespeare the key to
       Coriolanus's character--his relationship with his mother. His
       sense of all Rome's having deserted him and his vicious verbal
       attacks upon the tribunes and the common people reflect his

attempt, conscious or unconscious, to "censor and disguise his
intense preoccupation with his own merits" (p. 24). This mind
set is the result of his upbringing, of Volumnia's determination
to make him a man and to praise him only for martial exploits.
When she begs him to spare Rome, she creates a dilemma that he is
not trained to accommodate and destroys him as surely as she has
created him.

1027   BURKE, KENNETH. "Coriolanus--and the Delights of Faction."
        Arts in Society 2, no. 3 (1963). Reprinted in Hudson Review
        19 (1966):185-202.
            Describes the moral problem or social tension of Coriolanus
        to be a discord intrinsic to the distinction between upper and
        lower classes. Coriolanus's frankness and courage reflect his
        nobility, but his hubris constantly aggravates the situation.
        Caught between the clash of motivations of nation, class, family,
        and individual, his natural prowess has been twisted by his
        mother's training. His tragedy is a consequence not only of his
        individual flaw but also of the events and persons who conspire
        to produce it.

1028   BYRNE, M. ST. CLARE. "Classical Coriolanus." National
       Review 96 (1931):426-30.
            Questions why Coriolanus is the least loved, least studied,
       and least acted of the great tragedies, and then finds the answer
       in its structural incongruity. Whereas classical tragedy nor-
       mally provokes emotional interest by embodying the play's idea
       within the protagonist, here it is Volumnia who embodies the idea
       of Rome and its values. The plot creates for the spectator a
       strange emotional disjunction; the disappointment is much like
       that of an "enthusiastic but unlearned Shakespearian when taken
       to his first performance of a Greek play" (p. 430).

1029   CHAMBERS, R.W. "The Expression of Ideas--Particularly Polit-
       ical Ideas--in the Three Pages and in Shakespeare." In
       Shakespeare's Hand in the Play of "Sir Thomas More." Shake-
       speare Problem Series, 2. Cambridge: Cambridge University
       Press, 1923, pp. 142-87.
            Points out parallels in the 147 lines of Sir Thomas More
       believed to be by Shakespeare and in Coriolanus and Troilus and
       Cressida. For one thing, there is an extraordinary likeness in
       the general outlook on state affairs, for example in the fear of
       anarchy and the insistence on social order. For another, there
       are numerous parallel images, phrases, and words. More and
       Coriolanus have scenes in which an individual is rescued from
       the mob with similar metaphors; the scenes also use similar
       metaphors in describing the sanctity of the state and the
       rioters' need for repentance.

1030   COLMAN, E.A.M. "The End of Coriolanus." ELH 34 (1967):1-20.
        Asserts that Coriolanus illustrates a different kind of
tragic technique from that of the major tragedies, that much is
left unspoken but is established dramatically. Coriolanus's
choice at the end is between his self-respect and his humanity.
Given this choice earlier, there would have been no dilemma; now
his mother's implorations confuse him, and he opts for humanity.
His final outburst against Aufidius, however, gives evidence that
he dies continuing to aspire to personal integrity.

1031   DAVIDSON, CLIFFORD. "Coriolanus: A Study in Political Dis-
        location." Shakespeare Studies 4 (1968):263-74.
        Argues that Coriolanus remains unpopular because spectators
prefer tragedy tinged with melodrama rather than a more complex
resolution in which emotional identification with the protagonist
is impossible. Shakespeare in all of his political plays en-
courages a peaceful balance between patricians and plebeians and
places special emphasis on the moral responsibility of the leader.
Coriolanus as a leader is a miserable failure, a choleric man
guilty of such excessive pride that he considers the sacrifice of
his country a viable option.

1032   ENRIGHT, D.J. "Coriolanus: Tragedy of Debate?" Essays in
        Criticism 4 (1954):1-19. Reprinted in Discussions of Shake-
        speare's Roman Plays, ed. Maurice Charney (Boston: D.C.
        Heath, 1964), pp. 156-70.
        Notes that Coriolanus, a brilliant soldier but a disastrous
politician, is the most talked about character in Shakespeare.
The two sides of his personality are repeatedly discussed by
those favoring and those opposing him, and the result is a cold
accuracy that holds the spectators at emotional arm's length. In
the final analysis, the tragedy is that of Rome, of the failure
of self-understanding both in the people and in the leader.
While it is a successful play, it is of a lower order than that
of Macbeth.

1033   FABER, M.D. "Freud and Shakespeare's Mobs." Literature and
        Psychology 15 (1965):238-55.
        Investigates the extent to which Shakespeare's description
of mob behavior in Julius Caesar and Coriolanus accords with
Freudian mob psychology. The erotic nature of group ties is
central in Coriolanus, involving a mob that longs to be governed
lovingly. Coriolanus loathes the people, denying them the very
thing they desire. Brutus and Sicinius labor to prevent the
formation of any such erotic ties. When Coriolanus finally
agrees to woo the mob, the tribunes block it by whipping him
into a prideful frenzy.

1034   GOLDMAN, MICHAEL. "Characterizing Coriolanus." Shakespeare
        Survey 34 (1981):73-84.
            Questions the validity of our expectations of novelistic
        characters, problematic and psychologically penetrable, in lit-
        erary characters before the nineteenth century. Even so,
        Coriolanus offers in its protagonist a unique example in Shake-
        speare of distinctly modern characterization, with other charac-
        ters constantly attempting to explain his actions and with the
        spectators growing increasingly aware of how inadequate their
        analyses are. Surely Shakespeare intends for Coriolanus to be
        viewed as a problematic figure, a reflection of the paradox of a
        distinctive individual "who is at once incommunicably private and
        unavoidably social" (p. 84).

1035   GURR, ANDREW. "Coriolanus and the Body Politic." Shakespeare
        Survey 28 (1975):63-69.
            Attempts through Coriolanus to place in perspective the
        topical events of the Midlands riots of 1607 and the parliamen-
        tary quarrels of 1606. Specifically, Shakespeare exposes basic
        anomalies in the belly fable's concept of the body politic. The
        political realities of Rome constitute a parody of the concept,
        virtually a headless state. James, unlike Elizabeth, proclaimed
        that sovereignty rested in the king, not in the people; the play
        reflects the political realities, if not the popularity, of that
        tenet. (See entry 1048.)

1036   HALE, DAVID G. "Coriolanus: The Death of a Political Meta-
        phor." Shakespeare Quarterly 22 (1971):197-202.
            Describes the failure of the metaphor of the body politic
        in Coriolanus, the futility of attempting to comprehend a complex
        political situation by a simple analogy. Coriolanus's pride
        prevents his seeing himself as a part of the diseased body poli-
        tic, and thus he disqualifies himself as a functioning agent.
        The dilemma is that there is no solution to the political situa-
        tion. If Coriolanus is expelled, the city's defenses will be
        weakened; if he becomes consul, the tribunes' fear of tyranny
        will be justified.

1037   HALIO, JAY L. "Coriolanus: Shakespeare's 'Drama of Recon-
        ciliation.'" Shakespeare Studies 6 (1970):289-303.
            Claims that in Coriolanus's reconciliation with his own
        inner conflicts, with his family, and with Rome's structured
        society we see his growth from a flat, arrogant soldier to a
        complex and frustrated individual. This growth inevitably plays
        him into the hands of his manipulators. The tribunes abuse him
        by drawing a false antithesis between gods and men, and Aufidius
        does so by drawing an equally false distinction between man and
        boy. Ironically, Coriolanus makes the right decision--to spare
        Rome--but Aufidius provokes an immediate and fatal regression.

1038   HILL, R.F.   "Coriolanus: Violentest Contrariety." Essays
       and Studies, n.s. 17 (1964):12-23.
         Notes that Menenius's description of the opposition between
       Coriolanus and Aufidius as one of "violentest contrariety" aptly
       describes the structure of the play, a series of contrarieties
       both moral and physical. The knot of moral conflict is in
       Coriolanus himself, in whom pride is in conflict with duty and
       honor is set against policy. So, too, the plebeians are charac-
       terized by ambiguity in their vacillation between extremes in
       opinion and in action. Coriolanus's intransigence, compounded
       of folly and integrity, issues in both his failure and his
       nobility.

1039   HUFFMAN, CLIFFORD CHALMERS. "Coriolanus" in Context.
       Lewisburg: Bucknell University Press, 1971, 260 pp.
         Stresses the significance of the time of composition for
       Coriolanus, a period under James I in which the argument was
       intense between royal absolutism and limited monarchical power.
       The Jacobean age inherited from sixteenth-century discussions of
       the nature of English government an actively debated legal and
       political issue, and many in Shakespeare's audience would have
       had either theoretical or practical political experience. Shake-
       speare's position in Coriolanus is that both the immoral tribunes
       and the proudly intransigent Coriolanus are tyrannic extremes for
       a commonwealth desperately in need of an ethically temperate
       aristocracy.

1040   HUTCHINGS, W. "Beast or God: The Coriolanus Controversy."
       Critical Quarterly 24 (1982):35-50.
         Focuses on the perverted relationship between word and sub-
       ject, man and fellow man, that characterizes the civil life of
       Coriolanus. Menenius fails to respond meaningfully to the peo-
       ple's needs, just as the citizens fail to respond correctly to
       Caius's heroic deeds. When Coriolanus desires to befriend a
       citizen, he forgets the man's name. He dies with language at its
       lowest form, a base repetition of bestial noise, "Kill." The
       play reflects Aristotle's assertion in the Politics that man is
       meant for political association, that he is little more than an
       animal if isolated from law and justice, and that the isolated
       man is either a beast or a god.

1041   KNIGHTS, L.C. "Shakespeare and Political Wisdom: A Note on
       the Personalism of Julius Caesar and Coriolanus." Sewanee
       Review 61 (1953):43-55.
         Illustrates through Julius Caesar and Coriolanus how
       Shakespeare can enrich one's perceptions of perennial political
       issues. The value of Julius Caesar, for example, is to heighten
       our awareness of the potential conflict between public and private
       life. Coriolanus, on the other hand, insists on the human dimen-
       sion of politics. Both Volumnia and Coriolanus view the masses
       as an inanimate force unworthy of serious concern. Their

inability to relate to the plebeians as human beings produces
disruption in the state. Public crisis, in a word, is rooted in
one's personal orientation to the human condition.

1042   LEES, F.N. "Coriolanus, Aristotle, and Bacon." Review of
       English Studies, n.s. 1 (1950):114-25.
          Suggests that Coriolanus reflects a direct assimilation of
       passages from Aristotle's Politics, traceable to the English
       translation printed in 1598. The idea played an assimilative
       part with Plutarch in Shakespeare's version of the story.
       Aristotle's reference to one who is incapable of living in
       society as being a god or a beast is merely one example. Such
       a thought merged with Plutarch's description of Coriolanus as
       proud, great, and humanly incapacitated to produce the image of
       Shakespeare's spiritually houseless warrior. A similar embedding
       of an Aristotelian idea is noted in Bacon's "Of Friendship."

1043   McCANLES, MICHAEL. "The Dialectic of Transcendence in Shake-
       speare's Coriolanus." PMLA 82 (1967):44-53.
          States that one attempts to transcend something in order to
       escape it, to dominate it, to make it one's slave. In any attempt
       to transcend, ambiguity exists since positions are defined
       against and thus tied to each other. In Coriolanus praise and
       power are the controlling values, and the action depicts
       Coriolanus in a dialectical, and therefore ambiguous, relation
       with both friends and enemies. Coriolanus offers respect to
       Aufidius through a hatred that maintains his drive for superior-
       ity, and he is unable to accept the praise of the citizens be-
       cause to do so would represent a concession.

1044   MacLURE, MILLAR. "Shakespeare and the Lonely Dragon."
       University of Toronto Quarterly 24 (1955):109-20.
          Notes that Shakespeare's delineation of the hero in a
       political situation almost inevitably opens the plane between the
       private and the public consciousness of the leader. The inter-
       vention of the private self into the political arena produces
       sloth in Achilles, treason in Coriolanus, and apotheosis in
       Antony. Coriolanus loves to play his star role, but he refuses
       to join the company; he can bear neither blame nor praise because
       either suggests a kind of equality between him and other people.
       His pride may have an austere and monolithic beauty, but it is
       fatal to society.

1045   MURRY, JOHN MIDDLETON. "A Neglected Heroine of Shakespeare."
       In Countries of the Mind. London: W. Collins Sons, 1922,
       pp. 29-50.
          Describes Coriolanus as one of the most masterly of Shake-
       speare's plays, an example of magnificent creative control in its
       quality of Roman relentlessness and inevitability. Coriolanus
       himself is an alien figure; and, except for Virgilia, all the
       characters strike a chill to the heart. In her presence and in

the memory of her presence Coriolanus becomes a different being,
provoking his only soft and genuine moments. In her few words,
perhaps above all in her silences, she provides a foil for her
husband and manifests the power of love and the horror of
brutality and bloodshed.

1046   NEWMEYER, PETER F. "Ingratitude Is Monstrous: An Approach
        to Coriolanus." College English 26 (1964):192-98.
            Concentrates on the skillful interweaving of themes that
        gives Coriolanus the effect of tight dramatic unity. The prin-
        cipal theme is order, as it involves Menenius's attempt, for
        example, to prevent rebellion, the threat of the tribunes to sway
        the people, the threat of Coriolanus to turn all to anarchy. In-
        gratitude is also a violation of order reverberating throughout
        the play, in the mob's insistence that Coriolanus debase himself,
        in the patricians' willingness to force Coriolanus to terms, in
        Coriolanus and his towering egotism. A society and an individual
        consumed by such ingratitude must inevitably tear itself asunder.

1047   OLIVER, H.J. "Coriolanus as a Tragic Hero." Shakespeare
        Quarterly 10 (1959):53-60.
            Describes as fallacious the charge that Coriolanus is an
        unsatisfactory play because the central figure is unsympathetic.
        The play focuses on the place in a would-be democratic society
        of a pure aristocrat who refuses to compromise and who thus falls
        where a lesser person would survive. Both the tribunes' duplic-
        ity and Coriolanus's shock that his mother advises him to play
        the politician develop the spectators' fundamental sympathy for
        Coriolanus. Shakespeare's late tragic vision is that there are
        certain kinds of goodness that themselves lead to tragedy because
        they cannot adapt themselves to hard reality.

1048   PETTET, E.C. "Coriolanus and the Midlands Insurrection of
        1607." Shakespeare Survey 3 (1950):34-42.
            Notes that 7 May 1607 witnessed an outburst of desperate,
        ill-organized peasants in Northamptonshire that quickly spilled
        over into adjacent counties and just as quickly was brutally
        extinguished. The uprising, a marked demand for economic re-
        dress, was a struggle against enclosures. Something of this
        revolt is reflected in Coriolanus; as a landowner Shakespeare
        must have been confirmed in his attitude against the mob. The
        number of images of country life in an urban and political play
        not otherwise rich in imagery strongly suggest the correlation.
        (See entry 1035.)

1049   RABKIN, NORMAN. "Coriolanus: The Tragedy of Politics."
        Shakespeare Quarterly 17 (1966):195-212.
            Notes that Coriolanus and Antony and Cleopatra appear to
        be polar opposites, the one expansive in scope and championing
        the transcendent quality of romantic love, the other narrow in
        focus and cold in the utter absence of romantic passion. Yet,

paradoxically, the plays create almost identical visions of life; both create worlds in which we are forced to judge man's actions within the context of two opposing value systems. Coriolanus's virtue, for example, is also his vice; he is incomparably better and worse than anyone else in the play. Like Antony and Cleopatra the play rejects the optimism of the early tragedies in its vision of the impossibility of heroism in a corrupt play.

1050   ROUDA, F.H. "Coriolanus--A Tragedy of Youth." Shakespeare Quarterly 12 (1961):103-6.
       Asserts that Coriolanus is both an artistic success and genuinely moving theater. The key to the tragedy is Coriolanus's youth and the focus on the pathos of youth's chronic misapprehension of reality. He must be seen, not as a blustering, mature man, but as a high-minded, emotionally untried youngster. By nature chaste and chivalrous, he denies his nature in resolving upon vengeance against Rome, and he cannot but realize this fact. Hence, ironically in light of Aufidius's charge that he is a "Boy of tears," he does not die a boy.

1051   STCHERMAN, CAROL M. "Coriolanus: The Failure of Words." ELH 39 (1972):189-207.
       Views the central problem as the relation between word and meaning. Specifically, Coriolanus is incapable of wedding word and meaning in his communication with citizens, with his mother, and even with himself--as indicated in the awkward soliloquies. Not merely inarticulate, Coriolanus appears to have a defect in hearing as well. His language is either rampantly uncontrolled or uncommonly rigid. His speech is continually out of tune with his feeling, and the play ends in disharmony--"no common values, no common language, no consolation" (p. 207).

1052   SIMMONS, J.L. "Antony and Cleopatra and Coriolanus, Shakespeare's Heroic Tragedies: A Jacobean Adjustment." Shakespeare Survey 26 (1973):95-101.
       Notes that of all Shakespeare's plays only Coriolanus and Antony and Cleopatra are distinguished by definitively aristocratic appeals. Coriolanus's disgust at being displayed in the marketplace is not unlike Cleopatra's attitude toward being impersonated by mechanic slaves. This new set of appeals indicates a different kind of audience from those of his earlier plays, an audience becoming increasingly unsettled with social and moral fragmentation. To transcend this diversity Shakespeare incorporates the popular, didactic morality of the people with a heroic aspiration beyond that moralism.

1053   STOCKHOLDER, KATHERINE. "The Other Coriolanus." PMLA 85 (1970):228-36.
       Coriolanus, like Lear, is flawed by a blindness that renders him ridiculous as well as awesome. Both devote themselves to creating an image of virile masculinity that makes them dependent

on the choric response of their following for ratification of
that image. Ironically, Coriolanus's braggardism reveals his
amoral separation of valor and virtue. The play needs a scene of
anagnorisis between his leaving Rome and arriving at Corioles.
While Volumnia taught her son the qualities of strength essential
to a well-balanced leader, she failed to teach him the counter-
balance of humanity.

1054   TRAVERSI, DEREK A. "Coriolanus." Scrutiny 6 (1937):43–58.
        Observes that the superior quality of the verse in
Coriolanus belies the charge of Shakespeare's diminishing powers
or boredom, that indeed the language reveals that the consisten-
cies and the contradictions are intentional. A sense of social
stiffness and incompatibility is woven into Menenius's first
speech. A cruel and vulgar populace is set against a selfish and
irresponsible patrician class in a framework that permits no
contact, only repression on one side and animal discontent on the
other. Coriolanus is a failure in his insensitivity, but the
failure is actually one of society as a whole.

1055   WAITH, EUGENE M. The Herculean Hero in Marlowe, Chapman,
        Shakespeare, and Dryden. New York: Columbia University
        Press; London: Chatto & Windus, 1962, 224 pp.
        Examines the concept of the classical heroic image in the
protagonist of seven plays including Shakespeare's Antony and
Cleopatra and Coriolanus. Both plays set the hero against society but in different ways. Antony is a man of Herculean excess,
whether in battlefield achievements or in sensuality; much of the
play concentrates on his efforts to regain his heroic image of
the past. Shakespeare uses a dialectic method of contrasts
(choric conversations, parallelisms with other individuals) to
develop the character of Coriolanus. His greatness lies in his
rejection of anything contrary to his personal ideal of honor,
including his homeland itself; his tragedy lies in the fact that,
in despising a corrupt and petty world, he denies nature.

See also The Tragedies (entries 920–979) and 66, 104, 131, 136, 154,
212, 241, 258–59, 266–67, 269, 277, 281, 310, 329, 404, 1160, 1416,
1447.

HAMLET

Reference Works

1056   MARDER, LOUIS, comp. "Hamlet": A Supplementary Bibliography
        1867–1964. The New Variorum Shakespeare. New York: American
        Scholar Publications, 1965, 46 pp.
        Includes representative scholarship on Hamlet from 1877 to
1964 and is intended to supplement H.H. Furness's Variorum edition of 1877. The material is categorized under bibliographical

sources, reproductions of original folio editions, reproductions
and editions of Hamlet quartos, modern editions, and critical
studies (alphabetically arranged). While not exhaustive, the
material represents every major category of scholarship and
criticism.

1057   RAVEN, ANTON ADOLPH, comp. A "Hamlet" Bibliography and Ref-
       erence Guide: 1877-1935. Chicago: University of Chicago
       Press, 1936, 292 pp.
           Includes 2,167 entries representing Hamlet scholarship from
       1877 through 1935. The material is categorized under Hamlet and
       Hamlet; sources, early texts, and date; textual comments; charac-
       ters (other than Hamlet); editions; Hamlet on the stage, fiction
       (music, opera, burlesques, poems, novels); the influence of
       Hamlet; Hamlet and Elsinore; and miscellaneous. The first cate-
       gory covers items on Hamlet's character and on specialized topics
       such as his madness and his relationship with Ophelia.

1058   ROBINSON, RANDAL F., comp. "Hamlet" in the 1950s: An Anno-
       tated Bibliography. Garland Shakespeare Bibliographies, 7.
       New York and London: Garland Publishing, 1984, 383 pp.
           Contains 1,115 citations, representing virtually all pub-
       lications on the play from 1950 through 1959--books, chapters,
       articles, reviews, notices of stage production, accounts of
       writers and works directly influenced by the tragedy. The cate-
       gories, each arranged alphabetically, are divided into criticism,
       sources, dating, textual studies, bibliographies, editions, stage
       history, and adaptations and synopses. A brief introductory
       essay traces the most significant aspects of criticism during the
       decade.

Editions

1059   JENKINS, HAROLD, ed. Hamlet. The Arden Shakespeare. London
       and New York: Methuen, 1982, 574 pp.
           Includes discussion of the date, the publication, the texts
       (the first quarto, 1603; the second quarto, 1604; the First Folio,
       1623), the editorial problem and the present text, the sources, a
       discussion of Der Bestrafte Brudermord, and a critical introduc-
       tion. This edition is based primarily on the second quarto, but
       unique folio readings are allowed. The play was composed between
       the middle of 1599 and the end of 1601; a striking topical allu-
       sion seems to place it in 1601. The play is unique in having
       three substantive texts; the first quarto has its greatest value
       in suggesting the source of corruption where the other two texts
       vary. Hamlet is nothing if not problematic, made the more so by
       the critical practice of documentary fallacy, treating fiction as
       historical fact. The central problem obviously is the relation
       between Hamlet's task of revenge and the universal mysteries of
       man's being and its relation to cosmic powers and ethical
       premises.

1060   WEINER, ALBERT B., ed. "Hamlet": The First Quarto 1603.
       Great Neck, N.Y.: Baron's Educational Series, 1962, 176 pp.
           Argues that the first quarto, the first of three signifi-
       cantly different texts of Hamlet, is neither a reported (memorial
       reconstruction) text nor a pirated short-hand text, that, in fact,
       it is not a bad quarto at all. While the language of the 1603
       quarto is flat and the text is only slightly more than half as
       long as that of the second quarto and the folio, this Hamlet is
       decidedly Shakespeare's. Purged almost entirely of poetry and
       rhetoric, it is consistently and methodically cut with none of
       the action missing. Four characters--Hamlet, Corambis, the King,
       and Horatio--speak about seventy percent of the sixteen hundred
       lines, and the play could easily be produced by no more than
       twelve actors. This cut version was required for a touring per-
       formance by the Lord Chamberlain's Men during the summer of 1600,
       1601, or 1602. The abridgment-adaptation was based on Shake-
       speare's foul papers, and the textual corruptions result from
       the illegibility of the manuscript. (See entries 76, 77.)

1061   WILSON, JOHN DOVER, ed. The Tragedy of Hamlet, Prince of
       Denmark. Cambridge: Cambridge University Press, 1957,
       310 pp.
           Provides extensive textual notes, a critical introduction
       covering matters of text, dialogue, and plot, and a section on
       stage history. Four Hamlet texts are extant--Der Bestrafte
       Brudermord and the first quarto (1603), both corrupt (the former
       of degenerate English stock possibly pre-Shakespearean, the lat-
       ter a pirated memorial reconstruction), and the second quarto
       (1604) and the 1623 folio, both sound but differing in scores of
       lines. Copy for this edition is eclectic; the folio is the basic
       text but readings are allowed from the second quarto and, less
       frequently, the first. Hamlet, the longest of the plays, is con-
       sidered Shakespeare's spiritual and artistic turning point; so,
       too, it is the crossroads of Shakespearean criticism.

Textual Studies

1062   DUTHIE, GEORGE IAN. The Bad Quarto of "Hamlet": A Critical
       Study. Shakespeare Problems, 6. Cambridge: Cambridge Uni-
       versity Press, 1941, 279 pp.
           Argues that the quarto printed in 1603 is a memorial recon-
       struction for a provincial performance by an actor who had played
       the role of Marcellus (and perhaps others) in a full performance.
       While this version is dependent primarily on the text represented
       in the second quarto, printed in 1604, it also contains reminis-
       cences of the pre-Shakespearean Ur-Hamlet. A similar conglomer-
       ate type of memorial reconstruction is represented by Der
       Bestrafte Brudermord.

1063   WALKER, ALICE. "The Textual Problem of Hamlet: A Reconsid-
       eration." Review of English Studies, n.s. 2 (1951):328-38.
       Argues that since the first quarto was consulted where
autograph copy was illegible and since we have no idea how frequently that occurred, all readings where the second quarto
agrees with the first are suspect. Admittedly, analysis suggests
that the second quarto is an independent copy from the end of
act 1. If the folio was printed from a transcript of the promptbook, at least four agents are postulated--the compositors of the
second quarto and the folio, the scribe who prepared the promptbook, and the copyist who transcribed it for the folio. Only the
assumption that a corrected quarto was used as copy for the folio
provides an adequate explanation for the textual situation.

1064   WILSON, JOHN DOVER. The Manuscript of Shakespeare's "Hamlet"
       and the Problems of Its Transmission. Cambridge: Cambridge
       University Press, 1934, 437 pp.
       Examines the kind of manuscripts used for the printing of
the second quarto and the first folio and then attempts to re-
construct Shakespeare's autograph manuscript. Playhouse cuts and
revised stage directions in the folio point to a text corrupted
by playhouse interference and suggest that the printer's copy was
closely associated with, if not identical to, the Globe promptbook. Copy for the quarto was either Shakespeare's foul papers
or a faithful copy of them. In determining Shakespeare's original text, the second quarto must be granted authority; readings
from the folio can be allowed only in clearly justified
instances.

Criticism

1065   ALDUS, P.J. Mousetrap: Structure and Meaning in "Hamlet."
       Toronto and Buffalo: University of Toronto Press, 1976,
       235 pp.
       Argues that our response to Hamlet comes ultimately not
from the surface plot or some assumption about the poet's psyche
but from some mysterious power in the structure itself that
stirs our imagination at the subliminal level, "a controlling and
unifying metaphor on the grandest scale that embodies a heritage
of literary myths" (p. 20). The literal becomes figurative in a
mythic sense; two mythic patterns are entwined: one Greek, ending in death, and the other Christian, ending in Doomsday. At
the center of both are the metaphorical implications of the
mousetrap dumb shows, prologue, and play.

1066   ALEXANDER, NIGEL. Poison, Play, and Duel: A Study in
       "Hamlet." Lincon: University of Nebraska Press; London:
       Routledge & Kegan Paul, 1971, 212 pp.
       Suggests that the action of poisoning, playing, and duel-
ing, recurring at the beginning, middle, and end, forms the
structure of the play. The inner play, for example, represents

309

the past in such a way as to determine the future act. It forces
the members of the on-stage audience to reveal the roles they
intend to play in the future, ironically posing the question of
the relationship of Lucianus as murderer and Hamlet in his determination to assassinate Claudius. The play, in a word, functions as a complex moral reference for both the Prince and the
King.

1067   ALEXANDER, PETER. Hamlet: Father and Son. Oxford:
        Clarendon Press, 1955, 189 pp.
        Attacks the Hamletology that supposes that man is master of
his fate and an inhabitant of a world consciously governed by a
benevolent god, that Hamlet suffers from some flaw that justifies
his misfortune and reaffirms a providential design. To the contrary, the father-son relationship is but the metaphor for the
larger conflict between a young Wittenberg intellectual and an
old Elsinore soldier, between the humanistic and the ideal, the
perpetual struggle between the heart and the head.

1068   ALTICK, RICHARD D. "Hamlet and the Odor of Mortality."
        Shakespeare Quarterly 5 (1954):167-76.
        Describes Hamlet as a play enveloped in an atmosphere of
stench and a preoccupation with the corruption of mortal flesh.
Hamlet gives the generalized sense of sickness a specific connection with his second line, stating that he is too much in the sun;
so, too, the ghost relates his tale in language dominated by
images of rottenness and disease. The motif reaches its climax
in the graveyard scene. The sense of evil permeating the play is
a result not only of iterated allusions to corruption but also of
association with the most unpleasant of man's sensory perceptions.

1069   BATTENHOUSE, ROY W. "Hamlet's Apostrophe on Man: Clue to the
        Tragedy." PMLA 66 (1951):1073-1113.
        Describes Hamlet's noblest gift as the ability for specula-
tion, even though his reason is flawed, as evidenced in its con-
tinually defeating his actions as a man. His apostrophe on man
is noticeably lacking in reference to the supernatural; it,
rather, is grounded in natural reasoning. Since he sees nothing
for man beyond the natural condition, he is a man "deprived of
the light of grace" (p. 1081). The passage is a touchstone to
the entire play both in its mood and in its theme. It reflects
the psychology of frustration in man cut off from the Christian
faith.

1070   BOWERS, FREDSON T. "Hamlet as Minister and Scourge." PMLA
        70 (1955):740-49.
        Investigates Hamlet through the Elizabethan concept of how
God intervened externally in human affairs to punish crime--
either through an act of destruction committed by one already
damned (a scourge) or through a constructive act by one who is
spiritually healthy (a minister). Hamlet considers the ghost's

mandate to be a divine command to set right the disjointed times.
As a minister of God, however, he must act to secure a public
vengeance; unable to do so and at the point of committing himself
to private vengeance, he describes himself in 3.4 as scourge as
well as minister.

1071   CALDERWOOD, JAMES L.   To Be and Not to Be: Negation and
       Metadrama in "Hamlet." New York: Columbia University Press,
       1983, 222 pp.
           Examines the structure of Hamlet as a progression from
       coherence to paradox and negation and finally in turn to a rich
       and aesthetically rewarding coherence. This movement through
       deconstruction to reconstruction occurs simultaneously on several
       levels. Hamlet is compelled to seek his individual identity
       apart from his filial role as mourner-avenger; by determining his
       own path of action instead of sweeping to his revenge, he "de-
       names" himself as son and namesake and thereby "names" himself as
       his own distinct personality. At the same time, Shakespeare--by
       allowing his protagonist to assume this greater role than that of
       a Kydian revenger--"de-names" the strictures of traditional re-
       venge tragedy and creates an individually identifiable and highly
       ambiguous dramatic form for himself, the spectators at the Globe,
       and all future actor-Hamlets and spectators.

1072   CAMPBELL, LILY BESS. "Polonius: The Tyrant's Ear." In
       Joseph Quincy Adams Memorial Studies. Edited by James G.
       McManaway, Giles E. Dawson, and Edwin E. Willoughby. Washing-
       ton: Folger Shakespeare Library, 1948, pp. 295-313.
           Attacks the assumption that Polonius is an inconsistent
       figure, that it is virtually impossible to reconcile his wisdom
       with his folly. Polonius, we must remember, serves obsequiously
       a tyrant-usurper in a court rapidly preparing for war. Like
       Rosencrantz, Guildenstern, and Osric, Polonius is one of the
       King's "ears." Polonius is especially close to Claudius and is
       willing to use his own daughter as a spy. He, moreover, is con-
       sistent as a busybody. Claudius listens to him but never acts on
       his advice; such men are necessary to tyrants. (See entry 1133.)

1073   CHARNEY, MAURICE. Style in "Hamlet." Princeton: Princeton
       University Press, 1969, 333 pp.
           Explores the style of Hamlet in its broadest sense of the
       various means of expression by which Shakespeare attempts to
       achieve his dramatic ends--whether by puns, particular Eliza-
       bethan connotations, the imaginative embodiment of a theme, the
       contrapuntal quality of the various dramatic voices. The book is
       divided into three parts--imagery, staging and structure, and
       dramatic character. The first part focuses on the recurrent
       images of war, weapons, explosives, secrecy, poison, corruption,
       and limits. The middle section deals with imagery in nonverbal,
       presentational terms (gesture, music, sound effects, costumes,
       stage properties), and the final section is concerned with the

specific nature of the rhetorical roles that interact with Hamlet
and the rhetorical complexity of the protagonist. (See entry
1078.)

1074   CONKLIN, PAUL S. A History of "Hamlet" Criticism 1601-1821.
       New York: King's Crown Press, 1947, 176 pp.
           Chronicles the growth of Hamlet criticism from its begin-
       nings to 1821 and the manner in which this criticism reflects the
       climate of the times in the dominant trends of thought. The ma-
       terial is basically of three types--allusions to Hamlet, pri-
       marily imaginative reflections by some later writer; theatrical
       comments concerning actual stage productions; and critical anal-
       ysis involving an attempt to establish some sort of philosophic
       context for interpretation. Individual chapters address French
       and German criticism. Of special interest is the sharp dualism
       that develops in the late eighteenth century between the theatri-
       cal tradition and that of the closet or study.

1075   COX, LEE SHERIDAN. Figurative Design in "Hamlet": The Sig-
       nificance of the Dumb Show. Columbus: Ohio State University
       Press, 1973, 184 pp.
           Argues that Shakespeare intends the dumb show to function
       as an intrinsic component of the whole figurative and structural
       pattern. This dumb show, occupying a central structural posi-
       tion, is also thematically central; the symbolic importance of
       the mime provides an essential code for comprehending the entire
       play. Significant parallels exist between the "puppets" in the
       court entertainment and the characters in Hamlet, between the
       reiterated allusions to "dumbness" throughout the play and the
       muteness of the scene.

1076   DAVIS, ARTHUR G. Hamlet and the Eternal Problem of Man. New
       York: St. John's University Press, 1964, 227 pp.
           Asserts that Hamlet is the eternal mirror in whom individ-
       uals see reflections of their own struggle between good and evil,
       hope and despair. While his behavior is highly variable and com-
       plex, he is consistent in his imperfection or his human falli-
       bility. The spectators constantly perceive in him indications
       of something incomparably better, not indications of a pervasive
       wickedness. In his admission of failure to pursue his duty in
       the course of the play and his courage to act albeit with imper-
       fect knowledge in the final scenes, we are made to share with
       him the weakness and pain common to the human condition.

1077   DESSEN, ALAN C. "Hamlet's Poisoned Sword: A Study in
       Dramatic Imagery." Shakespeare Studies 5 (1969):53-69.
           Maintains that the visual image of Hamlet's poisoned sword
       is symbolic of his role as the tainted hero in a corrupt world.
       The sword appears throughout the play, in the cellarage scene, in
       the description of Priam's death, in the duel of the final scene.
       Its use, crossed, to ward off blasts from hell as an instrument

of justice contrasts with its later use, poisoned, to corrupt. Hamlet's tragedy is that he is unable to achieve his ends in a corrupt world without himself partaking of that corruption.

1078   DORAN, MADELEINE. "The Language of Hamlet." Huntington Library Quarterly 27 (1964):259-78.
      Examines Shakespeare's use of rhetoric for dramatic purposes in Hamlet. The conceits in the speeches in The Murder of Gonzago, for example, are formed and labored, the sententious passages commonplace and old fashioned. Such language tends not to call attention to itself, allowing interest to focus on how Hamlet, Claudius, and Gertrude are reacting. Similarly, the turgidly rhetorical speech of the player about Hecuba provokes a naturalistic response in Hamlet and thus furthers our identification with the prince as a real character. The cadences and imagery of his soliloquies help us to track his emotional progress through the play. (See entry 1073.)

1079   DRAPER, JOHN W. The "Hamlet" of Shakespeare's Audience. Durham: Duke University Press, 1939, 254 pp.
      Attempts to set Hamlet within its literary and historical context, examining the minor figures as individuals in a contemporary court. The play is envisioned as "a microcosm of the Renaissance state and of Renaissance society" (p. 229). In its cross-currents of action it illustrates current political, religious, and social themes--the inescapable consequences of sin, the consequences of the blind pursuit of duty, the loyalty to elders, the struggle between church and state, the problem of regicide, the struggle of the individual in a highly organized social structure.

1080   ELIOT, T.S. "Hamlet and His Problems." In The Sacred Wood. London: Methuen, 1920, pp. 95-103. Reprinted in Selected Essays: 1917-1932 (New York: Harcourt, Brace, 1932), pp. 121-26.
      Asserts that since Hamlet represents a stratification, the efforts of a series of men, we should treat it as Shakespeare's design superimposed upon much cruder material. The simple revenge motive, the difficulty of assassinating a monarch, and madness feigned for protection came from previous layers. While complicating these factors in terms of his protagonist, Shakespeare adds the principal motive of the effect of a mother's guilt upon her son. The play in failing to bring coherence to these varied elements is an artistic failure. To comprehend Hamlet completely we would "have to understand things which Shakespeare did not understand himself" (p. 126).

1081   ELLIOTT, GEORGE R. Scourge and Minister: A Study of "Hamlet"
        as a Tragedy of Revengefulness and Justice. Durham: Duke
        University Press, 1951, 208 pp.
            Describes Hamlet as the lineament of an intricate dramatic
        landscape contrasting true and false gentility. Claudius's con-
        science and his proud ambition provoke his ruin. He shrinks
        desperately from killing the Prince, just as Hamlet shrinks
        desperately from killing the King. At the first of the play
        Hamlet's attitude toward Claudius is vengeful; by the end it is
        largely impartial and just. While he is praised by Fortinbras
        as one who would have ruled wisely, justly, and courteously, his
        warfare was spiritual, the struggle of a Christian humanist to
        come to terms with the moral dualism of society.

1082   EMPSON, WILLIAM. "Hamlet When New." Sewanee Review 61
        (1953):15-42. Reprinted in Discussion of "Hamlet," ed. J.C.
        Levenson (Boston: D.C. Heath, 1960), pp. 96-109.
            Notes that there was no Hamlet problem until the eighteenth
        century. Critics would have us believe that Shakespeare wrote an
        extremely popular play that held the stage for nearly two hundred
        years before anyone perceived its essential enigmatic quality.
        Shakespeare's task was to capitalize on the popularity of the
        revenge play but to do so in a way that would be intriguing and
        exciting and not a laughing stock like the older Hamlet. Pos-
        sibly our text represents two Shakespearean versions, with the
        play evolving into its present shape.

1083   ERLICH, AVI. Hamlet's Absent Father. Princeton: Princeton
        University Press, 1977, 319 pp.
            Views Hamlet's problem as stemming in large part from the
        elder Hamlet's physical or emotional absence and thus the
        father's failure to provide an adequate role model for masculine
        identity in the crucial formative years. His obsessive desire
        is to prove his father (now the ghost figure) to be strong and
        dominant by discovering some means by which the spirit might
        exact his own revenge, hence the son's refusal or inability to
        accept the adult responsibility inherent in the mandate to kill
        and the rationalization for inactivity sought in near madness.

1084   FERGUSSON, FRANCIS. "Hamlet, Prince of Denmark: The Analogy
        of Action." In The Idea of a Theater: The Art of Drama in
        Changing Perspective. Princeton: Princeton University Press,
        1949, pp. 109-54. Portion reprinted in Interpreting "Hamlet":
        Materials for Analysis, ed. Russell E. Leavenworth (San
        Francisco: Howard Chandler, 1960), pp. 215-34.
            Maintains that Hamlet, if he is to be understood, must be
        accepted as a complex, many-sided individual caught in an equally
        ambiguous situation. The numerous critical evaluations serve
        simply as partial reflectors of the full picture. The major
        action, through each of its plot strands, is "the attempt to
        find and destroy the hidden 'impostume' which is poisoning the

life of Denmark" (p. 117). The various ritual scenes--the changing of the guards, Ophelia's mock rites, Claudius's black mass,
the play-within-the-play--focus attention on the hidden malady in
the body politic.

1085   FISCH, HAROLD. Hamlet and the Word: The Covenant Pattern in
       Shakespeare. New York: Frederick Ungar, 1971, 248 pp.
           Considers Hamlet's confrontation with the ghost in act 1 a
       conventional encounter in which he is elected to a unique re-
       sponsibility. His soliloquies through the middle acts reveal his
       "intestinal warfare," character defining itself in relation to
       destiny. Acting without soliloquy in the final act, he is re-
       warded with the recovery of a "faint but perceptible degree of
       faith in man and his future" (p. 75). In the tradition of Hel-
       lenic tragedy he is swept to his doom, but in the Hebraic tradi-
       tion he has also become the divine instrument of a moral purging.

1086   FLATTER, RICHARD. Hamlet's Father. New Haven: Yale Univer-
       sity Press, 1949, 207 pp.
           Asserts that the ghost of Hamlet's father is the true pro-
       tagonist of the play. As the motivating force, he sets the
       action in motion by directing his son to avenge his murder,
       intervening in person in act 4 when the son appears to be
       seriously digressing from his aim. Eventually the ghost succeeds
       through Hamlet's execution of Claudius as justice is victorious
       over covert evil. A key moment in the play is the spirit's for-
       giveness of Gertrude in the closet scene and his instructing the
       son to do likewise and to direct all vengeance against the usurp-
       ing king as the source of corruption.

1087   FRYE, ROLAND M. "Ladies, Gentlemen, and Skulls: Hamlet and
       the Iconographic Tradition." Shakespeare Quarterly 30 (1979):
       15-28.
           Asserts that the visual background of a graveyard and the
       allusions in Hamlet's reflections about Yorick help to prepare
       the audience for his new tranquility, sanity, and composure in
       the final scene. The iconographical tradition of a man contem-
       plating a skull functioned as a memento mori directed toward life
       that must be lived under the shadow of death but should be lived
       without anxiety and a preoccupation with transiency. The scene
       leads the spectators to assume that Hamlet has learned to accept
       such a view of life.

1088   ____. The Renaissance "Hamlet": Issues and Responses in
       1600. Princeton: Princeton University Press, 1984, 398 pp.
           Investigates the climate of opinion in which Hamlet took
       shape by analyzing contemporary response to events resembling
       those in the tragedy--for example, the Elizabethan response to
       death and funerals, to spiritual hauntings, to sexual misconduct.
       A king's untimely death and a queen's incest would be seen as
       sufficient to motivate Hamlet's distress; similarly, Catholics

and Protestants alike shared an ambivalence toward the supernatural that would lend credibility to Hamlet's tyrannicide.
Such problems of the play are examined and defined in historical
terms.

1089   GOLLANCZ, ISRAEL, ed. The Sources of "Hamlet": With Essays
        on the Legend. Shakespeare Classics. London: Frank Cass,
        1926, 321 pp.
        Examines the materials through which the Hamlet story
evolved prior to Shakespeare. The earliest known version appears
in an Icelandic saga depicting the tragic story of Snaebjorn the
Boar. Saxo Grammaticus's recording of this story in his twelfth-
century Historica Danica was also influenced by legendary Roman
history, specifically the tale of Lucius Junius Brutus. The next
stage of evolution is in Belleforest's Histoires tragiques in
1582. Inserted in the translated material are facing pages
carrying the Latin text of Saxo and the French text of Belleforest.

1090   GOTTSCHALK, PAUL. The Meanings of "Hamlet": Modes of Liter-
        ary Interpretation Since Bradley. Albuquerque: University
        of New Mexico Press, 1972, 197 pp.
        Notes the immense variety of interpretations of Hamlet,
especially in the post-Bradleyan era. Emphasis is on the evolu-
tionist critics who explain problems and inconsistencies in terms
of Shakespeare's adaptations of his sources; the psychological
critics, both those who analyze the Prince in terms of Elizabethan psychology and those who apply post-Freudian tactics; the
Christian and archetypal critics whose concern is with Hamlet's
accommodation to the moral imperatives of his world; and the
anagogical critics, who examine the play and the protagonist as
archetypes of human experience. In each case the focus is either
on the external struggle of hero and villain or on the struggle
within Hamlet's soul.

1091   GREBANIER, BERNARD. The Heart of "Hamlet." New York:
        Thomas Y. Crowell, 1960, 301 pp.
        Interprets Hamlet in its Elizabethan context, abjuring the
adaptation and attempts at modernity or peculiar contemporaneity
that have characterized so many recent productions. The weight
of criticism notwithstanding, Hamlet is perfectly sane and never
pretends to be otherwise. His delay is attributable, not to some
quirk of personality, but solely to the conventions of the revenge play. His tragedy results from defeated thought, not excessive thought, and it is a tragedy only because Hamlet in a
rash moment kills Polonius and sets destruction in motion. A
thirty-year-old athletic and intellectual man, he acts precipi-
tately and thus bring to nought the justifiable scheme of revenge
he has planned so carefully. Critics and actors alike would do
well to allow the play to speak for itself and to avoid the
labyrinthine bypaths of sheer speculation.

1092   HALLETT, CHARLES A., and HALLETT, ELAINE S. The Revenger's
       Madness: A Study of Revenge Tragedy Motifs. Lincoln:
       University of Nebraska Press, 1980, 349 pp.
            Claims that Shakespeare in Hamlet significantly alters and
       enhances several of the basic revenge play motifs established by
       Kyd. For one thing, the ghost, though presumably an embodiment
       of the spirit of revenge, epitomizes human dignity and majesty as
       well. Horatio's and Hamlet's reminiscences about the elder
       Hamlet's nobility and integrity in comparison with the character
       of Claudius, the ghost's solicitude for Gertrude, the fact that
       the ghost does not appear directly responsible for the multiple
       deaths in act 5--such touches lend the ghost a dimension of per-
       sonality quite absent in Andrea and Andrugio. For another thing,
       Shakespeare, through the protagonist's declared intention of
       assuming an antic disposition, is able to present Hamlet's mad-
       ness without degrading his character; the spectator on several
       occasions simply does not know where acting ends and passionate
       agony begins.

1093   HANSEN, WILLIAM F. Saxo Grammaticus and the Life of Hamlet:
       A Translation, History, and Commentary. Lincoln and London:
       University of Nebraska Press, 1983, 202 pp.
            Examines our knowledge of the tradition of Hamlet before
       and after Saxo, specifically how Saxo transforms the oral legend
       into a literary text and how the literary figure evolves from
       Danish to Latin to French. Considered also are Scandinavian and
       Roman legends as analogues of the Hamlet story and Shakespeare's
       transformation of the material for the stage in Renaissance
       England. Saxo's life of Hamlet from his History of the Danes is
       translated into idiomatic English prose.

1094   HARRISON, G.B. "Hamlet." In Shakespeare's Tragedies. New
       York: Oxford University Press, 1951, pp. 88-109. Reprinted
       in Hamlet, ed. Cyrus Hoy, Norton Critical Editions (New York:
       W.W. Norton, 1963), pp. 238-50.
            Stresses Hamlet as a play, not a treatise on philosophy,
       psychiatry, Elizabethan history, or social ethics. To the Eliza-
       bethan playgoer Hamlet was an exciting revenge play with a moral
       dimension. His melancholic disgust, his love-hate relationship
       with Ophelia, the play-within-the-play as an open declaration of
       war between Hamlet and Claudius, the counterrevenge of Laertes--
       all are methods of Shakespeare's transmutation of stock devices
       of the revenge play. When the armchair critic becomes obsessed
       with the problem of Hamlet's delay, he forgets that to the
       spectator in the theater there is no delay as the action develops
       at a fast pace.

1095   HUGHES, GEOFFREY. "The Tragedy of a Revenger's Loss of Con-
       science: A Study of Hamlet." English Studies 57 (1976):
       395-409.
            Argues that Hamlet, instigated by a supernatural agency
       whose moral nature is highly suspect, damns himself by

anticipating Heaven and assuming he is God's agent. Accepting
the ghost's integrity on nothing more than his own intuition, he
displays a blasphemous arrogance in refusing to kill Claudius at
prayer. The final proof of his damnation is his refusal to take
the opportunity to remain with pirates and thus escape the necessity of murder.

1096   JACK, ADOLPHUS ALFRED. Young Hamlet: A Conjectural Resolu-
       tion of Some of the Difficulties in the Plotting of Shake-
       speare's Play. Aberdeen: Aberdeen University Press, 1950,
       176 pp.
            Asserts that Hamlet is not a Goethe-like prince too gentle
       for his task or a Coleridge-like contemplative soul but a man who
       sweeps to his revenge as readily and as entertainingly as ob-
       stacles will allow. In the first quarto, Shakespeare's first
       version, Hamlet is about nineteen, and the lines of action are
       much clearer than in the second quarto, in which much speculation
       is added. Hamlet is a highly theatrical play of action; the
       spectator observes without identifying, and the "slaughter at the
       end is exciting but not moving" (p. 175).

1097   JOHNSON, S.F. "The Regeneration of Hamlet: A Reply to E.M.W.
       Tillyard With a Counter-Proposal." Shakespeare Quarterly 3
       (1952):187-207.
            Asserts that Hamlet, by accepting and obeying the dicatates
       of Providence in act 5, experiences a regeneration that is the
       counterpart to the antic dispostion he portrays earlier. As in
       the Morality play the conflict between divine and bestial nature
       brings Hamlet to the verge of despair. This conflict he tran-
       scends when he goes beyond reason in depending on Providence to
       provide the necessary opportunities for action. His spiritual
       renewal does not mitigate the tragedy; instead, it increases the
       spectators' sense of waste and heroic sacrifice. (See entry
       1119; for Tillyard's view, see entry 318.)

1098   JONES, ERNEST. Hamlet and Oedipus. New York: W.W. Norton,
       1949, 194 pp.
            Locates Hamlet's problem in the sphere of unconscious con-
       flicts known to Freudian psychologists as psychoneurosis; he
       suffers from an internal struggle inaccessible to his introspec-
       tion. As a child he viewed his father as a rival for his
       mother's affection. These repressed memories are revived by the
       realization of his father's death and his mother's remarriage.
       The more vigorously he berates his uncle, the more fully does he
       stimulate his own latent complexes. "In reality his uncle in-
       corporates the deepest and most buried part of his own person-
       ality, so that he cannot kill him without also killing himself"
       (p. 100). Only when he has received his own death wound from
       Laertes is he finally free from the constraints of his repressed
       memories; thus he can move against Claudius and avenge his
       father's murder. It is likely that Shakespeare, in molding the

old story anew, was giving artistic voice to "inspirations that
took their origin in the deepest and darkest regions of his mind"
(p. 178).

1099   JOSEPH, BERTRAM L. Conscience and the King: A Study of
        "Hamlet." London: Chatto & Windus, 1953, 176 pp.
             Insists that Hamlet, in its language and plot, be seen as
        an Elizabethan play, of which the elements (Hamlet's melancholy,
        his character, his relationship with his mother, his delay) be-
        come clear so long as we do not read it as a forerunner of modern
        sensibility. He does not delay, for example, because he examines
        the revenge code in the abstract and exposes its flaws; he delays
        for fear of damnation and constantly excoriates himself for doing
        so. He eventually becomes passive, an instrument of God, and is
        able to act, not fearing death but viewing it as a consummation.

1100   KERRIGAN, JOHN. "Heironimo, Hamlet and Remembrance." Essays
        in Criticism 31 (1981):105-26.
             Draws parallels among Hamlet, Kyd's The Spanish Tragedy,
        and Aeschylus's Orestes concerning remembrance and revenge, trac-
        ing the evolution of the motivation for revenge and noting how
        retrospection or remembrance draws the revenger back from his
        task or drives him toward it. Whereas in Greek tragedy, one
        either remembers or satisfies his vengeance, the Elizabethan has
        the third choice based on belief in God's providence. The last
        choice confounds Hamlet because the patience central to it fails
        to provide the catharsis achieved more easily through physical
        action.

1101   KING, WALTER N. Hamlet's Search for Meaning. Athens:
        University of Georgia Press, 1982, 180 pp.
             Claims that Christian thought is fraught with ambiguities,
        that it is far less rational than we normally tend to assume.
        Hamlet finally pursues his problem to the point of Christian
        certitude, but for the spectator with an omniscient perspective
        the fundamental ambivalences remain. In a real sense Hamlet's
        search for meaning ramifies outward and becomes the spectators'
        search as well. If it is enough in the play for Hamlet to recon-
        cile himself with himself, for us the rest is silence.

1102   KIRSCH, ARTHUR C. "Hamlet's Grief." ELH 48 (1981):17-36.
             Views Hamlet, not only as a study in revenge, but also as a
        study in grief. Hamlet's vow to the ghost intensifies his
        mourning and leads to pathological depression, preventing the ego
        to heal by emotionally coming to terms with the fact of the
        father's death; and he is deprived of sympathy from his mother,
        Ophelia, and Rosencrantz and Guildenstern. In act 5 Hamlet's
        state of mind changes as he completes the act of mourning by
        accepting his losses as an inevitable part of his own condition.

1103 KITTO, H.D.F. "Hamlet." In Form and Meaning in Drama: A
Study of Six Greek Plays and of "Hamlet." London: Methuen,
1956, pp. 246-337. Portion reprinted in Four Centuries of
Shakesperean Criticism, ed. Frank Kermode (New York: Avon,
1965), pp. 452-61.
Argues that Hamlet, like Oedipus, must be considered, not
as an individual tragedy of character, but as a religious drama
involving the all-pervading evil in Denmark. The individual
tragedies of Hamlet, Laertes, and Ophelia emanate from the murder
of a king and the corruption of his wife. Hamlet in a sense is
humanity itself; and, as in Greek tragedy, evil, "once it has
broken loose, will feed on itself and on anything else that it
can find until it reaches its natural end" (p. 337).

1104 KNIGHTS, L.C. An Approach to "Hamlet." Stanford: Stanford
University Press, 1961, 107 pp. Portion reprinted in Discussions of "Hamlet," ed. J.C. Levenson (Boston: D.C. Heath,
1960), pp. 77-83.
Asserts that Julius Caesar, Hamlet, and Othello were
written at a time Shakespeare was growing concerned with the
relationship between the mind and the world, more specifically
with various distortions in men's way of looking at the world.
In such plays the spectators are not required to take sides but
to observe the distortion of actuality by an abstracting, simpli-
fying habit of mind. In Hamlet we are drawn to look more closely
at the attitudes with which Hamlet confronts his world than the
actual evil in it. He represents a fixation of consciousness.

1105 LAW, ROBERT ADGER. "Belleforest, Shakespeare, and Kyd." In
Joseph Quincy Admas Memorial Studies. Edited by James G.
McManaway, Giles E. Dawson, and Edwin E. Willoughby. Wash-
ington: Folger Shakespeare Library, 1948, pp. 279-94.
Suggests that Shakespeare did not merely revise Kyd's Ur-
Hamlet within its own framework, that instead Shakespeare went
directly to Belleforest. The play opens at the beginning of
chapter 2 in Belleforest and concludes with events in chapter 5.
His development of the material into plot and subplot generally
parallels his method in handling the Leir story in King Lear.
The catastrophe, well prepared for in the last three scenes of
act 4, is typically Shakespearean. In a word, the theory of
Kyd's having authored a version of Hamlet is not untenable; but,
were there no such earlier play, Shakespeare's inventive genius
could well have acted upon the material in Belleforest.

1106 LAWLOR, JOHN J. "The Tragic Conflict in Hamlet." Review of
English Studies, n.s. 1 (1950):97-113.
Asserts that Hamlet delays simply because his nature is
such that he cannot perform the deed demanded of him; he is
reluctant to act on the grounds of moral scruples about the
justice of revenge. He endlessly seeks the cause of his aver-
sion, calling it by every other name, and never actually knows

it for what it is. The true tragedy of Hamlet is that he is a
man condemned to do what he has no assurance is right. He is
able to act only when responding to immediate and personal issues, not to the original mandate.

1107   LEVIN, HARRY. The Question of "Hamlet." New York: Oxford
        University Press, 1959, 178 pp.
            Emphasizes the universality of Hamlet, who--as a "man in a
        plight, a mind resisting its body's destiny, a fighter against
        cosmic odds" (p. 7)--commands our identification. The play like
        life is founded in mystery and question, and the protagonist is
        committed to a rite of initiation, hemmed in on all sides. Any
        attempt to locate and delimit his experience is at his peril be-
        cause, when will confronts fate, the odds confound his best-laid
        plans. The deflating tool in the play turns out to be Yorick,
        who beyond the grave mocks Hamlet's mortality at the same time
        he prompts in the Prince a sense of compassion for man's plight.

1108   LEVITSKY, RUTH M. "Rightly to Be Great." Shakespeare
        Studies 1 (1965):142-67.
            Observes that Hamlet's problem of how to behave with honor
        and dignity in an intolerable situation was especially critical
        to Elizabethans at the turn of the seventeenth century. His
        dilemma is occasioned by the fact that to members of the contem-
        porary audience the sometimes contradictory philosophies of
        Aristotelianism, Stoicism, and Christianity all held partial
        validity. Shakespeare dramatizes this dilemma by setting Hamlet
        within a Christian context but having him motivated to action by
        characters (the ghost, Horatio, Claudius, Laertes) who find their
        sanctions in the pagan philosophies of Greece or Rome. Ulti-
        mately, in gaining his revenge he transcends the received tradi-
        tions by combining passion and reason, faith in Divine Providence
        and in himself.

1109   LEWIS, C.S. Hamlet: The Prince or the Poem? London:
        Oxford University Press, 1942, 18 pp. Reprinted in Modern
        Shakespearean Criticism, ed. Alvin B. Kernan (New York:
        Harcourt, Brace & World, 1970), pp. 301-11.
            Finds the power of Hamlet, not in character and motive, the
        essence of which has boggled critical minds for three centuries,
        but in the play itself as mysterious, fascinating, at times even
        terrifying. Hamlet's speeches are spellbinding because they de-
        scribe spiritual regions through which most spectators themselves
        have passed. In a sense the play's subject is death; it is kept
        constantly before us, whether in terms of the soul's destiny or
        the body's. The ghost, like its play and like its chief charac-
        ter, is permanently ambiguous.

1110   LEWIS, CHARLTON M. The Genesis of "Hamlet." New York: Henry
        Holt, 1907, 133 pp.
            Views Hamlet as a blend of Kyd's figure and Shakespeare's;
        Kyd's is the actor largely responsible for the elements of plot,
        Shakespeare's the thinker who constitutes the character. From
        Kyd come the ghost, the feigned madness, the doubt of the ghost's
        veracity, the moustrap, the killing of Polonius, and the fencing
        bout. Shakespeare grafted a hero on this action who, as a tem-
        peramental, sensitive, and contemplative idealist, renders cer-
        tain features not merely irrelevant but incongruous. The causes
        for Hamlet's delay lie in these incongruities.

1111   LIDZ, THEODORE. Hamlet's Enemy: Madness and Myth in
        "Hamlet." New York: Basic Books, 1975, 258 pp.
            Examines Hamlet's madness both as a literal phenomenon
        within Shakespeare's play and as a symbolic phenomenon that sets
        off resonances within the audience about man's eternal struggle
        to tame his passion and to control human nature. Central issues
        include the corrupting nature of disillusionment, its preoccupa-
        tion with death and its destruction of the ability to love, and
        the ultimate loss of the human soul in passionate isolation. The
        tragedy in Hamlet stems from infractions of cardinal rules of
        family life blocking the normal development of both Hamlet and
        Ophelia, whose deaths are attributable to the transgressions of
        prior generations.

1112   LYONS, BRIDGET GELLERT. "The Iconography of Ophelia." ELH 44
        (1977):60-74.
            Observes that the ambiguity of Ophelia's character is re-
        flected in the ambivalence of her iconographic associations. As
        she stands reading a book, she symbolizes devoutness, but the
        appearance is hypocritical since she is being used as a spy by
        her father and Claudius. Also, in the flower scene she rever-
        berates both with positive associations with Flora, goddess of
        spring and love, and with Plutarch's Roman prostitute won for a
        night by Hercules in a wager. Her sexual confusion is seen in
        the contrast of her courtly language and her bawdy songs.

1113   _____. "Melancholy and Hamlet." In Voices of Melancholy:
        Studies in Literary Treatments of Melancholy in Renaissance
        England. London: Routledge & Kegan Paul, 1971, pp. 77-112.
            Notes that melancholy is central to Hamlet, not only in the
        images of disease and the graveyard scene, which in imagery and
        symbols support Hamlet's view of the world, but more functionally
        as a source of his superior imagination and in his role playing
        of a series of stereotyped melancholy parts (the political mal-
        content, the scholar and satirist, the madman). His role play-
        ing is expressive of his unwillingness to trust and communicate
        with others, and it is justified by the diseased world to which
        it is a response.

1114   McGINN, DONALD JOSEPH. Shakespeare's Influence on the Drama
       of His Age Studied in "Hamlet." New Brunswick: Rutgers
       University Press, 1938, 241 pp.
          Examines the influence of Hamlet on Shakespeare's contempo-
       raries, both specifically in regard to the revenge play itself
       and generally in allusions found in other plays written by 1642.
       John Marston's Antonio's Revenge, for example, is shown to be
       indebted to Hamlet in both plot and characterization. Major
       emphasis is on the portrayal of the melancholy Dane, the roman-
       tic conception of Ophelia, the nunnery and mad scenes, the re-
       pentant Queen, the wailing ghost, and the graveyard scene with
       its discussion of the transitoriness of human life.

1115   MACK, MAYNARD. "The Jacobean Shakespeare: Some Observations
       on the Construction of the Tragedies." In Jacobean Theatre.
       Edited by John Russell Brown and Bernard Harris. Stratford-
       upon-Avon Studies, 1. London: Edward Arnold; New York:
       Capricorn Books, 1960, pp. 11-42. Reprinted in Modern Shake-
       spearean Criticism, ed. Alvin B. Kernan (New York: Harcourt,
       Brace & World, 1970), pp. 323-50.
          Examines the essential components of Shakespeare's mature
       tragic vision. The protagonist and his foil (for example,
       Hamlet and Horatio) function as thesis and antithesis. The foil
       carries something of the function of the chorus in Greek tragedy
       in setting the voice of common sense against the instinct to be
       resolute and free. Toward the conclusion these two voices (as
       in Horatio's advice that Hamlet forego the duel) meet at spir-
       itual cross purposes. In the course of the play the hero's inner
       struggle is mirrored in various ways (Hamlet's confrontation with
       Rosencrantz and Guildenstern, his reaction to Fortinbras's ex-
       pedition, his madness).

1116   MACK, MAYNARD. "The World of Hamlet." Yale Review 41 (1952):
       502-23. Reprinted in Shakespeare: Modern Essays in Criti-
       cism, ed. Leonard F. Dean, rev. ed. (New York: Oxford Uni-
       versity Press, 1967), pp. 242-62.
          Focuses on the interrogative mood of the Hamlet world, a
       mysteriousness characterized by riddles of language and action
       and by the problematic nature of reality and the relation of
       reality to appearance. The nature of the ghost, Hamlet's mad-
       ness, Ophelia's innocence, Gertrude's guilt, the enigma of
       Claudius--all are essentially indeterminate matters to characters
       and spectators alike. Reinforcing these ambiguities are the
       frequent uses of "assume," "put on," "shape," "show," "act," and
       "play," and the verbal imagery of theatricality and painting. By
       the final act Hamlet has come to accept the ambivalence of the
       world and of life itself, and he is prepared for "the final con-
       test of mighty opposites" (p. 523).

1117   MADARIAGA, SALVADOR DE. On "Hamlet." London: Hollis &
        Carter, 1948, 145 pp.
            Claims that Hamlet is an egocentric, asserting his right to
        judge for himself, set in conflict with a society determined to
        master him. His prideful hauteur is registered in his relation-
        ship with Rosencrantz and Guildenstern, with Polonius, and with
        Laertes. He never truly loves Ophelia, indeed is incapable of
        loving anyone other than himself. A "full-bloodied and foul-
        mouthed man" (p. 55), he in entreating Horatio to report him and
        his cause aright can think only of himself even in the face of
        death. Various inconsistencies in the action reveal Shake-
        speare's willingness to pander to the worst tastes of the crowd.

1118   MALONE, KEMP. The Literary History of Hamlet: The Early
        Tradition. Anglistische Forschungen, 59. Heidelberg:
        C. Winter, 1923, 268 pp.
            Explores the literary history of Hamlet and the Hamlet
        saga, dealing with the origin and development of the hero and
        tale before the twelfth-century version in the Historia Danica.
        The origins probably lie in the Swedish king Onela, whom scops
        variously fashioned as a Danish, Norwegian, and Geatish folk
        hero. The major aspects of the legend--the mistreatment of
        Amleth's mother, Amleth's apparent acquiescence, and his attack
        on Fjalker-Feng--are traced through several Scandinavian tribes;
        and the hypothetical primitive plot, in its fullest form before
        Saxo, is constructed in the final chapter.

1119   MIRIAM JOSEPH, Sister. "Hamlet: A Christian Tragedy."
        Studies in Philology 59 (1962):119-40.
            Defines a Christian tragedy as one in which the hero's flaw
        and catharsis have explicitly Christian significance. The ghost,
        a soul from Purgatory acting as God's agent, orders Hamlet to
        dispatch Claudius but, in doing so, not to taint his mind with
        hatred. Hamlet does just that, however, in refusing to kill
        Claudius at prayer for fear of the King's repentant state. The
        result is a chain of deaths for which he is ultimately responsi-
        ble--Polonius, Ophelia, Laertes, Gertrude, Rosencrantz and
        Guildenstern. (See entry 1097.)

1120   MORRIS, HARRY. "Hamlet as a Memento Mori Poem." PMLA 85
        (1970):1035-40.
            Considers the similarity of the structure of Hamlet and
        that of the timor mortis-memento mori lyric. The gravediggers'
        scene in Hamlet (5.1) is a set piece involving three skulls and
        imagery of the instruments and furniture of burial and of flesh-
        stripped bones. Shakespeare's main source is Thomas Lord Vaux's
        memento mori lyric, but he also apparently uses St. Bernard's
        poem. The entire play is structured around this motif of remem-
        bering and preparing for death, both in Hamlet's desire for death
        and in his attempts to accomplish his duty without endangering
        his soul.

1121   NEWELL, ALEX. "The Dramatic Context and Meaning of Hamlet's
       'To Be or Not To Be' Soliloquy." PMLA 80 (1965):38-50.
          Insists on interpreting Hamlet's "To Be or Not To Be"
       soliloquy within its dramatic context. Specifically, this
       soliloquy involves his grappling with the idea of the presenta-
       tion of the mousetrap play that he has just previously discussed
       with the players. The opening question accrues meaning as Hamlet
       thinks through the situation, but it clearly concerns whether to
       act against Claudius or to suffer. By the time he comes to sense
       that thought may be a symptom of fear, he sees more deeply into
       the complexity of the human personality. The soliloquy moves
       from specific to general considerations.

1122   PROSSER, ELEANOR. "Hamlet" and Revenge. Stanford: Stanford
       University Press, 1967, 304 pp.
          Argues that Hamlet is the only revenger who seeks the
       damnation of his victim, that something is fundamentally wrong
       with the play if the protagonist is morally obligated to kill
       Claudius. Numerous stage cuts and critical treatises have
       attempted to explain away the difficulty. In truth, Shakespeare
       intends the spectator to be appalled by the savage course on
       which Hamlet embarks. The ghost, in a word, is a demonic spirit,
       appearing at midnight to a melancholic thirsting for revenge and
       presenting a temptation to Hamlet to resort to blood revenge at
       the expense of his own spiritual health.

1123   QUILLIAN, WILLIAM H. "Hamlet" and the New Poetic: James
       Joyce and T.S. Eliot. Studies in Modern Literature, 13. Ann
       Arbor: UMI Research Press, 1983, 171 pp.
          Examines the literary response to Hamlet in the decade from
       1911 to 1922 when the so-called "new poetic" was being forged in
       the work of Eliot and Joyce. Whereas the nineteenth century was
       fascinated with unraveling the heart of Hamlet's mystery, the
       present age focuses more frequently on the artistic techniques
       and the conditions of the age. So deeply has Hamlet become a
       part of Western consciousness that every new interpretation
       echoes the past and prefigures the future. Though ultimately
       not successful, both Joyce and Eliot attempted to free Hamlet
       from the vagaries of historical relativism, to see it as a play
       in its own historical context.

1124   REPLOGLE, CAROL. "Not Parody, Not Burlesque: The Play
       Within the Play in Hamlet." Modern Philology 67 (1969):
       150-59.
          Argues that the play-within-the-play in Hamlet, far from
       being burlesque and parody either stylistically or thematically,
       has a climactic function and that it is a serious and successful
       stylistic experiment. For one thing, The Murder of Gonzago is
       filled with sententiae that deal with love and loyalty, marriage
       and remarriage, and vacillations of purpose, thus reiterating
       the major themes of the play. For another, with its abundance

of monosyllabic words and closed couplets the action slows the
pace and suggests the passage of time.

1125   ROSE, MARK. "Hamlet and the Shape of Revenge." English
       Literary Renaissance 1 (1971):132-43.
          Views Hamlet as an individual whose freedom is sorely re-
       strained. Mentally and physically "tethered" in the play, he
       has come to envision Denmark as a prison. Claudius's refusal to
       permit him to return to Wittenberg prevents his leaving a court
       he now abhors, and God's decree against suicide blocks yet
       another avenue of escape. His major problem is to find a satis-
       factory shape for his revenge. Unlike Laertes, he refuses to be
       played upon; he must take the vulgar concept and refine it so
       that it no longer offends the modesty of nature or the dignity
       of man.

1126   ROWE, ELEANOR. "Hamlet": A Window on Russia. New York:
       New York University Press, 1976, 186 pp.
          Examines the impact of Hamlet on Russian life and litera-
       ture from 1748 to 1970. Used as a window to life's meaning, the
       play has shifted in focus from one age to another. Lermontov,
       Turgenev, Chekhov, and Pasternak, for example, attribute quali-
       ties of Hamlet to their own heroes, but the hero's plight and
       search for truth vary widely. Current Marxist interpretations
       generally stress Hamlet's victimization by two clashing ideolo-
       gies. For the very reason that Russians have consistently
       assigned to the play and its hero immediately applicable moral
       and social values, their critical and creative commentary pro-
       vides a significant insight into the Russian mind.

1127   SKULSKY, HAROLD. "Revenge, Honor, and Conscience in Hamlet."
       PMLA 85 (1970):78-87.
          Views Hamlet as a tragedy of spiritual decline caused by
       pride. Hamlet must choose between the law of the talon (the
       lustful determination to murder) and the code of honor (the de-
       sire through the duello to inflict injury). While Hamlet chooses
       the latter, both are motivated by the will; and Hamlet's linking
       of conscience to cowardice is an indication of his moral dete-
       rioration. He resolves his scruples by speciously determining
       that he is God's scourge and minister.

1128   SPENCER, THEODORE. "The Elizabethan Malcontent." In Joseph
       Quincy Adams Memorial Studies. Edited by James G. McManaway,
       Giles E. Dawson, and Edwin E. Willoughby. Washington:
       Folger Shakespeare Library, 1948, pp. 523-35.
          Maintains that Hamlet and the other major Shakespearean
       tragedies at least in part reflect the spirit of the times and
       that this spirit was triggered by a combination of factors in-
       cluding Essex's rebellion and execution, the plague visitations
       of 1602-3, and the old Queen's approaching death. The malcontent
       figure takes several different shapes--the physiologically

melancholy man, the diseased melancholy of Jaques and Hamlet, the
artificially melancholic, the malcontent (Malevole, Iago), and
the satirical ranter (Thersites, Apemantus).

1129 _____. "Hamlet and the Nature of Reality." ELH 5 (1938):
255-71.
Notes that the sense of enlargment in scope and dimension
in Shakespeare's major tragedies has its origin in Hamlet in the
playwright's sophisticated utilization of the difference between
appearance and reality in the creation of dramatic character and
situation. This motif capitalized on the implicit conflict between man's dignity and his wretchedness in the inherited Christian view of man and his universe. In Hamlet's soliloquies
Shakespeare weaves into the character a dialectical tension regarding morality and social duty based on this philosophic dual-
ism. His discovery of the differences between appearance and
reality is so disillusioning that it paralyzes the sources of
deliberate action.

1130 STOLL, ELMER EDGAR. "Hamlet": An Historical and Comparative
Study. Minneapolis: University of Minnesota Press, 1919,
76 pp. Portion reprinted in Hamlet, ed. Cyrus Hoy, Norton
Critical Editions (New York: W.W. Norton, 1963), pp. 181-85.
Aims to discover Shakespeare's intentions by analyzing the
techniques, characters, and sentiments of the play and by describing modifications Shakespeare makes in his source materials.
Above all, Shakespeare shifts the revenge itself into the background and labors to make the revenger a sympathetic figure, a
heroic--not pathetic--individual. The point of confusion is the
numerous transformations of Hamlet in later times that have
obscured his character, as each age attempts to remake him in
its own fashion.

1131 TAYLOR, MARION A. A New Look at the Old Sources of "Hamlet."
Studies in English Literature, 42. The Hague and Paris:
Mouton, 1968, 79 pp.
Finds the source of the Amleth-Hamlet story in the blending
of the Roman story of Junius Brutus with Byzantine tales carried
to Nordic lands by Scandinavian Varangians. While Hamlet was
legendary, his grandfather was the historical Rorick of Judland.
Gertrude, whether literal as daughter or mythical as mother of
Hamlet, was apparently vilified as the tales were caught up in a
wave of violent Christian antifeminism. Saxo's tale "blends
ancient literature and culture with the Roman-Byzantine and the
Russian-Varangian, overlaid with a strange veneer of Christianity" (p. 55).

1132   TAYLOR, MICHAEL. "The Conflict in Hamlet." Shakespeare
        Quarterly 22 (1971):147-61.
            Sees the conflict in Hamlet between free will and destiny
        as central to the philosophic ambivalence in Elizabethan England.
        The emphasis in acts 1-4, involving Claudius's plotting and
        Hamlet's countermoves to foil his plans, is on man as the con-
        triver of his own fate. In act 5, however, Hamlet comes to
        realize and to accept the limitations of man's freedom and the
        controlling hand of God. Thus, Hamlet dies in a state of inno-
        cence. The resolution, however, is psychologically unable to
        overcome the emphasis on free will in the first four acts, and
        it is difficult to reconcile the "sweet Prince" with the earlier
        ruthless Hamlet.

1133   TAYLOR, MYRON. "Tragic Justice and the House of Polonius."
        Studies in English Literature 8 (1968):273-81.
            Views Polonius as the purest symbol of all that is rotten
        in Denmark, a Machiavellian villain consumed by deceit whose main
        function is to act as Claudius's spy and who dies serving that
        purpose. Laertes, like his father, also engages in deceitful
        villainy, and Ophelia allows herself to be used for similar ends.
        In the deaths of Polonius and his children the clear hand of
        providence is at work. The activities of the household under-
        score the motif of appearance versus reality in the play. (See
        entry 1072.)

1134   TOLMAN, ALBERT H. The Views about "Hamlet" and Other Essays.
        Boston and New York: Houghton, Mifflin, 1904, 403 pp.
            Attempts to classify and interpret major critical theories
        concerning Hamlet under the categories of "Taint Not Thy Mind"
        (Hamlet's cowardice or effeminacy), "Nor Contrive Against Thy
        Mother Aught" (Hamlet's confusion of aim and motive), traces of
        an older play as an explanation for discrepancies and cruces, and
        Hamlet as the author's mouthpiece (obscurities resulting from too
        close an autobiographical connection). The study also includes
        essays on Macbeth, The Taming of the Shrew, and Love's Labor's
        Won.

1135   VAN LAAN, THOMAS F. "Ironic Reversal in Hamlet." Studies in
        English Literature 6 (1966):247-62.
            Observes that the primary conflict in Hamlet is the tension
        created by the view, on the one hand, that asserts a ubiquitous
        evil in a corrupt and fallen world and, on the other, that pro-
        claims a world controlled by a just and benevolent God. The ten-
        sion is for many critics resolved in act 5 with Hamlet's vision
        of the fallen sparrow and the purgation of evil through his self-
        sacrifice. But ironic reversal has operated throughout the play,
        and in the announced deaths of Rosencrantz and Guildenstern and
        the fact that Fortinbras arrives on the scene, having escaped all
        consequences of his actions, a dark ambiguity reasserts itself.

1136   WALDOCK, ARTHUR J.A.   "Hamlet": A Study in Critical Method.
       Cambridge: Cambridge University Press, 1931, 94 pp. Portion
       reprinted in Shakespeare's Tragedies, ed. Laurence Lerner
       (Baltimore: Penguin, 1963), pp. 78-85.
         Argues that Hamlet's so-called delay and all its ramifica-
       tions concerning the protagonist's personality are essentially
       fabrications of critical minds. Taken at a glance, or as the
       play is experienced in the theater, Hamlet's action occurs in a
       reasonable continuum. Problems of delay and motivations for
       delay aside, the play gives evidence of a fine harmony in "the
       portrait of a man who seems to express (and the more in his suf-
       ferings and his disasters) all that Shakespeare found of greatest
       beauty and worth in the human spirit" (p. 94).

1137   WALKER, ROY.   The Time Is Out of Joint: A Study of "Hamlet."
       London: Andrew Dakers, 1948, 157 pp.
         Asserts that it is disastrously erroneous to envision
       Hamlet as a maladjusted, obstinate, and self-centered individual.
       To the contrary, he has a transfiguring view of the decadent
       world, and his soul fights against time for immortality. Scene 1
       establishes the ghost as an objective phenomenon, and in the
       ensuing action we witness the crucifixion of the godlike in man,
       the pride in suffering man must pay for his idealism and his
       imagination. Hamlet does not delay; only in his weaker moments
       does he conceive his duty to be merely the murder of his uncle.
       His task is to await the proper moment to purge the entire king-
       dom of evil.

1138   WARHAFT, SIDNEY.   "The Mystery of Hamlet." ELH 30 (1963):
       193-208.
         Questions how Hamlet can provoke such a wide range of
       critical opinion, much of it flatly contradictory in nature, and
       suggests that the play was intended to comprehend such diversity.
       Hamlet, more specifically, might well have been intended as an
       inscrutable mystery dealing with the ambiguous predicament of a
       sensitive and intelligent individual caught in the providential
       workings of history. Heaven is ordinant in the fall of a corrupt
       dynasty, and this providential hand is dramatized in the actions
       of a baffled and tormented young prince.

1139   WEITZ, MORRIS.   "Hamlet" and the Philosophy of Literary Criti-
       cism. Chicago and London: University of Chicago Press, 1964,
       335 pp.
         Investigates the meaning of criticism by focusing on the
       critical paraphernalia surrounding Hamlet. Major attention is
       directed to the nature and the function, the relationship of
       poetics to aesthetics, the nature of disagreement, the conflict
       between schools or methods, and the problem of standards. The
       first part establishes the major critical approaches, while the
       second part attempts to articulate the twenty-four areas or is-
       sues of critical analysis. The multiple views complement rather

than discredit one another because the realm of literary interpretation defies an absolutist approach.

1140   WEST, REBECCA. The Court and the Castle: Some Treatments of
       a Recurrent Theme. New Haven: Yale University Press, 1957,
       319 pp. Portion reprinted in "Hamlet": Enter Critic, ed.
       Claire Sacks and Edgar Whan (New York: Appleton-Century-
       Crofts, 1960), pp. 254-66.
          Bemoans the tendency to read Hamlet as an inscrutable and
    mysterious drama with an equally enigmatic protagonist. Hamlet
    is, quite frankly, an exceptionally callous murderer. But he can
    kill only on his own behalf; he refuses the mandate of the ghost,
    who represents the values of tradition, preferring individual
    impulse as his motivation. Shakespeare's focus is also on the
    corruption of the entire court and of society. Calvinistic in
    its image of total depravity, Hamlet illustrates the impossi-
    bility of escape from the guilt of society and the human race.

1141   WILLIAMSON, CLAUDE C.H. Readings on the Character of Hamlet
       1661-1947. London: George Allen & Unwin, 1950, 783 pp.
          Provides representative criticism of Hamlet, through
    selected passages, for almost three hundred years. The items are
    arranged chronologically and comprise 332 entries by 264 differ-
    ent critics. While the study provides critical appraisal, a
    postscript also describes the major subjects of critical dispar-
    ity (for example, Hamlet's madness, his religion, his causes for
    delay). The material obviously illustrates shifting critical
    fashions, representing English, American, and European authors.
    The entries range in length from a single sentence to ten pages.

1142   WILSON, JOHN DOVER. What Happens in "Hamlet." Cambridge:
       Cambridge University Press, 1935, 357 pp.
          Provides a close and extensive analysis of Hamlet along
    with the background of Elizabethan beliefs. Hamlet's task is a
    family affair involving the honor of the entire family. That the
    ghost itself is seen by four persons nullifies the possibility of
    melancholic illusion though it does not remove the mystery con-
    cerning its nature. The four (Bernardo, Marcellus, Horatio,
    Hamlet) represent, in fact, the various contemporary assumptions
    about spirits--that they might be spirits of the departed,
    angels, or devils. Of special interest is the discussion of the
    dumb show, which--contrary to Greg's opinion--Claudius simply was
    not observing and which sorely annoyed Hamlet. Appendixes give
    special attention to such matters as Gertrude's adultery,
    Ophelia's funeral, the acting troupe, and Eliot's theory of
    Hamlet. (See entry 1080.)

Stage History

1143   BROWN, E. MARTIN. "English Hamlets of the Twentieth Century."
        Shakespeare Survey 9 (1956):16-23.
              Highlights some of the significant trends in Hamlet produc-
        tions in the twentieth century. The descriptive sketch covers
        the Forbes-Robertson staging at Drury Lane in 1913, a reading by
        H.B. Irving (son of Henry Irving), Brown's production in Sussex
        in 1923 with Robert Speaight as Hamlet, versions in 1925 in
        London with Ernest Milton, John Barrymore, and Barry Jackson,
        John Gielgud's in 1930 (entry 1144), Robert Helpmann's in 1948,
        and Alec Guiness's in 1951. Most memorable are Gielgud and
        Forbes-Robertson, those who have most fully interpreted the part.

1144   GILDER, ROSAMUND. John Gielgud's "Hamlet." New York and
        Toronto: Oxford University Press, 1937, 233 pp. Portion
        reprinted in Interpreting "Hamlet," ed. Russell E. Leavenworth
        (San Francisco: Howard Chandler, 1960), pp. 127-37.
              Compares John Gielgud with Burbage, Betterton, Garrick,
        Kean, and Booth in having the power to articulate a Hamlet that
        is both true to Shakespeare and pertinent to their own times.
        Complex, moody, by turns furious and dejected, Gielgud's Hamlet
        focuses on the conflict of the driving force of emotion neutral-
        ized by a contemplative, questioning, rational mind. Included
        are Gielgud's notes on costume, scenery, and stage business,
        along with--on pages facing the text--a scene-by-scene descrip-
        tion of his performance at the New Theatre, London, 1934-35, and
        at the St. James Theatre, New York, 1936-37.

1145   KLINAN, BERNICE. "Olivier's Hamlet: A Film-Infused Play."
        Literature/Film Quarterly 5 (1977):305-14.
              Observes that Olivier, by deciding not simply to film
        Shakespeare's play, gained freedom both of space and of perspec-
        tive. By using a flexible stage set (with movable stairways,
        pillars, and halls), a traveling camera to move from one angle
        to another, fade-outs, music, close-ups (at times several in
        rapid succession), and aural and visual transitions, Olivier
        achieves startling effects. His intention was to create, not a
        hybrid of film and stage, but a film-infused experience.

1146   REYNOLDS, GEORGE. "Hamlet at the Globe." Shakespeare Survey
        9 (1956):49-53. Reprinted in Interpreting "Hamlet," ed.
        Russell E. Leavenworth (San Francisco: Howard Chandler,
        1960), pp. 235-41.
              Notes that actors and directors are increasingly realizing
        that the absence of specific demands in the original text permits
        a wide latitude in the manner of staging Hamlet. It can, in
        fact, be played entirely on an arena stage without distortion.
        The difficulty of seeing and hearing when scenes are recessed and
        the question of whether there was even an inner, curtained stage
        at the Globe suggest that the action should be pulled forward on

the stage as far as practicable. The play-within-the-play scene,
for example, requires that Hamlet and Claudius be on opposite
sides of the main stage so that the spectators might watch both
the King's and the Prince's reaction to the playlet.

1147   ROSSI, ALFRED. Minneapolis Rehearsals: Tyrone Guthrie
        Directs "Hamlet." Berkeley: University of California Press,
        1970, 236 pp.
            Charts Tyrone Guthrie's direction of the Minnesota Theatre
        Company's production of Hamlet at the Tyrone Guthrie Theatre in
        Minneapolis in 1963. Prepared by a member of the Company and the
        Assistant to the Director for this production, the study includes
        a Hamlet log written during rehearsals and the postscript by
        Edward Payson Call, whose tendency to verbalize the action re-
        sults in a record of stage directions, not merely of stage move-
        ments. This production was in modern dress, with scenic and
        costume design by Tanya Moiseiwitsch, whose sketches are also
        included.

For discussion of the relationship of father and son, see entries
1067, 1083, 1086. For discussion of the imagery, see entries 1077,
1087, 1112. For discussion of revenge tragedy, see entries 1070,
1092, 1100. For discussion of the Hamlet saga, see entries 1093,
1105, 1118, 1131. See also The Tragedies (entries 920-979) and 25,
76, 79, 87, 89-90, 101, 103, 108, 115, 126, 131-34, 141, 144, 152,
171-72, 179, 213, 216, 221-22, 224, 228, 231, 238, 240, 243, 245,
250, 253, 263, 267, 272, 277, 286, 291, 294, 296, 302, 305-7, 312,
318-20, 323-24, 342-43, 627, 946, 991, 1164, 1258, 1483.

JULIUS CAESAR

Reference Works

1148   VELZ, JOHN W., comp. "The Tragedy of Julius Caesar": A
        Bibliography to Supplement the New Variorum Shakespeare Edi-
        tion of 1913. New York: Modern Language Association, 1977,
        58 pp.
            Includes 1,252 entries representing the scholarship on
        Julius Caesar from 1913 through 1972. The material is categorized
        alphabetically under editions, commentary, text, date, sources,
        criticism, and stage and stage history. Books with multiple focus
        are included in the criticism section; editions and book reviews
        are not included. The bibliography is intended to supplement
        entry 1150.

Editions

1149   DORSCH, T.S., ed. Julius Caesar. The Arden Shakespeare.
        London: Methuen; Cambridge, Mass.: Harvard University Press,
        1955, 166 pp.

Includes discussion of the text, date, contemporary allusions, Shakespeare's treatment of the sources, other Caesar
plays, the language and imagery, and the characterization, as
well as an appendix featuring a selection from Thomas Platter's
account of his visit to England. The text is based on the First
Folio, for which the copy was probably the promptbook. Apparently one of the first plays performed at the Globe in 1599,
Julius Caesar is effectively constructed with the balance of
power divided among the conflicting parties. Brutus is the
dramatic hero of the play, tragic because, for all his estimable
qualities, he is pompous, opinionated, and self-righteous;
Cassius is able to manipulate him for selfish and ignoble purposes.

1150   FURNESS, HENRY HOWARD, Jr., ed. The Tragedie of Julius
       Caesar. A New Variorum Edition of Shakespeare. Philadelphia:
       J.B. Lippincott, 1913, 482 pp.
          Uses the First Folio as the copy text. On each page, for
       that portion of the text, provides variant readings, textual
       notes, and general critical commentary. Following the text are
       sections on the nature of the text, the date of composition, the
       text of William Alexander's Julius Caesar, the individual char-
       acters, criticisms, stage history, the principal actors, drama-
       tic versions, and a list of works consulted.

1151   WILSON, JOHN DOVER, ed. Julius Caesar. Cambridge: Cambridge
       University Press, 1949, 219 pp.
          Provides extensive textual notes, a critical introduction,
       a discussion of the copy text, a section on stage history, and a
       glossary. This edition is based on the First Folio, the only
       substantive text, probably representing a transcription of the
       promptbook. The play in design reflects the proportion, sim-
       plicity, and restraint characteristic of classical art. The
       style, sparing of metaphor and wordplay, possesses a kind of
       Roman directness. While what is at stake is political--the fu-
       ture of Rome--the action is still played out among private
       thoughts, and the issues were of no small concern to the members
       of Shakespeare's audience.

Criticism

1152   ANSON, JOHN S. "Julius Caesar: The Politics of the Hardened
       Heart." Shakespeare Studies 2 (1966):11-33.
          Argues that Shakespeare in Julius Caesar develops the image
       of Rome as a body, an organism in which all parts have a neces-
       sary and significant function. Gradually this body, governed by
       a repressive ethic, loses its sensibility, and head is separated
       from hand. The contagion spreads from Caesar to the conspirators
       to the populace at large. Corporately the body loses compassion
       and the heart hardens, a political situation dramatized in the

play. Julius Caesar is a drama of rivalries, of "culture pur-
chased at the price of perpetual suffering" (p. 30).

1153   BONJOUR, ADRIEN. The Structure of "Julius Caesar." Liverpool:
       Liverpool University Press, 1958, 81 pp.
           Observes that--unlike the conscience-stricken criminal
       Henry IV or the repentant King John or the satanic slaughterer
       Richard III, all of whom commit murder for political ambition--
       Brutus is an intrinsically noble individual whose aims are polit-
       ically disinterested. He determines to sacrifice Caesar to a
       higher political imperative, but in that very act of subordinat-
       ing the human level to that of abstraction lie the seeds of his
       own destruction. Shakespeare forces the spectators' sympathies
       to fluctuate toward and away from Brutus as he focuses on certain
       ramifications of the political act.

1154   BOWDEN, WILLIAM R. "The Mind of Brutus." Shakespeare
       Quarterly 17 (1966):57-67.
           Maintains that deromanticizing Brutus yields a more real-
       istic figure consistent with the text. Brutus, for one thing,
       is not an intellectual; he is seduced by Cassius into joining the
       conspiracy, and his independent decisions are blunders. For
       another, it is impossible to focus on precisely the nature of
       Brutus's inner conflict, if indeed there is one. Finally, he
       experiences no anagnorisis, persisting to the point of death in
       refusal to admit moral culpability. He is a self-righteous do-
       gooder who is always wrong.

1155   BREYER, BERNARD. "A New Look at Julius Caesar." In Essays in
       Honor of Walter Clyde Curry. Vanderbilt Studies in the
       Humanities, 2. Nashville: Vanderbilt University Press, 1954,
       pp. 161-80. Reprinted in Shakespeare's "Julius Caesar," ed.
       Julian Markels (New York: Charles Scribner's Sons, 1961),
       pp. 45-54.
           Insists that Shakespeare and his contemporaries would view
       Caesar as a stereotypical tyrant. Brutus has no ideological ob-
       jections to monarchical government but fears what the office will
       do to Caesar. Two noted characteristics of the tyrant--boastful-
       ness and susceptibility to flattery--possess Caesar just before
       the assassination. That Brutus, the "good tyrannicide" (p. 178),
       falls at the hands of the tyrant's avengers is only one of the
       submerged ironies in the play.

1156   BURKE, KENNETH. "Antony in Behalf of the Play." Southern
       Review 1 (1935):308-19. Reprinted in The Philosophy of Lit-
       erary Form (New York: Vintage Books, 1957), pp. 279-90.
           Imagines Antony just after the murder addressing the spec-
       tators rather than the mob, explaining Shakespeare's method as
       variously stressing the Caesar principle and the Brutus principle.
       In Antony the Caesar principle is continued, and it continues to
       be problematic in the spectators' eyes through Antony's inciting

the mob to riotous and destructive action. Even so, the Brutus
principle degenerates even more strikingly through the quarrel
between Cassius and Brutus, his "descent to soft tearfulness"
(p. 290), and the prophetic appearance of Caesar's ghost as
Brutus's "evil spirit."

1157   FORTIN, RENÉ. "Julius Caesar: An Experiment in Point of
        View." Shakespeare Quarterly 19 (1968):341-47.
            Believes Julius Caesar is a deliberate experiment in point
        of view to reveal the limitations of human knowledge. Truth is
        at least partially subjective, modified by the individual's per-
        spective. The theme of misconstruing permeates the play. Each
        principal character has his own view of Caesar; but Brutus be-
        cause of his patrician pride allows himself to be seduced by
        Cassius, and his deception persists until the end of the play.

1158   GREENE, GAYLE. "'The Power of Speech to Stir Men's Blood':
        The Language of Tragedy in Shakespeare's Julius Caesar."
        Renaissance Drama, n.s. 11 (1980):67-83.
            Suggests that the rhetorical style of Julius Caesar is
        central to its tragic meaning, that the depiction of Rome as a
        society filled with speakers whose rhetorical skills mask moral
        and political truth demonstrates the use of language to pervert,
        conceal, and misconstrue. Particular focus is on Cassius's suc-
        cess in persuading Brutus to join the conspiracy, Brutus's self-
        justifying soliloquy, Brutus's funeral oration, and Antony's
        counteroration. Language, man's medium for coming to terms with
        his objective world, is turned inwardly and destructively back
        upon itself. (See entry 1172.)

1159   HARTSOCK, MILDRED. "The Complexity of Julius Caesar." PMLA
        81 (1966):56-62.
            Claims that a study of Shakespeare's use of sources in
        Julius Caesar reveals that he intends the play to be problematic
        and that any attempt to tilt the moral balance to a particular
        critical posture is false to the dramaturgical design. Altera-
        tions from Plutarch, more precisely, render ambiguous Caesar,
        Brutus, Cassius, and the Roman people. In such a manner Shake-
        speare effectively dramatizes the dilemma of being forced to act
        on what is inevitably a partial view and stimulates consideration
        of the nature of political realities.

1160   KIRSCHBAUM, LEO. "Shakespeare's Stage Blood and Its Critical
        Significance." PMLA 64 (1949):517-29.
            Observes that spectacular blood effects through concealed
        bladders, sponges, and animal entrails were relatively common on
        the Elizabethan stage. The bloody sergeant in Macbeth and the
        bleeding Coriolanus after the battle at Corioli are merely two
        examples. One of the most striking is in Julius Caesar where
        the assassination actualizes Calpurnia's dream that Caesar was a
        fountain spouting blood from many holes in which the conspirators

bathe their hands. Shakespeare not only excites the spectators
by such a scene; he also reflects the bloodthirstiness of the
conspirators.

1161   McALINDON, THOMAS. "The Numbering of Men and Days: Symbolic
        Design in The Tragedy of Julius Caesar." Studies in Philology
        81 (1984):372-93.
            Suggests that "mean" in the sense of both significance and
        intention is the key word in Julius Caesar. The most remarkable
        feature of the play is that Shakespeare involves the spectators
        in the hermeneutic problems, why Caesar pushed back the crown,
        why Brutus could join the conspiracy. Number symbolism also
        engages the spectators in a search for meaning, specifically the
        Pythagorean four (amity, justice) and eight (justice, regenera-
        tion). The numbers become reverberative through reiteration
        both verbal and visual. The observant minority in Shakespeare's
        audience would note that the characters in the play blandly dis-
        regard the signs of fate around them and that meaning is mock-
        ingly allusive.

1162   PAOLUCCI, A. "The Tragic Hero in Julius Caesar." Shakespeare
        Quarterly 11 (1960):329-33.
            Cautions that, even though there are problems with Brutus
        as the hero of Julius Caesar, the attempt to make Caesar the real
        or the nominal hero is fraught with danger. Perhaps Shakespeare
        named the play as he did to point up the fact that to understand
        the play properly we must see it through Brutus's eyes. Brutus
        saw more in Caesar than was there, and the discrepancy between
        his idealized conception and the real Caesar provoked his down-
        fall.

1163   PETERSON, DOUGLAS L. "'Wisdom Consumed in Confidence': An
        Examination of Shakespeare's Julius Caesar." Shakespeare
        Quarterly 16 (1965):19-28.
            States that Caesar's indifference to the omens and to
        Artemidorus's letter is not evidence of his contempt for super-
        stition or of his nobly placing matters of state above personal
        issues but of a character flaw invented by Shakespeare to account
        for his vulnerability to the conspirators' plot. While such a
        flaw explains how Caesar is manipulated into a situation cul-
        minating in his assassination, it in no way justifies his murder
        as a political tyrant. There is no trace of Plutarch's sugges-
        tion that Caesar's death is caused by an angry god in retribution
        for past crimes.

1164   PRIOR, MOODY E. "The Search for a Hero in Julius Caesar."
        Renaissance Drama, n.s. 2 (1969):81-101.
            Argues that, instead of viewing Brutus as an introspective
        tragic hero like Hamlet or Macbeth, Julius Caesar should be con-
        sidered as structurally akin to the history plays, which maintain
        a political theme while dividing the interest among the charac-

ters. Brutus and Cassius are the only figures of continual
interest. While Brutus attempts to maintain his moral integrity
as he confronts the issues raised by the conspiracy, Cassius
acts as a political realist who attempts to guide the course of
the rebellion by political consideration alone.

1165   RIBNER, IRVING. "Political Issues in <u>Julius Caesar</u>." <u>Journal</u>
       <u>of English and Germanic Philology</u> 56 (1957):10-22.
       Focuses on two fundamental political issues--the chaos that
results when a tyrant overthrows long-established governmental
institutions and the equally destructive consequences of noble
men violating their own natures to engage in political action for
what they assume will be the greater good. Caesar exemplifies
the first, claiming the prerogative of kingship with no legal
right; Brutus typifies the second, the inevitable failure of a
virtuous murderer. Shakespeare may well have been reflecting
anxieties about political succession in England.

1166   SCHANZER, ERNEST. "The Tragedy of Shakespeare's Brutus."
       ELH 22 (1955):1-15. Reprinted in <u>Discussions of Shakespeare's</u>
       <u>Roman Plays</u>, ed. Maurice Charney (Boston: D.C. Heath, 1964),
       pp. 65-76.
       Observes that the conception of Brutus's divided mind,
self-deception, and tragic disillusion are original with Shakespeare. Following his agreement to participate in the assassina-
tion, Brutus is subject to nightmarish doubt as his "whole in-
stinctive emotional and imaginative being rises in revulsion
against the decision which his intellect has made" (p. 5). His
later quarrel with Cassius reflects the tragic disillusionment of
a man who, by basing his rationale for acting on what Caesar
might have been, commits himself to the mercy of events.

1167   SMITH, GORDON ROSS. "Brutus, Virtue, and Will." <u>Shakespeare</u>
       <u>Quarterly</u> 10 (1959):367-79. Reprinted in <u>Shakespeare's</u>
       <u>"Julius Caesar,"</u> ed. Julian Markels (New York: Charles
       Scribner's Sons, 1961), pp. 103-12.
       Views Brutus as a character of internal psychological con-
sistency. Brutus's central quality is not his virtue but his
thoroughly egotistic will for which virtue serves as a splendid
muffling of self-justification. His insistence that the conspirators not swear an oath, that Cicero not be included, that
Antony not be slain, that Metullus Cimber be included, that
Antony be permitted to speak over Caesar's body, that Cassius
provide money for his troops, and that he and Cassius attack the
enemy at Phillipi--all such instances reveal a relentless will-
fulness. To the very end Brutus conceives of himself as capable
of mistake but not of fault.

1168   SMITH, WARREN D. "The Duplicate Revelation of Portia's
        Death." Shakespeare Quarterly 4 (1953):153-61. Reprinted in
        Shakespeare's "Julius Caesar," ed. Julian Markels (New York:
        Charles Scribner's Sons, 1961), pp. 113-19.
            Claims that the duplicate passages involving the revelation
        of Portia's death in 4.3 are textually authentic and are intended
        by Shakespeare to bear "unmistakable witness to the unselfishness,
        fortitude, and able generalship characteristic of Brutus in other
        parts of the play" (p. 154). Capitalizing on the variance of
        proscription figures and of the names of those slain in Rome as
        reported to Brutus, Shakespeare intends Messala's question about
        Portia to give Brutus desperate hope that she still lives. The
        remarkable manner in which he holds up under the double blow
        renders him highly heroic in the eyes of both the spectators and
        Cassius.

1169   VELZ, JOHN W. "Clemency, Will, and Just Cause in Julius
        Caesar." Shakespeare Survey 22 (1969):109-18.
            Notes that Caesar has a radically different conception of
        himself than do the conspirators, who brand him a present tyrant
        likely to grow far worse if allowed to assume the power of king-
        ship. According to Renaissance political thought (Pierre Charon,
        La Primaudaye) this view was essentially correct, and Brutus is
        thus neither hypocrite nor self-deceiver in his reasoning. That
        Brutus and his fellow conspirators fail exemplifies the tragic
        paradox that those who cleanse the body politic must sacrifice
        themselves in the holocaust.

1170   WELSH, ALEXANDER. "Brutus Is an Honorable Man." Yale Review
        64 (1975):496-513.
            Notes that honor is closely associated with one's identity
        as defined by what others think of him. Cassius, in this sense,
        convinces Brutus that his identity is being threatened by
        Caesar's putative ambition, that Caesar is bypassing the system
        of judgment by which social being is produced--ancestry and noble
        deeds. Brutus in turn acts purely from (and to protect) his code
        of honor, and the result is politically and humanly disastrous.
        Such autonomous action is revealed as a luxury society as a whole
        will not tolerate.

1171   WILKINSON, ANDREW M. "A Psychological Approach to Julius
        Caesar." Review of English Literature 7 (1966):65-78.
            Describes Caesar as a man who has totally identified with
        his ideal image of the ruler-king but who is subliminally plagued
        by a fear of incompetence and destruction. For one thing he
        constantly blames others--Calpurnia for her barrenness and for
        her interpretation of his dream, the soothsayer and Cassius at
        various times for the frustrations of his political ambition.
        His paranoia is reflected in this refusal to accept responsibil-
        ity, in his fear of persecution, and in his abnormal behavior
        when his delusion is touched upon.

1172   ZANDVOORT, R.W. "Brutus' Forum Speech in Julius Caesar."
        Review of English Studies 16 (1940):62-66. Reprinted in R.W.
        Zandvoort, Collected Papers, Groningen Studies in English, 5.
        (Groningen: Wolters, 1954), pp. 50-57.
           Describes the style of Brutus's speech as euphuistic in its
        deliberate elaboration and repetition of a number of stylistic
        patterns (schemata such as isocolon, parison, and paromion).
        Shakespeare probably assigned Brutus this highly rhetorical
        speech to mark it off from Antony's. Certainly, whereas Brutus's
        speech appeals to the intellect, Antony's appeals to the emo-
        tions. The speech is the most pronounced example in Shakespeare
        of the sustained use of rhetorical schemes. (See entry 1158.)

Stage History

1173   RIPLEY, JOHN. "Julius Caesar" on the Stage in England and
        America 1599-1973. Cambridge: Cambridge University Press,
        1980, 370 pp.
           Works from promptbooks, dramaturgical sketches, letters,
        diaries, biographies, reviews, and interviews to construct a
        stage history of Julius Caesar. The study focuses on four major
        areas--the texts and information they provide concerning the
        age's taste and sensibility; the stagings, involving matters
        such as sets, costumes, lighting, and crowd scenes; the inter-
        pretation of the four major roles, Caesar, Brutus, Cassius,
        Antony; and the extent to which academic theory and analysis
        have influenced the production.

For discussion of Julius Caesar as a problem play, see entries 1157,
1159, 1166. For discussion of Brutus as a tragic figure, see entries
1162, 1167, 1170; for a counterview, see entry 1154. See also The
Tragedies (entries 920-79) and 104, 137, 150, 182, 196, 227, 240,
245, 258, 266, 281, 294, 298, 304, 310, 342, 404, 1033, 1041, 1104.

KING LEAR

Reference Works

1174   CHAMPION, LARRY S., comp. "King Lear": An Annotated Bibliog-
        raphy. 2 vols. Garland Shakespeare Bibliographies, 1. New
        York and London: Garland Publishing, 1980, 909 pp.
           Contains 2,532 entries, representing virtually all publi-
        cations on King Lear from 1940 through 1978, along with the most
        significant items of scholarship prior to 1940. The categories,
        each arranged chronologically, are divided into criticism,
        sources, dating, textual studies, bibliographies, editions, stage
        history, and adaptations, influence, and synopses. An introduc-
        tory essay briefly traces the history of recent criticism and
        research. The explosion both of scholarly interest in the play
        and of stage productions of it reveals that, for many, it is the

tragedy for our time, a reflection of the postwar zeitgeist with
its lack of a center and the ever-present threat of nuclear
annihilation.

1175   MARDER, LOUIS, comp. "King Lear": A Supplementary Bibliog-
        raphy 1880-1965. The New Variorum Shakespeare. New York:
        American Scholar Publications, 1965, 30 pp.
            Includes representative scholarship on King Lear from 1880
        to 1965 and is intended to supplement H.H. Furness's Variorum
        edition of 1880. The material is categorized under reproductions
        of original folio editions, reproductions of original quarto edi-
        tions, bibliographical sources, modern editions, King Lear bib-
        liography, and critical studies (alphabetically arranged). While
        not exhaustive, the material represents every major category of
        scholarship and criticism.

1176   TANNENBAUM, SAMUEL A., and TANNENBAUM, DOROTHY R., comps.
        William Shakespeare: "King Lear." Elizabethan Bibliogra-
        phies, 16. New York: Privately Printed, 1940, 101 pp.
            Cites 1,934 unannotated items covering major scholarship on
        King Lear from the beginnings to 1938. The material is divided
        into the following categories and is arranged alphabetically by
        section--editions, adaptations; translations; music, songs,
        operas; commentary on music; illustrations, costumes; parodies,
        burlesques; old King Leir; King Lear in the theater; commentary
        on King Lear; book titles; addenda. The majority of the material
        (1,254 items) is loosely classified under commentary on the play.

Editions

1177   DUTHIE, GEORGE IAN, ed. Shakespeare's "King Lear": A Criti-
        cal Edition. Oxford: Basil Blackwell, 1949, 425 pp.
            Uses the First Folio as the principal copy text, but allows
        readings from the first quarto. In addition to a textual intro-
        duction, textual variants at the bottom of the page and textual
        notes are provided. The aim of this old-spelling edition is to
        establish a text "as near to what Shakespeare wrote as it is pos-
        sible to get" (p. 3). The folio text is a copy of the first
        quarto brought by an editor into general agreement with a theatri-
        cal manuscript containing a shortened version of the play, prob-
        ably the promptbook; the quarto text is a reported version by the
        entire company when the King's Men were on tour in 1606.

1178   DUTHIE, GEORGE IAN, and WILSON, JOHN DOVER, eds. King Lear.
        Cambridge: Cambridge University Press, 1960, 300 pp.
            Provides extensive notes, a discussion of the copy text, a
        critical introduction, sections on sources and date, Lear,
        Cordelia, Kent, the Fool, Lear's suffering, the subplot, nature,
        man's double nature, the play's "pessimism," and a glossary; C.B.
        Young provides notes on the stage history. Duthie abandons his
        earlier assumption that the first quarto is a memorial text

reconstructed by an entire company in favor of a modified view
that the source is two boy actors who played Goneril and Regan.
The folio text is probably a "conflation of 'good' pages from
[the first quarto] supplemented by inserted manuscript leaves to
replace corrupt passages of the quarto" (p. 128). The copy for
this edition is eclectic, with the folio as a base text.

1179   MUIR, KENNETH, ed. King Lear. The Arden Shakespeare.
       London: Methuen; Cambridge, Mass.: Harvard University Press,
       1952, 259 pp.
           Includes discussion of the text, date, sources, stage his-
       tory, and critical interpretation, as well as appendixes featur-
       ing selections from King Leir, Holinshed's Chronicles, Spenser's
       The Faerie Queene, The Mirror for Magistrates, and Sidney's
       Arcadia. The text is based on the First Folio, with quarto
       readings allowed where the folio text is corrupt. Current crit-
       icism fully accepts the tragic quality of the play, though opin-
       ions range from one polarity that it is set in a teleological
       universe in which suffering is redemptive to the other that
       Shakespeare is delineating the ultimate horror of an absurdist
       universe. Muir argues that Lear's experience leads to a stage of
       self-knowledge and that a new Lear is born from his reunion with
       Cordelia. Lear makes no concessions to sentimentality, however;
       it is logical that the innocent will suffer with the guilty once
       evil is unleashed.

                         Textual Studies

1180   DORAN, MADELEINE. The Text of "King Lear." Stanford:
       Stanford University Press, 1931, 148 pp.
           Notes that the order of the quartos is now settled, with
       the first quarto printed in 1608 and the second quarto printed in
       1619 but falsely dated 1608; the precise nature of the texts is,
       however, still a matter of debate. The first quarto is not a
       reported text but Shakespeare's original version considerably
       revised. The folio text, omitting three hundred lines from the
       quarto, is more regular and satisfactory; it is divided into acts
       and scenes, and the stage directions are more complete and pre-
       cise. The copy text for the folio was the promptbook, a tran-
       script revised and shortened by Shakespeare himself.

1181   DUTHIE, GEORGE IAN. Elizabethan Shorthand and the First
       Quarto of "King Lear." Oxford: Basil Blackwell, 1949, 82 pp.
           Argues that the folio text of King Lear was printed from a
       copy of the first quarto that had been brought by a scribe into
       general agreement with an authentic playhouse text, probably the
       promptbook. The quarto text bears the marks of memorial recon-
       struction. Theories that it was based on a shorthand account are
       not valid. A careful analysis of the three systems of shorthand
       available in 1608 reveals conclusively that none was sufficiently
       sophisticated to produce the text. A person might capture the

essence or summary through these systems, but nothing approaching
the verbal detail.

1182   GREG, W.W.   The Variants in the First Quarto of "King Lear."
       Oxford: Oxford University Press, 1940, 192 pp.
           Compares and analyzes the differences in the twelve extant
       copies of the first quarto. The text consists of ten sheets
       (twenty formes) and a single half-sheet containing the title
       page. Seven sheets involve variants (a total of 167), except for
       one instance confined to the outer formes. Of the seventy-two
       formes in all, thirty-two are in the original state, and forty-
       two are in corrected state. The variant readings are listed in
       one chart and compared to the superior folio reading in another.

1183   KIRSCHBAUM, LEO.   The True Text of "King Lear."   Baltimore:
       Johns Hopkins University Press, 1945, 81 pp.
           Views the quarto text of King Lear as a memorial recon-
       struction, while the folio text was printed from a copy of the
       quarto emended by reference to a transcript that derived from
       Shakespeare's associates. Any substantive difference between the
       quarto and the folio indicates a change deliberately introduced
       by someone directly connected with the company; hence, where the
       two texts differ, the folio reading must be adopted. A careful
       analysis of the two texts reveals that the quarto text is
       thoroughly undependable, plagued by omission, anticipation,
       recollection, assimilation, vulgarization, substitution, mis-
       understanding, and misinterpretation. The received text of Lear
       is the folio text except where omissions occur inadvertently or
       by design.

1184   STONE, P.W.K.   The Textual History of "King Lear."   London:
       Scolar Press, 1980, 280 pp.
           Argues that the first quarto is a reported text based on a
       longhand account developed during visits to several performances
       and that the folio is a refurbished version of the same report.
       It is impossible safely to select either the quarto or folio as
       the basis for a modern edition. Instead, a modern text must be
       "a judiciously compiled amalgam of selections from each, . . . an
       independent entity, the hypothetical reconstruction of a text
       which does not in fact exist, but which once did as the ancestor
       of the editions still surviving" (p. 163).

1185   TAYLOR, GARY, and WARREN, MICHAEL, eds.   The Division of the
       Kingdom: Shakespeare's Two Versions of "King Lear."   New
       York: Oxford University Press, 1984, 320 pp.
           Includes twelve original essays dealing with the current
       theories concerning the textual status of King Lear. The tragedy
       exists in two versions, the first quarto (1608) and the 1623
       folio, and virtually all editions are eclectic, conflating the
       two into a single text. Recent criticism has begun to challenge
       this view, arguing that the two versions represent different

stages in Shakespeare's composition and that the folio text
represents the form he finally intended. These essays examine
the question from both points of view; and, while they do not
settle the matter, they fully articulate it.

1186   URKOWITZ, STEVEN. Shakespeare's Revision of "King Lear."
         Princeton: Princeton University Press, 1980, 184 pp.
         Challenges the assumption that the first quarto and the
folio are blemished variations of the now lost text of King Lear
and that an eclectic, inclusive modern text best approximates
that original version. Instead, the quarto and folio texts
represent two stages of Shakespeare's composition, an early draft
and a final revision. Theatrical variants in the texts reveal
much about Shakespeare's sense of dramatic movement, rhythm, and
character development. The folio is clearly the superior text.

Criticism

1187   ALPERS, PAUL. "King Lear and the Theory of the 'Sight Pat-
         tern.'" In In Defense of Reading. Edited by Reuben Brower
         and Richard Poirier. New York: Dutton, 1962, pp. 133-52.
         Claims that studies stressing the pattern of sight imagery
as a metaphor issuing in moral insight and regeneration dilute
the intensity of the human suffering and love in the play. To
articulate the blinding of Gloucester as the culmination of such
a pattern, for example, is virtually to rewrite the scene;
Gloucester's supposed new understanding is nothing more than his
recognition that Edgar is not treacherous. Especially misleading
is the argument that the metaphor of sight mitigates our horror
at the brutality of the scene. What Gloucester must learn is not
the Platonic ideas proclaimed by the imagists but the truth of
the love of a real person and a real son. Similarly, to treat
Lear's recognition of Cordelia as a moral awareness is to assume
that his suffering has been good; to the contrary, the tragedy
tests man's experience, not his understanding.

1188   BAUER, ROBERT J. "'Despite of Mine Own Nature': Edmund and
         the Orders, Cosmic and Moral." Texas Studies in Literature
         and Language 10 (1968-69):359-66.
         Observes that Edmund, in the light of nominalism, skepti-
cism, and moral empiricism, exemplifies Renaissance individualism
defiant of all that would negate the primacy of self-interest in
legal, moral, or ethical circumstances. The dual concept of
nature--nomos, nature as law, and physis, nature as vital force--
is as old as the pre-Socratics, and the concept of nature as a
goddess exempt from moral law (physis) runs throughout the literature of the Middle Ages. Montaigne argues specifically that
laws originate not in nature but in man and social custom;
Machiavelli is a moral empiricist who maintains that human nature
admits of no laws; William of Ockham sees society as a unity that
thrives by competition and contention rather than by harmony and
cooperation. Edmund is the stark individualist whose relation

343

to society has been severed by society's brand of bastard and who
coolly and deliberately strives to prove his superior physical
and intellectual prowess. (See entry 1227.)

1189   BICKERSTETH, GEOFFREY LANGDALE. The Golden World of "King
        Lear." Oxford: Oxford University Press, 1946, 24 pp.
            Argues that Shakespeare's purpose in King Lear is essen-
        tially didactic, to reveal that morally evil elements and the
        suffering they provoke ultimately work for the cause of good.
        What we slowly realize is that all suffering, when accepted and
        patiently endured for another's sake and not for self-advantage,
        is sacrificial and redemptive. Cordelia's actions, more specif-
        ically, suggest Christ's Harrowing of Hell. Divine love enters
        a kingdom already divided, operating first as a disruptive force
        before restoring all things to order. It is Lear's conviction
        that she does live that causes his heart to break, not from
        sorrow, but "in an ecstasy of joy" (p. 25).

1190   BOOTH, STEPHEN. "King Lear," "Macbeth": Indefinition and
        Tragedy. New Haven: Yale University Press, 1983, 183 pp.
            Finds the key to Shakespeare's tragic power, not in meta-
        dramatic ramifications, but in the play's confrontation with
        inconclusiveness. By constantly sending false generic signals
        in King Lear, Shakespeare establishes expectations only to dash
        them and thus to stretch the audience out on the rack of this
        tough play. The Cinderella-like story of the banished younger
        daughter promises a happy ending; Gloucester's whorish boasting
        suggests a story in which he will be chastened and his illegiti-
        mate son morally enhanced; Lear's division of the kingdom points
        to a play about political folly. The sudden intrusion of tragic
        events aborts the play's suggested directions, and the spectators'
        response arises in part from the realization of the "folly of
        relying on artificial, arbitrary limits" (p. 61).

1191   BRANSON, JAMES. The Tragedy of King Lear. Oxford: Basil
        Blackwell, 1934, 227 pp.
            Views the major theme as the development and course of
        Lear's insanity. Following the King's initial outburst prompted
        by vanity, he is subjected to a series of strains with Goneril
        and Regan that precipitate his madness. His sanest moment is his
        willingness on the heath to acknowledge that he has been neglect-
        ful of his duty and that intellectual honesty, mercy, justice,
        and compassion represent the highest values. Throughout the
        tragedy Lear struggles between the pleasure principle and the
        reality principle; never is there a firm line between his percep-
        tion of reality and the distortions of his repressed wishes or
        repressed fantasies.

1192   BROOKE, NICHOLAS. "The Ending of King Lear." In Shakespeare
       1564-1964: A Collection of Modern Essays by Various Hands.
       Edited by E.A. Bloom. Providence: Brown University Press,
       1964, pp. 71-87.
          Asserts that the ending of play, specifically Cordelia's
       death, is as unbearable as Johnson claimed it to be. The pagans
       on stage suggest no benignity in the gods, and Lear hints at no
       further life for Cordelia either in heaven or on earth. Nor is
       there any profound wisdom in Lear's dying deluded. Every posi-
       tive act or assertion in the play is followed ironically by one
       that modifies or negates it. Lear's impassioned howls at the
       end are clearsighted. There is no affirmation in the final un-
       doing of the order implicit in repentance, forgiveness, redemp-
       tion, and regeneration, in the negation of all forms of hope.

1193   CAMPBELL, OSCAR JAMES. "The Salvation of Lear." ELH 15
       (1948):93-109. Reprinted in The "King Lear" Perplex, ed.
       Helmut Bonheim (Belmont, Calif.: Wadsworth, 1960),
       pp. 107-10.
          Describes King Lear as a sublime morality play involving
       man's finding true and eternal spiritual values at the very
       moment of death. Like the central figure in the Moralities, Lear
       must discover his true friends who will face death with him
       without fear; he must come to repudiate his kingdom, his re-
       tainers, and his creature comforts. Above all, he must master
       his passion of wrath. On his pilgrimage he is accompanied by
       two faithful companions, Kent and the Fool, both of whom are
       Cynic-Stoic commentators. Lear's suffering is purgatorial and
       allows him to realize the full dimensions of his own humanity.
       His moment of true redemption, when he awakens in Cordelia's
       arms, renders him forever independent of material circumstances.

1194   CHAMBERS, R.W. "King Lear." Glasgow University Publications
       54 (1940):20-52. Reprinted in His Infinite Variety: Major
       Shakespearean Criticism Since Johnson, ed. Paul N. Siegel
       (Philadelphia: J.B. Lippincott, 1964), pp. 353-75.
          Observes that Shakespeare remodels his sources to save
       Cordelia from despair and suicide. What really matters in the
       play is what is happening to Lear's soul under Cordelia's in-
       fluence and to Gloucester's soul under Edgar's influence. Lear
       is, like the Paradiso, a vast poem on the victory of true love.
       The old king ultimately dies in a moment of ecstasy, believing
       that Cordelia is alive; Gloucester also dies in the joy of the
       knowledge that his child lives, and Kent's strings of life begin
       to crack as he witnesses the death of Gloucester between joy and
       grief.

1195   DANBY, JOHN F.   Shakespeare's Doctrine of Nature: A Study of
        "King Lear."   London: Faber & Faber, 1949, 234 pp.   Portion
        reprinted in Shakespeare: Modern Essays in Criticism, ed.
        Leonard F. Dean, rev. ed.   (New York: Oxford University
        Press, 1967), pp. 377-88.
            Envisions in King Lear a dramatization of the two funda-
        mental meanings of nature in Shakespeare's day--the orderly,
        rational, and benevolent arrangement of the universe under God's
        control and the Hobbesian manifesto of superior enlightenment
        with man as king of the beasts and with Machiavelli's self-
        interest as the operable force.   The play is a Morality debate
        concerning the nature of man; as a kind of Everyman Lear must
        make his way through a conflict in nature that his own actions
        have instigated, and at the point of his greatest horror he
        achieves something of a religious insight.   The Fool is a synthe-
        sis; his heart is with Lear, but his head recognizes the logic by
        which Edmund, Goneril, and Regan operate.   Cordelia represents
        the kind of nature Edmund denies to exist and which Lear is un-
        able to perceive until the final moments of his life.   (See
        entry 1215.)

1196   DAVIS, ARTHUR G.   The Royalty of Lear.   New York: St. John's
        University Press, 1974, 168 pp.
            Maintains that to search for Lear's flaw in pride, misrule,
        or dotage is to distort Shakespeare's character.   In the opening
        scenes the King is regal, his political aim to divide the kingdom
        sound, and the love test a symbolic ritual.   When he reacts
        emotionally to Cordelia, Goneril and Regan seize the opportunity
        to gain political control.   Even Lear's madness is characterized
        by strength and aggressiveness, and his purgation and purifica-
        tion concern the exercise of authority in relation to love.
        Faced with Cordelia's death, he is utterly crushed by grief; and
        the tragedy is the destruction of a noble personality.   The
        atmosphere in the closing moments is grim, but not chaotic; the
        figures hovering over the dead king possess the capacity for
        rebuilding.

1197   DELANEY, PAUL.   "King Lear and the Decline of Feudalism."
        PMLA 92 (1977):429-40.
            Views the conflict as between the values of feudal aris-
        tocracy and those of an acquisitive and irreverent bourgeois
        class, reflecting the Tudor monarch's determination to establish
        central power in the throne by abolishing the right of the aris-
        tocracy to maintain an armed retinue.   Shakespeare, fundamentally
        unable to reconcile himself with these emerging forces, equates
        their predominance with the decay of feudal-heroic values.   Lear
        must tragically realize the horrible injustices of his earlier
        aristocratic views, but the sinister and avaricious schemes of
        Edmund, Goneril, and Regan offer no viable alternative.   The
        humanism of the play reflects the idealization of the glories of
        the old regime.

1198   ELLIS, JOHN. "The Gulling of Gloucester: Credibility in the
        Subplot of King Lear." Studies in English Literature 12
        (1972):275-89.
            Observes that Gloucester serves as a foil to Lear, empha-
        sizing the latter's titanic power and passion and making the old
        king's action more profoundly tragic. The action of the subplot
        is credibly motivated. Certainly Edmund's bastardy and Glouces-
        ter's discussion of it in his presence in the opening scene pro-
        vide adequate motivation for his villainy. Gloucester, moreover,
        is psychologically an ideal victim for slanderous intrigue be-
        cause his world has suddenly become chaotic, inverted, and pre-
        posterous as a consequence of Lear's actions and the disarray of
        the royal family. His later defiant move against Edgar is
        credible, considering what he believes to be the serious domestic
        crisis that confronts him at the very moment when he as a host
        must receive his feudal lord.

1199   ELTON, WILLIAM R. "King Lear" and the Gods. San Marino,
        Calif.: Huntington Library, 1966, 369 pp. Selections re-
        printed in The "King Lear" Perplex, ed. Helmut Bonheim
        (Belmont, Calif.: Wadsworth, 1960), pp. 174-76.
            Notes that the contention that King Lear is an optimisti-
        cally Christian drama is not supported by an examination of the
        intellectual milieu of the early seventeenth century in England.
        The four major pagan attitudes toward providence prevalent in the
        Renaissance are present both in Sidney's Arcadia and in Lear.
        The prisca theologica, reflected in Cordelia and Edgar, antici-
        pates the higher values of faith, hope, and charity through com-
        bining wisdom, knowledge, and understanding. Goneril, Regan, and
        Edmund adumbrate pagan atheism. Gloucester embodies pagan super-
        stition, and Lear represents the human reaction to the effects of
        a hidden providence, the Deus absconditus. Shakespeare places
        before his spectators a wide spectrum of contemporary pagan be-
        liefs, thus creating a masterful ambiguity that the less specu-
        lative devout would implicitly take as an affirmation of Chris-
        tian theology and the sophisticated auditors would see as an
        image of their own dilemma.

1200   EVERETT, BARBARA. "The New King Lear." Critical Quarterly 2
        (1960):325-39.
            Counters those critics who insist upon the profoundly
        Christian nature of Lear's experience, those who in effect are
        creating a new Lear whole cloth for the twentieth century.
        Lear's greatness emerges not from his choice of any moral quality
        but rather from the transformation of his suffering into some-
        thing vital and strong. This vitality is overwhelmed, however,
        by a sense of nihilism. The drama does not juxtapose the world
        against the spirit, but instead it mixes the two inextricably.

1201   FLAHIFF, F.T. "Edgar: Once and Future King." In Some Facets
        of "King Lear": Essays in Prismatic Criticism. Edited by
        Rosalie L. Colie and F.T. Flahiff. Toronto: University of
        Toronto Press, 1974, pp. 221-37.
            Observes that Thomas Elyot in The Book of the Governor de-
        scribes King Edgar as one who, like Moses, Agamemnon, and
        Augustus, imposed order and rule upon an "odiouse and uncomly"
        society. While Shakespeare's Edgar is not Elyot's Edgar, the
        playwright may well have been concerned with delineating that
        period in prehistory of the erosion of a primitive and paternal-
        istic social order and concomitantly the development of a concept
        of kingship involving a larger vision of social responsibility.
        Edgar alone survives as one capable of assuming such a responsi-
        bility; throughout the play he comes to act with a cunning and
        deliberateness that set him apart from the other characters.
        (See entry 1234.)

1202   FRASER, RUSSELL A. Shakespeare's Poetics in Relation to "King
        Lear." London: Routledge & Kegan Paul, 1962, 184 pp.
            Argues that stage characters in the Renaissance assumed
        life to a large degree through association with a stereotyped
        iconographical figure. The iconology in Lear is examined in the
        motifs of providence, kind, fortune, anarchy and order, reason
        and will, show against substance, and redemption. Evil consuming
        itself is emblematic of the destruction of Edmund, Goneril, and
        Regan, just as the role of time in the revelation of truth and
        the function of humility and affliction in the achievement of
        redemption are pictorial representations of Lear's experience.
        The spate of bestial images reflects the consequences of will's
        ascendency over reason. Renaissance man's familiarity with the
        motif's in emblem literature and his fondness for metaphor and
        symbol help to explain Shakespeare's poetics.

1203   FRENCH, CAROLYN. "Shakespeare's 'Folly': King Lear."
        Shakespeare Quarterly 10 (1959):523-29.
            Argues that the intellectual orientation for King Lear is
        derived for the original audiences from Christian theology, which
        orders the action upon a spiritual as well as an intellectual
        plane. Specifically, the play is about Christian folly; one
        achieves true wisdom and self-knowledge through actions the world
        considers foolish, through overcoming one's physical and emo-
        tional dependence on material values and objects. The Fool's
        function is to bring Lear to spiritual wisdom by deflating his
        pride with the bitter truth. Lear himself becomes the fool in
        his mad scene, admitting truths he could not face when sane.
        Cordelia replaces the Fool when Lear is able to acknowledge these
        same truths with his sanity restored.

1204   FROST, WILLIAM. "Shakespeare's Rituals and the Opening of
        King Lear." Hudson Review 10 (1957-58):577-85. Reprinted in
        Shakespeare: The Tragedies: A Collection of Essays, ed.

Clifford Leech (Chicago: University of Chicago Press, 1965), pp. 190-200.

Views the opening scene as overtly ritualistic--Lear's announcing his intention, the chronological parade of the daughters, the rejection of Cordelia, the banishment of Kent, the formal wooing by France. In itself the scene functions well as allegory with two tests of affection, one among the daughters and one between Burgundy and Kent; also it ironically amplifies Lear's sense of self-confidence and security. The storm scene involves one long parody of the ritual, the Fool and Tom sitting where Lear reigned a short while ago. The play returns to ritual at the conclusion as Albany and Edgar address the grievous wounds of the nation.

1205   FRYE, DEAN. "The Context of Lear's Unbuttoning." ELH 32
       (1965):17-31.
       Argues that the moment Lear sees Poor Tom, identifies with him, and begins to pull off his own clothes is fraught with significance because the gesture of undressing is related to the clothes imagery that runs throughout the play. This imagery functions as a kind of abstract language that lends universality to the situation. Dress in Elizabethan England had become a symbol of an ordered society, readily reflecting one's position and social rank. In Lear the villains force disguises upon their victims, and the disguises are symptomatic of the disorder let loose in the world. Lear must learn the extent to which his identity is dependent upon the external symbol of clothing, his lowest point being his rejection of all artifice in his denial of any difference between man and the beast, a point from which he must reconstruct a human perspective.

1206   CARDNER, HELEN. "King Lear." Oxford: Oxford University
       Press, 1967, 28 pp.
       Describes the integration of language, character, and action in King Lear. The opening scene is critical both in establishing a stylized tone and at the same time a powerfully destructive force in the central figure. The character of the Fool and the nature of the integration of the double plot, which both parallels and counterpoints, contribute to the dramatic effect. There is no blenching from the essential mystery of the play's conclusion. The Lear world can offer no consolation for the image of the old king holding the dead Cordelia in his arms. This secular pieta constitutes one of the most profound artistic visions of human suffering.

1207   GOLDBERG, SAMUEL LOUIS. An Essay on "King Lear." Cambridge:
       Cambridge University Press, 1974, 192 pp.
       States that the experience of King Lear refuses to be contained in a single interpretation, whether that of idealism, moralism, absurdism, or redemptionist sentimentality. For the spectator the play becomes all of these things as he is forced to

observe the various characters attempting to come to terms intellectually and emotionally with the welter of events. Ultimately
what the spectator must acknowledge is that his response is not
merely a matter of ambiguity, a concept suggesting multiple meanings within a coherent whole, but rather of divergent and contradictory realities, each of which he experiences. Like the play
as a whole the final scene evinces no clear and certain answers;
therein lies its most compelling quality.

1208   GRACE, WILLIAM J. "The Cosmic Sense in Shakespearean Tragedy."
        Shakespeare Review 50 (1942):433-45.
            Asserts that Shakespeare's concept of tragedy is based on
        the assumption that cosmic forces exist and that the actions of
        the individual are in a meaningful way related to these super-
        natural forces. King Lear is the most powerful and poetic ex-
        pression of this cosmic sense, delivering a crushing commentary
        on anthropocentric humanism, the assumption that man is the
        center of the universe and that the gods function merely as an
        extension of his wishes. The various characters in the tragedy
        assume the existence of gods who are extensions of their own
        assumptions.

1209   GREENFIELD, THELMA N. "The Clothing Motif in King Lear."
        Shakespeare Quarterly 5 (1954):281-86. Portion reprinted in
        The "King Lear" Perplex, ed. Helmut Bonheim (Belmont, Calif.:
        Wadsworth, 1960), pp. 149-52.
            Notes that, while in Medieval art the clothed figure--set
        against a naked figure--represents the superior value, Renais-
        sance iconography reverses this symbolism as nudity becomes the
        conventional representation of virtues such as temperance, forti-
        tude, truth, and chastity. Lear comes to the perception that Tom
        represents the poor naked wretches oppressed and destroyed by
        society, and he deliberately assumes the role of nakedness in
        recognition of his kinship with "unaccommodated man." This sym-
        bolic condition signals his self-recognition and points the way
        to his salvation.

1210   GREG, W.W. "Time, Place, and Politics in King Lear."
        Modern Language Review 35 (1940):431-36.
            Calls attention to the double time scheme operating in the
        play. Behind the immediate duration of each event as it unfolds
        on stage is a sequence of events that requires a considerably
        longer period of time. Otherwise, the French invasion of England
        must have occurred before the injustices perpetrated upon Lear.
        Perhaps a scene has been cut in which the King of France plans
        but then abandons an invasion to regain Cordelia's portion of the
        estate, with Cordelia then hastily employing the army that had
        been assembled for that purpose to aid her father.

1211   HARRIS, DUNCAN. "The End of Lear and a Shape for Shake-
        spearean Tragedy." Shakespeare Studies 9 (1976):253-68.
            Claims the closure of Lear is basically Christian, depend-
        ing for its astonishing effect upon the Christian notion of man's
        role in life and the meaning of death. Four resolutions comprise
        this closure--a resolution of justice (a meting out of reward and
        punishment according to merit), a resolution negating the first
        (through the suffering deaths of Cordelia, Lear, and Gloucester),
        a resolution returning those who have survived to a perilous and
        provisional order (in which Kent and Edgar, both annealed by
        their experiences, resume their own identities), and a resolution
        involving a catharsis of clarity in which audience and survivors
        share.

1212   HEILMAN, ROBERT B. This Great Stage: Image and Structure in
        "King Lear." Baton Rouge: Louisiana State University Press,
        1948, 339 pp. Selections reprinted in The "King Lear" Perplex,
        ed. Helmut Bonheim (Belmont, Calif.: Wadsworth, 1960),
        pp. 110-15.
            Sees in the play two types of human nature, the tradi-
        tional or religious and the rationalistic, individualistic, or
        opportunistic. These types of human nature also represent an age
        in turmoil and transition. The struggle focuses on Lear and
        Gloucester, who as representatives of the old order must come to
        realize that the egocentric values of the new generation actually
        are rooted in the arrogance, the indiscriminate action, the com-
        placency, and the loss of equilibrium of the old. Both old men
        are spiritually blind at the outset of the play; and Gloucester's
        physical blinding, which leads to genuine perception, is but the
        culminating physical moment of a multitude of images of sight and
        blindness through which this theme has been developing since the
        first scene.

1213   HOBSBAUM, PHILIP. "Survival Values." In Theory of Criticism.
        Bloomington: Indiana University Press, 1970, pp. 143-63.
            Proclaims that King Lear does not exist as a moral system;
        it depicts an appalling human paradox that reflects the human
        condition itself. The play is an aesthetic experience and makes
        its moral point in artistic terms, whereas the critic rewrites
        the play in his own analytic terminology, and the result is
        usually reductionistic. Lear's death, for example, can be seen
        as his ultimate reunion with Cordelia, a moral conclusion, an
        illusion that saves him, a release from pain, and blank despair.
        These are not necessarily alternatives. Lear finds love in
        death; survival values are affirmed even in the face of death.

1214   JAFFA, HARRY V. "The Limits of Politics: An Interpretation
        of King Lear, Act I, Scene i." American Political Science
        Review 51 (1957):405-27. Portion reprinted in The "King Lear"
        Perplex, ed. Helmut Bonheim (Belmont, Calif.: Wadsworth,
        1960), pp. 159-63.

Views Lear's decision to divide his kingdom as politically
prudent. Cornwall (in the south) and Albany (in the North)
represent the geographic extremities of the land, and English
kings found it impossible to rule the entire land without the
support of powerful nobles. Lear's intention was to gain support
of those nobles through a gift of land and to give Cordelia the
middle portion following her marriage to Burgundy. He would live
with her, continuing to reign with his one hundred knights, which
would have been a majority, not a minority, in a land maintained
by a foreigner who would have only a limited number of troops.

1215   JAMES, DAVID GWILYM. The Dream of Learning: An Essay on "The
       Advancement of Learning" and "King Lear." Oxford: Clarendon
       Press, 1951, 126 pp. Selections reprinted in The "King Lear"
       Perplex, ed. Helmut Bonheim (Belmont, Calif.: Wadsworth,
       1960), pp. 125-31.
          Claims that Bacon and Shakespeare, writing in an age of
       uncertainty and philosophic barrenness, set forth divergent vi-
       sions of life that are equally a repudiation of the theodicy of
       Medieval Christianity. Hamlet's mind falters before the wicked-
       ness of man and its implications; Lear is overwhelmed by it.
       Struggling between "blood" and "judgment," Hamlet is paralyzed by
       doubt in the face of life's awesome ambiguities; in Lear evil is
       the dominant force, and, though its vision is dark, suffering is
       a kind of proof against overwhelming odds. (See entry 1195.)

1216   JAYNE, SEARS. "Charity in King Lear." Shakespeare Quarterly
       15 (1964):277-88. Reprinted in Shakespeare 400: Essays by
       American Scholars on the Anniversary of the Poet's Birth, ed.
       James G. McManaway (New York: Holt, Rinehart & Winston,
       1964), pp. 277-88.
          Views Lear as a scathingly pessimistic statement of man's
       desperate need for love, but his inability to give it. While
       Cordelia's actions at the outset are immature, Lear's love could
       lead him through the crisis if it were sufficiently selfless.
       Kent, like Cordelia, defends truth over love and promptly in-
       herits a period of pain only his death will alleviate. Like
       Lear's, Gloucester's experience is a slow awakening to sensi-
       tivity and love, partly under loving and partly under brutal
       tutelage. But every character fails to reestablish social bonds
       based on charity.

1217   JORGENSEN, PAUL A. Lear's Self-Discovery. Berkeley: Univer-
       sity of California Press, 1966, 154 pp.
          Discusses the centrality of the concept of self-knowledge
       in contemporary philosophic treatises to Shakespeare's concept of
       the anagnorisis in the tragic hero. Pride and self-love are
       obstacles to such knowledge, and affliction is the purest guide
       to achieving it. As Lear progresses from arrogance, to rage, to
       self-pity, and to humble questioning, he must come to perceive
       the necessity for and true meaning of love. These perceptions

he eventually gains through his own suffering, his reduction in status, and his philosophic acceptance of unaccommodated man in the naked Edgar. Having journeyed through the purgatory of self-discovery, he returns to full sanity moments before his defiance in the final enigmatic scene.

1218   KIRSCHBAUM, LEO. "Banquo and Edgar: Character or Function?" Essays in Criticism 7 (1957):1-21.
       Views Edgar as a multifunctional character without psychological mimetic unity. His various roles contribute to Shakespeare's overall psychological unity, but as an individual he is a theatrical convention, a puppet manipulated in accordance with dramatic need. His roles include those of an incredibly naive son, the Bedlam beggar Tom, a peasant ministering to his blind father, the unknown and helmeted knight, and finally the son who reappears and stands ready to serve in the new day.

1219   KOZINTSEV, GRIGORI. "King Lear." In Shakespeare: Time and Conscience. Translated by Joyce Vining. New York: Hill & Wang, 1966, pp. 47-102.
       Considers words all important to Shakespeare since his plays were presented on nonrepresentational platforms. Imagery transferred the action into the midst of life, and the possibilities extended the limits of the theater into infinity. The storm is the key symbol in Lear, raging through the whole imagistic fabric of the tragedy. The events of the play occur in a real world of tyranny; indeed, additional emphasis is gained through the placement of a legendary hero into a society of contemporary processes, a world in which feudalism is passing into a new era governed by avarice and the cash nexus. Lear must evolve from a kind of moral infancy and spiritual self-gratification to the point of accepting love as a "martial concept, a challenge addressed to the ideas of the iron age" (p. 102).

1220   KREIDER, PAUL V. "Gloucester's Eyes." In Repetition in Shakespeare's Plays. Princeton: Princeton University Press, 1941, pp. 194-214.
       Considers the sight and blindness imagery central to the emotional pitch and harmony of the parallel Lear and Gloucester plots. The congestion of tone or theme words involving blindness is evident in key scenes in the drama. In the final scene Lear's faulty material vision fails him just as his moral vision has failed him throughout the play. His mad speeches constitute a veritable fanfare of references to sight. Through such a verbal and physical pattern Shakespeare creates a highly unified tragedy of moral and physical blindness.

353

1221   LASCELLES, MARY. "King Lear and Doomsday." Shakespeare
        Survey 26 (1973):69-79.
            Surmises that Shakespeare chose the figure of a Bedlamite
        for Edgar's disguise in order to provoke terror in the spectators
        through allusion to the commonplace Doomsday paintings dealing
        with the final judgment and also using the image of nakedness and
        defenselessness. Lear's calling on the gods to disclose the
        guilty, his awakening in Cordelia's arms and describing her as a
        "soul in bliss," his reference to the wheel of fire, and Kent's
        references to the "promis'd end" are further choric and allusive
        iconographical images.

1222   LINDHEIM, NANCY. "King Lear as Pastoral Tragedy." In Some
        Facets of King Lear": Essays in Prismatic Criticism.
        Edited by Rosalie L. Colie and F.T. Flahiff. Toronto:
        University of Toronto Press, 1974, pp. 169-84.
            Views Lear as related to pastoral literature in its basic
        concerns--the necessity for stripping man of all the accoutre-
        ments of society, the perception of the decadence and corruption
        of that society once the detachment has been achieved, and a
        determination of the minimal conditions conducive to a genuinely
        human existence. Once the play has utilized the pastoral struc-
        ture to develop the theme of man naturally purified and socially
        purged, it tragically forces the characters and the spectators
        beyond that point to the apocalyptic horror of act 5. There is
        no perception in that final scene of the pastoral's emphasis on
        cyclic rebirth.

1223   LOTHIAN, JOHN M. "King Lear": A Tragic Reading of Life.
        Toronto: Clark, Irwin, 1949, 101 pp.
            Claims that the play, dealing with the spiritual history
        of King Lear, is a celebration of man's capacity to endure suf-
        fering and to withstand the extremities of outrageous fortune.
        His development through wrath and madness to Stoic patience and
        humility is the constant focus of the play. The play's ultimate
        vision is not, however, one of religious consolation but one of
        chaos, of the chasm between reality and justice. Chapters are
        also included on the sources and on the character of the Fool
        and Edgar.

1224   MACK, MAYNARD. "King Lear" in our Time. Berkeley: Univer-
        sity of California Press, 1965, 126 pp.
            Addresses three major concerns--the stage history of King
        Lear, the play's sources in the most general sense of the term,
        and the play's compelling contemporaneity. Since in many ways
        our age (especially from 1930 to the present) is able to respond
        more fully to the jagged violence of the tragedy, we are not
        surprised that these years have been a period rich in notable
        Lears--Gielgud, Devlin, Ayrton, Wolfit, Olivier, Murray,
        Redgrave, Laughton, Scofield. Its current fascination is due in
        part to our interest in the antiheroism in which the capacity to

endure is admired more than the ability to act, our casual attitude toward death, and the play's apocalyptic implications and
its shattering experience of violence and pain. The dominant
mood of the play is imperative, and the emphasis is upon man's
exercise of free will for self-destruction. The end should not
be sentimentalized as a vision of either a Christian paradise or
an imbecilic universe; instead, it should be faced squarely as
victory and defeat ambiguously simultaneous and inseparable.

1225   McLAUGHLIN, JOHN J. "The Dynamics of Power in King Lear: An
       Adlerian Approach." Shakespeare Quarterly 29 (1978):37-43.
         Considers the psychology of power as the basis of the play,
with Lear, his three daughters, and Edmund all driven by the need
to achieve social, personal, and sexual power. Of these various
characters with distorted life plans, only Lear is cured of his
neurosis. On the heath he moves toward a social feeling with a
single act of generosity for his fellow man. By sharing the
Fool's and Poor Tom's misery in the storm, he reverses his life-
long aspiration for power and superiority.

1226   MacLEAN, NORMAN. "Episode, Scene, Speech, and Word: The
       Madness of Lear." In Critics and Criticism. Edited by R.S.
       Crane. Chicago: University of Chicago Press, 1952,
       pp. 595-615.
         Observes that Lear's descent into madness, treated as a
single tragic episode spanning from 3.1 to 4.6, reveals a vision
of a world that through adversity reduces a man to incoherent
helplessness--but for the purpose of creating a perspective and a
scale of values that can reveal his genuine magnificence. Through
such an experience Lear achieves new insights that ultimately
bring him to open and contrite communication with the daughter
whom he has wronged.

1227   McNEIR, WALDO. "The Role of Edmund in King Lear." Studies in
       English Literature 8 (1968):187-216.
         Views Edmund at the outset as an Iago-like manipulator with
only the limited objective of gaining Edgar's lands. As opportunity easily comes his way, he broadens his scope to include his
father's title and eventually the crown. When Goneril collapses
in the final act, he confesses his sins and appears duly remorse-
ful; but his repentance is aborted in the final stage. This
failure to achieve repentance is in stark contrast with the full
development in Lear and Gloucester; indeed, his moral vacillation
is directly responsible for the deaths of both Cordelia and Lear.
(See entry 1188.)

1228   MUIR, KENNETH. The Politics of "King Lear." Glasgow Univer-
       sity Publications, no. 72. Glasgow: Jackson, Son, 1947,
       24 pp.
         Views the theme as a confrontation between two social
orders, that of medieval communal values and that of modern

individualism. Goneril and Regan are exemplars of the new order,
soulless and amoral and driven by a lust for power that reduces
them to the level of animals; Edmund's ominous emergence fore-
shadows the rise of Fascism in later European history. The old
order, characterized by morality, duty, and responsibility,
possesses the capacity for compassion, pity, and humanitarian
concerns.

1229   MURPHY, JOHN L. Darkness and Devils: Exorcism in "King
       Lear." Athens: Ohio University Press, 1984, 267 pp.
         Examines the detailed connections between the world of King
Lear and the Papist exorcisings of the mid 1580s, the trial and
execution of Mary Queen of Scots, and Samuel Harsnett's antipapal
satire in A Declaration of Egregious Popish Imposters. Behind
the play lies the bitter rivalry among religious factions as to
the reality of spirits and demonic possession, specifically the
dramatic qualities of the Roman Catholic service of exorcism and
Harsnett's fierce attack on that practice. Many of the Fool's
and of Tom o'Bedlam's comments directly relate to the issue, the
most important of the "levels of intertextuality."

1230   NOVY, MARIANNE. "Patriarchy, Mutuality, and Forgiveness in
       King Lear." Southern Humanities Review 13 (1979):281-92.
         Considers the violation of the bonds of mutuality between
father and daughter central to Lear's tragic experience. Lear's
misuse of power provokes diverse reactions from Goneril and Regan,
who use deception to survive, and Cordelia, who attempts to maintain her integrity in a patriarchal world. The father's denun-
ciation of womankind in act 4 is in reality an acknowledgment of
his own guilt as well; and his reconciliation with Cordelia,
visualized in a parent's kneeling before the child, "suggests
that in a patriarchal society mutuality between man and woman
must include the mutuality of forgiveness and repentance"
(p. 288).

1231   OATES, JOYCE CAROL. "Is This the Promised End? The Tragedy
       Of King Lear." Journal of Aesthetics and Art Criticism 33
       (1974-75):19-32.
         Insists that King Lear is profoundly pessimistic, with
Shakespeare altering the conclusion to defeat the very forces of
salvation at work within the story. In one sense the tragedy
results from the lack of proper male-female balance in Lear and
in his society. In another it poses a vision of life related to
the social and political milieu of the times. In yet another
sense it dramatizes the soul's yearning for infinity, man's
desire to reach to a higher form of himself.

1232   ORWELL, GEORGE. "Lear, Tolstoy, and the Fool." In Shooting
       an Elephant and Other Essays. New York: Harcourt, Brace,
       1945, pp. 32-52. Reprinted in Four Centuries of Shakespearean
       Criticism, ed. Frank Kermode (New York: Avon, 1965),
       pp. 514-31.

Notes that Tolstoy's bitterly negative response to King Lear was probably occasioned by the resemblance between Lear's story and his own. Like Lear, Tolstoy renounced his estate in order to live like a peasant. He, too, acted on mistaken motives and was persecuted because of this renunciation. He, too, lacked humility and the ability to judge character. He, too, was inclined to revert to his earlier aristocratic attitudes and had two children who ultimately turned against him. Moreover, he shared Lear's revulsion toward sexuality. Tolstoy's examination of the play, in brief, is far from impartial; indeed, it is an exercise in misrepresentation.

1233   PECHTER, EDWARD. "On the Blinding of Gloucester." ELH 45 (1978):181-200.
Sees the basic pattern of the tragedy as the provocation of a passionately direct response, the need to justify that response through some form of philosophic assumption, and finally the painful realization of the deep-seated error in that assumption. The spectator, time and again, is made to pay for his attempts to escape suffering through rationalization. It is Gloucester's blinding that so painfully commits us to develop this pattern of anticipation. We like Gloucester must smell our way to Dover (our own assumptions that the action of the play will issue into a sense imposed by teleological control) only once again to be punished for our response. (See entry 1220.)

1234   PECK, RUSSEL A. "Edgar's Pilgrimage: High Comedy in King Lear." Studies in English Literature 7 (1967):219-37.
Views Edgar as a significant dynamic figure in the play, developing--through his various disguises as bedlamite, incognito stranger, Somersetshire peasant, and divine avenger--into "the Christian ideal in his large capacity to empathize with and take upon himself the afflictions of his fellow men" (p. 226). Through Christian analogues Edgar's journey lends a universality to that of Lear, and it serves a specifically choric function at the end of the play. By the conclusion of his pilgrimage, he among those remaining alive is most fit to rule. (See entry 1201.)

1235   REIBETANZ, JOHN. The Lear World: A Study of "King Lear" in Its Dramatic Context. Toronto: University of Toronto Press, 1977, 142 pp.
Insists that only by examining Lear within its Jacobean context will its full power be revealed. The grotesque world of love tests and wicked sisters lends a peculiar expositional quality unlike that of any previous Shakespearean tragedy. Like contemporary tragedies it abandons the Elizabethan concern for narrative continuity in favor of a structural unity based on scenic emphasis. There is no regard, for example, for developing the narrative line involving Cordelia's marriage, Edmund's relationship with Goneril and Regan, or the conflict between France

and England. Instead, the action, leaping from one scene to
another and focusing upon the evil natures of Goneril, Regan, and
Edmund along with the mounting suffering of Lear and Gloucester,
emphasizes the evolving anarchy at both the political and domestic level. Emblematic design and costuming reinforce this pattern of action. Another feature of contemporary drama, the fool,
is made the center of a moriae encomium,; he is the objective
viewpoint by which the folly of the surrounding figures is
measured.

1236   ROSENBERG, JOHN. "King Lear and His Comforters." Essays in
       Criticism 16 (1966):135-46.
           Argues that readings of King Lear as Christian allegory
       lead us away from the searing tragic center of the play. Further-
       more, the more the critics attempt to justify the existence and
       the action of the gods, the more appalling the gods become. By
       doubling the agony and perversion through the use of the Glouces-
       ter subplot, Shakespeare almost makes cosmic malevolence a char-
       acter in the play. The catastrophe is absolutely open-ended; a
       world of grace--or utter nothingness--may exist beyond the
       mortal's death.

1237   SEWALL, RICHARD B. The Vision of Tragedy. New Haven: Yale
       University Press, 1959, 178 pp.
           Observes that King Lear combines Greek, pagan, or human-
       istic values with Christian values to produce "a world of alter-
       natives, terrible in its inconclusiveness" (p. 68). Whatever is
       Christian about the play is psychological, not eschatological.
       Lear must win his redemption through his own efforts, and even
       then Cordelia's death must follow the moment of spiritual bliss.
       All one can ultimately say is that "human nature, in some of its
       manifestations, has transcended the destructive element and made
       notable salvage" (p. 78).

1238   STAMPFER, JUDAH. "The Catharsis of King Lear." Shakespeare
       Survey 13 (1960):1-10. Reprinted in Shakespeare's Tragedies,
       ed. Laurence Lerner (Baltimore: Penguin, 1963), pp. 147-60.
           Views the conclusion, with its tragic events and the mas-
       sive intrusion of Christian elements, as the central problem of
       King Lear. Neither Lamb's assertion that Lear's death was a
       "fair dismissal" from life in light of his great suffering nor
       Bradley's claim that Lear experiences a transfiguration of joy is
       supported by the full text (see entry 924). The true catharsis
       is the revelation of an imbecilic universe. The tragic hero
       "dies unreconciled and indifferent to society" (p. 7). Penance
       is proved to be impossible in a world without God--without
       charity, resilence, or harmony.

1239   WITTREICH, JOSEPH. "Image of That Horror": History,
        Prophecy, and Apocalypse in "King Lear." San Marino, Calif.:
        Huntington Library, 1984, 185 pp.
        Treats King Lear both within its historical context in
    relation to the political ideology of King James and within
    poetry's highest order, that of prophecy of the tragedy of human
    history. The play mirrors in its dialectic conflicting systems
    and contending attitudes towards the cosmos, but it also demands
    that some choices be made. If it is an encounter with incon-
    clusiveness, it is not itself altogether inconclusive. Most
    importantly, it draws upon apocalyptic prophecy in the Book of
    Revelation; in the literal action it is a "mind-transforming
    event that culminates in a king's redemption" (p. 22).

1240   ZAK, WILLIAM F. Sovereign Shame: A Study of "King Lear."
        Cranbury, N.J.: Rutgers University Press, 1982, 208 pp.
        Moves beyond the critical impasse of Lear as redeemed or
    absurd by arguing tht he suffers desperately from an ontological
    anxiety, a fear of personal worthlessness and doubt about deserv-
    ing love. This unacknowledged shame drives him from the absurd-
    ity of the love-action to the extreme distraction of his own
    madness and Cordelia's death. The man beneath Lear's outraged
    masks, then, is a king in disgrace; his tragedy is his inability
    to perceive what impels him to such desperate acts.

                              Stage History

1241   ROSENBERG, MARVIN. The Masks of "King Lear." Berkeley:
        University of California Press, 1972, 431 pp.
        Seeks an answer to the meaning of King Lear through the
    interpretations of American and European actors, directors, and
    critics. Sources include books, essays, periodical reports,
    memoirs, and acting versions. Additionally the author himself
    followed a production of Lear through two months of rehearsal.
    A firm artistic control gives to the ambiguities and paradoxes
    of the play a "system of reciprocating tensions" (p. 5). While
    the role of Lear, for example, can be performed in various ways,
    the actor must move generally from the pains of civilization with
    its robed furs to the austere position in which he can voice
    compassion for "unaccommodated man."

For counterviews of the conclusion, see entries 1189, 1193-94, 1203
versus entries 1192, 1199, 1238. See also The Tragedies (entries
920-979) and 15, 25, 79, 89, 98, 103, 125-26, 132, 134, 137, 160,
162, 171, 179, 189, 215-16, 223, 225, 232, 235, 238-40, 243, 246-47,
257, 260, 263, 266-67, 272, 277, 288, 291, 302, 304, 307, 312, 317,
328, 331, 333, 764, 848, 897, 981, 1378, 1384, 1483, 1485.

MACBETH

Reference Works

1242   TANNENBAUM, SAMUEL A., and TANNENBAUM, DOROTHY R., comps.
        William Shakespeare: "Macbeth." Elizabethan Bibliographies,
        9. New York: Privately Printed, 1939, 165 pp.
            Includes 3,153 unannotated entries covering major scholar-
        ship on Macbeth from the beginnings to 1937. The material is
        divided by the following categories and is arranged alphabetically
        by section--editions, translations; burlesques, satires, paro-
        dies; music, songs, operas, dances; commentary on music; illus-
        trations; Macbeth in the theater; commentary on Macbeth; book
        titles. The majority of the entries (1,936 items) is loosely
        classified under commentary on the play.

Editions

1243   MUIR, KENNETH, ed. Macbeth. The Arden Shakespeare. London:
        Methuen; Cambridge, Mass.: Harvard University Press, 1951,
        201 pp.
            Includes discussion of the text, date, interpolations,
        sources, stage history, and critical interpretations, as well as
        appendixes featuring selections from Holinshed's Chronicles and
        William Stewart's Book of the Chronicles of Scotland. The text
        is based on the First Folio, for which the copy was probably a
        transcript of the promptbook. Macbeth in many ways is Shake-
        speare's most profound vision of evil; its theme of damnation
        focuses on a struggle between creation and destruction and
        Macbeth's loss of soul. Any attempt to read fatalism into the
        work, however, is reductionistic. Macbeth, though a tragic hero,
        is a criminal; he is humanized by the fears that prove him to be
        all too human. Nor is Banquo without fault; he should have acted
        against the usurper before Malcolm's invasion.

1244   WILSON, JOHN DOVER, ed. Macbeth. Cambridge: Cambridge
        University Press, 1947, 186 pp.
            Provides extensive textual notes, a critical introduction,
        a discussion of the copy text, a section on stage history, and a
        glossary. This edition is based on the First Folio, for which the
        copy was probably a bookkeeper's transcript. Additions and
        alterations by Middleton are likely. Shakespeare's most striking
        departure from his source is the alteration of Banquo's charac-
        ter, a move that serves both his art and his design to compliment
        James I. The witches, representing the incarnation of evil in
        the universe, are appropriately monstrous. The extant text prob-
        ably represents Shakespeare's own revision and compression in
        1606. As for Macbeth himself, even as his soul dissolves, his
        personality becomes more portentous and more appealing.

Criticism

1245   ALLEN, MICHAEL. "Macbeth's Genial Porter." English Literary
       Renaissance 4 (1974):326-36.
       Argues that the porter scene possesses a structural and
thematic significance as a consequence of the etymology and the
semantic variants of the words porter and genius and of the
occult associations the Elizabethans attached to them. The
porter's language about heaven, hell gates, and devil porter
reinforce such associations, and his sudden appearance suggests
the presence of Macbeth's evil familiar. Moreover, the characters
mentioned by the porter signify the stages of Macbeth's degenera-
tion. Finally, when the porter opens the gate, he lets in
Macbeth's executioner who eventually sends his soul to hell.

1246   AMNEUS, DANIEL. "Macbeth's Greater Honor." Shakespeare
       Studies 6 (1970):223-30.
       Suggests that the original version of Macbeth included a
scene in which Macbeth is named Prince of Cumberland and thus is
heir apparent. This is probably the greater honor that Duncan
speaks of in 1.4 and is probably why Macbeth indicates to his
wife that he no longer plans to proceed with the regicide he has
discussed earlier. It probably also explains how Banquo without
dishonor can support Macbeth as king. In order to deny the
legitimacy of Macbeth's title and thus to praise James by elevating Banquo's position, Shakespeare is forced to substitute a
scene in which Duncan names Malcolm as Prince of Cumberland.

1247   ASP, CAROLYN. "'Be Bloody, Bold and Resolute': Tragic Action
       and Sexual Stereotyping in Macbeth." Studies in Philology 78
       (1981):153-69.
       Argues that sexual stereotyping plays a central role in
Macbeth. Lady Macbeth perceives that in her society femininity
is equated with weakness. Consciously rejecting her femininity
to adopt a masculine role, she pits herself against nature and
loses. Similarly, Macbeth by stretching courage and boldness beyond normal proportions pits himself against nature and loses.
By attempting to alter their fundamental nature, both Macbeth and
Lady Macbeth become inhuman symbols of sexual sterility. The
tension results from the conflict of the sexual roles they believe they must play in order to achieve their ambitions in moving beyond the limits imposed by nature and society. (See
entry 1276.)

1248   BERGER, HARRY J. "The Early Scenes of Macbeth: Preface to a
       New Interpretation." ELH 47 (1980):1-31.
       Argues that Scotland in the play suffers from instability,
conflict, sedition, murder, a general evil that moves beyond the
wickedness of one or two individuals. As a society that sanc-
tions violence and in which ferocity inspires, Scotland must
praise its heroes while suffering concern at the same time that

such actions will split the fabric of civil order. Duncan's un-
easiness is signaled in his rewards to Macbeth. Macbeth himself
is not so much the villain as is Scottish society that in its
very nature makes such regicide likely.

1249   BOOTH, WAYNE. "Macbeth as Tragic Hero." Journal of General
       Education 6 (1951):17-25. Reprinted in Shakespeare's Trage-
       dies, ed. Laurence Lerner (Baltimore: Penguin, 1963),
       pp. 180-90.
           Views Shakespeare's principal difficulty in Macbeth as
       maintaining the spectators' sympathy for the protagonist and at
       the same time depicting a credible path of moral degeneration.
       Shakespeare succeeds by emphasizing the genuine goodness of
       Macbeth at the beginning of the play, by portraying his mental
       anguish and self-torture immediately after each of his three
       murders, by endowing him with a highly poetic gift, and by indi-
       cating that his tragic error was provoked in part by outside
       forces (the witches, Lady Macbeth) and that he failed to compre-
       hend the effects of such action on his own character.

1250   BOYER, CLARENCE VALENTINE. The Villain as Hero in Elizabethan
       Tragedy. London: Routledge & Kegan Paul; New York: Dutton,
       1914, 264 pp.
           Traces to Seneca the concept of villain as hero, demon-
       strates the influence of Machiavelli on the type, and analyzes
       the nature of the emotion that the hero-villain arouses.
       Richard III, not the highest form of tragedy since there is no
       internal struggle, depicts the "perfect Machiavellian" with
       emphasis on his mental dexterity. The greatness of Macbeth re-
       sults from the protagonist's self-realization of the waste of
       magnificent courage and potential, from his imaginative power and
       the anguish of conscience. Macbeth is described as the only
       fully successful villain-hero tragedy.

1251   BROOKS, CLEANTH. "The Naked Babe and the Cloak of Manliness."
       In The Well-Wrought Urn. New York: Harcourt Brace Jovanovich,
       1947, pp. 22-49. Reprinted in Modern Shakespearean Criticism,
       ed. Alvin B. Kernan (New York: Harcourt, Brace & World,
       1970), pp. 385-403.
           Observes that two principal chains of imagery in Macbeth
       involve old clothes and babes. Banquo's comparison of Macbeth's
       "new honors" to "strange garments" in 1.3 and Macbeth's reference
       four scenes later to Duncan's conscience as like a "naked new-
       born babe" establish ideas that reverberate throughout the play.
       Ultimately, clothing represents the inhumane savagery with which
       Macbeth attempts to cover his humanity, and the babe symbolizes
       the future that Macbeth is unable to control.

1252   CHEUNG, KING-KOK. "Shakespeare and Kierkegaard: 'Dread' in
        Macbeth." Shakespeare Quarterly 35 (1984):430-39.
            Attempts to explain our ambiguous response to Macbeth by
        examining his decision to murder Duncan in the light of Kierke-
        gaard's concept of dread, that possibility of "being able" that
        produces sin in that state between possibility and reality, the
        desire to do what one fears that precedes one's leap into evil.
        Dread informs the very atmosphere of Macbeth; the witches, in
        creating the apprehension or dread of Macbeth's being king,
        create his fatal enticement to sin; and the spectators, too,
        under the spell of Shakespeare's poetry are caught in a shudder-
        ing complicity.

1253   COURSEN, HERBERT R., Jr. "In Deepest Consequence: Macbeth."
        Shakespeare Quarterly 18 (1971):375-88.
            Considers the archetype of man's fall from grace the source
        of the play's strength. Lady Macbeth encompasses both temptress
        (Eve) and victim, while Macbeth's role ranges from Lucifer to
        Adam. The myth like the play involves three aspects--the moral
        decision, the feminine persuasion, and the cosmic retribution.
        After Lady Macbeth has tempted Macbeth and he has made his fatal
        decision, images of darkness and destruction envelop Scotland.
        Malcolm's overthrow of Macbeth signals God's ultimate control.

1254   CUNNINGHAM, DOLORA G. "Macbeth: The Tragedy of the Hardened
        Heart." Shakespeare Quarterly 14 (1963):39-46.
            Argues that Macbeth through choice becomes a slave to evil,
        which feeds upon itself unto destruction. At the outset a good
        and sensitive man, he falls through error and goading to commit
        murder; then, overcome by guilt and resentment, he murders
        Banquo. At this point he determines to harden his heart against
        all reminders of his former self. His decision to murder
        Macduff's family indicates his confirmation in his new identity.
        The logical extreme of the hardened heart is insanity, enacted
        literally by Lady Macbeth and figuratively by Macbeth's courage
        and desperation.

1255   CURRY, WALTER CLYDE. Shakespeare's Philosophic Patterns.
        Baton Rouge: Louisiana State University Press, 1937, 244 pp.
        Selections reprinted in Twentieth Century Interpretations of
        "Macbeth," ed. Terence Hawkes, Twentieth Century Interpreta-
        tions (Englewood Cliffs: Prentice-Hall, 1977), pp. 30-33.
            Notes that evil in Shakespeare's day was considered not
        only as a subjective force but also as an objective power "in a
        metaphysical world whose existence depended in no degree upon
        the activities of the human mind" (p. 58). Shakespeare probably
        chose witches to convey this demonic power to avoid the comic
        associations that had developed with stage devils. No such
        demonic force can of itself actually penetrate the substance of
        the soul, but Macbeth's liberty of choice is progressively
        diminished by his increasing inclination toward evil; in this

sense fate compels him to certain destruction. Lady Macbeth, to
the contrary, is literally and willingly possessed of demons.

1256   DORAN, MADELEINE. "That Undiscovered Country: A Problem
       Concerning the Use of the Supernatural in Hamlet and Macbeth."
       Philological Quarterly 20 (1941):413-27.
              Explores the different responses of Elizabethan and modern
       audiences to the supernatural elements in Hamlet and Macbeth.
       While the witches in Macbeth, for example, in their grotesque
       contortions around a black pot have little more than a decorative
       function on the literal level to the modern spectator, the re-
       sponse of the Elizabethan was more complex. They represented
       genuine instruments of darkness and, even to the disbelievers,
       would evoke a sense of awe and wonder. Their real value to
       Elizabethans is symbolic of evil and fate; they were used not
       merely for decoration or sensation but to evoke a sense of tragic
       wonder.

1257   DOWNER, ALAN S. "The Life of Our Design." Hudson Review 2
       (1949-50):242-63. Selections reprinted in Shakespeare's
       Tragedies, ed. Laurence Lerner (Baltimore: Penguin, 1963),
       pp. 213-16.
              Notes that in great drama physical props also serve as
       dramatic symbols, thus intensifying and enriching the unity of
       the work. In Macbeth, for instance, Macbeth's change of costume
       symbolizes or reflects the change occurring in his state of mind.
       Dressed in armor, he is the honest warrior; but later, dressed in
       "borrowed robes," he is guilty of regicide. When he dons his
       armor in act 5, he is striving to regain his former status, but
       evil has corrupted him and made him infirm of purpose.

1258   DYSON, J.P. "The Structural Function of the Banquet Scene in
       Macbeth." Shakespeare Quarterly 14 (1963):369-78.
              Describes the banquet scene as important structurally be-
       cause it presents analogously the entire movement of the play,
       from order to chaos, from good to evil. Traditionally a symbol
       of harmony, fellowship, order, and hierarchy, the banquet scene
       is also the moment when Macbeth realizes that his world has
       turned upside down, that he has moved from the martlet world to
       the raven world. The ghost of Banquo is the catalyst of insight,
       the messenger from another world who forces Macbeth to realize
       that he has penetrated to a level of existence where nothingness
       has come to life. (See entry 1280.)

1259   ELLIOTT, GEORGE R. Dramatic Providence in "Macbeth": A Study
       of Shakespeare's Tragic Theme of Humanity and Grace. Prince-
       ton: Princeton University Press, 1958, 234 pp. Selections
       reprinted in Twentieth Century Interpretations of "Macbeth,"
       ed. Terence Hawkes, Twentieth Century Interpretations
       (Englewood Cliffs: Prentice-Hall, 1977), pp. 74-75.

Considers Macbeth as a tragedy dealing with the higher and the lower reaches of human nature, right volition and wrong desire, viewed from the Christian standpoint. Macbeth illustrates how infernal evil can destroy man unless he is upheld by supernal grace; the play is the epitome of tragic thought in the Renaissance, the cooperation of conscience and pride. His final opportunity for penance comes with Macduff's offer to allow him to live out his natural life in humiliating captivity, but his resurgent pride impels him to fight, his will swayed to the end by the ambitious evil at work in the depths of human nature.

1260   FERGUSSON, FRANCIS. "Macbeth as the Imitation of an Action." In English Institute Essays 1951. Edited by Alan S. Downer. New York: Columbia University Press, 1952, pp. 31-43. Selections reprinted in Twentieth Century Interpretations of "Macbeth," ed. Terence Hawkes, Twentieth Century Interpretations (Englewood Cliffs: Prentice-Hall, 1977), pp. 67-68.
Argues that the action of Macbeth demonstrates Aristotle's definition of the term. By praxis Aristotle means not so much the outward deed as the motive. When he speaks of tragedy as the imitation of an action, he refers to the motive that governs the psyche's life for a period of time. Plot, character, and diction all spring from this dominating thought. Macbeth, in each of these aspects, imitates action based on vaulting ambition that overthrows reason.

1261   FREUD, SIGMUND. "Those Wrecked by Success." In The Complete Psychological Works of Sigmund Freud. Edited and translated by James Strachey. Vol. 4. London: Hogarth Press and the Institute of Psycho-Analysis, 1957, pp. 318-24.
Cites Lady Macbeth as an example of one who strives for success with a single-minded energy and then collapses after receiving it. Prior to victory there is no sign whatsoever of an internal struggle, either at the knocking at the door or at the banquet scene. It is ultimately impossible to know whether she cracks from frustration or from some deeper motivation. Not impossibly her mental deterioration is due to her childlessness, and her crime (her unsexing of herself) has robbed Macbeth of the better part of his fruits.

1262   FRYE, ROLAND M. "Theological and Non-Theological Structure in Tragedy." Shakespeare Studies 4 (1969):132-48.
Distinguishes between plays dramatically structured upon theological doctrines (for example, Dr. Faustus, Samson Agonistes) and plays that are not (for example, Macbeth and Antony and Cleopatra). While both Faustus and Macbeth succumb to demonic temptation and are referred to as damned, Faustus's temptation is specifically linked with the doctrine of original sin, he signs a pact with the devil, and Lucifer himself appears to carry away his soul. In Macbeth the references are symbolic, and we are

left to ponder Macbeth's fate; his tragedy has been in the horror and wasted potential of his life.

1263   HEILMAN, ROBERT B. "The Criminal as Tragic Hero." Shake-
       speare Survey 19 (1966):12-24.
            Notes the critical indecisiveness about whether we are to
       view Macbeth at the end of the play as splendidly bold in des-
       perate valor or as monstrously evil. Clearly Shakespeare forces
       us to identify with Macbeth early in the play by drawing us
       within his psychic struggle. Even as his villainy deepens, his
       suffering makes him more than a murderer in our eyes. At every
       point at which our sympathy might end (for example, the Macduff
       murders), we are drawn back (by his sickness of heart, his wife's
       death, his role as underdog). To acknowledge our sympathy for
       Macbeth is not to deny our sympathy as well for Malcolm and the
       conquering party.

1264   HUNTLEY, FRANK L. "Macbeth and the Background of Jesuitical
       Equivocation." PMLA 79 (1964):390-400.
            Discusses the doctrine of equivocation developed in the
       seventeenth century by the Society of Jesus and clearly defined
       at the trial of Father Garnett, Superior of the Jesuits in
       England, on 28 March 1606. The doctrine was much in the minds
       of Shakespeare's spectators at the initial presentation of
       Macbeth shortly after the Gunpowder Plot and again at its revival
       in 1611 shortly after Henri IV had died in a Jesuit plot. The
       drunken porter refers to equivocators, but the theme is much more
       pervasive. Macbeth, originally brave and true, falls because he
       embraces the doctrine. (See entry 1273.)

1265   JAARSMA, RICHARD. "The Tragedy of Banquo." Literature and
       Psychology 17 (1967):87-94.
            Rejects the idea that Banquo is a static character who
       never succumbs to the evil in the play. While Banquo does re-
       sist temptation and serves as a foil early in the play, he
       changes after entering Macbeth's castle. He tells Macbeth of
       his own dream of the Weird Sisters, revealing inner suspicions
       and imaginings, suspecting Macbeth's intentions, suggesting after
       Duncan's murder that they remain silent until they put on clothes
       (and thus symbolically hide their true natures). Banquo, in a
       word, becomes Macbeth's silent accomplice.

1266   JACK, JANE H. "Macbeth, King James, and the Bible." ELH 22
       (1955):173-93.
            Claims that the fact that Macbeth was composed with direct
       connections to King James proved to be an artistic asset rather
       than a liability. The works of James, more specifically, are
       part of the background of the tragedy, particularly in the strong
       theological bias of James's mind and his constant references to
       certain passages in the Old and New Testaments. James's over-
       mastering theme is that the kingdom of evil lies very close to

that of Christianity; he saw life as a war between Grace and the Devil. The scriptural imagery supporting this argument provided Shakespeare a means of organizing the play.

1267   JAECH, SHARON L. JANSEN. "Political Prophecy and Macbeth's 'Sweet Bodements.'" Shakespeare Quarterly 34 (1983):290-97.
        Examines the meaning of the three mysterious apparitions that appear to Macbeth when he demands further information from the witches in light of their relationship to the long tradition of political prophecy in England. Each of the apparitions had a host of associated meanings in contemporary prophecy. While not necessarily indicating a single specific thing, these apparitions would have been recognized as powerful and ambiguous prophetic symbols, and the audience would immediately perceive the folly and danger of Macbeth's interpreting them according to his own desires.

1268   JORGENSEN, PAUL A. Our Naked Frailties: Sensational Art and Meaning in "Macbeth." Berkeley: University of California Press, 1971, 234 pp.
        Considers the most powerful and distinctive feature of the play to be the painfully dark atmosphere created by unparalleled sensational artistry—whether verbal ambivalence of fair and foul, the hints of metaphysical disarray, the haggish witches with their intent set on Macbeth, the brutal slaughter of Macduff's wife and children, or the illusionary dagger of Macbeth with its internal dagger and hideously real ghost. This constant emphasis on stark sensation renders Macbeth most ironically pitiable in his ultimate loss of all feeling.

1269   KERN, EDITH. "Ionesco and Shakespeare: Macbeth and the Modern Stage." South Atlantic Bulletin 39 (1974):1-16.
        Describes Ionesco's adaptation of Macbeth as a plea for mankind to abandon the madness of war and violence. Macbeth, more precisely, forces the spectator to take a detached view by depicting familiar things as extraordinary, estranged from their customary background. The action is based on Shakespeare's play, but it has no beginning, middle, or end; it is circular, creating a parallelism and circularity in which rebel kills tyrant, then in turn is killed by a tyrant.

1270   KNIGHTS, L.C. "Macbeth." In Some Shakespearean Themes. Stanford: Stanford University Press; London: Chatto & Windus, 1959, pp. 110-32. Reprinted in Shakespeare's Tragedies, ed. Laurence Lerner (Baltimore: Penguin, 1963), pp. 191-207.
        Maintains that the essential structure of Macbeth (and many other tragedies) is found in the poetry. Lady Macbeth's reference to dashing out the brains of a child to whom she has given suck, for example, is an image of unnatural violence that reverberates with others throughout the play. This interaction demands a liveliness of attention that forces the spectator to

respond fully through his active imagination as meanings below
the level of plot and character take form as a living structure.
Macbeth's lust for power is defined through a series of such
destructive and self-destructive patterns.

1271   LAWLOR, JOHN J. "Mind and Hand: Some Reflections on the
       Study of Shakespeare's Imagery." Shakespeare Quarterly 8
       (1957):179-93.
          Suggests that attention to imagery aids in one's sharing
       the authentic Shakespearean experience. It helps one to perceive
       that Macbeth, for example, is incapable of distinguishing bad
       acting from good, that he senses life as circular and meaning-
       less. The most powerful images are set, not in word alone, but
       in the interplay of character and stage effect as well. Duncan's
       comment about Macbeth's castle as a "pleasant seat" and the
       imagery concerned with Banquo's response about the martlet
       broaden the spectators' apprehension concerning Banquo's fate and
       the unnaturalness of Macbeth's desiring. Careful attention to
       the image in the mouth of the player challenges our habitual
       response to Shakespeare's text.

1272   McGEE, ARTHUR R. "Macbeth and the Furies." Shakespeare
       Survey 19 (1966):55-67.
          Examines the Elizabethan beliefs concerning the super-
       natural background of the play and Shakespeare's relation to it.
       The concept of witchcraft, on the one hand, had classical asso-
       ciations with mythological creatures from Greece and Rome like
       the Furies, Medusa, and the Harpies. It involved also the fairy
       world of trolls, genii, and satyrs. In their powers of operative
       magic, demon-Furies, witches, and fairies were virtually inter-
       changeable. They could prompt madness or diabolic possession;
       they could torture a man's conscience and inflict supernatural
       punishment upon the guilty. Our modern psychological approach
       falls far short of the horror that the spectators and Macbeth
       would have experienced concerning the witches.

1273   MULLANY, STEVEN. "Lying Like the Truth: Riddle, Representa-
       tion and Treason in Renaissance England." ELH 47 (1980):
       32-47.
          Concerns the language and representation of treason during
       the Renaissance, an age when society viewed traitors as treading
       a thin line between human and demonic, rational and possessed.
       Macbeth is the fullest literary representation of treason's
       amphibology, the use of double or doubtful language to confuse
       and deceive. The porter's use of equivocation has reference to
       Father Garnett's comments at his trial for complicity in the
       Gunpowder Plot. Macbeth gives himself up to amphibology in the
       course of the play; his head in the final scene is a kind of
       gruesome visual representation of a verbal pun. (See entry 1264.)

1274   MURRAY, W.A. "Why Was Duncan's Blood Golden?" Shakespeare
       Survey 19 (1966):34-44.
              Focuses on the line in which Macbeth refers to Duncan as
       lying with his "silver skin lac'd with his golden blood." The
       associative matrix of words from Paracelsus' De Sanguine Ultra
       Mortem (About the blood beyond death) would appear to provide
       the meaning that would have been clear to Shakespeare's audience.
       In Macbeth's imagination Duncan's blood assumes an alchemical
       tincture transforming the dross body into the spiritual; it is
       already in the hand of God.

1275   PAUL, HENRY N. The Royal Play of "Macbeth": When, Why, and
       How It Was Written by Shakespeare. New York: Macmillan,
       1948, 438 pp.
              Argues that Macbeth was written especially for performance
       before King James I, the occasion being the state visit of his
       brother-in-law King Christian of Denmark in 1606, and that the
       site was Hampton Court on 7 August. Inconsistencies are the
       result of haste in readying the material for this performance.
       James's delight at the presentation of Tres Sibyllae at Oxford in
       1603 prompted Shakespeare to consider whether the prophecy of
       Banquo could be set to stage. In doing so, Shakespeare used
       selections from Holinshed in combination with material from the
       King's Basilikon Doron and Daemonology.

1276   RAMSEY, JAROLD. "The Perversion of Manliness in Macbeth."
       Studies in English Literature 13 (1973):285-300.
              Describes the concept of manliness as one of the principal
       themes in the play, specifically the disjunction of aggressive
       manliness from humanness. At the outset Macbeth's manly actions
       are not devoid of kindness. His moral degeneracy is reflected in
       his progressive repudiation of all humane considerations, cul-
       minating in the savage slaying of Lady Macduff and her children.
       In the final moments Macbeth regains a vestige of human quality
       in his desire to avoid Macduff, who "cows" his reckless courage
       and rekindles a spark of remorse. (See entry 1247.)

1277   REID, B.L. "Macbeth and the Play of Absolutes." Sewanee
       Review 58 (1965):19-46.
              Considers Macbeth's attempt to disrupt the formal and
       orderly movement of time to be the action that leads to the
       emptiness and futility of his life and produces his ultimate
       damnation. Both Macbeth and Lady Macbeth pervert time, transport
       themselves past the "ignorant present," and base their vision on
       actions yet to be committed. Macbeth in 1.7 is in normal time,
       his moral outlook clear; but Lady Macbeth spurs him to commandeer
       time and misuse the moral order. Following Duncan's murder he
       wanders in a limbo devoid of time; and by the end time--and life
       itself--have lost all meaning.

1278   WAITH, EUGENE M. "Macbeth: Interpretation Versus Adapta-
       tion." In Shakespeare: Of an Age and for All Time. Edited
       by Charles T. Prouty. Hamden, Conn.: Shoe String Press,
       1954, pp. 103-22.
           Points out the difference between interpretation, which
       chooses between two or more possible meanings of a character or
       an incident, and adaptation, which rearranges, deletes, or ampli-
       fies. A flagrant example of such adaptation occurs in Macbeth in
       productions that omit 4.3, a long scene in which Macduff empha-
       sizes the divinity of kingship in conversation with Malcolm and
       implores the legitimate heir to cure the bleeding country. The
       concept is obviously a linchpin of the play. Yet Davenant in
       1674 greatly reduced the dialogue, and Garrick retained the cuts,
       as do many modern versions.

1279   WALKER, ROY. The Time Is Free: A Study of "Macbeth."
       London: Andrew Dakers, 1949, 234 pp. Selections reprinted
       in Twentieth Century Interpretations of "Macbeth," ed.
       Terence Hawkes, Twentieth Century Interpretations (Englewood
       Cliffs: Prentice-Hall, 1977), p. 60.
           Investigates Macbeth through the pattern of its poetic
       symbolism, focusing on Shakespeare's vision to much of which our
       changing world makes us strangers. The opening scene is apoca-
       lyptic, with meanings convoluted and distorted, in short, with
       an elemental convulsion. The fair-foul dichotomy establishes a
       poetic theme that reverberates throughout the play. Darkness
       also pervades the play both figuratively and literally; the sun
       apparently shines only twice in the entire play. The daybreak at
       the end is a new dawn signaling the mutual workings of the order
       of nature and the army of heaven.

1280   WILLSON, ROBERT F., Jr. "Macbeth the Player King: The
       Banquet Scene as Frustrated Play Within the Play." Shake-
       speare Jahrbuch (Weimar) 114 (1978):107-14.
           Describes the banquet scene as a play that goes wrong,
       revealing the process of change by which Macbeth hardens into
       villainy and suffers the psychological consequences and by which
       Lady Macbeth loses control of him. Banquo, whose ghost sits in
       Macbeth's seat, reasserts his right both as king and host. As
       Macbeth's birth into kingship the wine serves as a link between
       birth and death, representing not only the water of a baptismal
       celebration but also the blood of Christ-like victims. He is
       born into a world of death of his own creation. (See entry
       1258.)

Stage History

1281   BATHOLOMEUSZ, DENNIS. Macbeth and the Players. Cambridge:
       Cambridge University Press, 1969, 302 pp.
           Reconstructs and evaluates players' interpretations of
       Macbeth and Lady Macbeth, in terms of both thematic analysis and

the concrete realities of speech, costume, gesture, and expression. The discussion focuses on major figures such as Burbage, Betterton, Garrick, Kemble, Macready, and Irving. The closing chapters stress the return to Elizabethan stage techniques in the twentieth century and in that regard the importance of the work of Harley Granville-Barker. Olivier's production at Stratford in 1955 is described as the most successful in this century.

1282 ROSENBERG, MARVIN. The Masks of "Macbeth." Berkeley and Los Angeles: University of California Press, 1978, 802 pp.
Surveys important critical and theatrical interpretations of Macbeth from Europe, America, Asia, Africa, and Australia. By attempting to reexperience the conflicting emotions that ravage Macbeth's soul while at the same time being conscious of his outer mask by which he hides them, we can come to appreciate something of Shakespeare's art in characterization. The play's visual imagery and spectacle combine many multiple signals. This study moves through the play scene by scene interweaving the author's own interpretation with numerous references to critics and actors.

1283 SPENCER, CHRISTOPHER. Davenant's "Macbeth" from the Yale Manuscript: An Edition, with a Discussion of the Relation of Davenant's Text to Shakespeare's. Yale Studies in English, 146. New Haven: Yale University Press, 1961, 226 pp.
Focuses on the relationship of the various printed texts of Macbeth from 1623 to 1710 and on the manner in which Davenant adapted the play. Davenant's version, first published in 1674 and probably written in 1663-64, with its elaborate costuming, flying machines for the witches, singing and dancing, reflects his general efforts to establish opera on the Restoration stage. The women's roles are expanded, Lady Macduff becoming a foil for Lady Macbeth. The porter scene is omitted, probably to avoid the mixture of comedy and tragedy.

For discussion of Macbeth as a tragic figure, see entries 1249-50, 1263. See also The Tragedies (entries 920-79) and 25, 103, 115, 126, 128, 134, 136, 147, 149, 162, 171, 179, 189, 231, 245, 257, 259, 263, 266-67, 272, 286, 294, 297, 302, 304, 306, 311, 317, 320, 326, 329, 409, 434, 588, 1032, 1134, 1160, 1164, 1190, 1218, 1378.

OTHELLO

Reference Works

1284 TANNENBAUM, SAMUEL A., and TANNENBAUM, DOROTHY R., comps. William Shakespeare: "Othello." Elizabethan Bibliographies, 28. New York: Privately Printed, 1943, 132 pp.
Includes 3,100 unannotated entries covering major scholarship on Othello from the beginnings to 1941. The material is

divided by the following categories and is arranged alphabetically by section--English editions, adaptations, abstracts;
translations; travesties, parodies, imitations, continuations;
bibliography; sources; songs for Othello; incidental music;
Verdi's Otello; Rossini's Otello; electric and mechanical re-
cordings; commentary on Othello music; theatrical history;
Othello, Iago, Desdemona; commentary on the play; illustrations,
costumes; book titles; addenda. The majority of the material
(1,205 items) is loosely classified under commentary on the play.

Editions

1285   RIDLEY, M.R., ed. Othello. The Arden Shakespeare. London:
       Methuen; Cambridge, Mass.: Harvard University Press; 1958,
       246 pp.
           Includes discussion of the text, date, sources, the "double
       time" scheme, and critical interpretations, as well as appendixes
       on Cinthio's narrative and on various textual problems. The text
       is based on the first quarto (1622), for which the copy was
       probably a transcript of Shakespeare's foul papers. Othello may
       well be Shakespeare's greatest theatrical production. Through
       the soliloquies of both Othello and Iago Shakespeare forces the
       spectators to become involved in the action. Othello is a mag-
       nificently conceived figure, a black man of great dignity and
       bravery but possessed of a vulnerability to the intellectual and
       psychological stratagems of Iago. Iago himself is the supreme
       opportunist. Shakespeare's task was to create a psychological
       sense of sufficient time for the deeds of darkness to be consum-
       mated.

1286   WALKER, ALICE, and WILSON, JOHN DOVER, eds. Othello.
       Cambridge: Cambridge University Press, 1957, 246 pp.
           Provides extensive textual notes, a critical introduction
       (including discussion of Othello as a Moor, the date and sources,
       Cinthio's novella and Shakespeare's Othello, Iago, the "double
       time" in the play, Othello's temptation and fall, the imagery,
       and the various interpretations of the final scene), a discussion
       of the copy text, a section on stage history, and a glossary.
       This edition is eclectic, based primarily on the First Folio but
       with quarto readings allowed. In Shakespeare, unlike Cinthio,
       the Moor as a stern judge offers Desdemona as a sacrifice to
       outraged chastity. His dignity and nobility are preserved in the
       final scene through his sense of remorse earned through agony and
       his equally stern justice upon himself.

Criticism

1287   ADAMSON, JANE. "Othello" as Tragedy: Some Problems of Judg-
       ment and Feeling. Cambridge: Cambridge University Press,
       1980, 301 pp.
           Insists that critical appreciation for Othello has been
crippled between arguments that the protagonist is noble and

arguments that he is a creature of monstrous ego. The play is
tragic in the fullest sense of the word, the supposed limitations
reflecting the readers' restricting moral and artistic preconcep-
tions. The play, more specifically, focuses powerfully on each
character's perception of reality so that we tend painfully to
identify with a partial view of truth instead of recognizing the
fallibility that links us with the other characters as well and
universalizes the tragedy.

1288   BABCOCK, WESTON. "Iago--An Extraordinary Honest Man."
        Shakespeare Quarterly 16 (1965):297-301.
            Observes that "honest" and "honesty" are applied to Iago
        ten times in Othello. These references, however, have a pejora-
        tive connotation; they are used in a patronizing way to an in-
        ferior and serve to intensify Iago's hatred and his determination
        to strike back at those who subtly denigrate him. The use of
        "thee" and "thou" (fifty-five times) and "fellow" function sim-
        ilarly in the play. Such social snobbery exacerbates his emo-
        tions, combining with his native shrewdness and intelligence to
        form a notable villain.

1289   BAYLEY, JOHN. "Love and Identity: Othello." In The Charac-
        ters of Love: A Study in the Literature of Personality.
        London: Constable, 1960, pp. 125-201.
            Notes that Othello focuses intensely on problems of domes-
        ticity and daily living with something of the familiarity of a
        novel or a newspaper. Reflecting the many sides of love, it is
        above all highly personal, culminating in a total loneliness of
        spirit that leaves the spectators with a similar sense of soli-
        tude. The spectators are made to see both with the eye of love
        and without it, sympathetically and judgmentally. At the end
        Othello assures us that suicide will cut him off from the last
        hope of mercy, and in that act his love endures, if not triumphs.

1290   BERRY, RALPH. "Pattern in Othello." Shakespeare Quarterly 23
        (1972):3-19.
            Asserts that an overly rigid symbolic interpretation of
        Othello destroys vitality and plausibility by smothering the
        naturalistic and psychological human qualities. These qualities
        are apparent in the pattern of interaction Shakespeare sets up
        among individuals. Brabantio, for example, moves from calm
        assurance to shock and outrage under the careful guidance of
        Iago, and the pattern is repeated in Othello. Iago's methods
        and motives are revealed through his relationship with Roderigo.
        Shakespeare through the surrounding characters refuses to offer
        an absolute judgment of Othello's character.

1291   BETHELL, S.L. "Shakespeare's Imagery: The Diabolical Images
        in Othello." Shakespeare Survey 5 (1952):62-80.
           Observes that functional imagery assists in clarifying the
        meaning of a passage, possibly helping to develop character or
        theme. Othello, more specifically, is built on a theological
        structure, and pervasive diabolic imagery reinforces the spiritual
        struggle for the Moor's soul. Interestingly, these images apply
        only to Iago in the early acts, but they attach themselves to
        Othello in 4.5. His sin is essentially that of Adam in that pas-
        sion usurps reason. Since he is a Christian, his suicide seals
        his fate.

1292   BODKIN, MAUD. "The Image of the Devil, of the Hero, and of
        God." In Archetypal Patterns in Poetry. Oxford: Oxford
        University Press, 1934, pp. 217-70. Selections reprinted in
        Shakespeare's Tragedies, ed. Laurence Lerner (Baltimore:
        Penguin, 1963), pp. 99-105.
           Views Iago as an archetype of the devil concentrating on
        hunting in order to destroy his hero, the destined prey. Once
        Othello wrenches himself free of Iago's power, his sense of the
        villain's deviltry is overwhelming. Othello, a romantic symbol
        of faith in human values of love and war, and Desdemona, not so
        much an individual woman as a symbol of the female divinity of
        love, are also archetypal conceptions. Iago is a limitless,
        formless, negative denial of all romantic values whose only
        pleasure is to destroy. (See entry 1308.)

1293   BOOSE, LYNDA E. "Othello's Handkerchief: The Recognition
        and Pledge of Love." English Literary Renaissance 5 (1975):
        360-74.
           Focuses on the strawberry-red fruit embroidered on
        Desdemona's handkerchief and its symbolic significance as the
        virgin blood of her consummated marriage. When she is unable to
        produce the handkerchief, Othello's passion mounts steadily to
        the point of his murdering her for what he assumes to be whore-
        dom. By using the handkerchief as the visual symbol of
        Desdemona's fidelity, Shakespeare emphasizes for the spectator
        the significance in the play of concepts and misconcepts of
        vision.

1294   BURGESS, C.F. "Othello's Occupation." Shakespeare Quarterly
        26 (1975):208-13.
           Observes that Othello's military code, under which he has
        prospered, fails to educate him to double-dealing. Unprepared
        for the subtleties of the Venetian world, he cannot accept ambi-
        guity or equivocation. Even in his final moments his demeanor is
        military as he reminds the audience of the services he has ren-
        dered and then kills himself. Traditional among the military is
        the belief that one has a right to kill himself before being
        killed. His greatest military flaw is his breaking of the code
        of ethics in discussing Cassio with Iago, a subordinate.

1295   CAMDEN, CARROLL. "Iago on Women." Journal of English and
        Germanic Philology 48 (1949):57-71.
            Traces the main points of antifeminism through the period
        and describes Iago's conversation with Desdemona as they await
        Othello's arrival at Cyprus as in the main current of this tra-
        dition, reflecting many Elizabethan conceptions. Since Shake-
        speare is at such pains to depict Desdemona as an example of the
        ideal wife, Iago's words have sharply ironic force, just as her
        precise wifely devotion in the bedchamber scene adds horrible
        poignancy to the murder.

1296   DOEBLER, BETTIE ANNE. "Othello's Angels: The Ars Moriendi."
        ELH 34 (1967):156-72.
            Asserts that Shakespeare evokes the ars moriendi tradition
        in 5.2, following Desdemona's murder, in Gratiano's reference to
        Brabantio's death. This tradition, which views the death-bed
        scene as a climactic struggle between the forces of evil and the
        forces of good for the possession of man's soul, is used to sig-
        nal Othello's struggle with the temptation to despair. The
        juxtaposition of the art of dying well with Othello's actual
        death suggests Othello's damnation, but the suffering resulting
        from recognition and admission of his guilt also generates in-
        tense dramatic sympathy for the hero.

1297   DORAN, MADELEINE. "Good Name in Othello." Studies in English
        Literature 7 (1967):195-217.
            Traces the still-current meanings of reputation and slander
        to illustrate a central motif in the play. In the pattern of the
        former, Iago warns Othello of the consequences of the loss of his
        good name, Cassio laments the loss of reputation, and Othello in
        his final moments is concerned that his deeds be related in the
        proper spirit. Slander in each case is the destructive agent.
        Othello's final speech is best understood as akin to the medieval
        purgatio canonica, in which he is asking to be relieved of the
        infamia facti, the undeserved infamy.

1298   DRAPER, JOHN W. The "Othello" of Shakespeare's Audience.
        Paris: Marcel Didier, 1952, 246 pp.
            Aims to bring into perspective the background pertinent to
        the individual characters Brabantio, Desdemona, Emilia and
        Bianca, Roderigo, Cassio, Iago, and Othello, along with units on
        significant aspects of the background--military, political, so-
        cial (marriage customs, laws concerning infidelity). With jeal-
        ousy as a principal motive, Othello's actions and reactions are
        most fully understood in light of the family mores of the English
        and the Italian. This tragedy of love is built on chronic mis-
        understanding at all social levels.

1299   ELIOT, T.S. "Shakespeare and the Stoicism of Seneca." In
        Selected Essays of T.S. Eliot. New York: Harcourt, Brace,
        1932, pp. 107-20. Selections reprinted in A Casebook on
        "Othello," ed. Leonard F. Dean (New York: Thomas Y. Crowell,
        1961), pp. 153-55.
             Argues that Othello, and to a lesser degree Coriolanus and
        Antony, in their final moments adopt a Stoic attitude of self-
        dramatization in order not to have to admit failure. Othello's
        words express, not the greatness in defeat of a noble, erring
        nature, but a determination to envision himself against his
        environment. He is "cheering himself up," adopting an aesthetic
        rather than moral posture in an endeavor to escape reality.
        (See entry 1322.)

1300   ELLIOTT, GEORGE R. Flaming Minister: A Study of "Othello"
        as a Tragedy of Love and Hate. Durham: Duke University
        Press, 1953, 245 pp.
             Argues that Othello, not Iago, is the moving force of the
        tragedy and that his motive is a subtle and deadly pride that
        nullifies the humility essential to human development. Indeed,
        the theme of pride is the central unifying theme in all Shake-
        spearean tragedy. In Othello, more specifically, the divinely
        magnanimous and the diabolically brutish clash with disastrous
        consequences in a domestic context. His pride forces him to hide
        his jealousy, and his refusal to tell the truth prevents his
        discovering it.

1301   EVANS, K.W. "The Racial Factor in Othello." Shakespeare
        Studies 5 (1969):124-40.
             Regards the racial factor as the fatal point of Othello
        and as the source of much of its philosophic significance.
        Blacks on the Elizabethan stage traditionally play upon social
        and religious prejudices, as well as satisfying a taste for the
        strange and exotic. Through the opening comments of Iago and
        Brabantio the spectators are conditioned to expect a fierce and
        violent individual, but Othello's appearance is just the oppo-
        site. In acts 3-5, however, the hero degenerates from nobility
        to the condition prejudicially associated with the race. His
        tragic nobility arises from the fact that, true to his Moorish
        nature, his judgment upon himself is as harsh as it had been upon
        Desdemona.

1302   EMPSON, WILLIAM. "Honest in Othello." In The Structure of
        Complex Words. London: Chatto & Windus, 1957, pp. 218-49.
        Reprinted in Four Centuries of Shakespearian Criticism, ed.
        Frank Kermode (New York: Avon, 1965), pp. 475-90.
             Explores the interplay of meaning with the word "honest"
        as a key to understanding the relationship of Othello and Iago.
        The word appears fifty-two times in the play, used divergently
        by the main characters in a kind of symbolic charade. Other
        characters use the word to describe Iago, but with Othello it

becomes an obsession. All elements of Iago's character are
represented in its range of meanings as is the range of moral
values that an audience would experience about him.

1303   FLATTER, RICHARD. The Moor of Venice. London: William
       Heinemann, 1950, 225 pp.
          Maintains that to view Othello as a caged animal without
       the nobility and intelligence to be a match for the conniving
       Iago is totally to miss Shakespeare's intention. Othello, to be
       sure, is trusting, nobly so; and as such he is relatively easy
       prey for Iago. The complexity of the protagonist, though, is
       evident in the final act. Confident that he is a minister of
       justice, he falls to despair when he learns of Desdemona's inno-
       cence; but, when he learns further of Iago's machinations, he
       emerges from despair to a new sense of self-esteem and of love
       for his wife. When he "dies upon a kiss," he is joyously wel-
       coming death as a reunion, combining the frenzy of death with the
       rapture of love.

1304   GARDNER, HELEN. "The Noble Moor." Proceedings of the British
       Academy 41 (1955):189-205.
          Asserts that Othello has a supreme beauty, sensuous, in-
       tellectual, and moral, qualities arising from the nature of the
       hero. The living personalities defeat any efforts at allegoriz-
       ing, and scatalogical concerns bow to attraction for human pas-
       sion. As a drama of passion and love, it fails to sustain the
       height of noon. Iago is monstrous, motivated by a detestation
       of superiority. The theme involves Othello's loss of faith at a
       sexual level where body meets spirit. His assassination of
       Desdemona is heroic in its absoluteness, committed to save her
       from herself. The godlike is mingled with the brutal.

1305   GARDNER, S.N. "Shakespeare's Desdemona." Shakespeare Studies
       9 (1976):233-52.
          Describes Desdemona's character as fully human, neither a
       goddess nor a slut. Divergent views reinforce her human com-
       plexity. Brabantio idealizes her; but Othello indicates that she
       invited his kisses, and she confirms this attitude in her request
       to travel with him to Cyprus where they may enjoy the full rites
       of marriage. The view that sexuality leads her to marry a black
       man is countered by her assertion that she claimed him for his
       dignity, energy, and power.

1306   GERARD, A. "'Egregiously an Ass': The Dark Side of the Moor:
       A View of Othello's Mind." Shakespeare Survey 10 (1957):
       98-106.
          Suggests that a new look at Shakespeare's transmutation of
       Cinthio's material might provide insight into the playwright's
       intentions. As a study in the relationships between the moral
       and the intellectual, Othello depicts the ultimate responsibility
       for the fateful developments as resting with the Moor. The

fundamental tragic flaw is a shortcoming in his intellect in that
he fails to distinguish between the ideal and the actual. In his
anagnorisis he recognizes this flaw and sees himself for what he
is, a fool. Yet he remains barbarian to the end in condemning
his soul to hell.

1307   HALLSTEAD, R.N. "Idolatrous Love: A New Approach to
       Othello." Shakespeare Quarterly 19 (1968):107-24.
           Examines Othello as a story of idolatrous love that in-
       evitably ends tragically. The first sign that Othello has become
       consumed by love is his gross neglect of public duty. Following
       the consummation of the marriage, he emerges a changed man,
       annoyed and angered by the brawl. By making an idol of Desdemona,
       he turns his carnal knowledge of her to grounds for suspicion of
       her infidelity. In the final moments he confesses his idolatry
       and his renunciation of the Christian faith.

1308   HEILMAN, ROBERT B. Magic in the Web: Action and Language in
       "Othello." Lexington: University of Kentucky Press, 1956,
       298 pp. Selections reprinted in Shakespeare: Modern Essays
       in Criticism, ed. Leonard F. Dean, rev. ed. (New York:
       Oxford University Press, 1967), pp. 329-45.
           Observes that in Othello verbal drama (poetic language)
       and actional drama (the narrative line) combine to form a har-
       monious structure of meaning. Iago is no abstraction, but an
       individual who carries impulses to such a logical fullness that
       the character becomes humanly fascinating; he operates primarily
       by manipulating appearances through insinuation, thus inducing a
       kind of blindness, and his major imagistic mode is one of light-
       darkness. He also repeatedly expresses his views in terms of
       bodily functions, dehumanizing love by treating it as mechanical
       animality. Othello's breakdown in 3.3 is a consequence of his
       loss of position and of a sense of being loved. His plurality
       of motives consistently reflects both the noble Moor bent on
       justice and a loathsome monster of self-deception. Othello,
       Iago, Roderigo, and Cassio all act out versions of the lover sick
       with loss, with the characters enunciating several doctrines of
       love that help to clarify the symbolic import of the action.
       (See entry 1292.)

1309   HIBBARD, G.R. "Othello and the Pattern of Shakespearian
       Tragedy." Shakespeare Survey 21 (1968):39-46.
           Argues the atypicality of Othello as Shakespearean tragedy
       in that there is no public eulogy, little comment about his suc-
       cessor and the disposal of his estate, and no close interconnec-
       tion of the public and the private. The play's action seems to
       contract rather than expand. Othello's painful and private loss
       emphasizes a sense of wanton waste; he suffers brutal degradation
       at the hands of an outside force and so privately has he become
       the focus of his tragedy that he alone is able to speak his own
       valediction.

1310   HUBLER, EDWARD. "The Damnation of Othello: Some Limitations
        on the Christian View of the Play." Shakespeare Quarterly 9
        (1958):295-300.
            Concerns the danger of utilizing selected points of Chris-
        tianity as a handle upon which to hang clusters of images or
        symbols and then claiming to have perceived Shakespeare's deepest
        dramatic intentions. Both Bethell (entry 1291) and Siegel
        (entry 1326), for example, send Othello's soul to hell. Whether
        his soul goes to heaven or hell is peripheral to the play.
        Shakespeare's audience was diverse, living in a time of rapid
        change and doubt. It is foolish to insist on any kind of doc-
        trinaire consistency; a hallmark of Shakespeare and his audience
        was the ability to see the many-sidedness of things.

1311   HYMAN, STANLEY EDGAR. Iago: Some Approaches to the Illusion
        of His Motivation. New York: Atheneum, 1970, 181 pp.
            Displays the pluralism of literary analysis through five
        schools of interpretation of Iago--genre criticism, Iago as a
        stage villain descended from the Vice character; theological
        criticism, Iago as Satan with Desdemona having Christological
        overtones; symbolic criticism, with Iago as a partial portrait of
        the artist; psychoanalytic criticism, with Iago as a latent homo-
        sexual; and historical criticism, with Iago as a Machiavel. Any
        single view is reductive and partial; only taken together do they
        produce a full understanding of the complex imaginative creation.

1312   JORGENSEN, PAUL A. "Honesty in Othello." Studies in
        Philology (1950):557-67.
            Explores the connotation of "honest" that relates language
        to theme in Othello, specifically the mystery of how to distin-
        guish an honest man from a knave. Traces this theme through
        several Morality and early Elizabethan plays. Iago, one must
        note, is active in his surface role as the honest man, most
        skillful in creating the appearance that Desdemona and Cassio are
        but "seeming honest." His pose is complex in that he is a knave
        posing as honesty, a hunter of knaves.

1313   _____. "'Perplexed in the Extreme': The Role of Thought in
        Othello." Shakespeare Quarterly 15 (1964):265-75. Reprinted
        in Shakespeare 400: Essays by American Scholars on the Anni-
        versary of the Poet's Birth, ed. James G. McManaway (New York:
        Holt, Rinehart & Winston, 1964), pp. 265-75.
            Views the role of thought as central to Othello. Othello
        himself is torn between two kinds of reason, the ratiocinative
        and the intuitive; when he is confronted by the mentality of
        Iago, his faith in his intuition collapses, and his ratiocinative
        thought is duped. Iago, believed by others to be a thoughtful
        man, is in reality psychopathically incoherent and unreasonable,
        sexually perverted, and voyeuristic. While the role of thought
        is perverted in the two principals, Othello does gain a degree
        of self-knowledge through his tragedy.

1314   KAY, CAROL McGINNIS. "Othello's Need for Mirrors. <u>Shake-</u>
        <u>speare Quarterly</u> 34 (1983):261-70.
            Points out that Othello's suicide is staged as a public
        event. Both his first (interrupted) attempt that he has called
        Gratiano to witness and his second (successful) attempt involve
        his recalling his military accomplishments, his blaming the
        events on external forces, and his claims of honorable but mis-
        directed intentions. Reaction to the deed is horror and regret,
        as Othello would have wished. Whatever his ability, bravery,
        and eloquence, this hero here and throughout the play is charac-
        terized by an immature ego.

1315   KIRSCHBAUM, LEO. "The Modern Othello." <u>ELH</u> 11 (1944):
        283-96. Reprinted in <u>A Casebook on "Othello</u>," ed. Leonard F.
        Dean (New York: Thomas Y. Crowell, 1961), pp. 156-68.
            Disagrees with modern criticism that places the central
        cause of Othello's collapse in Iago. Instead, Othello like
        Shakespeare's other protagonists is nobly tragic in part because
        he is very much the maker of his own destiny. A romantic ideal-
        ist who overidealizes both himself and Desdemona, he also readily
        shifts to suspicion at the least provocation. His refusal to
        face his crime squarely in act 5 and to see himself as ordi-
        narily human is what makes him psychologically consistent. In a
        word, Iago succeeds with Othello because the Moor is tragically
        and nobly susceptible, not because Iago is a Devil-man against
        whom one is doomed to failure.

1316   LEAVIS, F.R. "Diabolic Intellect and the Noble Hero." In
        <u>The Common Pursuit</u>. London: Chatto & Windus, 1952,
        pp. 136-59.
            Claims that, even though it is the simplest of Shakespeare's
        tragedies, <u>Othello</u> suffers from an essential and denaturing
        falsification. Bradley's mistaken notion of the play as the un-
        doing of a noble Moor (entry 920) is largely responsible.
        Othello, instead, is the supreme egotist given from first to
        last to self-approving self-dramatization. His own mind, not
        Iago's, undoes him. "Self-pride becomes stupidity, ferocious
        stupidity, an insane and self-deceiving passion" (pp. 146-47).
        At the end there is no tragic self-discovery, only the <u>coup</u> de
        <u>theatre</u> of Othello's contemplating the spectacle of himself.
        (See entry 1322.)

1317   LERNER, LAURENCE. "The Machiavel and the Moor." <u>Essays in</u>
        <u>Criticism</u> 9 (1959):339-60.
            Describes Iago as a mixture of the subhuman metaphor of
        evil from the medieval Morality plays and the super-subtle human
        Machiavel who calculates and conceals behind his honest facade.
        This mixture of the symbolic and the naturalistic was a phenom-
        enon of characterization, a transitional stage, in the literature
        of Shakespeare's day. Similarly, there are two Othellos, the
        stylized noble Moor of the first half and the realistic passionate

Moor of the last half. The Othello of the final scene is a
reversion to the noble figure.

1318   LEVIN, RICHARD. "The Indian/Iudean Crux in Othello."
        Shakespeare Quarterly 33 (1982):60-67.
            Reviews arguments concerning the preferred reading in
        Othello's final speech about the base "Indian" (first quarto,
        1622) or "Iudean" (First Folio, 1623) who threw a pearl away and
        describes how the critics' preference is frequently a consequence
        of their predetermined interpretation of the play. Since Othello
        is attempting to explain his state of perplexity when he has
        killed Desdemona, the word "Indian" would be dramatically appro-
        priate in that the Indian was ignorant of the pearl's value. But
        such logic is unlikely to dissuade those who insist on "Iudean"
        because the reference to Judas becomes a theological metaphor for
        one who like Othello rejects grace through his suicide.

1319   LEVITSKY, RUTH M. "All-in-All Sufficiency in Othello."
        Shakespeare Studies 6 (1972):209-21.
            Analyzes Othello's weakness in terms of the Pelagianism
        inherent in Iago's comments on will and reason. Specifically,
        Othello is more about the weakness of the mind and the under-
        standing than of the body. Faulty reason, not drunkenness and
        adultery, wreaks the havoc in the play. Othello is a character
        of self-sufficiency, but as such his Stoicism sacrifices a part
        of his humanity and requires a subjugation of human emotions.
        He murders his wife according to his belief in strict justice,
        never humbling himself before man or God, more antique Roman than
        Christian.

1320   McCLOSKY, JOHN C. "The Motivation of Iago." College English
        3 (1941):25-30.
            Observes that Iago's basic motivation is hatred, a coales-
        cence of wounded pride, a sense of personal injustice, and jeal-
        ous suspicion. His tragic practice begins in his determination
        to gain satisfaction for the personal wrong of his not being
        promoted. In the execution of his method he employs the method
        of psychological suggestion. In his very consistency of motiva-
        tion and his dedication to achieve his ends lie his greatness as
        a literary creation. To see his evil as motiveless is highly
        reductionistic.

1321   McGEE, ARTHUR R. "Othello's Motive for Murder." Shakespeare
        Quarterly 15 (1964):45-54.
            Focuses on the time problem in Othello, in which it appears
        that the Moor is led to suspect infidelity in Desdemona for which
        there was no possible time, the insinuations of adultery and the
        murder they lead to all occurring two days after the wedding.
        Iago's insinuations, however, imply that Cassio has been
        Desdemona's lover prior to Othello; since adultery to Shake-
        speare's audience meant sexual infidelity after the moment of

betrothal, Othello suspects Desdemonoa of unfaithfulness in
Cyprus before the actual marriage.

1322   MERCER, PETER. "Othello and the Form of Heroic Tragedy."
       Critical Quarterly 11 (1969):45-61.
           Complains that Leavis (entry 1316) in locating the reason
       for Othello's collapse in the Moor himself has reduced the play
       to a rather arbitrary intrigue against a self-deceiving egotist.
       Likewise, to view Othello in his final word as merely cheering
       himself up, as Eliot (entry 1299) does, is to neglect the nature
       of heroic tragedy in favor of psychological peculiarities. In-
       stead, Othello's progress is "from heroic certainty to total un-
       bearable uncertainty" (p. 50), with the play turning upon dis-
       tinctions between the linguistic and existential worlds and a
       general movement toward rhetorical reassertion.

1323   NOWOTTNY, WINIFRED M.T. "Justice and Love in Othello.
       University of Toronto Quarterly 21 (1951-52):330-44. Re-
       printed in A Casebook on "Othello," ed. Leonard F. Dean (New
       York: Thomas Y. Crowell, 1961), pp. 169-84.
           Maintains that the play turns upon a conflict between
       justice and love, hence the significance of Othello's claim in
       act 5 that he is a minister of justice. His agony results from
       the simultaneous growing intensity in his realization of con-
       tinued love for Desdemona and his growing compulsivenes to enact
       the sanctions of justice. His tragic error is that, in applying
       judgment to love, he attempts to join two concepts incompatible
       in their essential natures. In that he accepts justice as life's
       supreme value, it is wholly consistent that ultimately he executes
       himself.

1324   RICE, JULIAN C. "Desdemona Unpinned: Universal Guilt in
       Othello." Shakespeare Studies 7 (1974):209-26.
           Rebuts the traditional view of Desdemona as a Christ-like
       innocent victim and points to a significant flaw of psychological
       dishonesty. Her Neoplatonic view of Othello in 1.3, for example,
       denies a sexual basis for their relationship; she later needs
       reassurance from Iago of her virtue; she is blind to her own
       pride in her ready willingness to help Cassio regain office; and
       she is excessively naive in her response to Othello's charges of
       infidelity. In the unpinning scene (4.3) Shakespeare uses the
       conventional topos of clothing to symbolize Desdemona's psycho-
       logical exposure.

1325   ROGERS, ROBERT. "Endopsychic Drama in Othello." Shakespeare
       Quarterly 20 (1969):205-15.
           Argues that Othello stresses the conflict within, as dis-
       tinct from between, human beings, that the conflict between
       Othello and Iago is a dramatic portrayal of what is fundamentally
       an endopsychic conflict in the Moor. Othello's conscious adora-
       tion of Desdemona betokens an unrealistic and precarious assessment

of womankind. Othello, moreover, is a composite personality--a
normal character, a romanticist, and a psychotic. Iago hates
women, and he successfully plays upon Othello's contrasting
temperaments in turning the Moor against his wife.

1326   SIEGEL, PAUL N. "The Damnation of Othello." PMLA 68 (1953):
       1068-78. Reprinted in His Infinite Variety: Major Shake-
       spearean Criticism Since Johnson, ed. Paul N. Siegel (Phila-
       delphia: J.B. Lippincott, 1964), pp. 309-22.
           Draws an analogy between Othello and the fall of man, with
       Desdemona reminiscent of Christ in her purity and Iago of Satan
       in his destructiveness. Othello must choose between Christian
       love and Satanic hate and vengefulness. As his passion takes
       control, Othello assumes Faustian qualities, and Iago like Satan
       is conveniently on hand to spur the Moor to his final act of
       damnation. Ultimately Iago is sentenced to unnatural earthly
       torments as a prelude to his future suffering in hell, while
       Othello attempts to execute poetic justice on himself and brings
       perdition to his soul.

1327   STEMPEL, DANIEL. "The Silence of Iago." PMLA 84 (1969):
       252-63.
           Envisions Iago as a "Jesuitical Machiavel," Shakespeare's
       capitalizing on a combination of the Elizabethan concept of
       Machiavelli and of the Jesuit priest. Seventeenth-century re-
       ligious and political sources speak of an "Ignatian Matchivell"
       who justified his villainy by an appeal to faith and piety.
       Specifically, Iago symbolizes the doctrine of the autonomous
       will, a doctrine advocated by the Spanish Jesuit Luis de Molina
       and denounced by Protestantism and Catholicism alike. Iago's
       silence is reflective of the usual obdurate resistence of im-
       prisoned Jesuits.

1328   STOLL, ELMER EDGAR. "Another Othello Too Modern." In Joseph
       Quincy Adams Memorial Studies. Edited by James C. McManaway,
       Giles E. Dawson, and Edwin E. Willoughby. Washington: Folger
       Shakespeare Library, 1948, 351-71.
           Attacks G.G. Sedgewick's interpretation of the play, which
       views the seed of tragedy in the miscegenation even though (save
       Iago and Brabantio) no one in Venice or Cyprus seems surprised.
       Sedgewick's view supposes that the black's infatuation with the
       white, though in fact Desdemona is the aggressor, attributes to
       Othello a predisposition to jealousy, though in fact Shakespeare
       stresses just the opposite. Actually, Othello is duped by Iago
       no more than the other characters, including Iago's own wife.
       Shakespeare's audience did not, as Sedgewick suggests, expect
       tragedy because of the marriage itself and thus sit in ironic
       judgment on all that happened. (See entry 309.)

1329   TANNENBAUM, SAMUEL A. "The Wronged Iago." Shakespeare
        Association Bulletin 12 (1937):57-62.
            Suggests that Iago is angered at the opening of Othello,
        not only because he has been passed over for promotion, but be-
        cause he does indeed believe that Othello has cuckolded him.
        Shakespeare apparently would have us believe so, too. The accu-
        sation occurs in the exposition, and nothing elsewhere makes it
        improbable. Certainly, Emelia is not the type of woman who would
        immediately remove all suspicion. Othello's interview with
        Emelia in act 4 furnishes veritable proof of their relationship.

1330   WEISINGER, HERBERT. "Iago's Iago." University Review 20
        (1954):83-90.
            Observes that the main confusion about Iago's character is
        a consequence of his stated motivations--frustrated ambitions,
        revenge for cuckoldry, unrequited love for Desdemona--not fully
        justifying the depths and passion of his villainy. Iago has been
        a man of faith, but it has been shattered before the play begins;
        and he now turns his fierce intellect to the development of a
        materialistic and individualistic philosophy. Both Iago and
        Othello are incomplete men; the intellect of the one united with
        the passion of the other would result in a human and humane in-
        dividual.

Stage History

1331   ROSENBERG, MARVIN. The Masks of "Othello." Berkeley:
        University of California Press, 1961, 313 pp.
            Provides a stage history of Othello. Described as a play
        ripe for the era of sexual promiscuity in James's Court, Othello
        also warmly accommodated the appearance of women on stage in the
        Restoration but suffered from the censors and the charges of in-
        decorum in the eighteenth century. Major nineteenth-century
        Othellos are discussed in some detail--Kean, Macready, Fechter,
        Irving, Booth, Forrest, Salvini. Desdemona during this period
        steadily gained in courage, dignity, and tenderness. While the
        present century has produced no great interpretations, those
        particularly notable in the role of the Moor have been Laurence
        Olivier, Godfrey Tearle, Wilifred Walter, and Paul Robeson.

For discussion of Iago, see entries 1288, 1295, 1320, 1327, 1329-30.
For discussion of Othello, see entries 1304, 1315 versus 1316. See
also The Tragedies (entries 920-79) and 25, 83, 89-90, 103, 134,
143, 160, 223, 228, 230, 240-41, 243, 246, 250, 257-59, 263, 270,
272, 278, 302, 304, 307, 309, 317, 326, 328, 611, 878, 981, 991,
1104, 1384.

ROMEO AND JULIET

Reference Works

1332   MARDER, LOUIS, comp. "Romeo and Juliet": A Supplementary
       Bibliography 1871-1964. The New Variorum Shakespeare. New
       York: American Scholar Publications, 1965, 20 pp.
          Includes representative scholarship on Romeo and Juliet
       from 1871 through 1964 and is intended to supplement H.H.
       Furness's Variorum edition of 1871. The material is categorized
       under folio facsimiles, quarto facsimiles, editions of the play
       in chronological order, and critical studies (alphabetically
       arranged). While not exhaustive, the material represents every
       major category of scholarship and criticism.

1333   TANNENBAUM, SAMUEL A., and TANNENBAUM, DOROTHY R., comps.
       William Shakespeare: "Romeo and Juliet." Elizabethan Bib-
       liographies, 41. New York: Privately printed, 1940, 107 pp.
          Includes 2,354 unannotated entries covering major scholar-
       ship from the beginnings to 1938. The material is divided by the
       following categories and is arranged alphabetically by section--
       editions, adaptations; translations; selections; sources; theat-
       rical history; music; recordings; ballet; travesties, burlesques;
       Juliet, Romeo; commentary; addenda not indexed. The majority of
       the material (1,225 items) is loosely classified under commentary.

Editions

1334   DUTHIE, GEORGE IAN, and WILSON, JOHN DOVER, eds. Romeo and
       Juliet. Cambridge: Cambridge University Press, 1955, 249 pp.
          Provides extensive textual notes, a critical introduction,
       a discussion of the copy text, a section on stage history, and a
       glossary. This edition is based on the second quarto, with occa-
       sional readings allowed from the memorially contaminated first
       quarto; this situation arises from numerous compositorial errors
       in the second quarto that on occasion can be corrected against
       the first quarto. Romeo and Juliet, one of the most popular love
       stories in the Medieval and Renaissance periods, came to Shake-
       speare directly from Arthur Brooke's long poem The Tragical His-
       tory of Romeus and Juliet. Shakespeare's alterations for dra-
       matic effect are considered at length as is the quality of his
       verse, which in some ways developed more rapidly than his powers
       as a playwright.

1335   EVANS, G. BLAKEMORE, ed. Romeo and Juliet. The New Cambridge.
       Cambridge: Cambridge University Press, 1984, 249 pp.
          Represents a re-edition and redesigning of entry 1334 to
       reflect current critical and theatrical opinion. The introduc-
       tion discusses the date, sources and structure, tragic pattern,
       language and style, characters, and stage history. A textual
       analysis addresses both the nature of the first quarto (a bad

quarto) and the manner in which the second quarto (set from
Shakespeare's foul papers and the copy text for this edition) is
tainted by the first. Supplementary notes and excerpts from
Arthur Brooke's The Tragical History of Romeus and Juliet are
also included.

1336   GIBBONS, BRIAN, ed. Romeo and Juliet. The Arden Shakespeare.
       London: Methuen; Cambridge, Mass.: Harvard University Press,
       1980, 280 pp.
          Includes discussion of the text, the date, sources, and
       critical interpretations, as well as appendixes on the Queen Mab
       speech in the first quarto and a selection from Arthur Brooke's
       Romeus and Juliet. The text is based on the second quarto, for
       which the copy was probably Shakespeare's foul papers. The first
       quarto is clearly a memorial reconstruction. For Shakespeare
       this stage world is an exploration of various kinds of love
       poetry. Speed in the play is a matter of fate, and the awesome
       final scene stands as grim testimony to the impetuous rashness
       of youth.

Textual Studies

1337   HOPPE, HARRY R. The Bad Quarto of "Romeo and Juliet": A
       Bibliographical and Textual Study. Ithaca: Cornell Univer-
       sity Press, 1948, 230 pp.
          Argues that the first quarto (1597) is a memorial recon-
       struction of a version represented in substantially correct form
       in the second quarto (1599). External evidence includes the
       nature of the stage directions, errors in versification, omitted
       scenes, wordy passages, and attributions of speeches to the wrong
       characters, while internal evidence includes shifting of words,
       lines, or passages to another part of the play, appropriations
       from other plays, and anticipations of words and phrases. Prob-
       ably the text was reconstructed by Gabriel Spencer and William
       Bird, who deserted the Chamberlain's Company for Pembroke's in
       1597.

1338   THOMAS, SIDNEY. "The Queen Mab Speech in Romeo and Juliet."
       Shakespeare Survey 25 (1972):73-80.
          Argues that the Queen Mab speech was not in Shakespeare's
       original draft of the play, that it was added at a later date to
       enlarge Mercutio's role. Moreover, the version of the speech
       found in the first quarto is to be preferred to that in the
       second. While the second quarto is generally the superior text,
       peculiarities in spelling, word substitution, speech heading,
       and the substitution of prose for verse suggest textual corrup-
       tion. The first quarto text for this speech should be used in
       future editions.

Criticism

1339   ADAMS, BARRY. "The Prudence of Prince Escalus." ELH 35
        (1968):32-50.
            Deals with the dramatic function of Escalus and how his
        action, to some extent, leads to the tragedy of the play. The
        Prince's first appearance establishes him as a mediator between
        the play world and the audience. His second appearance follows
        Tybalt's death, and his final appearance follows the suicides of
        Romeo and Juliet. In each case he brings order to prevailing
        confusion. But Escalus, like all men lacking sufficient under-
        standing of the past to make completely reliable inferences about
        the future, is forced to make key decisions that play into the
        hand of evil fortune.

1340   BLACK, JAMES. "The Visual Artistry of Romeo and Juliet."
        Studies in English Literature 15 (1975):245-56.
            Views Romeo and Juliet as an exercise suiting action to
        words in such a manner as to produce special intensity. Scenes,
        for example, are repeated for visual effect and striking con-
        trasts. The first balcony scene is marked by delight and sweet
        anticipation, ending in "sweet sorrow"; the second is altered by
        Romeo's banishment and his engagement in bloodshed, ending in
        desperation. So, too, in the friar's cell scenes; the first
        finds Romeo seeking advice for love while the second finds
        Juliet seeking a remedy for it. Yet other examples are the
        framing scenes with Prince Escalus. In all cases the scenes
        stand on opposing sides of Mercutio's death.

1341   BONNARD, GEORGES A. "Romeo and Juliet: A Possible Signifi-
        cance." Review of English Studies, n.s. 2 (1951):319-27.
            Examines those deviations from Brooke's Romeus and Juliet
        that appear to be Shakespeare's efforts to lend the material
        tragic dignity. Most striking is the treatment of time, com-
        pressed by Shakespeare from nine months to five days. Such re-
        duction stresses the irresistible character of Romeo and Juliet's
        passion. Whereas Brooke tells the story of the fickleness of
        fortune, Shakespeare adds elements that make the principals more
        responsible agents, at the same time removing Romeo from involve-
        ment in the family feud. Above all, Romeo and Juliet are made to
        represent an opposite force to the hatred that consumes the
        Veronese society.

1342   BOWLING, LAWRENCE E. "The Thematic Framework of Romeo and
        Juliet." PMLA 64 (1949):208-20.
            Disagrees with the view that Romeo and Juliet as a work of
        Shakespeare's adolescence lacks a central theme. To the con-
        trary, the unifying motif is that character after character must
        come to the realization of the complexity of things, the mixture
        of good and evil. Such paradoxicalness is signalled in the
        prologue in Friar Lawrence's soliloquy, Juliet's "dove-feathered

raven" speech, Capulet's festival-funeral speech, Romeo's "loving
hate" speech, and his speech about gold as a cordial poison.
Both Romeo and Juliet mature in the course of the action through
the acceptance of this duality, as to a lesser extent do their
parents.

1343   BRENNER, GERRY. "Shakespeare's Politically Ambitious Friar."
        Shakespeare Studies 13 (1980):47-58.
        Argues that, in marrying Romeo and Juliet without parental
consent, failing to acquaint Prince Escalus with his plan, and
using a sleeping potion when removing Juliet to Mantua would be
far simpler, Friar Lawrence acts from self-aggrandizing political
ambitions. He views Romeo and Juliet as political tools by which
to "assert his superiority over domestic and civil authorities"
(p. 52). In doing so, he oversteps the bounds of religious
responsibilities. His flight from the tomb results from "fear of
social exposure lest he be punished" (p. 55).

1344   BRYANT, J.C. "The Problematic Friar in Romeo and Juliet."
        English Studies 55 (1974):340-50.
        Argues that, in light of Friar Lawrence's questionable con-
duct in the drama, one must judge him as an ecclesiastic, the
stereotype of comical friars derived from medieval fabliaux and
commedia erudita. The friar becomes comic and problematic at the
very points at which he deviates from his spiritual functions.
In having Lawrence disregard the canon law forbidding clandestine
marriage, marry minors without parental consent, and counsel
Juliet to engage in deliberate lying, Shakespeare strips him of
priestly dignity and leaves him in the final scene little more
than a coward.

1345   CAIN, H. "Romeo and Juliet: A Reinterpretation." Shake-
        speare Association Bulletin 22 (1947):163-92.
        Views Romeo and Juliet as a study in the passion of anger,
providing first an overview of medieval and Elizabethan ethics
concerning anger and the use of the theme in The Faerie Queene
and Romeus and Juliet. Shakespeare's Romeo first gives evidence
of inordinate passion in his obsession with Rosaline and then
with Juliet; similarly, he succumbs to passion in his duel with
Tybalt, and the final scenes depict in him a fury akin to madness. Romeo through his passion makes himself Fortune's fool,
not having attained the maturity of mind necessary to withstand
temptation.

1346   CARROLL, WILLIAM C. "'We Were Born to Die': Romeo and
        Juliet." Comparative Drama 15 (1981):54-71.
        Notes that the ending of the play represents what the
action has pointed to from the outset, the consummation of the
love of Romeo and Juliet in the tomb. Romeo and Juliet appear
alone on stage on only three occasions, at the beginning of their
love, at its consummation, and at their death. All three scenes

are nocturnal, and each represents their extreme sense of isolation while suggesting the three ages of man in passing from life
to death. Not only does the play include several allusions to
journeys and pilgrims; image clusters of wombs and tombs, sex and
death, also link the idea of the beginning to the end.

1347   CHANG, JOSEPH, S.M.J. "The Language of Paradox in Romeo and
        Juliet." Shakespeare Studies 3 (1967):22-42.
        Argues that the structure of Romeo and Juliet is controlled
by its Petrarchan contrarieties, realized in both its rhetoric
and its action. The play is only secondarily about love; like
the sonnet sequences it develops a love-centered situation as a
means of exploring the larger issues of time, death, and immortal
aspiration. Paradoxically, true love, though brief, can create
values not subject to measurement; beyond time, it creates a
value for life and a means of sustaining it.

1348   EVANS, BERTRAND. "The Brevity of Friar Lawrence." PMLA 65
        (1950):841-65.
        Describes Romeo and Juliet as more than any other of
Shakespeare's plays a tragedy of unawareness. The full force of
fate as the operative agent in the play comes in Friar Lawrence's
final speech, filled with dramatic irony since the spectators
know the full range of events and no one of the characters is
aware of all the details. Most stand in awe at the unexplained
carnage. Friar Lawrence can explain much, but Balthazar must
relate why Romeo was in the tomb and a page tells why Paris was
there. Only as the events unfold do the characters become aware
of their individual actions that make a part of the fatalistic
design.

1349   EVANS, ROBERT. The Osier Cage. Lexington: University of
        Kentucky Press, 1966, 108 pp.
        Offers a rhetorical analysis of Romeo and Juliet with spe-
cific attention to the dramatic function of Friar Lawrence and of
Mercutio's Queen Mab speech. The oxymoron, in particular, allows
Shakespeare to weave together the inexorably bound motifs of the
tragedy--the combination of love and violence, the imagery of
darkness and light, and the ambiguous relationship of reality and
appearance, of passion and rationality. Even in this highly
rhetorical play, Shakespeare seldom utilized ornament for its own
sake. Mercutio's speech, for example, totally preoccupied with
rhetoric, both points forward to the dramatic action and also
illustrates the fullness of Mercutio's character.

1350   EVERETT, BARBARA. "Romeo and Juliet: The Nurses's Story."
        Critical Quarterly 14 (1972):129-39.
        Suggests that the nurse's story in 1.3 involving her re-
membrance of her husband and her own daughter is significant in
that it provides both a chronological framework and a leitmotiv
on death for the tragic events of the play. Acting almost as a

choric commentary, in close conjunction with the chorus's remarks
in the prologue, she concentrates attention on Juliet's age, her
weaning, and her fall.

1351   FABER, M.D. "The Adolescent Suicide of Romeo and Juliet."
        Psychoanalytic Review 59 (1972):169-82.
            Maintains that the suicide of Romeo and Juliet is caused by
        the thwarting of an adolescent's attempt to transfer his libidi-
        nal energies to a nonincestuous object, thereby achieving the
        successful separation of the sexually mature child from the par-
        ent. The Montague-Capulet feud is narcissistic and restrictive,
        blocking the attempt of Romeo and Juliet to unite in a healthy
        complementary relationship. Romeo in taking his life desires
        both to unite with Juliet and to take out his aggression against
        the world and against his parents' association with the feud.

1352   LEVIN, HARRY. "Form and Formality in Romeo and Juliet."
        Shakespeare Quarterly 11 (1960):1-11. Reprinted in Four
        Centuries of Shakespearian Criticism, ed. Frank Kermode (New
        York: Avon, 1965), pp. 386-99.
            Calls the mutuality of the love of Romeo and Juliet the one
        organic relationship in the midst of highly stylized expressions
        and attitudes. Romeo at the outset is the traditional Petrarchan
        lover, doting on Rosaline, and even his first encounter with
        Juliet is set within the literary restrictions of the sonnet
        form. The quarrel at the opening is highly stylized with ser-
        vants, young members of the feuding families, the heads, and
        finally the Prince entering in seriatim fashion. Romeo's viola-
        tion of tradition by overhearing Juliet's soliloquy signals the
        naturalness of their love; after their death their private world
        disappears, and the social ambience closes around them.

1353   McARTHUR, HERBERT. "Romeo's Loquacious Friend." Shakespeare
        Quarterly 10 (1959):35-44.
            Describes earlier criticism of Mercutio as focusing on his
        bawdiness or his inconsistency and, thus, on Shakespeare's de-
        ficiency in developing a tragic tone as long as he is on stage.
        To the contrary, his function as a foil to Romeo is critical to
        the structure of the play. In his attempt to dislodge Romeo's
        melancholy in the Queen Mab speech, he prompts his friend out of
        his role as a fashionable lover, and Romeo catches a somber and
        prophetic glimpse of the future. In a word, Romeo's own destruc-
        tion is prefigured in the vulgarization and death of Mercutio.
        (See entry 1363.)

1354   MOORE, OLIN H. The Legend of "Romeo and Juliet." Columbus:
        Ohio State University Press, 1950, 167 pp.
            Records that the Montecchi family existed as a family in
        Verona in the twelfth century, but after 1207 the term refers
        only to a political party. The Cappelletti were a faction in
        Verona associated with the political affairs of Cremona. Dante

was the first author to mention the two together. One of the
most important sources of the Romeo and Juliet legend is
Boccaccio's Filocolo and Decameron (premature burial, sleeping
potion, corrupt abbot). Other authors involved in the accretion
of the legend before it reached Shakespeare are Masuccio, Luigi
da Porta, Adrien Sevin, Bandello, Boaistuau, and Arthur Brooke.

1355   . "Shakespeare's Deviations from Romeo and Juliet."
          PMLA 52 (1937):68-74.
          Notes that, whereas the general assumption is that Shake-
speare altered his source for Romeo and Juliet only in terms of
the minor characters, there are four significant modifications in
the roles of the major characters--in Romeo's object in attending
the Capulet's ball, in Romeo's motivation for killing Tybalt, in
Juliet's attending her wedding without the nurse, and in the
balcony scene in which Romeo and Juliet first exchange their love
vows. Apparently Shakespeare had direct access to the story as
treated in Italian by Luigi da Porta.

1356   NEVO, RUTH. "Tragic Form in Romeo and Juliet." Studies in
         English Literature 9 (1969):241-58.
         Observes that, as a drama stressing the accidental, Romeo
and Juliet could have failed either through the excessively melodramatic or the excessively didactic. The network of ironies and
the paradoxical effects of coincidences prevent the former, while
Romeo's initial effort to avoid a confrontation with Tybalt combined with his engagement only to avenge a friend prevents the
latter. The friar's Christian counsel of moderation is tragically useless in the face of Romeo and Juliet's conviction that
love fulfills the needs of both flesh and spirit.

1357   NOSWORTHY, J.M. "Two Angry Families of Verona." Shakespeare
         Quarterly 3 (1952):219-26.
         Argues that Romeo and Juliet was influenced by Henry
Porter's farce The Two Angry Women of Abingdon and that this
influence is responsible for the lack of tragic tone and substance in Shakespeare's play. Parallels of tone and style are
far more significant than parallels in language. Specifically,
Romeo and Juliet never develop as characters, the feud is more
comic than tragic, fate and tragic necessity are not blended,
the divergent styles are incongruous, and the surrounding action
is so filled with the frivolous and the trivial that no tragedy
can carry it.

1358   PETTET, E.C. "The Imagery of Romeo and Juliet." English 8
         (1950):121-26.
         Observes that the note of fate or premonition affects every
character and development in the narrative of Romeo and Juliet,
for example, Romeo's sudden misgiving mind in act 1, Juliet's
chilling comment about having no joy of her newfound love in
act 2, or Friar Lawrence's admonition against haste. With such

emphasis on fate Shakespeare not surprisingly makes frequent use
of star imagery; also, the pilot image recurs at three key
points--when Romeo decides to attend Capulet's ball, when he
first gains Juliet's love, and when he defies the stars in
act 5. The imagery of darkness also appears at significant
moments throughout the action.

1359   PORTER, JOSEPH A. "Mercutio's Brother." South Atlantic
       Review 49 (1984):31-41.
         Investigates the ghost character of Valentine, who is de-
scribed in Capulet's guest list as brother of Mercutio, but who
never appears in the play. While Shakespeare's source Arthur
Brooke is of no direct help, he does indirectly provide the
answer, for Brooke's Romeus is the source of minor incidents for
Shakespeare's Valentine. Romeo and Valentine were paired in
Shakespeare's mind; and in transforming Mercutio into a fuller
character, the playwright added Valentine to enhance the character's quality of brotherly affection.

1360   SIEGEL, PAUL N. "Christianity and the Religion of Love in
       Romeo and Juliet." Shakespeare Quarterly 12 (1961):371-92.
       Reprinted in Shakespeare in His Own Time and Ours, ed. Paul N.
       Siegel (South Bend, Ind.: Notre Dame University Press, 1969),
       pp. 69-107.
         Asserts that Shakespeare in Romeo and Juliet employs the
Renaissance concept that sexual love is a manifestation of divine
love to fuse the doctrine of the religion of love and the Christian concept of love into a complex unified pattern. At the conclusion of the play it is the lovers' paradise of the religion of
love rather than the Christian afterlife (with its associated
judgment on despair and suicide) that is envisioned. Romeo's
suicide, more specifically, is depicted as an act of meditative
deliberation in which love triumphs over death and hate, uniting
Romeo and his enemies in general reconciliation.

1361   SMITH, WARREN D. "Romeo's Final Dream." Modern Language
       Review 62 (1967):579-83.
         Asserts that the key to the resolution in Romeo and Juliet
is found in Romeo's dream in 5.1, in which he joyously recounts
that his lady found him dead and breathed life into him, making
him an emperor. These lines are not tragically ironic, as they
are usually regarded, but are symbolically true. Romeo in spirit
is revived by Juliet's kiss and becomes an emperor by the side of
his dead bride. In death and timeless bliss, they need no
golden statues as mortal mementos.

1362   SNYDER, SUSAN. "Romeo and Juliet: Comedy into Tragedy."
       Essays in Criticism 20 (1970):391-402.
         Claims that Romeo and Juliet contains a generic transforma-
tion from comedy to tragedy. Mercutio's death marks the turning
point from the comic game of the sexes to a sacrifice with the

lovers as its marked victims. The play has dramatic unity, despite the tonal shifts, in that the spectators are aware that premonitions of disaster precede Mercutio's death and hopes for avoiding disaster persist until the conclusion. The friar's attempt to adjust the situation to serve the course of love is the final hope for comedy.

1363   UTTERBACK, RAYMOND. "The Death of Mercutio." Shakespeare
       Quarterly 24 (1973):105-16.
          Views Mercutio's death as structurally significant in that it establishes a chain of events culminating in the final catastrophe. Specifically, his death (the tragic consequence) occurs because of a threatening situation, a provocation that actualizes the threat, the response to the provocation, the tragic consequence, and a blurring of the sense of responsibility. The same pattern occurs in three different instances--the death of Juliet, the death of Romeo, and the actions of Friar Lawrence. The force of destiny and the force of moral choice are delicately balanced throughout these patterns.

For discussion of Friar Lawrence, see entries 1343-44, 1348. For discussion of the language, see entries 1347, 1349, 1358. See also The Tragedies (entries 920-79) and 50, 56, 76, 78-79, 87, 93, 109, 125, 141-42, 150, 152, 172, 179, 182, 211, 231-32, 237-38, 242, 245, 256, 259, 263, 302, 317, 324, 545, 585, 711, 715, 799, 878, 1394.

TIMON OF ATHENS

Editions

1364   MAXWELL, J.C., ed. Timon of Athens. Cambridge: Cambridge
       University Press, 1957, 189 pp. Introduction reprinted in
       Shakespeare's Tragedies, ed. Laurence Lerner (Baltimore:
       Penguin, 1963), pp. 265-78.
          Provides extensive textual notes, a critical introduction, a discussion of the copy text, a section on stage history, and a glossary. This edition is based on the First Folio, for which the copy was probably Shakespeare's incomplete draft. Since the character of Timon is less individualized than those of other Shakespearean tragic protagonists, our response depends to a large extent on perceiving the figure as an example of a moral category, the abstract and general design. In technique the play mixes the quality of the moral and the realistic, and the result is, albeit imperfectly, to provoke the spectator's judgment, but not in Jonson's satiric spirit.

1365   OLIVER, H.J., ed. Timon of Athens. The Arden Shakespeare.
       London: Methuen; Cambridge, Mass.: Harvard University Press,
       1969, 155 pp.
            Includes discussion of the text, theories of authorship,
       the unfinished state of the play, sources, the date, and critical
       interpretations, as well as appendixes covering the stage history
       and selections from North's Life of Marcus Antonius and Life of
       Alcibiades and from Lucian's dialogue Timon the Misantrope. The
       text is based on the First Folio, for which the copy was a com-
       bination of Shakespeare's foul papers and Ralph Crane's transcript
       of them. Inconsistencies in major figures and in the verse has
       long prompted the observation that Timon is an unfinished play,
       as has the assumption that it was inserted in the folio only when
       the printers thought they would be unable to include Troilus and
       Cressida. Timon was probably either a first attempt at Lear or
       a harbinger of the romances. It was left unfinished, not because
       Shakespeare experienced emotional problems himself but because of
       dramatic problems in the subject and the essentially nondramatic
       nature of the narrative.

                                  Criticism

1366   BERGERON, DAVID M. "Alchemy and Timon of Athens." College
       Language Association Journal 13 (1970):364-73.
            Observes that the practice of alchemy is a kind of analogue
       for Timon of Athens, that in a metaphorical sense Timon is an
       alchemist who fails to achieve his goals and thus is unable to
       perceive the various distortions in the lives of the characters.
       Like the alchemical process of transformation, the play has a
       tripartite structure--Timon as a philanthropist, Timon in need,
       and Timon as misanthropist. Timon's life is an inversion of the
       alchemical process; debasement leads to despair from which there
       is no escape since there is no transmuting elixir.

1367   BRADBROOK, MURIEL C. "The Comedy of Timon: A Reveling Play
       of the Inner Temple." Renaissance Drama 9 (1966):83-103.
            Suggests that the anonymous play The Comedy of Timon is a
       law students' burlesque of Timon of Athens, probably presented
       at a Christmas revel at the Inner Temple. In order to create
       this reaction Shakespeare's play must obviously have been staged.
       Timon of Athens is a novel experiment, a spectacular pageant or
       show presented as a series of tableaux rather than a drama. The
       Comedy, probably presented in 1611, burlesques Shakespeare in the
       presentation of the excesses of the student cast as Christmas
       Lord.

1368   _____. The Tragic Pageant of Timon. Cambridge: Cambridge
       University Press, 1966, 38 pp. Reprinted in Muriel C.
       Bradbrook, Shakespeare The Craftsman (New York: Barnes &
       Noble; London: Chatto & Windus, 1969), pp. 144-67.

Suggests that Timon of Athens is perhaps not a full play at all, that it represents in its pageantic qualities Shakespeare's response to the challenge of moving to the new indoor theater at Blackfriars in 1609. This rough but corrupt draft experiments with the possibilities of the indoor lighted stage. Much is made of the scenic contrast between the city and the woods, and there are no battle scenes or mobs. Timon is a role, not a character, offering Burbage in the succession of moods the opportunity for a virtuoso performance.

1369   BUTLER, FRANCELIA. The Strange Critical Fortunes of "Timon of Athens." Ames: Iowa State University Press, 1966, 188 pp.
        Traces the history of diametrically opposed critical opinions of Timon of Athens concerning structure, characterization, meaning, whether Shakespeare left the play unfinished, whether Shakespeare wrote the play, and whether the play is a success. Such critical polarities suggest that two sets of critical values have been employed for analysis. Structural critics have adjudged the work clumsy, unfinished, perhaps a collaboration. Thematic critics, to the contrary, either disregard the structure of praise it as experimental, shaped to contain the thought. Through the structural diptych and the starkly drawn characterization, Shakespeare was perhaps attempting to force the spectator to participate actively in resolving the question of how the idealist fits into society.

1370   COOK, DAVID. "Timon of Athens." Shakespeare Survey 16 (1963):83-94.
        Asserts that Timon of Athens handles the theme of pride more objectively and offers less resolution of the issues raised than any other Shakespearean play. Timon's polar extremes prevent his gaining self-knowledge. He is in both halves of the play a study in human aberrations provoked by subtle pride. From playing the role of the god of men, he moves to the role of animal; in neither case will he accept man's real condition. The resolution comes not in Timon but in Alcibiades, who acts on having learned to accept and love the human condition for what it is.

1371   DRAPER, JOHN W. "The Psychology of Shakespeare's Timon." Modern Language Review 35 (1940):521-25.
        Observes that, whereas in the old Timon story the figure is suddenly transformed from a philanthrope to a misanthrope who wishes only ill on mankind, Shakespeare is concerned with lending the protagonist heroic qualities. Hence, more fault must fall on the people and the society who provoke his response and on Timon's fault as one of virtuous liberality rather than wasteful extravagance. Shakespeare also provides psychological credibility, describing Timon as a figure of sanguine humor. The quality in dire adversity gives way to choleric humor and in turn produces the melancholy attendant to his suicide.

1372   DRAPER, JOHN W. "Timon of Athens." Shakespeare Quarterly 8
        (1957):195-200.
            Describes Timon of Athens as a transitional play in which
        Shakespeare was experimenting with the destructive clash of the
        ideal and the real that informs the final tragedies. Nature's
        powers of healing and regeneration are also being explored.
        Timon is a larger-than-life character. Not only does his exces-
        sive reaction reflect man's individual flaws; he also reflects
        the impecunious lords ruined by extravagance in Shakespeare's
        own day. The drift of the later part of the play is toward a
        restoration of order in Alcibiades, though it leaves unsatis-
        factory the psychological evolution of Timon.

1373   ELLIS-FERMOR, UNA. "Timon of Athens: An Unfinished Play."
        Review of English Studies 18 (1942):270-83.
            Argues that Timon of Athens is either Shakespeare's re-
        working of an older play, his unfinished play completed by some-
        one else, an incredibly cut and corrupted folio text, or Shake-
        speare's unfinished work. Most likely it is the last, roughed
        out, worked over in part, and then abandoned. Such a theory
        accommodates the fact that the power of Shakespeare is felt
        throughout but that there are undeniable fragments and loose
        ends--primarily in the character of Timon, who is inadequate to
        the theme, and in the action, which does not integrate his fate
        and that of the other characters.

1374   GOMME, ANDOR. "Timon of Athens." Essays in Criticism 9
        (1959):107-25.
            Admits that Timon of Athens with its mood of cynicism that
        informs the whole movement of the verse seems to represent Shake-
        speare writing in a genre he did not find wholly congenial. The
        problem, in part, is our constant attempt to sentimentalize
        Shakespeare's tragic heroes and to sympathize with them; this we
        find difficult with Timon because his personality is unattractive.
        His failure to come to terms with his society is at once intel-
        lectual and moral. Timon and his society, in a word, appear too
        decadent for Shakespeare's purpose.

1375   HONIGMANN, E.A.J. "Timon of Athens." Shakespeare Quarterly
        12 (1961):3-20.
            Observes that two Timon traditions meet in Shakespeare's
        tragedy--Plutarch's account of his misanthropy and Lucian's de-
        scription of his prodigality reduced to poverty. Timon also
        mirrors details from Plutarch's accounts of both Antony and
        Coriolanus, a fact that reduces the possibility of a lost source
        for the play. Supposed structural weaknesses, if examined care-
        fully, prove fragmentary--the unsympathetic character of Timon,
        the episodic structure, the intellectual quality of the play.
        Quite probably Shakespeare was striving for a new kind of tragic
        effect for a coterie audience.

1376   KERNAN, ALVIN. The Cankered Muse: Satire of the English
        Renaissance. New Haven: Yale University Press, 1959, 261 pp.
            Describes Thersites (Troilus and Cressida) as the most in-
        tense image of the satiric character in English literature. Com-
        posed only of the fundamental energy that drives the satirist, he
        is developed unchecked to a point of loathing for all other char-
        acters. In Timon the satirist occupies center stage; a mutation
        from a creature of love, he is a penetrating analysis of the
        satiric sense of life. The grandeur of his titanic loathing is
        emphasized through the contrast with two lesser satiric figures,
        the poet and Apemantus. Since Timon cannot obliterate the world,
        he turns upon himself in suicide.

1377   MERCHANT, W. MOELWYN. "Timon of Athens and the Conceit of
        Art." Shakespeare Quarterly 6 (1955):249-57.
            Claims that the poet and the painter in their discussion
        and rivalry have an integral relationship to the major themes of
        Timon of Athens. In this technical flyting in which two profes-
        sionals argue the mystery of their crafts by stating the case for
        the status of their arts in society's intellectual economy,
        Shakespeare may echo da Vinci's argument that painting is a lib-
        eral art and that it provides an insight into reality not unlike
        philosophy and poetry. Timon in his generosity commends these
        artists for their ability; but, when he turns misanthropist, he
        banishes both, claiming that neither is capable of depicting the
        corruption that lies beneath the surface.

1378   PARROTT, THOMAS MARC. The Problem of "Timon of Athens."
        Oxford: Oxford University Press, 1923, 34 pp.
            Describes Timon of Athens as, at once, fascinating, per-
        plexing, and disappointing. It must forever remain a play for
        the study rather than the stage because it lacks sufficient
        creative power. Shakespeare probably started work on the play
        just after Lear in 1606, writing Timon's monologues in the last
        acts and sketching out the early acts. He then put it aside and
        moved on to Macbeth. After Shakespeare left the company Chapman
        was perhaps assigned to complete the play. Later the company had
        to overhaul it yet again. The resultant folio text is almost
        unintelligible.

1379   SCOTT, WILLIAM O. "The Paradox of Timon's Self-Consuming."
        Shakespeare Quarterly 35 (1984):290-304.
            Examines Timon's curses as an undoing of the verbal form he
        purports to observe. His effusions in prosperity invite being
        turned back on themselves, and he in a sense creates the shock of
        his friends' infidelity during his time of need. His anger
        quickly turns to bitterness, but he is ineffectual in buying with
        gold the enactment of his curse of a general destruction. His
        curses include himself in all mankind as well as the audience.
        Even in death he curses mankind in his epitaph, but he invites
        the continued curses of others as well.

1380   SOELLNER, ROLF. "Timon of Athens": Shakespeare's Pessimistic
       Tragedy. Columbus: Ohio State University Press, 1979,
       245 pp.
            Attempts to demonstrate that Timon of Athens is artistically
       deserving of its recent popularity as a play that speaks directly
       to our times. The play is not textually flawed; it is not some
       form of spiritual autobiography reflecting the neurotic state of
       the author; it does not require special pleading as a satire, a
       morality play, a domestic drama, or a pageant. On the other
       hand, neither does it represent the culmination of Shakespeare's
       artistry, as the rhapsodizing of G.W. Knight claims (entry 945).
       It is a tragedy set in the Renaissance context of the contemptus
       mundi of Christian humanism, a context best reflected in works
       like Pierre Boaistuau's Theatrum Mundi and Richard Barkley's A
       Discourse on the Felicity of Man. Timon's rejection of the world
       represents not merely the obverse of his flawed idealism but an
       awakening to the evil in rapacious and exploitative society. The
       tragedy lies in his failure to recognize his own overreactions,
       his inability to live with this knowledge without developing a
       misanthropy that is both microcosmic and macrocosmic.

1381   SWIGG, R. "Timon of Athens and the Growth of Discrimination."
       Modern Language Review 62 (1967):387-94.
            Believes that Timon of Athens delineates a moral scheme
       that demands the development of discrimination, the critical
       sense to determine the true from the false amidst mixed motives
       and ambiguous associations. Timon is the point of disequilibrium
       in the play, moving from mindless philanthropy to equally mind-
       less misanthropy. His diatribes in the woods illustrate his
       inability to perceive reality. The remedy is found in Alcibiades,
       who at the end combines youthful compassion with aged authority.

1382   WRIGHT, ERNEST HUNTER. The Authorship of "Timon of Athens."
       New York: Columbia University Press, 1910, 104 pp.
            Views Timon of Athens as one of Shakespeare's most per-
       plexing plays in its corrupt text, its indeterminate date, its
       questions of authorship, its relationship to Shakespeare's other
       work, its stage history, its wide variations in style, and its
       eccentric form. Evidence suggests divided authorship with some-
       one of limited talent reworking Shakespeare's original and un-
       finished material. The alien hand is far more visible in 1-3
       than 4-5, with spurious additions accounting for approximately
       one-third of the play.

See also The Tragedies (entries 920-79) and 80, 181, 205, 209, 212,
232, 995, 1447.

TITUS ANDRONICUS

Editions

1383   ADAMS, JOSEPH QUINCY, ed. Shakespeare's "Titus Andronicus":
       The First Quarto, 1594. New York and London: Charles
       Scribner's Sons, 1936, 122 pp.
           Reproduces in facsimile the unique copy in the Folger
       Shakespeare Library. The copy was discovered in 1904 in Sweden
       and was purchased by Henry Clay Folger. Ownership of the volume
       can be traced from the seller, Petrus Johannes Krafft, back
       through three generations to Charles Robson (d. 1794), who came
       to Sweden from Scotland. The quarto text is now able to correct
       emended lines in the last three leaves of the previously pub-
       lished second quarto (1600). Also discussed are the date, the
       Longleat manuscript with the sketch of Alarbus, and the newly
       discovered source--a chapbook entitled The History of Titus
       Andronicus (preserved in an eighteenth-century version).

1384   MAXWELL, J.C., ed. Titus Andronicus. The Arden Shakespeare.
       London: Methuen; Cambridge, Mass.: Harvard University Press,
       1953, 132 pp.
           Includes discussion of the text, date, authorship, source,
       and literary interpretations. The text is based on the first
       quarto, for which the copy was probably Shakespeare's foul
       papers. The Longleat manuscript contains a drawing representing
       Tamora and her two sons on their knees pleading to Titus. No
       source survives in a form that we know to have been available to
       Shakespeare but a mid-eighteenth century chapbook (The History
       of Titus Andronicus) may reflect a pre-Shakespearean version of
       the story. Titus as a tragic figure foreshadows both Othello and
       Lear. Shakespeare has both a sense of the play as a whole and a
       sense of the individual episode, though he still has not mastered
       the interrelationship; it was not yet determined whether he would
       "steer clear of violent episodic melodrama on the one hand and
       exagerratedly Ovidian narrative in dialogue on the other"
       (p. xxxviii).

1385   WILSON, JOHN DOVER, ed. Titus Andronicus. Cambridge:
       Cambridge University Press, 1948, 173 pp.
           Provides extensive textual notes, a critical introduction,
       a discussion of the copy text, a section on stage history, and a
       glossary. This edition is based on the first quarto, for which
       the copy was probably Shakespeare's foul papers. Titus Androni-
       cus is a tragedy of blood, a kind of crude melodrama that grew
       in the hands of Shakespeare and Webster to tragedy of the highest
       order. The hands of both Peele and Shakespeare are evident in
       the play. While there are human touches such as Aaron's protec-
       tive instincts for his black child and Lavinia's pleas to Tamora
       for mercy, much of the action seems to represent a burlesquing of
       the popular melodramatic form.

Criticism

1386   BAKER, HOWARD. Induction to Tragedy: A Study in the Develop-
        ment of Form in "Gorboduc," "The Spanish Tragedy," and "Titus
        Andronicus." Baton Rouge: Louisiana State University Press,
        1939, 247 pp.
            Describes Titus Andronicus as an Elizabethan transformation
        of the Philomela story, the transformation occurring through ad-
        ditions of plot fragments from the stories of Virginia, Lucrece,
        and Coriolanus. Rhetorical flourishes are derived from Virgil,
        and Aaron stems from the Vice of the morality plays. The flaw
        is that the treatment of character is superficial with Titus
        largely impotent before Aaron's wickedness. The claim for ex-
        tensive and specific Senecan influence is seriously questioned;
        the pyramidal de casibus structure of medieval drama is clearly
        exemplified in the play.

1387   BOLTON, JOSEPH H.G. "Titus Andronicus: Shakespeare at
        Thirty." Studies in Philology 30 (1933):208-24.
            Argues that Shakespeare in Titus Andronicus was carefully
        and systematically revising the work of another writer, that four
        acts of the play (1-4) reflect his artistic ability on the eve of
        his thirtieth birthday. The original was probably written for
        Pembroke's Men and, sold to Henslowe in 1593, was revised by
        Shakespeare. Acted by Sussex's Men early in 1594, it was then
        submitted to John Danter for publication. While critics have
        attacked crudities of action, they have failed to appreciate the
        careful and complex plotting of a young playwright in an age of
        general immaturity in drama. (See entry 1392.)

1388   BROUDE, RONALD. "Four Forms of Vengeance in Titus Andronicus."
        Journal of English and Germanic Philology 78 (1979):494-507.
            Asserts that the play is an anatomy of revenge exemplifying
        four forms of vengeance--human sacrifice to placate ghosts of the
        slain, the vendetta of blood revenge to avenge past injury, state
        justice or a civic response to transgression to maintain civil
        order, and divine vengeance by heavenly intervention. The gen-
        eral movement in the play is away from the self-government whose
        tenets underlie the first two to the principles of state justice
        that Lucius proclaims at the end, made possible by the actions of
        Titus that he perceives as divinely ordered.

1389   CUTTS, JOHN P. "Shadow and Substance: Structural Unity in
        Titus Andronicus." Comparative Drama 2 (1968):161-72.
            Suggests that the unifying dramatic pattern in Titus
        Andronicus is based on the Renaissance topos frequently found in
        iconography: the mistaking of the shadow for the substance.
        Titus, in making mistake after mistake, is unaware that his
        comprehension is faulty. In allowing Alarbus to be butchered,
        for example, he in fact is attempting to appease the shadow of

his own ambitions. When Tamora, disguised as Revenge, speaks to
him, he fails to recognize the shadow of his own vengeful heart.

1390   ETTIN, ANDREW V. "Shakespeare's First Roman Tragedy." ELH 37
        (1970):325-41.
            Views Titus Andronicus as both an acceptance and a testing
        of the literary tradition of Rome as representative of the values
        of civilization, especially those concerning law, justice, and
        political order. While embodying these concepts in the opening
        scenes describing Rome as conqueror of a warring tribe and in
        Tamora and Aaron's bestial revenge against Titus, Shakespeare
        also utilizes Ovidian and Senecan allusions to signify darkness,
        cruelty, and barbarism in Rome as well. The Roman characters
        progressively come to hide human passion behind Senecan stoicism
        and Ovidian rhetoric.

1391   HAMILTON, A.C. "Titus Andronicus: The Form of Shakespearean
        Tragedy." Shakespeare Quarterly 14 (1963):201-13.
            Finds thematic unity in the development of Titus as a
        tragic figure. Honored as a conquering hero in act 1, he over-
        reaches himself in his godlike decision to allow the sacrifice of
        Alarbus. Following a period of fury and grief, he recognizes his
        responsibility for placing the tyrant on the throne and seeks
        justice. He is pitied by both the messenger who brings his hand
        and his sons' heads and by Lucius and his grandson at the end of
        the play. Albeit in sketchy terms, Titus is humanized in the
        course of the action.

1392   HASTINGS, WILLIAM T. "The Hard-Boiled Shakespeare."
        Shakespeare Association Bulletin 17 (1942):114-25.
            Claims in the face of those who argue that Shakespeare
        could never have penned the atrocities of Titus Andronicus that
        the play is rewarding because of this very uncharacteristic na-
        ture. Shakespeare in other plays certainly does not eschew hor-
        rors. The key is the playwright's young age and the nature of
        the other tragedy being written at this time. Both the general
        structure and the nature of the characterization are a cut above
        it, and it is a mistake to assume that Shakespeare was incapable
        of the hard-boiled mood of the play. It is an excellent example
        of youthful creative power. (See entry 1387.)

1393   HUFFMAN, CLIFFORD CHALMERS. "Titus Andronicus: Metamorphosis
        and Renewal." Modern Language Review 67 (1972):730-41.
            Considers the resolution of Titus Andronicus to consist of
        Rome's returning from an Iron Age of injustice and violence to a
        Golden Age of justice and peace. Barbarous Roman justice against
        Alarbus at the outset sets in motion a chain of atrocities, and
        Lucius pointedly pursues the initial act of cruelty. When he
        returns as leader of an army of the Goths in act 5, he brings not
        warfare but a restoration of order. He has no direct association
        with Titus's vindictive actions and thus stands relatively

untainted at the end of the play as a spokesman for the new day
in Rome.

1394   HUNTER, G.K. "Shakespeare's Earliest Tragedies: Titus
        Andronicus and Romeo and Juliet." Shakespeare Survey 27
        (1974):1-9.
            Views Titus Andronicus and Romeo and Juliet as experiments
        in which Shakespeare marks out the opposite poles of his tragic
        boundaries, with Titus reflecting Senecan influence and Romeo the
        influence of the Italian novella. The structure of the plays is
        similar in several ways. Both open with a scene of discord into
        which an authority figure enters (Titus, Prince Escalus); both
        involve families in conflict; and in both a tomb is a central
        physical and symbolic prop.

1395   MOWAT, BARBARA A. "Lavinia's Message: Shakespeare and Myth."
        Renaissance Papers, 1981, pp. 55-69.
            Sees the scene in which Lavinia turns the pages of Ovid to
        the tale of Philomela as Shakespeare's calling attention to the
        deliberate parallels in that account and his play. Since the
        incident occurs halfway through the action, it encourages the
        spectators to anticipate events that will follow and to attribute
        to Titus and Lavinia the anguish and desperation of Procne and
        Philomela as they move toward their revenge. It is the most
        obvious of Shakespeare's many uses of myth for structural pur-
        poses. The Merchant of Venice is also considered in some detail.

1396   PRICE, HEREWARD T. "The Authorship of Titus Andronicus."
        Journal of English and Germanic Philology 42 (1943):55-81.
            Reexamines the evidence of Shakespeare's authorship of
        Titus Andronicus, reviewing the work of disclaimers since
        Ravenscroft in 1687, especially that of the revisionists in the
        early twentieth century. The parallels in Titus and other
        Shakespearean works in style, meter, and construction are numer-
        ous and convincing. The acknowledged fact about Shakespeare's
        early work is its unevenness. Unlike the work of Marlowe,
        Greene, or Peele, the play possesses "intensity of conflict, the
        power to give variety to unity" (p. 81).

1397   REESE, JACK E. "The Formalization of Horror in Titus
        Andronicus." Shakespeare Quarterly 21 (1970):77-84.
            Suggests that Shakespeare deliberately utilizes several
        methods of formalization to abate the impact of wanton bloodshed
        and horror in Titus Andronicus. The characters, for example, are
        highly stylized as good or evil; also there is a careful and con-
        sistent system of balances in the plot, both in the elements of
        the action and in the symmetry of stage scenes. Finally, repeti-
        tion of words, phrases, scenes, and images functions as a form of
        stylization. (See entry 1401.)

1398   SARGENT, RALPH M.   "The Source of Titus Andronicus." Studies
        in Philology 46 (1949):167-83.
            Examines the prose history, The History of Titus Androni-
        cus, extant in an eighteenth-century chapbook, as the source for
        Shakespeare's play. Most probably the chapbook is a reprint of
        the actual prose history and ballad that existed in the sixteenth
        century. Clearly its origin is independent of the play. A care-
        ful consideration of the work strengthens the supposition that
        Shakespeare worked from it, although he markedly alters the
        political significance, making the dominant motif the injustices
        suffered by the loyal Andronici at the hands of a wicked queen
        and her iniquitous paramour.

1399   SOMMERS, ALAN.   "'Wilderness of Tigers': Structure and
        Symbolism in Titus Andronicus." Essays in Criticism 10
        (1960):275-89.
            Views the conflict in Titus Andronicus as a struggle be-
        tween Rome (civilization) and primitive nature (barbarism).
        Titus, by committing errors, releases the conflict, and chaos
        ensues in his mind and in Rome. Tamora and Aaron, agents of
        barbarism, are triumphant; but eventually order is restored
        through Titus's revenge--the sacrifice of Lavinia and the death
        ritual of the feast. Lavinia's mutilation symbolizes the frus-
        tration of self-conscious virtue, and Tamora's cannibalistic meal
        symbolizes self-devouring appetite.

1400   TOOLE, WILLIAM B.   "The Collision of Action and Character
        Patterns in Titus Andronicus." Renaissance Papers, 1971,
        pp. 25-39.
            Finds Titus Andronicus structurally flawed in that the
        pattern of the spectators' mounting sympathy for Titus is blocked
        by a similar pattern depicting his mounting horrors. The pattern
        of action, more specifically, based on revenge and counter-
        revenge, involves the sacrifice of Alarbus, the murder of his own
        son, and the cannibalistic banquet for Tamora. The pattern of
        character, on the other hand, involves our increasing pity for
        Titus in his grief and seeming madness. The two patterns artis-
        tically work at cross-purposes.

1401   WAITH, EUGENE M.   "The Metamorphosis of Violence in Titus
        Andronicus." Shakespeare Survey 10 (1957):34-49.
            Asserts that Shakespeare's extreme use of violence and the
        excessive adornment of language in Titus Andronicus is the con-
        sequence of Shakespeare's attempting, with only partial success,
        to adapt Ovidian narrative techniques to the stage. The tales
        in the Metamorphoses describe the power of intense emotional
        states to transform individuals beyond their normal selves.
        Similarly, Shakespeare in Titus and Lavinia depicts the dehuman-
        izing effects of passion produced by extreme outrage, a movement
        toward a metamorphosis of character that transcends the limits of

individuality and becomes a phenomenon of nature or personified
emotion.   (See entry 1397.)

Stage History

1402   METZ, G. HAROLD. "The Stage History of Titus Andronicus."
       Shakespeare Quarterly 27 (1976):154-69.
            Notes that, while Titus Andronicus has been among the least
       frequently produced of Shakespeare's plays, there have been four
       periods of relative popularity--in the years around the turn of
       the seventeenth century by Sussex's, Chamberlain's, and the
       King's Men, in the Restoration period as revised by Edward
       Ravenscroft, in the 1840s as revised by the black actor Ira
       Aldridge, and in the twentieth century, especially the last
       thirty years. Among the most significant productions are those
       directed by Peter Brook in 1955 by the Royal Shakespeare Company
       (with Laurence Olivier and Vivien Leigh) and by Joseph Papp in
       1967 by the New York Shakespeare Festival Theater.

See also The Tragedies (entries 920-79) and 78, 97, 211, 215, 219,
229, 281, 323-24, 488, 499, 589.

VI. The Romances

1403   CUTTS, JOHN P.   Rich and Strange: A Study of Shakespeare's
       Last Plays. Pullman: Washington State University Press,
       1968, 106 pp.
            Views the final plays as an extension of the experience of
       the major tragedies in that they utilize dream texture, mirror
       techniques, and visions heightened by masque, song, and dance--
       in a word, the framework of a romance--to heighten man's vision
       of himself. This juxtaposition of style and rhetoric, of fanci-
       ful elegance and vulgar grotesqueness, dramatizes man's desire to
       hide his true nature behind a mask of putative innocence.
       Pericles, Cymbeline, Posthumous, Leontes, Prospero are all
       flawed; they suffer a sea change that permits them to accept life
       for the paradoxical mixture of good and evil that it is.

1404   EDWARDS, PHILIP.   "Shakespeare's Romances: 1900-1957."
       Shakespeare Survey 11 (1958):1-18.
            Describes twentieth-century criticism of the romances as
       showing no continuous course but rather as a series of different
       vectors from a different starting point. Some thirty studies are
       discussed, not so much to focus on a particular critic as to
       illustrate the four or five critical approaches and the divergent
       conclusions reached by some critics using the same method. Ap-
       proaches include the biographical, the theatrical, the myth-
       symbol-allegorical, the post-tragic and Christian interpretation,
       and the romantic with emphasis on form and structure.

1405   FELPERIN, HOWARD.   Shakespearean Romance. Princeton:
       Princeton University Press, 1972, 319 pp.
            Explores the poetics and problematics of Shakespeare's
       romances. Part 1 deals with the specific definition and de-
       lineation of the form, part 2 with the relationship to the re-
       mainder of the canon. Three modes of romance converge in Shake-
       speare--the classical Greek romance of the third century, the
       chivalric romance of the Middle Ages, and the romance of medieval
       religious drama. Basically Shakespeare's romances involve

stories in which characters overcome difficulties against enor-
mous odds; near or at the center are figures resembling the
morality hero. Salvation or reconciliation and sexual union are
inevitably accompanied by family reunion and international
alliance.

1406   FRYE, NORTHROP. A Natural Perspective: The Development of
        Shakespearean Comedy and Romance. New York: Columbia Univer-
        sity Press, 1965, 159 pp.
            Focuses on the recurring images and structural devices of
        Shakespeare's romances, the genuine culmination of Shakespeare's
        dramatic achievement. Declaring himself an Odyssean critic
        attracted to comedy and romance, Frye observes that Shakespearean
        comedy is highly stylized, nondidactic, and consciously primitive
        in its origins both dramatically and psychologically. The in-
        ternal structure is consistent with its logic, utilizing the
        rhythms of atonement, saturnalia, and festivity. In the romances
        the dramatic conventions are descended from myths--all moving
        from anticomic to comic, from loss to discovery of identity--and
        all involving a movement through the green world toward the
        "rebirth and renewal of the powers of nature" (p. 119).

1407   GESNER, CAROL. Shakespeare and the Greek Romance: A Study of
        Origins. Lexington: University Press of Kentucky, 1970,
        216 pp.
            Examines the Greek romance tradition in Boccaccio and
        Cervantes and then relates Shakespeare to the overall tradition.
        This material is a major strand of Renaissance narrative prose
        and drama; many of the motifs and patterns of marvelously ad-
        venturous story, especially those calculated to produce horror or
        some spectacular effect, derive from the Greek romances. Shake-
        speare's romances, unified in tone, theme, and incident, all make
        direct use of the tradition, Pericles, for example, adapting the
        narrative of Apollonius of Tyre; Cymbeline, a mixture of several;
        The Winter's Tale, Heliodorus's Aethiopica (by way of Greene's
        Pandosto); and The Tempest, Daphnis and Chloe along with pastoral
        motifs from Longus.

1408   HARTWIG, JOAN. Shakespeare's Tragicomic Vision. Baton Rouge:
        Louisiana State University Press, 1972, 196 pp.
            Stresses the artifice in the romances and the ambivalence
        of response provoked by these plays. Each contains similar nar-
        rative characteristics--a lost child, sea journeys, characters
        miraculously resurrected, a reconciliation through the agency of
        young people, the fulfillment of aspirations in a manner that
        leaves characters and spectators amazed. Elements of comedy and
        tragedy are mixed to produce a kind of emotional dislocation.
        The dramatic logic is that conventional modes of representation
        are inadequate for the values of these plays. The stylized
        theatrical fiction becomes a metaphor for examining genuine emo-
        tional issues of familial and marital relationships.

1409   KNIGHT, G. WILSON. The Crown of Life: Essays in Interpreta-
        tion of Shakespeare's Final Plays. Oxford: Oxford University
        Press, 1947, 336 pp.
             Argues that the final plays, far from being an artistic
        retrogression, represent an advancement beyond tragedy to Shake-
        speare's deepest reading of human affairs against destiny. The
        binding principles of tempest-music opposition and Elizabethan
        nationalism are vital to any full appreciation of these plays.
        In The Winter's Tale Leontes as a consequence of his sin must
        endure a kind of purgatory; by act 5 a figure of accomplished
        repentance, he is prepared for reunion with the resurrected
        Hermione. For all its narrative untidiness, Shakespeare "offers
        nothing greater in tragic psychology, humour, pastoral romance"
        (p. 128). The Tempest traces the spiritual progress from pain
        and despairing thought through Stoic acceptance to a serene and
        mystic joy; it is, in effect, an interpretation of Shakespeare's
        personal world, a personification of poetry itself.

1410   LONG, JOHN H. Shakespeare's Use of Music: The Final Comedies.
        Gainesville: University of Florida Press, 1961, 159 pp.
             Observes that Shakespeare uses music in the comedies to
        underscore climactic or crucial scenes, to render supernatural
        effects more sharply, and to symbolize abstract or psychological
        ideas. All three uses converge in the romances, dealing with a
        character's recognition of a truth concerning divine providence.
        Pericles's perception of divine intercession, for example, is
        signaled by the music of the spheres; so, too, music in Cymbeline
        occurs when members of Posthumous's family importune Jupiter's
        intercession. Music throughout the romances is used to indicate
        harmony, whether within oneself, between men, or between men and
        the gods.

1411   McFARLAND, THOMAS. Shakespeare's Pastoral Comedy. Chapel
        Hill: University of North Carolina Press, 1972, 218 pp.
             Argues that the pastoral element is not merely superimposed
        on comedy by Shakespeare but that it is fused with it to create a
        stronger and deeper vision of life uniquely capable of artisti-
        cally depicting a paradise. In Shakespeare's pastoral comedies
        the common thematic thread is that characters must come to terms
        with the reciprocity of social and religious concerns. The stuff
        of tragedy at the outset of As You Like It, transferred to Arden,
        is softened to deviance and resolved by marriage. In The Tempest
        the ambience of the isle provides a favorable setting for trans-
        forming crimes to willful faults subject to correction by tem-
        pered punishment.

1412   MOWAT, BARBARA A. The Dramaturgy of Shakespeare's Romances.
        Athens: University of Georgia Press, 1976, 163 pp.
             Views Shakespeare's romances as a conscious blend of
        representational and presentational modes, creating "open form"
        drama with special theatrical experiences. Comic devices con-
        front tragic passions; the realistic or mimetic action, the

artificial or spectacular; the dramatic, the narrative. Generically, stylistically, dramaturgically, the romances combine the joy and vivacity of romantic comedy with the passion and power of the tragedies. Individual chapters are devoted to Cymbeline, The Winter's Tale, and The Tempest.

1413   PETERSON, DOUGLAS L. Time, Tide, and Tempest: A Study of Shakespeare's Romances. San Marino, Calif.: Huntington Library, 1973, 259 pp.
        Argues that Shakespeare in the romances was not following the style of Beaumont and Fletcher or retreating into the happy comedy of his youth but instead was seeking for an effective manner of dealing with metaphysical and epistemological problems broached by the tragedies. The result, a radically new form of tragicomedy, by appropriating the improbable fictions of romance to plots depicting genuinely destructive evil celebrates the restorative power of human love in the vision of a morally coherent universe that defies growing Jacobean skepticism.

1414   SMITH, HALLETT. Shakespeare's Romances: A Study of Some Ways of the Imagination. San Marino, Calif.: Huntington Library, 1972, 244 pp.
        Views the romances as a natural outgrowth of Shakespeare's experience in writing comedy and tragedy. Full of theatrical spectacle and elaborate devices, these plays were written with an eye for the court and the private stage as well as for the Globe. Particular attention is also directed to the heroine, her symbolic names, the relationship between her innocence and pastoralism, and to the romantic tradition in general. In the tragedies and problem comedies, the sacrifice of the younger generation leads to redemption and salvation. In the romances, in which the appearance is evil but the reality is good, the younger generation is the full recipient of the cathartic wisdom and joy of the older.

1415   THORNDIKE, ASHLEY H. The Influence of Beaumont and Fletcher upon Shakespeare. Worcester, Mass.: Wood, 1901, 176 pp.
        Maintains that the romances written by Beaumont and Fletcher and by Shakespeare were not the end results of the development of current forms or of manifest dramatic tendencies, but were an altogether new artistic form. An examination of the order of composition of the plays and especially of the influence of Philaster on Cymbeline reveals that Beaumont and Fletcher initiated this movement and that Shakespeare was their debtor. Shakespeare, writing with a keen eye for theatrical success, was willing to adapt his work to follow current fashions, and this fashion under his genius produced The Winter's Tale and The Tempest. (See entries 173A, 276.)

1416   TILLYARD, E.M.W. Shakespeare's Last Plays. London: Chatto &
        Windus, 1938, 85 pp.
            Views Shakespeare's purpose in the romances as to supple-
        ment tragedy, a process begun in Antony and Cleopatra and
        Coriolanus. This concentration on the regenerative process in
        tragedy involves a destruction of the old order and the reshaping
        into a new. Specifically, the pattern in each romance moves from
        prosperity to destruction to recreation. The motifs of repen-
        tance and regeneration lend a tone of religious mystery.

1417   TRAVERSI, DEREK A. Shakespeare: The Last Phase. New York:
        Harcourt, Brace, 1954, 272 pp.
            Stresses the significance in the romances of poetic drama,
        a movement away from realism and toward a subsuming of character
        and action in a symbolic unity or expanded image. The dominant
        pattern is a movement from loss to reconciliation, involving the
        "divisions created in love and friendship by the passage of time
        and the action of 'blood' and of the final healing of these
        divisions" (p. 107). Characters and the situation in The Tempest,
        the logical consummation of Shakespeare's art, are clearly sym-
        bolic with tragedy of human passion followed by a period of trial
        issuing in redemption.

1418   UPHAUS, ROBERT W. Beyond Tragedy: Structure and Experience
        in Shakespeare's Romances. Lexington: University Press of
        Kentucky, 1981, 150 pp.
            Argues that Shakespeare's romances develop a concept of
        life beyond tragedy by placing a greater value upon the process
        of the life cycle than upon individual life. Inherent to this
        continuing cycle is a sense in which time is reversible and
        characters are offered a means of expiation short of death.
        Pericles is a skeletal romance, utilizing all of the features but
        without counterpoint or complication. Cymbeline parodies the
        very conventions upon which it is constructed. The Winter's Tale
        invests the elements of romance with a profound human signifi-
        cance by directly juxtaposing the tragic perspective of 1-3 with
        the providential view of 5 and developing the pastoral comedy of
        4 as a means of transition between the two. The Tempest enacts
        the imaginative descent of the experience of romance into areas
        more accessible to reason; if the sea change for Alonso and
        Sebastian is mental, it is physical for Prospero, who must aban-
        don his magic in order to be fully reabsorbed into human society.

1419   YATES, FRANCES A. Shakespeare's Last Phase: A New Approach.
        London: Routledge & Kegan Paul, 1975, 140 pp.
            Theorizes that the imagery of the last plays directly
        relates them to a conscious and nostalgic revival of Elizabethan-
        ism centered on Prince Henry and Elizabeth, children of James I.
        Cymbeline, for example, is seen symbolically as a reenactment of
        the Tudor mythology and the analysis of Henry VIII focuses on
        imperial reform. The mystical atmosphere of the romances suggests

the influence of the Rosicrucian movement in Germany, and in
Prospero one sees a renewed respect for the magus figure.

See also entries 72, 233, 255, 265, 272, 312, 315, 322, 333, 512, 516.

CYMBELINE

Reference Works

1420   JACOBS, HENRY E., comp. Cymbeline. Garland Shakespeare
        Bibliographies, 3. New York and London: Garland Publishing,
        1982, 591 pp.
            Contains 1,379 annotated entries, representing virtually
        all publications on the play from 1940 through 1980, along with
        the most significant items of scholarship prior to 1940. The
        categories, each arranged chronologically, are criticism, sources,
        dating, textual studies, bibliographies, editions, productions,
        and translations. A brief introductory essay traces the history
        of recent criticism and research.

Editions

1421   FURNESS, HENRY HOWARD, ed. The Tragedie of Cymbeline. A New
        Variorum Edition of Shakespeare. Philadelphia: J.B. Lippin-
        cott, 1913, 523 pp.
            Uses the First Folio as the copy text. On each page, for
        that portion of the text, provides variant readings, textual
        notes, and general critical commentary. Following the text are
        sections on the date of composition, the sources, the text of
        Durfey's version, and criticisms.

1422   MAXWELL, J.C., ed. Cymbeline. Cambridge: Cambridge Univer-
        sity Press, 1960, 246 pp.
            Provides extensive textual notes, a critical introduction
        (covering matters of date and authenticity, sources, and the play
        itself), a discussion of the copy text, a section on stage his-
        tory, and a glossary. This edition is based on the First Folio,
        for which the copy was probably a transcript of the promptbook.
        The term tragicomedy has been found useful to describe the play's
        unusual combination of elements; the serious matter is undercut
        by the comic and pastoral. Like the other last plays it is con-
        cerned with loss and recovery, reconciliation and rebirth, the
        sense of the deeper rhythms of life.

1423   NOSWORTHY, J.M., ed. Cymbeline. The Arden Shakespeare.
        London: Methuen; Cambridge, Mass.: Harvard University Press,
        1955, 216 pp.
            Includes discussion of the text, sources, authenticity, the
        experimental quality, style, imagery, significance, the relation-
        ship to Philaster, and literary interpretations, as well as

appendixes featuring information on the stage history and the
songs and selections from Holinshed and other sources. The text
is based on the First Folio, for which the copy was probably a
scribe's transcript of difficult foul papers which had preceded
the promptbook. Shakespeare, in fashioning a straightforward
romantic plot, apparently worked from a variety of sources in a
colonizing effort without a reputable model, one that influenced
Fletcher's Philaster. As a romance the play is highly experimental; at times a tragic view of life dominates his portrayal of
character, and on occasion symbolic characters lapse into a
realism that is detrimental to the comic tone. Clearly he is
moving toward a new kind of tragicomic expression.

Criticism

1424   BROCKBANK, J.P. "History and Histrionics in Cymbeline."
        Shakespeare Survey 11 (1958):42-49. Reprinted in Four Cen-
        turies of Shakespearian Criticism, ed. Frank Kermode (New
        York: Avon, 1965), pp. 277-89.
        Argues that Cymbeline should be regarded primarily as a
historical romance in that it attempts to express certain truths
about the processes that have shaped Britain's past. Cymbeline,
more particularly, describes a brazen world transmuted to golden
by the agency of miraculous providence. Along with Henry VIII it
is the last chronicle fruits of Shakespeare's art. Cloten and
the Queen represent a range of views threatening the integrity of
the court. Imogen represents an innocence that must pass through
animal barbarism (Cloten) and duplicity (Posthumous), and the
agreement to pay tribute to Rome signals the approach of the
Golden Age.

1425   HOENIGER, F. DAVID. "Irony and Romance in Cymbeline."
        Studies in English Literature 2 (1962):219-28.
        Argues that the pervasively ironic perspective in Cymbeline
affects the play's characterization and tone, its structure, and
its vision. Dramatic irony may be comforting and amusing in matters such as the spectators' knowledge of the true identity of
the King's sons, but it is something else again when it provokes
Imogen's despair over the headless body of what she presumes to
be Posthumous but we know to be Cloten or when it underscores the
vulnerability of honest women in the bedchamber scene. Only at
the end does mockery yield to vision, appearance to reality and
joy, as irony dissolves into romance.

1426   JONES, EMRYS. "Stuart Cymbeline." Essays in Criticism 11
        (1961):84-99.
        Acknowledges that Cymbeline appears to abound in wild in-
congruities and apparent absurdities. For Shakespeare's audience,
however, the play had special meaning. Not only does the action
of the play, moving from division and war to harmony and peace,
prepare historically for the universal time of peace at Christ's

birth; it also pays topical tribute to James's strenuous peace-
making policy. The arrival of James was a fulfillment of prophecy; a second Arthur, uniting England and Scotland, James
delighted in also being called a second Augustus, the pacific
emperor under whom Christ was born.

1427   KIRSCH, ARTHUR C. "Cymbeline and Coterie Dramaturgy." ELH 34
       (1967):285-306.
       Maintains that the characteristics of Cymbeline and other
romances are determined in part through the developing pattern of
drama in the private theater. Central to such drama is the
principle of discontinuity, a sensationally mingled tone creating
both empathy and critical detachment. Cymbeline is frankly experimental, exploring the techniques and implications of self-
conscious dramaturgy in Posthumous's sudden change and counter-
change, the arrant villainy of Iachimo, the melodramatic exploitation of Imogen's distress, the bewildering montage of events.
(See entry 1430.)

1428   LAWRENCE, JUDIANA. "Natural Bonds and Artistic Coherence in
       the Ending of Cymbeline." Shakespeare Quarterly 35 (1984):
       440-60.
       Considers the concluding scenes of Cymbeline to be neither
straight romance nor parody, but an examination of the means and
ends of fiction. Balancing on the edge between solemnity and
farce, these scenes hold in delicate suspense a response of
affirmation and skepticism, a tension between engagement and
detachment that informs all of his work and much of the literary
output of the Renaissance. The play's ironic and elusive tone
constitutes through its constant emphasis on chance and changed
perceptions an artistic triumph over both the unreality of the
mode and the rigidity of its form.

1429   MARSH, D.R.C. The Recurring Miracle: A Study of "Cymbeline"
       and the Last Plays. Pietermaritzburg: University of Natal
       Press, 1962, 197 pp.
       Argues that Cymbeline is an affirmation of life, revealing
death to be an illusion primarily through the influence of Imogen
as the active agent of truth and her role in the restoration of
the younger generation. Neither botched work as a trial run for
later drama nor the efforts of boredom, Cymbeline like all the
romances is a stylized examination of love as self-denial and
self-discipline that produces a miraculous sense of renewal.

1430   MOWAT, BARBARA A. "Cymbeline: Crude Dramaturgy and Aesthetic
       Distance." Renaissance Papers, 1967, pp. 39-48.
       Notes that in many respects Cymbeline appears to be, how-
ever artful in plot, deficient in dramatic technique. Repeated
use of expository direct address to set forth the story, soliloquies scattered among minor figures, undisguised entrance an-
nouncements and exit signals--such devices seem to be a throwback

to the presentational drama of Shakespeare's early years. Instead, they are deliberate theatrical devices that force the
spectator to recognize the dramatic illusion and thus to view the
romance from a distance that prevents close emotional identification. (See entry 1427.)

1431   SMITH, WARREN D. "Cloten with Caius Lucius." Studies in
        Philology 49 (1952):185-94.
             Argues that Cloten is not inconsistent as a despicable lout
        who suddenly assumes political prudence in refusing to pay trib-
        ute to Rome, that in defying Rome and advocating war he is acting
        contrary to the desires of Cymbeline. His attitude toward
        Lucius, moreover, directly opposes the traditional courtesy
        afforded visiting dignitaries, and all of his speeches fall far
        below the ideal of modesty. His attitude toward Lucius is
        totally consistent with his villainous character elsewhere in the
        play.

1432   STEPHENSON, A.A. "The Significance of Cymbeline." Scrutiny
        10 (1942):329-38.
             Explores the unusual nature of the imagery in Cymbeline,
        more specifically its vagueness and triteness. The pervading
        idea is that of worth or value as applied to honor, fidelity, and
        chastity. The contrast of inner and outer, real and apparent
        worth is constantly held before the spectator--that between birth
        and position, that between beauty and integrity of spirit. The
        persistence of this value imagery reveals Shakespeare's pre-
        occupation with the idea of human perfection, a vision involving
        the rejection of dualism and the humanization of experience.

1433   SWANDER, HOMER. "Cymbeline and the 'Blameless Hero.'" ELH 31
        (1964):259-70.
             Observes that W.W. Lawrence is correct in describing
        Posthumous as a variation of the blameless hero of popular story
        who reacts ethically and courteously to the accusation of in-
        fidelity in the betrothed and who eventually is reunited with
        her. In certain respects, though, Posthumous is quite unlike the
        hero of tradition. Shakespeare exposes in acts 1-4 an essential
        meanness in the man that makes him unworthy of Imogen, and only
        in act 5 when he overcomes the inadequacies of the convention
        itself does he achieve a truly excellent quality.

1434   THORNE, WILLIAM BARRY. "Cymbeline: 'Lopp'd Branches' and the
        Concept of Regeneration." Shakespeare Quarterly 20 (1960):
        143-59.
             Views Cymbeline as a sophisticated extension of themes from
        the early comedies interweaving a serious element in that, with
        its folk materials and national orientation, it is deliberately
        holding up a glass to Elizabethan culture. It is "a patriotic
        affirmation of national unity and a sentimental extolling of
        established social mores" (p. 144). Concerned with the

restoration of both the king and his realm, the action is not
unlike that of a mummers' play with its mock ritualistic death.
Impulses toward regeneration and reconciliation in the young
transcend the evil forces within and without and revitalize the
whole kingdom.

1435   TINKLER, F.C. "Cymbeline." Scrutiny 7 (1938):5-19.
            Views Cymbeline as an enigmatic extension of the achieve-
ment of the tragedies in another form. There is throughout a
brutal and harsh strain in the verse for the ear and an exaggera-
tion of dramatic gesture for the eye, combined with the melodramatic element of the plot. The result is an unresolved tension or duality that pervades the entire play. Cymbeline cannot,
then, be regarded as lighthearted romance. While the final scene
evolves a kind of static tableau, it is not an unqualified resolution. There is still a touch of irony in the reconciliation of
England and Rome.

See also The Romances (entries 1403-19) and 240, 246, 254, 258, 262,
272, 281, 516, 610-11, 976.

PERICLES

Editions

1436   HOENIGER, F.E., ed. Pericles. The Arden Shakespeare. London:
            Methuen; Cambridge, Mass.: Harvard University Press, 1963,
            188 pp.
            Includes discussion of the text, sources, authorship, stage
history, and literary interpretations, as well as appendixes
featuring material from Lawrence Twine, evidence for collaboration with John Day, conjectural reconstructions of episodes, and
conjectural rearrangements of verse. The text is based on the
first quarto (1609), from which the third folio is derived.
Since the quarto text is seriously corrupt (a reported copy
further tainted by careless compositors), Hoeniger has adopted
emendations whenever a reading can be attributed convincingly to
compositor's error. The majority of contemporary critics believe
Shakespeare had little or nothing to do with acts 1-2 but that
he wrote either completely or in large part acts 3-4. Shakespeare was clearly preoccupied with certain areas of experience
that were to be crucial in the final plays with the greater
emphasis on evil, on man's subservience to supernatural forces,
and on the restorative and redemptive qualities of love.

1437   MAXWELL, J.C., ed. Pericles. Cambridge: Cambridge Univer-
            sity Press, 1956, 211 pp.
            Provides extensive textual notes, a critical introduction
(covering the story, the problem of authorship, Shakespeare's
contribution), a discussion of the copy text, a section on stage

history, and a glossary. This edition is based on the first
quarto, for which the copy was probably a reported text. George
Wilkins's novel The Painfull Adventures of Pericles Prince of
Tyre (1608), was most likely based on the same version of the
play that the quarto reports. Shakespeare, apparently partially
reworking a rather crude and rambling story, was beginning to
move toward the hints of larger themes behind the literal
action--life as a journey, patience, regeneration, the cycle of
life.

Criticism

1438   ARTHOS, JOHN. "Pericles, Prince of Tyre: A Study in the
        Dramatic Use of Romantic Narrative." Shakespeare Quarterly 4
        (1953):257-70.
           Advocates approaching Pericles as a structurally sound plot
        in order to focus on how Shakespeare was turning romantic narra-
        tive material to dramatic use. The play explores a wide world
        stocked with mysteries and riddles, and its fundamental wisdom
        rests in Pericles's trials testing his patience to the utmost.
        It explores, also, a world of miracles and visions that resonate
        with something beyond the immediacy of our flawed existence.
        Gower's choruses lend a fictive distance, placing the story far
        in the past and triggering our willing suspension of disbelief.

1439   BARBER, C.L. "'Thou That Beget'st Him That Did Beget':
        Transformation in Pericles and The Winter's Tale." Shake-
        speare Survey 22 (1969):59-67.
           Notes that, whereas the festive comedies stress freeing the
        younger generation from the blockage of the older, the romances
        involve reconciliation of the two. In both Pericles and The
        Winter's Tale the recovery of a daughter precipitates the dis-
        covery of a wife. In the process Marina and Perdita temporarily
        become objects of wonder to a father, and the relationship thera-
        peutically prepares the father for a penitent reunion and recon-
        ciliation with his family.

1440   CRAIG, HARDIN. "Pericles and The Painfull Adventures."
        Studies in Philology 45 (1948):600-605.
           Calls recent neglect of Pericles surprising in light of the
        fact that a novel exists by George Wilkins based on the play.
        Wilkins apparently worked from notes based on a theatrical per-
        formance. The notable difference in the handling of the brothel
        scenes suggests that the play was revised after Wilkins wrote
        his account. These revised sections are universally attributed
        to Shakespeare. Probably the extant text of Pericles is not a
        bad quarto, but a "painstaking and successful revision"
        (p. 604).

1441   CUTTS, JOHN P. "Pericles' 'Downright Violence.'" Shakespeare
        Studies 4 (1968):275-93.
            Asserts that Pericles is not an innocent Job-like plaything
        of Fortune but instead is flawed with impetuosity, rashness, and
        infatuation. Imagistically, from the first of the play until his
        reunion with Marina at which time he hears the music of the
        spheres, he destroys musical harmony. The five knights who vie
        with him at Antiochus's tournament emblematically suggest the
        stages through which he has passed. Only Marina's song makes him
        feel sympathetic for another and cease boasting of his great en-
        durance. Impurities of material impediments are purged at
        Diana's temple, and his acknowledged infirmities glorify the
        blessed gods.

1442   FELPERIN, HOWARD. "Shakespeare's Miracle Play." Shakespeare
        Quarterly 18 (1967):363-74.
            Focuses on the marked dramaturgic changes that occur in
        Pericles and set the scene for the other romances. Projecting a
        beneficent supernature that presides over the natural world of
        action, Pericles is a kind of idealized Everyman, reflecting in
        Pericles's personal experiences the universal condition of man-
        kind. Here, however, the salvation is translated into an earthly
        destiny, the fruit of faith, charity, chastity, and patience.
        Each of the late plays fuses elements of allegorical-religious
        drama with elements of naturalistic-secular drama.

1443   GREENFIELD, THELMA N. "A Re-Examination of the 'Patient'
        Pericles." Shakespeare Studies 3 (1967):51-61.
            Notes that, whereas recent critics have focused on
        Pericles's patience, the more salient feature is his wisdom, his
        ability to survive as a solver of riddles and a master of escape.
        Like Odysseus and Oedipus, Pericles travels and learns to use his
        wits. Marina reenacts this role through her dangerous adventures
        and, sharing his virtue, is the true heir to the father. To
        overstress Pericles's patience is to minimize his courage and
        wisdom that help him to endure his tribulations.

1444   HASTINGS, WILLIAM T. "Shakespeare's Part in Pericles."
        Shakespeare Association Bulletin 14 (1939):67-85.
            Focuses on Shakespeare's contribution to the composition of
        Pericles. Since active collaboration by Shakespeare is highly
        unlikely the only tenable view is that Shakespeare worked over a
        completed play. He apparently added little to acts 1-2; metrical
        tests reveal a sharp distinction between 1-2 and 3-5. Much of
        acts 3-5 can safely be attributed to Shakespeare, including the
        brothel scenes. Of the eight choruses, Shakespeare's hand is
        present in all except the second.

1445   HOENIGER, F. DAVID. "Gower and Shakespeare in Pericles."
       Shakespeare Quarterly 33 (1982):461-79.
            Argues that the immense popularity of Pericles in Shake-
       speare's day and the strikingly successful productions of the
       past thirty years must make us question the academic quibbling
       about incongruities in the character and the action. The effect
       of Gower as chorus is one of enchantment, and the sense of illu-
       sion remains strong even after he calls actors upon the stage.
       With him on stage on six subsequent occasions, the action seems
       to be a series of adventures or spectacles, a show of colorful
       episodes. Shakespeare in recreating an old tale turned to a bold
       and different style and technique, in large part imitating the
       very manner of early storytelling.

1446   PARROTT, THOMAS MARC. "Pericles: The Play and the Novel."
       Shakespeare Association Bulletin 23 (1948):105-13.
            Reviews the relationship between Shakespeare's Pericles and
       George Wilkins's The Painfull Adventures of Pericles Prince of
       Tyre (1608). As a highly successful stage play, Pericles drama-
       tizes chronicle-action of a popular legend replete with dumb show
       and spectacle. Wilkins attempted the unprecedented task of turn-
       ing play into novel and then of capitalizing on its popularity;
       in effect, it is curious and amusing hack work. The corner on
       the market for Wilkins's novel was cut short by the unauthorized
       publication of a reported version of Shakespeare's play by Henry
       Gosson in 1609.

1447   THOMPKINS, J.M.S. "Why Pericles?" Review of English Studies,
       n.s. 3 (1952):315-24.
            Questions why Shakespeare chose to write Pericles imme-
       diately after his most profound tragedies. The admitted finan-
       cial success, its popularity, its affinity with the romances to
       come--nothing explains why he opted to develop this old-fashioned
       play with its chronological sequence of disconnected adventures
       and its virtually static protagonist. Perhaps in working up
       Coriolanus and Alcibiades from Plutarch he took note of the two
       patient men (Pericles and Fabius Maximus) who were juxtaposed
       with the impatient and determined to dramatize in Pericles the
       patience that saves.

See also The Romances (entries 1403-19) and 29, 87, 209, 847, 1487,
1506.

THE TEMPEST

                          Reference Works

1448   MARDER, LOUIS, comp. "The Tempest": A Supplementary Bibliog-
       raphy 1892-1965. The New Variorum Shakespeare. New York:
       American Scholar Publications, 1965, 23 pp.

Includes representative scholarship on The Tempest from
1892 to 1965 and is intended to supplement H.H. Furness's Variorum edition of 1892. The material is categorized under reproductions of original folio editions, bibliographical sources, modern
editions, and critical studies (arranged alphabetically). While
not exhaustive, the material represents every major category of
scholarship and criticism.

Editions

1449   KERMODE, FRANK, ed. The Tempest. The Arden Shakespeare.
        London: Methuen; Cambridge, Mass.: Harvard University Press,
        1954, 173 pp.
           Includes discussion of the text, date, themes of the play,
        the concept of the New World, of nature, of art, pastoral tragi-
        comedy, analogous literature, structure, verse, and critical
        interpretations, as well as appendixes on Ariel, Montaigne,
        music, lineation, the Jacobean stage, and selections from
        Strachey, Jourdain, and Ovid (Golding's translation). The text is
        based on the First Folio, for which the copy was probably a
        transcript by Ralph Crane of Shakespeare's foul papers. The
        Tempest is a pastoral drama juxtaposing Prospero's world of art
        with Caliban's world of nature. The New World stimulated inter-
        est in nature, and the events of 1609 (the voyage of the Virginia
        Company) seem to contain the whole situation in little. Caliban
        represents a measure of the superiority of art, but also in a
        measure its corruption. Prospero in one sense is a magus re-
        flecting the disciplined exercise of virtuous knowledge; in an-
        other sense he symbolically stands for the world of better nature
        and its qualities. Shakespeare, in effect, offers an exposition
        of the themes of the Fall and Redemption by means of analogous
        narrative.

1450   QUILLER-COUCH, ARTHUR, and WILSON, JOHN DOVER, eds. The
        Tempest. Cambridge: Cambridge University Press, 1921,
        116 pp. Introductions reprinted in Twentieth Century Inter-
        pretations of "The Tempest," ed. Hallett Smith, Twentieth
        Century Views (Englewood Cliffs: Prentice-Hall, 1969),
        pp. 12-19.
           Provides extensive textual notes, a critical introduction,
        a discussion of the copy text, a section on stage history, and a
        glossary. This edition is based on the First Folio, for which
        the copy was Shakespeare's foul papers that had served as a
        promptbook. An additional general introduction (covering a his-
        torical sketch of criticism and an analysis of the state of
        textual research) serves to introduce the New Cambridge Shake-
        speare edition. The play marches to marital music, celebrating
        betrothal, like A Midsummer Night's Dream, with music, dance, and
        fairies. It celebrates, as well, the dream of reconciliation and
        the perennial trust in young love.

Criticism

1451   ABRAMS, RICHARD. "The Tempest and the Concept of the
       Machiavellian Playwright." English Literary Renaissance 8
       (1978):43-66.
       Compares the playwright to a Machiavellian politician,
capable through role casting of manipulating artistic time just
as history is subject to manipulation. Prospero, who identifies
himself with the author through references to "my project" in the
epilogue, is a powerful protagonist, standing behind the action
as a supernatural force and prime mover. Manipulating the action
against Antonio, who himself has seized Prospero's dukedom through
Machiavellian means, he acts as a benevolent despot; but like the
playwright he realizes that he can sustain the dreamworld for only
a short time.

1452   ALLEN, DON CAMERON. "The Tempest." In Image and Meaning:
       Metaphoric Traditions in Renaissance Poetry. Baltimore:
       Johns Hopkins University Press, 1960, pp. 42-62. Reprinted in
       Twentieth Century Interpretations of "The Tempest," ed.
       Hallett Smith, Twentieth Century Views (Englewood Cliffs:
       Prentice-Hall, 1969), pp. 68-78.
       Describes The Tempest as mellow with ripeness of knowledge,
a marriage of the inner and the outer world. The imaginative
setting is enhanced by strict adherence to the classical unities.
The journey across water to a magic island is an age-old symbolic
motif with allegorical overtones concerning moral testing and
education. The masque is one of the dramatic centers of the
play, presenting in microcosm the theme of immortality through
generation.

1453   BERGER, KAROL. "Prospero's Art." Shakespeare Studies 10
       (1977):211-39.
       Compares Prospero's art to Ficino's theories of music in
that it centers on man's imagination through the instrument of
the spirit utilizing the imagery of both words and music to
transmit its influences. The garment, staff, and book are also
characteristic of Ficinian magic. While Prospero could easily
have avenged himself through his power, his "political wisdom"
is his recognition of the necessity of forgiveness and of leading the surrounding figures (Alonso, Miranda) to similar action.

1454   BOUGHNER, DANIEL C. "Jonsonian Structure in The Tempest."
       Shakespeare Quarterly 21 (1970):3-10.
       Observes that Shakespeare in The Tempest utilizes not only
the neoclassical unities of time, place, and action but also a
modified version of five-act structure. The protasis sets in
motion the several plot strands that are developed in the epit-
asis (Prospero's controlling action with Alonso's increasing
misery, the conspiracy of Antonio and Sebastian, the parodic
conspiracy of Trinculo and Caliban, the romance of Ferdinand and

Miranda). The catastasis or false conclusion is the potential
vindictiveness of Prospero, and the catastrophe emerges when
Ariel persuades him to exercise mercy and reunites the storm-
scattered community. The marriage of the young people is the
joyous capstone.

1455 BOWLING, LAWRENCE E. "The Theme of Natural Order in The
      Tempest." College English 12 (1951):203-9.
          Considers The Tempest a significant commentary on practical
      government in a modern civilized state. The violation of natural
      order and pirority leads inevitably to discord. Examples of in-
      fractions of natural order include Prospero's misjudgment both
      in Milan and on the island; the conspiracy of Caliban, Trinculo,
      and Stephano; and the conspiracy of Antonio and Sebastian. The
      whole series of individuals--Prospero to Caliban--find them-
      selves, after violating natural order, harmoniously readjusted
      by returning to their proper sphere in the great chain of being.

1456 BROCKBANK, PHILIP. "The Tempest: Conventions in Art and
      Empire." In Later Shakespeare. Edited by John Russell Brown
      and Bernard Harris. Stratford-upon-Avon Studies, 8. London:
      Edward Arnold, 1966, pp. 183-202.
          Views The Tempest as complex allegory dealing simultaneously
      with the social and moral nature of man, with providential de-
      sign, and with the aims and methods of art itself. Moral growth
      is envisioned as a seasonal process requiring strange mutations
      and interventions of magical nature imposed by a figure who is at
      once godlike and theatrical. Harmony in the world can be
      achieved only by allowing to providence and to Prospero the
      powers of a playwright skilled in masque. Beyond the play
      Antonio and Sebastian will return to their hard nature in Milan
      and Prospero will return to human vulnerability.

1457 BROWER, REUBEN A. "The Heresy of Plot." In English Institute
      Essays 1951. Edited by Alan S. Downer. New York: Columbia
      University Press, 1952, pp. 44-69.
          Describes the heresy of plot as the Aristotelian tendency
      to discuss elements of drama in abstract terms, in isolation from
      the other structures that exist in the play. The Tempest, 5.1,
      effectively illustrates how words and action combine to achieve
      the effect of dramatic fact and metaphorical qualification.
      Prospero describes the behavior of the king and his courtiers as
      they are released from the magic spell and regain their senses.
      The metaphoric sea change is fully experienced only in the
      atmosphere of music and songs and dissolving storm. The Aris-
      totelian sense of "poetic" directs us to technical movements of
      the play; the modern sense of "poetic" directs us to a perception
      of the close interactions of meaning at various levels.

1458   ___ \. "The Mirror of Analogy: The Tempest." In Fields of
        Light: An Experiment in Critical Reading. New York: Oxford
        University Press, 1951, pp. 95-122. Reprinted in Shakespeare:
        Modern Essays in Criticism, ed. Leonard F. Dean, rev. ed.
        (New York: Oxford University Press, 1967), pp. 162-66.
            Observes that the harmony of The Tempest lies in its meta-
        phorical design, its linking of images through almost inexhaust-
        ible analogies. The six main recurrent patterns are "strange-
        wondrous," "sleep-dream," "sea-tempest," "music-noise," "earth-
        air," "slavery-freedom," and "sovereignty-conspiracy." The
        characters at various levels of the plot experience these di-
        chotomies in a world controlled by Prospero's magic. The key
        metaphor is "sea-change," and the play's design takes visible
        form at the point of Alonso's transformation, action that gives
        philosophic depth to the Ovidian theme of metamorphosis.

1459   COLLINS, J. CHURTON. "Poetry and Symbolism: A Study of The
        Tempest." Contemporary Review 93 (1908):65-83.
            Observes that the power of poetry rests far more surely on
        what it suggests than what it expresses. Shakespeare in Prospero
        has symbolically depicted his latter days. The full vision of
        the romances unfolds in The Tempest, where one perceives a faith
        that the "moral government of the world is a system tempering
        justice and righteousness with mercy and benevolence" (p. 76).
        In its fullest extension the island symbolizes the world; the
        characters, mankind; Prospero and his intentions, life's control
        by heaven. Caliban represents man before his elements were
        harmonized.

1460   COURSEN, HERBERT R., Jr. "Prospero and the Drama of the
        Soul." Shakespeare Studies 4 (1968):316-33.
            Observes that, whereas the romantic comedies deal with the
        exposure of human folly, Prospero's play exposes sin and aims at
        redemption of the soul. In the course of his project, human
        feeling overtakes intellectual pursuit, and Prospero himself is
        redeemed through the development of compassion for his enemies.
        At this point he ceases playing God and recognizes his full
        humanity. The epilogue asks the same thing of the spectators
        (forgiveness) that the play does of its characters.

1461   DOBRÉE, BONAMY. "The Tempest." Essays and Studies, n.s. 5
        (1952):13-25. Reprinted in Twentieth Century Interpretations
        of "The Tempest," ed. Hallett Smith, Twentieth Century Views
        (Englewood Cliffs: Prentice-Hall, 1969), pp. 47-59.
            Admits that the romances must be considered as a group and
        that the general theme is the necessity of forgiveness as the
        rarer virtue. The Tempest, however, moves beyond this theme.
        Repentance and forgiveness seem to be fossils rather than active
        principles in the play. The Tempest, in a word, while grouped
        with the other plays, is not infused with the same sentiment
        about life. It is composed of the impulses of love and

forgiveness, of fear of destiny and the immortality of our
existence and the brutality of matter--all brought into a harmony
that belies contradiction.

1462   EGAN, ROBERT. "'This Rough Magic' Perspectives of Art and
        Morality in The Tempest." Shakespeare Quarterly 23 (1972):
        171-82.
            Argues that Prospero's mistake, as protagonist-magician-
        dramatist, is to uphold his warped view of morality by which he
        in his self-righteousness would purify Caliban, Antonio, Alonso,
        Sebastian, and even Ferdinand. Until Ariel forces him to relent,
        he is vengeful and vindictive. In drowning his book he drowns
        his idealism and joins the world of humanity. Yet, Prospero's
        and Shakespeare's project remains unfinished unless the specta-
        tors accept Prospero's vision of love as an act of love on their
        own part. Prospero, Shakespeare, and the spectators join at the
        end in a celebration of shared humanity.

1463   GESNER, CAROL. "The Tempest as Pastoral Romance." Shake-
        speare Quarterly 10 (1959):531-39.
            Notes that the key factor in Shakespeare's art in The
        Tempest is the composite quality of the plot, with Longus's
        romance of Daphnis and Chloe a significant influence. The
        omission of the malcontent element and the addition of the super-
        natural machinery point to Longus as a direct source rather than
        an intermediary one. The coincidences of the chief characters in
        the storm and in the wedding festivities strongly support this
        supposition. Evidence suggests further that Shakespeare used the
        French translation of Jacques Amyot (1559, 1594, 1596, 1609)
        rather than the English translation of Angel Day (1587).

1464   GILBERT, ALLAN. "The Tempest: Parallelism in Characters and
        Situations." Journal of English and Germanic Philology 14
        (1915):63-74.
            Calls attention to Shakespeare's doubling of action and
        character in The Tempest to reinforce by contrast or by similar-
        ity. Both Prospero and Gonzalo are virtuous men from the court,
        for example, but one for neglect of his duty in favor of retired
        study has brought evil on himself and others. Prospero and
        Sycorax exercise magical powers in diametrically different man-
        ners. Caliban and Ariel are contrasted as creatures beyond the
        human. The two conspiracies (Stephano, Trinculo, and Caliban
        against Prospero; Antonio and Sebastian against Alonso) emphasize
        one another even in details. The main theme is that people are
        good or bad by virtue of that which is within, not the external
        situation or appearance.

1465   GILMAN, ERNEST B. "'All Eyes': Prospero's Inverted Masque."
        Renaissance Quarterly 33 (1980):214-30.
            Suggests that the nuptial masque presented by Prospero for
        Ferdinand and Miranda shapes our response to the play as a whole,

especially in the crucial factor of its sudden collapse and dissolution. The sequence of the disrupted masque followed by the
reappearance of evil in Caliban constitutes an exact reversal of
the contemporary court masque. This deliberate reversal of
masque-antimasque motifs reflects the play's coherent structure
by pointing us to the thematic center of the play--"that the cure
for distemper lies not in withdrawing from time's sometimes violent jars but in tempering oneself to them" (p. 223).

1466   GRUDIN, ROBERT. "Prospero's Masque and the Structure of The
       Tempest." South Atlantic Quarterly 71 (1972):401-9.
            Focuses on the masque in 4.1, in its language and its con-
       figuration of goddesses, as a mirror of Prospero's perspective in
       the first three acts and as an axis shifting his view to a more
       realistic one. Venus and Caliban, representing disruptive cosmic
       and human forces, are banished from the masque, a vision of na-
       ture purified by knowledge and art. Following the masque, how-
       ever, Prospero realizes social order requires that knowledge and
       art coexist with human baseness.

1467   HANKINS, JOHN E. "Caliban the Bestial Man." PMLA 62 (1947):
       793-801.
            Describes "caliban" as a metathesis of "cannibal" and sug-
       gests that Shakespeare in this figure was depicting, not specifi-
       cally a red Indian from the New World, but primitive man as a
       type. Probably his physical appearance is derived from a freak
       of nature described by voyagers; the idea of the appearance of
       spirits in conjunction with him apparently was drawn from Ludwig
       Lavater's Of Ghosts and Spirits Walking by Night (1572). While
       Shakespeare clearly does not share Montaigne's enthusiasm for
       primitive man, Caliban is something more than the savage of the
       voyagers' narratives.

1468   HENZE, RICHARD. "The Tempest: Rejection of a Vanity."
       Shakespeare Quarterly 23 (1972):420-34.
            Envisons a growth in Prospero that leads him to reject the
       masque as a vanity of his art in particular and the concept of a
       passive life that attempts to live apart from the world in gen-
       eral. He is able to make the island, a physical and symbolic
       representation of his ducal deficiencies, a place for blessed
       recognition; and he returns to his dukedom a different man be-
       cause he has learned patience, control of the flesh, the neces-
       sary balance between learning and public responsibility.

1469   HILLMAN, RICHARD. "Chaucer's Franklin's Magician and The
       Tempest: An Influence Beyond Appearances." Shakespeare
       Quarterly 34 (1983):426-32.
            Examines the relationship between Chaucer's "The Franklin's
       Tale" and The Tempest, both of which concern the role of gener-
       osity and compassion in ideal relationships and both of which
       conclude a scene of magical illusion with essentially the same

words.   The main magical event in Chaucer--an illusion of protec-
tion from shipwreck--virtually mirrors Prospero's trick.   Both
illusions of destruction become means of redemption in that each
provokes a generous response from the magician himself.   In both
cases the magician is the agent of forgiveness as he releases
his control; in both his role has providential overtones.

1470   HOMAN, SIDNEY R.   "The Tempest and Shakespeare's Last Plays:
        The Aesthetic Dimensions."   Shakespeare Quarterly 24 (1973):
        69-76.
            Speculates that The Tempest offers the most expansive
statement not only of Shakespeare's dramatic themes but also of
the aesthetic principles that form the basis of his art, more
specifically the ability to achieve universal human statements
through the fiction of imaginative creation.   The play reflects
Shakespeare as a balance between the extremes of practical playwrights who sacrifice thematic substance to sensationalism and
aesthetic playwrights whose plays convey specialized themes to a
coterie group but lack appeal to the popular audience.

1471   HUNT, JOHN D.   A Critical Commentary on Shakespeare's "The
        Tempest."   London: Macmillan, 1968, 76 pp.
            Observes that the ideal comprehension of a work of art
mediates between a sense of the details and a retrospective view
of the whole.   The Tempest summarizes and recapitulates much of
Shakespeare's vision of the world.   The controlling theme of the
play is art, both that of civil order and that of providence; it
translates delight into instruction and philosophic speculation
into entertainment.

1472   JAMES, DAVID GWILYM.   The Dream of Prospero.   Oxford:
        Clarendon Press, 1967, 174 pp.
            Considers The Tempest Shakespeare's mature philosophic
response to the dark vision of life expressed in King Lear,
depicting in Prospero the tension between the love of the inner
life and the desperate need of a culture for a spiritual basis.
Chastened by his exile, Prospero will return to Europe and his
political responsibilities, not because evil has been destroyed
but for the very reason that it will continue to exist and must
be countered in the best manner possible by humane individuals
willing to be involved in the public life.   The Tempest does not
negate the horror of King Lear; it asserts that man's answer be
conscientious constructive efforts and prayer rather than
despair.

1473   JOHNSON, W. STACY.   "The Genesis of Ariel."   Shakespeare
        Quarterly 2 (1951):205-10.
            Considers the Elizabethan belief that spirits are either
affiliated in some way with God or Satan (medieval Christianity)
or with a wise man ascending toward spiritual unity with the
divine (Neoplatonic).   Ariel's function is benevolent rather than

diabolic. The name is that of an angelic epithet and, whatever
its direct source, is appropriate for this creature of air. The
spirit is primarily elemental, associated with the spirit-
operated phenomenal world of Neoplatonism, but Shakespeare en-
dows him with the personality of a familiar and thus makes him
more than merely inhuman.

1474   KNOX, BERNARD. "The Tempest and the Ancient Comic Tradition."
       In English Institute Essays 1954. Edited by W.K. Wimsatt, Jr.
       New York: Columbia University Press, 1955, pp. 52-73. Re-
       printed in Virginia Quarterly Review 31 (1955):73-89.
          Observes that in The Tempest the fantasy and originality of
       the setting are counterbalanced by close adherence to tradition
       in character and plot. While the play projects the most fantas-
       tic of all of Shakespeare's settings in its geographically un-
       locatable nameless isle, the pattern of action and character is
       a virtual paradigm of classical comedy. The old man with a
       marriageable daughter controls the other principal characters.
       Caliban and Ariel are variations of the clever servant. The
       action culminates in release, reconciliation, and marriage.

1475   McPEEK, JAMES A.S. "The Genesis of Caliban." Philological
       Quarterly 25 (1946):378-81.
          Finds the source of Caliban in Spenser's The Faerie Queene,
       specifically in Chorle, the son of the witch Hag. Florimell
       comes to their hut to escape a tempest, whereupon the slothful
       and ragged-haired creature brings her gifts and begs to be her
       thrall, a pose that covers his lustful desires. Both poets con-
       sistently use the terms "monster" and "beast" in describing them,
       and Shakespeare quite possibly got from Spenser the name itself
       since Chorle is something of a cannibal in his desire to devour
       woman's flesh.

1476   NUTTALL, ANTHONY DAVID. Two Concepts of Allegory: A Study of
       Shakespeare's "The Tempest" and the Logic of Allegorical Ex-
       pression. London: Routledge & Kegan Paul; New York: Barnes
       & Noble, 1967, 175 pp. Selections reprinted in Twentieth
       Century Interpretations of "The Tempest," ed. Hallett Smith,
       Twentieth Century Views (Englewood Cliffs: Prentice-Hall,
       1969), pp. 79-85.
          Reviews and rejects nineteenth-century attempts to make The
       Tempest allegorical in the sense that a system of specified meta-
       physical significancies is consistently adumbrated in the text.
       Instead, the peculiar wedding of the marvellous and the circum-
       stantial creates a "pre-allegorical" (p. 159) quality in which
       paradisiacal intuitions are undermined by a doubt about reality.
       The vision of Prospero may transcend objective facts, but it
       does not obliterate them. Shakespeare throughout the play
       fleshes out allegorical inclinations with a minutely perceptive
       skepticism.

1477   SEMON, KENNETH. "Shakespeare's Tempest: Beyond a Common
       Joy." ELH 40 (1973):24-43.
          Describes the sense of wonder that infuses the play as a
       consequence of Prospero's magic and the sense of wonder that in-
       fuses the spectators when he gives over his magic at the end of
       the play to return to the ambiguities of a fully human life. The
       spectators enjoy with Prospero the therapeutic amazement he vis-
       its upon the European travellers during the storm, upon Ferdinand
       when he first meets Miranda, and on Alonso when he discovers his
       son alive. Because of the shared level of perception throughout
       the play, the spectators also share his sense of mystery and
       apprehension for what awaits him beyond his art.

1478   SISSON, C.J. "The Magic of Prospero." Shakespeare Survey 11
       (1958):70-77.
          Describes the terrifyingly real quality of magic to Shake-
       speare and his contemporaries. Whereas Sycorax as a witch repre-
       sents the world of black magic and the power of Satan, Prospero
       works in white magic, its power emanating from a study of the
       liberal arts. The Tempest is a companion play to Measure for
       Measure, in which a duke also dispenses justice by opposing
       wrongs by mysterious means. Both may have been designed to flat-
       ter King James through the image of the powerful and benevolent
       ruler.

1479   STOLL, ELMER EDGAR. "The Tempest." PMLA 47 (1932):699-726.
       Portion reprinted in Twentieth Century Interpretations of
       "The Tempest," ed. Hallett Smith, Twentieth Century Views
       (Englewood Cliffs: Prentice-Hall, 1969), pp. 25-33.
          Denies the presence of allegorical intent in The Tempest.
       Ariel, sprung out of popular superstition, is simply an Eliza-
       bethan sprite, Caliban but a creature of earth, Prospero but a
       man with knowledge of magic, The Tempest but a play for stage
       enjoyment. Nor is the play serene, Shakespeare's harmonious
       farewell to his art. Critics who fail to perceive the ugly and
       the monstrous in the last plays are "not reading but reading in"
       (p. 723). A tendency to enjoy a mood of reverie has indeed
       grown upon the poet, and there is something less than vital,
       less than clear-cut.

1480   TRAVERSI, DEREK A. "The Tempest." Scrutiny 16 (1949):127-57.
          Asserts that The Tempest represents a logical development
       in Shakespeare's symbolic technique in the last plays. While The
       Winter's Tale delineates characters in the process of an expe-
       rience that will lead them to assume symbolic values, The Tempest
       begins after such an experience has already occurred, and the
       characters exist entirely in their symbolic function. Alonso,
       like Lear, becomes penitent, and Prospero declares that it is
       time for the past to be set aside for a harmony all the richer
       for their experience. Gonzalo as the voice of destiny proclaims
       a newborn vision of humanity, a second, redeemed, and reasonable
       life.

1481   WICKHAM, GLYNNE. "Masque and Anti-Masque in The Tempest."
       Essays and Studies, n.s. 28 (1975):1-14.
            Argues that The Tempest operates on three levels--theatri-
       cal romance, political commentary, and metaphysical allusion.
       The phantom banquet of act 3 serves as antimasque, the heavenly
       vision of act 4 as the masque. Prospero controls both, haunting
       Alonso and Antonio in the one and rewarding Miranda and Ferdinand
       in the other. On the political level, alluded to in the prologue
       and the epilogue, reference is to the wedding and prosperity of
       Scotland and England through King James and to the hope for the
       future in the younger generation of Henry, Prince of Wales, and
       Princess Elizabeth.

1482   WILLIAM, DAVID. "The Tempest on the Stage." In Jacobean
       Theatre. Edited by John Russell Brown and Bernard Harris.
       Stratford-upon-Avon Studies, 1. London: Edward Arnold, 1960,
       pp. 133-57.
            Notes that no other Shakespearean play so tempts a director
       to such exaggerated emphasis on scenery, spectacle, and costume.
       The danger lies in blurring the play's major focus on Prospero,
       whose moral decision to renounce vengeance provides the resolu-
       tion of the action. An effective production must reveal the ten-
       sion between his rational desire to tell the story objectively
       and the passion that both his recollections and the contemporary
       action sporadically generate. The play is abundantly rich in
       music and dance, accommodating a wide variety of costumes; but
       all elements must cohesively yield a primary dramatic interest
       in Prospero and the impact of past and present events on his de-
       cision concerning Alonso and Antonio.

1483   WILSON, JOHN DOVER. The Meaning of "The Tempest." Newcastle
       upon Tyne: Literary and Philosophical Society, 1936, 23 pp.
       Reprinted in His Infinite Variety: Major Shakespearean
       Criticism Since Johnson, ed. Paul N. Siegel (Philadelphia:
       J.B. Lippincott, 1964), pp. 397-412.
            Locates the meaning of The Tempest in its spiritual mood,
       a mood all the more significant because Shakespeare's mind has
       already experienced Hamlet and King Lear. There can be little
       doubt that the play is Shakespeare's valedictory; that he himself
       probably played the role of Prospero at a court performance lends
       added poignancy to the epilogue. Above all the last plays in
       their treatment of reconciliation and forgiveness, The Tempest
       has an atmosphere of serenity and peace. Shakespeare's tragic
       vision of life in act 1 is confronted with his new vision in the
       resolution.

1484   ZIMBARDO, ROSE. "Form and Disorder in The Tempest."
       Shakespeare Quarterly 14 (1963):49-56.
            Does not consider The Tempest a part of the last plays
       dealing with the theme of regeneration. The play focuses, in-
       stead, on the continuous conflict between order and chaos,

specifically on the limited ability of art to impose form on that
which is chaotic. Prospero is a very human artist, irascible at
times in his confrontation with evil that he cannot control. He
is able to subject the travellers to the ordering influence of
his art; but it is at best temporary, and Caliban, the "incarnation of chaos," defies even that degree of order.

Stage History

1485   SUMMERS, MONTAGUE, ed. Shakespeare's Adaptations: "The
       Tempest," "The Mock Tempest," and "King Lear." London:
       J. Cape, 1922, 282 pp.
          Includes William Davenant and John Dryden's The Tempest, or
       the Enchanted Island (1670) and Thomas Duffet's The Mock Tempest:
       or the Enchanted Castle (1675), and Nahum Tate's The History of
       King Lear (1681). The preface describes the nature of the three
       texts, and the extensive introduction traces the popularity of
       Shakespeare's plays in the Restoration and the general manner in
       which they were modified. While it is proper to condemn altera-
       tions in Shakespeare's texts, we must remember that it is still
       frequently done today. Generally, the Restoration adaptations
       were the works of "playwrights of practical knowledge and no in-
       considerable talent" (p. cviii).

For discussion of the character of Prospero, see entries 1453, 1460,
1467-68. For discussion of the function of the masque, see entries
1465-66, 1468, 1481. See also The Romances (entries 1403-19) and 63,
66, 128, 134, 141, 159, 171, 189, 196, 208, 221, 223, 225, 228-30,
241, 245-46, 248, 250, 254-55, 261, 267, 285, 302, 304, 306, 312-13,
315, 324-25, 333, 342, 515, 609, 753, 1487.

THE WINTER'S TALE

Reference Works

1486   MARDER, LOUIS, comp. "The Winter's Tale": A Supplementary
       Bibliography 1898-1965. The New Shakespeare Variorum. New
       York: American Scholar Publications, 1965, 17 pp.
          Includes representative scholarship on The Winter's Tale
       from 1898 to 1965 and is intended to supplement H.H. Furness's
       Variorum edition of 1898. The material is categorized under
       reproductions of original folio editions, bibliographical sources,
       modern editions, and critical studies (arranged alphabetically).
       While not exhaustive, the material represents every major cate-
       gory of scholarship and criticism.

Editions

1487   PAFFORD, J.H.F., ed. The Winter's Tale. The Arden Shake-
        peare. London: Methuen; Cambridge, Mass.: Harvard Univer-
        sity Press, 1963, 225 pp.
            Includes discussion of the text, date and authorship,
        sources, and critical interpretations, as well as appendixes
        covering music and the songs, the stage history, and a selection
        from Greene's Pandosto. The text is based on the First Folio,
        for which the copy was probably an edited transcript made by the
        scrivener Ralph Crane possibly from Shakespeare's foul papers.
        For The Winter's Tale, which shares common characteristics with
        Pericles, Cymbeline, and The Tempest, the keynote of modern crit-
        icism is that it is experimental, directed to the new tastes for
        the court masque or for the private theater or for variations of
        the theme of reconciliation. Both time and a second generation
        are vital components of the healing process in the play. Con-
        trastive use of prose and poetry and variations in the verse
        effectively counterpoint both the major sections of the play
        divided by sixteen years and the principal figures.

1488   QUILLER-COUCH, ARTHUR, and WILSON, JOHN DOVER, eds. The
        Winter's Tale. Cambridge: Cambridge University Press, 1931
        206 pp.
            Provides extensive textual notes, a discussion of the copy
        text, a critical introduction, a section on stage history, and a
        glossary. This edition is based on the First Folio, for which
        the copy was probably an assembled text prepared from individual
        parts by the scrivener Ralph Crane. Shakespeare's alterations
        from Greene's Pandosto are discussed at length, for example the
        acceleration of Leontes's jealousy, the interchange of kingdoms,
        the removal of Leontes's incestuous desire, the "resurrection"
        of Hermione. Generally the play reflects Shakespeare's declining
        dramatic powers, but the beauty of the setting, the language, and
        the theme of reconciliation amply redeem it.

Criticism

1489   BETHELL, S.L. "The Winter's Tale": A Study. New York and
        London: Staples Press, 1947, 128 pp.
            Describes The Winter's Tale, with its synthesis of natural
        and supernatural and its elevation of the natural to a genuine
        and universal symbolism, as "the supreme literary example of the
        Baroque" (p. 110). In it the medieval and the classical coexist
        in both form and matter. The Hellenic-Medieval romance (Florizel-
        Perdita) has been fused with the otherworldliness of orthodox
        Medieval religion (Leontes-Hermione). The natural virtue of
        Florizel and Perdita restores family and kingdom, but that virtue
        has been earned by Hermione's submission and Leontes's penitence.

1490   BIGGINS, DENNIS. "'Exit Pursued by a Bear': A Problem in The
         Winter's Tale." Shakespeare Quarterly 13 (1962):3-13.
         Argues that Shakespeare's audience would have reacted
seriously to the bear scene in The Winter's Tale. Indeed, the
scene has a tonal, symbolic, and structural function. It focuses
on Leontes's brutality and false suspicion on Antigonus and
dramatically destroys those qualities, symbolically purging the
tragic world. Antigonus in his own words has reduced himself to
a level of wild beasts in agreeing to carry out Leontes's tyran-
nical command, and it is ironically appropriate that he should be
killed by such a beast. Occurring in a storm that reflects an
angry providence, this action both spares the innocent child and
destroys the corrupt agent of tyranny. (See entry 1499.)

1491   BLISSETT, WILLIAM. "This Wide Gap of Time: The Winter's
         Tale." English Literary Renaissance 1 (1971):52-70.
         Concentrates on the contrast between the tragic and comic
halves of the play with Leontes offending and Polixenes in a
state of innocence in the first and Polixenes offending and
Leontes in a state of penitence in the second. Time's gesture of
turning the hourglass marks the division between the two. Destructive time characterizes acts 1-3; redeeming time, acts 4-5.
Leontes's final words about the "wide gap" of sixteen years re-
fer to the redemption involved in his penitential process but
echo as well Ovid's reference to time as an engulfing mouth of
destruction. (See entry 1496.)

1492   BONJOUR, ADRIEN. "Polixenes and the Winter of His Discontent."
         English Studies 50 (1969):206-12.
         Focuses on the parallel outbursts of temper by Leontes in
act 1 and by Polixenes in act 4 of The Winter's Tale. Previous
critics have erred in stressing the similarities rather than the
differences. Whereas Leontes is in dead earnest in his threats
against Polixenes and his wife and we fear for the life of the
newborn infant, Polixenes's threats are but shadows. Since the
spectators know Florizel's decision to be true to Perdita and the
real identity of Perdita, their attitudes and feelings are con-
ditioned and controlled in a manner totally unlike the situation
in act 1.

1493   BRYANT, JERRY H. "The Winter's Tale and the Pastoral Tradi-
         tion." Shakespeare Quarterly 14 (1963):387-98.
         Asserts that Shakespeare transcends the Greek, Roman, and
Italian pastoral tradition in The Winter's Tale by transforming
its conventions into a subtle commentary on the nature of truth,
specifically the dangers of assuming appearance to be reality.
Both Florizel's ability to see truth through pastoral disguise
and Autolycus's recognition of himself as a knave serve as a foil
to Leontes's blindness and delusions. The pastoral episode in
act 4 prepares the cure for Leontes's infected mind in act 5.

1494   BRYANT, JOSEPH A., Jr. "Shakespeare's Allegory: The Winter's
        Tale." Sewanee Review 63 (1955):202-22.
           Views The Winter's Tale as a parable of sin and redemption,
        a Pauline pattern for salvation, with Hermione symbolizing St.
        Paul's Christ who saves by grace, Leontes the Jew, Mamillius the
        Jewish church in his death, and Perdita the true church. The
        play thus participates in an action which is "Christian, divine,
        and eternal." In act 4 Shakespeare uses the same metaphor of
        grafting regarding the relationship of Florizel and Perdita that
        Paul used to refer to the union of the Gentile and the church.

1495   COX, LEE SHERIDAN. "The Role of Autolycus in The Winter's
        Tale." Studies in English Literature 9 (1969):283-301.
           Perceives Autolycus, a taleteller and singer, rogue agent
        of providence, man of masks and busy clothes-changer, as furnish-
        ing an important counterpart to the story of Leontes and as
        serving to advance the theme of appearance versus reality. Since
        it is by his interference that Perdita's revelation occurs, he
        can be seen as an agent of a superior power for good. His first
        appearance--as a victim robbed by Autolycus--parallels the self-
        destructive nature of Leontes's wrongdoing. (See entry 1501.)

1496   EWBANK, INGA-STINA. "The Triumph of Time in The Winter's
        Tale." Review of English Literature 5 (1964):83-100.
           Sees the structure serving as a means of examining what
        time does to man, the sixteen-year gap juxtaposing past and pres-
        ent. The three aspects of time are natural growth, destruction,
        and revelation of truth. While these aspects are present through-
        out, they coalesce powerfully in the final act. Destruction is
        present in Leontes's retrospection and Mamillius's absence,
        natural growth in the appearance at court of Florizel and Perdita,
        and the revelation of truth in the discovery of Perdita's iden-
        tity and the reunion with Hermione. (See entry 1491.)

1497   FREY, CHARLES. Shakespeare's Vast Romance: A Study of "The
        Winter's Tale." Columbia and London: University of Missouri
        Press, 1980, 174 pp.
           Consists of three major sections--a selective history of
        critical responses to the play, a discussion of the play in the
        context of Shakespeare's development and of his use of Greene's
        Pandosto as a source, and an anlysis of the play itself. The
        Winter's Tale, quite the opposite of a philosophic play, is a
        drama of sudden, spontaneous, and manifold action demanding both
        aesthetic and intellectual assent. The vastness of its design
        forces us to realize that, if it is a work of admiration and
        delight, it also radically shocks in its vision of regeneration
        and redemption.

1498   FRYE, NORTHROP. "Recognition in The Winter's Tale." In
        Essays on Shakespeare and Elizabethan Drama in Honor of Hardin
        Craig. Edited by Richard Hosley. Columbia: University of
        Missouri Press, 1962, pp. 235-46.
            Observes that the two halves of The Winter's Tale form a
        diptych of parallel or contrasting actions. The first deals with
        age, jealousy, winter, and death; the other with youth, summer,
        love, and life. Symbolically central to the action is the natural
        cycle of seasons from winter to summer and the human cycle of the
        passage of sixteen years. The play ends with a double recogni-
        tion--that of Perdita's parentage and that of the awakened statue
        of Hermione and her reunion with daughter and husband. Leontes
        and the spectators share in a sense of participation in the re-
        deeming and relative power of nature.

1499   GURR, ANDREW. "The Bear, the Statue, and Hysteria in The
        Winter's Tale." Shakespeare Quarterly 34 (1983):420-25.
            Focuses on the significance of the bear and statue episodes
        as matching counterparts that conclude respectively the tragic
        and comic halves of the play. Both events blatantly challenge
        credulity and transform tragedy into comedy through the exploita-
        tion of theatrical illusion. In the first half passions prevail
        at court; in the last half art prevails in the natural world of
        the shepherds. This art used to disguise nature is comically
        symbolized by Autolycus, who on three occasions deceives the same
        audience with disguises. (See entry 1490.)

1500   HOENIGER, F. DAVID. "The Meaning of The Winter's Tale."
        University of Toronto Quarterly 20 (1950):11-26.
            Asserts that only an allegorical approach can do justice
        to the greatness of The Winter's Tale since no literal interpre-
        tation can satisfactorily explain the profound impact of the play
        upon the reader or spectator. The core of the meaning is con-
        tained in the discussion of art and nature in act 4. The theme
        of identity pervades the whole play. Symbolically, Perdita and
        Mamillius are parts of the changing personality of Leontes. The
        theme of changing seasons is interwoven with that of youth and
        age, of death and resurrection. Leontes passes from youth into
        a state of sin, suffering the loss of Mamillius; his repentance
        is accompanied by a new and creative love, culminating in the
        rediscovery of his wife and daughter.

1501   HUGHES, MERRITT Y. "A Classical Versus a Social Approach to
        Shakespeare's Autolycus." Shakespeare Association Bulletin
        15 (1940):219-26.
            Finds the source of Autolycus, not in social causes in
        England, but in classical lore, specifically in the popular
        mythology of Rome, in which the figure became something of a
        Paul Bunyan character, as references by both Plautus and Martial
        indicate. Standard editions of these writers in the sixteenth
        century duly note the derivation of the name from the Odyssey,

but Renaissance mythographers like Natale Conti were more
fascinated by his virtuosity as a rogue. It was this spirit that
found its way into Shakespeare's creation. (See entry 1495.)

1502   LAWLOR, JOHN J. "Pandosto and the Nature of Dramatic Provi-
       dence." Philological Quarterly 41 (1962):96-113.
       Explores the major differences between Greene's Pandosto
and The Winter's Tale as an aid to addressing the characteristics
of romance as a dramatic form. Shakespeare's major changes involve the development in Leontes of jealous passion followed by
lengthy repentance, the omission of crude low comedy, the use of
the sheepshearing festival as a meeting place for the young and
old. Most important, he invests Greene's subtitle "The Triumph
of Time" with new meaning in preserving Hermione and allowing
Leontes to be reconciled with her and his daughter. Both the
story of Leontes and Hermione and that of Perdita and Florizel
gain richest meaning in the complex manner in which they are
interwoven.

1503   NATHAN, NORMAN. "Leontes' Provocation." Shakespeare Quar-
       terly 19 (1968):19-24.
       Argues that Shakespeare does not suggest jealousy in
Leontes anterior to the play, that his passion is sudden and well
motivated. Since Polixenes is Leontes's close friend, Hermione
treats him with less reserve and greater personal regard than
other men. This action--combined with Hermione's witty play on
the phrase "kind hostess," on the idea that Polixenes must be
either her "guest" or her "prisoner," and Polixenes' willingness
to stay at her request--credibly explains Leontes's sudden jealous explosion. (See entry 1507.)

1504   PAFFORD, J.H.F. "Music, and the Songs in The Winter's Tale."
       Shakespeare Quarterly 10 (1950):161-75.
       Notes that the chief musical element in The Winter's Tale
is in the singing roles of Autolycus, Dorcas, and Mopsa. The
songs in the text, the numerous references to songs and ballads,
and the dances constitute a variety of musical styles from the
period. The music, moreover, is integral to the play, contribut-
ing much to the spirit of the sheepshearing scene and much to the
personality of the clown. Seventeenth-century musical texts
exist for "Whoop do me no harm good man," "Jog on," and "Lawn as
white as driven snow." The songs are in Shakespeare's late style
and help to date the composition.

1505   PYLE, FITZROY. "The Winter's Tale": A Commentary on the
       Structure. London: Routledge & Kegan Paul; New York: Barnes
       & Noble, 1969, 195 pp.
       Offers a scene-by-scene analysis of The Winter's Tale as a
transmutation of the source, Robert Greene's Pandosto. The
highly unified play combines courtly and popular elements in a
setting of pastoral romance. By keeping Leontes alive, restoring

Hermione to life, and linking Hermione's return with the discovery of Perdita, Shakespeare gives organic character to
Greene's welter of events. Hermione's apparent resurrection from
the dead, a shock of amazement to Leontes and to the spectators
as well, effectively characterizes the power of the human spirit
to achieve the miraculous.

1506   SCHANZER, ERNEST. "The Structural Pattern of The Winter's
       Tale." Review of English Literature 5 (1964):72-82.
          Claims that Pericles provides a model for The Winter's Tale
       in structure, plot, and imagery. In both cases acts 1-3 focus on
       a royal father; act 4, following a great lapse of time, is de-
       voted to the daughter; and act 5 fuses the two elements through a
       double reunion. In both cases the first half is basically de-
       structive and the second half constructive. In both instances a
       harmonious relationship is shattered, and the early acts are
       marked by images of uprooting, blight, and infection. "Great
       creating nature" becomes virtually a character in itself in the
       final acts.

1507   SCHWARTZ, MURRAY M. "Leontes' Jealousy in The Winter's Tale."
       American Imago 30 (1974):250-73.
          Claims that Leontes's sudden jealousy in act 1 is a result
       of a repressed homosexual interest in Polixenes that precipitates
       the development of paranoia. This paranoia is a form of psychic
       imprisonment that perverts the mutuality and innocence of their
       boyhood friendship. Leontes tries desperately to exclude himself
       from the fantasies he projects onto both Hermione and Polixenes.
       The focus of the final act is on the process of recovery. (See
       entry 1503.)

1508   TAYLOR, JOHN. The Patience of The Winter's Tale." Essays in
       Criticism 23 (1973):333-56.
          Describes the structure of the play as a series of four
       emotional peaks (Leontes's jealousy, Polixenes's rage against his
       son, Perdita's sudden acceptance of her role as mistress of the
       sheepshearing feast, and Leontes's outburst of love before the
       living Hermione), all the result of a long passage of time and of
       something beyond human design. The great lesson of these events
       is the virtue of patience. The spectators, too, gain patience as
       the play progresses, almost expecting a miracle in act 5 by which
       the resolution will be effected.

1509   WILLIAMS, JOHN A. The Natural Work of Art: The Experience of
       Romance in Shakespeare's "The Winter's Tale." Cambridge,
       Mass.: Harvard University Press, 1967, 47 pp.
          Describes Shakespearean romance as a poetic solution to the
       metaphysical problem of mutability in human life. Shakespeare in
       The Winter's Tale replaces Leontes's experience of pain with that
       of wonder, guiding him to a new perception of man at the center
       of a beneficent creation. Nature in this vision of art becomes

the means by which hope and happiness are sustained even in the midst of pain and death, namely in the multiple generations of life. The transformation of Hermione's statue caps Leontes's realization of the necessity of patience in the attunement to the harmony of the natural order.

1510   WILSON, HAROLD S. "'Nature and Art' in The Winter's Tale." Shakespeare Association Bulletin 18 (1943):114-20.
        Describes the passage in which Perdita and Polixenes dis-cuss the merits of artificial flowers (4.4.79 ff.), a variation of the relative merits of nature and art, as commonplace both in antiquity and in the Renaissance. Examples are cited from Plato, Aristotle, Cicero, Petrarch, Daniello, Peletier, Sidney, and Daniel. A particular passage is quoted at length from George Puttenham's Art of English Poetry as the probable source for Shakespeare's dialogue. Drawn from agriculture, it describes art as an alterer and surmounter of nature's skill.

Stage History

1511   BARTHOLOMEUSZ, DENNIS. "The Winter's Tale" in Performance in England and America 1611-1976. Cambridge: Cambridge Univer-sity Press, 1982, 279 pp.
        Traces major performances of The Winter's Tale from Jacobean England through the mid-twentieth century. Particular attention is directed to productions by John Philip Kemble, William Charles Macready, Samuel Phelps, Charles Kean, Lawrence Barrett, Herbert Beerbohm Tree, Trevor Nunn, and Peter Brook. Analysis of textual cuts, costuming, set designs, and music re-flects the various stage interpretations and the shifting impact of the play's theme. A table of performances and theaters rele-vant to the study is included.

See also The Romances (entries 1403-19) and 115, 131, 141, 152, 225, 229, 245-46, 251, 254, 306, 312, 317, 320, 324-25, 333, 609, 613, 632, 1439, 1487.

Index

Note: References are to entry numbers; underscored numbers in listings for play titles indicate entries specifically on that play.

Crick, John, 817
Criticism, history of Shake-
    spearean, 64-72, 1057-58,
    1074, 1141, 1174. See also
    under individual titles
Croyland Manuscript, the, 579
Crutwell, Patrick, 218
Cummings, E.E., 355
Cunliffe, Richard John, 7
Cunningham, Dolora, 1254
Cunningham, James V., 345, 936
Curry, Walter Clyde, 1155, 1255
Cutts, John P., 219, 1389, 1403,
    1441
Cymbeline, 240, 246, 254, 258,
    262, 276, 281, 516, 610, 615,
    953, 976, 1407, 1410, 1412,
    1415, 1418-19, 1420-35, 1487;
    blend of comedy and realism,
    1423, 1425, 1428, 1434-35;
    Cloten, 1431; criticism,
    1424-35; editions, 1421-23;
    historical romance, 1424;
    imagery, 1423, 1432;
    influence of the private
    stage, 1427; reference works,
    1420; sources, 1423-24;
    structural technique, 1430;
    theme of renewal, 1428;
    topicality, 1426

Daiches, David, 993
Damon and Pithias, 907
Danby, John F., 911, 994, 1195
Dance, 207, 1482
Daniel, Samuel, 454, 538, 1510
Daniello, Bernardino, 1510
Danse macabre, 117
Danson, Lawrence N., 143, 471,
    761
Danter, John, 1387
Dash, Irene, 220
Davenant, Anne, 350, 352
Davenant, John, 350, 352
Davenant, William, 189, 812,
    1278, 1283, 1485; The Law
    Against Lovers, 812;
    Macbeth, 189, 1283; The
    Tempest (with Dryden), 1485
Davenport, Edward Loomis, 186
David, Richard, 172, 696

Davidson, Clifford, 1031
Davies, John, 789
Davis, Arthur G., 1076, 1196
Davis, Walter R., 817, 823, 826,
    833, 835
Dawson, Anthony B., 221
Dawson, Giles E., 393, 435, 488,
    528, 542, 737, 1019, 1072,
    1105, 1128, 1328
Day, Angel, 1463
Day, John, 1436
Dean, Leonard, 394, 412, 547,
    671, 856, 905-6, 1007, 1116,
    1195, 1299, 1308, 1315, 1323,
    1458
Dean, Paul, 487
Dekker, Thomas, 30
Delaney, Paul, 1197
Dennis, Carl, 641
Dennis, John, 70
Dent, Edward J., 14
Dent, R.W., 8
Dessen, Alan C., 222, 1077
Devlin, William, 1224
Dickey, Franklin, 937
Dobrée, Bonamy, 14, 1461
Dodds, W.M.T., 726
Doebler, Bettie Anne, 583, 1296
Dollimore, Jonathan, 938
Donatus, Aelius, 109, 616
Donaworth, Jane, 144
Donne, John, 218, 364, 367, 369
Donno, Elizabeth Story, 995
Donow, Herbert S., 763
Doran, Madeleine, 114, 417, 503,
    1078, 1180, 1256, 1297
Dorius, R.J., 478, 548
Dorsch, T.S., 3, 1149
Dowden, Edmund, 64
Downer, Alan S., 887, 1257, 1260,
    1457
Drake, Alfred, 833
Dramatic companies, 165, 183,
    174, 180
Draper, John W., 309, 418, 888,
    1074, 1298, 1371-72
Drayton, Michael, 579
Dreams, 236, 312
Driscoll, James P., 223
Driver, T.F., 115
Droeshout engraving, the, 58

Kokeritz, Helge, 17–18, 38, 41
Kott, Jan, 190, 267, 602
Kozintsev, Grigori, 179, 182,
    1219
Krafft, Petrus Johannes, 1383
Kreider, Paul, V., 672, 1220
Krieger, Murray, 363, 732
Kuhl, Ernest P., 843
Kurosawa, Akira, 182
Kyd, Thomas, 1, 590, 909, 922,
    1092, 1100, 1105, 1110; The
    Spanish Tragedy, 909, 922,
    1100, 1386; Soliman and
    Perseda, 909; Ur-Hamlet,
    1059, 1105

La Primaudaye, Pierre de, 148,
    1169; The French Academy,
    148
Laguardia, Eric, 645
Lamb, Charles, 64, 885, 1238
Lamb, Margaret, 1021
Landen, Jack, 833
Landino (Francesco Landini), 109
Landry, Hilton, 364–65
Lanier, William, 55
Lascelles, Mary, 733, 1221
Latham, Agnes, 661
Latomus, 109
Laughton, Charles, 1224
Lavater, Ludwig, 1467; Of Ghosts
    and Spirits Walking by Night,
    1467
Law, Robert Adger, 397, 428,
    1105
Lawlor, John J., 952, 1106,
    1502
Lawrence, Judiana, 1428
Lawrence, William W., 612, 646,
    728, 730, 734, 864, 1433
Leavenworth, Russell E., 1084,
    1144, 1146
Leavis, F.R., 190, 735, 1002,
    1316, 1322
Lee, Sidney, 52, 268, 712
Leech, Clifford, 384, 460, 613,
    647, 736, 907, 1204
Lees, F.N., 1042
Leggatt, Alexander, 614, 648
Legge, Thomas, 97, 579;
    Richardus Tertius, 97

Leigh, Vivian, 1402
Leishman, J.B., 366
Lelyveld, Toby, 780
Lermontov, Mihail Yurievich,
    1126
Lerner, Laurence, 663, 708, 760,
    793, 803, 1011, 1136, 1238,
    1249, 1257, 1270, 1292, 1311,
    1384
Lessing, Gotthold Ephraim, 64, 68
Levenson, J.C., 1082, 1104
Lever, J.W., 22, 375, 716, 769,
    998
Levin, Harry, 37, 269, 1107, 1352
Levin, Richard, 1318
Levitsky, Ruth M., 1108, 1319
Lewalski, Barbara, 770, 825, 895
Lewis, C.S., 1109
Lewis, Charlton M., 64, 1110
Lewis, Cynthia, 771
Lewis, Wyndham, 270
Lidz, Theodore, 1111
Lindenbaum, Peter, 913
Lindheim, Nancy, 1222
Lindsay, Marshall, 365
Lloyd, Michael, 1003
Locrine, 34, 279
Lodge, Thomas, 660–61, 664, 673,
    675, 679; Rosalynde, 660,
    662, 664, 673, 675, 679; A
    Margarite of America, 675
Logan, Thad Jenkins, 896
Long, John H., 271, 1418
Longus, 1407, 1463; Daphnis and
    Chloe, 1407, 1463
Lothian, John M., 883, 1223
Love, John, 649
Love's Labor's Lost, 56, 66,
    144–46, 211, 215, 240, 250,
    290, 304, 351, 357, 594,
    608–9, 618, 622, 624, 626–27,
    632, 694–714; conclusion,
    710; criticism, 699–714; Don
    Armado, 702; editions,
    696–98; possible revision,
    696, 709, 713; reference
    works, 694–95; satiric theme,
    700, 706, 708, 711; struc-
    ture, 701; style and lan-
    guage, 696, 704–5, 707;
    topicality, 698, 703, 714

102831